Mapping the Political Landscape

an introduction to political science

Second Edition

Reeta Chowdhari Tremblay
Memorial University

André Lecours
Concordia University

Csaba Nikolényi
Concordia University

Bassel Salloukh
Lebanese American University (Beirut)

Francesca Scala
Concordia University

NELSON / EDUCATION

NELSON / EDUCATION

Mapping the Political Landscape:
An Introduction to Political Science, Second Edition

by Reeta Chowdhari Tremblay, André Lecours,
Csaba Nikolényi, Bassel Salloukh, and Francesca Scala

Associate Vice President,
Editorial Director:
Evelyn Veitch

Editor-in-Chief, Higher Education:
Anne Williams

Executive Editor:
Cara Yarzab

Acquisitions Editor:
Bram Sepers

Senior Marketing Manager:
Lenore Taylor-Atkins

Developmental Editor:
Linda Sparks

Photo Researcher and Permissions
Coordinator:
Patricia Buckley

Content Production Manager:
Tammy Scherer

Production Service:
Gunjan Chandola,
ICC Macmillan Inc.

Copy Editor:
Karen Rolfe

Proofreader:
Dianne Fowlie

Indexer:
Colleen Dunham

Manufacturing Coordinator:
Ferial Suleman

Design Director:
Ken Phipps

Interior Design:
Tammy Gay

Cover Design:
Fernanda Pisani

Cover Image:
© Andrew Judd/Masterfile

Compositor:
ICC Macmillan Inc.

Printer:
RR Donnelley

Library and Archives Canada
Cataloguing in Publication Data

Mapping the political landscape :
an introduction to political science /
Reeta Chowdhari Tremblay . . .
[et al.].—2nd ed.

Includes bibliographical references
and index.

ISBN-13: 978-0-17-642413-8
ISBN-10: 0-17-642413-X

1. Political science. I. Tremblay,
Reeta Chowdhari

JA66.M35 2006   320
C2006-905374-X

TABLE OF CONTENTS

PREFACE

We are delighted to present the second edition of our introductory text/reader. This edition has benefited a great deal from the responses of the instructors and students who have used the text during the past three years. Consistent with the first edition, our text/reader has four goals: (1) to introduce students to the major concepts, themes, and vocabulary of political science; (2) to expose students to classical and contemporary readings on the particular subject matter; (3) to acquaint students with the contemporary debates and critiques; and (4) to evaluate concepts and themes in light of the differing experiences of advanced industrial and less-developed societies, of democratic and various other regimes, of modern and traditional cultures, and of humans as distinguished by gender. This text/reader is divided into four major sections: Politics as Discipline; Politics as Ideas; Politics as Institutions; and Politics as Change. Each section is further divided into chapters. Each chapter has a thematic commentary that includes a definition of the concept, its philosophical and historical context, and the application of the concept to differing regional, cultural and, when relevant, gender contexts. A small section of classical and contemporary readings follow. We have attempted to provide a short introduction to the readings that should assist students in relating the thematic commentary to the readings. In the new edition, all chapters—thematic summaries as well as readings—have been updated. In some chapters, such as Democracy and Democratization and Religion and Politics, new readings have been introduced.

The idea for this text/reader initially emerged from an extended discussion among us about the introductory courses taught in our department at Concordia and what we perceived as a number of major gaps in the existing materials. The first edition of this text/reader was our response to our own needs that, as we have discovered through the usage of this book in other universities, are not very different from those of introductory political science courses offered in most other universities. We hope that, as with the first edition, within the context of a large and diverse Canadian population and with increasing globalization, our strategy to relate the classical concepts to differing political and cultural experiences should be productive for both instructors and students. In addition, our section on Politics as Change will provide instructors an opportunity to introduce timely conceptual debates.

Collaborative works are generally difficult to execute, but our team of five has enjoyed initially putting together this text/reader and now working on the second edition. Part of the pleasure of this collaboration is due to the fact that the members of the team not only have different methodological approaches to the study of political science, but also possess differing areas of expertise covering different regions in the world. We hope that this introductory book will give students an opportunity to learn that politics is complex and that the study of politics does not lend itself to one methodological approach. Moreover, we hope what will also come across is that the concepts in our discipline consistently evolve and are reformulated in light of the regional, cultural, and global experiences.

Several individuals have graciously and generously assisted us in the preparation of this book. To begin with, we would like to acknowledge the advice given to us by several reviewers, providing us with us with detailed comments on our text/reader and the selection of our readings. Our sincerest thanks go to Douglas Long of the University of Western Ontario; Marlene Hancock of Douglas College; George MacLean of the University of Manitoba, and Nergis Canefe of York University. We owe a great deal to the team at Thomson Nelson, including Bram Sepers, Acquisitions Editor; Tammy Scherer, Content Production Manager; and Karen Rolfe, Copy Editor. We remain indebted to Chris Carson who was the Executive Editor at the time of the publication of the first edition of this text/reader. He guided us from conception to the completion of the earlier project. Linda Sparks, Developmental Editor, has been marvellous in coordinating the production and in keeping us on track with regard to every aspect of the process. We have relied upon her sound advice and counsel, and she has taken us smoothly through the whole project without any interference in the revision of the second edition. Since we have benefited from such able guidance and assistance, the traditional acknowledgment is all the more true that the responsibility for any remaining errors is ours.

Reeta Chowdhari Tremblay
André Lecours
Csaba Nikolényi
Bassel Salloukh
Francesca Scala

PART 1

POLITICS AS DISCIPLINE

Section 1 offers the reader a general introduction to political science as a discipline. The intention is to highlight the necessarily cumulative, diverse, and often contested nature of the study of politics. Chapter 1 opens with a discussion of the contemporary study of politics as the inheritor of a historical tradition of philosophical speculation and inquiry, and a description of the rise of the first departments of politics in North America, and hence the emergence of political science as a discipline. In Chapter 2, the diversity of the discipline is explored through a discussion of contending approaches in the study of politics. The different approaches are explored historically, beginning with the legal-formal approach, passing through behaviourism, and concluding with rational choice and the new institutionalism. The basic assumptions and criticisms of each approach will be explained respectively. Chapter 3 addresses differing methodologies in political science. Here the reader is introduced to the basic methods, concepts, and terminologies employed in the study of politics.

CHAPTER 1

TRADITION, DISCIPLINE, AND DEFINITION

Politics—the subject matter of the discipline of Political Science—underlies a great variety of human interactions. Whether we think about it consciously or not, government decisions impinge on our daily lives. Most are routine decisions about everyday matters, but they range in importance all the way up to those momentous decisions that affect the nation's peace and prosperity. Some of us participate directly and others submit passively in the making of these decisions. Those who choose to be active in politics do so for different reasons, usually a mixture of two types of considerations: to make a living or to strive idealistically for a better polity. Through the study of **political science**, we can be better informed about how people govern themselves, how policies are made, and how we can improve our government policies at the local, state, national, and international levels. At a minimum, the study of politics is likely to form citizens who are better able to evaluate their political systems, ask critical questions about decisions made by their leaders, and demand actions which are not on the agenda of the politicians.

Political science revolves around a discussion of central concepts such as government, power, conflict, state, state–society relations and public policy. While there is contention and an on-going debate among the students of political science about what is political and whether political science is really a science, there is a general consensus that politics constitutes the core content of the discipline. In this introductory chapter, we explore three themes: the tradition of political science; the history of the discipline; and the subject matter of the discipline—"what is politics."

THE TRADITION OF POLITICAL SCIENCE

The tradition of political science is based in Western civilization. The development of our political institutions, the systems of political thought, the questions underlying the political enquiry (for example, what is a good government, the role of a citizen, the concept of justice) are deeply rooted in the Greek, Roman, and Judeo-Christian traditions. To understand contemporary institutions and belief systems, we must be familiar with the ideas of past thinkers and the history of political events. In our discipline, knowledge is cumulative and an understanding of the cumulative Western experience is essential to locate the current debates on politics and its processes. For example, it was the Greeks (Plato: 427–347 B.C., Aristotle: 384–322 B.C.) who introduced to us the notion of democracy, and the development of democracy in Athens was to become both a model and an inspiration for succeeding generations to the present time. Despite the changed nature of our polity within an increasingly globalized world, the concern of the Greeks with issues such as citizenship, justice, and the relationship between the state and the individual remains relevant in our contemporary context. Ultimately, Plato and Aristotle's writings laid the foundations of political enquiry, introducing us to both a philosophical and scientific understanding of the political—not only what politics is, but what politics ought to be.

The Stoic philosophers emphasized the importance of individuality and human dignity. The concept of citizenship and rights is associated with the Romans, who also linked ancient with medieval thought. Cicero (106–43 B.C.) interpreted Roman history in terms of Greek political theory. His contribution to contemporary thought can be attributed to his systematizing and transmitting Greek thought to the medieval world and thus to the modern world. The contributions of St. Augustine (A.D. 354–430) and St. Thomas Aquinas (1225–74) relate to the relationship between religion and politics. Our own contemporary debates about Islam and its role in politics, the role of liberation theology in bringing about democratic transition in the authoritarian regimes of Latin America, the rise of Christian fundamentalism in the United States, or the rise of Hindu fundamentalism in India can find resonance in medieval experience and thought. The medieval period witnessed political contests between the Catholic Church and the monarchy on the one hand, and between the feudal lords and the monarchs on the other.

Plato

The modern concept of the state, as well as the notion of separation of church and state and the commitment to a secular polity, can be traced to philosophical thinking and historical events of the sixteenth century. While Niccolo Machiavelli (1469–1527) took for granted the concept of state sovereignty, Jean Bodin (1530–1596) and Thomas Hobbes (1588–1679) wrote of sovereignty as the inalienable right of the monarch, which no other authority, either temporal or spiritual, could override. It is interesting that, despite so many developments over the centuries and a changed political context, we still speak of sovereignty or a sovereign state in Bodin's terms. While Henry VIII of England (1491–1547) and Louis XIV of France (1638–1715) established absolute authority over their respective kingdoms, John Locke (1632–1704) introduced the notions of limited government, individual rights, and political tolerance. The American Revolution (1776) and the French Revolution (1789) were premised on the principles of individual rights of life, liberty, and equality. As Western societies moved from the absolute authority and sovereignty of the monarch and established the principles of popular sovereignty, the thoughts of John Stuart Mill (1806–1873), building on those of Locke, formed the foundation of democratic ideologies. Karl Marx (1818–1883) had a profound influence in raising our consciousness to structural inequalities in society, thereby resulting in the broadening of our notion of citizenry and eventually to the rise of the welfare state. Not only were women and other populations, previously excluded from the electoral process on the basis of education and property, now brought into the participatory state, but the state transformed itself and took up the responsibility to assist the underprivileged sections of the society. By the mid-twentieth century, this expansion of the democratic ideology saw the independence of the colonized

CONFUCIUS
Le plus célèbre Philosophe de la Chine.

Confucius

countries of Asia and Africa. Similarly, since the end of the Cold War, democracy has emerged as by far the most acceptable form of government. This brief excursion into Western history and civilization illustrates that knowledge in political science is indeed cumulative and that it is rooted in the political thought and experiences of the West.[1]

We should point out here that, while non-Western civilizations may have had substantial traditions of political thought and of political experience, these have remained, until recently, largely peripheral to the tradition of political science. Among the non-Western traditions, we may point to major figures such as Confucius, Kautilya, Avicenna, and Gandhi. Confucius (551–479 B.C.), China's most famous teacher, philosopher, and political theorist, has influenced political and social thought throughout East Asia. In South Asia, Kautilya's (321–296 B.C.) *Artha-shastra*, the Hindu philosopher's classic treatise on polity, is compared by many to Machiavelli's *Prince*, Plato's *Republic*, or Aristotle's *Politics*. It is generally believed that Kautilya's political realism was largely responsible for the consolidation and success of the Mauryan empire under Chandragupta (321–297 B.C.) and Ashoka (265–238 B.C.). Avicenna (980–1037) was one of the most famous and influential of the philosopher-scientists of Islam. His own personal philosophic views were close those of the Greeks. Gandhi's (1869–1948) nationalism, based on the principles of non-violence, acquired an ethical universalism, influencing followers both within and outside India.

Feminist scholars have questioned the tradition of political science, which, they believe, has ignored the question of gender. The experience, history, and alleged universal norms of Western political thought are called into question. Through a reformulation of the concepts of agency, power, and sites of political resistance, feminist scholars—in a variety of often contending ways—are exploring the centrality of gender as an analytic category in the discipline of politics. It is important to point out that, once at the periphery of political science, the feminist debates and the non-Western experiences have begun to enrich its tradition.

THE DISCIPLINE OF POLITICAL SCIENCE

While the tradition of political science is ancient, the professionalization of the discipline is a recent phenomenon. Until the late-nineteenth century, political science, as an academic discipline, was subsumed under moral philosophy, political economy, history, or law. The first North American political science department, the School of Political Science, was established at Columbia University in New York City in 1880. In 1886 it inaugurated the journal

Political Science Quarterly, which became the main outlet for major scholarly writings in the discipline. Between the two world wars, there was a steady expansion of the departments in the United States, although in Canada the establishment of political science departments in universities and colleges is largely a post–World War II phenomenon. The 1960s witnessed the rise of separate political science or politics departments, and, accordingly, in 1967 the *Canadian Journal of Economics and Political Science* was split into two journals—one for economics and one for political science. At present, there are fifty-eight departments of political science in Canadian universities and colleges.

The United States has had a tremendous influence in defining the discipline of political science. During the 1930s and 1940s, under the influence of European scholars who had migrated to the United States, the study of political science was largely based on an explanation and understanding of the legal and institutional aspects of a government, such as the constitution, the law-making process, and the structure of governments. The method often employed to study the institutions was historical-comparative. After World War II, attempts by a new generation of American scholars to enlarge the discipline beyond purely institutional and legal perspectives added such themes as the political process and the behaviour of political actors. American political scientists began to explore a wide range of subjects such as the role of interest groups; the content of political power, authority, and legitimacy; individual and collective behaviour; electoral politics; political culture; etc. As a result, American political science has come to exercise a hegemonic influence in determining the content of political science all around the world. The United States' rise as a superpower during the second half of the twentieth century largely explains why we study political science the way we do. The new nations in Asia and Africa, which had gained their independence from the colonial empires after World War II, were facing challenges of nation-building and political and economic development. Their dependence upon foreign assistance resulted in acceptance of the models of development of the aid donors. Not only did their political institutions reflect these models, but their university education followed the so-called universally accepted curricula. Canadian political science has also been influenced by the American enterprise.[2] There are a substantial number of political scientists teaching in Canadian universities who are trained in the United States. We have seen a similar shift in Canada from an institutional and legal emphasis to the study of political process, although in this country the study of political economy continues to be emphasized. Moreover, given the strong role played by the state in the Canadian society and its commitment to policies such as universal health care, the study of institutions has remained parallel to the study of political behaviour and political process.

One of the major impacts of the professionalization of the discipline of political science has been its division into several sub-fields or sub-disciplines. Generally, the discipline is divided into the specializations of political theory and philosophy, domestic politics (in our case Canadian politics), comparative politics, and international politics. To these are also added the sub-disciplines of political economy, public policy, and public administration. Recently, gender and politics has begun to assert itself as another specialization.

THE DEFINITION OF POLITICAL SCIENCE

Political science is now generally understood to be the study of the governmental processes—the dynamics and institutions of public governance. In short, it is a study of politics, where politics is the process of making binding decisions to allocate scarce resources within the society. David Easton has described this process as "the **authoritative allocation**

of values."[3] Harold Lasswell's phrase "who gets what, when, and how" captures this process more succinctly.

There are two universal characteristics of politics: conflict and power that are inextricably linked. Conflict emerges in a society for two reasons—first, through competition for scarce resources, and second, through competition for differing goals and values. In a society, different individuals and groups compete for the same resources—whether economic or social. Our public policies reflect a choice made by the government at a particular period of time with regard to the allocation of the limited resources available to it. All governments are constantly pushed toward making choices: Should more money be diverted to health or education or defense? Should personal taxes be lowered or corporate taxes be raised? These choices are directly related to the second type of conflict: competition for differing values and goals. Different worldviews or different ideological commitments prescribe varying models for the organization of political systems and state–society relations. Political leaders compete for positions of political power so that they can influence the allocation of resources in conformity with their ideological positions. Conflict, thus, is directly related to the exercise of power. Power enables the government to make binding decisions to allocate scarce values.

Power can be defined as the ability of a person to make the others do something that he or she might not otherwise do. There are three variants of power: influence, coercion, and authority. In a polity, all these three variants are used, but it is authority that has the greatest significance for political governance. Influence and coercion have limited value so far as government is concerned, although both are used extensively in all political systems. A government can use influence to persuade the citizens of a country to do something, but the obedience of the citizen is voluntary and there is no assurance that the goals of the government will be implemented. Coercion, on the other hand, uses force to make citizens comply with its orders. Although it is a successful strategy in the short run (and it is a last resort for all governments), no government can rely upon it exclusively and for an extended period of time for fear of losing legitimacy. It is the third variation of power, **authority**, that all political systems can count on to make binding decisions regarding the allocation of resources. Authority is vested in individuals by virtue of their office. For example, police officers have the authority to hand someone a ticket with a fine and impose demerit points if a driver, say, fails to stop at a stop sign. Police officers' authority is a product of their office, which vests them with the power to hand over a ticket for a traffic infraction. It should be noted that authority is only possible if it is accompanied by legitimacy. If authority is the right to command, **legitimacy** is the response to command. In order for the authority of a government to be successful, it must be obeyed. That is why we speak about politics involving binding decisions. Max Weber (1864–1920) points out that the basis of authority differs according to the nature of authority. He distinguishes between charismatic, traditional, and legal authority. While the legitimacy in the **traditional authority** structure is derived from a respect for the sanctity of tradition, in **charismatic authority** it is based on the extraordinary qualities and mission of the charismatic leader. Conversely, **legal authority** is based on legal principles, and it is the rule of law that legitimizes the authority.

Politics, as defined here, as the authoritative allocation of resources, can be found in all organizations, for example, a family, a church, a union, a corporation. We call these groups para-political organizations. In our discipline we are generally interested in a larger system called the state, and politics in a state needs to be distinguished from that of smaller and limited organizations. Although binding decisions occur in para-political organizations within the context of power and conflict, the scope of these organizations is narrow. Their decisions pertain exclusively to the members of these organizations and do not have an impact on non-members. Moreover, the members of these organizations can always opt out of the organization if they do not want to obey its authority. On the other hand, the government of a state has comprehensive authority over its involuntary membership. Rules of government are binding on its citizens. If there is conflict between the rules of the government and those of para-political organizations, it is the rules of the former that are considered binding upon the citizens. Moreover, the citizens cannot easily opt in or out of the membership of a state.

Sub-Fields of Political Science

The discipline of political science encompasses the study of such a broad range of political processes and other political phenomena that specialization has been unavoidable. In order for students of politics to get a firmer and deeper grasp of their subject, this complex subject wound up being divided into smaller, more manageable parts. It has become traditional to categorize Political Science according to five major sub-fields: Political Theory, Comparative Politics, International Politics, Canadian (National or Domestic) Politics, Public Policy and Public Administration.

Political Theory: This field encompasses both normative political philosophy and empirically oriented theory. While the latter attempts to explain political behaviour and to account for individual decisions and collective outcomes, political philosophy concerns itself with the ends or purposes of political action. It addresses normative issues such as: what is a good citizen? What is the best form of political system or a government? What should be the relationship between authority and citizens? What makes a government legitimate? What rights and duties must a citizen have in order to fully participate in a state and make its authority legitimate? Western political thought can be divided into five major historical periods: classical (Greeks and Romans), medieval (Christian Thinkers), enlightenment (social contract theorists such as Hobbes, Locke and Rousseau), late modern thought (Marx, Weber etc.) and contemporary political theory (racism, multiculturalism, gender, democratic theory). Non-Western political thought includes the Islamic philosophy and the eastern traditions such as Hinduism, Buddhism, and Confucianism. Recently there has been a rising interest in reviewing the works of Arab thinkers such as the twelfth-century Islamic theologian, Averroes, who interpreted Greek thought and wrote commentaries on Aristotle.

Comparative Politics: This sub-field of political science studies different political systems in the world, comparing different forms of government and their functioning in order to develop an understanding of some of the world's diverse political structures and practices. Major topics covered generally in this subfield are: political culture, ideologies and institutions (e.g. constitutions, political parties, electoral systems, democracy, interest groups etc.) There is a perennial debate in comparative politics about whether this sub-field should concentrate on area studies (dealing with particular regions or countries in depth) or should generalize common principles which govern diverse political systems by conducting so-called large "n" studies. Comparative politics is further divided into the study of developing societies and of advanced industrial nations. Given the fast pace of globalization and the emerging global powers (China and India), some feel that this distinction no longer makes sense.

International Politics: Whereas the sub-field of comparative politics deals with the domestic politics of different countries, international politics studies the relations between different states and their foreign policies. Major topics covered are: foreign policy, war and peace, strategic and security studies, international organizations, and globalization. The dominant schools of thought in international politics are: realism and neo-realism (sovereign states are the principal actors in the international arena and states maximize their power to pursue their national interests), liberalism and neoliberalism (international outcomes are explained by placing emphasis on the domestic structure of states rather than the distribution of power), constructivism (emphasis on the selection, transmission, and effects of ideas to explain changes in social and state identity), feminism (while mainstream feminist theories examine the contrasting roles of male and female ideations and use their proportion in a polity to explain foreign policy and international systemic outcomes, critical feminism challenges the cause-effect assumptions of the positivist social scientific method, and its usefulness for studying the international system).

Canadian or Domestic Politics: In this sub-field, students focus upon the political processes and politics of their own country. Topics studied range from local to national politics, the nature of intergovernmental relations, bureaucracy, public policy, political culture, leaders, electoral systems, political parties, minority representation etc. Generally the approaches to the study of domestic politics parallel those of comparative politics.

Public Policy and Public Administration: This sub-field focuses on the making and the implementation of public policy. It addresses issues such as: what governments do or do not do (i.e., it includes both decisions and non-decisions), what processes underlie these governmental actions and inactions, and what consequences can be attributed to them. The topics studied can range from local to national and comparative public policies. Public administration addresses the functioning of the bureaucracy, its role in the making and the implementation of public policy, its accountability to the citizenry and to the elected institutions of the government.

In addition to these five subfields, some would include as well political economy, political sociology, and gender and politics. In political economy, the interactions between politics and economy are emphasized: what is studied is either the influence of political processes on economic policy, or the influence of economic factors on political outcomes. On the other hand, political sociology focuses on the non-institutionalized, societal context of politics, for example the role of citizens in politics. Topics studied could include a study of individual attitudes and behaviour, citizens' participation in voluntary associations, such as interest groups or parties, or social movements such as anti-globalization movements. Recently, due to the success of the feminist movement, another vibrant sub-field has emerged: Gender and Politics. It approaches the study of political science from a non-masculine point of view and attempts to deconstruct the patriarchal nature of our discipline: why have women been absent from the profession and discipline of political science? Why is the masculine gender so often an attribute of those in power? What are the effects of a polity's gendered makeup on a political system and its policies? In short, what are the gender dynamics of politics?

Some political scientists question the categorization of our discipline in sub-fields as we have described above. For them, political science deals with complex political phenomena where economic, political and social realties are intertwined. They claim that it is a disservice to our discipline which is by nature interdisciplinary to define it by artificially defined specializations and categories. In conformity with the interdisciplinarity of politics, these scholars suggest defining the discipline of political science by themes rather by sub-fields. Themes might include citizenship, globalization, nationalism, race and gender etc. The advocates of interdisciplinary political science point to two advantages in using themes: first, our observations about political phenomena would benefit a great deal as we went beyond the narrow categorizations based on artificially created boundaries; second, it allows us to shift the study of politics from one set of themes to another in response to emerging political realities. The latter is in keeping with the tradition of political science which maintains that knowledge is cumulative and grows or changes in response to different historical realities.

ENDNOTES

1. Dwight Waldo, "Political Science: Tradition, Discipline, Profession, Science, Enterprise," in *Handbook of Political Science*, ed. I. Fred Greenstein (Reading, MA: Addison-Wesley, 1975), 1–43.
2. Alan Cairns, "Alternative Styles in the Study of Canadian Politics," *Canadian Journal of Political Science* 7, no. 1 (March 1974).
3. David Easton, "Some Fundamental Categories of Analysis," in *A Systems Analysis of Political Life* (New York: John Wiley and Sons, 1965), 29–33.

READINGS

In this chapter we illustrated how, although the profession of political science is relatively recent, our discipline is embedded within much older Western Judeo-Christian practices and traditions. We went on to define the concept of politics within the contemporary context. For this chapter we have selected two readings as introductions to the concept of politics: a small excerpt from Max Weber's essay "Politics as a Vocation" and the first chapter from Bernard Crick's book *In Defence of Politics*.

Weber's reading is an excellent piece to begin with, as it helps establish the framework for politics. It not only speaks to politics as an activity, but it also points to the institution of the state as the exclusive domain within which the activity of politics occurs. (Pay attention to his definition of the state as a human community that claims the monopoly of the legitimate use of force. You will come across it again in Chapter 8.) Weber then goes on to define politics as striving to share power to influence the distribution of power. He cautions us not to confuse the political activities of para-political institutions with those of the state, the political community central to our discipline. After defining politics and relating it to the exercise of power (or domination, as he calls it), he asks how power is exercised and consequently why individuals obey the decisions made by persons in positions of power. He goes on to describe three bases for legitimate (which Weber calls "pure type") authority. The essay ends with the role of political leadership and the notion of politics as avocation (practised by all those for whom "politics is, neither materially nor ideally, their life") and vocation (practised by all those who are dedicated wholly and exclusively to the profession of politics). In distinguishing the profession of politics in terms of those who live for politics and those who live off politics, Weber concludes by suggesting that economic independence allows a politician to live for politics. We can ask whether, in contemporary politics, this is possible or is just wishful thinking.

Bernard Crick, in "The Nature of Political Rule," defines politics as freedom as well as an activity by which different interests are conciliated. Invoking Aristotle, he reminds us that politics arises in "organized states" where different interests and groups are represented. Politics is fundamentally the activity of conciliating these interests through a sharing of power. This activity occurs within the domain of a political system whose goal is to maintain both order and stability. Thus, government is an essential instrument in fulfilling the objectives of community survival, maintenance of order and stability, and providing mechanisms for tolerance and diversity, thereby enabling the conciliation of differing interests. We should note that, much like Weber, Crick's discussion of politics refers to the activity of politics within the domain of the state and not within para-political organizations (which he refers to as small groups).

POLITICS AS A VOCATION

Max Weber

This lecture, which I give at your request, will necessarily disappoint you in a number of ways. You will naturally expect me to take a position on actual problems of the day. But that will be the case only in a purely formal way and toward the end, when I shall raise certain questions concerning the significance of political action in the whole way of life. In today's lecture, all questions that refer to what policy and what content one should give one's political activity must be eliminated. For such questions have nothing to do with the general question of what politics as a vocation means and what it can mean. Now to our subject matter.

What do we understand by politics? The concept is extremely broad and comprises any kind of *independent* leadership in action. One speaks of the currency policy of the banks, of the discounting policy of the Reichsbank, of the strike policy of a trade union; one may speak of the educational policy of a municipality or a township, of the policy of the president of a voluntary association, and, finally, even of the policy of a prudent wife who seeks to guide her husband. Tonight, our reflections are, of course, not based upon such a broad concept. We wish to understand by politics only the leadership, or the influencing of the leadership, of a *political* association, hence today, of a *state*.

But what is a "political" association from the sociological point of view? What is a "state"? Sociologically, the state cannot be defined in terms of its ends. There is scarcely any task that some political association has not taken in hand, and there is no task that one could say has always

been exclusive and peculiar to those associations which are designated as political ones: today the state, or historically, those associations which have been the predecessors of the modern state. Ultimately, one can define the modern state sociologically only in terms of the specific *means* peculiar to it, as to every political association, namely, the use of physical force.

"Every state is founded on force," said Trotsky at Brest-Litovsk. That is indeed right. If no social institutions existed which knew the use of violence, then the concept of "state" would be eliminated, and a condition would emerge that could be designated as "anarchy," in the specific sense of this word. Of course, force is certainly not the normal or the only means of the state—nobody says that—but force is a means specific to the state. Today the relation between the state and violence is an especially intimate one. In the past, the most varied institutions—beginning with the sib—have known the use of physical force as quite normal. Today, however, we have to say that a state is a human community that (successfully) claims the *monopoly of the legitimate use of physical force* within a given territory. Note that "territory" is one of the characteristics of the state. Specifically, at the present time, the right to use physical force is ascribed to other institutions or to individuals only to the extent to which the state permits it. The state is considered the sole source of the "right" to use violence. Hence, "politics" for us means striving to share power or striving to influence the distribution of power, either among states or among groups within a state.

This corresponds essentially to ordinary usage. When a question is said to be a "political" question, when a cabinet minister or an official is said to be a "political" official, or when a decision is said to be "politically" determined, what is always meant is that interests in the distribution, maintenance, or transfer of power are decisive for answering the questions and determining the decision or the official's sphere of activity. He who is active in politics strives for power either as a means in serving other aims, ideal or egoistic, or as "power for power's sake," that is, in order to enjoy the prestige-feeling that power gives.

Like the political institutions historically preceding it, the state is a relation of men dominating men, a relation supported by means of legitimate (i.e., considered to be legitimate) violence. If the state is to exist, the dominated must obey the authority claimed by the powers that be. When and why do men obey? Upon what inner justifications and upon what external means does this domination rest?

To begin with, in principle, there are three inner justifications, hence basic *legitimations* of domination.

First, the authority of the "eternal yesterday," i.e., of the mores sanctified through the unimaginably ancient recognition and habitual orientation to conform. This is "traditional" domination exercised by the patriarch and the patrimonial prince of yore.

There is the authority of the extraordinary and personal *gift of grace* (charisma), the absolutely personal devotion and personal confidence in revelation, heroism, or other qualities of individual leadership. This is "charismatic" domination, as exercised by the prophet or in the field of politics by the elected war lord, the plebiscitarian ruler, the great demagogue, or the political party leader.

Finally, there is domination by virtue of "legality," by virtue of the belief in the validity of legal statute and functional "competence" based on rationally created *rules*. In this case, obedience is expected in discharging statutory obligations. This is domination as exercised by the modern "servant of the state" and by all those bearers of power who in this respect resemble him.

It is understood that, in reality, obedience is determined by highly robust motives of fear and hope—fear of the vengeance of magical powers or of the power-holder, hope for reward in this world or in the beyond—and besides all this, by

interests of the most varied sort. Of this we shall speak presently. However, in asking for the "legitimations" of this obedience, one meets with these three "pure" types: "traditional," "charismatic," and "legal."

These conceptions of legitimacy and their inner justifications are of very great significance for the structure of domination. To be sure, the pure types are rarely found in reality. But today we cannot deal with the highly complex variants, transitions, and combinations of these pure types, which problems belong to "political science." Here we are interested above all in the second of these types: domination by virtue of the devotion of those who obey the purely personal "charisma" of the "leader." For this is the root of the idea of a *calling* in its highest expression.

Devotion to the charisma of the prophet, or the leader in war, or to the great demagogue in the *ecclesia* or in parliament, means that the leader is personally recognized as the innerly "called" leader of men. Men do not obey him by virtue of tradition or statute, but because they believe in him. If he is more than a narrow and vain upstart of the moment, the leader lives for his cause and "strives for his work."[1] The devotion of his disciples, his followers, his personal party friends is oriented to his person and to its qualities.

Charismatic leadership has emerged in all places and in all historical epochs. Most importantly in the past, it has emerged in the two figures of the magician and the prophet on the one hand, and in the elected war lord, the gang leader and *condotierre* on the other hand. Political leadership in the form of the free "demagogue" who grew from the soil of the city state is of greater concern to us; like the city state, the demagogue is peculiar to the Occident and especially to Mediterranean culture. Furthermore, political leadership in the form of the parliamentary "party leader" has grown on the soil of the constitutional state, which is also indigenous only to the Occident.

These politicians by virtue of a "calling," in the most genuine sense of the word, are of course nowhere the only decisive figures in the cross-currents of the political struggle for power. The sort of auxiliary means that are at their disposal is also highly decisive. How do the politically dominant powers manage to maintain their domination? The question pertains to any kind of domination, hence also to political domination in all its forms, traditional as well as legal and charismatic.

Organized domination, which calls for continuous administration, requires that human conduct be conditioned to obedience towards those masters who claim to be the bearers of legitimate power. On the other hand, by virtue of this obedience, organized domination requires the control of those material goods which in a given case are necessary for the use of physical violence. Thus, organized domination requires control of the personal executive staff and the material implements of administration.

***

Today we do not take a stand on this question. I state only the purely *conceptual* aspect for our consideration: the modern state is a compulsory association which organizes domination. It has been successful in seeking to monopolize the legitimate use of physical force as a means of domination within a territory. To this end the state has combined the material means of organization in the hands of its leaders, and it has expropriated all autonomous functionaries of estates who formerly controlled these means in their own right. The state has taken their positions and now stands in the top place.

During this process of political expropriation, which has occurred with varying success in all countries on earth, "professional politicians" in another sense have emerged. They arose first in the service of a prince. They have been men who, unlike the charismatic leader, have not wished to be lords themselves, but who have entered the *service* of political lords. In the struggle of expropriation, they placed themselves at the princes' disposal and by managing the princes' politics they earned on the one hand a living and on the other hand an ideal content of life. Again, it is *only* in the Occident that we find this kind of professional politician in the service of powers other than the princes. In the past, they have been the most important power instrument of the prince and his instrument of political expropriation.

Before discussing "professional politicians" in detail, let us clarify in all its aspects the state of affairs their existence presents. Politics, just as economic pursuits, may be a man's avocation or his vocation. One may engage in politics, and hence seek to influence the distribution of power within and between political structures, as an "occasional" politician. We are all "occasional" politicians when we cast our ballot or consummate a similar expression of intention, such as applauding or protesting in a "political" meeting, or delivering a "political" speech, etc. The whole relation of many people to politics is restricted to this. Politics as an avocation is today practiced by all those party agents and heads of voluntary political associations who, as a rule, are politically active only in case of need and for whom politics is, neither materially nor ideally, "their life" in the first place. The same holds for those members of state counsels and similar deliberative bodies that function only when summoned. It also holds for rather broad strata of our members of parliament who are politically active only during sessions. In the past, such strata were found especially among the estates. Proprietors of military implements in their own right, or proprietors of goods important for the administration, or proprietors of personal prerogatives may be called "estates." A large portion of them were far from giving their lives wholly, or merely preferentially, or more than occasionally, to the service of politics. Rather, they exploited their prerogatives in the interest of gaining rent or even profits; and they became active in the service of political associations only when the overlord of their status-equals especially demanded it. It was not different in the case of some of the auxiliary forces which the prince drew into the struggle for the creation of a political organization to be exclusively at his disposal. This was the nature of the *Räte von Haus aus* [councillors] and, still further back, of a considerable part of the councillors assembling in the "Curia" and other deliberating bodies of the princes. But these merely occasional auxiliary forces engaging in politics on the side were naturally not sufficient for the prince. Of necessity, the prince sought to create a staff of helpers dedicated wholly and exclusively to serving him, hence making this their major vocation. The structure of the emerging dynastic political organization, and not only this but the whole articulation of the culture, depended to a considerable degree upon the question of where the prince recruited agents.

A staff was also necessary for those political associations whose members constituted themselves politically as (so-called) "free" communes under the complete abolition or the far-going restriction of princely power.

They were "free" not in the sense of freedom from domination by force, but in the sense that princely power legitimized by tradition (mostly religiously sanctified) as the exclusive source of all authority was absent. These communities have their historical home in the Occident. Their nucleus was the city as a body politic, the form in which the city first emerged in the Mediterranean culture area. In all these cases, what did the politicians who made politics their major vocation look like?

There are two ways of making politics one's vocation: Either one lives "for" politics or one lives "off" politics. By no means is this contrast an exclusive one. The rule is, rather, that man does both, at least in thought, and certainly he also does both in practice. He who lives "for" politics makes politics his life, in an internal sense. Either he enjoys the naked possession of the power he exerts, or he nourishes his inner balance and self-feeling by the consciousness that his life has *meaning* in the service of a "cause." In this internal sense, every sincere man who lives for a cause also lives off this cause. The distinction hence refers to a much more substantial aspect of the matter, namely, to the economic. He who strives to make politics a permanent source of income lives "off" politics as a vocation, whereas he who does not do this lives "for" politics. Under the dominance of the private property order, some—if you wish—very trivial preconditions must exist in order for a person to be able to live "for" politics in this economic sense. Under normal conditions, the politician must be economically independent of the income politics can bring him. This means, quite simply, that the politician must be wealthy or must have a personal position in life which yields a sufficient income.

Reading Note

1. "Politik als Beruf," *Gesammelte Politische Schriften* (Muenchen, 1921), pp. 396–450. Originally a speech at Munich University, 1918, published in 1919 by Duncker & Humblodt, Munich.

THE NATURE OF POLITICAL RULE

Bernard Crick

Who has not often felt the distaste with democratic politics which Salazar expressed when he said that he "detested politics from the bottom of his heart; all those noisy and incoherent promises, the impossible demands, the hotchpotch of unfounded ideas and impractical plans . . . opportunism that cares neither for truth nor justice, the inglorious chase after unmerited fame, the unleashing of uncontrollable passions, the exploitation of the lowest instincts, the distortion of facts . . . all that feverish and sterile fuss?" (J.H. Huizinga in The Times, *16 November 1961)*

Boredom with established truths is a great enemy of free men. So there is some excuse in troubled times not to be clever and inventive in redefining things, or to pretend to academic unconcern or scientific detachment, but simply to try to make some old platitudes pregnant. This essay simply seeks to help in the task of restoring confidence in the virtues of politics as a great and civilizing human activity. Politics, like Antaeus in the Greek myth, can remain perpetually young, strong, and lively so long as it can keep its feet firmly on the ground of Mother Earth. We live in a human condition, so we cannot through politics grasp for an absolute ideal, as Plato taught with bewitching single-mindedness. But the surface of the earth varies greatly, and being human we are restless and have many different ideals and are forced to plan for the future as well as to enjoy the fruits of the past, so equally politics cannot be a "purely practical and immediate" activity, as those who cannot see beyond the end of their own noses praise themselves by claiming.

Politics is too often regarded as a poor relation, inherently dependent and subsidiary; it is rarely praised as something with a life and character of its own. Politics is not religion, ethics, law, science, history, or economics; it neither solves everything, nor is it present everywhere; and it is not any one political doctrine, such as conservatism, liberalism, socialism, communism, or nationalism, though it can contain elements of most of these things. Politics is politics, to be valued as itself, not because it is "like" or "really is" something else more respectable or peculiar. Politics is politics. The person who wishes not to be troubled by politics and to be left alone finds himself the unwitting ally of those to whom politics is a troublesome obstacle to their well-meant intentions to leave nothing alone.

To some this may seem very obvious. But then there will be no harm in reminding them how few they are. All over the world there are men aspiring to power and there are actual rulers who, however many different names they go by, have in common a rejection of politics. Many Frenchmen in 1958, warm defenders of the Republic, argued that General de Gaulle was saving the French nation from the politicians; in 1961 an army rebellion broke out in Algeria in which the same General was then accused of seeking a "purely political solution" to the Algerian problem, and the rebel Generals went on to deny that they themselves had any "political ambitions." Fidel Castro told a reporter in 1961: "We are not politicians. We made our revolution to get the politicians out. We are social people. This is a social revolution." In so many places the cry has gone up that *the* party or *the* leader is defending *the* people against the politicians. "Politics, ill understood, have been defined," wrote Isaac D'Israeli, "as 'the art of governing mankind by deceiving them.'" Many people, of course, even in régimes which are clearly political, think that they are not interested in politics, and even act as if they are not; but they are probably few compared to the many who think that politics is fiddled, contradictory, self-defeatingly recurrent, unprogressive, unpatriotic, inefficient, mere compromise, or even a sham or conspiracy by which political parties seek to preserve some particular and peculiar social systems against the challenge of the inevitable future, etc. The anti-political are very right to think that politics is an achievement far more limited in time and place than politically-minded men, or men who practise this odd thing politics, normally presume.

Many politicians, publicists, and scholars in Western cultures are apt to leap to the defence, or the propagandizing, of words like "liberty," "democracy," "free-government," and then to be puzzled and distraught when, even if their voices are heard at all elsewhere, they are only answered by proud and sincere assurances that indeed all these good things exist and are honoured in styles of government as different as my Soviet Union, my China, my Spain, my Egypt, my Cuba, my Ghana, my Northern Ireland, or my South Africa. Even if precise meanings can be attached to these words, they are too important as symbols of prestige to be readily conceded. Publicists would perhaps do better simply to defend the activity of politics itself. For it is a very much more precise thing than is commonly supposed; it is essential to genuine freedom; it is unknown in any but advanced and complex societies; and it has specific origins only found in European experience. It is something to be valued almost as a pearl beyond price in the history of the human condition, though, in fact, to overvalue it can be to destroy it utterly.

Perhaps there is something to be said for writing in praise of an activity which seems so general that few people can feel any great passion to appropriate it, or to nationalize it, as the exclusive property of any one group of men or of any particular programme of government.

It is Aristotle who first states what should be recognized as the fundamental, elementary proposition of any possible political science. He is, as it were, the anthropologist who first characterizes and distinguishes what still appears to be a unique invention or discovery of the Greek world. At one point in the second book of his *Politics*, where he examines and criticizes schemes for ideal states, he says that Plato in his *Republic* makes the mistake of trying to reduce everything in the *polis* (or the political type of state) to a unity; rather it is the case that: "there is a point at which a *polis*, by advancing in unity, will cease to be a *polis*: there is another point, short of that, at which it may still remain a *polis*, but will none the less come near to losing its essence, and will thus be a worse *polis*. It is as if you were to turn harmony into mere unison, or to reduce a theme to a single beat. The truth is that the *polis* is an aggregate of many members."[1] Politics arises then, according to great Aristotle, in organized states which recognize themselves to be an aggregate of many members, not a single tribe, religion, interest, or tradition. Politics arises from accepting the fact of the simultaneous existence of different groups, hence different interests and different traditions, within a territorial unit under a common rule. It does not matter much how that unit came to be—by custom, conquest, or geographical circumstance. What does matter is that its social structure, unlike some primitive societies, is sufficiently complex and divided to make politics a plausible response to the problem of governing it, the problem of maintaining order at all. But the establishing of political order is not just any order at all; it marks the birth, or the recognition, of freedom. For politics represents at least some tolerance of differing truths, some recognition that government is possible, indeed best conducted, amid the open canvassing of rival interests. Politics are the public actions of free men. Freedom is the privacy of men from public actions.

Common usage of the word might encourage one to think that politics is a real force in every organized state. But a moment's reflection should reveal that this common usage can be highly misleading. For politics, as Aristotle points out, is only one possible solution to the problem of order. It is by no means the most usual. Tyranny is the most obvious alternative—the rule of one strong man in his own interest; and oligarchy is the next most obvious alternative—the rule of one group in their own interest. The method of rule of the tyrant and the oligarch is quite simply to clobber, coerce, or overawe all or most of these other groups in the interest of their own. The political method of rule is to listen to these other groups so as to conciliate them as far as possible, and to give them a legal position, a sense of security, some clear and reasonably safe means of articulation, by which these other groups can and will speak freely. Ideally politics draws all these groups into each other so that they each and together can make a positive contribution towards the general business of government, the maintaining of order. The different ways in which this can be done are obviously many, even in any one particular circumstance of competing social interests; and in view of the many different states and changes of circumstance there have been, are, and will be, possible variations on the theme of political rule appear to be infinite. But, however imperfectly this process of deliberate conciliation works, it is nevertheless radically different from tyranny, oligarchy, kingship, dictatorship, despotism, and—what is probably the only distinctively modern type of rule—totalitarianism.

Certainly it may sometimes seem odd, in the light of contemporary usage, to say that there is no politics in totalitarian or tyrannical régimes. To some it would be clearer to assert that while there is plainly some politics in all systems of government, yet some systems of government are themselves political systems: they function by or for politics. But usage does not destroy real

distinctions. And this distinction has a great tradition behind it.[2] When Chief Justice Fortescue in the mid fifteenth century said that England was both *dominium politicum et regale*, he meant that the King could declare law only by the consultation and consent of Parliament, although he was absolute in power to enforce the law and to defend the realm. But a régime purely *regale* or royal would not be *politicum* at all. In the early modern period "polity" or "mixed government," that is the Aristotelean blending of the aristocratic with the democratic principle, were terms commonly used in contrast both to tyranny or despotism and to "democracy"—even when democracy was just a speculative fear, or a theoretical extension of what might happen if all men acted like the Anabaptists or the Levellers. In the eighteenth century in England "politics" was commonly contrasted to the principle of "establishment." Politicians were people who challenged the established order of Crown, Court, and Church; and they challenged it in a peculiar way, not by the Palace intrigues of despotism, but by trying to create clear issues of policy *and* by making them public. Politicians were people, whether high-minded like Pitt the Elder, or low-minded like Jack Wilkes, who tried to assert the power of "the public" and "the people" (in reality, of course, always publics and peoples) against what Dr. Johnson called "the powers by law established." The term was pejorative. The Tory squires called the Whig magnates "politicians" because they enlisted the help of people like Wilkes; and the "big Whigs" themselves regarded people like Wilkes as politicians because he made use of "the mob," or rather the skilled urban workers. So being political in fact usually meant recognizing a wider "constituency," than did the powers-that-be of the moment, whom it was felt to be necessary to consult if government was to be effectively conducted, not in the past, but in the present which was the emerging future.

So in trying to understand the many forms of government that there are, of which political rule is only one, it is particularly easy to mistake rhetoric for theory. To say that all governing involves politics is either rhetoric or muddle. Why call, for instance, a struggle for power "politics" when it is simply a struggle for power? Two or more factions within a single party, or the clients of two great men, struggle for a monopoly of power: there may be no political or constitutional procedures whatever to contain this struggle, or powerful enough to do so, and the contestants will regard any compromise as a pure tactic or breathing-space on the way to the complete victory of one faction and the suppression of the other. Certainly there is a sense in which, even in a tyranny or totalitarian regime, politics exists up to the moment when the ruler finds himself free to act alone. While he is not free to act alone, while he is forced to consult other people whom he regards as his enemies, either through necessity or through a temporary ignorance of their real power, he is in some kind of a political relationship. But it is essentially fragile and unwanted. The ruler will not, nor may anyone else, regard it as normal, even if it could be shown that it is perennial. Politics is then regarded simply as an obstacle—and, in a sense, it is an obstacle, but it may not be an at all secure or effective one. Some politics may exist in unfree régimes, but it is unwanted—a measure to their rulers of inadequate progress towards unity; and every effort will be made to keep such disputes secret from the ruled, to prevent the formation of a "public." For Palace politics is private politics, almost a contradiction in terms. The unique character of political activity lies, quite literally, in its publicity.

There is no need, then, to deny that elements of politics can exist in tyrannical and other régimes—rather the contrary. Sophocles makes this point in the *Antigone*:

CREON: Then she is not breaking the law?

HAEMON: Your fellow-citizens would deny it, to a man.

CREON: And the *polis* proposes to teach me how to rule?

HAEMON: Ah. Who is it that's talking like a boy now?

CREON: Can any voice but mine give orders in this *polis*?

HAEMON: It is no *polis* if it takes orders from one voice.

CREON: But custom gives possession to the ruler.

HAEMON: You'd rule a desert beautifully alone.

Suppose I had made my point less strongly by rendering *polis* as simply "city"; we would still see a word being contested for by two different theories of government—call it "civil society" or "political society." Both claim that their theory is inherent in the concept—the primacy of autocracy or citizenship respectively.

And which is the more realistic? The great hope for the political way of Haemon is that it is, in the long run, a more workable way of maintaining order than the one Creon chose or stuck to. Politics thus arises from a recognition of restraints. The character of this recognition may be moral, but more often it is simply prudential, a recognition of the power of social groups and interests, a product of being unable, without more violence and risk than one can stomach, to rule alone. (An anti-political moral heroine like Antigone may arouse the city, but it is the power of the city that counts. Creon is a bad man to refuse to let her bury her rebel brother, but he is a bad ruler because he does not allow for the power of the city on this issue.) It is, of course, often possible to rule alone. But it is always highly difficult and highly dangerous. "To make a desert and to call it peace" is not impossible, nor is it uncommon. But fortunately most ordinary politicians realize the incalculability of violence, and do not always need to wreck the State in learning this lesson.

Politics, then, can be simply defined as the activity by which differing interests within a given unit of rule are conciliated by giving them a share in power in proportion to their importance to the welfare and the survival of the whole community. And, to complete the formal definition, a political system is that type of government where politics proves successful in ensuring reasonable stability and order. Aristotle attempted to argue that these compromises of politics must in some sense be creative of future benefits—that each exists for a further purpose. But it is probably wiser to keep what we want to defend as simple as possible and simply to point out that no finality is implied in any act of conciliation or compromise. Each compromise has at least served some purpose, teleological or not, if at the time it is made it enables orderly government to be carried on at all. Orderly government is, after all, a civilized value compared to anarchy or arbitrary rule; and political government, other things being equal, clearly remains more acceptable to more people if they are ever given any chance or choice in the matter. Advocates of particular political doctrines—as will be seen—should beware of denying the context in which their doctrines can operate politically: their claims can never be exclusive. The political process is not tied to any particular doctrine. Genuine political doctrines, rather, are the attempt to find particular and workable solutions to this perpetual and shifty problem of conciliation.

Why cannot a good ruler do this, without all the muddle and certainty of politics?—it will always be asked. When the academic is asked this question by an ordinary person in urgency or innocence, he coughs and blushes, feels that he is meant to utter a platitude and tries to remember correctly Lord Acton's words about all power corrupting. Aristotle, however, took this as a perfectly serious issue of principle. If there was a "perfectly just man" he should, by right and reason, be made king (just as we *should* obey any party which could prove that it knows which way the iron laws of history are unfolding for our future benefit). This for some is at least a theoretical possibility—and an interesting one. There is no similar hope for an absolute justification of political rule. The answer is a practical one; Aristotle thinks, not surprisingly, that such a man is not very likely to be found. We have no particular need to take his word for that when faced with our own modern gallery of moralistic autocrats, dictators promising the moon and various "fathers of their people." Many of these men are not, in any ordinary sense, bad men; but few, to put it mildly, could be described as "perfectly good." And to Aristotle the slightest flaw will disqualify one, will put one in need of some restraint. It was only the *perfectly* good man who would not need to listen to his fellows, who would not need to have rival powers so firmly entrenched that he has to listen. Indeed, he remarks that the man who can live outside the *polis* is either a beast or a god. God is the only possible being who does not need to consult, having no fellows; God is the only possible being whose command is identical with law and justice. Aristotle's sometime pupil, Alexander, had to try to become a god in order to solve the problem of finding the authority—and hence the power—to rule, not merely conquer, diverse types of *polis*, indeed whole empires which had never known politics at all. Plato's philosopher king, in the parable of the *Republic*, after all his intense scientific training, has to undergo a mystical experience of illumination or conversion, an utter change of quality, before he is fit to rule the ideal state. The Caesars were to find deification a practical response to the problem of authority in consolidating an empire gained by conquest. And the notion of descent from God has been typical of Oriental and of pre-Hispanic American empires (an "imperium" or empire being kingship which aspires to govern men of different histories and cultures, and thus has need of a greater authority than can stem from custom alone). The utility of such a notion for rulers is less surprising than the willingness of many followers, even in our own times, to treat their leaders as if they were God: the declarer of the law, the one above criticism, above the need to consult, the only truly self-sufficient man.

Politics, then, to Aristotle, was something natural, not of divine origin, simply the "master science" among men. Politics was the master-science not in the sense that it includes or explains all other "sciences" (all skills, social activities, and group interests), but in that it gives them some priority, some order in their rival claims on the always scarce resources of any given community. The way of establishing these priorities is by allowing the right institutions to develop by which the various "sciences" can demonstrate their actual importance in the common task of survival. Politics are, as it were, the market place and the price mechanism of all social demands—though there is no guarantee that a just price will be struck; and there is nothing spontaneous about politics—it depends on deliberate and continuous individual activity.

Now it is often thought that for this "master science" to function, there must be already in existence some shared idea of a "common good," some "consensus" or *consensus juris*. But this common good is itself the process of practical reconciliation of the interests of the various "sciences," aggregates, or groups which compose a state; it is not some external and intangible spiritual adhesive, or some allegedly objective "general will" or "public interest." These are misleading and pretentious explanations of how a community holds together; worse, they can even be justifications for the sudden destruction of some elements in the community in favour of others—there is no right to obstruct the general will, it is said. But diverse groups hold together, firstly, because they have a common interest in sheer survival and, secondly, because they practise politics—not because they agree about "fundamentals," or some such concept too vague, too personal, or too divine ever to do the job of politics for it. The moral consensus of a free state is not something mysteriously prior to or above politics: it is the activity (the civilizing activity) of politics itself.

Now, of course, our aspirations and actions will be sadly disembodied spirits if they cannot go beyond a mere appreciation of what politics is all about. We shall all want to do something with it.

Those who sit tight and drift, murmuring incantations which did not wreck us yesterday, are apt to be cast away on hostile shores. Those who urge us to remember that our only clearly demonstrable task is simply to keep the ship afloat have a rather curious view of the purpose of ships. Even if there is no single predetermined port of destination, clearly all directions are still not equally preferable. "What politics is" does not destroy or exhaust the question "What do we want to get out of it?" But we may not go about trying to get what we want in a political manner at all.

For politics is to be seen neither as a set of fixed principles to be realized in the near future, nor yet as a set of traditional habits to be preserved, but as an activity, a sociological activity which has the anthropological function of preserving a community grown too complicated for either tradition alone or pure arbitrary rule to preserve it without the undue use of coercion. Burke's aphorism about the need to reform in order to preserve is a characterization of the political method of rule far more profound than that of those conservatives who hold that politics is simply a communication received from tradition.

Politics is, then, an *activity*—and this platitude must be brought to life: it is not a thing, like a natural object or a work of art, which could exist if individuals did not continue to act upon it. And it is a *complex activity*; it is not simply the grasping for an ideal, for then the ideals of others may be threatened; but it is not pure self-interest either, simply because the more realistically one construes self-interest the more one is involved in relationships with others, and because, after all, some men in most part, most men in some part, have certain standards of conduct which do not always fit circumstances too exactly. The more one is involved in relationships with others, the more conflicts of interest, or of character and circumstance, will arise. These conflicts, when personal, create the activity we call "ethics" (or else that type of action, as arbitrary as it is irresponsible, called "selfish"); and such conflicts, when public, create political activity (or else some type of rule in the selfish interest of a single group).

Consider another human *activity*, almost as famous as politics—something which is again neither an implementation of principles nor a matter of pure expediency: sexuality. They are both activities in which the tacit understanding of presuppositions often makes more formal propositions unnecessary; the sympathies that are a product of experience are better than the doctrines that are learnt from books. Sexuality, granted, is a more widespread activity than politics, but again the suspicion remains that the man who can live without either is either acting the beast or aping the god. Both have much the same character of necessity in essence and unpredictability in form. Both are activities which must be carried on if the community is to perpetuate itself at all, both serve this wider purpose, and yet both can become enjoyable ends in themselves for any one individual. Both activities can be repeated in an almost infinite variety of forms and different circumstances; and yet in both, the activity often becomes attached to a quite arbitrary or fortuitous individual instance, which we then proceed to treat as if that he or she, or Fatherland or Motherland, were the most perfect example ever found of the whole great enterprise. And both are activities in which the range of possible conduct is far greater than any conceivably desirable range of actual conduct. Both are activities in which the human group maintains itself amid the utmost variations in, for the actors involved, success and failure, tragedy and joy, passion and prudence, and in those dialectic syntheses more often domestic and familiar. Politics, then, like sexuality is an activity which must be carried on; one does not create it or decide to join in—one simply becomes more and more aware that one is involved in it as part of the human condition. One can only forsake, renounce, or do without it by doing oneself (which can easily be done—and on the highest principles) unnatural injury. To renounce or destroy politics is to destroy the very thing which gives order to the pluralism and variety of civilized society, the thing which enables us to enjoy variety without suffering either anarchy or the tyranny of single truths, which become the desperate salvation from anarchy—just as misogamy and celibacy are forms of salvation for the overly passionate mind.

For political rule must be preceded by public order just as love must be preceded by social acquaintance and contained by social conventions. Politics and love are the only forms of constraint possible between free people. Rule or government preserve and often even create communities. "Electoral representation," "liberty," "rights" and even, or especially—as we will see, "democracy" are specific and subsequent achievements of a civilization which has already established order and constraint in a known territory. Those who glibly say that all government is based on consent, as if that settles anything, are being as passionately vague as those who say, for instance, that all love must be based on the absolute freedom of the partners in love. If there were absolute freedom, there could be no love; if there is absolute consent, there could be no government. But people have every right to say that all government is based on consent, and there may be no harm in their saying so, so long as the small word "all" is taken seriously. For this shows us that the assertion can have little to do with any possible distinction between freedom and oppression—the most absolute tyrant must have his faithful dogs around him.

And equally the word "government" must be taken seriously and recognized for what it is: the organization of a group of men in a given community for survival. Thomas Hobbes, after all, spent a great deal of time arguing the massively simple point that if one does not survive, there is no knowing whether one has made the right choice. But there are good grounds for thinking that politics is often a more effective way of ensuring survival than the absolute rule of Leviathan. Whether Leviathan is a monarch, a dictator, a party, or a "nation in arms," he is apt to be a pretty clumsy fellow who has few reliable ways of knowing what is really going on (representative electoral institutions, for instance, seem a fairly good way by which a government can find out what people will do and what they will stand for). But this ignorance on the part of autocracy only arises because one part of survival is a continuous process of adaptation to complicated social changes, economic and technological; this need to consult cannot eliminate the other type of survival which is military, or at least militant, the capacity to act without compromise or normal consultation in a state of emergency, whether flood, famine, pestilence, or war itself. Leviathan must be there already—he cannot be created in a hurry, but he is the guarantor of politics, neither the single leader nor the negation. His authority, like that of the two Dictators of Republican Rome, ceases with the end of the emergency. *Quis custodiet custodes*? Who, indeed, shall guard the guardians? There is, perhaps it should be simply said, no possible general answer to this question. History is rich with experiment and examples, some relatively successful, some complete failures. Only the problem is clear enough. As Lincoln put it amid the agony of Civil War: "It has long been a grave question whether any government not too strong for the liberties of its people, can be strong enough to maintain its liberties in great emergencies."

The guardians may, indeed, try to carry on ruling the country after the end of the emergency or, more often, by prolonging the emergency—if they can get away with it. There is no possible "right" of revolution to check this, as John Locke tried to argue: revolution is the destruction of a particular order of rights. But, thinking in sociological rather than legal terms, Locke had an obvious point; there may come a time when people are driven to rebel by the failure of a government to govern politically at all. The state of emergency is the time of sovereignty—when all power has to go to and to come from one source, if the community is to survive at all. "Those republics," wrote Machiavelli, "which in time of danger cannot resort to a dictatorship will generally be ruined when grave occasions occur." But in normal times in some fortunate states the "sovereignty" of governments is a very formal abstract thing compared to the reality of politics. Hobbes's *Leviathan* saw government as a perpetual state of emergency. Hobbes may have been frightened in the womb by the guns of the Spanish Armada, and he may have thought sixty years later that there was nothing more terrible than Englishmen killing Englishmen in civil war, but that is no excuse for not studying, as Machiavelli did, the problem of how to maintain a state through time (which is a problem of spreading power), as well as how to preserve it in crisis (which is a problem of concentrating power). Surely we have less excuse. Some modern states in times of infinitely greater threat have been able to preserve politics, even to recreate it, as even in part of Germany where for a generation it was wiped out with a unique and deliberate fury. "The secret of liberty is courage," as Pericles declaimed. It is not a very safe world anyhow. Free men stick their necks out.

Even with luck and courage, we must not hope for too much from politics, or believe that we see it everywhere. It can exist only where it has been preceded by sovereignty or where sovereignty can be quickly called into being. So if politics, to be a stable and possible method of rule, requires some settled order, as well as tolerance and diversity, then the relationships between states themselves can be seen at their best only as a kind of quasi-politics. The will to conciliate and compromise may actually be stronger at times in international relations simply because it is more difficult to calculate whether one is powerful enough to ignore diplomacy, than it is to know whether one can govern unpolitically in a single, settled country. But the possibility of politicizing an established order is largely absent simply because there is no established order—only a speculative and doubtful common interest in peace, or some more certain, but more abstract, moral fact of human brotherhood. The agony of international relations is the need to try to practise politics without the basic conditions for political order. The "cold war" would not have surprised Hobbes, for he defined "War" simply as "time men live without common power to keep them all in awe." International society was no society at all, but simply the state of nature—war. For "the nature of War consisteth not in actual fighting, but in the known disposition thereto, during all the time there is no assurance to the contrary." And there are no assurances to the contrary, outside the realm of a particular sovereign or "common power." This I take to be the case of "international politics." One wishes it were otherwise, but it is not. Certainly diplomacy and politics have much in common: the urge to conciliate and act prudently are much alike, indeed can be, as we have said, actually stronger in diplomacy. But in diplomacy the basic fact of order is lacking. Even in times of emergency, of threat to what international order there is, there may not be a clearly superior and effective power. In a territorial society, government makes politics possible; but in an international "society," politics (or rather diplomacy) has to try to make any even minimal government or order possible. Political maxims and experience (even though as aspirations and not an established activity) will be some help in international problems. Clearly, for instance, a country powerful enough to threaten world peace cannot be permanently excluded from any institution which even purports to be concerned with world order. But genuine politics remains an ideal in international relations. Distinctions can be in fact drawn. The United Nations Organization is not, for instance, a political assembly because it is not a sovereign assembly. There are, strictly speaking, no politicians at the United Nations; there are only "statesmen" and "ambassadors" who are mere delegates of bodies regarded as sovereign. Unlike politicians, they cannot settle issues of government among themselves; they depend upon instructions. For the politician is not a delegate; the politician has power to act in conjunction with other politicians; his power is limited by acceptance of periodic elections, but is not bound by daily instructions. Where government is impossible, politics is impossible. Once again, distinctions can in fact be drawn. Everything is not politics. Struggles for power are struggles for power. And the task of diplomacy is a somewhat different task from that of politics. Certainly it can be a universal activity among states—whereas politics is not a universal activity even within states. Let us defend politics, then, as an actual activity without thinking that so-called international politics is more than, at the best, a kind of aspirant, quasi-politics.

Similarly, common usage may encourage us to talk about politics in the small group—in the trade union, in the office, and even in the family; and anthropologists find that many tribal societies are more "political" and less "autocratic" than once supposed. Some social scientists, perhaps being a little too clever, make quite a song and dance about "the politics of small groups." They hope by studying the microcosm to understand the macrocosm. But the difference is not just one of scale: a valuable qualitative distinction is lost. If all discussion, conflict, rivalry, struggle, and even conciliation is called politics, then it is forgotten, once more, that politics depends on some settled order. Small groups are subordinate parts of that order. They may help to create politics, but their internal behaviour is not political simply because their individual function is quite different from that of the state itself. And, unlike the state, they have no acknowledged legal right to use force if all else fails.

If the argument is, then, that politics is simply the activity by which government is made possible when differing interests in an area to be governed grow powerful enough to need to be conciliated, the obvious objection will be: "why do certain interests have to be conciliated?" And the answer is, of course, that they do not have to be. Other paths are always open. Politics is simply when they are conciliated—that solution to the problem of order which chooses conciliation rather than violence and coercion, and chooses it as an effective way by which varying interests can discover that level of compromise best suited to their common interest in survival. Politics allows various types of power within a community to find some reasonable level of mutual tolerance and support. Coercion (or secession or migration) need arise only when one group or interest feels that it has no common interest in survival with the rest. Put at its most obvious, most men would simply agree that coercion needs justification: conciliation justifies itself if it works. There may not be any absolute justification of politics. Let us be brazen and simply say, "We prefer politics." But such modesty had better be somewhat truculent. For it is, after all, too hard (indeed perverse) to respect the morality and wisdom of any who, when politics is possible, refuse to act politically.

Political rule, then, because it arises from the problem of diversity, and does not try to reduce all things to a single unity, necessarily creates or allows some freedom. Political freedom is a response to a need of government— it is not, as so many sentimentally think, an external impetus that somehow forces, or persuades, governments to act tolerantly. The freedom of a group will be established at the moment when its power or its existence cannot be denied and must be reckoned with in governing a country as it actually is. The American Revolution took place, for instance, not because people suddenly became super-sensitive to their rights, or—an even more unlikely theory— because they suddenly became nationalistic, but because the existing government broke down. The British Government had failed to recognize the peculiar interests and the peculiar character of the colonies which it suddenly tried to govern, with the Stamp Act of 1765, after a long century of what Burke had called "wise and salutary neglect." And it failed to recognize their interests because they were not represented. If they were "virtually represented" in Parliament, this was in numbers so few compared to their real power and commercial importance that they were not taken seriously until too late, until they had been driven into revolutionary violence. Political representation is, then, a device of government before ever it can be sensibly viewed as a "right" of the governed. If it is not made use of, a government may not be able to govern at all—unless it is willing to practise coercion and to suffer fear to the degree that it is ignorant of the interests of the governed. Almost any system of representation, however ramshackle, incomplete, and at times even corrupt, is better than none; and is better than one that will represent only an alleged single interest of the governed. The English Reform Bills of 1832 and 1867 did not take place because old Whig

gentlemen in Westminster suddenly became convinced, out of some movement in abstract ideas, that those Radical fellows were morally right, but because it became increasingly clear that government could not be carried on in an industrialized society unless the power and existence first of the entrepreneur and then of the skilled manual worker were recognized and represented.

"Politics," then, simply summarizes an activity whose history is a mixture of accident and deliberate achievement, and whose social basis is to be found only in quite complicated societies. It is not as such motivated by principle, except in a dislike of coercion which can, in turn, be simply thought to be a matter of prudence. (To debate too hotly the rival integrity of different motives which lead to the same action is academic—either political folly or the luxury of an already established political order.) Political principles are, whatever they are, principles held within politics. Now the holding of political principles or doctrines, at some level, with some degree of consistency, seems quite inevitable for any but the beast or the god—and why not? There is a touch of doctrinaire absurdity in those conservatives who would argue that all political doctrines become doctrinaire. A political doctrine is only doctrinaire, firstly, if it refuses to recognize the power and existence of other forces and ideas within an established political order; or, secondly—and more obviously—when it seeks to argue that some of these groups must be eliminated urgently, illegally, and unpolitically if other great benefits are to follow. Political doctrines must, in fact, be genuinely political (Marxism, for instance, as we shall see, is clearly and explicitly an anti-political doctrine).

A political doctrine I take to be simply a coherently related set of proposals for the conciliation of actual social demands in relation to a scarcity of resources. As such, a political doctrine should make short shrift with the old and barren academic controversy over "fact" and "value"— for it is necessarily both evaluative and predictive. For a political doctrine always offers some generalizations about the nature of actual, or possible, political societies, but it always also offers some grounds, however disputable, for thinking some such possibilities desirable. By prediction I do not mean something that is necessarily measurable as in natural science, but merely something that guides our present actions according to our expectations of what will happen in the future (or, of course, of what we shall find in the past). And it is evaluative not merely because all thought is an act of selection from a potentially infinite range of relevant factors, but because we do in fact seek to justify some act of selection as in some way significant. A political doctrine will state some purpose, but it will claim to be a realizable purpose; or it may state some sociological generalization. But argument, if not analysis, will always reveal some ethical significance in wanting this relationship to be true, or to remain true. A political doctrine is thus just an attempt to strike a particular harmony in an actual political situation, one harmony out of many possible different (temporary) resolutions of the basic problem of unity and diversity in a society with complex and entrenched rival social interests. This problem is the germ of politics and freedom.

Some freedom, at least, must exist wherever there is political rule. For politics is a process of discussion, and discussion demands, in the original Greek sense, dialectic. For discussion to be genuine and fruitful when something is maintained, the opposite or some contrary case must be considered or—better—maintained by someone who believes it. The hall-mark of free government everywhere, it is an old but clear enough test, is whether public criticism is allowed in a manner conceivably effective—in other words, whether opposition is tolerated. Politics needs men who will act freely, but men cannot act freely without politics. Politics is a way of ruling divided societies without undue violence—and most societies are divided, though some think that that is the very trouble. We can do much worse than honour "mere politics" so we must examine very carefully the claims of those who would do better.

Reading Notes

1. Aristotle: The Politics, trans. by Sir Ernest Barker (London: Oxford University Press, 1981–82), p. 51.

2. See further "Semantic Digression" in the first Appendix, in Bernard R. Crick, In Defence of Politics (Chicago: University of Chicago Press, 1972), pp. 168–69.

KEY TERMS

Authoritative Allocation of Values   This phrase, coined by David Easton, refers to the binding decisions made by a government to distribute scarce resources.

Authority   The ability to command. It is vested in individuals by virtue of their office.

Charismatic Authority   Authority based on the extraordinary qualities and mission of the charismatic leader. Legitimacy of this authority is possible because the followers believe in that mission and those qualities.

Legal Authority   The rule of law determines who exercises power. The obedience of the citizens and their acceptance of governmental decisions are due to their loyalty to the constitution.

Legitimacy   The acceptance by citizens of a political system of governmental policies or of a set of public authorities as proper and deserving obedience. Legitimacy is a response to authority.

Political Science   The study of politics, where politics is understood as the process of making binding decisions to allocate scarce resources within the society.

Politics   An activity pertaining to the authoritative allocation of resources. Power and conflict are embedded in the activity of politics.

Power   The ability of a person to make others do something that they might not otherwise do.

Traditional Authority   Authority (power) based on the inheritance of position such as a hereditary monarchy; a system legitimated by the sanction and prestige of tradition.

FURTHER READINGS

Dahl, Robert. *Modern Political Analysis*. Englewood Cliffs, NJ: Prentice Hall, 1991.

Lasswell, Harold D. *Politics, Who Gets What, When and How*. New York: Peter Smith, 1950.

Waldo, Dwight. "Political Science: Tradition, Discipline, Profession, Science, Enterprise." In *Handbook of Political Science*, edited by I. Fred Greenstein. Reading, MA: Addison-Wesley, 1975.

WEB LINKS

Research Political Science at the World's Largest Online Library:
www.questia.com/Index.jsp?CRID=political_science&OFFID=se1

Search the 32-volume Encyclopaedia Britannica:
www.britannica.com

Verstehen-Max Weber's Home Page:
www.faculty.rsu.edu/~felwell/Theorists/Weber/Whome.htm

CHAPTER 2

CONTENDING APPROACHES

Political science is a divided discipline. Political scientists use a variety of often contending approaches to study politics; that is, they have different assumptions, focuses, concepts, and perspectives. In this chapter, we will discuss the most important of these approaches and point out their strengths and weaknesses. We will begin by looking at the formal-legal approach that dominated political science before World War II. We then explain how criticism of that approach led behaviouralism, aimed at making political science more scientific, and describe two approaches that developed from this movement: systems analysis and structural-functionalism. We follow with a review of the political culture and political economy approaches. The chapter continues with a discussion of two recent and very popular approaches: rational choice and new institutionalism. It concludes with a presentation of two "critical" and more controversial approaches: feminism and postmodernism. Prior to the 1950s, political science was dominated by the formal-legal approach, retrospectively called the "old institutionalism," which centred on the formal institutions of politics: constitutions, parliaments, cabinets, bureaucracies, and so on. It described the workings of the state through an exploration of the structure of these institutions and their relationships with one another. For example, political scientists using this approach examined the interactions between the executive and legislative branches of the state; they conducted detailed analysis of constitutional documents; and they looked into the role of the head of state in a political system. In short, the formal-legal approach sought to explain politics by specifying how political institutions worked.

This approach came under criticism in the 1950s.[1] It was deemed to be weak for five reasons. First, it was descriptive rather than explanatory as it did not substantially address the issue of *why* institutions worked the way they did. Second, the formal-legal approach was criticized for being atheoretical, that is, for not looking to formulate generalizations. Third, its focus on institutions led to a narrow view of politics. In other words, critics argued that understanding politics, as well as being able to explain and put forward generalizations, involved turning away from institutions to focus instead on society and political actors. A fourth criticism of the formal-legal approach held that it simply led to the description of particular case studies and was therefore non-comparative. Finally, this approach was also criticized for being parochial; that is, for looking almost exclusively at Western developed countries as opposed to non-Western and developing ones. Here again, the focus on institutions was seen as the major culprit since, in the context of the 1950s, political scientists could not find, in many parts of the world, institutional frameworks they could recognize, let alone deal with.

In reaction to the formal-legal approach and its perceived failures, a new way of thinking about and practising political science developed, called behaviouralism. The central objective of the behaviouralist movement was to make the study of politics truly scientific. This task involved formulating general theories for political outcomes and phenomena through systematic, often large-scale, comparisons and the use of quantitative methods. In this context, the emphasis was put on individual actors and, more specifically, their behaviour, rather than institutions. Two approaches, systems analysis and structural-functionalism, were developed in the 1960s and proved very influential; they took from behaviouralism a commitment toward the formulation of general theories and models, and a distaste for the particularism involved in institutional analysis.

SYSTEMS ANALYSIS

The first approach devised to make political science more scientific and more theoretical consisted of viewing politics as a system. This approach, simply called "systems analysis" or "systems theory" was developed primarily by David Easton.[2] **Systems analysis** represented a break with earlier work in political science for at least three reasons. First, it focused on political actors rather than on institutions. Second, it provided a theoretical model of politics, that is, a simplified representation of political life that specified its logic and detailed its workings. Third, this model was said to be general. In other words, systems analysis was presented as being valid for understanding politics in virtually any country at almost any time.

The heart of systems analysis is, of course, the concept of system. For Easton, a system involves the interrelation of individual components. As such, it represents a whole, but only in a minimalist fashion: it is the sum of its parts, no more, no less. A political system, Easton argued, is constituted by interactions that lead to the "authoritative allocation of values" where values can take many different forms: material (financial and other) as well as symbolic (prestige, recognition, etc.). This is Easton's famous definition of politics. The political system exists within an environment. This "environment" also comprises systems. More specifically, there are two types of systems in the political system's environment: intrasocietal and extrasocietal. The distinction roughly follows the dichotomy between domestic and international politics. Intrasocietal systems include other domestic systems: economic systems, cultural systems, and ideological systems. Extrasocietal systems lie outside the realm of domestic politics and include the international political system and the international economic system.

The key principle behind systems analysis is equilibrium. The political system is self-adjusting; it continuously seeks to maintain a balance and, when disturbed, moves to recapture an equilibrium. At the heart of this equilibrium are input and output mechanisms.[3] Inputs take the form of demands or support. Demands are claims for money, services, recognition, moral values, etc. They are often conflictual and in competition, which means political systems need to filter demands and select the most worthy. Supports are inputs of loyalty toward the system; they strengthen the legitimacy of the filtering process, thereby enabling the system to manage demands and maintain an equilibrium. These inputs are transformed into outputs by a "black box" of governmental institutions. Outputs are the decisions, actions, and policies of political authorities. When they are considered satisfactory by society, they come back as inputs in the form of feedback. When they are considered unsatisfactory, they add to the demand side of the inputs.

Systems analysis aspired to provide political science with an approach that could be used to study politics in all societies in a scientific manner. Indeed, systems analysis brought to the discipline attributes of generality, consistency, and universality. However, it has, by and large, fallen out of favour with political scientists. Four main criticisms have been directed at this approach. First, it has often been said that systems analysis, in an attempt to get away from the old institutionalism and its focus on political institutionalism, has completely evacuated the state from political analysis and therefore misses an important element of politics. Indeed, Easton was very reluctant to use concepts such as the state, institutions, or even government. Systems analysis does not explain the conversion of inputs into outputs; we know only that it occurs in an institutional "black box" whose workings are not explored. Second, this approach gives the impression that politics takes place in the context of a classless society. This comment, which has been made most forcefully by neo-Marxist scholars, suggests that systems analysis gives a rosy and unrealistic picture of politics in industrialized societies. Third, the model generated by systems analysis is fairly static. The political system shows a strong bias toward equilibrium; it can change but only incrementally, that is, through small adjustments. For this reason, political scientists have argued that it is fundamentally unable to deal with political change, especially in its most radical and dramatic forms. Finally, many critics of systems analysis have argued that it is not explanatory in nature. They suggest that it does not shed light on the fundamental workings of politics, but rather simply gives a new terminology to *describe* (not explain) the political process.

STRUCTURAL-FUNCTIONALISM

Structural-functionalism was popularized in the 1960s by another American political scientist, Gabriel Almond.[4] Functionalist approaches to politics and society were not developed in this decade; they had been present in the work of social scientists from earlier generations (for example, Talcott Parsons, Robert Merton, and Emile Durkheim), but Almond made structural-functionalism one of the foremost approaches to politics during the 1960s and 1970s.

Much like systems analysis, **structural-functionalism** views politics and social life in systemic terms: a political system coexists with other types of systems. However, the theory states that the structures of politics (formal institutions, rules, practices, etc.) exist because they have a social function. In other words, social needs determine the structure of politics. Consequently, explaining these structures requires an understanding of the social roles they play. Almond identified seven functions found in every political system: political socialization, interest articulation, interest aggregation, political communication, rule making, rule application, and rule adjudication.

The analogy most frequently drawn when considering the political system from a structural-functionalism perspective is to human life. Medical scientists understand the workings of the human body through the complex interaction of its vital organs. They posit that each of these organs needs to adequately perform a certain function for the body to survive. Similarly, structural-functionalism suggests that politics and society hold together because their different parts are performing vital functions. Politics is therefore an organic whole; it cannot be reduced to the sum of its parts, and altering or removing a part necessarily leads to fundamental changes for the whole. This is quite different from Easton's more mechanistic systems analysis, where political components can be changed and removed without fundamentally affecting the political system.

As was the case with systems analysis, structural-functionalism proved attractive to many political scientists because it offered an elegant, straightforward view of politics. Also, because it was not tied to any particular institutional design, it could be used to study politics in developing as well as developed countries. Indeed, structural-functionalists argued that institutions were country-specific, but that functions were universal. However, structural-functionalism is criticized for the same reason as systems analysis is. Critics state that the explanatory power of each approach is poor. Critics of structural-functionalism also suggest that its proponents produce a list of functions (enumerated above) and then, predictably, justify the existence of structures by relating them to the different functions. There is, in this criticism, the idea that structural-functionalism presupposes a meaning to action; political and social actors need to behave a certain way because they are fulfilling a particular function. Structural-functionalism has also been criticized for hiding or forgetting class and other cleavages and for a bias toward stability and the status quo.

POLITICAL CULTURE

Gabriel Almond, along with his co-writer Sidney Verba, was also a central figure in the articulation of a **political culture** approach. The idea behind this approach is that political systems can be explained by a society's culture. The research questions that prompted the development of the political culture approach centred on democracy. As the colonies in Asia and Africa became independent after World War II, and as most of the early post-colonization governments were authoritarian, political scientists began thinking about democracy in these societies. Some suggested that democracy was linked to certain norms, values, beliefs, and attitudes toward power, politics, personal behaviour, and life in society. These factors, taken together, form political culture. In their analysis of democracy, scholars using the political culture approach have suggested that tolerance, individual freedom, a distrust of political authority, and a belief in the ability of individuals to shape history are the values/attitudes most conducive to democracy.[5] By and large, studies conducted using this approach tend to suggest that these values are stronger in the Western world and weaker, or even absent, elsewhere.

In the North American context, the best known expression of the political culture approach is the so-called fragment theory. In looking to explain American politics, particularly the absence of socialism and the bias toward limited government, historian Louis Hartz suggested that American society should be understood as a transplanted fragment from seventeenth-century Europe. From this perspective, one can account for certain characteristics in U.S. society. For instance, the influence of socialism is marginal in the United States because the industrial revolution occurred in Europe after settlement in the American colony took place, and there is a distrust of government and an attachment to individual freedoms because those who went to America left Europe to escape political arbitrariness and religious persecution.[6] Fragment theory has also been applied to Canada. Here, the traditional-conservative structures of pre-1960 French Canada are explained by the settlement being established before liberal ideas emerged in Europe, while the liberal traditions of English Canada are traced to later waves of immigration, particularly the one that saw British Loyalists coming from the United States.

The political culture approach delves into the cultural and psychological dimension of politics. As such, it brings a different type of insight to the study of politics when compared with approaches that stress institutions, the political process, the economy, etc. However, this emphasis on culture also introduces problems. The first concerns the issue of change. If a society has a particular culture, and if this culture brings specific political outcomes, then how can there be political change? For instance, if African or Asian cultures are deemed not conducive to democracy, what does this mean for democratization in these areas? Political culture scholars could argue that there can be cultural change, which can then lead to political change, but they are generally at pains to explain how cultural change occurs. Second, there is evidence that culture is not the sole determinant of political outcomes. For example, there are stable democracies in societies (Japan, India, Botswana) that do not exhibit the values found in Western societies. Third, political culture approaches can lead to stereotyping and oversimplifications. One example of this danger is the tendency to draw on "national character" to explain politics: Canadians as polite and tolerant, Americans as individualistic, Germans as militaristic, etc. These "national characters" tend to be clichés that leave the analyst with more questions than answers. Finally, it can be misleading to speak of national political cultures because in many states there are arguably regional sub-cultures. In Canada, for example, a good case can be made that political cultures in Quebec, Ontario, the Maritimes, and the West are all fairly different.

POLITICAL ECONOMY

Scholars looking to explain politics can focus on elements other than institutions, the polit-ical process, social functions, or political culture. One option is to look at economic factors and relationships. This is the perspective of the **political economy** approach, which has a long and rich tradition in Canadian political science, as you will see in the excerpt below by Janine Brodie. At the broadest level, political economy is concerned with the relationship between states and markets. It works under the assumption that politics is shaped, or even completely determined, by economics. Some political economists are content to state that the economy is a crucial force in politics, leaving the door open to considering other fac-tors such as institutions and culture; others go further and argue that political relationships are in fact economic relationships.

Political economy as an approach to politics is divided into two branches.[7] The first branch draws from Marx's theory of class conflict, which suggests that in a capitalist economy there are two antagonistic classes, and that these classes are determined by ownership of the means of production. The classes consist of the bourgeoisie, wealthy and powerful merchants and industrialists who control the means of production, and the proletariat, the poor and weak who work for them. The contemporary political economy that rests on Marxist thought suggests that politics is best understood in terms of the inequalities in wealth and power pro-duced by the capitalist economy. It is openly critical of capitalism; in fact, it tends, explicitly or implicitly, to advocate a fundamentally different type of economic system. For example, this branch of political economy will usually see globalization and free trade as favouring the already wealthy and powerful. It also tends to look at issues of uneven development, poverty, and so on. Some of its proponents will include other factors such as gender and culture in their analysis, suggesting that economic classes often overlap with other categories, for example, women and cultural/racial minorities as the poor and the exploited.

The second branch of political economy derives from the work of classical economists such as Adam Smith. Smith suggested that the free market was the best tool of social and economic development. He argued that individuals, whom he described as rational and self-interested, worked for the common good in looking to improve their own condition. The free market, Smith argued, increases collective wealth. Contemporary political economists in this tradition are committed to the market, free trade, and deregulation. They do identify losers and winners from particular economic/financial arrangements, but view capitalism and the market economy as fluid enough to correct, with the occasional help of the state, its worst consequences. As a result, their research questions tend to be geared toward smoothing the workings of the market economy: identifying dysfunctions, proposing improvements, etc. They are interested, much like their neo-Marxist counterparts, in issues of trade, finance, and development, but with a perspective of adjustment rather than radical change.

The political economy approach, in either form, seems increasingly relevant as a tool of analysis of the contemporary world. Indeed, contemporary politics gives an increasingly important place to the market. East European countries have made the transition to market economies; we are witnessing free trade arrangements and economic integration in Europe and the Americas; Western states have, in the last decade, cut spending in order to eliminate deficit and reduce debt; and non-Western states have been encouraged to adopt Western policies by Western countries as well as international trade and financial institutions. However, this focus on the economy to explain politics is also seen as a weakness. Some scholars suggest that politics as a sphere of activity is, at least partially, autonomous from economics. These critics argue that political phenomena are not entirely, nor even primarily, conditioned by economic forces.

RATIONAL CHOICE

The **rational choice** approach is most squarely in line with the behavioural project of making political science truly scientific. First articulated by William Riker,[8] rational choice has become one of the most popular approaches to politics, especially in the United States. At the broadest level, it is committed to seeking the formulation of general value-free laws of politics through the study of individual behaviour. Rational choice has proven very influential in many areas of political science, but particularly in the study of elections, voting, and the formation of party coalitions.

Rational choice theorists assume that individuals are rational, strategic, and self-interested, that they naturally look to maximize their own wealth or power, and that they are constantly making decisions by weighing costs and benefits. They suggest that political actors are players in a game; they are looking to win and will act strategically to achieve the desired outcome. Therefore, from the rational choice perspective, politics is fundamentally about strategic action, and it should be understood as the aggregate of rational individual decisions.

At its core, the world of rational choice is one of individuals making strategic decisions in the context of available information and expectations regarding the behaviour of other actors. However, rational choice theorists also recognize the existence of groups. They suggest that individuals may, for strategic reasons, choose to join or form a group (party, association, interest group, etc.); these groups are then treated as rational actors just like individuals. Rational choice theorists have also integrated institutions, defined in terms of both formal structures such as parliaments and executives and more informal ones such as electoral systems and political rules, into their framework. They are not interested in conducting formal-legal analyses of institutions as did the "old institutionalists"; rather, they conceptualize institutions as part of the individual or the group's strategic context. For example, a country's electoral system can provide parties with incentives to adopt certain policy positions, and/or to form electoral coalitions.

Rational choice presents two great strengths as an approach to politics. The first is its straightforwardness. Studying politics through the rational decisions of individuals avoids the pitfalls of elusive concepts such as political culture or even social functions. The second is its wide applicability. By basing its analysis on what it suggests is a universal characteristic of human beings, rationality, the rational choice approach positions itself to tackle political phenomena in any country at any time.

Rational choice has been criticized for at least three reasons. First, strategic decision making never occurs in undistorted conditions. Information, for example, is rarely complete. Second, and more important, rational choice looks to explain strategy, but takes objectives and preferences as given. In other words, rationality may be useful in explaining the means to an end, but not the end itself. Third, critics question the very foundation of rational choice, that is, rationality. Can individuals be adequately described as self-interested maximizers? Is politics only and always about strategic decision making? Some scholars suggest that reducing politics to individual rationality is an oversimplification. They argue that there are other dimensions to politics (culture, religion, and identity, for example) that are not captured by rational choice.

NEW INSTITUTIONALISM

In the last decade or so, institutions have made a comeback in political science.[9] Some scholars felt that criticism of the old institutionalism had taken the discipline too far in the direction of society-centred approaches at the expense of a proper consideration of political institutions. This was much more the case in the United States than in Canada, where institutionalist analysis was never discredited, as you will see in the excerpt by Alan Cairns below. Nevertheless, in the United States as in Canada, scholars were critical of approaches such as systems analysis and structural-functionalism for their conceptualization of state institutions either as a neutral "black box" or as the product of social needs. Many of them, often called "new institutionalists," suggested instead that the state, and political institutions more generally, should be given theoretical importance, that is, be considered important variables in explaining political phenomena.

The **new institutionalism** is different from the old in that it focuses on how institutions impact on political outcomes, rather than simply on how institutions work. New institutionalists also hold a different perspective from systems analysis, political culture, and even rational choice theorists. Instead of viewing social factors as conditioning institutional frameworks, new institutionalists reverse the causal arrows and suggest that institutions weigh heavily on society. They argue that political scientists can explain political phenomena better if they start with institutions rather than society. New institutionalists are particularly interested in explaining differences in outcomes across countries. They argue that these differences tend to be the product of different institutional frameworks. For example, from a new institutionalist perspective, the difference in behaviour and strategies of interest groups in Canada and the United States is largely the result of the different systems of government. The parliamentary system in Canada and the presidential system in the United States encourage distinct forms of lobbying. Still, from a new institutionalist perspective, policy making in federal and unitary states would have fundamentally different outlooks and, in all likelihood, would yield different results. Few new institutionalists would claim that only institutions are important in explaining politics. They do argue, however, that institutions matter heavily and that they should be given primary importance in political analysis.

New institutionalism presents an interesting approach to politics insofar as institutions are part of any political landscape and, therefore, seem important to consider when analyzing political phenomena. With new institutionalism, political actors and social forces (economic, ideological, cultural, etc.) are no longer studied as if they operate in an institutional vacuum. However, the boldness of the new institutionalist approach can also be a weakness. In insisting that institutions shape society and political phenomena rather, or at least more, than vice versa, new institutionalists are often accused of ignoring or marginalizing variables other than institutional ones. Politics, critics state, is multidimensional and cannot be reduced to the weight of institutions. Some political scientists are uncomfortable with the return of institutionalist analysis because of its association with a more historically minded type of scholarship. They argue that emphasizing institutions hampers possibilities for formulating general theories of political science because institutions, contrary to the individual rationality stressed by the rational choice approach, for example, are different across countries and historical periods.

FEMINISM AND POSTMODERNISM

Some recent approaches to politics, often termed "critical," present a fundamental challenge not only to existing "traditional" approaches, but to the discipline in general. Two of these approaches are feminism and postmodernism. They are called critical because they argue that traditional approaches are not neutral and value free as they claim to be; rather, they represent and promote a particular view about politics. More generally, these critical theorists believe that the process of theorizing, far from being detached from politics, is grounded in power relationships. For example, they would say that the political picture presented by systems analysis and structural-functionalism of a cleavage-free society (be it class, race, gender, or other), where everyone seems to have equal access to the political process, serves to mask the inequalities of liberal-capitalist societies and to promote political structures with which those political scientists are comfortable.

Feminist approaches rest on the idea that traditional approaches remain silent on the power relationships between the genders. Feminist theorists adopt a gender-specific standpoint when looking at politics.[10] At the broadest level, they seek to "bring women into the study of politics," that is, to situate them within different political phenomena and processes. For example, traditional studies on nationalism do not tackle the issue of gender. Recently, however, scholars using a feminist approach have suggested that nationalism has particular consequences for women,[11] or at least that it involves women in a different fashion than men. Feminist scholars note that women, as the reproducers of the nation, are encouraged to have large families, and they often suffer most in the context of violent nationalist conflicts (through rape, for example). By and large, scholars using feminist approaches tend to conclude that existing political orders are male dominated and oppressive for women. In this context, they usually favour fundamental political change and do not hide that their studies and theories represent a first step toward doing just that.

Postmodernism is perhaps the most controversial approach to politics.[12] Postmodernists argue that there is no political reality per se, but rather that politics is simply "discursive practices," or discourse. As such, they focus on discourse, and consider theories of politics to be a part of this discourse. Postmodernist scholars are concerned with connecting discourse to power. They argue, for example, that a dominant political discourse represents a claim to power and hides a particular conception of politics, if not an agenda and interests. Their approach consists of "deconstructing" discourse so as to show its power dimension. Postmodernists are also critical of existing political orders; however, unlike feminist scholars, they do not believe that a new, different order can be established since power relationships, and therefore oppression, are unavoidable. In fact, as they believe that everything, including theorizing, is discourse and power claims, they question the very idea of the possibility of generating knowledge.

Feminism and postmodernism have encountered severe criticism from many political scientists. Feminism is criticized for favouring a political science that is not neutral, objective, and value free. Of course, feminist scholars argue that there is no such thing and that traditional approaches are in fact gendered and therefore not neutral or unbiased. This answer, however, does not prove satisfactory for most political scientists, many of whom are skeptical at the idea of an approach that specifically seeks to look at women. The criticism directed at postmodernism is even harsher. As postmodernists do not seek to explain politics (any theories or explanation being just another oppressive power claim), but rather prefer to interpret discourse, they are often called relativist and nihilist. In other words, critics state that postmodernism threatens all the perceived gains made by the discipline of political science in the last fifty years and beyond.

ENDNOTES

1. Roy Macridis, *The Study of Comparative Government* (New York: Random, 1955).
2. David Easton, *A Framework for Political Analysis* (Englewood Cliffs, NJ: Prentice-Hall, 1965).
3. Bernard Susser, ed., *Approaches to the Study of Politics* (New York: Macmillan, 1992), 183–85.
4. Gabriel Almond and Bingham Powell, Jr., *Comparative Politics: A Developmental Approach* (Boston: Little Brown, 1966).
5. See, for example, Gabriel Almond and Sidney Verba, *The Civic Culture* (Princeton: Princeton University Press, 1963).
6. Louis Hartz, *The Founding of Societies* (New York: Harcourt and Brace, 1964).
7. An example of the traditional/liberal branch would be Robert Gilpin, *The Political Economy of International Relations* (Princeton: Princeton University Press, 1989). For the critical/neo-Marxist branch, see Robert Cox, *Production, Power and World Order* (New York: Columbia University, 1967); Leo Panitch, *The Canadian State: Political Economy and Political Power* (Toronto: Toronto University Press, 1977); Glen Williams, *Not for Export: Toward a Political Economy of Canada's Arrested Industrialization* (Toronto: McClelland and Stewart, 1986).
8. William Riker, *The Theory of Political Coalitions* (New Haven: Yale University Press, 1962).
9. See B. Guy Peters, *Institutional Theory in Political Science: The "New Institutionalism"* (New York: Continuum, 1999).
10. See, for example, Mary McIntosh, "The State and the Oppression of Women," in Annette Kuhn and Ann Marie Wolpe, eds., *Feminism and Materialism: Women and Modes of Production* (London: Routledge, 1978).
11. F. Anthias and Nira Yuval-Davis, eds., *Woman-Nation-State* (London: Macmillan, 1989).
12. The origins of postmodernism are usually traced to French philosopher Michel Foucault. See, for example, *Madness and Civilization: A History of Insanity in the Age of Reason* (London: Tavistock, 1967).

READINGS

This chapter emphasizes the idea that political science is a divided discipline and demonstrates that there is not one single accepted approach to politics, but rather a variety of contending approaches. The two readings selected for this section highlight some of this theoretical diversity: the first features the political economy approach and the second makes an argument for an institutionalist approach. Since Canadian political science has a particularly strong tradition of political economy and institutionalist analysis, it seems appropriate to have these two approaches introduced by Canadian authors.

The first reading, an excerpt by Janine Brodie, discusses various efforts to explain regionalism in Canada from a political economy approach. This article was chosen because it reflects a larger political economy scholarship that has been very important to Canadian political science. Brodie is primarily concerned with regional disparities, that is, with the uneven territorial development of the Canadian economy. This understanding of regionalism involves a rejection of the idea that regions correspond simply to geographical boundaries; rather, here they are viewed as the product of social and political relationships in the context of a historical process of development. Brodie reviews early and more recent political economy works on regionalism in Canada. Her examination of early works focuses on Harold Innis, generally recognized (along with W.A. Mackintosh) as the pioneer of the political economy approach in Canada, and his famous staples theory. At the broadest level, Innis's staples theory suggests that the historical economic development of Canada was driven by foreign powers (first France, then Britain, and finally the United States) that wished to exploit its raw materials. It has often been said that the type of dependent relationships pictured by Innis makes him a precursor to the dependency theories of the 1970s that sought to explain underdevelopment in Latin America and Africa. Staples theory, Brodie argues, sheds light on regionalism in Canada since, for Innis, the staple of a region's economy conditions the nature and level of development and, in turn, patterns of social relations (for example, between Natives and non-Natives through the fur trade). Brodie then looks at more recent works on the political economy of regionalism. She explains how many of these works applied dependency theory to the relationship between Atlantic and Central Canada, thereby explaining the underdevelopment of the Atlantic provinces through control and even exploitation by Central Canada. In a similar vein, she discusses a slightly different type of research that focuses on conflicting federal and provincial development strategies. This excerpt should be read not so much for understanding the political economy of regionalism in Canada (although this would certainly be a good thing!), but rather for gaining insight into a type of research and scholarship that has been central to political science in Canada.

The second piece is an excerpt from a presidential address to the Canadian Political Science Association delivered in 1977 by one of Canada's best-known political scientists, Alan Cairns. It underlines the distinctiveness of Canadian political science in relation to the discipline in the United States. As we said earlier, Canadian political science never embraced behaviouralism and the rejection of institutions it advocated, perhaps partly because Canada's linguistic and regional cleavages lead to a preoccupation with the federal nature of the Canadian state. Cairns's scholarship is reflective of this larger Canadian political science tradition. From this perspective, Cairns could be considered an early proponent of the new institutionalist approach formally developed in the 1980s by American political scientists. In the present piece Cairns argues that while the impact of society on government is the subject of much scholarly attention, the same cannot be said about the weight of government on society. Cairns focuses more specifically on federalism and seeks to reject the argument (or assumption) that the nature and dynamic of federal structures are to be found in society. In this context, he discusses the position of provinces in Canadian federalism and referendum politics in Quebec. On the first issue, Cairns argues that "provincial survival and growth" in English Canada makes no sense from a society-centred perspective because sociologically the populations of these provinces are fundamentally similar. It is more comprehensible, Cairns suggests, if we consider that provincial structures and the people attached to them seek to maintain or bolster their power and status. On the second issue, Cairns writes that the period leading to the Quebec sovereignty referendum in 1980 would feature a sustained effort by the Parti Québécois (through the timing of the vote, the wording of the question, the control of mobilization, etc.) to convince a majority of the population to back its option. This process, he suggests, shows that the weight of institutions on political outcomes should not be ignored.

THE POLITICAL ECONOMY OF REGIONALISM

Janine Brodie

Few political economists would disagree with the assertion that regionalism is a "profound and fundamental" feature of Canadian political life.[1] Canadian politics revolves around persistent and divisive conflicts about the spatial distribution of economic development, state activity, living standards, governmental services, and political power. And, unlike the experience of other advanced capitalist countries, spatially based conflict in Canada has not decreased as the pace of development accelerates. The centrality of regionalism to Canada's collective political experience has prompted many scholars, especially revisionist historians, to advocate a fundamental reorientation in thinking about Canada, one in which region would "rival, if not replace, the nation-state as the central construction in Canadian studies."[2]

The revisionists argue that the most popular interpretations of Canadian history, the so-called national schools, are centralist in bias and contain a vision of economic, social, and political development that is profoundly at odds with the Canadian experience. Recently, similar charges have been levelled against the current generation of Canadian political economists.[3] Both the "old" and "new" schools of Canadian political economy incorporate considerations of space and geography in their analysis. Unlike its predecessor, however, the new political economy, especially the class and dependency streams, has not been particularly self-conscious about questions of regional definition and integration, that is, explaining what a region is and how regions relate to one another and to the nation-state of which they are a part.[4] This essay examines selected contributions of the old and new political economies to the study of Canadian regionalism. It attempts to show that the early political economists, particularly Harold Innis and Vernon Fowke, provide a useful point of departure for a future political economy that is sensitive to the spatial dimension of Canadian development and politics.

***

CREATION OF REGIONS: THE EARLY TRADITION

Innis's Staple Theory

We begin our survey of the early political economy with Harold Innis's staples theory. This may seem a questionable point of departure. Some have argued that staples theory is not a relational approach to regional definition and integration but, instead, an example of vulgar geographic and resource determinism.[5] This accusation is largely, though not entirely, unwarranted and appears to derive from two sources in particular. The first source is Innis himself. Innis's work is often frustratingly imprecise and makes sweeping assertions about the importance of geography, staples, and technology. Critics have taken some of these assertions as

evidence that Innis was a determinist who allowed little room for political agency in the explanation of regionalism.[6] Admittedly, strong currents of determinism do run through his work, but they are not sufficiently deep to dismiss Innis's potential contribution to the study of Canadian regionalism.

Second, more often than not, the charge that Innis's work is little more than vulgar resource determinism results not from a close reading of Innis but rather from the liberal laundering of his staples theory. This "laundering" coincided with the growth in popularity of quantitative economics and reduced Innis's staples theory to little more than a neoclassical theory of international trade and comparative advantage.[7] Not surprisingly, this interpretation of staples theory has been embraced by such conservative think-tanks as the Economic Council of Canada. In a major study on regionalism in Canada, it concluded: "The varying economic fortunes of different areas of Canada are . . . explained, according to the staples approach, by varying availability and marketability of natural resources."[8] Similarly, Pomfret, an economic historian following in this tradition, argues: "Staples theory asserts that the pace and nature of an area's economic growth is determined by the characteristics of its staple product."[9] These interpretations of staples theory do provide examples of vulgar resource determinism but bear little resemblance to the complexity of Innis's argument.

Innis was not the first Canadian political economist to emphasize the centrality of staples production in Canadian history. Mackintosh, who argued that the exploitation of staples was a necessary transitional stage on the path to economic maturity, first alerted him to the idea of the staple.[10] Innis, however, doubted that staples trade would inevitably lead to industrialization. In fact, he disagreed strongly with the assumption that the course of economic development in a new country would eventually parallel that of Britain or Europe. For Innis, it was simply defective thinking to attempt "to fit the phenomena of new countries into the economic theories of old countries."[11]

A central thread underlying Innis's work is that Canadian political economy must be understood in relation to its unique historical antecedents.[12] The experience of North America was simply different from that of Europe. It came into contact with the old world only after capitalism had emerged as the dominant model of social organization. Innis, like Marx, was acutely aware that geography is continuously shaped and reshaped by explicitly historical and social forces such as the organization of production and new technologies.[13] For him, the key to understanding the pattern of Canadian development was to trace how the invasion of European culture and the price system left its imprint on a geography that previously corresponded to the non-capitalist forms of social organization of the Aboriginal peoples.

According to Innis, the new white settler colonies of North America were, by definition, economically weak and were forced to engage in staples trade with a series of imperial centres, first France and later Britain and the United States, in order to obtain necessary material and technological goods. The form and location of economic activity within these colonies, however, were determined by the centre's demand for staple products. The exploitation of a series of staples—fish, fur, timber, wheat, and minerals—meant that different areas of the country developed at different times as the demands of the centre as well as technology and transportation made them accessible. New countries, in other words, developed in relation to old countries.[14] However, it was not the staple itself that stimulated growth but rather prices, markets, and the monopoly of markets, all of which are defined historically.

Innis argued that the succession of staples exploitation explained much more of Canadian history than simply the location of economic activity at any given period. Each staple was also characterized by specific patterns of settlement, linkages to other economic activities, interactions with the centre, culture, and institutional arrangements. "Concentration on the production of staples for export to more highly industrialized areas in Europe and later in the U.S.," he writes, "had broad implications for the Canadian economic, political and social structure. Each staple in turn left its stamp, and the shift to a new staple invariably produced periods of crises." Moreover, "the tendency has been cumulative."[15]

Innis provides us with a relational and diachronic analysis of the link between uneven development and political arrangements in Canada. Each staple was characterized by a complex web of forms located in geographic space that changed across time. Innis asked us to think about geographic space abstractly and relationally. It was as if Canadian history could be represented as a series of transparencies, each representing a different matrix of economic growth and political organization, laid on geographic space, one on top of the other, as the international political economy changed. Each staple led to different geographic configurations that were unstable across time. Boundaries—whether national or regional—were not "in the land" but rather tied to the pattern of staples exploitation.[16]

Some have argued that Innis's work is anti-regional because he concentrates on patterns of national development—the whole rather than the parts. But his work is also valuable in illuminating the historical relationships among imperial centres and Canadian regional centres, between imperial centres and Canadian hinterlands, and between Canadian regional centres and Canadian hinterlands. In *The Cod Fisheries*, for example, he describes how the nature of the fish staple made Nova Scotia, and in particular Halifax, a regional centre in the Maritime provinces. "Her position, sensitive alike to competition from New England and to the effects of Imperial commercial policy, gave Nova Scotia a great influence with the administration in Great Britain."[17] Innis also recognized that the diversity of the Ontario economy gave it "undue weight on the less favoured areas of the Dominion."[18]

Innis saw political forms as necessarily emanating from the demands of staple production. This is because he ascribed the state a major role in facilitating the extraction of the staple. Thus, the east-west unity of Canada originated in the fur trade and trading ties with Europe, while the political form, Confederation, was tied to the wheat staple. The regions joined together at Confederation had developed independently in relation to Britain but were drawn into a new constitutional arrangement largely to underwrite the transportation costs necessitated by expansion to the interior. Heavy expenditures involved the development of a strong centralized government in Canada. They also placed the federal state at the heart of political conflict over the distribution of resources across geographic space.

Innis's analysis of state policy and political conflict is not particularly sophisticated, but he did acknowledge that the role played by the federal state in the economy was "unique" and more interventionist than most countries because of Canada's dependence on staples exploitation. During the development of the wheat staple, in particular, "heavy expenditures on transport improvements including railways and canals, . . . involved government grants, subsidies, and guarantees to an exceptional degree."[19] Moreover, the costs and benefits accruing from government intervention were not distributed equally among the regions. "Western Canada," he wrote in 1923, "has paid for the development of the Canadian nationality, and it would appear that it must continue to pay. The acquisitiveness of eastern Canada shows little sign of abatement."[20] National policies, in other words, were often little more than thinly disguised regional policies, which, in turn, gave content to regional conflict.[21] "In regions bearing the burden of fixed charges and dependent on staples which fluctuate widely in yield and price, political activity became more intense. Relief was obtained by political pressure." "A less kindly critic," he confesses, "might say that currents of hot air flowed upwards from regions with sharp fluctuations in income."[22] Innis attributed regional conflict to the vagaries of staples exploitation and provided a point of departure for later work on regional protest movements in western Canada. More important, however, he suggested that the contours of regional protest changed with the pattern of staples exploitation.

Innis was especially concerned with the institutional maladjustments and regional conflict engendered by the shift from one staple to another. He argued that Confederation became obsolete when the wheat economy, complete with its east-west linkages, had run its course and staple production shifted to a north-south linkage, supplying pulpwood, minerals, and energy to the American market[23]—a theme adopted by Garth Stevenson in his treatment of federal-provincial relations.[24] Innis wrote:

> The dangers to Canada have been increased by disturbances to the Canadian constitutional structure which have followed the rise of new industries developed in special relation to the American market . . . A division has emerged between the attitude of provinces which have been particularly fortunate in the possession of natural resources in which the American market is interested and that of the

> provinces more largely dependent on European markets . . . The strains imposed on a constitution specifically designed for an economy built up in relation to Great Britain and Europe have been evident in the emergence of regionalism.[25]

Innis's observations seem especially prescient in the late 1980s as Canada undertakes constitutional reform that corresponds to the realities of continental economic integration. His analysis of regionalism suggests that the form and content of regional protest change as major development strategies change. Moreover, the process is cumulative, as new symbols, forms, and tensions are layered onto older ones. In other words, the story of the spatial dimension of Canadian politics is not, as many now argue, that while once regions protested, provinces now do.[26] Instead, Innis argued that, with shifts in international demand for staples, certain *groups* of producing provinces would be placed in a new relationship with the United States and with central Canada, that is with the imperial centre and regional centres. The wheat staple had produced a particular pattern of regional definition, integration, and conflict, while the new staples, destined for the American market, produced another. This shift created tensions between the old and new orders and inevitably led to institutional crisis and adjustment. The position of Canada in the international political economy changed and, with it, the pattern and form of regional politics.

Innis suggests a necessary connection between economic development strategies, institutional and policy formation, and regional conflict. His formulations, however, are rudimentary and reveal one of the major weaknesses of his work. Innis's history, as history, is largely dehumanized.[27] Although he gave passing recognition to the impact of politics and policy in sustaining uneven regional economic development, the forces of the imperial centre and the price system always took conceptual priority. Staples exploitation limited the options and opportunities for a more equitable and controlled distribution of economic development, invariably leading the country deeper and deeper into a "staples trap" of dependency and stagnation. In this respect, Berger, Richards, Pratt, and others have grounds to judge him a determinist. Yet, as Berger explains, "paradoxically, to understand the magnitude and character of deterministic elements was for him to establish the margin, invariably narrow, in which men were free to make their own history."[28] In sum, Innis's contribution to the study of Canadian regionalism was his emphasis on an indigenous interpretation of regional development and the links between spatial configurations within Canada and changes in the international economic order.

***

CURRENT TRENDS

Unlike its predecessor, the new Canadian political economy has not devoted much attention to uneven spatial development within Canada or to regional politics. Recently, there has been renewed interest in the political economy of Canadian regionalism, especially among radical scholars working outside central Canada. They have examined the uneven spatial development of Canada, but their approach has been eclectic. We can, however, discern two distinct trends in the current literature. The first borrows from neo-Marxist dependency theory and is an extension of the centre-periphery tradition in Canadian scholarship. The second stream, echoing Innis, examines the impact of continental economic integration on resource production and the activities of resource-producing provinces. This "provincialist" literature has provided rich historical analysis of the attempts by various provincial governments to promote accumulation and diversification within their respective boundaries. Neither stream, however, has elaborated a coherent theoretical approach to the spatial dimension of Canadian politics.

Scholars seeking to explain the persistent problem of underdevelopment in Atlantic Canada have relied heavily on various dependency models borrowed from South America. It would be impossible to review all this work here, but useful summaries are available for those wishing to pursue this theme.[29] In one of these, Barrett identifies three distinct trends in Atlantic scholarship which have emerged over the past two decades from debates and research in the dependency tradition: the Frankian model of the "development of underdevelopment," the "new dependency" (or dependent capitalist development) approach and the "modes of production" perspective.[30]

Archibald was the first to apply a modern theory of dependency, specifically, Frank's "development of underdevelopment" thesis, systematically to Atlantic Canada. According to Archibald, Atlantic Canada was reduced to the status of a satellite economy by a series of metropoles, first by Britain and then by central Canada and the United States. These metropoles drained surplus from the region, controlled patterns of development, and blocked industrial diversification of its resource-based economy.[31] Archibald's work shares the weaknesses of a centre-periphery model as described above and has been criticized for historical inaccuracy, especially for ignoring the fact that the Maritimes were not underdeveloped as much as they were deindustrialized.[32]

The "dependent capitalist development" school argues that the "development of underdevelopment" thesis misinterprets the nature of development in the periphery because it concerns itself with exchange relations rather than relations of production. Veltmeyer has been the key proponent for the incorporation of class in dependency models of Atlantic Canada. He argues that regional underdevelopment can be understood in terms of the universal tendencies of capitalism, especially the declining rate of profit and capital's requirement for an industrial reserve army. Atlantic Canada, he suggests, has been reduced to an industrial reserve army for central Canada.[33] He does not explain, however, why capital in Canada, but not elsewhere, requires such a peculiar spatial distribution of the industrial reserve army. He also fails to recognize the significant force of unemployed within the industrial heartland.

The "modes of production" approach also incorporates Marxist class analysis but departs considerably from popular dependency models. Employing this perspective, Sacouman argues that the underdevelopment of the rural Maritimes over the last century has been based on the "structural articulation of two apparent modes of production," petty primary production and monopoly capitalism. He uses this model to trace how the petty primary producer unit (tied seasonally to farming, lumber, and fishing) and the relative surplus population have been increasingly exploited by the strictly capitalist mode of production.[34] While more credible, his analysis is limited in scope, addressing only the issue of rural underdevelopment.

In a somewhat different vein, Clement has examined the interrelationship among three factors: Canada's dependence on the United States and multinational enterprises, its "distorted" class structure, and its uneven development. He argues that this external dependence causes internal spatial asymmetries because the weight of capitalist activities is located at the centre. He seeks to demonstrate how Ontario, with its disproportionate share of capitalists, multinationals, and corporate activity, dominates and exploits the rest of Canada.[35]

Clement's initial attempt to incorporate class and region provides little more than a description of a few of the consequences of uneven development and not an explanation of its causes. He and others working within this genre often confuse structural dualism (vertical class inequalities) with spatial dualism (uneven development across space). This confusion is evident in discussions of the transfer of surplus, which has very different meanings in class and regional analysis: extraction of surplus within capitalist relations of production and movement of capital across space, respectively. Evidence that more capitalists are located in Ontario than elsewhere may indicate spatial dominance—but it could indicate instead that capital in other regions is simply concentrated. In other words, a relatively few capitalists may be extracting surplus from workers within a region (names like Irving, McCain, Sobey, and Jodrey come to mind), and the capital thereby derived may or may not remain in the region.

Clement's work on Canadian regionalism has shifted emphasis in recent years, but he maintains a dependency perspective, arguing that "a region can only be underdeveloped if it is tied to an external economy which is responsible for its underdevelopment."[36] But a general confusion about structural and spatial dualism remains when he argues that "true" development is achieved only when "all those on site who participate in development share equally in the surplus produced."[37] By this latter criterion, regions identified as exploitative through the dependency lens, such as Ontario, cannot be considered developed, nor for that matter can any capitalist economy. This logical inconsistency can result only from the conceptual fusion of uneven spatial development and class exploitation.

Dependency models can be seductive, particularly when, as Williams points out, they conform to one's political objectives.[38] There are a number of reasons, however, why we should hesitate to employ them in an analysis of regionalism. First, there are logical problems with the dependency perspective's crude application of the spatial transfer of surplus. Flows of surplus are extremely difficult to measure empirically, and dependency theory ignores questions about the use of the surplus transferred.[39] Contrary to the assumptions of the dependency model, the region that gains value is not necessarily the one in which value is capitalized.[40] In fact, surplus may be used for takeovers and mergers and thereby actually contribute to contraction at the centre.

Massey's objections to the use of dependency models to explain intranational uneven spatial development are equally instructive. The dependency perspective was developed as a response to modernization theory in order to explain the effect of imperialism on a global scale. Massey, however, argues that it is a fallacy to "simply transplant" these models "to a lower level of spatial disaggregation." The interrelationships among nation states within world imperialism cannot be equated with inter-regional relations within a nation. In so doing, we ignore social divisions of territory and socially different types of territorial division.[41] In particular, we eliminate the role of national politics and policies and the state in the creation of uneven spatial development.

Clow has criticized the dependency literature on Maritime underdevelopment precisely on this point. He points to the detailed empirical work of revisionist historians such as Acheson and Forbes to demonstrate that politics, beginning with Confederation and the National Policy, profoundly influenced Maritime underdevelopment. "The options for Maritime development were narrowed and channelled by the political fact" of Confederation and the National Policy, which "crystallized around rival strategies of economic development."[42] By the 1920s, the Maritimes had been effectively "deindustrialized" and suffered from the related maladies of depopulation and the loss of political power.[43]

The work on Maritime deindustrialization suggests a quite different perspective on regional development than that provided by centre-periphery models and dependency theory, both of which tend to assume that once a core-periphery structure is established it is resistant to change. Instead, the experience of the Maritime provinces demonstrates that as capitalists and government shift their developmental strategies to correspond to the changing international political economy and to internal political pressures, certain localities for accumulation are favoured over others. As suggested by Innis and Fowke, each phase of accumulation tends to have its own geography, distinct from the geography of earlier phases. As a result, "the existing pattern of regions at any time is the result of the overlaying of these various phases of accumulation."[44] Capital, population, and political power also shift, but the structure is not immutable. Thriving industrial centres are deindustrialized by shifts in developmental strategies, a point that is currently being argued by opponents of free trade with the United States.

Revisionist Maritime historiography has begun to chart the interaction between politics, policy, and regionalism, but it remains largely a liberal history, which discounts the role of social classes in human agency. The conceptual priority given to class analysis, more than anything else, distinguishes the new political economy from the old. And it is precisely the historical coincidence of space, class, and politics that informs some of the most notable contributions of the new political economy to the study of regionalism. Several studies have appeared in recent years that examine the efforts of various coalitions of provincial elites and business interests to implement provincially based developmental strategies.

Nelles was one of the first to examine the class bases of provincialism, although, as we have seen, this theme also runs through the work of Innis. In *The Politics of Development*, he describes how, at the turn of the century, Ontario business interests, responding to American demand for energy and raw materials and unfavourable federal policies, joined in a coalition with political actors to engage in province-building. They pursued a combination of policies designed to promote a "manufacturing condition" and, thereby, ensured limited industrial diversification within the province.[45]

As Nelles demonstrates, Ontario's elites were the first to use the provincial state to construct regional development policies in response to continental and national pressures. Attempts by provincial governments, especially in the resource-rich provinces, to foster capital accumulation and economic diversification have accelerated since 1945 and have stimulated a number of important studies in the "provincialist" stream of the new political economy. Echoing the

concerns of Innis, for example, Stevenson has argued that provincial governments have established close relations with resource capital and that federal-provincial conflict in Canada is an expression of conflict between competing fractions of the bourgeoisie.[46] Similarly, Marchak has explored how the pull of the international market, especially the United States, has shaped class conflict in British Columbia and the policies of the provincial government in periods of growth and decline.[47] Richards and Pratt, examining prairie capitalism, grant the provincial governments of Saskatchewan and Alberta more autonomy from resource capital than others working in this genre. They argue that the relationship between the provincial state elite and foreign capital changes over time, from dependence to inter-dependence, as provincial officials move up what they term a "learning curve" of skills, information, and expertise.[48] Finally, Coleman has examined the independence movement in Quebec as a shifting coalition of class forces that has promoted the continued integration of Quebec into the continental economy and the growth of an indigenous capitalist class.[49]

We cannot hope to survey the richness of this research here, but it does highlight one aspect of the spatial dimension of Canadian politics that has become increasingly evident over the past three decades, namely, the conflict between provincial and federal economic development strategies. In many ways this work reflects Innis, in its concern with resource production, continental integration, and the resulting political forms. This is, nonetheless, only one dimension of spatial politics experienced in Canada over the past century. The nation-state, sub-central units of government, and electoral politics are all organized around territory. Any one of these may be a vehicle for territorial conflict when classes or fractions of the same class centred disproportionately in one space bear the costs of a particular development strategy or wish to use political mechanisms to pursue alternative strategies.

Those working within the provincialist tradition therefore should be particularly cautious not to interpret the specifically conjunctural elements of the last few decades as being immune from the forces of history. The recent experiences of provincial governments, in fact, provide students of the political economy of regionalism with a number of important lessons. First, provincial developmental strategies are created within the contexts of national developmental policy and the international political economy and thus are vulnerable to change or failure when conditions at either of the other two levels shift. As Coleman argues in this volume, the federal government should not be discounted in the analysis of provincialism. Second, while an analysis of the class forces and political coalitions behind regional initiatives is essential, these coalitions are temporal. Local capital will behave just like foreign capital when the locations for accumulation shift in space. Finally, while recognizing the apparent movement to province-building in the past two decades, we should not imbue provincial governments with excessive powers or consider them in isolation. The growth of provincial bureaucracies and their expertise is real, but their powers to effect change independent of the economic and political forces around them is limited, especially in a laissez-faire environment. The ability to break out of past accumulation patterns and construct a new geography requires a broader political base than a tacit coalition between regional capital and bourgeois political parties dedicated to creating favourable investment climates. It also requires more radical state developmental strategies than partnership with the private sector.

Reading Notes

1. Elkins and Simeon, eds., *Small Worlds*, viii.
2. Westfall, "On the Concept of Region," 3. This insightful essay is valuable reading for all interested in this topic.
3. See, for example, Clow, "Politics and Uneven Capitalist Development"; Sacouman, "The 'Peripheral' Maritimes."
4. See Westfall, "The Concept of Region," 6.
5. See, for example, G. Kealey et al., "Canada's Eastern Question," 37.
6. Most often cited as evidence of determinism is Innis, *The Fur Trade in Canada*, 392, beginning: "The present Dominion emerged not in spite of geography but because of it." Also see Innis, "The Economic Development of Canada," 670.
7. For a discussion see Clement and Drache, *A Practical Guide*, 28–30: also Neil, "The Passing of Canadian Economic History," 73.
8. Economic Council of Canada, *Living Together*, 23.
9. Pomfret, *The Economic Development of Canada*, 33.
10. See Carl Berger, *The Writing of Canadian History*, 92.
11. Innis, "The Teaching of Economic History," 10.
12. See ibid., 85.
13. See Drache, "Harold Innis and Canadian Capitalist Development," 39; Marx, *Grundisse*, 740.
14. See Carl Berger, *Writing*, 91.
15. Innis, *Empire and Communications*, 5; Innis, *The Fur Trade*, 385.
16. Westfall, "The Ambivalent Verdict," 48.
17. Innis, *The Cod Fisheries*, 490. I would like to thank Glen Williams for helping me develop this point.
18. Innis, *Essays*, 122.
19. Innis, *The Fur Trade*, 388.
20. Innis, *A History of the Canadian Pacific Railway*, 290–4, as cited in Carl Berger, *Writing*, 88.
21. See Westfall, "Ambivalent Verdict," 48; see also Innis's condemnation of the Rowell-Sirois Report in Review.
22. Innis, *Essays*, 396.
23. See ibid., 370.
24. See Garth Stevenson, *Unfulfilled Union*.
25. Innis, *Essays*, 396.
26. This is essentially the argument of Gibbons in *Prairie Politics and Society*, chap. 1.
27. See Carl Berger, *Writing*, 98.
28. Ibid., 102.
29. See, for example, Clow, "Politics"; Brym and Sacouman, eds., *Underdevelopment*; and *Canadian Review of Sociology and Anthropology* (Aug. 1980).
30. L.G. Barrett, "Perspectives," 277.
31. See Archibald, "Atlantic Regional Underdevelopment."
32. For example, see Acheson, "The National Policy."
33. Veltmeyer, "Capitalist Underdevelopment."
34. See Sacouman, "Semi-proletarianization."

35. See Clement, "A Political Economy of Regionalism."
36. Clement, "Regionalism as Uneven Development."
37. Ibid.
38. See Glen Williams, "Centre-Margin Dependency."
39. See Gore, *Regions*, 198.
40. See Webber, "Agglomeration," 4.
41. Massey, "Regionalism."
42. Clow, "Politics," 124, 125.
43. For a description of Maritime deindustrialization see Acheson, "The National Policy"; Forbes, *The Maritime Rights Movement*; Alexander, *Atlantic Canada and Confederation*.
44. Webber, "Agglomeration," 5.
45. See Nelles, *The Politics of Development*.
46. Garth Stevenson, *Unfulfilled Union*.
47. See Marchak, "Rise and Fall."
48. Richards and Pratt, *Prairie Capitalism*.
49. Coleman, *The Independence Movement*.

Reading References

Acheson, T., "The National Policy and Industrialization of the Maritimes," *Acadiensis*, 1, 1972.

Alexander, D., *Atlantic Canada and Confederation* (Toronto: University of Toronto Press, 1983).

Archibald, B., "Atlantic Regional Underdevelopment and Socialism," in LaPierre et al., *Essays on the Left* (Toronto: McClelland and Stewart, 1971).

Barrett, L.G., "Perspectives on Dependency and Underdevelopment in the Atlantic Region," *Canadian Review of Sociology and Anthropology* (August 1980).

Berger, Carl, *The Writing of Canadian History* (Toronto: Oxford University Press, 1976).

Brym, R. and Sacouman, J. eds., *Underdevelopment and Social Movement in Atlantic Canada* (Toronto: New Hogtown Press, 1979).

Clement, Wallace, "A Political Economy of Regionalism," D. Glenday et al., *Modernization and the Canadian State* (Toronto: Macmillan, 1978).

Clement, Wallace, "Regionalism as Uneven Development: Class and Region in Canada," *Canadian Issues*, 5 (1983).

Clement, Wallace and Daniel Drache, *A Practical Guide to Canadian Political Economy* (Toronto: Lorimer, 1978).

Clow, Michael, "Politics and Uneven Capitalist Development: the Maritime Challenge to the Study of Canadian Political Economy," *Studies in Political Economy* (summer 1984).

Coleman, William, *The Independence Movement in Quebec 1945-1980* (Toronto: University of Toronto Press, 1984).

Drache, Daniel, "Harold Innis and Canadian Capitalist Development," *Canadian Journal of Political and Social Theory* 6 (winter/spring 1982).

Economic Council of Canada, *Living Together: A Study of Regional Disparities* (Ottawa: Supply and Services, 1977).

Elkins, David and Richard Simeon (eds), *Small Worlds: Provinces and Parties in Canadian Politics* (Toronto: Methuen, 1980).

Forbes, E.R., *The Maritime Rights Movement* (Montreal and Kingston: McGill-Queen's University Press, 1979).

Gibbons, Roger, *Prairie Politics and Society: Regionalism in Decline* (Toronto: Butterworths, 1980).

Gore, Charles, *Regions in Question* (London: Methuen, 1984).

Innis, H.A., *The Fur Trade in Canada* (Toronto: Toronto University Press, 1956).

Innis, H.A., "The Economic Development of Canada, 1867-1921: The Maritime Provinces." In J. H. Rose et al., *The Cambridge History of the British Empire* (Cambridge: Cambridge University Press, 1930).

Innis, H.A., *The Cod Fisheries* (Toronto: Toronto University Press, 1954).

Innis, H.A., *Empire and Communications* (Toronto: University of Toronto Press, 1972).

Innis, H.A., "The Teaching of Economic History in Canada," in Mary Q. Innis, *Essays in Canadian Economic History* (Toronto: University of Toronto Press, 1956).

Innis, H.A., *A History of the Canadian Pacific Railway* (London: McClelland, 1923).

Innis, H.A., *Essays in Canadian Economic History* (Toronto: Toronto University Press, 1956).

Kealey, G. et al., "Canada's Eastern Question," *Canadian Dimension* 13:2 (1978).

Neil, Robin, "The Passing of Canadian Economic History," *Journal of Canadian Studies* 12:5 (1977).

Nelles, H.V., *The Politics of Development. Forest, Mines and Hydro-Electric Power in Ontario, 1840-1941* (Toronto: Macmillan, 1974).

Marchak, Patricia, "The Rise and Fall of the Peripheral State: The Case of British Columbia," in R. Brym (ed), *Regionalism in Canada* (Toronto: Methuen, 1986).

Marx, E, *Grundrisse* (London: Penguin Books, 1973).

Massey, Doreen, "Regionalism: Some Issues," *Capital and Class* 6 (1978).

Pomfret, Richard, *The Economic Development of Canada* (Toronto: Methuen, 1981).

Richards, J. and L. Pratt, *Prairie Capitalism. Power and Influence in the New West* (Toronto: McClelland and Stewart, 1979).

Sacouman, R.J., "The 'Peripheral' Maritimes and Canada-wide Marxist Political Economy," *Studies in Political Economy* 6 (autumn 1981).

Sacouman, R.J., "Semi-proletarianization and Rural Underdevelovment in the Maritimes," *Canadian Review of Sociology and Anthropology* (August 1980).

Stevenson, Garth, *Unfulfilled Union* (Toronto: Macmillan, 1979).

Veltmeyer, H., "Capitalist Underdevelopment of Atlantic Canada," in Brym, R. and Sacouman, J. eds., *Underdevelopment and Social Movement in Atlantic Canada* (Toronto: New Hogtown Press, 1979).

Webber, M.J., "Agglomeration and the Regional Question," *Antipode* 17:2 (1984).

Westfall, William, "The Ambivalent Verdict: Harold Innis and Canadian History," in W. Melody et al., *Culture, Communications and Dependency* (New Jersey, 1981).

Westfall, William, "On the Concept of Region in Canadian History and Literature," *Journal of Canadian Studies* (summer 1980).

Williams, Glen, "Centre-Margin Dependency, and the State in the New Canadian Political Economy," Paper presented to the Canadian Political Science Association Meetings, Winnipeg 1986.

THE GOVERNMENTS AND SOCIETIES OF CANADIAN FEDERALISM

Alan C. Cairns

If you marry the Spirit of your generation you will be a widow in the next.

(Dean Inge)

The Canadian political system, now in its second century, can no longer be taken for granted. It is altogether possible, some would say probable, and some would say desirable, that major institutional change, not excluding the fragmentation of Canada, is on the immediate horizon. It is therefore an opportune time to reflect on the century-long interaction between government and society in Canada. I use the word "reflect" advisedly, for this is not the type of interaction about which hard statements can be confidently made.

The impact of society on government is a common theme in the study of democratic polities. Less common is an approach stressing the impact of government on the functioning of society. I have chosen the latter for the guiding theme of my remarks, because I am convinced that our approach to the study of Canadian politics pays inadequate attention to the capacity of government to make society responsive to its demands.

With some exceptions, my remarks will be confined to senior governments operating in the institutional framework of federalism. Particular institutions, such as the electoral system, the Senate, and many others will be ignored or given only minor attention.

***

The great mystery for students of Canadian federalism has been the survival and growth of provincial governments, particularly those of

English Canada. Sociologically focused inquiries, with Quebec as an implicit model, have looked for vital, inward-looking provincial societies on which governments could be based and, finding none, have been puzzled why these governmental superstructures, seemingly lacking a necessary foundation, have not faded away.

The sociological perspective pays inadequate attention to the possibility that the support for powerful, independent provincial governments is a product of the political system itself, that it is fostered and created by provincial government elites employing the policy-making apparatus of their jurisdictions, and that such support need not take the form of a distinct culture, society, or nation as these are conventionally understood. More specifically, the search for an underlying sociological base, whatever its nature and source, as the necessary sustenance for viable provincial political systems, deflects us from considering the prior question of how much support is necessary. Passivity, indifference, or the absence of strong opposition from their environment may be all that provincial governments need in order to thrive and grow. The significant question, after all, is the survival of provincial governments, not of provincial societies, and it is not self-evident that the existence and support of the latter is necessary to the functioning and aggrandisement of the former. Their sources of survival, renewal, and vitality may well lie within themselves and in their capacity to mould their environment in accordance with their own governmental purposes.

In the analysis of contemporary party systems much has been made of the extent to which today's parties represent the historic residue of the cleavages of yesteryear. In the Canadian case the freezing of party alternatives fades into insignificance compared with the freezing by the federal system of initially five and now eleven constitutionally distinct and separate governments. The enduring stability of these governments contrasts sharply with the fluctuating fortunes of all parties and the disappearance of many. Governments, as persisting constellations of interests, constitute the permanent elements of the Canadian polity that thus far have ridden out the storms of social, economic, and political change.

The decision to establish a federal system in 1867 was a first-order macro decision concerning the basic institutional features of the new polity. It created competitive political and bureaucratic elites at two levels of government endowed with an impressive array of jurisdictional, financial, administrative, and political resources to deploy in the pursuit of their objectives. The post-Confederation history of Canadian federalism is little more than the record of the efforts of governing elites to pyramid their resources and of the uses to which they have put them. Possessed of tenacious instincts for their own preservation and growth, the governments of Canadian federalism have endowed the cleavages between provinces, and between provinces and nation that attended their birth, with an ever more comprehensive political meaning.

The crucial, minimum prerequisites for provincial survival and growth have been the preservation of jurisdictional competence and of territorial integrity. In terms of the former, it is notable that explicit change in the constitutional responsibilities of the two levels of government has been minimal, in spite of strong centralizing pressure on occasion. The division of powers has been altered to federal advantage only three times, in each of which unanimous provincial consent was obtained, and in two of which provincial paramountcy was respected. Provincial pressure has ensured the *de facto* acceptance of the principle that the concurrence of all provincial governments is necessary for any amendment that would reduce their formal constitutional authority. Even in their periods of greatest weakness provincial governments steadfastly resisted and thwarted all efforts to accord explicit constitutional recognition to a more flexible amendment procedure dealing with the division of powers. By their self-interested obstinacy they preserved their basic bargaining power for the future and formally protected the jurisdictional integrity essential for subsequent increases in their governmental potency. Although the proposed amendment procedures in the Victoria Charter of 1971 departed from the principle of provincial unanimity for formal changes in the distribution of legislative powers, the Charter was rejected by the Bourassa government of Quebec.[1] The principle of unanimous provincial consent for constitutional amendments in this area thus remains as part of the operating constitution. The paucity of amendments dealing with the division of power and the long-standing opposition of provincial governments to any formally agreed amendment procedures that might diminish their lawmaking authority without their express consent strikingly reveal an entrenched governmental conservatism where the constitutional base of provincial governing capacity is concerned.

Equally indicative of provincial tenacity in self-preservation is the integrity of provincial boundaries. No province has given up territory to which it had clear and undisputed possession. Where territorial "loss" has occurred, as in the 1872 case of the San Juan boundary settlement by the German Emperor, which denied the claims of British Columbia, or in the case of Labrador decided by judicial determination in favour of Newfoundland in 1927, provincial frustrations have been pronounced, and in the latter case long-lived. Half a century later the claim of Quebec to Labrador remains a live issue to the Quebec government.[2] Disputed cases, such as offshore mineral resources caught between the counterclaim of federal and provincial governments, illustrate the vigour with which provincial positions are defended, even in the face of adverse court decisions. Where the possibility of territorial expansion has existed, or still exists, with respect to contiguous territory outside provincial boundaries, the provinces have consistently manifested a revolution of rising expectations not yet dead. It has not only been the federal government assiduously extending the range of its jurisdiction from the limited Canada of 1867 to the ten-province Canada of 1949, and now extending its effective writ over Canada's Arctic frontiers, which displays a well-developed drive for territorial acquisition. The original boundaries of Quebec, Ontario, and Manitoba contained only a small portion of the land masses they now control. On occasion, interprovincial controversy over disputed territory has even produced mini border conflicts, as in the case of Manitoba and Ontario in the thirty-year period preceding the final determination of their boundary in 1912.[3]

The three Maritime provinces, doomed by location to be deprived of attainable territorial ambitions, have been tenacious in not giving up the political control over defined territories they individually possess. They resisted amalgamation in the 1860s, and in spite of the urgings of the Deutsch Report, they resist it today. "By any administrative logic," stated The Economist, "the three provinces should be bundled into one. But nobody will be crazy enough to try."[4] The hostile stance of Newfoundland to any possible reopening of the Labrador case by an independent Quebec further attests to the territorial conservatism of the provinces, tightly holding on to what they have won in the historical lottery of land acquisition. The provincial protection of and search for Lebensraum comprise a relatively unexamined aspect of federal-provincial history deserving as much scholarly investigation as their better-known safeguarding of their formal jurisdictional authority. The protection of jurisdictional authority and the protection and expansion of provincial territory have been accompanied by an ever more vigorous employment of provincial legislative competence. Related to this as both cause and effect has been a concomitant increase in government personnel. A similar expansion of personnel and a no less aggressive exploration of the limits of its constitutional responsibilities have been displayed by the federal government.

It would be a serious mistake to view these governmental mountains as molehills. The several hundred political officeholders constitute only a trivial minority of those who wield government power and/or derive their income directly from public positions. The growth of one federal and ten provincial governments has produced large and powerful complexes of institutions and personnel with their own professional and personal interests, and their own official purposes for the provincial and federal populations they govern. At the elementary level of numbers, the figures are staggeringly impressive. Total provincial government personnel, including provincial government enterprises, as of September, 1976, reached 519,000,[5] while the federal government sustains a veritable army of various shades and categories of civil service and crown corporation personnel, totalling 557,000 persons, a figure that includes the armed forces.[6] Nearly one out of every nine members of the Canadian work force is employed by the two senior levels of government,[7] while municipal government employs a further 256,000.[8] They are not indifferent to the fate of the governments they serve.

The astute observation of Alexander Hamilton in Federalist Paper No. 1, two centuries ago, has not declined in relevance: "Among the most formidable of the obstacles which the new Constitution will have to encounter may readily be distinguished the obvious interest of a certain class of men in every State to resist all changes which may hazard a diminution of the power, emolument, and consequence of the offices they hold under the State establishments."[9] Another certain class of men has attached itself to the central government.

It makes little sense to think of these impressive concentrations of power and personnel as superstructures whose existence and purposes are largely derivative of the electorate, the class structure, the pressure group system, or whatever. Even if we ignore their functions, the more than one million Canadians who work for federal and provincial governments, and their dependents, constitute an immense component of Canadian society directly tied to government. When we do consider their functions of policy-making, service-provision, regulation, and protection, extending to the most specialized activities where government monopolizes the expertise in a given field, we are made aware that we live in a period of convulsive change in government-society relations. In the evolution of the division of labour between those who govern and those who are governed, the energizing, proselytizing, and entrepreneurial role increasingly rests with those civil servants and politicians with the capacity to influence policy and its administration.

While the sheer fact of large numbers directly dependent on government should not be underestimated as a crucial, if elementary, factor in government survival, that contribution is multiplied by the ramifying effects of the institutional and organizational complexes in which these employees work and have their being. The ministries, departments, agencies, bureaus, and field offices to which they daily report constitute partially self-contained entities, valued for their own sake, and possessed of their own life and interests. Their minimum desire is for a steady level of activity. Typically, however, they seek to enlarge the scope of their functions. If the environment offers new opportunities for expansion in emergent problem areas they will compete with other bureaucracies for the prizes of status and growth offered by enhancement of their activity. If major challenges are made to their organizational identity, purpose, or cohesion, they will fight back against unsympathetic political superiors and other menacing figures and forces in their environment.[10] If their functions decline in social utility or their expertise becomes obsolescent, they will scan the horizon of alternative possibilities in an aggressive search

for new justifications for continued existence.[11] While they are subject to political control and direction they have impressive capacities to get their own way and to bend their political superiors to their will. Although their functions relate them to particular sectors of society, they are not puppets or simple reflections of the interests of the groups they control, regulate, or service. "[B]oth the sector served and political leaders come to be forces in the environment which public servants must manage and manipulate so that they will demand or agree to expansion of the bureaucracy."[12] Their basic strength resides in the expertise that makes them indispensable to their political superiors and in the support of the external interests that have positively adapted to their policies. They represent a permanent, expansive aspect of government. They are the necessary instruments of an administered society that could not, without major disruption, survive their disappearance from the scene.

The presence in the Canadian federal system of eleven governments, each honeycombed with bureaucratic interests and desires of the nature just described, helps explain the expansion of each level of government, the frequent competition and duplication of activity between governments, and the growing impact of government on society. It is impossible to think clearly about Canadian federalism without devoting extensive attention to the one million Canadians parcelled out in eleven jurisdictions and committed by loyalty, the terms of their employment, and self-interest to the particular government they serve.

These pyramids of bureaucratic power and ambition are capped by political authorities also possessed of protectionist and expansionist tendencies. The eleven governments of the federal system endow the incumbents of political office with the primary task of defending and advancing the basic interests of crucial sectors of the provincial or national economy and society. Each political office, particularly those of prime ministers and premiers, has a history that influences and constrains the succession of incumbents who briefly possess it. Thus, as André Bernard says: "No political leader in Quebec would ever dare voice a doubt about the sacrosanct objective of 'la survivance française en Amérique'. Survival of the French-Canadian people is an obligation, an article of faith. It has been so for 200 years. It is basic, fundamental."[13] Since 1871 the political leaders of British Columbia have consistently pressed economic claims on Ottawa demanding compensation for the chronically alleged financial maltreatment they have suffered from the federal government. The special needs and expenses associated with the harsh facts of geography and a primary resource-based economy have been reiterated in countless briefs. Other provinces also have "fairly durable and persisting interests"[14] reflecting the relatively unchanging factors of society, economy, and basic position in the federal system. The claims derived from the preceding are nourished by the constantly refurbished memory of past grievances.

Provincial political elites not only seek to further the long-range interests of their society and economy, they also have "a vested interest in provincial status and power which the several provincial electorates perhaps do not share fully."[15] Their policy determinations reflect a varying mix of goals for their provincial citizenry and an institutional concern for the long-term survival of the political and bureaucratic power of government itself. On the other side of the bargaining table they encounter Ottawa, a larger version of their own expansionist tendencies, which, in the slightly jaundiced words of Claude Morin, "is quite simply loyal to a solidly-rooted historical tradition, the unmistakable outlines of which could already be discerned in John A. Macdonald's remarks at the time the federation was put together."[16]

The inertia of the political and bureaucratic momentum of the governments they join inducts new recruits into prevailing definitions of the situation. This is instanced by the frequency with which staunch provincialists, from Joseph Howe onwards, become staunch federalists on entering the federal government. Thus, it is not surprising that the representatives of "French power" in Ottawa will seek solutions to French-English problems by policies that do not weaken the central government. They will try and make the federal government and, indeed, the whole country a more congenial environment for Francophones rather than opt for a solution that enhances the power of the government in Quebec City. It is also not surprising that such efforts are looked on with little favour by government elites in Quebec City. French Canadians in federal politics and in the federal civil service are conditioned to see the world through different eyes than their Quebec City counterparts.[17] What is attractive to the latter is often a direct threat to the polit-

ical and bureaucratic needs of the former. Profound governmental constraints minimize the possibility of ethnic solidarity across jurisdictional boundaries.

Federal and provincial governments are not neutral containers, or reflecting mirrors, but aggressive actors steadily extending their tentacles of control, regulation, and manipulation into society—playing, in Deutsch's terminology, a steering role—and thus fostering sets of integrated relationships between themselves and the various socio-economic forces and interests in their jurisdictions. Governing elites view their task as the injection of provincial or federal meaning into society, giving it a degree of coherence and a pattern of interdependence more suited for government purposes than what would emerge from the unhindered working of social and market forces. Each government's policies pull the affected interests into relations of dependence and attachment to the power centre that manipulates their existence. Each government seeks policy coherence in order to minimize internal contradictions leading to the frustration of its own policies. The inadequacies of the theory and advice on which decision-makers rely produce major discrepancies between governmental ambition and actual achievement. The byzantine complexity of internal government structures and the sluggishness of the diffuse bureaucratic instrumentalities on which policy-makers depend create additional obstacles to the coherence in policy and society that each government seeks. Nevertheless, given these limitations, each government transmits cues and pressures to the environment, thus tending to group the interests manipulated by its policies into webs of interdependence springing from the particular version of socio-economic integration it is pursuing. Provincial governments work toward the creation of limited versions of a politically created provincial society and economy, and the national government works toward the creation of a country-wide society and economy.

Federal policies are responses to nation-wide considerations. From the perspective of Ottawa the provinces constitute concentrations of governmental power whose manipulation is difficult but nevertheless must be attempted where necessary. In pursuing its mission as a national government from 1867 to the present, Ottawa has not hesitated to interfere with provincial policies by the disallowance of provincial legislation and, more recently, by the adroit and extensive employment of the spending power. The mission of provincial political elites is necessarily more restricted, being territorially confined by provincial boundaries, often restrained by weaknesses of financial capacity, and, formerly, hampered by administrative shortcomings. Nevertheless, the British North America Act gives the provinces jurisdictional authority in functional areas of expanding significance, and, most importantly, gives them control of the natural resource base of their economies. While the jurisdiction of a province lacks the comprehensive coverage enjoyed by the government of a unitary state, it is a sufficiently impressive base of governmental power to elicit visions of futures to be pursued. It cannot be doubted, to cite only the more obvious examples, that Lesage, Smallwood, Douglas, W.A.C. Bennett, and Manning had coherent sets of public purposes for the provincial societies they governed. From their perspective the federal government and its policies constituted environmental uncertainties that had to be managed, exploited, or reduced, and in some cases bitterly attacked in the defence of the provincial futures whose creation they envisaged.

As they pursue their specific goals, federal and provincial elites unwittingly serve the profound trend toward the increasing politicization of society. What Léon Dion calls the "political invasion of our daily lives . . . a new phenomenon in history,"[18] has a particular significance for a federal polity. In almost every conceivable aspect of our existence, from the workaday world of our daily occupation to the private intimate worlds of sex and love, our conduct is affected by the larger, pervasive world of federal and provincial competition and co-operation. We are light years away from the relatively apolitical, nongovernmentalized societies of 1867. No national society existed in 1867, and provincial societies were expected to be relatively free from extensive government controls by the newly created provincial governments. A century later we have governmentalized societies, both federal and provincial, interwoven with each other in relations of competitive interdependence.

The institutionalization of government,[19] the construction of a sphere of political and bureaucratic existence differentiated from other spheres of collective life, automatically reduces the relative importance of non-government groups, interests, and individuals in policy-

making. There is impressive unanimity from students of Canadian government that members of the public are little more than spectators, mobilized by competing elites at three- to five-year intervals for electoral purposes and then returned to their accustomed role as objects of government policy. "Canada," observes Richard Simeon, "combines the British tradition of a strong executive and centralized leadership with a *relative* freedom from mass pressure and popular constraint."[20] Even bitter and well-publicized intergovernmental conflict may take place in the face of almost complete public indifference or ignorance, as Claude Morin asserts was true of the recent Ottawa-Quebec hostilities over the latter's role at international conferences.[21]

Paradoxically, the institutionalization process acting as a barrier to public influence on decision making is the instrumentality for political and bureaucratic elites to bring society under ever more comprehensive government control and guidance. If socialism is about equality, contemporary Canadian federalism is about governments, governments that are possessed of massive human and financial resources, that are driven by purposes fashioned by elites, and that accord high priority to their own long-term institutional self-interest. We should not be surprised, therefore, to be told that in the early years of the Lesage regime "most governmental activity . . . was initiated by the government itself,"[22] to be reminded of the various federal government programs introduced by political and bureaucratic elites in the absence of strong demands,[23] and to read that the "demands on government have been in large part self-created."[24] It is abundantly clear that the massive impact of government on society at the output stage does not require a prior massive impact of society on government at the input stage.

By and large, the above analysis also applies to Quebec. The Quebec government, like the others, attempts to mould society in terms of its conception of a desirable future. Here, too, bureaucrats and politicians have the same disproportionate capacity to influence policy evident in other jurisdictions. But important differences exist. In recent years the political system they manage has been repeatedly shaken by social transformations, often government induced. Further, the society to which elites respond is not simply the provincial segment of an English-speaking North American culture that, with variations, dominates the rest of the country and the neighbour to the south. Although clusters of French culture exist elsewhere in Canada, its primary concentration in the province of Quebec necessarily involves the government of that province in a host of specific national questions. The government of Quebec is not in the business of controlling and directing the provincial segment of a larger society but of fostering and stimulating a "full blown society"[25] infused with nationalistic fervour by two centuries of minority status. This is a society in which the major groups, associations, and organizations increasingly "tend . . . to fall back on the Quebec government."[26]

The singular importance of provincial government in contemporary Quebec is partly a delayed compensation for the long era of negative government under Duplessis and his predecessors, which bequeathed the modernizing governments of the past two decades a heritage of daunting problems. Also, the relative weakness of the Francophone role in the private economic sector generates pressure to employ the majority-controlled provincial state to redress this no longer acceptable ethnic imbalance. Thus, although in contemporary Quebec, as elsewhere in Canada, the political debate centres on the precise nature of the leading role to be played by government, it is a debate with a difference. In recent years it has focused with growing intensity on the fundamental question of the relationship of the people and government of Quebec with the rest of Canada. Specifically, the debate centres on the question of whether a sovereign Quebec government is the best instrument to satisfy the profound desire of Francophone Quebecers for a modern, secure community. The existing system of political authorities is not taken for granted. The opponents of Confederation claim that it constitutes a mobilization of governmental bias hostile to national survival.

As a consequence of the particular circumstances just outlined, government-society relations in Quebec are characterized by a special intensity and passion. Further, the commitment of the present provincial leadership to hold a referendum on the constitutional future of the province involves the provincial population in the determination of the most crucial issue facing the society. The situation, therefore, is fundamentally different from the first sixty years of this century when the goal of provincial autonomy was standard fare in elite political rhetoric but left the masses "largely unmoved."[27] Nevertheless, in the process leading up to the referendum a key role will be played by the political leaders of the government. Their clear and professed task is to employ the levers of government power to persuade a majority of the population to support independence. They will control the wording and the timing of this carefully controlled exercise in democratic participation. And, confident that time is on their side, they have told the population of Quebec, and Canadians outside the province, that if the first effort fails they will try and try again.

The vanguard role of the governing Parti Québécois in actively changing attitudes to the political system is, from the perspective of this paper, no more than a particular manifestation of the managerial role I have attributed to all governments of the federal system. The creative leadership role of the Quebec government is a necessary consequence of the simple fact that it is deeply committed to an objective for which popular support is, in relative terms, lacking.

Before the referendum there will be intergovernmental competition of a particularly aggressive nature, for the issues at stake relate not to a particular program or to the next election, but to opposed constitutional futures. The erosion of support for the federal regime involves the federal government in extraordinary efforts to preserve its legitimacy,[28] particularly by maximizing direct links with individuals clearly seen to be profitable by the Quebec citizenry. The federal system, as Morin observes, "divides Quebecers against themselves."[29] The constitutional referendum that has been under way in Quebec for a decade and a half, which accelerated in tempo after November 15, 1976, and which will be formalized in the near future, involves a competition orchestrated by the government elites in Quebec City and Ottawa to shift or stabilize the dividing line in individuals and in the society as a whole. Further, it is evident that whatever its outcome the referendum will only constitute an ephemeral plebiscitarian interruption of the intergovernmental contest that will resume immediately after the votes are counted. The results of the referendum will instantly be transformed into political resources by federal and provincial prime ministers and cabinet ministers who will fasten conflicting interpretations on the nature of the message the electorate has transmitted. And even should that message be unequivocally positive in support of independence it will still be the task of governments to manage the next stage of partial or complete disengagement.

Reading Notes

1. D.V. Smiley, *Canada in Question: Federalism in the Seventies* (2nd ed.; Toronto, 1976), pp. 10–11, and chapter 2.

2. See Luce Patenaude, *Le Labrador à l'heure de la contestation* (Montreal, 1972), and Jacques Brossard et al., *Le Territoire Québécois* (Montreal, 1970), pp. 17–19, for materials and analysis from a Quebec perspective on the Labrador dispute.

3. For an excellent technical description of boundary changes, see Norman L. Nicholson, *The Boundaries of Canada, Its Provinces and Territories*, Canada, Department of Mines and Technical Surveys, Geographical Branch, Memoir no. 2 (Ottawa, 1964).

4. February 12, 1972, cited in Edgar Gallant, "Maritime Cooperation and Integration—A Progress Report," in O.J. Firestone, ed., *Regional Economic Development* (Ottawa, 1974), p. 167.

5. This is the combined total of 349,063 wage-earners, full-time and other, excluding B.C., but including Yukon and the Northwest Territories, for general government services, Statistics Canada, *Provincial Government Employment October–December 1976* (Ottawa, 1977), p. 6; 136,463 salary-earners and wage-earners, full-time and other, for provincial government enterprises, ibid., p. 28; and 33,197 employees of the B.C. government, excluding B.C. Ferries, *Public Service Commission Annual Report* (Victoria, 1977), p. 23, for a total of 518,723.

6. Statistics Canada, *Federal Government Employment July–September 1976* (Ottawa, 1977), p. 11.

7. Based on unadjusted employment figures of 9,688,000 for September, 1976. *Canadian Statistical Review* (February, 1977), p. 49.

8. Statistics Canada, *Local Government Employment July–September 1976* (Ottawa, 1977), p. 5. "If we add to the list of civil servants . . . [at all three levels] those employed in a vast array of nondepartmental agencies, boards, commissions, enterprises, and teachers and hospital employees, we would find that at least one in every five in the labour force in the country is on a public payroll." J.E. Hodgetts and O.P. Dwivedi, *Provincial Governments as Employers* (Montreal and London, 1974), p. 2.

9. Roy P. Fairfield, ed., *The Federalist Papers* (2nd ed.; Garden City, N.Y., 1966), p. 2.

10. For a relevant case study, see A. Paul Pross, "Input versus Withinput: Pressure Group Demands and Administrative Survival," in A. Paul Pross, ed., *Pressure Group Behaviour in Canadian Politics* (Toronto, 1975).

11. "A classic case [of the survival capacity of public organizations] is the Halifax Disaster Relief Commission, established to handle claims arising from the Halifax explosion of 1917. In late 1975, the federal government introduced a bill to repeal the act respecting the Commission and to transfer authority for continuation of pensions and allowances to the Canadian Pension Commission. So long-lived was the commission that the bill winding it up had to make pension provisions for employees of the Commission itself." Donald Gow, "Rebuilding Canada's Bureaucracy," edited and revised by Edwin R. Black and Michael J. Prince (Kingston, 1976), mimeo, p. 40.

12. Ibid.

13. André Bernard, "The Quebec Perspective on Canada: The Last Quarter Century—Language Strife," a paper prepared for the University of Saskatchewan Conference on Political Change in Canada, March 17, 1977, p. 1. This leadership role is a response to the social and political fact that "No power in the world can prevent Francophone Quebecers from perceiving themselves as a society and as a nation, original and distinct from the Canadian whole." Léon Dion, *Québec: The Unfinished Revolution* (Montreal and London, 1976), p. 45.

14. Smiley, *Canada in Question,* p. 108.

15. Corry, "Constitutional Trends and Federalism," p. 101.

16. Claude Morin, *Quebec versus Ottawa: The Struggle for Self-government 1960–1972* (Toronto, 1976), p. 95.

17. Ibid., chapter 13.

18. Dion, *Québec: The Unfinished Revolution*, p. 86.

19. For an extremely helpful discussion of institutionalization, see Samuel P. Huntington, "Political Development and Political Decay," in Norman J. Vig and Rodney J. Stiefbold, eds., *Politics in Advanced Nations* (Englewood

Cliffs, N.J., 1974). "Institutionalization is the process by which organizations and procedures acquire value and stability. The level of institutionalization of any political system can be defined by the adaptability, complexity, autonomy, and coherence of its organizations and procedures" (p. 115). In comparative terms, the Canadian political system is highly institutionalized.

20. Richard Simeon, "The 'Overload Thesis' and Canadian Government," *Canadian Public Policy*, 2 (1976), p. 550, italics in original. Similar statements abound in the literature. "For today's citizens," states Dion, "as for their fathers, the State is still a distant 'they,' alien and almost inimical . . . " (*Québec: The Unfinished Revolution*, p. 87). Smiley speculates that "elites are somewhat unresponsive to popular attitudes and that the citizenry for whatever reasons has a considerable tolerance for this unresponsiveness" (*Canada in Question*, p. 201). J.R. Mallory observes that "the mass of citizenry is perhaps as far away from the real decisions of government as they were two hundred years ago, and the cabinet system provides strong institutional barriers to the development of more democratic ways of doing things" ("Responsive and Responsible Government," *Transactions of the Royal Society of Canada*, Fourth Series, xii [1974], p. 208). A recent volume on pressure groups documents instances in which government agencies withstood "considerable input pressure from the external environment, and that they may significantly influence that environment, if not dominate it" (A. Paul Pross, "Pressure Groups: Adaptive Instruments of Political Communication," in Pross, ed., *Pressure Group Behaviour in Canadian Politics*, p. 21). J.E. Anderson suggests "that in Canada the relations between civil servants and pressure groups are usually dominated by civil servants" ("Pressure Groups and the Canadian Bureaucracy," in W.D.K. Kernaghan, ed., *Bureaucracy in Canadian Government* [2nd ed.; Toronto, 1973], p. 99).

21. Morin, *Quebec versus Ottawa*, p. 43.

22. Dion, *Québec: The Unfinished Revolution*, p. 138.

23. John Meisel, "Citizen Demands and Government Response," *Canadian Public Policy*, 2 (1976), p. 568.

24. Simeon, "The 'Overload Thesis' and Canadian Government," p. 546.

25. Bernard, "Quebec Perspective on Canada," p. 1.

26. Dion, *Québec: The Unfinished Revolution*, p. 156.

27. Ibid., pp. 124, 169–70.

28. Ibid., p. 156.

29. Morin, *Quebec versus Ottawa*, p. 130.

KEY TERMS

Feminism Politics   Politics conceptualized in terms of gender relations.

New Institutionalism   Politics is seen as heavily shaped by political institutions.

Political Culture   The pattern of individual attitudes and orientations toward politics among the members of a political system. It is the subjective realm that underlies and gives meaning to political action.

Political Economy   Politics is conceptualized in terms of state–market relations.

Postmodernism   Politics is constructed by discourse.

Rational Choice   Political outcomes are viewed as the product of strategic decision making.

Structural-Functionalism   Political structures are viewed as developing in response to social needs.

Systems Analysis (Theory)   Politics is conceptualized as a system with inputs, outputs, and feedback.

FURTHER READINGS

Bill, James A., and Robert L. Hargrave, Jr. *Comparative Politics: The Quest for Theory.* 2nd ed. Lanham: University Press of America, 1981.

Knuttila, Murray. *State Theories: From Liberalism to the Challenge of Feminism.* Toronto: Garamond Press, 1987.

Lecours, André (ed). *New Institutionalism. Theory and Analysis.* Toronto: University of Toronto Press, 2005.

CHAPTER 3

METHODOLOGY

Whether or not one subscribes to the notion that the study of politics is a scientific enterprise modelled on the hard sciences, methodology is unquestionably a central component of the study of political science. A self-conscious reflexive awareness of how we go about conducting research in political science is essential. What kind of questions about political phenomena do we ask? What kind of data do we collect, and how do we collect it? What kind of generalizations can we make about the political world? These are all questions that fall under the label of methodology. This chapter introduces students of political science to the basic terminologies, concepts, and methodologies of the discipline. It opens with a discussion of the language of politics. This is followed by an explanation of the basic concepts and terms employed by political scientists. The chapter closes with an exploration of the different methodologies used in the discipline.

THE LANGUAGE OF POLITICS

The quest to explain political puzzles is at the heart of the study of political science. Political scientists often organize their research in a manner conducive to explaining differences within a state, or between a number of states. In so doing, they typically explore different political institutions, electoral systems, party systems, federal structures, or political actors within states or across them. However, this research employs a particular language that allows for consistency in research and comparative analysis. It is probably best to explore this language of politics through an example.

Let us assume that we are interested in democracy as a political system, and that we want to explain why it exists in some countries but not in others. We will probably start our research by selecting two countries, one of which represents a functioning and durable democracy, and one that does not. The objective of our research is to explain this puzzle. We may also want to try to see whether or not our conclusions may be generalizable to a larger number of countries within a certain geographic region—the Middle East, Latin America, Europe, or North America—or across them. And if we want to challenge ourselves, we might start this exercise by selecting two countries from two different regions of the world, say Latin America and East Asia.

In the above example, "democracy" is what in the language of politics is labelled the **dependent variable**, or the political phenomenon we are trying to explain. It is called a dependent variable because our explanation of it will depend on other factors, which are in turn called **independent variables**. Independent variables are labelled thus because it is presumed that they cause the dependent variable, and because they are independent of anything else. Consequently, independent variables are also referred to as "explanatory" variables, while the dependent variable is also labelled as "what needs to be explained." One way to think about dependent and independent variables is to think of the independent variable as a cause, and the dependent variable as the effect, i.e., the political phenomenon we are trying to explain.

Thus, in our quest to answer the puzzle mentioned above, we might suggest a number of independent variables. One possible independent variable that helps explain the existence of democracy in some countries, but not in others, is the level of economic development. In fact, we may suggest a **hypothesis** that encapsulates the relationship between democracy and different levels of economic development. A hypothesis is defined as a conjectural statement about the relationship between two variables. In this case, we may represent our hypothesis in the following way:

(if) high level of economic development ⟶ (then) democracy

In other words, this hypothesis suggests that we should expect democratic political systems in those countries with high levels of economic development. Alternatively, if we have low levels of economic development we might then expect a lack of democracy, or authoritarianism. All hypotheses should thus be stated in terms of a relation between two variables, and they must relate changes in the dependent variable to changes in the independent variable(s). Schematically this means

(if) A ⟶ (then) B

However, the most useful hypotheses are those that relate the independent variable and the dependent variable in a dynamic way. They do so by investigating how changes in the independent variables affect changes in the dependent variable. The following examples may help explain these relations.

1. For example, we may hypothesize that the more economic development in a certain country, the more the prospects for political stability in that country. The logic of the argument suggests that greater economic development allows for the emergence of a substantial middle class in the country. Consequently, the professional nature of the middle class often militates for political stability rather than instability. Notice that the value of the dependent variable (political stability) changes as a function of change in the value of the independent variable (economic development).

2. We may also want to investigate how religious belief impacts upon support for abortion. Here we may argue that the more religious you are, the more you believe in the sanctity of life, and the less you support abortion. In this particular hypothesis the label "belief in the sanctity of life" is called an intervening variable, because it intervenes between the independent and dependent variables and influences the relation between them in a positive or negative way. Thus,

independent variable ⟶ intervening variable ⟶ dependent variable

3. Finally, we may want to investigate the relation between poverty and political alienation. Here the logic of the argument suggests that the poorer you are, the more you perceive the system to be unresponsive to your needs, and thus the more politically alienated you are. Here also "system unresponsiveness" is an intervening variable because it reinforces the relationship between the independent and dependent variables (in this case) in a positive manner.

Having explored independent and dependent variables, a caveat is required. Constructing a useful and testable hypothesis may sometimes be a deceptively simple exercise. Indeed, many students of politics lapse into a common error when constructing hypotheses: a relationship is assumed to exist between two variables that actually have no causal interaction. For example, consider the following statement: Armed conflict between Lebanon's different sects produced a bitter civil war. The problem with this hypothesis is that the dependent variable may also serve as an independent variable and may account for it (the independent variable) as well. Thus the independent and dependent variables are easily interchangeable. In the language of politics, such a statement is labelled a "tautology." After all, armed conflict and civil war are one and the same. Consequently, this hypothesis is devoid of any explanatory power because the independent variable does not explain the dependent variable. Rather, possible independent variables to explain the civil war in Lebanon may include such factors as intersectarian animosity, political inertia, or regional crisis.

Another pitfall that should be avoided when constructing hypotheses is that of spurious correlations. In this case, two variables appear to be correlated when in fact there is no relationship between them. The famous example of this methodological pitfall concerns the fairy tale that babies are delivered by storks. Statistical data from northern Europe does suggest that human births increased whenever stork births increased, and vice versa. The problem with this correlation is that stork births and human births are causally unconnected. Spurious correlations are thus those types of correlations where two variables seem to be correlated, but in reality neither causes the other.

Alternatively, a spurious correlation can exist when two variables seem to be positively correlated, but in reality they are both caused by a third variable. For example, ice cream sales tend to increase with increases in the use of air conditioners. However, these two variables are not directly correlated. Rather, they are both caused by an alternative variable: increase in temperature. This language of variables is the language of the study of politics. Whether or not one subscribes to the argument that the study of politics is a scientific enterprise, this language of variables is essential to our research; otherwise, our quest for comparative research conclusions would be very difficult indeed. Having said this, we should always be careful lest we get carried away with causal statements. Because the study of politics is unlike that of the hard sciences, and because analysis of political phenomena involves looking at complex topics (war, voting, political systems, political culture) that are difficult to replicate in the manner in which scientific experiments are replicated, many students of politics tend to avoid causal statements (A causes B), and instead satisfy themselves with tendency statements. Instead of arguing that high levels of economic development cause democracy, political scientists are more comfortable arguing that "countries with high income levels tend to be more likely to have democratic institutions." After all, exceptions to the causal statement are not in short supply. Saudi Arabia is one such exception, where a very high gross domestic product (GDP) rate is not correlated with the existence of democratic political institutions.

The language of methodology in politics also contains a number of additional important terms that are commonly used in political science. These include the following:

Taxonomy A subject divided into classes distinct from one another. For example, we may want to classify European political systems into either presidential or parliamentary systems.

Typology That kind of taxonomy in which classificatory distinctions are graded or ordered. In other words, a typology is a more advanced and complex taxonomy that involves classifying phenomena based on a number of variables. A famous typology in political science is that developed by Arend Lijphart. Lijphart's typology classified Western democratic political systems according to the structure of the society and the nature of the behaviour of the political elite. Moreover, each variable was subdivided into two types: homogeneous or plural societies, and coalescent or competitive behaviour by the political elite. The result of this fourfold scheme is a typology that arranged Western democratic political systems according to the matrix shown in Figure 3.1.[1]

Model A theoretical and simplified representation of the real world, helping us represent and understand what are otherwise complex processes. Models are deliberate simplifications of an otherwise very complex process. However, they do allow us to organize complex patterns of political interaction

Figure 3.1 **LIJPHART'S TYPOLOGY**

	Structure of Society	
	Homogeneous	**Plural**
Coalescent	Austria (1966–)	Belgium Netherlands Switzerland Austria (1945–1966)
Competitive	Finland UK, US Sweden West Germany	France Italy Canada

(Row label to the left, spanning both rows: **Elite Behaviour**)

and thus study political dynamics in an orderly fashion. One famous model in the study of politics is that developed by David Easton in the mid-1960s. This model attempts to represent the world of Western politics as a set of interrelated components whose sum total forms a political system. This system has inputs that go into the political system in the form of values, pressures by interest groups, and political parties. These inputs or demands are then processed by the institutions of the state, which ultimately lead to outputs in the form of domestic or foreign policies. In turn, these government policies feed back into the system in two ways: (1) as support for the state's policies and hence for the government if the policies agree with the demands of certain segments of the population and (2) in the form of new demands if the policies raise objections from segments of the population. For a fuller discussion of Easton's model and systems theory, see Chapter 2.

Theory A set of systematically related generalizations suggesting new observations for empirical testing. The construction of theories is a central objective for the scientific enterprise. But in political science, theories are not as common as in the hard sciences. This is the case because in physics, chemistry, or biology it is not too difficult to control measurements and thus replicate experiments. This allows for exact tests, which ultimately generate verifiable results. The complexity of the political world makes the kind of rigorous testing common in the hard sciences very difficult, if not impossible. Nevertheless, contemporary political scientists aspire to generate verifiable theories. The most recent attempt in political science to construct a theory from a hypothesis involves rigorous testing of the generalization that democracies—or more accurately, democratic dyads (pairs)—do not go to war against each other. Proponents of this "democratic peace" argument argue that the similar institutional composition of democratic dyads—transparent decision-making processes, division of powers, public debates, the potential for electoral defeat—constrains political elites and hence permits the peaceful resolution of conflict among democracies.[2]

METHODOLOGY IN POLITICAL SCIENCE

The study of political science is guided not only by the language and concepts that we have partially explored above, but also by a set of systematic research techniques. These techniques shape the particular methodology researchers employ in the study of political science: that is, what political puzzles do we want to answer? What kind of data and evidence do we collect to answer these puzzles? How do we collect the data to allow for comparative analysis and conclusions? There are two main types of inquiry in the study of political science.

Normative

This type of inquiry is concerned with normative questions. That is, how should we act and live and organize our lives to achieve greater justice, equality, democracy, and freedom for all. These philosophical or *how* questions about politics, individuals, and society have pre-occupied political philosophers for millennia, and they continue to do so today. They are the concern of the sub-discipline of political philosophy.

Empirical

This type of inquiry is concerned with *why* things happen rather than with what *should* happen. It seeks to establish testable and verifiable relationships between the independent and dependent variables.

A normative approach to the 1978–79 Iranian revolution is concerned mainly with whether or not revolutions are inherently good or bad agents of change, a topic thoughtfully dissected a long time ago by Edmund Burke in his classic *Reflections on the Revolution in France* (1790). By contrast, an empirical approach to the study of the Iranian revolution of 1978–79 would rather ask a different question: "Why did a revolution take place in Iran in 1978–79?" This question would invite an investigation of the empirical reasons that can best explain why the Iranian revolution occurred at a specific point in time. Influenced by political culture analysis you would argue that the rapid pace of modernization in Iran under Reza Shah undermined the existing traditional institutions of authority and alienated most Iranians from the monarchy, paving the way for the Shah's ouster. Alternatively, a political economic analysis would suggest that the Shah's despotism and refusal to modernize the authoritarian institution of the monarchy alienated a critical mass of the population, while his socio-economic reforms alienated the religious establishment, which retaliated by radicalizing religion—in a manner not very unlike the way the Church in Latin America preached a radical brand of religion through liberation theology. The convergence of these pressures mobilized a critical mass against the Shah and successfully ousted him from power. Whether one deploys a political culture or a political economic analysis, the explanation of the Iranian revolution is nevertheless based on empirical observations rather than normative questions.

The empirical approach is at the heart of the contemporary study of political science and particularly the study of comparative politics and international relations. Within this approach, there are a number of different methods for collecting data and suggesting testable explanations of political puzzles, hence the following different methodologies.[3]

CASE STUDY METHOD

This method emphasizes the in-depth study of a single country, or a single political institution or political behaviour in a single country. Examples include the study of political development in Tanzania, parliament in Great Britain, or voting behaviour in France. Its advantage is that it allows for a truly detailed and intensive analysis of the case under investigation. The drawback of the case study pertains to the generalizability of its findings. This is so because such findings are based on the study of a single case. Consequently, case study research contributes the least to theory building in political science. It is often deployed to confirm or debunk existing theories.

STATISTICAL METHOD

This method involves a large number of cases. Often it is used to evaluate the validity of rival hypotheses and explanations against a large number of cases (or countries). It involves the use of a variety of statistical techniques to measure observations and collect data. At the heart of the statistical method is the mathematical manipulation of empirically observed data to test or discover certain relationships among the independent and dependent variables. For example, the statistical method is very useful to test hypotheses relating economic development (independent variable) and political stability (dependent variable). Mathematical coding techniques allow scholars to test the relation between these variables over hundreds of cases, and thus use their findings to confirm or debunk hypotheses. The most serious weakness of the statistical method rests in the difficulty encountered by scholars trying to develop variables that can travel easily across different regions and cases. Say you are testing the relation between democracies and war: do all democracies share the same institutional structures? Or do they vary in certain ways across cultures and societies? The obstacles encountered when developing truly representative variables often expose the statistical method to some loss in the accuracy of its findings. Consequently, scholars may be skeptical about the validity of its findings.

COMPARATIVE METHOD

Perhaps the most popular method in the study of comparative politics, this method involves the analysis of a small number of cases, usually two or three, but at least two, to discover empirical relationships between variables and to test hypotheses. The comparative method is best explained via an example. Let us assume that you are a comparative scholar interested in the study of revolutions (the dependent variable), and your aim is to develop a general explanation of why revolutions take place. To do so, you will undertake an intensive comparative study of revolutions in a number of countries that have actually undergone such experiences. To be sure, the universe of your cases is not infinite. Consequently, you may decide to undertake a comparative study of revolutions in China, Russia, and France. By comparing the revolutionary experiences in these three countries, you may then be able to generate a theory of revolutions. Indeed, Theda Skocpol undertook such a comparative study in her classic study of revolutions.[4]

One of the main strengths of the comparative method rests in the flexibility it allows researchers when selecting their cases. Indeed, case selection is an important aspect of comparative methodology. The objective of advertent case selection is to establish empirical relationships between two variables while all other variables are controlled or held constant. This may be achieved by selecting two or more cases that share a similar political puzzle or phenomenon (the dependent variable), and are similar in many aspects except on the independent variable. This methodology allows the researcher to control for as many variables as possible between the cases under study, thus discovering empirical relationships between the independent and dependent variables. There are two general case selection approaches in political science:

Most-similar-systems approach Employing this approach, the researcher selects two cases that are similar in as many ways as possible. The objective is to control for as many variables as possible between the two cases to explain variation on the dependent variable through a single independent variable. For example, a researcher might be interested in resolving the following puzzle: Despite their oil wealth, Saudi Arabia and Kuwait differ in that the former is an absolutist monarchy while the latter boasts of having a vocal opposition. What explains this puzzle? In search of an answer, the researcher attempts to control for as many similar variables between the two countries. Both countries are Arab Muslim, and hence share a similar political cultural orientation; both have substantial oil reserves and have used oil revenues to buy political support from their populations; and both have roughly similar population structures. However, Saudi Arabia did not experience direct colonization by a foreign power. Kuwait, on the other hand, was colonized by the British, who encouraged the emergence of a powerful merchant class that gradually came to represent the opposition. Thus the colonial experience may be considered as a possible independent variable explaining the variation on the dependent variable between Saudi Arabia and Kuwait.

Most-different-systems approach Unlike the most-similar-systems approach, this approach seeks to explain variations on the dependent variable by selecting cases that are dissimilar in many respects. Consequently, the one variable shared by these cases tends to explain the variation on the dependent variable. The literature on democratization and political liberalization uses this approach. It tries to explain why very different countries, belonging to different cultural traditions, went through similar transitions from authoritarianism to democratization or political liberalization. Comparative research suggests that democratization and political liberalization is often engineered from above as a result of differences among the ruling elite and/or to contain the political consequences of difficult economic crises.[5]

Comparative research may also be undertaken either within a state or across states. Here, two broad types may be delineated:

Diachronic comparisons These compare political dynamics or a political institution in one country, but during different periods of time. A study of the powers of the executive in France in 1950 and 1990 is an example of **diachronic comparisons**.

Synchronic comparisons These compare a political institution or political behaviour across countries, usually during the same period of time. A study of the role of the state in the economic development of Chile and Singapore is an example of **synchronic comparisons**. The most-similar-systems approach is associated with these types of comparisons.

EXPERIMENTAL METHOD

The methods outlined above—the case study, the statistical, and the comparative method—are, in political science, labelled non-experimental methods because they are based on observation and measurement of variables within or between cases. In contrast, the experimental method, the ideal method for scientific explanations, is based on the manipulation of variables. In this case, two equivalent groups are set up, one of which (the experimental group) is exposed to a stimulus while the other (the control group) is not. The results among the two groups of this test are then compared, with the difference between them attributed to the stimulus. Of course, this assumes that all other variables are held constant or are being controlled for. However, the practical and ethical impediments confronting this method make it the least employed in political science research. After all, the complexity of the political world, and of the human beings that inhabit it, makes it extremely difficult to undertake controlled experiments of the type used in the experimental method. Nevertheless, some researchers, principally social psychologists, have used this method to study aspects of human behaviour relevant to political scientists such as risk perception, reactions to symbols, selective memory, and so on.

ENDNOTES

1. See Arend Lijphart, *Democracy in Plural Societies* (New Haven: Yale University Press, 1977), 106.
2. See Bruce Russett, *Grasping the Democratic Peace* (Princeton, NJ: Princeton University Press, 1993).
3. For an overview see Arend Lijphart, "Comparative Politics and the Comparative Method," *American Political Science Review* 65, no. 3 (September 1971): 682–93.
4. See Theda Skocpol, *State and Social Revolutions: A Comparative Analysis of France, Russia, and China* (Cambridge: Cambridge University Press, 1979).

5. See Guillermo O'Donnell and Philippe C. Schmitter, *Transitions from Authoritarian Rule: Tentative Conclusions about Uncertain Democracies* (Baltimore: The Johns Hopkins University Press, 1986).

READING

An excerpt from Michael Sodaro's book on comparative politics offers a very interactive application of most of the concepts and themes discussed in this chapter. The examples presented on the following pages should be particularly valuable to enhance your understanding and ability to apply the key concepts discussed in this chapter. As with the chapter itself, the relatively large number of definitions and concepts encountered in Sodaro's reading will be much more manageable with an instructor's guidance as to which he or she considers important.

The point of departure for the reading is the difference made in political science between normative and empirical explanations. The analysis then turns to a discussion of the objectives involved in the study of political science: namely, the explanation of political phenomena, and a certain level of generalization about political processes. As the opening line in this chapter suggests, this does not imply that *all* political scientists share the same quest for generalization in the study of politics, in the way that all physicists, chemists, or biologists seek generalizations in the study of nature. What they do share—and this is especially true for students of comparative politics and international relations—is a common language to describe, code, analyze, and perhaps disagree about political phenomena. The reading applies these concepts to some interesting examples pertaining to the relation between different levels of annual income (independent variable) and voter turnout (dependent variable), as well as different degrees of alienation (independent variable) and voter turnout (dependent variable). Such examples help students explore the different types of correlation that may exist between independent and dependent variables. The reading also explores the theme of spurious correlation, a common pitfall in the analysis of political phenomena.

The rest of Sodaro's reading is dedicated to an analysis of the terms already introduced in this chapter. These include taxonomy, typology, model, and theory. It also discusses some additional concepts, such as "laws" and "paradigms." Like the preceding concepts, these are considered basic to the language of politics. The reading closes with an instructive discussion of logical fallacies in the study of political science. We have already encountered in this chapter one such fallacy: tautology. Sodaro's reading introduces students to some additional fallacies. While different instructors will no doubt make different choices as to which of these fallacies to concentrate on, all of them, of course, should be avoided.

CRITICAL THINKING ABOUT POLITICS

Michael Sodaro

(I) ANALYTICAL TECHNIQUES OF POLITICAL SCIENCE

Political science . . . is a science to the extent that its practitioners engage in the following tasks:

- *Definition*: as political scientists, we *define* terms and concepts as precisely as possible;

- *Description*: we *observe*, *collect* and *describe* facts systematically, make relevant descriptive comparisons, and build descriptive models;

- *Explanation*: we *explain* the phenomena being studied, often by making *generalizations* about them in the form of *hypotheses* and *theories* and *testing* these generalizations against reality;

- *Probabilistic prediction*: without predicting future events precisely, we seek to project future trends and tendencies in a *probabilistic* manner, often by specifying various *conditions* for future development; and
- *Prescription*: depending on the issue, we can sometimes *prescribe* policies or actions that address the real-world problems of political life.

Ought-questions and is-questions As a general rule, political science asks two broad types of questions: *is*-questions (What *is* political reality?) and *ought*-questions (What *ought* to be done about political reality?). The two sets of questions are intimately related: we cannot adequately determine what ought to be done through practical political activity without a thorough comprehension of the realities we are facing. Good policy prescription requires good analysis. We must always keep in mind, however, that is-questions and ought-questions are fundamentally different. Is-questions concentrate on *facts* and *explanations* of facts, whereas ought-questions frequently deal with *personal preferences* and *values*. The systematic analysis of facts is called *empirical analysis*. Before turning our attention to that subject, however, we need to clarify the relationship between is- questions and ought-questions a bit further.

"WHAT IS?": A GUIDE TO EMPIRICAL POLITICAL ANALYSIS

In addition to being interested in what people ought to do in the realm of politics, political science is concerned with *describing* and *explaining* political realities. To this end it takes a close look at the facts of political life and searches for patterns or relationships that help explain those facts. What is democracy and how does it work? What are the various connections between politics and the economy? How do people behave in politics? What is a military dictatorship? How does it differ from other forms of authoritarianism? Why does it tend to occur in some countries but not in others? Questions such as these probe the *what*, the *how*, and the *why* of political reality.

Empirical analysis is centered on facts. It seeks to discover, describe, and explain facts and factual relationships, to the extent that the facts are knowable.

The term *empirical* derives from the ancient Greek word for experience. Empirical analysis is based strictly on what we can experience or perceive through our senses: namely, *facts*. Empirical analysis is not concerned with our values, ideals, or preferences. It does not make value judgments.

At least in principle, when we study politics empirically we are supposed to put aside our personal preferences and religious faith and just stick to the observable facts. As a consequence, empirical political science is sometimes called *value-free* political science: it requires us to keep our investigations of political reality free from our own particular values and biases, no matter how well-intentioned or well-reasoned our convictions may be. If we favor democracy, for example, we must not allow this preference to intrude into our efforts to understand how democracies work in actual fact. Otherwise, we may blind ourselves to certain realities about democracies that we may find unpalatable. The same admonition applies to adherents of all political persuasions. In practice, however, it can be quite difficult to keep our subjective inclinations completely separate from our fact-centered analyses. Personal values and preferences sometimes creep into the way we select the topics we are interested in and the ways we look at them. The canons of science require us to acknowledge our biases and make sure that they do not get in the way of our quest for objective truth when conducting empirical investigations.

Definition

All sciences must strive for definitional clarity with respect to the phenomena they study and the terms and concepts they employ. Unless we are clear about the meanings of the terms we use, we may end up in a conceptual muddle. The same terms may mean different things to different people, or they may have several different meanings that depend on the context in which they are used. The meanings we attach to key terms and concepts may also change over time. Biologists, for example, must be as precise as they can about the meaning of such concepts as cellular metabolism, evolution, and even life itself. These basic concepts do not lend themselves to simple definitions that are valid for all time and circumstances. Biologists may have to revise their definitions from time to time, and they may even disagree among themselves about what these and other biological concepts actually mean.

As political scientists, we too must define our concepts and refine our definitions so that they accurately apply to reality and clearly reflect our ideas and preferences about political reality. *A concept is a word, a term, or a label that applies to a whole class or category of phenomena or ideas.* In political science, such terms as *freedom, power, democracy, liberalism, conservatism, socialism,* and *interdependence* are concepts whose meanings need to be carefully spelled out if we are to be able to talk about them intelligibly and consistently. Like many political concepts, each of them can be defined in more than one way. For James Madison and the framers of the U.S. constitution, for example, freedom meant above all freedom from the tyranny of an excessively powerful state. For Karl Marx, however, it meant freedom from economic exploitation by private industrialists. In early twentieth-century Germany, a conservative was a staunch opponent of democracy who favored a militarily powerful authoritarian state. Conservatives in contemporary Germany, by contrast, favor both democracy and civilian control over the military. Conceptual clarity is imperative whether we are discussing political values (e.g., freedom) or describing political facts (e.g., German conservatism). Achieving such clarity is one of the principal aims of political science.

Description: Observing, Collecting, Comparing

Natural scientists must be keen observers of nature. They must look very closely at natural phenomena, record their observations, and gather them together in some systematic fashion. Political scientists must be equally acute observers of politics. To understand how the facts of political life fit together, they must record and gather the facts at hand as systematically as they can.

To study things *systematically* means *to employ a particular method.* One of the oldest ways of studying the natural world has involved the comparative method. Biologists, for example, compare various forms of animal and plant life and group them into categories, such as kingdom, genus, and species. In a roughly similar manner, political scientists can examine systems of government, describe their similarities and differences, and classify them in various categories. Starting

with democracy and authoritarianism as the two broadest categories, we can group different types of democracy under the first rubric and different forms of authoritarian government under the second. Gabriel Almond, a pioneering figure in the study of comparative politics, once suggested that it is especially interesting to look for *dissimilarities* between *similar* forms of government (such as democracies) and *similarities* between *dissimilar* forms of government (such as democracies and non-democracies). By employing these descriptive and comparative techniques, we can get a better understanding of how governments work. In the process, we might also gain some insight into how we can improve the way governments work, employing scientific description in the cause of policy prescription. We can use these same techniques to understand other political phenomena as well, such as power, political behavior, political economy, and so forth.

The precise methods we use to carry out our observations and comparisons will vary from case to case, usually depending on the specific topic we are interested in exploring. If we are interested in the way people vote, we will want to gather election returns as well as relevant information about the voters, such as their social class, religion, ethnicity and the like. If we want to understand how political elites view politics, it may be helpful to conduct interviews with relevant officials, such as parliamentarians or bureaucrats, to see how they perceive politics and their own role in political affairs. To increase the breadth and depth of these observations on a comparative basis, we may wish to examine voting patterns or elite attitudes in a variety of countries over extended periods of time. The more information we observe, the more likely it is that patterns will emerge that will permit us to go beyond merely describing reality. It will then be possible to *make generalizations* about reality with the aim of *explaining* it.

Explanation and Generalization

Are American voters becoming less loyal to political parties over time? Are similar tendencies occurring in other democracies? If so, then why?

Do political elites in democratizing countries share similar conceptions of democracy, or do they differ? What accounts for these similarities or differences? Are these attitudes conducive to stabilizing democracy or might they tend to undermine it?

Questions such as these take us beyond merely isolated facts about politics in this or that country, however intriguing they may be. They prompt us to *generalize* from those facts in order to gain a broader perspective on political reality. One of the central purposes of studying politics systematically is to make sense out of the bewildering array of political facts that constantly barrage us in newspapers and on television screens. By themselves, facts are not especially meaningful. (As one wag put it, "History is just one damned thing after another!") The facts of political life, whether historical or contemporary in nature, assume meaning only when we visualize them as general patterns, tendencies, or relationships.

. . . if we want to comprehend the significance of discrete facts or events in political life, we must integrate them into larger processes or frameworks. Today's headlines, for example, may announce that the prime minister of a major democratic country has resigned, that the government's central bank in a leading trading nation has just raised interest rates, or that the military in a country struggling to establish democracy has seized power in a coup d'état. Governments, private businesses, journalists, and other interested parties around the world must pay instant attention to these occurrences and assess their implications for decision makers or average citizens. As political scientists, we too may be interested in the immediate practical effects of these events. But we will also be interested in what they tell us about *politics* more generally.

What does the prime minister's resignation tell us about how democracies work? What does the central bank's actions tell us about the relationship between politics and economics? What does the latest coup tell us about military intervention in politics? Our aim in this more conceptual endeavor is to deepen our understanding of democracy *in general*, political economy *in general*, and military authoritarianism *in general*. Generalization is a central purpose of science. At the same time, we can apply our understanding of these general processes and tendencies to sharpen our understanding of the specific events at hand.

In order to construct meaningful generalizations from a welter of political events and information and in order to determine how accurate these generalizations are, we must use scientific methods of analyzing facts and testing general propositions. Many students of science maintain that *the essence of science lies in its methods of analysis.*[1]

Analysis *is simply the quest for understanding through close observation and broad generalization.* In pursuit of this objective, scientific analysis makes use of a number of concepts and procedural operations. Variables, correlations, laws, theories, hypotheses, models, and paradigms are some of the most important ones, and they are particularly important in political science. They sharpen our critical-thinking skills and enable us to understand the real world of politics by applying scientific logic. What follows is a brief explanation of each of these terms, coupled with some elementary examples of how they can be employed in political science.

VARIABLES

A variable is something that can vary or change. That is, it can take different forms or be a changeable characteristic of a phenomenon.

Suppose we want to understand democracy. Democracy has many different characteristics that can vary or come in different forms. For example, there are *stable* democracies that endure over long periods of time with few major alterations (such as the United States); there are *unstable* democracies that experience frequent changes of government (e.g., Italy) or that alternate over time with non-democratic modes of government (e.g., Argentina). *Stability* is thus a characteristic of democracy that can vary. We can focus on stability as one among several variables about democracy that can be analyzed systematically. We can define exactly what we mean by stability and instability, we can collect information on stable and unstable democracies, compare different cases of each variant, and look for possible *explanations* of why some democracies are stable and others are not. The explanatory factors that account for stability or instability are also variables. For example, we may find that, of all the possible characteristics of a given country, national wealth is the variable that best explains democratic stability: rich democracies may turn out to be the most stable, poor ones the most unstable.

Suppose we want to learn more about political elites in a newly democratizing country such as South Africa. Members of the South African political elite can vary in a number of ways: they come from different racial or tribal groups, they have different levels of education, they may have different attitudes on political and social issues, and so forth. By conducting attitude surveys, we can gather information on various attitudes held by these elites on such issues as democracy or race relations in South Africa. We can then categorize different types of attitudes among various members of South Africa's political elite. Some may be categorized as "hostile to other racial groups," others as "open to cooperation with other racial groups," and so on. Further study may reveal that a cooperative racial attitude on the part of a large number of white and non-white South African elites is an *explanatory variable* that accounts for the relative stability of the country's fledgling multiracial democracy in the 1990s. We could conduct similar studies of elite attitudes in other newly democratizing countries such as South Korea or Russia in order to assess the prospects for democracy in those countries. And by comparing elite attitudes in several newly democratizing countries, we may be able to make some broad generalizations that apply across the board to democratization processes in general.

Just about any general topic in political science has characteristics that can vary, such as types of government (e.g., democracy, authoritarianism), governmental institutions (e.g., unicameral and bicameral legislatures), or the political behavior of people (e.g., mass voting behavior, elite decision-making behavior). When we engage in the scientific study of politics, it is these variables that occupy our most direct analytical attention. In some cases we may wish simply to *observe* these phenomena, collecting information about them and perhaps classifying them in some way. Things get especially interesting, however, when we find *relationships* between two or more observed variables.

Is there perhaps a relationship between *democratic stability* and a country's *level of economic development*? (Are stable democracies predominantly rich countries? Are poor countries doomed to authoritarianism?) Is there a relationship between *voting for conservative candidates* and the voters' *income level* or *religion* or *ethnic group* or *gender*? (Do upper-income voters, whether in the United States or other countries, tend to vote mainly for conservatives?) Is there a relationship between peoples' *willingness to compromise* in a newly democratizing country and their *educational level*? (Are better educated people more willing to compromise than less well educated ones?) One of the first ways of generalizing about politics is to look for relationships of these kinds.

Dependent and independent variables Whenever we are looking for patterns or connections between two variables: one variable is the *dependent variable* and the other is the *independent variable*.

> *The dependent variable is the variable we are most interested in examining or explaining; it is the main object of our study. It is the effect or outcome that is influenced or caused by another variable or variables. It is the variable whose value changes in response to changes in the value of other variables (viz., independent variables).*

Let's say that we are interested in understanding voting behavior in the United States and other democracies. One variable characteristic of voting behavior is *turnout*, in other words, the number of people who turn out to vote. Some voters go the polls but others stay home. Electoral statistics over the past fifty years show that Americans tend to vote at consistently lower rates than West Europeans or the Japanese. What explains these differences? Are there any patterns we can find that might be associated with the level of voter turnout? Put another way, on what factors is turnout *dependent*? Turnout is thus our *dependent* variable. It is the variable we seek to explain; we want to see what it *depends* on.

> *The independent variable is the factor or characteristic that influences or causes the dependent variable. In cause-and-effect relationships, it is the causal or explanatory variable. Changes in the value of the independent variable may produce changes in the value of the dependent variable.*

In our hypothetical study of voting behavior, the independent variables are various characteristics of the electorate that may help account for variations in voter turnout. These characteristics would include income level, age, education level, ideological proclivities, and other pertinent factors. For example, low income voters may be less inclined to vote than upper-income voters; younger voters may be less

Figure 3.1 **INDEPENDENT AND DEPENDENT VARIABLES**

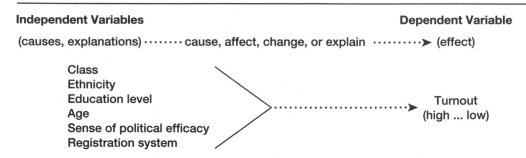

inclined to turn out than older ones; and so on. Independent variables could also include different attitudes about politics, as evidenced in public opinion surveys. Some people may not vote because they believe their vote doesn't really matter and that voters can't change anything for the better; they therefore have a low sense of political efficacy and feel alienated from the political system. By contrast, others may have a high sense of political efficacy: they believe that "every vote counts" and that voters can in fact influence politicians to make desirable decisions while in office. Turnout might also hinge on registration procedures: it may be higher in countries where registering to vote is easy and lower where it is more inconvenient (as in the United States). Just about anything that might affect turnout can be an independent variable in our investigation. Figure 3.1 illustrates these variables.

We can try out our independent variables individually to see to what extent each one is associated with our dependent variable, or we can try different combinations of independent variables. For example, we can focus first on the relationship between ethnicity and turnout in the United States, examining turnout levels for whites, blacks, Asians, Hispanics, and so on. We can do the same for the income-level variable, the religious variable, and so on. In these instances we are engaging in *single-variable analysis*. We can also examine two or more independent variables in combination against the dependent variable (e.g., rich whites, poor blacks; Protestants who attend church regularly and Protestants who do not attend church regularly, and so on). Such analyses are *multi-variable analyses*.

Our aim in this study is to determine whether, or to what extent, there are any connections between the independent variables and our dependent variable, voter turnout. Such

connections between variables are called correlations, or associations.

CORRELATIONS

A correlation (or association) is a relationship in which two or more variables change together.

Variables are positively correlated when they vary in the same direction. Two variables are positively correlated when they go up or down together (i.e., they *increase together* or *decrease together*).

If our variables are quantifiable, we can plot them on a graph. Usually we plot the dependent variable along the y-axis (vertical axis), and the independent variable along the x-axis (horizontal axis). Let's measure the relationship between turnout and the electorate's income levels in a hypothetical country. Figure 3.2 illustrates a *positive correlation* between the voters' income levels (the independent variable) and the percentage of people who turn out to vote (the dependent variable). The higher the income level, the higher the turnout; the lower the income level, the lower the turnout. Ninety percent of people in the highest income bracket turn out to vote, but only 5 percent of the people in the lowest income level show up at the polls. Note that when the correlation is positive, the plotted line goes from bottom left to top right.

Variables are inversely correlated when they vary in opposite or reverse directions. In quantitative terms, an inverse correlation occurs when one variable *increases* and the other variable *decreases*, or vice versa. We can illustrate an inverse correlation rather easily by looking at the relationship between turnout (the dependent variable) and the voters' sense of *alienation* from the political system (the independent variable). (Alienation means a low sense of political

Figure 3.2 **POSITIVE CORRELATION BETWEEN INCOME LEVELS AND TURNOUT**

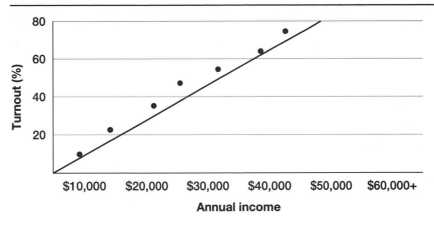

Figure 3.3 **INVERSE (NEGATIVE) CORRELATION BETWEEN ALIENATION AND TURNOUT**

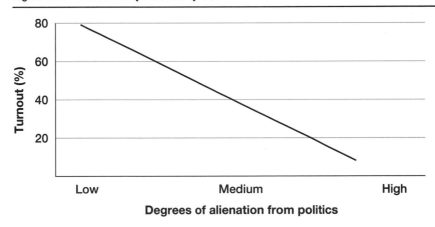

efficacy and a basic distrust of politicians and government officials.) As Figure 3.3 illustrates, voters with the lowest sense of alienation have the highest turnout rates; voters with the highest sense of alienation have the lowest turnout rates. Thus there is an *inverse correlation* between alienation and turnout. Inverse correlations are also called negative correlations. Note that when the correlation is negative, the plotted line goes from top left to bottom right.

In some cases we cannot chart quantifiable degrees of variation on a graph, but we can display different examples of the variable on a histogram. Figure 3.4 shows the relationship between turnout and voter registration in the United States. Because we cannot distinguish among different magnitudes of "registered-ness," we cannot plot variations in turnout rates *within* these two groups. The histogram compares the percentage of registered voters who have turned out to vote in elections to the House of

Representatives with the percentage of total eligible voters who have turned out.

Conceivably, we could undertake a different research project by taking one of the independent variables just listed and making it our dependent variable. Suppose, for example, we are primarily interested in focusing on the phenomenon of political alienation: what factors might affect or cause it? In this study, political alienation becomes the dependent variable, and we then try out various independent variables to see if they are correlated with it. To what extent (if any) is political alienation dependent on race or ethnicity? on religious orientation? on income level? on education level? on psychological factors? on other variables? on some combination of variables? Figure 3.5 shows a negative (inverse) correlation between alienation (the dependent variable) and education level (the independent variable). The less educated people are, the higher their sense of alienation; the more

Figure 3.4 **HISTOGRAM COMPARING TURNOUT RATES OF REGISTERED AND UNREGISTERED U.S. VOTERS (ELECTIONS TO HOUSE OF REPRESENTATIVES, (1986–96)**

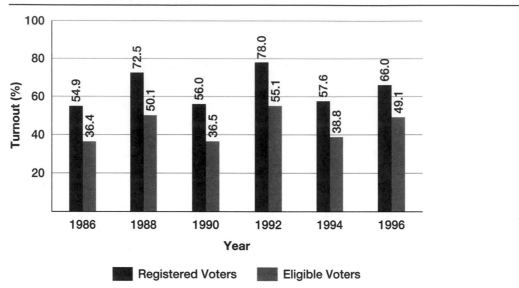

Figure 3.5 **CORRELATION BETWEEN ALIENATION AND EDUCATION LEVEL**

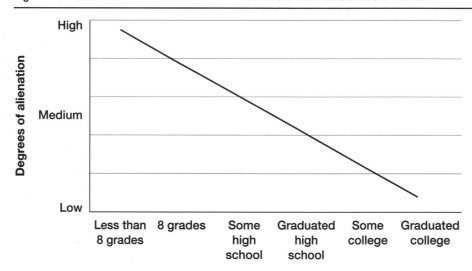

educated people are, the lower their sense of alienation. Our point here is that, depending on the main focus of our analysis—that is, the main effect we wish to understand or explain—alienation can be either an independent variable or a dependent variable. Many other variables can also be used either way.

Keep in mind that *correlations are not explanations*. Even though our data may show a clear correlation, positive or negative, between the dependent and independent variables, they do not explain *why* the variables are related. Let's

take another look at Figure 3.2, which shows a positive correlation between voter turnout and income levels. *Why* do higher-income people vote at higher rates than less well-off citizens? We cannot get answers to this question just by looking at the graph depicting the correlation.

To find out why higher-income voters come out on election day at higher rates than the less well-to-do voters do, we will have to extend our investigations by conducting surveys of voter attributes and attitudes. These surveys may reveal that wealthier citizens tend to be better

Figure 3.6 INTERVENING VARIABLES

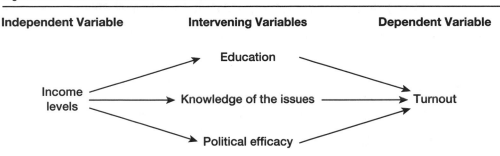

educated than poorer ones and thus more knowledgeable about political issues. They may also have a higher sense of their own political efficacy, that is, their ability to have a real impact on government policies. The surveys may further reveal that poor citizens tend to be poorly educated, display less knowledge of the issues of the day, and have a markedly lower sense of political efficacy. These results suggest that income levels (the independent variable) affect election day turnout (the dependent variable) by working through such intermediary factors as education, knowledge of the issues, and a citizen's sense of political efficacy. These intermediary factors are called intervening variables. As Figure 3.6 shows, intervening variables *are located in between the independent and dependent variables.*

As a general rule, *correlations do not prove that one variable* (i.e., income level) *actually causes the other variable* (i.e., voter turnout). In other words, correlations do not conclusively demonstrate *causality.* All a correlation does is to *suggest* or *imply* that there *may be* a cause-and-effect relationship between the variables under observation. Of course, in order to show that a causal relationship does in fact exist, it is first necessary to demonstrate that a correlation exists. Correlations are *necessary* to demonstrate causality, but by themselves they are not *sufficient* to do so.

LAWS

In science, a law is a regularly occurring association (or correlation) between two or more variables.

A *deterministic law* means that whenever X occurs, Y *always* occurs. The laws of gravity are an example. Starting with the simple observation that what goes up must come down (at least within the Earth's atmosphere), Sir Isaac Newton showed with mathematical precision that phys-

ical bodies have a general tendency to be pulled toward one another in patterns determined by their mass and distance. Albert Einstein's famous equation, $E = mc^2$, is a law specifying that energy always occurs as the product of mass times the square of the speed of light.

A less stringent type of scientific law is a *probabilistic law.* In this case, whenever A occurs, B *sometimes* occurs. Occasionally we can calculate the *degree of probability* with which B is likely to occur. In the natural world, weather predictions are frequently based on probabilistic laws. Given certain temperatures, humidity levels, and other atmospheric conditions, we can predict when snow will probably fall. Depending on the accuracy of our weather data and the sophistication of our computer models, we may be able to make accurate forecasts with a very high degree of probability. Nevertheless, so many variables are at work that we cannot be absolutely certain when it will snow, or if it does, we cannot be completely sure how much will fall on which spots.

Human behaviour is not as law-bound as inanimate nature. Unlike the planets or atomic particles, human beings are capable of conscious volitional behaviour as well as completely erratic irrational behaviour. We can make decisions about how we wish to behave by choosing from a menu of alternative courses of action. We can change our minds. We can act singly or in all sorts of groups; we can act cooperatively or at cross-purposes. Moreover, our social or political behaviour can be affected by a multitude of variables (ethnic group, religion, economic interests, parents, peers, etc.). Sometimes we miscalculate, acting on the basis of false assumptions, inadequate information, or faulty logic. Sometimes we may not even be consciously aware of the factors that induce us to behave in certain ways, as when our biases, emotions, or subconscious impulses intrude on our actions.

As a consequence, human behavior is extremely variable and unpredictable. Hence the social sciences, which focus on human behavior (especially in large social groups), cannot predict the future with unfailing accuracy. Whereas the planets and other celestial bodies obligingly conform to the laws of gravitational motion, making it possible to pinpoint with mathematical precision the position of the moon or Halley's comet hundreds or even thousands of years from now, human behavior is so variegated that no one can foretell what political, social, or economic realities will look like ten years from now or even ten months from now. Perhaps for this reason Einstein also declared, "Politics is more difficult than physics."

Hence there are no *deterministic* laws in political science. Nevertheless, in political science as in other social sciences (such as sociology, economics, and social psychology), researchers can frequently discern real patterns and tendencies in human social activity. And even though we cannot foretell with any degree of certainty exactly what the future will bring, social scientists can sometimes suggest which future developments are more probable or less probable, at least in the near term.

Prediction of the future in the social sciences is thus suggestive or probabilistic in nature. If we can identify regularities in a population's voting patterns, for example, we can *suggest* how people *may* vote in the next elections. The closer we get to election day, the greater the confidence we may have in our estimation of *probable* outcomes. Even the most sophisticated statistical analyses of the most comprehensive polling data we can obtain, however, may not be sufficient to predict the way people actually will vote the very next day. Many pollsters were as surprised as virtually everyone else by Harry Truman's upset victory over Thomas Dewey in 1948 and by the magnitude of the Republicans' sweeping takeover of the U.S. Senate and House of Representatives in 1994. Similarly, experts on the Soviet Union were shocked at the USSR's complete collapse in 1991; veteran China-watchers did not foresee the eruption of pro-democracy student demonstrations in Beijing in 1989; and specialists on South Africa could scarcely have predicted in the early 1980s that the white minority would finally allow multi-racial elections to take place there in the early 1990s, bringing Nelson Mandela, a black man, to the presidency.

Only in a suggestive and probabilistic sense, therefore, can we speak of laws in social science. Actually, social scientists rarely use the term at all. In a few cases, they apply the term to certain patterns of social behavior that occur with considerable frequency and in a relatively regularized manner. Even these cases, however, are probabilistic rather than deterministic laws.

In political science, Duverger's law, named after a French political scientist, stipulates that an electoral system in which the voters choose competing candidates by a simple majority (i.e., the highest number of votes) in a single ballot tends to produce a two-party system. Examples would include elections to the U.S. House of Representatives and the British House of Commons.

Virtually every scientific law has its exceptions, as even natural scientists acknowledge with respect to nature. This reality is especially true in the social sciences. Economists therefore recognize that the law of supply and demand, although a general tendency, does not always operate perfectly. Even in a market economy, factors such as monopolies or fluctuating consumer demands may interfere with it. Similarly, Duverger's law may not apply in all circumstances, as Duverger himself acknowledged.[2] (Britain, for example, has more than two parties represented in the House of Commons.) Any so-called law in the social sciences must be constantly put to the test against the evidence of reality to determine whether, or to what extent, it holds true. In social science as in the physical sciences, laws are occasionally broken.

Moreover, laws—like correlations—are not *explanations*. They simply point out that two or more variables generally go together, but they do not explain why. To find out why these patterns exist, social scientists must conduct other exploratory investigations. The principal ways of explaining political realities scientifically are by formulating *theories* and *hypotheses*.

THEORIES

The term *theory* can have several different meanings in political science.

1. In its broadest sense, theory simply refers to *thinking about politics as opposed to practicing it.* As such, it is an *abstract intellectual exercise.* Theorizing can mean nothing more than *making generalizations* about politics, whether in accordance with strict scientific

rules or far more informally, as in latenight political discussions with friends. In this elementary definition of the term, theory also refers to *general principles or abstract ideas* that may not necessarily be true in actual fact. For example, when we say, "In theory, democracy is government by the people," we are referring to some general principle or idea of democracy; we are not explaining how democracy actually works in practice.

2. More restrictively, theory can mean *normative theory*: that is, valuecentered political philosophy (or political thought), as we defined these terms earlier in this chapter.

3. In the natural and social sciences, theory most frequently means a *generalization, or set of generalizations, that seeks to explain, and perhaps predict, relationships among variables.* This is explanatory theory.

Explanation is the main aim of theory in empirical political science. The word *because* is stated or implied in just about every explanatory theory.

As a general rule, explanations that merit the term theory have usually gained wide acceptance over long periods of time because their ability to explain the facts has been confirmed in repeated scientific investigations. Theories thus tend to be more solidly grounded in empirical reality than hypotheses, which are typically assumptions that have yet to be sufficiently tested. Nevertheless, even the most widely respected theories are not unchallengeable truths. They are meant to be constantly challenged against the hard facts of reality. In political science as in the natural sciences, *explanatory theories are not abstractions that are divorced from reality; on the contrary, they seek to explain reality.* Theories are valid only as long as they are consistent with the facts they endeavor to explain. If new evidence comes to light that contradicts the theory, then the theory is probably either partially or entirely wrong. It must then be modified or discarded and replaced by a better theory that fits the facts. All explanatory theories must therefore be regarded as tentatively valid explanations of empirical reality. They need to be repeatedly subjected to verification against the hard data of reality. The main way of accomplishing this task is by breaking theories down into hypotheses and testing them against the available evidence.

HYPOTHESES

A hypothesis is an assumption or supposition that needs to be tested against relevant evidence.

In some cases hypotheses can be purely *descriptive* in nature. For example, we can hypothesize that democracy has broad popular support in Russia. We can then test this hypothesis by surveying a large number of Russians and asking them whether they support democracy, and if so, how strongly. After we've collected and analyzed our research data we will end up with a description, a picture, of mass attitudes toward Russian democracy. The data will permit us to describe the Russian electorate as mostly supportive of democracy or mostly unsupportive of it by providing statistical readings of the proportion of the voters who support it strongly, the percentage of those who support it with less conviction, and the percentage of those who don't support it very much or not at all.

This descriptive hypothesis simply proposes certain facts about the Russian electorate, and the hypothesis-testing survey seeks to determine whether and to what extent those facts are really occurring. The descriptive hypothesis does not suggest an *explanation* as to *why* the proposed phenomena might be occurring, however. It is not an *explanatory* hypothesis that explains *why* Russians feel as they do about democracy. But in political science as in the physical sciences, *explanation is the ultimate goal.*

Explanatory hypotheses posit a cause and effect relationship between dependent and independent variables that can be tested empirically (i.e., against factual evidence).

By formulating explanatory hypotheses about politics, we force ourselves to specify our dependent and independent variables and to be clear about the sharp difference between cause and effect. By *testing* hypotheses empirically, we submit them to a reality check: we take a close look at all the available facts to see if they substantiate or contradict the relationships we propose in our hypotheses. For example, we might find that, contrary to our hypothesis, popular support for democracy in Russia is in fact much weaker than we had originally surmised. We must then formulate explanatory hypotheses that might suggest possible reasons for this phenomenon. We could hypothesize that public

Figure 3.7   **INDEPENDENT VARIABLES AFFECTING NEGATIVE ATTITUDES TOWARD DEMOCRACY**

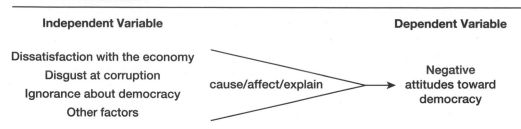

Independent Variable   **Dependent Variable**

Dissatisfaction with the economy
Disgust at corruption   cause/affect/explain   Negative
Ignorance about democracy   attitudes toward
Other factors   democracy

dissatisfaction with the economy is causing people to turn against democracy; or we could hypothesize that disgust at political corruption may be the main explanatory variable accounting for Russian attitudes; or we could assume that public ignorance about democracy may be the explanation; or we could develop a host of other possible explanations, whether singly or in combination.

We could then test these various explanatory hypotheses by going back to Russia and resurveying the electorate, asking them more specific questions about their attitudes on the economy, corruption, and so forth. After analyzing our survey data, we can then come to some conclusions about which of these explanatory variables explain why many Russians are suspicious of democracy. We may find, for example, that all of them play a role, albeit to varying degrees, among the voters. In these explanatory hypotheses, *"negative attitudes toward democracy"* is the *dependent variable. The possible explanations* to be tested are the *independent variables.* (See Figure 3.7.)

MODELS

In political science, a model is a simplified representation of reality in descriptive or abstract form.

A desktop scale model of a Stealth bomber can neither fly nor drop bombs. Its sleek proportions, however, provide some understanding of how the real aircraft is able to avoid radar detection. An auto designer's computer model of next year's dream car indicates how all its components will mesh together in perfect harmony once the vehicle hits the road. Environmental scientists have built a large model of the Chesapeake Bay designed to replicate the bay's complex ecological system. Economists construct graphical and

mathematical models of various dynamic economic processes, such as a perfectly competitive market economy or a global free trade system.

Though the composition of these models is different, they all serve the same function: they enable us to understand some aspect of reality, whether aerodynamics or the economy, by *representing* some of its essential features in a simplified or idealized form. Obviously, these scaled down physical or mathematical models cannot be perfect copies of the realities they represent. The car designer does not plan for the car to malfunction, but at some point it probably will. Economists know that purely free market systems, which are devoid of any governmental interference or monopolies, exist nowhere in today's world.

The purpose of a model is not to represent reality perfectly but to enable us to understand reality by allowing us to compare it against some standard or pattern. If the car has stalling problems, the computer design can help us find the source. If world trade is declining, the mathematical model of how a free trade system works in theory may help us understand how to deal with existing trade barriers in the global economy. When viewed against the model, the complexities of the real world stand out all the more prominently by comparison with the simplified version. As one economist put it, "Models are to be used, not believed." They are to be used, more specifically, as guides to further understanding. As learning devices, models serve a *heuristic* purpose, a term that derives from the Greek word meaning "to find out."

In roughly similar fashion, political scientists use models of various kinds to help us understand political realities. Sometimes these models are purely descriptive. For example, we can construct a model of democracy just by listing its characteristic features: a competitive electoral system, legal guarantees of certain freedoms and rights, and so forth. Although many democracies of today's world may actually diverge from this model of an "ideal" democracy in one way or another, these divergences will tend to stand out when compared with the model, prompting us to investigate how and why they occur.

A descriptive model of this sort is known as an *ideal type*. An *ideal type is a model of a political or social phenomenon that describes its main characteristic features*. The term was coined by the German sociologist Max Weber (1864–1920), one of the founders of modern sociology. Weber was among the first students of modern bureaucracy. Based on his observations of European bureaucracies in the early twentieth century, Weber devised an ideal type of a modern bureaucracy that specified the features most commonly found in them. He described this standard (or ideal typical) bureaucracy as a highly impersonal organization run in accordance with strict rules and legal procedures. Not all bureaucracies in Europe conformed exactly to this standard type in every respect, however. For Weber, an ideal type is not just a carbon copy of one or two real world examples of the phenomenon it represents. Rather, it is an abstract conception constructed from a variety of observations and trends. Weber used it as a conceptual standard against which social scientists could study and compare the world's bureaucracies and come to a better understanding of the phenomenon of bureaucracy itself. The concept of the ideal type is very useful in describing all sorts of political phenomena.

PARADIGMS

The term paradigm has two meanings in political science:

> *In one sense, a paradigm is a prime example of a particular phenomenon or pattern.*

For example, the British system of government is a paradigm of parliamentary democracy. This is not to say that all parliamentary governments are exactly like Britain's in every respect. Italy, Israel, and other parliamentary political systems differ from the British version (and from one another) in various ways. Still, they are all close to the British example in certain fundamental respects. We can understand how these various governments work more clearly by comparing them to the British paradigm.

Paradigms are quite useful in comparative politics because they help us observe and analyze variations on a theme (such as parliamentary democracy). In this respect they serve the same purpose as models. The difference is that whereas models tend to be abstract or intellectually idealized representations of reality, paradigms are usually real world phenomena (like Britain's governmental system).

> *In another sense, a paradigm is a particular way of looking at phenomena, formulating questions and generalizations, and conducting research.*

This second definition of paradigm construes it as a particular form of intellectual inquiry or a specific approach to scientific investigation. This meaning of the term was popularized by Thomas Kuhn, a philosopher interested in the nature of scientific thought. Kuhn argued that over the centuries Western science developed several radically different paradigms of scientific thinking, based on very different assumptions about the natural world and about how to study it. Ptolemaic astronomy, for example, held that the sun and planets revolve around the Earth. Only in the sixteenth century did Ptolemy's ancient paradigm give way to the heliocentric astronomy of Copernicus, based on more precise methods of observing the solar system. Similarly, Aristotle's views on physics were eventually supplanted by Newton's laws of mechanics; Newton's paradigm gave way to twentieth-century relativity theory and quantum mechanics; and so on.[3]

This meaning of paradigm also applies to political science. The paradigm of political science presented in this chapter conforms in its essential features to the rules of scientific logic that emerged from the empirical approach to scientific inquiry pioneered by Copernicus, Newton, and other seminal contributors to modern science. This scientific approach to studying politics is a fairly recent development, however. It emerged slowly in the United States in the 1930s and 1940s and increasingly shaped the way American political scientists were trained to think about politics in the 1950s and subsequently. Earlier, the dominant paradigm of political science research was largely descriptive and tended to concentrate on governmental institutions and constitutional law. It was less concerned with studying how people behave in political life, and it did not employ such concepts as variables, hypotheses, correlations, and other nuts and bolts of modern scientific thinking. It was also considerably less quantitative. Even today, many important books and articles are written about politics that employ the more traditional descriptive approach.

LOGICAL FALLACIES

To round out this chapter's introduction to critical thinking about politics, we must warn against certain logical fallacies that are commonly committed in political argumentation. Our list can be only a partial one, given space limitations, and it cannot substitute for a book on logic.

Fallacy of composition We commit this fallacy when we assume that the whole is exactly the same as its parts. Beware of ascribing attributes (such as attitudes, behaviors, etc.) to an entire class or group when those attributes may apply only to a portion of that group. For example, do not say, "The Germans are highly disciplined" or "Americans are well off," when in fact only some Germans may be highly disciplined and not all Americans are well off. This fallacy is the basis of stereotyping, that is, regarding all individuals of a particular group as similar while overlooking their differences.

Tautology (circular reasoning) ascribes causation to the very phenomenon whose causes we are trying to explain. (To put it another way, beware of using your dependent variable as an independent variable that accounts for it.) The term comes from the ancient Greek word for "the same." Here's an example: "Armed conflict among Yugoslavia's contending groups produced a bitter civil war." The statement is tautological because civil war is armed conflict among a country's contending groups. The two points are essentially the same thing; hence, the one cannot cause the other. To ascertain the causes of the civil war, we must look at real explanatory variables such as ethnic and religious hatreds. One of the most famous tautologies ever attributed to a politician was the remark allegedly uttered by President Calvin Coolidge, "When a great many people are unable to find work, unemployment results."

Post hoc ergo propter hoc ("After it, therefore because of it") is the fallacy of concluding that A *caused* B just because A *preceded* B. For example, "The U.S.–led victory over Iraq in the Persian Gulf War at the start of 1991 precipitated the collapse of the Soviet Union later that same year." The statement does not explain *why* the war was a cause of the USSR's demise but simply assumes that it was. In fact, the war had no demonstrable effect on the Soviet collapse.

A fortiori ("All the more") assumes that what is true of a phenomenon at one level or degree is automatically true of the same phenomenon at larger levels or degrees. The statement, "The more private enterprise there is in the economy, the more democracy will flourish," assumes without empirical evidence that, just because a certain amount of private enterprise may be good for democracy, then a totally private economy, with no government involvement in economic affairs whatsoever, will be even better for democracy. It overlooks the possibility that a completely private economy, with no government sponsored safety net to help the poor and the middle class, could create great disparities in wealth and perhaps lead to intense social conflicts capable of destroying democracy.

False analogy is the fallacy of making inappropriate or inexact analogies or comparisons between one phenomenon or situation and another. One example is the statement "Political systems are like organisms: they are born, they grow, and they inevitably decay and die." This "organic" analogy does not stand up to the facts. Historical analogies are also frequently misused. Here's an example: "The Persian Gulf War was exactly like World War II: Saddam Hussein was another Hitler, and Hitler showed that we must not appease dictators." Despite some evident similarities, the two cases are not exactly similar. (For one thing, Hitler's army was far more militarily prepared for a long war than Saddam's.) Prior to the successful U.S.–led attack against Iraqi troops occupying Kuwait in 1991, some people warned that such an invasion would result in a protracted military standoff similar to the Vietnam War. Once again, the analogy was incorrect: the Persian Gulf War lasted only a few weeks. In fact, no two historical cases are ever *exactly* alike in all respects, and one must pay as much attention to dissimilarities as to similarities when comparing them.[4]

Reading Notes

1. In *The Grammar of Science*, written in 1892, the scientist and philosopher Karl Pearson wrote, "The unity of all science consists alone in its method, not its material."

2. Maurice Duverger, *Political Parties*, rev. ed., translated by Barbara and Robert North (London: Methuen, 1959), 217. Duverger asserted that the correlation between single ballot plurality electoral procedures and two party systems "approaches the most nearly perhaps to a true sociological law." He observed, however, that this electoral system "does not necessarily and absolutely lead to bipartism in all cases." It was with this caveat in mind that he called the correlation a "brazen law" (228). For a description of the electoral system, see Chapter 9; for further discussion of Duverger's law, see Chapter 11.

3. Thomas Kuhn, *The Structure of Scientific Revolutions*, 2nd ed. (Chicago: University of Chicago Press, 1970).

4. For a study of the dangers of false historical analogies, see Richard E. Neustadt and Ernest R. May, *Thinking in Time: The Uses of History for Decision-Makers* (New York: Free Press, 1986).

KEY TERMS

Dependent Variable The political phenomenon we are trying to explain.

Diachronic Comparisons Comparing within the same country but during different periods.

Hypothesis A conjectural statement about the relationship between two variables. It gives a direction to a study before it has begun.

Independent Variable A factor that affects or causes the dependent variable.

Model A theoretical and simplified representation of the real world. An operationalized theory.

Synchronic Comparisons Comparing across countries but during the same period.

Taxonomy A subject divided into classes that are distinct from one another.

Theory A set of systematically related generalizations suggesting new observations for empirical testing.

Typology A more advanced and complex taxonomy that involves classifying phenomena based on a number of variables.

FURTHER READINGS

George, Alexander L., and Andrew Bennet. *Case Studies and Theory Development in the Social Sciences*. Cambridge, MA.: MIT Press, 2005.

Goodin, Robert E., and Hans-Dieter Klingsmann. *A New Handbook of Political Science*. Oxford: Oxford University Press, 1996.

King, Gary, Robert O. Keohane, and Sidney Verba. *Designing Social Inquiry: Scientific Inference in Qualitative Research*. Princeton: Princeton University Press, 1994.

Lijphart, Arend. "The Comparative-Case Strategy in Comparative Research." *Comparative Political Studies* 8, no. 2 (July 1975): 158–77.

Symposium, "Where is Political Science Going?" *PSOnline* (October 2004) at http://www.apsanet.org.

Tsebelis, George. *Nested Games: Rational Choice in Comparative Politics.* Berkeley: University of California Press, 1990.

Van Evera, Stephen. *Guide to Methods for Students of Political Science.* Ithaca, NY: Cornell University Press, 1997.

WEB LINKS

Political Science Resources on the Web:
www.lib.umich.edu/govdocs/polisci.html

Richard Kimber's Political Science Resources—Political Theory Links:
www.psr.keele.ac.uk/theory.htm

Political Methodology and Survey Research:
http://polmeth.wustl.edu

PART 2

POLITICS AS IDEAS

At the broadest level, the objective of this section is to convey to the reader that ideas are as much a part of politics as institutions or unfolding processes. The specific objective of this section is to introduce the most important ideologies of contemporary political life: liberalism, conservatism, democratic socialism, scientific socialism (communism), fascism, feminism, and environmentalism. This is done by developing the following themes: (1) main tenets; (2) historical origins, context, and development; (3) main theorists; (4) internal divisions; (5) contemporary manifestations and representational forms. This last theme is explored through an overview of different regional areas and the different meanings given to the ideologies in those various regions. This section of the book is divided into four chapters. Chapter 4 describes liberalism and conservatism as the two main ideologies of democratic societies or, more specifically, as ideologies that accept democracy and whose contemporary tenets and representational forms are compatible with democratic frameworks. Chapter 5 continues this discussion and introduces the reader to the third variant of a democratic ideology—socialism—and distinguishes it from its non-democratic variant, communism. Chapter 6 expands on the non-democratic ideologies, and examines fascism. Chapter 7 explores emerging ideologies, namely **feminism** and environmentalism, which tend to be critical of contemporary democracies and put forward their own version of democratic principles and of the democratic process.

CHAPTER 4

LIBERALISM AND CONSERVATISM

When asked what is involved in politics, many people would intuitively mention ideology. This is not to say that they would be able to define the concept, but they would perhaps associate it with specific political discourses, parties, and public policies. The French word "idéologie" was first used by French philosopher Destutt de Tracy (1754–1836) to denote a science of ideas. From a more normative standpoint, Karl Marx equated ideology with "false consciousness" that saw the poor deceive themselves about their true interests, thereby remaining bonded to their subjugation. Another theorist, Karl Mannheim (1893–1947), suggested distinguishing between ideology and utopia, where the former has a conservative nature while the latter involves revolutionary ideas.

In contemporary political science, ideology refers to a coherent and articulated system of ideas, consisting of values and concepts that simplify how we perceive the complex sociopolitical reality. Ideology interprets that reality and recommends how it could be changed or improved. In other words, ideologies provide lenses for understanding societal (social, political, and economic) issues and point to the way society ought to be structured. Consciously or not, they frequently guide the political choices of citizens, determining, for example, whether Canadian voters prefer the New Democratic Party or the Conservative party; or whether Canadians prefer a universal, tax-subsidized health care system to one that is privately funded. Moreover, the choices affected by ideologies may carry great consequences. For example, during the twentieth century, nationalist ideologies became the basis for mobilizing the populations of several colonies to achieve independence from their colonial masters, but they have also been responsible for wars aimed at conquest or ethnic cleansing.

Frequently ideologies, as systematic expressions of ideas, emerge from identifiable philosophical traditions. For example, one might say that the roots of the liberal ideology are based on the political thought of John Locke or that modern-day conservatism originates with the writings of Edmund Burke. Ideologies tend to last through time, but they are not fixed. Rather, they represent social and historical constructions that respond to and inform the context of the day.

Liberalism and conservatism are ideological references that tend to feature prominently in discussions about politics, both within and outside academic circles. Pundits and journalists speak of "triumphant liberalism," the "liberal order," and "neoliberal policies," some approvingly and others critically. They refer to politicians and parties as having a "conservative agenda," or as being "conservative forces." What do all these expressions really mean? Or, more generally, what is it to be liberal or conservative? This chapter provides an answer to these questions by discussing the historical origins of these ideologies, their key proponents, their main tenets, their evolution, and their place in contemporary politics.

LIBERALISM

Liberalism first emerged as an ideology in seventeenth-century Britain. The defining feature of British politics in this period was a political struggle between a rapidly growing bourgeoisie and the monarchy. At the centre of this struggle was the issue of political power: to what extent was this bourgeoisie of merchants and traders going to have a say in political decision making? They had formed an assembly (also called parliament, although there were no elections) to discuss public affairs and were seeking to make this institution politically relevant.

Early in the century, British kings (James I and Charles I) had ruled according to the absolutist doctrine, which held that political power rested with the monarchy only. However, as the assembly became more assertive, and in the wake of a civil war in which Charles I was beheaded, future monarchs would have to accept some forms of consultation. This was a matter of great practical importance for the British bourgeoisie since many political decisions (for example, declaring wars or levying taxes) had major repercussions on their business interests. So, when James II rejected the assembly in favour of absolute rule, he was forced out in what became known as the Glorious Revolution (1688). It was "glorious" because it was nonviolent, and it was a revolution because it forever changed British politics: the input of parliament into political decision making was never again to be denied. In other words, the Glorious Revolution ushered in a liberal era in Britain, as "good" political power was no longer seen as absolute and concentrated, but instead to be fragmented and held in check.

The liberal ideology that came out of this context is known as **classical liberalism**. Classical liberalism is defined in relation to a later version of the ideology, reform liberalism, which emerged in the nineteenth century. The context for the development of reform liberalism was much different than for classical liberalism. Reform liberalism was the product of the inequalities of the Industrial Revolution, more specifically of the perceived need to reduce them, and of the rise of democratic ideas. Let us examine both branches of the liberal ideology.

Classical liberalism has four main principles. The first is this idea of limited political power. Liberals argue that political power that is absolute, extensive, and arbitrary is problematical since it prevents individuals from fully using their intelligence and creative capabilities to better their own lives and the future of society as a whole. They argue that this type of political power tends to be corrupt, self-serving, and unpredictable. Instead, they advocate limited and accountable government. John Locke (1632–1704) was the theorist who con-tributed most to the development of this idea. Locke argued that government needed the consent of the governed. He suggested that the governed had the right—in fact, the responsibility—to withdraw their consent and to repudiate a government that stopped acting in their best interests. Therefore, liberalism is closely linked with the notion of government by representation. Liberals also argue that the state should play only a minimal role in society. Earlier, Thomas Hobbes (1588–1679) had suggested that the state was the product of a social contract whereby individuals agreed to delegate authority to a sovereign for the purpose of maintaining law and order or, simply put, to avoid violent conflict. Locke argued that

John Locke

the state had the further crucial role of protecting private property. Liberals argue for a "small" state because they think individuals need to be free of constraints to fully develop their potential. They also argue that individuals, not governments, know best what to do with financial resources. In politics, these positions translate into preferences for weak economic regulation and low levels of taxation.

This position on the role of the state is anchored in a particular view of human nature. For Liberals, human beings are rational and self-interested. They look after themselves first and have the capabilities to do so better than anyone else. They are autonomous actors, which means that they have the power to choose and are therefore responsible for their actions. This view is now widely accepted in Western societies, but it was not always. For the longest time, self-interested behaviour was frequently viewed as immoral, and individuals were seen as part of a society in which submission to authority, whether political, religious, or intellectual, was a central value. The submissive position was opposed by Liberals, who instead stressed the rationality, autonomy, creativity, and imagination of individuals. Liberals advocated the *secularization* of society, that is, the separation of religion and politics, thereby frequently alienating religious establishments. The liberal state is not only small and associated with limited and accountable government, it is also secular.

The second principle of liberalism has to do with freedom. Freedom is the most important value for Liberals because it allows individuals to fully use their intellectual capacities and creativity. If individuals are free, Liberals argue, society's wealth, prosperity, and the "good life" will follow. This emphasis on freedom is coherent with the idea of a small, unobtrusive state. Early Liberals conceptualized freedom in terms of the absence of obstacles. Scholars have called this *negative freedom*.[1] Negative freedom is freedom "from something," which in politics translates into freedom from state interference. In liberal states, negative freedom is reflected in the protection of fundamental liberties (thought, religion, association, and speech) and by such legal provisions as *habeas corpus*, which protects against arbitrary searches and seizures.

The third principle of liberalism is equality of rights. In addition to battling absolutism and Church power, early Liberals opposed the societal model of institutionalized inequalities through privileges, which characterized feudal Europe. Instead, they argued for equality before the law. In doing so, a primary concern was that political leaders be legally treated no differently from private citizens. Liberals call this the rule of law; it means that nobody is above the law, not even those who make it. While liberalism puts great emphasis on equality of rights, it must be said that early Liberals failed to make this a political reality or even to give it serious meaning except for a limited segment of the population. They were not true democrats since, for example, they limited the right to vote to males who owned property. Even when these restrictions had disappeared, suffrage did not immediately become universal since women were still denied the vote. Equality of rights was not a political reality in most Western states until the mid-twentieth century.

The fourth principle of liberalism is the free-market economy. Liberals believe that capitalism is the economic system that complements best the political principles of their ideology. If individuals are guaranteed the political freedoms necessary to fully exploit their intellectual capacities and creativity, they should enjoy a similar treatment in the economic sphere. For Liberals, political freedoms set the stage for a competition between ideas, a process that can only be favourable to the common good since the more worthy ideas will tend to prevail. They apply a similar logic when it comes to economics, arguing that competition generates wealth and prosperity. Liberalism holds that the market itself—not the state—is the most efficient instrument of economic regulation. Adam Smith (1723–90) argued that individuals, while selfishly pursuing their own interests, are actually working toward the common good.[2] There was, he suggested, something like an *invisible hand* that guided participants in a free market to promote the common good whether it was their intention or not. This made the market the most proficient distributor of jobs and wealth. This positive view of the market makes liberalism favour economic competition and free trade.

As we have already mentioned, liberalism in contemporary politics is not limited to the ideological perspective we have just described. Ideologies evolve, and liberalism has changed since it was first articulated. Of course, there are Liberals who still abide strictly by the principal tenets of classical liberalism. However, for others these principles are worthy and necessary but insufficient. These people would identify with *reform liberalism*.

Reform liberalism refashioned the ideology in four ways. First, it added the idea of positive freedom to classical liberalism's emphasis on negative freedom. Positive freedom is not "freedom from" but "freedom to." It entails the capacity and power to do something, rather than merely the legal right to act. The notion of positive freedom was added to liberalism in the context of the socio-economic discrepancies exacerbated by European industrialization during the nineteenth century and, later, by the Great Depression early in the twentieth century. Indeed, the meaning of negative freedom was brought into question by these inequalities. Were the very poor really free? Could it be said that they were in any meaningful sense as free as the very rich even if they were guaranteed similar freedoms? Answering "yes" to these questions was problematic, so to the notion of freedom reform Liberals added the notion of empowerment.

Second, reform Liberals boosted classical liberalism's conception of equality. For classical Liberals, equality was a legal matter. However, in the social context of industrialization this perspective was questioned, just as negative freedom was questioned. How meaningful is equality before the law if there exist such significant socio-economic inequalities? It is in facing this issue that liberalism added to equality of rights the concept of equality of opportunity. The idea was that meaningful equality involved levelling the playing field, that is, creating conditions that would allow individuals to effectively exploit their legal entitlements.

Third, reform liberalism looks more favourably toward state intervention than does classical liberalism. This is an unavoidable consequence of the reformulation of the concepts of freedom and equality. Industrialization suggested that the market alone would not provide individuals with positive freedom and equality of opportunity. This could be done only through state intervention, more specifically, using mechanisms of redistribution such as progressive taxation (the wealthier you are, the higher your tax rate) and welfare/unemployment policies. In other words, reform Liberals advocated a welfare state as conceptualized by, among others, John Maynard Keynes (1883–1946).

Fourth, reform Liberals advocated universal suffrage, thereby reconciling the liberal ideology with democracy. For example, liberal theorist John Stuart Mill (1806–73) was one of the first voices to call for women's suffrage. For Mill, extending the right to vote to women was a logical implication of the liberal ideology.[3] Liberalism and democracy are often considered to be the same thing. Political scientists often speak of "liberal democracies." However, liberal and democratic thought and practice have different roots and manifestations. As already mentioned, early Liberals were not democrats. Moreover, liberal political systems are not necessarily democratic, and vice versa. On the one hand, when Hong Kong was administered by the United Kingdom before 1997, it was governed by a governor appointed by London; therefore, it was not a democracy since there were no meaningful elections. It was, however, a liberal society where basic rights and freedoms were respected. On the other hand, many countries that have recently undergone democratic transitions (in Eastern Europe, for example) are not liberal. They may hold elections that are reasonably free and fair, but in many cases the power of political leaders is virtually unchecked (e.g., President Putin in Russia) and fundamental rights and freedoms are often curtailed.

LIBERALISM IN CONTEMPORARY POLITICS

Liberalism is the dominant ideology in Western societies. In Canada, politics unfolds within a predominantly liberal context. Several mechanisms have been put in place to control and limit political power: responsible government, whereby the executive needs to explain, justify, and defend its actions to a legislative assembly; federalism, which in formally dividing power between federal and provincial governments fragments political power and provides a check on the power of both levels of governments; and the Charter of Rights and Freedoms, which offers a judiciary check on political power. The Charter is a strong liberal feature of Canadian politics as it also assures the rule of law and guarantees liberal rights and freedoms. On the economic front, Canada is committed to a market economy, albeit not without government intervention. Also, Canadian political parties operate largely within a liberal ideological framework. Here it is important not to be misled by political labels such as the names of political parties. The fact that there is only one party called "Liberal" in Canada does not mean that it is the only party that is liberal in the ideological sense. The four major federal parties, for example, all agree with the main principles of liberalism, although with qualifications in some cases: the Conservative party exhibits strong shades of conservatism while the NDP is close to **democratic socialism**. Arguably the central ideological debate in Canada is between classical and reform Liberals. Classical Liberals speak of lowering taxes, eliminating deficit, reducing the debt, controlling public spending, privatizing Crown corporations, and creating a good business environment. Many Liberal Party members of Parliament are classical Liberals, as are most elected representatives from the Conservative party. Reform Liberals put more emphasis on social spending and rely on the state to redistribute wealth and correct the deficiencies of the market. They speak of social justice and equality. An important wing of the Liberal party falls under this category.

A striking example of a liberal tradition of politics is the United States. The 1776 revolution, which led to the creation of the United States, was underpinned by the liberal ideology. Thomas Jefferson, who wrote the Declaration of Independence, borrowed heavily from John Locke. He explained that the British monarch (George III) was not being fair toward the American colony, acting arbitrarily and levying taxes in the absence of political representation, and that its settlers therefore had the right and the duty to cut its ties with Britain. Liberal principles were at the centre of the United States' institutional design, as the major preoccupation of the new state was to avoid tyranny and arbitrary rule. A presidential system of government featuring a rigid separation of powers was created. Power was fragmented territorially through federalism. The Bill of Rights was drafted to guarantee the basic rights and freedoms of American citizens. American political parties, Republican and Democratic, are ideologically very similar, that is, close to classical liberalism, although the Republican party is also strongly influenced by conservatism. The American commitment to the market economy and to a small state is also strongly reflective of classical liberalism. One caveat is in order when discussing liberalism in American politics: the term "liberal" often comes up in political discussions and debates, but its meaning is slightly skewed since it generally refers to specific positions on particular issues, most notably, support for multiculturalism, gender equality, legal abortion, gay rights, and pacifism in international affairs.

Liberalism is not as dominant in Western Europe as it is in North America. The political institutions of west European countries are liberal in nature but many of their parties are, in their own way, critical of liberalism: environmental and social democratic parties are skeptical about the market as an agent of social and economic regulation; far-right parties tend to be antithetical to the egalitarian discourse of liberalism; and communist parties, which are now weak but were quite strong in the 1960s and 1970s, particularly in Italy and France, prefer state planning to the market. Also, the contemporary history of such Western European countries as Germany, Italy, Spain, Portugal, and Greece features authoritarian or totalitarian regimes that opposed the most fundamental principles of liberalism. Other states have deeper liberal traditions. It is obviously the case of Great Britain but also of France, whose 1789 revolution, although it eventually turned violent and authoritarian, destroyed a sociopolitical order of privileges and absolutism in the name of freedom and equality.

The fact that Canada, Western European countries, and, most importantly, the United States are liberal societies has far-reaching implications for world politics. The "West," as these states as a whole are often dubbed, strongly promotes, even imposes, free-market economics and free trade, both directly and through international financial economic institutions. This is often called the neoliberal position. Neoliberalism is classical liberalism with the added element of international free trade, which was not discussed to the same degree by early Liberals. Since the end of the Cold War, neoliberalists are also increasingly pressuring developing countries to adopt the political elements of liberalism, such as a guarantee of rights and freedoms. Indeed, there has been an important "human rights" discourse coming from Western states since the 1990s. Western states suggest that the fall of the Soviet Union marks the triumph of liberalism, and that it has left the world the potential for a global liberal order. In this context, they are actively trying to export liberalism. Whether this is desirable is a matter of debate. Many political scientists argue that pushing liberalism onto developing societies is wrong, not only because it constrains the choices available to these societies about their own politics, but also because transplanting a Western ideology into Africa or the Middle East might lead to severe social and cultural dislocations. There are political scientists who are more enthusiastic about the potential of liberalism to better the fate of developing societies. However, these scholars do not see such a transition as easy; they recognize that there are important obstacles.

Developing societies have their own political culture and traditions, which are often at odds with liberalism. In China, for example, the social and political thought of Confucianism values order through hierarchy and deference toward authority. This is very different from the liberal emphasis on equality of rights and limited power. Confucianism also speaks of duties and responsibilities. This partly explains why Chinese leaders do not accept the liberal notion of rights, or at least the idea of human or universal rights. They argue that the concept of right is culture specific, that is, Western, and that Chinese society is comfortable with its own guiding principles.

In other parts of Asia, such as Pakistan, the Middle East, and some African countries, religion clashes with liberalism. In societies where Islam is central to political power and legitimacy, in addition to often representing the source of law, the liberal discourse of secularization is problematic. So is liberalism's view of human beings as rational and autonomous actors, since it challenges the authority of religion. In some Muslim countries such as Iran or Afghanistan, under the Taliban, it is more accurate to speak of the rule of religion (which claims to be the rule of God) rather than the rule of law. In Africa, ethnic ties and loyalties offer a stark contrast to the strongly individualist nature of liberalism. This is especially the case in the many countries (Nigeria, Rwanda, Burundi, Zaire/Congo) where political power has a history of being exercised by a particular ethnic group and on behalf of this group's members. In these situations, power is concentrated, exercised arbitrarily, and favours certain citizens at the expense of others. Liberals in the West would suggest that there is no rule of law, no formal guarantees of rights and freedoms, and no meaningful legal equality in these countries.

CONSERVATISM

The conservative ideology is strongly rooted in the sociopolitical order of European feudalism. Feudal societies were hierarchically structured and functioned according to well-defined sets of relationships. At the top was an absolute monarch, whose legitimacy rested in his or her lineage rather than with popular support, and the Church, whose moral authority permeated politics and society. Also in positions of authority were aristocratic landowners, who had the privilege, or the birthright, to keep the product of the serfs' labour. Serfs were at the bottom of this hierarchical pyramid. They worked the land—without having the right to own it or to enjoy the fruit of their labour—in exchange for the benevolent protection offered by their masters. Feudalism presents a picture of a rigid society with institutionalized inequalities, where political power is unchallenged and change is unwelcomed. This is the

type of society against which Liberals reacted: they did not like the absolute power of the monarch, the institutionalization of social inequalities, and the influence of the Church on politics and society. In this context, liberalism was the main ideological adversary of conservatism from the seventeenth to the late-nineteenth century.

The French Revolution was a decisive moment in the articulation of **classical conservatism**. The Revolution represented a rupture with the feudal order: it abolished the monarchy, stripped aristocrats of their special privileges, and sought to destroy the power and influence of the Church. It proposed to build a new order on the ideas of equality of rights, freedom, and popular sovereignty. The transition was not smooth. It occurred in violence and chaos, and was marked by purges, terror, and eventually the dictatorship of Napoleon Bonaparte, who proceeded to invade France's neighbours in hope of

Edmund Burke

destroying their monarchies. Observing these events from Britain was Edmund Burke (1729–97), a member of Parliament, who was to become a key theorist of conservatism. In 1790 Burke wrote *Reflections on the Revolution in France*, in which he expressed serious doubts about the project of French revolutionaries. He argued that such a radical break with the past could result only in turmoil and dictatorship. Burke believed that you could not break with the past without paying a price, since society was held together by custom and traditions. Moreover, Burke was comfortable with the differentiated legal status found in feudal societies, which he saw as the foundation for an orderly society, that is, a society where everyone knew their place and their function. From this perspective, the democratic ideals of the French Revolution appeared frightening.

The conservative ideology underpinned feudalism but was formally articulated primarily as a response to the perceived danger of the ideas behind the French Revolution. Its core principles are decidedly different from those of liberalism. The first distinctive feature of conservatism is the importance it gives to order. Order, rather than freedom or equality, is the key value for Conservatives. Without order, they suggest, societies fall into anarchy and tyranny. Therefore, conservatism has a positive bias for the status quo. It holds that things that have existed for a long time (for example, political institutions, social structures, and practices) have an inherent value. It is wary of rapid and/or radical change because it sees change as leading to disorder. Despite this suspicion toward change, it would not be fair to say that the conservative ideology is against any type of change, although some forms of conservatism could certainly be described this way. Indeed, conservatism can be reactionary, that is, it can seek to undo change and come back to a previously existing situation. However, by and large, it is more accurate to say that conservatism accepts change if it is slow and gradual.

The second distinctive feature of conservatism is its conceptualization of individuals and society. Conservatives view society as an organic whole, which means that they consider it akin to a living organism, or to the human body, where one organ cannot function without the others. Therefore, they reject the liberal view that society is simply a collection of individuals. In other words, Conservatives argue that there is such a thing as "society," whereas Liberals focus more strictly on individuals. Similarly, Conservatives speak much more readily of "the nation" than do Liberals. In fact, conservatism tends to glorify the nation and emphasize its unity. The conservative ideology also suggests that liberalism exaggerates the autonomy and rationality of individuals. Instead, they suggest that individuals need to be grounded in custom and tradition to make sense of the world around them and to fit into society. If you suddenly remove this fabric and alter the existing social structure, Conservatives argue, the supposedly autonomous and rational individual will be lost. The importance that Conservatives give to tradition and structure is reflected in the institutions they value, namely the Church, the army, and the family.

The third distinctive feature of conservatism is the belief in the existence of an objective moral order. Liberals tend to judge the virtues of an idea or policy in utilitarian terms: does this idea or policy work? Conservatives contemplate their righteousness, their moral standard. This concern with morality explains the importance of religion in conservative thought. Conservatives are skeptical toward the rigid secularism of Liberals. Rather, they believe that politics must be imbued with the moral guidance provided by religion; politicians must do the right thing. In contemporary politics, this aspect of conservatism typically translates into an anti-abortion position, the rejection of gay rights (which, in addition to going against religious doctrine, is viewed as undermining the family), and opposition to such things as reproductive technology and cloning.

Finally, conservatism involves a distinctive view of the state as a benevolent and slightly paternalistic entity. Conservatives believe that the state has a substantial role to play in society. At the broadest level, this role is the protection of society, both in terms of physical security and socio-economic needs. Conservatives are in agreement with Liberals that the state must maintain law and order in society and protect it from external threats. In fact, conservatism puts a great deal of stress on these two state functions. For example, Conservatives in contemporary politics speak of the need for an expanded police presence and a tough justice system. They also argue for a strong army and increased military spending. On socio-economic issues, they are different from classical Liberals since they do not shy away from using the state as an agent of redistribution. The perspective here is not one of equality but rather one of social compassion; providing for the needy is the right, moral thing to do.

Characterizing the evolution of conservative thought is not as straightforward as for liberalism. In Western societies, Conservatives no longer advocate institutionalizing inequalities. Rather, they support democracy. A strand of contemporary conservatism, often dubbed "neoconservatism," has abandoned the organic view of society in favour of an individualist conception. **Neoconservatism** also has a much less positive view of the state than its original version, preferring to limit the state to law-and-order duties and minimal social protection. This translates into positions that are often called "fiscally conservative": lowering taxes, controlling or reducing spending, eliminating deficits, and reducing the debt. In this sense, neoconservatism is very close to classical or neoliberalism. However, Neoconservatives have often retained the ideology's stress on morality, which produces a unique outlook on politics. Conservative thought has also evolved in a different way. In this embodiment, represented, for example, by European Christian Democracy, conservatism has kept its traditional view of the state as an agent of redistribution. On social issues, it has relaxed its positions, evacuating much of the religious discourse while at the same time maintaining its concern for the unity and well-being of society as a whole.

CONSERVATISM IN CONTEMPORARY POLITICS

As we previously mentioned, liberalism, not conservatism, is the dominant ideology in the Western world. Nevertheless, politics in Western countries do exhibit, albeit in varying degrees, conservative trends. This is strongest in the United States, where politics is imbued with a strong sense of righteous morality. This is perhaps most striking in foreign policy, where the American government's view tends to be one of "good" versus "evil," from its struggle against the Soviet Union during the Cold War to its recent campaign against terrorism. Presidential electoral campaigns are also indicative of the presence of conservative thought in American politics. Candidates often have to answer questions about their "character": Are they loyal? Are they truthful? Can they provide strong moral guidance to the country? They have to take a position on the issue of abortion. They are usually questioned about their personal and family life. Conservatism is most significant in the Republican party, where many influential members are close to the religious establishment. Typically, Republicans are anti-abortion; they stress family values, and the importance of moral leadership; they advocate a strong military; they also favour a small state, with low taxes and minimum redistribution.

In Canada, these types of positions were articulated by the Reform/Canadian Alliance party. The rise of Reform in the early-to-mid-1990s brought conservative thought to the forefront of the Canadian political scene. Several of its stands or policy proposals represented a significant departure from Canadian politics. Some, such as institutional change (for a "Triple E" Senate, referenda, recalls of members of Parliament), had nothing to do with the conservative ideology and were in fact quite antithetical to it. However, others clearly flowed from conservative thought. Reform promised to "get tough on crime" by, among other things, reforming the Young Offenders Act to carry stricter sentences. It argued for increased military spending. It opposed the federal government making any concessions to or alliance with Quebec nationalists, arguing that those strategies undermined the cohesion of the nation. It spoke of the importance of the family as a cornerstone of Canadian society. It brought, albeit briefly and involuntarily, the issue of abortion to political debates. Fiscally, it advocated lowering taxes, eliminating the deficit, and paying down the debt. Therefore, much like the Republican party in the United States, Reform combined elements of traditional and neoconservatism.

Conservative thought existed in Canada before Reform came onto the political scene. The party's views were strongly embedded in the political culture and politics of many parts of Western Canada, particularly Alberta. There was also a Tory tradition, politically embodied by the Conservative party, which took some elements from traditional conservative thought, such as the emphasis on the unity of the nation (the Conservative party was central to the nation-building process in Canada through, among other things, the construction of the railway) and the attachment to long-standing institutions (for example, the British Crown). But perhaps most strikingly representative of traditional conservatism was Quebec before the Quiet Revolution of the 1960s. The province, or more specifically its Francophone majority, was a profoundly religious society. In fact, political power found legitimacy in the Catholic religion, and the Catholic Church had much influence on politics. As a result, political leaders promoted "Catholic values": large families, a rural lifestyle and economy (capitalism and industrialization were seen as morally bankrupt), the non-involvement of masses in politics (another morally bankrupt activity). They celebrated the unity of the French-Canadian "nation." They also found comfort in the status quo and resisted change.

Conservatism is also part of the European political landscape. The connection between the Church and politics is embodied by a family of parties generally known as "Christian Democracy." Christian Democratic parties, which are very strong in countries such as Germany and Belgium, take political stances that are informed by the conservative ideology: a stress on moral and family issues (marriage, divorce, birth control, abortion); state interventionism for purposes of enforcing morality (for example, in education), strengthening traditional institutions (the family), supporting small businesses, farms, and so on; and a suspicion toward change and politics that challenge the status quo. Christian Democracy in Western Europe has been strikingly pro-European, that is, in favour of European integration. Perhaps this political ideology's association with a community, Christianity, that is transnational in nature renders it more open to the European project than socialism or even liberalism.

Some developing societies have also been shaped by conservatism. Colonization was an important vehicle for the exportation of this ideology, more specifically, the religious messianism that accompanied much of it. Indeed, colonial powers such as France and Spain justified their presence in Africa and Latin America partly by suggesting that they were performing, through conversions to Catholicism, functions of moral education and spiritual redemption. The religious dimension of colonization left many former colonies with societies strongly penetrated by the Catholic religion. This is the case in Latin America where, as a result, politics has a "morality" dimension that translates into positions on social issues that often follow the official position of the Church. Politics in Latin America also exhibits other features of the conservative ideology. Society tends to be viewed as organic rather than as the sum of individuals, and there is a strong emphasis on the glory and unity of the nation. The army commands utmost respect and is often very involved in political life.

As we have already said, conservatism is a Western ideology. However, some non-Western political thoughts do resemble the conservative ideology. Confucianism, for example, is built upon well-defined sets of relationships (husband–wife, father–son, etc.) that structure a society hierarchically and where authority is accepted and respected. It values social harmony, which is deemed possible only through order. Similarly, Islam and Hinduism emphasize the value of the family, the organic unity of society, and the concept of obligation.

ENDNOTES

1. Isaiah Berlin, *Four Essays on Liberty* (London: Oxford University Press, 1969).
2. Adam Smith, *An Inquiry into the Nature and Causes of the Wealth of Nations* (Oxford: Clarendon Press, 1979).
3. John Stuart Mill, *The Subjection of Women* (London: Longmans, Green, Reader and Dyer, 1878).

READINGS

The preceding discussion explained the historical origins, main tenets, evolution, and contemporary relevance of liberalism and conservatism. It stressed that these two ideologies are themselves plural in the sense that "branches" or "streams" can be identified within each. The readings selected for this chapter are drawn from the work of two theorists who have been instrumental in articulating liberalism and conservatism, and who are associated with a particular version of the ideology: Edmund Burke, the father of conservative thought, and John Stuart Mill, a central influence behind reform liberalism.

The first reading is an excerpt from John Stuart Mill's *Considerations on Representative Government*. Mill (1806–73) made several significant contributions to liberal thought. He developed the notion of utilitarianism, which suggests that the appropriateness of an action depends upon its ability to promote happiness. He discussed at length the importance of individual liberty as a social and political value (*On Liberty*, 1859), suggesting that it should be constrained only when it is harmful to others. He advocated women's suffrage (*On the Subjection of Women*, 1869) earlier than most other theorists and politicians. He strongly argued that representative government is preferable to other types of government in which political power is concentrated in the hands of one person, no matter how wise and enlightened that person may be. Typical of Liberals, Mill strongly values individual rights, freedom, and the opportunity to achieve prosperity. For him, individual rights are best protected when citizens are able to defend these rights, and prosperity is greater if they enjoy the freedom to use their creativity and their energy. This is best achieved, Mill argues, in political systems where citizens can take part in government. This argument is developed in the section entitled "That the Ideally Best Form of Government is Representative Government," which is partially reproduced here.

Born in Ireland, Edmund Burke (1729–97) is generally considered the leading theorist of conservative thought. Burke never really synthesized his political philosophy in one comprehensive work. Rather, his ideas can be found in various letters and political speeches. Burke was more than a political pundit; he also sat as a member of Parliament, where he advocated an attitude of conciliation toward the American colonies, which were growing increasingly dissatisfied with Britain's rule. However, Burke is most famous for his virulent criticism of the French Revolution, which upset his predilection for order and slow, gradual change. In fact, Burke foresaw much of the chaos and violence that would afflict revolutionary France. The second reading is drawn from Burke's best-known writing, *Reflections on the Revolution in France* (1790). In it, Burke engages in a discussion in which he takes a cautious approach to liberty. Indeed, for Burke, liberty may be good in the abstract, but it becomes problematic when used to break away from the past, its traditions, and customs, because it threatens societal order. Burke was also critical of the French Revolution for its secular character. In the reading, he declares man a "religious animal" and proclaims that Great Britain shall keep its church, monarchy, and aristocracy.

THAT THE IDEALLY BEST FORM OF GOVERNMENT IS REPRESENTATIVE GOVERNMENT

John Stuart Mill

It has long (perhaps throughout the entire duration of British freedom) been a common saying that, if a good despot could be ensured, despotic monarchy would be the best form of government. I look upon this as a radical and most pernicious misconception of what good government is; which, until it can be got rid of, will fatally vitiate all our speculations on government.

The supposition is that absolute power, in the hands of an eminent individual, would ensure a virtuous and intelligent performance of all the duties of government. Good laws would be established and enforced, bad laws would be reformed; the best men would be placed in all situations of trust; justice would be as well administered, the public burdens would be as light and as judiciously imposed, every branch of administration would be as purely and as intelligently conducted as the circumstances of the country and its degree of intellectual and moral cultivation would admit. I am willing, for the sake of the argument, to concede all this; but I must point out how great the concession is, how much more is needed to produce even an approximation to these results than is conveyed in the simple expression "a good despot." Their realization would in fact imply, not merely a good monarch, but an all-seeing one. He must be at all times informed correctly, in considerable detail, of the conduct and working of every branch of administration, in every district of the country, and must be able, in the twenty-four hours per day which are all that is granted to a king as to the humblest laborer, to give an effective share of attention and superintendence to all parts of this vast field; or he must at least be capable of discerning and choosing out, from among the mass of his subjects, not only a large abundance of honest and able men, fit to conduct every branch of public administration under supervision and control, but also the small number of men of eminent virtues and talents who can be trusted not only to do without that supervision, but to exercise it themselves over others. So extraordinary are the faculties and energies required for performing this task in any supportable manner that the good despot whom we are supposing can hardly be imagined as consenting to undertake it, unless as a refuge from intolerable evils and a transitional preparation for something beyond. But the argument can do without even this immense item in the account. Suppose the difficulty vanquished. What should we then have? One man of superhuman mental activity managing the entire affairs of a mentally passive people. Their passivity is implied in the very idea of absolute power. The nation as a whole and every individual composing it are without any potential voice in their own destiny. They exercise no will in respect to their collective interests. All is decided for them by a will not their own, which it is legally a crime for them to disobey. What sort of human beings can be formed under such a regimen? What development can either their thinking or their active faculties attain under it? On matters of pure theory they might perhaps be allowed to speculate, so long as their speculations either did not approach politics or had not the remotest connection with its practice. On practical affairs they could at most be only suffered to suggest; and even under the most moderate of despots, none but persons of already admitted or reputed superiority could hope that their suggestions would be known to, much less regarded by, those who had the management of affairs. A person must have a very unusual taste for intellectual exercise in and for itself, who will put himself to the trouble of thought when it is to have no outward effect, or qualify himself for functions which he has no chance of being allowed to exercise. The only sufficient incitement to mental exertion, in any but a few minds in a generation, is the prospect of some practical use to be made of its results. It does not follow that the nation will be wholly destitute of intellectual power. The common business of life, which must necessarily be performed by each individual or family for themselves, will call forth some amount of intelligence and practical ability, within a certain narrow range of ideas. There may be a select class of *savants* who cultivate science with a view to its physical uses or for the pleasure of the pursuit. There will be a bureaucracy, and persons in training for the bureaucracy, who will be taught at least some empirical maxims of government and public administration. There may be, and often has been, a systematic organization of the best mental power in the country in some special direction (commonly military) to promote the grandeur of the despot. But the public at large remains without information and without interest on all the greater matters of practice; or, if they have any knowledge of them, it is but a *dilettante* knowledge, like that which people have of the mechanical arts who have never handled a tool. Nor is it only in their intelligence that they suffer. Their moral capacities are equally stunted. Wherever the sphere of action of human beings is artificially circumscribed, their sentiments are narrowed and dwarfed in the same proportion.

The food of feeling is action: even domestic affection lives upon voluntary good offices. Let a person have nothing to do for his country, and he will not care for it. It has been said of old that in a despotism there is at most but one patriot, the despot himself; and the saying rests on a just appreciation of the effects of absolute subjection, even to a good and wise master. Religion remains: and here at least, it may be thought, is an agency that may be relied on for lifting men's eyes and minds above the dust at their feet. But religion, even supposing it to escape perversion for the purposes of despotism, ceases in these circumstances to be a social concern and narrows into a personal affair between an individual and his Maker in which the issue at stake is but his private salvation. Religion in this shape is quite consistent with the most selfish and contracted egoism and identifies the votary as little in feeling with the rest of his kind as sensuality itself.

A good despotism means a government in which, so far as depends on the despot, there is no positive oppression by officers of state, but in which all the collective interests of the people are managed for them, all the thinking that has relation to collective interests done for them, and in which their minds are formed by, and consenting to, this abdication of their own energies. Leaving things to the Government, like leaving them to Providence, is synonymous with caring nothing about them and accepting their results, when disagreeable, as visitations of Nature. With the exception, therefore, of a few studious men who take an intellectual interest in speculation for its own sake, the intelligence and sentiments of the whole people are given up to the material interests and, when these are provided for, to the amusement and ornamentation of private life. But to say this is to say, if the whole testimony of history is worth anything, that the era of national decline has arrived; that is, if the nation had ever attained anything to decline from. If it has never risen above the condition of an Oriental people, in that condition it continues to stagnate. But if, like Greece or Rome, it had realized anything higher, through the energy, patriotism, and enlargement of mind, which as national qualities are the fruits solely of freedom, it relapses in a few generations into the Oriental state. And that state does not mean stupid tranquillity, with security against change for the worse; it often means being overrun, conquered, and reduced to domestic slavery, either by a stronger despot or by the nearest barbarous people who retain along with their savage rudeness the energies of freedom.

Such are not merely the natural tendencies, but the inherent necessities of despotic government; from which there is no outlet unless in so far as the despotism consents not to be despotism; in so far as the supposed good despot abstains from exercising his power and, though holding it in reserve, allows the general business of government to go on as if the people really governed themselves. However little probable it may be, we may imagine a despot observing many of the rules and restraints of constitutional government. He might allow such freedom of the press and of discussion as would enable a public opinion to form and express itself on national affairs. He might suffer local interests to be managed, without the interference of authority, by the people themselves. He might even surround himself with a council or councils of government, freely chosen by the whole or some portion of the nation, retaining in his own hands the power of taxation and the supreme legislative as well as executive authority. Were he to act thus, and so far abdicate as a despot, he would do away with a considerable part of the evils characteristic of despotism. Political activity and capacity for public affairs would no longer be prevented from growing up in the body of the nation, and a public opinion would form itself not the mere echo of the government. But such improvement would be the beginning of new difficulties. This public opinion, independent of the monarch's dictation, must be either with him or against him; if not the one, it will be the other. All governments must displease many persons, and these having now regular organs and being able to express their sentiments, opinions adverse to the measures of government would often be expressed. What is the monarch to do when these unfavorable opinions happen to be in the majority? Is he to alter his course? Is he to defer to the nation? If so, he is no longer a despot, but a constitutional king—an organ or first minister of the people, distinguished only by being irremovable. If not, he must either put down opposition by his despotic power, or there will arise a permanent antagonism between the people and one man, which can have but one possible ending. Not even a religious principle of passive obedience and "right divine" would long ward

off the natural consequences of such a position. The monarch would have to succumb and conform to the conditions of constitutional royalty, or give place to someone who would. The despotism, being thus chiefly nominal, would possess few of the advantages supposed to belong to absolute monarchy, while it would realize in a very imperfect degree those of a free government; since, however great an amount of liberty the citizens might practically enjoy, they could never forget that they held it on sufferance and by a concession which under the existing constitution of the state might at any moment be resumed; that they were legally slaves, though of a prudent, or indulgent, master.

It is not much to be wondered at if impatient or disappointed reformers, groaning under the impediments opposed to the most salutary public improvements by the ignorance, the indifference, the intractableness, the perverse obstinacy of a people, and the corrupt combinations of selfish private interests armed with the powerful weapons afforded by free institutions, should at times sigh for a strong hand to bear down all these obstacles and compel a recalcitrant people to be better governed. But (setting aside the fact that for one despot who now and then reforms an abuse, there are ninety-nine who do nothing but create them) those who look in any such direction for the realization of their hopes leave out of the idea of good government its principal element, the improvement of the people themselves. One of the benefits of freedom is that under it the ruler cannot pass by the people's minds and amend their affairs for them without amending them. If it were possible for the people to be well governed in spite of themselves, their good government would last no longer than the freedom of a people usually lasts who have been liberated by foreign arms without their own co-operation. It is true, a despot may educate the people; and to do so really would be the best apology for his despotism. But any education which aims at making human beings other than machines in the long run makes them claim to have the control of their own actions. The leaders of French philosophy in the eighteenth century had been educated by the Jesuits. Even Jesuit education, it seems, was sufficiently real to call forth the appetite for freedom. Whatever invigorates the faculties, in however small a measure, creates an increased desire for their more unimpeded exercise; and a popular education is a failure if it educates the people for any state but that which it will certainly induce them to desire, and most probably to demand.

I am far from condemning, in cases of extreme exigency, the assumption of absolute power in the form of a temporary dictatorship. Free nations have, in times of old, conferred such power by their own choice, as a necessary medicine for diseases of the body politic which could not be got rid of by less violent means. But its acceptance, even for a time strictly limited, can only be excused if, like Solon or Pittacus, the dictator employs the whole power he assumes in removing the obstacles which debar the nation from the enjoyment of freedom. A good despotism is an altogether false ideal, which practically (except as a means to some temporary purpose) becomes the most senseless and dangerous of chimeras. Evil for evil, a good despotism in a country at all advanced in civilization is more noxious than a bad one; for it is far more relaxing and enervating to the thoughts, feelings, and energies of the people. The despotism of Augustus prepared the Romans for Tiberius. If the whole tone of their character had not first been prostrated by nearly two generations of that mild slavery, they would probably have had spirit enough left to rebel against the more odious one.

There is no difficulty in showing that the ideally best form of government is that in which the sovereignty, or supreme controlling power in the last resort, is vested in the entire aggregate of the community, every citizen not only having a voice in the exercise of that ultimate sovereignty, but being, at least occasionally, called on to take an actual part in the government by the personal discharge of some public function, local or general.

To test this proposition, it has to be examined in reference to the two branches into which, as pointed out . . . the inquiry into the goodness of a government conveniently divides itself—namely, how far it promotes the good management of the affairs of society by means of the existing faculties, moral, intellectual, and active, of its various members, and what is its effect in improving or deteriorating those faculties.

The ideally best form of government, it is scarcely necessary to say, does not mean one which is practicable or eligible in all states of civilization, but the one which, in the circumstances in which it is practicable and eligible, is attended with the greatest amount of beneficial consequences, immediate and prospective. A completely popular government is the only polity which can make out any claim to this character. It is pre-eminent in both the departments between which the excellence of a political constitution is divided. It is both more favorable to present good government and promotes a better and higher form of national character than any other polity whatsoever.

Its superiority in reference to present well-being rests upon two principles of as universal truth and applicability as any general propositions which can be laid down respecting human affairs. The first is that the rights and interests of every or any person are only secure from being disregarded when the person interested is himself able, and habitually disposed, to stand up for them. The second is that the general prosperity attains a greater height and is more widely diffused in proportion to the amount and variety of the personal energies enlisted in promoting it.

Putting these two propositions into a shape more special to their present application: human beings are only secure from evil at the hands of others in proportion as they have the power of being, and are, self-*protecting*; and they only achieve a high degree of success in their struggle with nature in proportion as they are self-*dependent*, relying on what they themselves can do, either separately or in concert, rather than on what others do for them.

The former proposition—that each is the only safe guardian of his own rights and interests—is one of those elementary maxims of prudence which every person capable of conducting his own affairs implicitly acts upon wherever he himself is interested. Many, indeed, have a great dislike to it as a political doctrine and are fond of holding it up to obloquy as a doctrine of universal selfishness. To which we may answer that whenever it ceases to be true that mankind, as a rule, prefer themselves to others, and those nearest to them to those more remote, from that moment Communism is not only practicable but the only defensible form of society, and will, when that time arrives, be assuredly carried into effect. For my own part, not believing in universal selfishness, I have no difficulty in admitting that Communism[1] would even now be practicable among the *élite* of mankind, and may become so among the rest. But as this opinion is anything but popular with those defenders of existing institutions who find fault with the doctrine of the general predominance of self-interest, I am inclined to think they do in reality believe that most men consider themselves before other people. It is not, however, necessary to affirm even thus much in order to support the claim of all to participate in the sovereign power. We need not suppose that when power resides in an exclusive class, that class will knowingly and deliberately sacrifice the other classes to themselves; it suffices that, in the absence of its natural defenders, the interest of the excluded is always in danger of being overlooked, and, when looked at, is seen with very different eyes from those of the persons whom it directly concerns. In this country, for example, what are called the working classes may be considered as excluded from all direct participation in the government. I do not believe that the classes who do participate in it have in general any intention of sacrificing the working classes to themselves. They once had that intention—witness the persevering attempts so long made to keep down wages by law. But in the present day their ordinary disposition is the very opposite: they willingly make considerable sacrifices, especially of their pecuniary interest, for the benefit of the working classes, and err rather by too lavish and indiscriminating beneficence; nor do I believe that any rulers in history have been actuated by a more sincere desire to do their duty toward the poorer portion of their countrymen. Yet does Parliament, or almost any of the members composing it, ever for an instant look at any question with the eyes of a workingman? When a subject arises in which the laborers as such have an interest, is it regarded from any point of view but that of the employers of labor? I do not say that the workingmen's view of these questions is in general nearer to the truth than the other, but it is sometimes quite as near; and in any case it ought to be respectfully listened to instead of being, as it is, not merely turned away from, but ignored. On the question of strikes, for instance, it is doubtful if there is so much as one among the leading members of either House who is not firmly convinced that the reason of the matter is unqualifiedly on the side of the masters, and that the men's view of it is simply absurd. Those who have studied the question know well how far this is from being the case, and in how different and how infinitely less superficial a manner the point would have to be argued if the classes who strike were able to make themselves heard in Parliament.

It is an adherent condition of human affairs that no intention, however sincere, of protecting the interests of others can make it safe or salutary to tie up their own hands. Still more obviously true is it that by their own hands only can any positive and durable improvement of their circumstances in life be worked out. Through the joint influence of these two principles, all free communities have both been more exempt from social injustice and crime, and have attained more brilliant prosperity, than any others, or than they themselves after they lost their freedom. Contrast the free states of the world, while their freedom lasted, with the contemporary subjects of monarchical or oligarchical despotism: the Greek cities with the Persian satrapies; the Italian republics and the free towns of Flanders and Germany with the feudal monarchies of Europe; Switzerland, Holland, and England with Austria or ante-revolutionary France. Their superior prosperity was too obvious ever to have been gainsaid, while their superiority in good government and social relations is proved by the prosperity, and is manifest besides in every page of history. If we compare, not one age with another, but the different governments which coexisted in the same age, no amount of disorder which exaggeration itself can pretend to have existed amidst the publicity of the free states can be compared for a moment with the contemptuous trampling upon the mass of the people which pervaded the whole life of the monarchical countries, or the disgusting individual tyranny which was of more than daily occurrence under the systems of plunder which they called fiscal arrangements and in the secrecy of their frightful courts of justice.

Reading Note

1. By Communism, Mill means pre-Marxian socialism. Nowhere in his writings does Mill indicate any awareness of Marxian socialism, which was formulated during his lifetime. (The first volume of Marx's *Das Kapital* appeared in 1867.) He often speaks sympathetically of the various pre-Marxian schools of socialism represented by Claude

Henri de Rouvroy, Comte de Saint-Simon (1760–1825 . . .), François Marie Charles Fourier (1772–1837), Robert Owen (1771–1858), Pierre Joseph Proudhon (1809–1865), and others whom the Marxians dismissed as unscientific and utopian.

REFLECTIONS ON THE REVOLUTION IN FRANCE

Edmund Burke

I flatter myself that I love a manly, moral, regulated liberty as well as any gentleman of that society, be he who he will; and perhaps I have given as good proofs of my attachment to that cause, in the whole course of my public conduct. I think I envy liberty as little as they do, to any other nation. But I cannot stand forward, and give praise or blame to anything which relates to human actions, and human concerns, on a simple view of the object, as it stands stripped of every relation, in all the nakedness and solitude of metaphysical abstraction. Circumstances (which with some gentlemen pass for nothing) give in reality to every political principle its distinguishing colour and discriminating effect. The circumstances are what render every civil and political scheme beneficial or noxious to mankind. Abstractedly speaking, government, as well as liberty, is good; yet could I, in common sense, ten years ago, have felicitated France on her enjoyment of a government (for she then had a government) without inquiry what the nature of that government was, or how it was administered? Can I now congratulate the same nation upon its freedom? Is it because liberty in the abstract may be classed amongst the blessings of mankind, that I am seriously to felicitate a madman, who has escaped from the protecting restraint and wholesome darkness of his cell, on his restoration to the enjoyment of light and liberty? Am I to congratulate a highwayman and murderer, who has broke prison, upon the recovery of his natural rights? This would be to act over again the scene of the criminals condemned to the galleys, and their heroic deliverer, the metaphysic knight of the sorrowful countenance.

When I see the spirit of liberty in action, I see a strong principle at work; and this, for a while, is all I can possibly know of it. The wild *gas*, the fixed air, is plainly broke loose: but we ought to suspend our judgment until the first effervescence is a little subsided, till the liquor is cleared, and until we see something deeper than the agitation of a troubled and frothy surface. I must be tolerably sure, before I venture publicly to congratulate men upon a blessing, that they have really received one. Flattery corrupts both the receiver and the giver; and adulation is not of more service to the people than to kings. I should therefore suspend my congratulations on the new liberty of France, until I was informed how it had been combined with government; with public force; with the discipline and obedience of armies; with the collection of an effective and well-distributed revenue; with morality and religion; with the solidity of property; with peace and order; with civil and social manners. All these (in their way) are good things too; and, without them, liberty is not a benefit whilst it lasts, and is not likely to continue long. The effect of liberty to individuals is, that they may do what they please: we ought to see what it will please them to do, before we risk congratulations, which may be soon turned into complaints. Prudence would dictate this in the case of separate, insulated, private men; but liberty, when men act in bodies, is *power*. Considerate people, before they declare themselves, will observe the use which is made of *power*; and particularly of so trying a thing as *new* power in *new* persons, of whose principles, tempers, and dispositions they have little or no experience, and in situations, where those who appear the most stirring in the scene may possibly not be the real movers.

***

We know, and what is better, we feel inwardly, that religion is the basis of civil society and the source of all good and of all comfort. In England we are so convinced of this, that there is no rust of superstition, with which the accumulated absurdity of the human mind might have crusted it over in the course of ages, that ninety-nine in a hundred of the people of England would not prefer to impiety. We shall never be such fools as to call in an enemy to the substance of any system to remove its corruptions, to supply its defects, or to perfect its construction.

If our religious tenets should ever want a further elucidation, we shall not call on atheism to explain them. We shall not light up our temple from that unhallowed fire. It will be illuminated with other lights. It will be perfumed with other incense, than the infectious stuff which is imported by the smugglers of adulterated metaphysics. If our ecclesiastical establishment should want a revision, it is not avarice or rapacity, public or private, that we shall employ for the audit, or receipt, or application of its consecrated revenue. Violently condemning neither the Greek nor the Armenian, nor, since heats are subsided, the Roman system of religion, we prefer the Protestant; not because we think it has less of the Christian religion in it, but because, in our judgment, it has more. We are Protestants, not from indifference, but from zeal.

We know, and it is our pride to know, that man is by his constitution a religious animal; that atheism is against, not only our reason, but our instincts; and that it cannot prevail long. But if, in the moment of riot, and in a drunken delirium from the hot spirit drawn out of the alembic of hell, which in France is now so furiously boiling, we should uncover our nakedness, by throwing off that Christian religion which has hitherto been our boast and comfort, and one great source of civilization amongst us, and amongst many other nations, we are apprehensive (being well aware that the mind will not endure a void) that

some uncouth, pernicious, and degrading superstition might take place of it.

For that reason, before we take from our establishment the natural, human means of estimation, and give it up to contempt, as you have done, and in doing it have incurred the penalties you well deserve to suffer, we desire that some other may be presented to us in the place of it. We shall then form our judgment.

On these ideas, instead of quarrelling with establishments, as some do, who have made a philosophy and a religion of their hostility to such institutions, we cleave closely to them. We are resolved to keep an established church, an established monarchy, an established aristocracy, and an established democracy, each in the degree it exists, and in no greater. I shall show you presently how much of each of these we possess.

It has been the misfortune (not, as these gentlemen think it, the glory) of this age, that everything is to be discussed, as if the constitution of our country were to be always a subject rather of altercation, than enjoyment. For this reason, as well as for the satisfaction of those among you (if any such you have among you) who may wish to profit of examples, I venture to trouble you with a few thoughts upon each of these establishments. I do not think they were unwise in ancient Rome, who, when they wished to new-model their laws, set commissioners to examine the best constituted republics within their reach.

KEY TERMS

Classical Conservatism   Original version of conservatism, often associated with British theorist Edmund Burke, which emphasizes order, morality, and traditions. It also stresses the organic nature of society, adopts a paternalistic view of the state's role in society, and advocates slow and gradual, as opposed to radical, change.

Classical Liberalism   Original version of liberalism that emphasizes equality of rights, negative freedom, and a minimal role for the state in society.

Democratic Socialism   Branch of socialist thought that accepts to work within a liberal-capitalist order, but seeks to soften the effects of the market through regulation and redistribution.

Neoconservatism   Stream of conservative thought that sheds the organic view of society in favour of an individualist conception, and that advocates a minimal state, i.e., less government and a small bureaucracy.

Reform Liberalism   Stream of liberal thought, articulated in the nineteenth century, that advocates equality of rights and opportunity, negative and positive freedom, and some degree of state welfarism and interventionism. Also known as modern liberalism or welfare liberalism.

FURTHER READINGS

Gibbins, Roger and Loleen Youngman. *Mindscapes: Political Ideologies Towards the 21st Century.* Toronto: McGraw-Hill Ryerson, 1996.

Qualter, Terence. *Conflicting Political Ideas in Liberal Democracies.* Toronto: Methuen, 1986.

WEB LINKS

Liberal International:
www.liberal-international.org

Movement for Christian Democracy:
http://concise.britannica.com/ebc/article-9360712/Christian-Democracy

National Citizens' Coalition:
www.morefreedom.org

CHAPTER 5

SOCIALISM AND COMMUNISM

The relevance of socialism in contemporary politics has been a topic of debate since the end of the Cold War. Some have declared socialism to be dead, buried alongside the totalitarian regimes of the former Soviet Union and Eastern European countries. Others, however, argue that socialism's class-based politics and egalitarian principles are even more relevant today than they were in the past. A discussion of socialism also has to distinguish between two of its branches: communism and social democracy. While the influence and saliency of communism may have diminished in the past decades, social democracy continues to influence government policies throughout the world. This chapter examines the ideas, practice, and history of socialism and its two variants, communism and social democracy. We begin with an overview of socialist and Marxist theory—the intellectual foundation of socialism—and then outline the basic tenets of socialism, providing a comparison between social democracy and communism. Next, we examine the influence of Marxist theory in Communist regimes and highlight some of the ways Marxism was reformulated and adapted in different parts of the world. The chapter ends with a look at the influence of social democracy and communism in contemporary politics.

SOCIALIST AND MARXIST THOUGHT

Social democracy and communism have their ideological roots in nineteenth-century socialism and the work of Karl Marx and Friedrich Engels. They emerged during a period of great economic and social transformation brought about by the Industrial Revolution of eighteenth-century Europe. Born out of technological progress that allowed goods to be produced on a much larger scale than had previously been possible, the Industrial Revolution radically transformed the relations of production (relations between owners and workers) and the social conditions of workers. In the cities, where people were flocking to find employment in factories, working conditions were extremely difficult and often dangerous, and wages very low. The very wide gap between rich and poor was increasing. There was virtually no regulation of labour conditions, and no mechanism to reduce the disparity between those who owned the **means of production** (the machines and factories) and those who did not.

Socialist ideas and movements sprang up in many European countries, as political thinkers critical of the consequences of an unfettered capitalist economy began to speak out and press for reform. In the eighteenth and nineteenth centuries, social reformers and theorists such as Gracchus Babeuf and Robert Owen drew attention to the political and social problems created by industrialization. They argued that liberal principles of individual freedoms and political rights did nothing to alleviate poverty, oppression, and the increasing polarization between rich and poor. Rejecting the liberal conception of human beings as self-interested and competitive individuals, socialists argued that people could achieve self-fulfillment and happiness only as members of a cooperative community.[1] They called for a new social order, a utopian society, where goods would be produced and distributed to advance the overall good of society. Some of these early socialist reformers advocated the creation of self-sufficient cooperative communities in order to attain their socialist goals.

Karl Marx

Others called for better treatment of workers and radical improvements to their living conditions.

However, the most important work in socialist theory came from Karl Marx. The publication of Marx's *Communist Manifesto* in 1848 was a watershed event in the history of socialist thought. It provided protest movements with a socio-economic explanation for understanding the plight of the working class and a road map for political action. Marxist theories soon dominated socialist thought in Europe. Marx advanced an economic interpretation of human history in which all social processes and institutions are founded on the dominant **mode of production** (i.e., ancient civilization, feudalism, and capitalism) and the consequent class struggle. He argued that in every society, irrespective of its economic structure, there exist two "warring" **classes**: the dominant class, which owns the means of production (e.g., land, raw material, machines, money), and the subject class, whose members are exploited for their labour. Under capitalism there are two classes: the **proletariat**, or working class, and the **bourgeoisie**, or capitalist class. The relationship between the workers and capitalists is by necessity an exploitative one. The worker is exploited, dehumanized, and treated like a commodity. As Marx explained, "His work is not voluntary but imposed, forced labour. It is not the satisfaction of a need, but only a means for satisfying other needs. Its alien character is clearly shown by the fact that as soon as there is no physical or other compulsion it is avoided like the plague . . ."[2] Workers are alienated from their work and from each other, while the employer reaps the rewards of their labour.

Drawing from the **labour theory of value**, which proposes that the price of a commodity directly reflects the labour time used to produce it, Marx argued that capitalism contained its own seed of self-destruction. Because capitalists strive to achieve surplus value in order to attain profits, workers' wages represent only a portion of the value of the product they have produced. He argued that as the profits of factory owners steadily increased while the living conditions of workers deteriorated, it was only a question of time before the workers would realize their common plight, revolt, and ultimately overthrow the capitalist economic order. According to Marx, capitalism would be overthrown by a proletariat revolution and replaced by socialism. Socialism was to be a temporary and transitional stage on the road to the final destination, communism. Under **communism**, the means of production would be publicly owned, private property would be abolished, and the state would wither away. He predicted that capitalism would self-destruct due to its internal contradictions, which would culminate in a proletariat revolution and the creation of a classless society. Essentially, Marx advanced a scientific interpretation of history that saw social evolution as being governed by scientific laws.

Influenced by Marx's class-based view of politics and society, **socialism** views the capitalist relations of production as the primary causes of social and political inequalities in society and advances political projects to eliminate social injustices. Socialism does not view human nature as fixed, but as flexible and capable of adapting to the surrounding environment. It rejects the liberal conception of individuals as naturally competitive and self-interested and instead argues that human beings, under the right conditions, are cooperative and interested in pursuing the common good.

Socialism places the greatest importance on equality, not freedom or order as is the case for Liberals and Conservatives, respectively. **Social democracy** considers the equality of rights cherished by classical Liberals to be nice but insufficient. Its own view of equality is closer to reform liberalism's equality of opportunity, although this last notion does not go far enough and constitutes only a minimum position for socialism. Indeed, socialism strives for some measure of equality of conditions. In other words, it is not quite sufficient to "level the playing field"; for equality to be meaningful, there cannot be major discrepancies between actual living conditions, even if everyone has a roughly similar opportunity to accumulate wealth. Accordingly, social democracy stresses positive rather than simply negative freedom. Socialists argue, much like reform Liberals but even more forcefully, that basic rights and liberties fall short of providing individuals living in difficult socio-economic conditions with meaningful freedom. They suggest that freedom involves dimensions of empowerment that can result only from state action.

This is the second key idea of democratic socialist thought: the state playing an active and positive role in society. Socialists advocate substantial redistribution of wealth in society. As we said earlier, reform liberalism also favours redistribution but is reluctant to go as far as social democracy. For example, Liberals would hesitate having high taxes on corporations for fear that this policy would hurt the economy; typically Socialists have no such qualms as they see large, presumably profitable companies paying high taxes as a matter of social justice. They harbour a suspicion, often a distrust, of the market. This is why they see a need for the state to act not only as an agent of redistribution, but also as a regulator of the economy.

Socialism also pays particular attention to minority and disadvantaged groups in society. For example, it supports the traditional demands of women's groups (the right to an abortion, pay equity, and so on); the claim of homosexual couples to have a similar legal status as heterosexual couples; and the right for immigrant communities to preserve and promote their native culture. These positions reflect socialism's emphasis on the notions of equality, social justice, and tolerance.

Like liberalism and conservatism, socialism is divided into different branches, the most important ones being social democracy and communism. Both branches, to varying degrees, adhere to the main tenets of socialism, such as equality, social justice, and centralized planning of the economy. However, they differ considerably in their views on property and collective ownership, revolutionary change, and constitutional democracy. For example, social democrats are reformists, who want to bring about change through democratic means, while Communists represent the most radical faction of the socialist movement, which advocates revolutionary action. Differences between social democracy and communism are discussed in the next section.

SOCIAL DEMOCRACY AND COMMUNISM COMPARED

Both communism and socialism favour public ownership of the means of production in order to eliminate economic inequalities. Socialism, however, views the move toward public ownership as a gradual process, involving key industries or sectors considered vital to the economic well-being of a society. For socialists, public ownership is a means to an end; socialists decide to nationalize industries if they are experiencing financial difficulty, if they are a monopoly, or if they are considered vital to the national economy.[3] Communism, on the other hand, advocates the elimination of all private enterprise in favour of complete state control of the means of production, distribution, and exchange. It seeks to eliminate private property, even property that is personal in nature, so that one group cannot have an economic advantage over another group. Socialism, however, safeguards the rights of individuals to own consumer goods. It is only the means of producing these consumer goods, i.e., factories, machinery, etc., that are publicly owned. As stated by Ebenstein et al., "communism stands for the complete sharing of all things, while classical socialism seeks only collective ownership of the means of production."[4]

Another difference between social democracy and communism concerns the issue of income distribution. While social democracy upholds the principle of equality and seeks to diminish economic disparities, it stops short of eliminating them altogether. Social democrats would distribute resources according to a person's "*deeds*," that is, according to the type of work performed. This means that not everyone will make the same wages. Communism, on the other hand, adheres to Marx's famous slogan, "From each according to his ability, to each according to his *needs*." The ultimate goal of communism is a classless society, which rests on the complete elimination of economic inequalities. Individuals would cooperate freely and equally in the production of goods and services and in turn, would share the fruits of their labour with others, regardless of the work performed.

Social democracy and communism also distinguish themselves by the means used to achieve social change. Early social democrats viewed Marxism as a force liberating human beings from economic and political exploitation. They were dedicated to the realization of individual liberty, albeit in a socialist framework. Social democrats believe that socialism could naturally evolve, over time, within democratic institutions and processes. They form parties and participate in elections in order to effect change benefiting the working class. While communism seeks to abolish capitalist economic relations, socialists work within the system and introduce reforms that curtail the negative consequences of the market. Social democrats are concerned with providing workers with legal protections (a minimum wage, safe working conditions, the right to strike in the context of collective bargaining, and so on). Historically, they have been the crucial force behind the creation and empowerment of trade unions. In the context of international economic relations the social democratic distrust of the market typically translates into a cautious approach toward free trade, if not outright opposition. Social democrats argue that free trade, as it involves deregulating the economy and giving primacy to the market in economic life, hampers the ability of the state to act as an agent of redistribution and to protect workers.

For communism, social change, i.e., a classless society, can occur only through a revolution of the proletariat. Parliamentary democracy is regarded as a sham, a product of the capitalist system, benefiting the interests of the bourgeoisie. Trade unionism and electoral politics undermine the development of class consciousness as vehicles for social change and therefore are doomed to failure because they did not transform the underlying social and economic structures. The state itself is perceived as an instrument of the exploitation of the subject class, and, as such, should be dismantled through violent resistance. The transition from capitalism to socialism, Communists argue, can occur only through a dictatorship of the proletariat.

Social democracy and communism are also associated with different types of political regimes. Social democracy is found in constitutional democracies, where people directly or through their representatives take part in making policies. In the democratic system of government, working-class interests are represented by political parties that compete in elections to form governments. Social democrats play by the rules of the game and adhere to democratic principles such as civil liberties and political rights, free elections, and freedom of the press. Communism, on the other hand, is associated with totalitarian forms of government, such as those found in the former Soviet Union, China, and North Korea. Totalitarian regimes are ruled by a single mass party that completely controls political and social institutions in an effort to attain an ideologically driven goal. A distinctive feature of Communist regimes is a centrally planned economy founded on state-owned industry and collectively owned agriculture. Dissent is quashed and controlled through the use of terror, censorship, a secret police, and military force. Democratic ideals of individual rights and freedoms could be sacrificed for the needs of the class revolution.[5]

MARXIST DOCTRINE AND COMMUNIST REGIMES

While Marxist theory inspired the revolutions that took place in Communist countries, the totalitarian regimes that were created afterward significantly transformed the content of Marxism to suit their needs and circumstances. The Communist regime of the former Soviet Union was influenced by Marxism-Leninism, a reformulation or reinterpretation of Marxist ideas advanced by Vladimir Lenin. While Marx had predicted that a Communist revolution would occur in Europe, where capitalism was most developed, in fact it occurred in Russia, an economically backward country. The Bolshevik revolution of 1917, led by Vladimir Lenin, solidified the power of the revolutionary faction in Russia, which then went on to form the Communist party in 1918.

According to Marx's economic interpretation of social change, socialism was to occur in advanced capitalist societies, given that capitalism was the necessary precursor to socialism. Lenin, however, believed that socialism could be achieved without going through the capitalist stage. Unlike Marx, who argued that class-consciousness had to develop before a proletarian revolution could take place, Lenin believed in "revolution from above," with a small vanguard of party elites leading the working class to realize its true interests. The Communist party played an instrumental role in bringing about this transition. According to Lenin, workers on their own could not move beyond the petty issues of "trade-union consciousness" to foster class consciousness and organize themselves effectively to initiate a socialist revolution. The average worker was unable to fully understand the true nature of the forces at work. A hierarchically organized and highly disciplined party would have to develop a clear program of action. The Communist party would be the vanguard of the proletariat, leading the workers to an understanding of their true class interests.

In 1919, Lenin formed the Third International or the Comintern, an international organization, controlled by Moscow, that would provide direction for Communist parties and promote anti-imperialist revolutions around the world. Lenin regarded imperialism as the final stage of capitalism, characterized by the exploitation of economically underdeveloped societies by a small number of imperialist powers. He argued that capitalists in industrialized countries were able to forestall a socialist revolution at home through imperial expansionism and colonization. Capitalists in a small number of countries were deriving huge profits from the exploitation of workers in colonies. However, Lenin contended that the expansionism of imperialism would ultimately bring these countries into mutual conflict, paving the way for a global proletariat revolution.

Lenin's views of imperialism proved quite attractive to many underdeveloped countries that would reinterpret and modify the Marxist-Leninist doctrine to fit their own unique circumstances. For example, while the Comintern strategy focused on industrial workers as the base for revolutions in colonial areas, the Chinese Communist party under Mao Zedong looked to the peasantry rather than the urban proletariat to bring about a Communist revolution in that country. The support base he developed in China's countryside largely aided his rise to power in the 1930s and 1940s and the subsequent establishment of the Communist state in 1949. In Fidel Castro's Cuba, a guerrilla band took on the functions that were to be performed by the party.[6] Like most ideologies, communism developed in a variety of countries according to their own unique national traditions and circumstances.

SOCIAL DEMOCRACY AND COMMUNISM IN CONTEMPORARY POLITICS

Social democracy has had a great influence in Western societies over the last century. This ideology was behind the development of trade unions and work legislation. It was also central to the rise of the welfare state, which has been paramount to the politics of Western states in the last fifty years. The welfare state comprises social benefits and services that provide a safety net for citizens in order to maintain a certain standard of living in the event of economic uncertainty. In countries with a strong social democratic tradition, such as Sweden, the welfare state offers extensive and universal services and benefits to all citizens. Conversely, in countries where social democracy does not enjoy a strong presence, such as the United States, the welfare state tends to be "residual," with social programs available only to the poor and most in need.

In Canada, the influence of social democracy is noticeable in the social programs/ protection available to Canadians, from employment insurance and universal health care to a system of equalization payments that redistributes wealth from richer to poorer provinces. Canada also has a party, the New Democratic Party (NDP), that most observers would argue is social democratic. Indeed, the NDP takes positions that are coherent with the social democratic ideology. For example, it has advocated, even in the context of fiscal constraints, expanding the welfare state by instituting a national daycare system. It also suggested, when all the other federal parties were proposing tax cuts, to raise taxes to corporations and wealthy individuals. It opposes free trade and is suspicious of globalization. It also dedicates itself to issues that concern women and cultural minorities.

The influence of social democracy has been uneven in the Western world. This ideology is almost foreign to American politics. The United States has only a minimal welfare state and no social democratic party. More generally, U.S. politics and society are permeated by a negative view of the state, which tends to be perceived as constraining, inefficient, and mired in bureaucratic red tape. The picture is much different in Western Europe, where state intervention is viewed much more positively. This is reflected in a substantial welfare state and significant economic regulation. Many countries—for example France, Italy, and Spain—were governed by social democratic–led coalitions or parties for much of the 1980s and 1990s. However, several social democratic parties in Western Europe have recently undergone important transformations. Led by the United Kingdom's Labour party headed by Tony Blair, they have embraced the so-called Third Way, which basically represents something close to a reform liberal approach to politics: attempting to reconcile business-friendly policies (low taxes, balanced budgets, and so on) with strong social programs.

Social democracy has also been central to the politics of many developing countries. In Latin America, this ideology has long been associated with a distrust of American influence in the region. Its proponents have typically described the situation of Latin American countries as one of dependence vis-à-vis the United States, particularly on the economic front, and have argued that interaction with the United States served only to accentuate the region's underdevelopment. Consequently, they suggested attempting to rid Latin America of U.S. influence by, among other things, adopting protectionist policies. Social democrats in that region are now much more favourable to free trade, with the possible exception of Venezuela's Hugo Chavez, having adopted a "Third Way" similar to their West European counterparts. It is important to note that, as elsewhere in the developing world, social democracy was often overshadowed during the Cold War by its non-democratic counterpart—communism. This was obviously the case in Eastern Europe, where the Soviet Union imposed this Marxist version of socialism as official doctrine. Communism is now marginal in the region but the old political elite has, in many countries, continued its involvement in politics through social democratic parties.

After World War II, the strength of communism increased with the expansionist policy of the Soviet Union in Eastern Europe, encompassing Poland, Hungary, Romania, and Czechoslovakia. The 1950s also witnessed the emergence of a number of Soviet-style Communist regimes in other parts of the world, including China and North Korea. From the end of World War II, international relations were dominated by the political and ideological struggles between the Soviet-led Communist bloc countries and the liberal democratic world, led by the United States. By 1989, however, Communist regimes in Eastern Europe collapsed and the Soviet Union disintegrated due to nationalist movements in the republics and economic troubles.

While the recent demise of the former Soviet Union and Eastern European Communist regimes has tended to discredit communism, it is important to note that Marxist-Leninist thought is still a significant ideological force in China, Cuba, North Korea, and Vietnam. However, these countries are not immune to economic and political forces brought about by globalization. In the past two decades, China has introduced economic liberalization reforms that encourage multiple forms of ownership, thereby lessening the state's total control over the economy. Some argue that advancing economic freedom in China will lead to more personal freedoms for its citizens.

Communist parties continue to be politically important in former Soviet bloc countries. Most, however, have changed their names and adopted a more social democratic program.[7] Outside these countries, there are only a few countries where Communist parties have had any degree of electoral success. In France and Italy, Communist parties typically win under 10 percent of the votes, allowing them to participate in coalition governments. In the 1996 Japanese national elections, the Communist party gained 12 percent of the popular vote and twenty-six of the 500 seats, allowing the party to submit a bill to the House of Representatives.[8] In Canada and the United States, however, Communist parties continue to have little if any impact on the politics of the two countries.

ENDNOTES

1. Marvin Perry, *An Intellectual History of Modern Europe* (Boston: Houghton Mifflin, 1993).
2. Karl Marx, "Economic and Philosophical Manuscripts" in *Karl Marx: Early Writings*, ed. T.B. Bottomore (New York: McGraw-Hill, 1963), 122.

3. Alan O. Ebenstein, William Ebenstein, and Edwin Fogelman, *Today's Isms: Socialism, Capitalism, Fascism and communism*, 3rd ed. (Englewood Cliffs: Prentice Hall), 1994.
4. Ibid., 19.
5. Marvin Perry, *An Intellectual History of Modern Europe* (Boston: Houghton Mifflin, 1992).
6. Paul Brooker, *Non-Democratic Regimes: Theory, Government and Politics* (New York: St. Martin's Press, 1999).
7. Exceptions include the Russian Communist party and the Communist party of the Czech Republic.
8. The Party can introduce only bills that do not require budgetary decisions.

READINGS

This chapter has explored the main tenets of socialism's two branches: social democracy and communism. While both view society in terms of class conflict, they differ considerably in the means used to achieve greater economic and political equality. Social democracy is more reform-minded and seeks to improve the plight of economically disadvantaged groups through democratic institutions. Communism, on the other hand, seeks to fundamentally transform economic and political institutions through revolutionary action. It sacrifices individual freedoms in its effort to create a classless society. The two selected readings in this chapter represent the two branches of socialism. "What Canadian Social Democrats Need to Know about Sweden, and Why" discusses social democratic ideas and recent debates in the Canadian context. The excerpt from "What Is to Be Done?", by Vladimir Lenin, outlines the revolutionary route to social change.

The first reading, drawn from a collection of essays published in 1991 under the title *Social Democracy without Illusions: Renewal of the Canadian Left*, critically rethinks social democracy in Canada and the discourse of the New Democratic Party (NDP). This exercise is still being conducted today as the Canadian left, and more specifically the NDP, is facing the dilemma of emphasizing its socialist roots or moving toward the ideological centre. The piece, by Henry Milner, nicely exemplifies the difference between Marxism/communism and social democracy. The author makes a case for Canadian social democrats rejecting the more radical Marxist position. Milner suggests that the Marxist ideal of a classless society is utopian and that social democrats should adopt pragmatic objectives such as fostering a more egalitarian society where individual freedoms are respected. He also argues, in opposition to Marxists, that centrally planned economies do not work and that social democrats should accept the principles of private property and the market, and indeed support the efforts of corporations to increase their productivity within certain social, environmental, and cultural parameters. However, this acceptance of a market economy has to be complemented by a strong welfare state. For Milner, it is possible to reach an acceptable level of social justice and equality through progressive social and redistributive policies.

The second reading is a seminal document of Marxism-Leninism written by Lenin himself in 1902, fifteen years before the overthrow of the Russian tsar. In this pamphlet, Lenin addresses important questions facing Marxists in Russia (in the text referred to as Social Democrats) regarding how to mobilize workers and peasants and foster working-class consciousness. Here, Lenin expresses his belief that the working class cannot rise above the trivial concerns of trade unions and launch a successful revolution without the leadership of a highly organized group of trained revolutionaries. He argues that centralization of authority and secrecy are important organizational principles of an effective revolutionary movement. The ideas in this passage helped shape the Communist regime of the former Soviet Union.

WHAT CANADIAN SOCIAL DEMOCRATS NEED TO KNOW ABOUT SWEDEN, AND WHY

Henry Milner

INTRODUCTION

This essay is intended for those who care about social equality in this country and want to do something lasting about it—even if it means dirtying their hands in muddy political waters. I mean to be provocative; I have little interest in social democracy as after dinner-conversation. The point, said Marx, is to change the world, not just to interpret it. Ironically, Marxism, which indirectly has a major influence on contemporary Canadian social democratic thinking, has inhibited Canadian social democrats from changing the world! Now that Marxist-inspired socialism has proven itself so dramatic a failure in Eastern Europe and the Soviet Union, we can turn to the building of a socialist vision free of Marxist baggage.

What I intend to argue is that the most relevant example of building a workable socialism without Marxism is what the Swedes did long ago—as have others in northern Europe. The post-war British left has been unable or unwilling to pull it off (see Jenkins, 1988). Here in Canada we have never tried, except—partially and fleetingly—in the Prairies and Quebec.

It is consistent with their world view for Marxists to reject the Swedish approach to politics. It violates the fundamental tenet of their credo that class interests are irreconcilable. Many in and around the NDP, who perceive themselves as anything but Marxists, implicitly accept this Marxist tenet about class irreconcilability and have failed to pursue, or even really to examine, the social democratic alternative. The essence of a social democratic—as distinct from a Marxist—credo is faith that a principled reconciliation of classes is feasible or, in other words, that collective political activity can achieve an acceptable degree of equality without seeking to eliminate private employers who hire salaried workers and who exchange goods and services in markets.

While Canadian social democrats express superficial admiration for Swedish accomplishments, they make little effort to understand how they came about. They leave their followers with the impression that the Swedish approach is inapplicable to Canada. Attentive Canadians are likely to see and hear repeated comparisons to Sweden, in which Canada invariably comes out the worse. Yet, if they look for analysis, it is available only from the right or the Marxist left (e.g., Gill, 1989), both of which have their own separate reasons for dismissing the Swedish "model." In dismissing the relevance of Swedish experience to Canada, Canadian socialists are in effect dismissing social democracy.

This is not a play on words. Social democracy means democratic egalitarianism. The levels of economic productivity, equality at work, and social guarantees achieved by the Swedes are the best Canadians can hope to achieve for a long way down the road. To realize that this is so, Canadian socialists should leave their academic lecture halls, put down their union songbooks, and look at the day-to-day lives of "ordinary" (to use the NDP's favourite adjective) Swedes. Socialism cannot be based on utopian theories of the perfect man, nor on the peaks of worker solidarity achieved at moments of social activism. Scandinavian achievements in combining egalitarian communal goals with a respect for individual liberty, and the pragmatic pursuit of economic self-interest by workers and owners within private firms, cannot be dismissed. Quite the opposite, they force us to look at our very notion of change, of melding theory and practice.

Ironically, it is the Marxists with their utopian agenda who are often cited to prove that social democracy is unrealistic and inapplicable to Canada. In dismissing the "fallacy" of the "exportability" to Canada of European systems based on social partnership, Stephen Brooks

(1989, pp. 234–35) in his introductory public policy textbook approvingly cites Leo Panitch, a Marxist. Reportedly, Panitch was also influential in the Macdonald Commission's refusal to consider such approaches seriously. In light of the immense changes under way in Europe—dismantling command economies in the East, planning economic integration in the West—it is surely absurd for us as social democrats to accept uncritically the negative opinion of Marxists and conservatives on the "exportability" of what is, undeniably, the most successful of social democratic societies.

In a democratic society, lasting changes that substantially improve the lives of ordinary people can come only as the result of gradual, consensual choices. There are no shortcuts to social democracy. Human beings are the object of social democratic goals, but also their subject. Social democratic reforms can achieve their intended egalitarian effects only if complemented by carefully considered, freely made individual choices. At best, winning political power is a step in this direction.

At the level of national politics Canadian socialists have never given much attention to the day-to-day requirements of a social democratic society. One such requirement is the need to pay for generous social programs and income redistribution. In order to gain (probably fleeting) popular approval, NDPers gleefully jumped on the bandwagon against the federal goods and services tax (GST), giving little heed to the dangers of fomenting a tax revolt that erodes popular willingness to fund redistributive programs. It is essential to criticize the Conservatives for unfair tax policies, such as tax-free capital gains for the rich. But what is a "fair" alternative to the GST? Most industrial countries—including social democratic regimes in Scandinavia—impose broad sales taxes (usually described as "value added taxes") like the GST. With few exceptions, left-wing answers to this question remain a vague footnote to the attack.[1]

I am not asking for self-delusion with regard to social democracy; it, too, deserves critical assessment. But before we criticize, the least we can do is devote some creative talent to thinking about social democratic institutions. One shudders at how many fine minds and idealistic impulses have been deflected by contemporary Marxism from the practical work of identifying the strategic reforms for advancing society toward socialist goals.

CLEARING THE UNDERBRUSH

There is a lot of underbrush to clear away if we are ever to harvest a good crop. We social democrats need freshly cleared intellectual land. We cannot find it in the jargon-filled, convoluted prose of academic Marxist writing, nor in slogan-filled NDP resolution books. We need to work toward the 1990 equivalent of the Regina Manifesto as if there were no NDP candidates to elect, no CLC bureaucrats to reconcile, no feminist, ecological, or other progressive interest group to appease with the correct choice of language. Can we get our strategy out from under our sacred cows?

Our ideals remain those of 1933 when the Regina Manifesto was adopted. But we hopefully have learned not only about the murderous aberration of "actually existing socialism" that was Stalin, but also about the everyday grey frustrations of life under Brezhnev, Jaruzelski, Honecker, and all the rest. In our modest Canadian way, we need to be as ruthless in exploring new ideas as are contemporary Soviets in debating new political and economic options for their country. (For surveys of contemporary Soviet debates, see Åslund, 1989; Nove, 1989.)

Whether in Eastern Europe or Canada, we now know that central planners cannot manage successfully a complex industrial economy. We now know that, even if democratically elected socialist governments could appoint the most unselfish and competent economic managers imaginable, they would in the long run lower our living standard if they attempted the wholesale substitution of political criteria for profit maximization by privately owned firms based on market prices. *Private ownership can take many forms.* In many industries, worker collectives and co-operatives may be more efficient than shareholder-owned firms; and unions can enhance the productivity of shareholder-owned companies. The lesson that we have learned since 1933 is that, subject to important exceptions (collectively known as "market failures" in economics texts), the aggregate wealth of the community is maximized when firms obey the basic rules of markets. Whatever the form of ownership, the managers of firms should seek to maximize profit based on market prices for the products produced and for the factors of production, including labour. In turn, the basis for market prices must be the equating of supply and demand in markets where buyers can select among alternate sellers.

New firms must be able to enter an industry and—with public aid for the transition—inefficient firms must be allowed to go bankrupt.

We on the left do not need to be convinced of the limits of markets. What is harder for us to accept are the fundamental limits of a planned economy. To paraphrase Sir Winston Churchill's assessment of democracy, individual firms competing in markets may be the worst means of organizing economic activity—except for the alternatives.

Realizing the productive potential of modern industry requires that each firm undertake thousands of discrete managerial decisions with respect to hiring and firing of workers, buying inputs, investing in plant and equipment, etc. Inescapably, many of these decisions entail socially difficult choices; others entail uncertainty with respect to their outcome. Under any economic system, firing workers is a tough decision. While laying off workers may increase productivity, it violates the natural sense of community among workers. However, if firms avoid the issue of productivity and they overstaff, aggregate productivity in the economy obviously suffers. The decision to buy an expensive piece of equipment generates a current cost and may generate no net financial benefits if the future fails to conform to expectations. Again, no economic system can escape costly decisions under conditions of uncertainty, and everyone will—with hindsight—regret some of them.

The authors of the Regina Manifesto entertained unabashed enthusiasm for central planning as the panacea for the woes of capitalist depression. As did far too many on the left in the 1930s, they uncritically hailed the successes of five-year plans in the Soviet Union. They were prescient in insisting that macroeconomic planning was essential to counter instability of aggregate demand. They also realized planning to be necessary to address economic problems where markets, even under ideal conditions, would perform badly—problems such as pollution, the provision of services like education and health, or the organization of industrial research.

But as the twentieth century draws to a close, social democrats must unambiguously understand that well-functioning markets are necessary to realize a productive industrial economy. In general, firms will not make the painful decisions required to realize a productive economy unless their owners face a "hard" financial constraint that forces the firm—be it a humble farm or a large corporation—to bear the financial consequences of decisions made. I repeat, once again, that the owners of the firm need not be financial investors. They may also be workers within the firm or the firm's customers, as with consumer co-operatives.

No centrally planned economy has succeeded in forcing its state-owned firms to respect "hard" financial constraints. Even in countries such as Hungary, where the Communist government abandoned centrally imposed quotas and introduced a significant measure of market discipline on all state-owned firms, the financial constraints remained "soft." Firm managers could, if necessary, obtain subsidies from the state in order to balance accounts. Firms did not go bankrupt; very few new firms succeeded in competing with existing firms. In the case of traditional centrally planned economies, firms too frequently meet their quotas by lowering quality; markets do not function to impose a financial penalty for such behaviour (see Kornai, 1986; Brus and Laski, 1989).

Even with modern computers and the best of intentions, central planners cannot hope to substitute their decisions for those of managers in the field. In order to render the financial constraints on managers "hard," there is unfortunately no substitute for an economy based on firms exchanging goods and services in markets at prices negotiated voluntarily. These firms will realize financial profits when they are efficient and losses—even bankruptcy—when they are inefficient. Price competition among firms, supplemented by some discretionary regulation and progressive taxation, can be relied on to check excess profitability.

An elected social democratic government could proceed to socialize the means of production nonetheless, hoping to persuade the people that there would be no sacrifice in productivity or that any loss of productivity would be worth it because of other achievements, such as greater equality of income. But we know that we would soon face electoral defeat and have our policies reversed—unless, of course, we made sure the people only heard what we had to tell them and could vote only for approved candidates. As social democrats, we reject this scenario in advance.

In ruling out major socialization, we evidently do not embrace the neo-conservative objective of the minimal state where market forces rule in all spheres. Yet, as John Richards makes dramatically clear in his introduction, social democrats must engage neo-conservatives in serious debate, just as we do Marxists. Thatcherism is not just a religious cult to be condemned. The British voted for Thatcherism because it seemed the only workable alternative. By 1979, when her Conservative Party defeated the Labour government, the post-war Keynesian welfare state was not doing the job. British per capita incomes were on average only two-thirds those in Germany and France; unemployment and inflation were consistently worse.

Yet the Keynesian welfare state and mixed economy—to use two shorthand descriptions of post-war society—are the starting point for any practical alternative to Anglo-American neo-conservatism. To be blunt, in our new manifesto we must not only be prepared to live with capitalism; we should welcome it where it contributes to the real wealth of the community!

In his important essay on the ills of British society, David Marquand (1988, p. 172) emphasizes a distinction made as early as John Locke, namely that between active and passive property.

> *The notion of active property—of property justified by the personal abstinence and entrepreneurial flair of the heroic, self-reliant owner manager, who built up his own capital, risked his own substance, lured his own labour, found his own markets and, in the process, created a new and more productive economic system—had a moral appeal extending far beyond the entrepreneurial middle class itself. It had about it an almost Promethean quality, which forced the paternalist, noblesse oblige ethic of the aristocracy onto the defensive, and which the group ethic of the working class could not match. The switch to passive property—to the view of property which makes it possible to treat industrial enterprises like . . . "bits of real estate"—destroyed the moral basis of the industrial order.*

The instinct of many on the left is to assume all property has become passive, to deny the significance of active property. To indulge this instinct is to substitute dogma for thought.

If social democrats accept the limits of planning and the benefits of competitive markets in a mixed economy, what remains of our aspirations for an egalitarian co-operative commonwealth? What happens to the impassioned cry for social justice and an end to exploitation? In their place we can only offer the truth as we see it, a comprehensive program composed of concrete policies and the rationale for them. Our manifesto thus begins, in effect, with the realization that we cannot achieve a communal utopia. We do not have policies that can by themselves change people's conditions. Such policies do not exist. In particular, policies that suppress competitive markets will lower, not increase, average wealth. Moreover, they offer no guarantee of equalizing income distribution. In a well-functioning mixed economy, however, markets, in which consumers and private firms engage in voluntary exchange, and the state, in which agencies operate subject to democratic political control, are not in competition but are complementary. Social democrats must reinforce that complementarity. The idea that we can improve overall welfare by using the state against productive private firms is, ultimately, wrong.

As Canadians currently practice politics, the "parliamentary game" is just that, a game. The government proposes; the opposition, self-righteous trumpets blaring, opposes. Within the realm of the possible, we social democrats must rise above this game. We have an obligation to enlist popular participation—at all levels from municipal councils to Parliament, and from Canadians acting both as individuals and through popular-based organizations. If we are successful—a big "if"—the result will be a social democratic Canada. Whatever name we take, we must continue to think of ourselves as a labour-oriented party. We shall continue to stress full employment and base our support on the mobilized majority of Canadian people.

This is not simply a statement of traditional left-wing ideology. Among the structural changes required is that in the future any Canadian social democratic political party must be able to formulate policy independently of organized labour. Both unions and a social democratic party will be prominent in any future Canadian social democracy. But, just as unions in communist countries were traditionally hollow shells that echoed party propaganda and ignored controversial worker demands, there is an analogous danger in the Anglo-Saxon tradition. The British Labour Party was the child of trade unions. One reason for the failure of British social democracy relative to the Scandinavian experience is that the Labour Party has rarely been able to act at arm's length from organized labour. A trade union is the natural response of a group of workers to promote the collective interests of their trade or their industry. Inevitably, these collective instincts run counter to the general interest of society in well-functioning, productive markets. Neo-conservatives see no problem in this conflict; they are on the side of the market.

For social democrats life is not so simple. We recognize the value of unions, both as institutions to promote equality at work and, if well organized, to promote worker satisfaction and hence productivity. But we also recognize the value of competitive markets. Most people, including most union members, appreciate this tension. A social democratic party that denies its existence and fails to define independent economic policy is electorally doomed. Social democracy needs a powerful social democratic party able to effect reasonable compromises between the logic of trade union demands and that of competitive markets.

If we can become such a force, we will be in a position to seek a principled collaboration with private capital in achieving national economic objectives. Our new manifesto should contain language addressed to business circles: "We will support you in your efforts to make your firms more productive, to invest in those activities where profits await. We will co-ordinate in those efforts where needed: research and development, manpower training, long-run resource development. We specify at the outset those areas of overriding national concern—environmental protection, cultural industries, basic human services—where we believe markets cannot adequately provide. We commit ourselves elsewhere in the economy to allow firms to do what they think best, to respond to market signals in deciding what products and services to supply, and how to do so."

In return, we will insist that the benefits of a productive economy be distributed as equitably as possible. We will implement programs to complement, not inhibit, industrial development. We will fairly compensate the "losers" from changes in technology and market prices, through temporary income support and comprehensive on-the-job and in-house retraining. We will settle for no less than full employment—unemployment levels below 3 percent—one-third the current Canadian level of 9 percent. We will redistribute through transfers and generous public services, in enhanced access to education and to leisure-time and cultural pursuits, in improved working and environmental standards. We will pursue generous international policies with respect to aid, trade, technology transfer, and refugees.

Our manifesto must be clear that, if elected to office, a social democratic government will not attempt to govern alone. It will promote institutional reforms that allow far more effective collaboration in public policy by relevant interest groups. On many issues business and labour have shared interests and should speak with one voice. We will organize permanent forums, advisory commissions, and agencies where representatives of both will sit.

While we believe there to be a creative role for collaboration, we take seriously the distinction between active and passive property. Tax laws will foster productive industry but will aggressively seek to stamp out "paper entrepreneurship" based on real estate flips, stock exchange manoeuvres, and other types of short-term financial speculation that seemingly took on a life of its own in the 1980s. We take seriously government's role to foster unionization through supportive labour codes. In particular, we will encourage unionization in the private sector to promote a greater equilibrium between work conditions in the public and private sectors.

We intend to reform political structures to enhance political discussion and rational compromise as opposed to rhetorical polarization. One reform that may merit serious consideration—Ontario NDP, please take note—is an electoral system based on proportional representation. If poorly constituted such systems may be unstable, as in Israel, but they have the great virtue of allowing parties representing diverse views to win legislative representation. Because no one party usually enjoys an overall parliamentary majority, coalition governments are the norm. In putting together coalitions, politicians make publicly debated compromise an inherent characteristic of government. Thereby Canadians could be spared the worst of the "black-and-white" parliamentary charade according to which there are but two sides—one right and the other wrong—to political debates. (Proportional representation would also lessen the regional polarization of Parliament. The present first-past-the-post electoral system frequently allows a party to capture a near monopoly of seats from a region in which it commands a plurality of voter support. Throughout most of our generation our electoral system has, for example, eliminated Liberals from western Canada and New Democrats from Quebec.)

Given traditional attitudes, Canadian business leaders will likely be little interested in the structured partnership we propose—unless they feel it is in their interest. But businessmen are pragmatic. If we can win solid, visible electoral support from "ordinary Canadians" and are able to effect a new relationship with organized labour, business leaders will pay attention. So, the first task is to rally the majority of "ordinary Canadians." Since our manifesto promises neither the usual pie in the sky nor the stirring old left-wing rallying cries, how do we win a large constituency? How do we break through the

various vicious circles that preserve the status quo. Using imported British Labour Party traditions, the NDP cannot expect to break through to majority status, but it can assure itself of 15–20 percent of the vote. Canadians are accustomed to strident politicians feigning indignation over the hot topic of the day. Would Canadians pay attention to a new breed of aspiring politician who talks in depth about issues and complex policies to deal with them?

To free ourselves from these vicious circles is the reason for evoking the politics of 1933, a world where possibilities had yet to be closed off. In 1933 the political consciousness of most Canadians was not trapped by Madison Avenue sales techniques. J.S. Woodsworth did not have to break his speeches into seventeen-second sound bites and scramble after photo opportunities.

I indulge the luxury of imagining that Canadians may still be willing to think about the complexities of "actually existing social democracy." More particularly, that means a willingness to look seriously at those countries that have painstakingly constructed social democratic societies.

Reading Note

1. When it is fully in place, in 1992–93, the federal government expects to capture $21.9 billion annually from the GST (Wilson, 1990, p. 135). Subtracting the enhanced GST-tax credit for low-income earners, $1.3 billion annually, leaves net revenue of $20.6 billion. What are the alternatives? We could preserve the current manufacturers' sales tax, which will preserve an estimated $20.4 billion in annual revenue. But everyone agrees the present sales tax is more inequitable and induces more distortions than the proposed GST. Theoretically, we could increase personal and corporate income taxes. But the required increases would be astronomical and politically impossible to impose. To realize an additional $20.6 billion from higher personal income taxes would require they rise by a third. To realize an additional $20.6 billion from corporate income taxes would require them to rise one and a half times! If we could generate a social consensus—which the Conservatives are incapable of doing—to balance the budget and pay for our social policies, Canadians would enjoy a significant indirect benefit. Investors would have less fear of inflation and the Bank of Canada would have no excuse to pursue a high interest rate policy. This, in turn, would lower the cost of servicing the public debt, which currently absorbs twenty-five cents of every dollar of Ottawa's expenditure.

Reading References

Åslund, A. (1989). *Gorbachev's Struggle for Economic Reform*. Ithaca, NY: Cornell University Press.

Brooks, S. (1989). *Public Policy in Canada: An Introduction*. Toronto: McClelland and Stewart.

Brus, W., and K. Laski (1989). *From Marx to the Market: Socialism in Search of an Economic System*. Oxford: Clarendon Press.

Gill, L. (1989). *Les limites du partenariat*. Montréal: Boréal.

Jenkins, P. (1988). *Mrs. Thatcher's Revolution: The Ending of the Socialist Era*. Cambridge, MA: Harvard University Press.

Kornai, J. (1986). "The Hungarian Reform Process: Visions, Hopes, and Reality," *Journal of Economic Literature*, XXIV, pp. 1687–1737.

Marquand, D. (1988). *The Unprincipled Society: New Demands and Old Politics*. London: Fontana Press.

Nove, A. (1989). Glasnost in Action. London: Unwin Hyman.

WHAT IS TO BE DONE?

Vladimir Lenin

Without revolutionary theory there can be no revolutionary movement. This idea cannot be insisted upon too strongly at a time when the fashionable preaching of opportunism goes hand in hand with an infatuation for the narrowest forms of practical activity. Yet, for Russian Social-Democrats the importance of theory is enhanced by three other circumstances, which are often forgotten: first, by the fact that our Party is only in process of formation, its features are only just becoming defined, and it has as yet far from settled accounts with the other trends of revolutionary thought that threaten to divert the movement from the correct path. On the contrary, precisely the very recent past was marked by a revival of non-Social-Democratic revolutionary trends (an eventuation regarding which Axelrod long ago warned the Economists). Under these circumstances, what at first sight appears to be an "unimportant" error may lead to most deplorable consequences, and only short-sighted people can consider factional disputes and a strict differentiation between shades of opinion inopportune or superfluous. The fate of Russian Social-Democracy for very many years to come may depend on the strengthening of one or the other "shade."

Secondly, the Social-Democratic movement is in its very essence an international movement. This means, not only that we must combat national chauvinism, but that an incipient movement in a young country can be successful only if it makes use of the experiences of other countries. In order to make use of these experiences it is not enough merely to be acquainted with them, or simply to copy out the latest resolutions. What is required is the ability to treat these experiences critically and to test them independently. He who realises how enormously the modern working-class movement has grown and branched out will understand what a reserve of theoretical forces and political (as well as revolutionary) experience is required to carry out this task.

Thirdly, the national tasks of Russian Social-Democracy are such as have never confronted any other socialist party in the world. We shall have occasion further on to deal with the political and organisational duties which the task of emancipating the whole people from the yoke of autocracy imposes upon us. At this point, we wish to state only that the *role of vanguard fighter can be fulfilled only by a party that is guided by the most advanced theory*. To have a concrete understanding of what this means, let the reader recall such predecessors of Russian Social-Democracy as Herzen, Belinsky, Chernyshevsky, and the brilliant galaxy of revolutionaries of the seventies; let him ponder over the world significance which Russian literature is now acquiring; let him . . . but be that enough!

***

. . . [D]emagogues are the worst enemies of the working class. The worst enemies, because they arouse base instincts in the masses, because the unenlightened worker is unable to recognise his enemies in men who represent themselves, and sometimes sincerely so, as his friends. The worst enemies, because in the period of disunity and vacillation, when our movement is just beginning to take shape, nothing is easier than to employ demagogic methods to mislead the masses, who can realise their error only later by bitter experience.

***

As far as "deep roots" are concerned, we cannot be "unearthed" even now, despite all our amateurism, and yet we all complain, and cannot but complain, that the "*organisations*" are being unearthed and as a result it is impossible to maintain continuity in the movement. But since you raise the question of *organisations* being unearthed and persist in your opinion, I assert that it is far more difficult to unearth a dozen wise men than a hundred fools. This position I will defend, no matter how much you instigate the masses against me for my "anti-democratic" views, etc. As I have stated repeatedly, by "wise men," in connection with organisation, I mean *professional revolutionaries*, irrespective of whether they have developed from among students or working men. I assert: (1) that no revolutionary movement can endure without a stable organisation of leaders maintaining continuity; (2) that the broader the popular mass drawn spontaneously into the struggle, which forms the basis of the movement and participates in it, the more urgent the need for such an organisation, and the more solid this organisation must be (for it is much easier for all sorts of demagogues to side-track the more backward sections of the masses); (3) that such organisation must consist chiefly of people professionally engaged in revolutionary activity; (4) that in an autocratic state, the more we *confine* the membership of such an organisation to people who are professionally engaged to revolutionary activity and who have been professionally trained in the art of combating the political police, the more difficult will it be to unearth the organisation; and (5) the *greater* will be the number of people from the working class and from the other social classes who will be able to join the movement and perform active work in it.

I invite our Economists, terrorists, and "Economists-terrorists"[1] to confute these propositions. At the moment, I shall deal only with the last two points. The question as to whether it is easier to wipe out "a dozen wise men" or "a hundred fools" reduces itself to the question, above considered, whether it is possible to have a mass *organisation* when the maintenance of strict secrecy is essential. We can never give a mass organisation that degree of secrecy without which there can be no question of persistent and continuous struggle against the government. To concentrate all secret functions in the hands of as small a number of professional revolutionaries as possible does not mean that the latter will "do the thinking for all" and that the rank and file will not take an active part in the *movement*. On the contrary, the membership will promote increasing

numbers of the professional revolutionaries from its ranks; for it will know that it is not enough for a few students and for a few working men waging the economic struggle to gather in order to form a "committee," but that it takes years to train oneself to be a professional revolutionary; and the rank and file will "think," not only of amateurish methods, but of such training. Centralisation of the secret functions of the *organisation* by no means implies centralisation of all the functions of the *movement*. Active participation of the widest masses in the illegal press will not diminish because a "dozen" professional revolutionaries centralise the secret functions connected with this work; on the contrary, it will *increase* tenfold. In this way, and in this way alone, shall we ensure that reading the illegal press, writing for it, and to some extent even distributing it, will *almost cease to be secret work*, for the police will soon come to realise the folly and impossibility of judicial and administrative red-tape procedure over every copy of a publication that is being distributed in the thousands. This holds not only for the press, but for every function of the movement, even for demonstrations. The active and widespread participation of the masses will not suffer; on the contrary, it will benefit by the fact that a "dozen" experienced revolutionaries, trained professionally no less than the police, will centralise all the secret aspects of the work—the drawing up of leaflets, the working out of approximate plans; and the appointing of bodies of leaders for each urban district, for each factory district, and for each educational institution, etc. (I know that exception will be taken to my "undemocratic" views, but I shall reply below fully to this anything but intelligent objection.) Centralisation of the most secret functions in an organisation of revolutionaries will not diminish, but rather increase the extent and enhance the quality of the activity of a large number of other organisations that are intended for a broad public and are therefore as loose and as non-secret as possible, such as workers' trade unions; workers' self-education circles and circles for reading illegal literature; and socialist, as well as democratic, circles among *all* other sections of the population; etc., etc. We must have such circles, trade unions, and organisations everywhere in *as large a number as possible* and with the widest variety of functions; but it would be absurd and harmful to *confound* them with the organisation of *revolutionaries*, to efface the border-line between them, to make still more hazy the all too faint recognition of the fact that in order to "serve" the mass movement we must have people who will devote themselves exclusively to Social-Democratic activities, and that such people must *train* themselves patiently and steadfastly to be professional revolutionaries.

Yes, this recognition is incredibly dim. Our worst sin with regard to organisation consists in the fact that *by our primitiveness we have lowered the prestige of revolutionaries in Russia.* A person who is flabby and shaky on questions of theory, who has a narrow outlook, who pleads the spontaneity of the masses as an excuse for his own sluggishness, who resembles a trade union secretary more than a spokesman of the people, who is unable to conceive of a broad and bold plan that would command the respect even of opponents, and who is inexperienced and clumsy in his own professional art—the art of combating the political police—such a man is not a revolutionary, but a wretched amateur!

Reading Note

1. This term is perhaps more applicable to *Svoboda* than the former, for in an article entitled "The Regeneration of Revolutionism" the publication defends terrorism, while in the article at present under review it defends Economism. One might say of *Svoboda* that "it would if it could, but it can't." Its wishes and intentions are of the very best—but the result is utter confusion; this is chiefly due to the fact that, while *Svoboda* advocates continuity of organisation, it refuses to recognise continuity of revolutionary thought and Social-Democratic theory. It wants to revive the professional revolutionary ("the Regeneration of Revolutionism"), and to that end proposes, first, excitative terrorism, and, secondly, "an organisation of average workers" (*Svoboda*, No. 1, p. 66, et seq.), as less likely to be "pushed on from outside." In other words, it proposes to pull the house down to use the timber for heating it. [Lenin]

KEY TERMS

Bourgeoisie (Capitalist Class)   The dominant class, which owns the means of production.

Class   Members of a society who share a common economic or social position or, in Marxist terms, common relations to the means of production.

Communism   An ideology and political system that seeks to establish a classless society through revolutionary action. It calls for the collective ownership of goods and property.

Labour Theory of Value   The value (i.e., price) of a commodity is equal to the quantity of labour time required to produce it.

Means of Production   The instruments and raw materials used to produce a commodity, e.g., equipment, buildings, and labour.

Mode of Production   The method used to produce the necessities of life. It includes both the means of production and the relations of production, i.e., the social relations through which goods and services are produced.

Proletariat (Working Class)   The subject class, which lives from the sale of its labour power.

Social Democracy   A branch of socialism that aims to reduce economic and social equality and diminish class distinctions by democratic means. It supports some level of state ownership of the means of production to accomplish these goals. The type of democracy that emphasizes the importance of collective, as opposed to individual, rights and development.

Socialism   An ideology that seeks to eliminate class divisions and social and economic inequalities in society through the collective ownership of the means of production, distribution, and exchange.

FURTHER READINGS

Brzezinski, Zbigniew. *The Grand Failure: The Birth and Death of communism in the Twentieth Century.* New York: Collier Books, 1990.

Harrington, Michael. *Socialism: Past and Future.* New York: Penguin Books, 1989.

Marx, Karl. *Capital: A Critique of Political Economy.* London: Lawrence & Wishart, 1954–1959.

Marx, Karl, and Friedrich Engels. *Communist Manifesto.* London: Allen & Unwin, 1848.

WEB LINKS

Website of the Communist Party of Canada:
http://www.communist-party.ca

Website of Canada's New Democratic Party:
http://www.ndp.ca

Constitution of the Communist Party of China (1982):
http://www.politics.ubc.ca/chab/p321/private/cpcon.htm

CHAPTER 6

FASCISM

Fascism, and its variant, social nationalism, is a non-democratic ideology found at the extreme right of the political spectrum. Emerging in Europe, fascist doctrine was embodied in the totalitarian regimes of Adolf Hitler and Benito Mussolini in the early twentieth century. In theory and in practice, fascism contradicts liberal democratic ideals and principles. It adheres to one-party states, government by force, the use of coercion to quash freedom of expression, and control over instruments of communication. It rejects individual freedoms and rights in favour of national unity and assigns a privileged status to an elite group who are deemed to be the only ones qualified to govern society. This chapter examines the ideology of fascism, outlining its historical origins and basic tenets. It discusses fascism's anti-democratic traits and the political projects of fascist totalitarian regimes, and concludes with a discussion of the impact of fascism on contemporary politics.

HISTORICAL ORIGINS OF FASCISM

Fascism, as a political and ideological movement, originated in the 1920s in Italy, Germany, and several other European countries. It emerged after World War I during a period of great social and political upheaval brought about by the post-war economic crisis and the spread of communism and socialism. The success of the Bolshevik revolution in 1917 and the growing popularity of socialist movements in European countries instilled fear among property owners and government officials, who stood to lose under a Soviet-style regime. The alternative—parliamentary democracy—was also rejected because it was perceived as an ineffective vehicle for resolving the economic difficulties facing much of post-war Europe. Support for fascism was also found among the lower middle classes, who "dreaded the prospect of joining (or rejoining) the paid-by-the-hour working class and looked to fascism for salvation of their status and prestige."[1] Disillusioned with democratic values and institutions, people turned to the strong leadership represented by fascist parties. Discontented World War I veterans, the unemployed, and certain segments of the working class joined fascist movements, drawn by fascism's appeal to nationalist sentiments. Ultimately, fascism cut across all social groups.

Mussolini's Italy and Nazi Germany are regarded as the exemplary cases of fascism. Italian fascism first emerged in 1919 when revolutionary nationalists, led by Benito Mussolini, formed the organization *Fasci di combattimento*, which was later transformed into the new Fascist Party in 1921. Mussolini was a former activist in the socialist movement who had been expelled from the party for his nationalist views and for his support of Italy's entry into World War I. In 1921 Mussolini, along with thirty-three other party members, was elected to Parliament. In October 1922, tens of thousands of Fascists marched to Rome, demanding power for their party. The king, fearing a civil war, handed power over to Mussolini. By 1925, Mussolini's position as dictator and head of state was secured after he abolished the Italian parliamentary system and outlawed all other political parties. He used terror, in the form of a paramilitary group called the "Black Shirts," to preserve his power.

Mussolini's fascist regime emerged during a very tumultuous time in Italy's history. After World War I, Italy faced rising unemployment and growing social unrest in the cities. Labour

Benito Mussolini

militancy, in the form of riots, strikes, and factory occupations, was high, and public support for communists was on the increase. Italian coalition governments, rife with strong internal divisions and unable to alleviate the post-war hardships, were viewed as ineffectual and corrupt by many segments of Italian society. Nationalist sentiments were also on the rise after the allies' promise to support Italian territorial demands in Austria-Hungary after the war was not kept. National revival and Italian expansionism became the rallying cry of romantic nationalists who harked back to the glory days of the Roman Empire.

The fascist movement was able to exploit the economic and political weaknesses and social divisions besetting Italy in the inter-war period. Mussolini aligned himself with the more conservative elements of Italian society whose economic interests were threatened by the growing popularity of the Communist Party among workers. Landowners and industrialists turned to Mussolini's fascist "action squads" to crush peasant revolts in the countryside and labour strikes in the cities. At the same time, however, he presented himself as sympathetic to the plight of workers. His nationalist orientation and his encouragement of revolutionary change also found broad appeal among the masses. Through pageantry, propaganda, and terror, Mussolini presented himself as Italy's hero, capable of solving national problems and restoring social order when others before him had failed.

Under Mussolini's reign, the Italian economy was reorganized into a corporatist arrangement, in which the state regulated economic affairs by incorporating labour and industry groups in the state apparatus with **fascist corporatism**. Important sectors of the economy, including banking and steel, were brought under the control of the fascist state. The corporatist state was a central feature of Mussolini's fascist regime. In an effort to undermine class alliances in favour of national unity, Mussolini sought to manage class conflict through a national network of corporations or councils representing trade unions and industry associations from every sector of the Italian economy. The state was to mediate among competing interest groups on behalf of the national interest. The corporatist state represented the third way between laissez-faire capitalism and communism. It provided the state with unlimited control over economic life while still keeping intact the capitalist system of private ownership. Labour disputes and strikes were rendered illegal, and industry had to take direction from state agencies responsible for setting prices and wages and for establishing the terms of employment, production, and distribution for individual sectors. By 1934, the fascist regime had reorganized trade unions and industry associations into twenty-two corporations. The corporatist arrangements generally preserved the interests of the wealthy class. However, workers derived some benefits from the corporatist state. For example, during the Depression the fascist regime introduced public works programs to alleviate the unemployment problem. Fascist movements made contradictory promises to satisfy all supporters.[2]

The economic and political viability of the fascist state and corporatist arrangement began disintegrating with Italian expansionism in Ethiopia and Italy's alignment with Hitler's Germany in World War II. In the process of losing the war, the Fascist grand council rebelled against Mussolini, who was later dismissed by Victor Emmanuel III. Soon after, the Fascist Party was disbanded and Italy surrendered to the allied forces. Mussolini was captured and executed in April 1945.

NATIONAL SOCIALISM AND NAZISM

Like Italian fascism, **national socialism** or what is most commonly referred to as Nazism, emerged in Germany after World War I as a reaction against communism and the liberal-rational tradition. One year after its founding in 1918, the Weimar Republic, headed by democratic socialists, was under attack by both left- and right-wing segments of German society. Radical Marxists, who wanted to establish a proletarian state, attempted to overthrow the new republic in 1919 but were quickly suppressed. Their attempt, however, inspired fear among members of the middle and upper classes. As it did in Italy, the fear of communism inspired the conservative segment of German society to join ultra-nationalist right-wing parties and organizations aimed at bringing about the downfall of the Weimar Republic. Disillusioned by democracy, conservatives—including landowners, industrialists, and army officials—wanted a strong government that would ward off the threat of communism in Germany and protect their economic and political interests. The 1929 Great Depression and the political and social tensions that ensued would further undermine the viability of the Weimar Republic.

One of the groups that sprang up during this time was Adolf Hitler's National Socialist German Workers' Party, otherwise known as the Nazi Party. Hitler opportunistically exploited German dissatisfaction with the 1919 Versailles Treaty, which had assigned responsibility for the war on Germany and ordered the country to pay huge and extraordinarily onerous reparations to the allied nations.[3] He also exploited the misery of the German people during the Great Depression, appealing to their frustrations and insecurities. In March 1933, Hitler was elected into office, and soon after, he introduced the Enabling Act, which essentially outlawed the Communist Party and, more importantly, conferred to him total dictatorial powers.

Between 1933 and 1937, Hitler established a well-organized party structure and para-military secret police, the Gestapo, to ensure compliance with his totalitarian regime. Nazi doctrine was institutionalized in Germany's laws and court system. Like Mussolini, Hitler established a corporatist state, disbanding trade unions and strictly controlling the country's economic affairs. In the late 1930s, the Nazi Party also regulated all aspects of cultural life, including schools and the press, in an effort to quash dissent and strengthen the racial consciousness of the German people. The party also created youth groups, like the Hitler Youth and the League of German Girls, and organized youth ceremonies to indoctrinate children and adolescents (ten- to eighteen-year-olds) in its racist worldview. Propaganda was also an important tool of the Nazi regime, which used words and images in art, literature, and film to exalt the status of the Party and its leader.

Hitler espoused an extreme racial nationalism, wanting to establish a new empire that would unite all German-speaking *Volk* ("people") in Central and Eastern Europe. Consistent with the Nazis' doctrine of racial superiority, the empire would lay claim to the superiority of the Aryan race and domination of "inferior" races. Under Hitler's regime, Jews were conceived as the embodiment of evil and the mortal enemy of racial nationalism. They represented values of the Enlightenment tradition, such as reason, equality, and individualism, values that threatened the "Volkish" union. This anti-semitism congealed into the Holocaust, wherein six million European Jews were exterminated.

In 1939, Hitler's aggressive bid to dominate Europe precipitated World War II. In the early years of the war, Germany succeeded in conquering many parts of Europe, including Poland, Denmark, Norway, Belgium, France, and the Balkan states. By 1942, the tide began to turn, and the Allied forces successfully defeated the German army in the U.S.S.R. and North Africa. Germany was defeated in April 1945, putting an end to Hitler's Nazi regime.

BASIC TENETS OF FASCISM

Fascism, as an ideology and political movement, is located at the extreme right of the ideological spectrum. The term itself comes from the Italian word *fascio*, which means "union." It also derives from the ancient Roman symbol of power, the *fasces*, represented by a bundle of rods tied together around an axe. The symbol represented power and unity in Roman times and became the emblem for fascist political movements in the early 1900s.

Unity and power are central features of fascist doctrine. In contrast to liberalism, fascism rejects the Enlightenment ideals of rationality and individual liberty, and champions a collectivist ideology that focuses on the needs and aspirations of the national community. This ideology is all embracing and, as Hannah Arendt explains, "pretends to know the mysteries of the whole historical process—the secrets of the past, the intricacies of the present, the uncertainties of the future."[4] Critical analysis and rational debate are dismissed in favour of instinct, feeling, and will. Fascism appeals to emotions rather than reason, and glorifies instinctive, aggressive action as a creative force.

Fascism depicts liberal society as spiritually empty, because it forces individuals to compete with one another in their pursuit of material ends. Fascism rejects materialism as the basic goal of human existence. Human beings are perceived as spiritual beings, striving to achieve not only material ends but also spiritual ones, which can be only achieved collectively, as a people. A *people*, in fascist doctrine, is defined as a distinct faction or group within a society that is united through language, culture, tradition, or territory. Life, according to fascism, is not about pursuing material wealth for oneself but rather is conceived as duty—duty to the state, the nation, and future generations of the collective. As Mussolini stated, " . . . the Fascist accepts life and loves it, knowing nothing of and despising suicide: he rather conceives of life as duty and struggle and conquest, life which should be high and full, lived for oneself, but above all for others—those who are at hand and those who are far distant, contemporaries, and those who will come after."[5]

At first glance, there would appear to be several similarities between conservatism and fascism. Both ideologies reject the principle of equality, affirming "the immutable, beneficial and fruitful inequality of mankind."[6] They are also critical of rationalism and the liberal society that exalts the supremacy of the individual over the community. Like conservatism, fascism also promulgates an idealized vision of the past in an effort to arouse national rebirth. However, fascism's call for the creation of a new society or community and the dismantling of traditional institutions (e.g., religious institutions) stands in direct contrast to conservatism's dislike of radical political change and its commitment to the democratic process.

Fascism's political goal is to establish a new social and political order based on a unified national and/or ethnic identity. For this reason, it rejects Marxism's class-based politics, arguing that it promotes allegiances that divide and weaken the national community. Under fascism, class conflict is institutionalized and managed through *corporatism,* an arrangement in which labour and business groups are integrated within the state apparatus. The economic interests and agendas of labour and industry become subordinate to the needs and objectives of the state. The economy is heavily regulated and controlled by the state through this corporatist structure.

The fascist state controls not only the economy but also other spheres of life. The fascist state is a totalitarian state due to the extensive control it exerts on its individual citizens. While liberalism assigns great importance to the individual and calls for a "small" state, fascism views the state as having ultimate moral and political authority. Fascism regards the state and the individual as inseparable, making no distinction between the private and public spheres of life. The individual does not exist without the state. Individual desires and aspirations are regarded as subservient to the needs and goals of society, as defined by the state. As Rocco explains:

> *For Liberalism, the individual is the end and society the means; nor is it conceivable that the individual, considered in the dignity of an ultimate finality, be lowered to mere instrumentality. For Fascism, society is the end, individuals the means, and its whole life consists in using individuals as instruments for its social ends.*[7]

Fascism glorifies the state and the leader that represents it. The leader is seen as invincible and infallible, embodying the aspirations and will of the people. Rejecting democratic institutions, like parliament and elections, authority is concentrated in the hands of a dictatorial cult figure. The leader's authority does not derive from any legal-rational deliberations or institutions, but rather derives from his perceived extraordinary skills or personal powers. A fascist leader makes use of myths and rituals to mobilize and manipulate the masses. His reign is also maintained through a totalitarian regime of propaganda and terror. The fascist dictator is the epitome of Weber's charismatic authority, receiving religious-like adulation from the masses. Given the lack of democratic institutions, the leader is not subject to any checks or controls.

As a variant of fascism, Nazism rejects materialism and the Enlightenment traditions and espouses the virtues of leadership and corporatism. It glorifies irrational instincts and will, dismissing the virtues of reason and responsible action. Despite these common elements, however, Nazism distinguishes itself by its extreme or radical nationalism based on race. Joseph Gobineau, a French conservative, who wrote *Essay on the Inequality of the Human Races* in 1853, heavily influenced German radical nationalist thought. Gobineau placed race at the centre of world history and attributed the decline of civilizations to racial degeneration rather than class conflict or economic decline. He claimed that there exists a hierarchy of races, with the "Aryan race" ascribed superior characteristics. Nazi ideology embraced these racist ideas, calling for the revitalization of the German racial community and its dominance over "inferior" races. For Nazism, duty is owed not to the state, but to the race. The corporatist state, foreign policy, and war become instruments for preserving racial purity and establishing a new world order based on racial nationalism. As Hitler wrote in *Mein Kampf,* "A state which in this age of racial poisoning dedicates itself to the care of its best racial elements must some day become lord of the earth."[8]

FASCISM TODAY

Racial nationalism, a key component of fascism, has re-emerged in Eastern Europe, represented by the drive for "ethnic cleansing" in the former nation of Yugoslavia. Political parties spewing anti-immigrant and xenophobic sentiments have also gained popularity in recent years. In France, an ultra-rightist politician, Jean-Marie Le Pen, who advocated that preference be given to French citizens in the area of employment and social benefits, placed second in the first round of voting for president. Belgium's Flemish Bloc, an anti-immigration party, received approximately 25 percent of the vote during the 1991 general election. Italy's Lombard League achieved electoral success at the municipal level in the early 1990s, winning a majority of votes in the city of Brescia.[9] Neo-Nazi movements and organizations targeting minority groups have sprung up in several countries, including Germany and the United States. These developments and events reveal that while the fascist regimes of Mussolini and Hitler are defunct, elements of fascist ideology have not disappeared.

ENDNOTES

1. Alan O. Ebenstein et al., *Today's Isms: Socialism, Capitalism, Fascism, and Communism* (Englewood Cliffs: Prentice Hall, 1994).
2. Ibid.
3. Ibid.
4. Hannah Arendt, *The Origins of Totalitarianism* (New York: Meridean Books, 1958), 469.
5. From Benito Mussolini, "The Political and Social Doctrine of Fascism," in *International Conciliation*: 306 (January 1935) 5–17, passim.
6. Ibid.
7. Alfredo Rocco, "The Political Doctrine of Fascism." An address delivered at Perugia, Aug. 30, 1925. Reprinted in *Readings on Fascism and National Socialism* (Denver: A. Swallow, 1958), 34–35.
8. Adolf Hitler, *Mein Kampf*, trans. Ralph Mannheim (Boston: Houghton Mifflin, 1962), 289.
9. Ebenstein et al., *Today's Isms.*

READING

This chapter discussed fascism's rejection of liberal democratic principles such as individual freedom and majority rule in favour of duty to a fascist state. The fascist state is regarded as the symbol of the needs and aspirations of the national community. The chapter also explored fascism's exaltation of violence and emotion over reason. These fascist principles are articulated in the following excerpt by Benito Mussolini.

The reading is a passage written by Mussolini and submitted to the *Italian Encyclopedia* in which he outlines several key features of fascist political doctrine. In the piece, Mussolini denounces both liberal democracy and Marxism, the former for promoting individual freedom at the expense of the national community and the latter for dividing the nation along class lines. He rejects the democratic principles of majority rule and basic human equality, and instead categorizes political inequalities as natural and indeed desirable elements of humanity. Another important idea advanced by Mussolini in this piece is the role of the fascist state. Unlike the liberal state, which just "records" voter preferences, the fascist state is regarded as the agent of national social integration. The fascist state, through its strong leadership, rises above petty group interests to represent the "true" aspirations of present and future generations of the social collectivity. It alone determines what is best for its members, including which freedoms individuals should exercise. The fascist state requires unity and power, not individual freedom. Finally, Mussolini also expresses the fascist exaltation of violence in his discussion of imperialism, which he regards as an expression of a people's greatness. Critics of the imperialist regime, both Liberal and Socialist, would be severely reprimanded for undermining the fascist principle of unity and duty.

FUNDAMENTAL IDEAS

Benito Mussolini

Like all sound political conceptions, Fascism is action and it is thought; action in which doctrine is immanent, and doctrine arising from a given system of historical forces in which it is inserted, and working on them from within. It has therefore a form correlated to contingencies of time and space; but it has also an ideal content which makes it an expression of truth in the higher region of the history of thought. There is no way of exercising a spiritual influence in the world as a human will dominating the will of others, unless one has a conception both of the transient and the specific reality on which that action is to be exercised, and of the permanent and universal reality in which the transient dwells and has its being. To know men one must know man; and to know man one must be acquainted with reality and its laws. There can be no conception of the State which is not fundamentally a conception of life: philosophy or intuition, system of ideas evolving within the framework of logic or concentrated in a vision or a faith, but always, at least potentially, an organic conception of the world.

Thus many of the practical expressions of Fascism—such as party organisation, system of education, discipline—can only be understood when considered in relation to its general attitude toward life. A spiritual attitude. Fascism sees in the world not only those superficial, material aspects in which man appears as an individual, standing by himself, self-centred, subject to natural law which instinctively urges him toward a life of selfish momentary pleasure; it sees not only the individual but the nation and the country; individuals and generations bound together by a moral law, with common traditions and a mission which suppressing the instinct for life closed in a brief circle of pleasure, builds up a higher life, founded on duty, a life free from the limitations of time and space, in which the individual, by self-sacrifice, the renunciation of self-interest, by death itself, can achieve that purely spiritual existence in which his value as a man consists.

The conception is therefore a spiritual one, arising from the general reaction of the century against the flacid [*sic*] materialistic positivism of the XIXth century. Anti-positivistic but positive; neither sceptical nor agnostic; neither pessimistic nor supinely optimistic as are, generally speaking, the doctrines (all negative) which place the centre of life outside man; whereas, by the exercise of his free will, man can and must create his own world.

Fascism wants man to be active and to engage in action with all his energies; it wants him to be manfully aware of the difficulties besetting him and ready to face them. It conceives of life as a struggle in which it behoves a man to win for himself a really worthy place, first of all by fitting himself (physically, morally, intellectually) to become the implement required for winning it. As for the individual, so for the nation, and so for mankind. Hence the high value of culture in all its forms (artistic, religious, scientific), and the outstanding importance of education. Hence also the essential value of work, by which man subjugates nature and creates the human world (economic, political, ethical, intellectual).

This positive conception of life is obviously an ethical one. It invests the whole field of reality as well as the human activities which master it. No action is exempt from moral judgement; no activity can be despoiled of the value which a moral purpose confers on all things. Therefore life, as conceived of by the Fascist, is serious, austere, religious; all its manifestations are poised in a world sustained by moral forces and subject to spiritual responsibilities. The Fascist disdains an "easy" life.

The Fascist conception of life is a religious one, in which man is viewed in his immanent relation to a higher law, endowed with an objective will transcending the individual and raising him to conscious membership of a spiritual society. Those who perceive nothing beyond opportunistic considerations in the religious policy of the Fascist régime fail to realise that Fascism is not only a system of government but also and above all a system of thought.

In the Fascist conception of history, man is man only by virtue of the spiritual process to which he contributes as a member of the family, the social group, the nation, and in function of history to which all nations bring their contribution. Hence the great value of tradition in records, in language, in customs, in the rules of social life. Outside history man is a nonentity. Fascism is therefore opposed to all individualistic abstractions based on eighteenth century materialism; and it is opposed to all Jacobinistic utopias and innovations. It does not believe in the possibility of "happiness" on earth as conceived by the economistic literature of the XVIIIth century, and it therefore rejects the teleological notion that at some future time the human family will secure a final settlement of all its difficulties. This notion runs counter to experience which teaches that life is in continual flux and in process of evolution. In politics Fascism aims at realism; in practice it desires to deal only with those problems which are the spontaneous product of historic conditions and which find or suggest their own solutions. Only by entering in to the process of reality and taking possession of the forces at work within it, can man act on man and on nature.

Anti-individualistic, the Fascist conception of life stresses the importance of the State and accepts the individual only in so far as his interests coincide with those of the State, which stands for the conscience and the universal will of man as a historic entity. It is opposed to classical liberalism which arose as a reaction to absolutism and exhausted its historical function when the State became the expression of the conscience and will of the people. Liberalism denied the State in the name of the individual; Fascism reasserts the rights of the State as expressing the real essence of the individual. And if liberty is to be the attribute of living men and not of abstract

dummies invented by individualistic liberalism, then Fascism stands for liberty, and for the only liberty worth having, the liberty of the State and of the individual within the State. The Fascist conception of the State is all-embracing; outside of it no human or spiritual values can exist, much less have value. Thus understood, Fascism, is totalitarian; and the Fascist State—a synthesis and a unit inclusive of all values—interprets, develops, and potentiates the whole life of a people.

No individuals or groups (political parties, cultural associations, economic unions, social classes) outside the State. Fascism is therefore opposed to Socialism to which unity within the State (which amalgamates classes into a single economic and ethical reality) is unknown, and which sees in history nothing but the class struggle. Fascism is likewise opposed to trade-unionism as a class weapon. But when brought within the orbit of the State, Fascism recognises the real needs which gave rise to socialism and trade-unionism, giving them due weight in the guild or corporative system in which divergent interests are coordinated and harmonised in the unity of the State.

***

Fascism will have nothing to do with universal embraces; as a member of the community of nations it looks other peoples straight in the eyes; it is vigilant and on its guard; it follows others in all their manifestations and notes any changes in their interests; and it does not allow itself to be deceived by mutable and fallacious appearances.

Such a conception of life makes Fascism the resolute negation of the doctrine underlying so-called scientific and Marxian socialism, the doctrine of historic materialism which would explain the history of mankind in terms of the class-struggle and by changes in the processes and instruments of production, to the exclusion of all else.

That the vicissitudes of economic life— discoveries of raw materials, new technical processes, scientific inventions—have their importance, no one denies; but that they suffice to explain human history to the exclusion of other factors is absurd. Fascism believes now and always in sanctity and heroism, that is to say in acts in which no economic motive—remote or immediate—is at work. Having denied historic materialism, which sees in men mere puppets on the surface of history, appearing and disappearing on the crest of the waves while in the depths the real directing forces move and work, Fascism also denies the immutable and irreparable character of the class struggle which is the natural outcome of this economic conception of history; above all it denies that the class struggle is the preponderating agent in social transformations. Having thus struck a blow at socialism in the two main points of its doctrine, all that remains of it is the sentimental aspiration—old as humanity itself—toward social relations in which the sufferings and sorrows of the humbler folk will be alleviated. But here again Fascism rejects the economic interpretation of felicity as something to be secured socialistically, almost automatically, at a given stage of economic evolution when all will be assured a maximum of material comfort. Fascism denies the materialistic conception of happiness as a possibility, and abandons it to the economists of the mid-eighteenth century. This means that Fascism denies the equation: well-being = happiness, which sees in men mere animals, content when they can feed and fatten, thus reducing them to a vegetative existence pure and simple.

After socialism, Fascism trains its guns on the whole block of democratic ideologies, and rejects both their premises and their practical applications and implements. Fascism denies that numbers, as such, can be the determining factor in human society; it denies the right of numbers to govern by means of periodical consultations; it asserts the irremediable and fertile and beneficent inequality of men who cannot be levelled by any such mechanical and extrinsic device as universal suffrage. Democratic régimes may be described as those under which the people are, from time to time, deluded into the belief that they exercise sovereignty, while all the time real sovereignty resides in and is exercised by other and sometimes irresponsible and secret forces. Democracy is a kingless régime infested by many kings who are sometimes more exclusive, tyrannical, and destructive than one, even if he be a tyrant. This explains why Fascism—although, for contingent reasons, it was republican in tendency prior to 1922—abandoned that stand before the March on Rome, convinced that the form of government is no longer a matter of preeminent importance, and because the study of past and present monarchies and past and present republics shows that neither monarchy nor republic can be judged *sub specie aeternitatis*, but that each

stands for a form of government expressing the political evolution, the history, the traditions, and the psychology of a given country.

Fascism has outgrown the dilemma: monarchy v. republic, over which democratic régimes too long dallied, attributing all insufficiencies to the former and proning the latter as a régime of perfection, whereas experience teaches that some republics are inherently reactionary and absolutist while some monarchies accept the most daring political and social experiments.

***

. . . In rejecting democracy Fascism rejects the absurd conventional lie of political equalitarianism, the habit of collective irresponsibility, the myth of felicity and indefinite progress. But if democracy be understood as meaning a régime in which the masses are not driven back to the margin of the State, then the writer of these pages has already defined Fascism as an organised, centralised, authoritarian democracy.

Fascism is definitely and absolutely opposed to the doctrines of liberalism, both in the political and the economic sphere. The importance of liberalism in the XIXth century should not be exaggerated for present-day polemical purposes, nor should we make of one of the many doctrines which flourished in that century a religion for mankind for the present and for all time to come.

***

From beneath the ruins of liberal, socialist, and democratic doctrines, Fascism extracts those elements which are still vital. It preserves what may be described as "the acquired facts" of history; it rejects all else. That is to say, it rejects the idea of a doctrine suited to all times and to all people. Granted that the XIXth century was the century of socialism, liberalism, and democracy, this does not mean that the XXth century must also be the century of socialism, liberalism, and democracy. Political doctrines pass; nations remain. We are free to believe that this is the century of authority, a century of tending to the "right," a Fascist century. If the XIXth century was the century of the individual (liberalism implied individualism) we are free to believe that this is the "collective" century, and therefore the century of the State.

***

The Fascist State expresses the will to exercise power and to command. Here the Roman tradition is embodied in a conception of strength. Imperial power, as understood by the Fascist doctrine, is not only territorial, or military, or commercial; it is also spiritual and ethical. An imperial nation, that is to say a nation which directly or indirectly is a leader of others, can exist without the need of conquering a single square mile of territory. Fascism sees in the imperialistic spirit—i.e., in the tendency of nations to expand—a manifestation of their vitality. In the opposite tendency, which would limit their interests to the home country, it sees a symptom of decadence. Peoples who rise or rearise are imperialistic; renunciation is characteristic of dying peoples. The Fascist doctrine is that best suited to the tendencies and feelings of a people which, like the Italians, after laying fallow during centuries of servitude, is now reassuring itself in the world.

But imperialism implies discipline, the coordination of efforts, a deep sense of duty and a spirit of self-sacrifice. This fact explains many aspects of the practical activity of the regime, and the direction taken by many of the forces in the State, as also the severity which has to be exercised towards those who would oppose this spontaneous and inevitable movement . . . by agitating the outgrown ideologies of the XIXth century, ideologies rejected wherever great experiments in political and social transformations are being dared.

Never before have the peoples thirsted for authority, direction, order, as they do now. If each age has its doctrine, then innumerable symptoms indicate that the doctrine of our age is the Fascist. That it is vital is shown by the fact that it has aroused a faith; that this faith has conquered souls is shown by the fact that Fascism can point to fallen heroes and its martyrs.

Fascism has now acquired throughout the world that universality which belongs to all doctrines which by achieving self-expression represent a moment in the history of human thought.

KEY TERMS

Fascism   An extreme-right ideology that rejects the ideals of rationality and individual liberty and champions a collectivist ideology that focuses on the needs and aspirations of a national community. Anti-materialist and anti-democratic, fascism rejects basic human equality as an ideal and espouses government by an elite group.

Fascist Corporatism   One way of organizing state–society relations in autocratic, capitalist societies. An economic system divided into state-controlled associations representing labour, business, and professionals. Each association has a monopoly of representation and organization in its respective field. The economic interests of labour and industry are subordinate to the needs and objectives of the state.

National Socialism   (Nazism) An extreme branch of fascism that espouses extreme or radical nationalism based on race. State policies aim to preserve racial purity and establish a new world order based on racial nationalism.

FURTHER READINGS

Arendt, Hannah. *Origins of Totalitarianism.* New York: Harcourt Brace Jovanovich, 1966.

De Felice, Renzo. *Interpretations of Fascism.* Cambridge: Harvard University Press, 1977.

Griffin, Roger. *The Nature of Fascism.* New York: Routledge, 1991.

Nolte, Ernst. *Three Faces of Fascism.* New York: Holt, Rinehart, & Winston, 1966.

CHAPTER 7

FEMINISM AND ENVIRONMENTALISM

While ideological debate for the past two centuries has largely been dominated by the ideas and political projects of conservatism, liberalism, and socialism, the past decades have witnessed the broadening of the ideological landscape with the emergence of new political ideologies, including feminism and environmentalism. These ideologies, advanced by new social movements, offer new ways of thinking about identity and society that often challenge the traditional left–right spectrum. Moreover, as political projects, they strive to influence policy decisions as well as change values in civil society on the issues of gender and the environment in an effort to create a more just society. Feminism and environmentalism distinguish themselves from the traditional ideologies by the diversity of views and strategies they encompass. This chapter provides a general overview of the historical origins, basic concepts, and diverse branches of feminism and environmentalism.

FEMINISM

Concepts and Themes

The term "feminism" has different meanings for different people. Broadly defined, **feminism** is an ideology and political project based on the belief that men and women are treated unequally socially, politically, and economically. It aims to identify and abolish the sources of women's oppression in all spheres of life. It is important to note, however, that there is not one feminism but rather many feminisms. Like other ideologies, there exist different strands of feminism that propose a broad range of strategies for ameliorating the status of women in society. These strands, however, all agree that women, as a social class, are oppressed by virtue of their gender.

The term "gender" is one of the most fundamental concepts in feminism. While "sex" refers to the physiological differences between males and females, "**gender**" is used to describe those characteristics of men and women that are socially constructed rather than biologically determined. Through socialization, men and women learn what the appropriate behaviour, attitudes, and roles are for them and how they should relate to one another. For example, women are often regarded as more emotional, intuitive, and passive while men are viewed as assertive, competent, and rational. For many feminists, these stereotypes are one of the main culprits for women's subordinate status in society.

Another important concept in feminism is patriarchy. **Patriarchy** is an institutionalized system of male domination and power, which subordinates and marginalizes women. Patriarchy is maintained by a number of institutions and processes in society, including motherhood, compulsory heterosexuality, notions of femininity, and the traditional nuclear family. Feminism seeks to abolish patriarchy and other systems of subordination and privilege, such as racism, through social and political activism. The specific strategies used to eliminate patriarchal power vary among the different branches of feminism.

Feminism also seeks to challenge the separation of the public and private spheres of life that have their origins in classical Greek thought. The *public/private dichotomy* is an important concept in feminism because it distinguishes public or political concerns from private or personal matters. The dichotomy also rests on a division of labour between the sexes, with men responsible for issues dealing with economic and political life and women with private matters related to family life. This dichotomy, feminists argue, is a false one and ignores the power dynamics found in the personal sphere of sexuality, housework, and the family. Indeed, feminism has been successful in politicizing issues once deemed to be personal and private matters, such as domestic violence and child abuse.

"HERSTORY": A BRIEF OVERVIEW OF THE WOMEN'S MOVEMENT

The women's movement emerged in North America and Britain in the mid-1800s. During this first wave of women's activism, women began to demand equal civil and political rights when their attempts to participate equally in the anti-slavery movement and temperance movements were rejected. During this time, married women had neither property rights nor the right to vote, and husbands had legal power over and responsibility for their wives and children. Women were also barred from going to college or university and from entering professions such as medicine or law. These early feminists were calling for a number of reforms that would ameliorate women's status in society. Eventually, the right to vote emerged as the central issue, since it would provide the means to achieve other important reforms. Women gained the right to vote in national elections in 1920 in the United States and in 1921 in Canada.

While the first-wave feminist movement focused on equal rights, second-wave feminism of the 1960s argued that women needed economic opportunities as well as civil liberties to achieve equality. National organizations like the National Organization for Women in the United States and the National Action Committee on the Status of Women in Canada were formed in the 1960s and sought not only equality before the law but also equal employment opportunities, child care, and reproductive rights. The movement became more ideologically diverse, especially in Canada, as more branches of feminism began to emerge, with their own ideological insights and political projects. Many of these branches were critical of the mainstream women's movement, arguing that it reflected the experiences and aspirations of white, middle-class women. Working-class and minority women felt their "voices" were marginalized within the movement.

The 1990s ushered in the third wave of the feminist movement, which gives greater recognition to diversity and identity, focusing on the unique experiences of women. Often called post-modern feminism, the third wave challenges the beliefs of grand political theories and encourages the recognition and celebration of women's multiple identities, e.g., immigrant, mother, lesbian, worker, person with disabilities, etc. While second-wave feminism sought to unite women through consciousness raising and creating a shared experience, the third wave is more interested in how differences among women shape their political and personal views on issues.

The recognition of diversity is an important issue for feminists in developing countries, who criticize the women's movement as a Western construct that neglects the specificity of culture and tradition in other parts of the world. Third World feminists assert that "women" and "women's problems" cannot be examined in a homogeneous manner. Women in different societies experience subjugation resulting from patriarchy in varying forms due to racism, class, ethnicity, historical processes, colonialism, and imperialism. For this group of feminists, even the usage of the term "Third World Feminism" is problematic because it depicts "third world women as a singular monolithic subject," for a "discursive colonization."[1] Categorizing all Third World women as a non-Western "other" obfuscates the differences amongst women's experiences and creates an ahistorical feminist discourse. They therefore view the Western feminist discourse, and the strategies it proposes for women's liberation, as another form of cultural imperialism and domination. While recognizing some commonalities with the struggle of women in the West, Third World feminists contend that strategies should be cognizant of their unique experiences and traditions. The tensions and differences between Western feminism and Third World feminism are illustrated by the debate over the hijab, a veil worn by Muslim women to cover their heads and faces. While Western feminists regard it as a symbol of women's oppression, some Muslim women regard it as a symbol of freedom from Western cultural imperialism and domination. This debate and others like it remind us that feminism is not a homogenous and monolithic movement and that the struggle for women's emancipation must be culturally and historically grounded.

STRANDS OF FEMINISM

As mentioned earlier, feminism encompasses a variety of perspectives on the nature of gender relations, the source of women's subordination, and the strategies to overcome it. Given that an exhaustive survey of contemporary feminist thought falls beyond the scope of this chapter, we will focus on three major strands of feminism: Liberal feminism, Marxist-feminism, and Radical feminism.

Liberal Feminism The Liberal feminist perspective is informed by the principles of equality, fairness, and individual autonomy. Influenced by the works of nineteenth-century liberal thinkers, **Liberal feminism** adheres to the humanist conception of the individual as a rational, autonomous agent.[2] One of the earliest and most influential Liberal feminist theorists was Mary Wollstonecraft, an English Liberal theorist, who wrote *A Vindication of the Rights of Woman* in 1770. She criticized the lack of educational opportunities for women, claiming that it kept them in a state of ignorance and rendered them dependent on their husbands. Wollstonecraft argued that women should be treated as autonomous, rational decision makers and given the same political rights as men. Other Liberal theorists, such as John Stuart Mill and Harriet Taylor Mill, also wrote in favour of education and equal rights for women. In *The Subjection of Women*, Mill conceptualizes men and women as equally rational and recommends greater educational opportunities for women so they can fully participate in the social and political

Mary Wollstonecraft Godwin

life of their communities. However, both Mill and Taylor differed from Wollstonecraft in their belief that society should provide women with the same civil rights and economic opportunities bestowed to men.

The principles of equality and rationality continue to inform contemporary liberal feminism. Liberal feminists argue that women, as rational beings, are entitled to the same rights and opportunities enjoyed by men. Betty Friedan, a proponent of Liberal feminism and author of the 1974 book *The Feminine Mystique*, maintained that women's inferior position in society is due to gender socialization and notions of femininity that place exclusive value on women's roles as housewives and mothers. Friedan dispelled the myth that women find complete satisfaction in marriage and motherhood, a myth that legitimized gender discrimination in the workplace and in the home. Because of this myth, women are relegated to low-paying and low-status occupations, such as clerical and service work, and continue to be primarily responsible for housework and child care. Liberal feminists also want to abolish the formal discrimination that undermines women's legal rights, such as property rights and equal pay for work of equal value.

In general, Liberal feminism locates its political project in the public realm, where politics is conceptualized in terms of activities that occur within formal political institutions and processes. Primarily reformist in theory and in practice, Liberal feminists seek to improve women's status through legislative measures and by working within existing decision-making structures. However, there is some debate between classical Liberal feminists and welfare Liberal feminists regarding the appropriate strategy to achieve this end. Classical Liberal feminists focus on changing laws that discriminate against women and that deny them formal equality before the law. Welfare Liberal feminists, on the other hand, argue that the feminist project should also focus on eliminating socio-economic barriers that impede women from realizing their true human potential. Employment equity would be the type of policy that welfare Liberal feminists would support but classical Liberal feminists would reject because it would entail a level of government intervention that they are uncomfortable with.

In Canada and in the United States, Liberal feminists have been instrumental in bringing about significant reforms, including maternity leave, equal pay for equal work, matrimonial property rights, and human rights legislation. The goal of liberal feminism is to reform existing decision-making institutions to ensure the representation and participation of women. While women have made significant gains in this area, they continue to be underrepresented in key political institutions.

Marxist-Socialist Feminism Socialist feminists offer a class perspective regarding the root of women's oppression in society that originates in the nineteenth-century works of Karl Marx and Friedrich Engels. Marx argued that the organization of social relations is heavily influenced by material conditions. Society is divided into two basic economic classes, each having conflicting interests to the another. The bourgeoisie is the wealthy ruling class that owns the means of production while the proletariat, or working class, is forced to sell its labour in order to survive. These differences in the relationship to the means of production create conditions of exploitation that lead to inequality of power and ultimately class conflict in society. According to Marx, the capitalist economy also determines the elements that compose the superstructure of society, such as politics, religion, law, art, and philosophy. These elements ultimately work to legitimize the existing economic order.

Viewing inequality between the sexes in structural terms, **Marxist-socialist feminism** argues that women's subordination is rooted in both patriarchy and capitalism. The starting point for Marxist-socialist feminism is Friedrich Engels' 1884 piece, *The Origins of the Family, Private Property and the State*. Engels contended that gender relations and the inferior status of women in society are inextricably linked to the capitalist economy. In capitalist societies, men and women have different relations to the means of production. While men are involved in the production of goods that are bought and sold in the marketplace, women's work primarily takes place outside the market economy, that is, in the home. As a consequence, domestic labour and child care are not considered real work and are therefore not remunerated. According to Engels, this sexual division of labour serves the interests of men and of the capitalist economy. Women's unpaid work, such as child rearing, household tasks, and taking care of the aged and the sick, allows the male worker to freely pursue full-time paid work, thus encouraging economic productivity. Engels argued that women's oppression would end only with the collectivization of child care and domestic tasks and women's entrance into the paid labour force.

Engels' solution to the sexual division of labour has its critics. Today's Marxist-socialist feminists argue that women's participation in the labour force has not liberated them but rather has led to working women performing "double duty," that is, working for wages in the labour market while still undertaking many of the domestic chores in the household. Women employed outside the home are also disadvantaged in terms of wages and occupational standing. Women as a group are usually employed in low-paying and low-status jobs, often on a part-time basis. The conceptualization of men as the primary "breadwinner" in the family further justifies differentials in wages as women's paid labour is regarded only as supplementing the husband's income. Women who do not belong to a traditional nuclear family, such as single women and lesbian couples, are further disadvantaged because they do not have access to this "family wage."[3] Moreover, because of their care-taker position in the family, women are often regarded as a "reserve army of labour," called upon to enter the labour force when they are needed and sent home when that need ceases to exist.[4] This was the case during World War II, when American and Canadian women were recruited to take on jobs left behind by men who entered the army, only to be sent home once the war was over.

For Marxist-socialist feminists, patriarchy and capitalism are inextricably linked, therefore requiring the reorganization of institutions found in both the public and private spheres. The liberation of women can occur only under socialism, which would bring about the massive restructuring of existing institutions, such as the economic order and the patriarchal, nuclear family. For the most part, Marxist-socialist feminists do not advocate revolutionary change to existing political and economic institutions; rather, they call for reforms that would improve women's economic independence. In North America, Marxist-socialist feminists have been instrumental in placing on the public agenda a variety of important issues, including affordable and effective daycare, equal pay for equal work, and wages for housework.

Radical Feminism While the preceding strands of feminism are tied to the old ideologies of liberalism and socialism, **Radical feminism** provides a fairly new perspective on the oppression of women. It has helped define the second-wave feminist movement. Radical feminism originated in the late 1960s out of the civil rights and New Left movements in North America, Britain, and France. Women involved in these movements became increasingly disillusioned because they were treated as clerical assistants or sex objects by their male coworkers rather than as equal partners in the organization.[5] From these personal experiences, women began to understand their situation in terms of patriarchy and gender oppression. Unlike Marxist-socialist feminists, who view both capitalism and patriarchy as the source of women's subjugation, Radical feminists point out that women around the world are oppressed regardless of the economic system they live under. They argue instead that women's oppression, in fact all forms of oppression such as racism, ageism, and even environmental degradation, are rooted in patriarchy.

Radical feminism focuses on the relationship between biology and women's status in society. Proponents of this feminist position, however, have contradictory views on the relationship between biology and women's oppression and subsequent strategies to overcome it. Some Radical feminists argue that biological reproduction is the primary source of women's oppression. Motherhood and compulsory heterosexuality, they argue, allow men to control every aspect of women's lives. Sexual politics is a primary focus of Radical feminism. Sex is viewed as the foremost form of oppression, allowing men control over women's bodies, sexuality, and reproduction. This group advocates an androgynous society where gender differences no longer exist and individuals are free to assume both "male" and "female" characteristics. Some Radical feminists, like Shulamith Firestone, are in favour of reproductive technologies, like in vitro fertilization and assisted insemination, arguing that they liberate women from the "oppressive chains" of motherhood and childbirth. Others contend that women's liberation can occur only by rejecting traditional heterosexual relationships and striving toward female separatism. An alternative radical feminist perspective takes a very different view of reproduction, regarding it as a source of power for women. This perspective calls for the affirmation of a "women's culture" that celebrates women's reproductive and sexual powers.

Radical feminists have made significant contributions in broadening our understanding of politics. They coined the term "the personal is political," referring to the need to politicize issues traditionally relegated to the private sphere, especially in the area of sexual and familial relationships. Indeed, they were instrumental in placing a number of issues on the public agenda that were once considered private matters, such as domestic violence, rape, incest, sexual harassment, and pornography. Unlike reform-minded Liberal feminists who work within the system for change, Radical feminists often choose to work outside the system, seeking radical personal and social transformations.

FEMINISM IN CONTEMPORARY POLITICS

As an ideology and political project, feminism has introduced gender as an important unit of analysis in the study of politics. Its different branches have highlighted the political nature of gender relations and their consequences for women. Indeed, feminism has also broadened our understanding of the political. Like other ideologies, feminism is concerned with the affairs of the state. It informs the demands and identities of groups and individuals seeking to influence government decisions. As an activity, feminist politics strives to achieve a more equitable distribution of resources between men and women. However, feminism's conception of the political also goes beyond the arenas of public life (i.e., the state, political parties) to include the gendered politics of personal life.[6] The Radical feminist slogan "the personal is political" exemplifies feminism's blurring of the boundaries between political issues and personal matters. Feminism's conception of politics therefore includes a wide range of activity from lobbying government officials for particular policies to the organization of "take back the night" marches to end violence against women.

While feminism has expanded our notion of the political, in recent decades the relevance of feminism in contemporary politics has been questioned, as evidenced by a 1998 cover story in *Time* magazine that asked "Is Feminism Dead?" Some critics argue that greater equality between men and women has been achieved, therefore rendering feminism, as an ideological and political force, obsolete. Others contend that feminism no longer speaks to the reality of ordinary women's lives. The New Right political era of the 1980s and 1990s also saw a backlash against feminism, with the emergence of conservative organizations and anti-feminist women's groups espousing the return to traditional family values. In terms of policy, government cutbacks in the area of welfare programs have significantly impacted women, who tend to make up the majority of the poor in Canadian and American society. The New Right's political agenda, which emphasizes a minimal state, stands in sharp contrast to feminism's reliance on government intervention in economic and social matters.[7] It is not surprising, therefore, that feminists tend not to support right-wing political parties during elections.

While feminism has encountered many challenges in recent decades, it remains an important force in contemporary politics. Liberal and Radical feminism have been especially influential in raising awareness and compelling government action on a number of issues that affect women's lives, including reproductive rights, educational and workplace equity, political representation, and domestic violence. While progress has been made on a number of fronts, there continues to be room for improvement. Women in almost all countries continue to be underrepresented in the upper echelons of political and economic power. In North America women, in particular single mothers, are overrepresented among the poor. Moreover, due to familial responsibilities and lack of opportunities, women continue to be concentrated in low-paying, low-status jobs. These issues remind us of the importance of including "gender" in the political equation.

ENVIRONMENTALISM

Concepts and Themes

There is not one single way to define environmentalism. It is an all-embracing term used to describe a number of different themes, activities, and perspectives related to the issue of the environment. For the purpose of this discussion, **environmentalism** is defined as a belief system and political project that seeks to protect the quality and continuity of life through the conservation, preservation, or protection of the natural environment and its inhabitants. Like feminism, there are many branches of environmentalism, which offer alternative and sometimes conflicting perspectives on the root causes of the environmental problem and the appropriate course of action. However, they all seek to place environmental concerns on the political agenda.

Two central concepts used to classify different ideological perspectives within environmentalism are anthropocentrism and ecocentrism. **Anthropocentrism** is based on the principle of a human-centred world, where humans are assigned a superior status in their relationship with nature. The natural environment exists to serve the needs of human beings. **Ecocentrism**, on the other hand, rejects this hierarchical relationship and offers a more organic view of the world that recognizes the interdependence and interconnection between humans and nonhumans. An ecocentric perspective does not view the environment in instrumental terms but rather regards it as having intrinsic value. These two different philosophical worldviews have led to considerable debate within environmentalism over appropriate strategies for resolving environmental problems.

Sustainable development is also an important concept in environmentalism. The World Commission on Environment and Development (the Brundtland Commission) defined sustainable development as "development that meets the needs of the present without compromising the ability of future generations to meet their own needs."[8] It represents the reconciliation of economic development with the integrity of the ecological system. Some have expanded the term to include not only economic development but also cultural and social development. Sustainable development, however, has met with criticism. While international resolutions for sustainable development have been embraced by Western countries (at least in principle), they have been criticized by developing countries that believe economic development can occur only with the exploitation of the country's natural resources.

HISTORICAL OVERVIEW OF THE ENVIRONMENTAL MOVEMENT

The first wave of environmentalism can be traced back to the eighteenth-century conservation movement in the West. Early conservationists and preservationists were concerned with the impact of industrialization and European colonialism on the natural environment. They had romantic ideals of unspoiled landscapes and sought to protect natural resources and wildlife for future generations. Conservationists wanted to protect natural resources to ensure future development while preservationists wanted to protect wildlife for recreational and spiritual purposes. Early conservationists and preservationists, like John Muir, had an anthropocentric view of the environment. They wanted to protect nature and wildlife for the spiritual, recreational, or economic pursuits of human beings. In North America, preservationists were instrumental in the creation of national parks, which preserved forests and wildlife from exploitation. The creation of Yellowstone National Park in 1872 and the first wildlife sanctuary in California were a result of the activism and lobbying efforts of upper-class preservationists who wanted large tracts of public lands left essentially alone. In 1892 these wilderness lovers, led by John Muir and others, founded the Sierra Club, an organization that continues to be active in today's environmental movement.

The second wave of the environmental movement began with the publication of Rachel Carson's *Silent Spring* in 1962. Carson challenged the notion that human beings were destined to control nature and instead portrayed humans and nature as intertwined in the complex web of life. Her book raised the public's awareness of the detrimental effects of pesticides on both the natural environment and the health of humans. Carson concluded that the continued use of certain pesticides on agricultural land would irrevocably harm birds and animals and contaminate the world's food supply.[9] Her findings prompted a government inquiry in the United States and the creation of the Environmental Protection Agency in 1970. Carson's work and that of other scientists heightened the public's awareness of environmental problems that cut across national borders, such as air pollution and acid rain. It was during the 1960s and 1970s that the environmental movement was institutionalized and transformed from a local, grassroots project to a global movement. Growing public support for environmental issues culminated in the Earth Day demonstrations of 1970. We also saw the emergence of Green parties in many Western countries, the most notable and successful of which is Germany's Green Party, which entered a coalition government with the Social Democratic Party in the 1990s. In 2002, the Green Party occupied 55 seats (8.8 percent) in the German Parliament.

The 1980s and 1990s witnessed the third wave of the environmental movement, which sought to harmonize environmentalism with free markets and economic growth. The 1987 report of the World Commission on Environment and Development,[10] titled *Our Common Future*, characterized sustainable development as a legitimate compromise between economic interests and environmental protection, as did the Rio Summit of 1992. The environment and economy were no longer viewed as irreconcilable. Natural resources could be managed to ensure economic growth while still achieving environmental goals. The recent Kyoto Accord is the latest international effort to address climate change and establish emission limits for participating countries. However, several countries, including the United States—which is responsible for approximately 30 percent of the world's emissions—have opposed the treaty.

While "sustainable development" has become the dominant paradigm in environmental policy, it is not without its critics. Environmentalists influenced by the ideas of ecologism are critical of the principle of sustainable development, claiming there are limits to economic growth. They argue that fundamental changes need to be made to the modern political economy as well as to civil society. Grassroots environmental movements are also emerging, especially in developing countries, that make the link between environmental problems and issues of poverty and cultural survival.

BRANCHES OF ENVIRONMENTALISM

Like feminism, there exist several strands of environmentalism, which offer different views on the relationship between the environment and the economy, the linkage of the environment to other social and political issues, and the appropriate course of action. Norwegian philosopher Arne Naess' 1972 article "The Shallow and the Deep, Long-Range Ecology Movement" distinguished between the "**shallow ecology**" perspective, which seeks to achieve short-term environmental objectives within existing institutions and processes, and "**deep ecology**," which calls for the long-term, radical transformation of ideological, economic, and political principles that underpin industrial capitalism. The different branches of environmentalism that exist can be placed on this "shallow ecology–deep ecology" spectrum, depending on whether they have an anthropocentric or ecocentric view of the world and whether they call for reforms or for a more radical transformation of existing values and institutions.

"Shallow Ecology" Branches

At the "shallow" end of the spectrum are reformist branches of environmentalism, including personal environmentalism and reform environmentalism. The least political of the branches, personal environmentalism seeks to make a positive impact on the environment through individuals incorporating sensible and earth-friendly practices in their day-to-day lives. Recycling, carpooling, driving fuel-efficient cars, and cutting down on water use are the type of strategies that make up a good "environmental citizen." Personal environmentalism is the least political of the branches because it does not delve into the link between environmentally conscious behaviour and broader political or economic issues.

While personal environmentalism seeks to achieve environmental objectives through non-political, individual action, reform environmentalism has a political mandate and seeks to achieve these objectives within the policy process. Commonly associated with the environmental movement of the 1970s and 1980s, reform environmentalism seeks legislative and policy changes such as anti-pollution legislation, bans on the use of certain pesticides, waste disposal strategies, stopping nuclear testing, etc., in an effort to protect the local or global environment. While reform environmentalists tackle a myriad of issues and causes, they do not seek radical changes. Rather, their intent is to "fix" the current state of the environment without overhauling the prevailing political and economic order.[11]

"Deep Ecology" Branches

Dissatisfied with the reformist environmental movement of the 1970s and 1980s, proponents of "deep ecology" call for a fundamental change in the relationship between humans and the environment. Today's environmental problems, they argue, are rooted in industrial capitalism, which itself is based on the domination of nature. Deep ecology is a new worldview that rejects the notion of atomistic individuals separated from the natural environment. Instead, it views individuals as interconnected and interdependent with other living beings. Within this framework, human beings are " . . . just one particular strand in the web of life."[12] Human beings are not assigned a superior status but rather are placed on equal footing with other living beings. Deep ecology takes an ecocentric view of the world, in that nonhuman life is viewed as having intrinsic value, independent of its usefulness to human beings. It is a political ideology based on the position that nature and wildlife are worthy of moral consideration, and that this principle should govern social, economic, and political relations. In terms of policies, it calls for changes in basic economic, technological, and ideological structures in an effort to preserve and restore ecosystems. Deep ecology in developing countries makes the link between ecological integrity and social justice, and between ecological diversity and cultural diversity. Emphasizing the importance of place and community, developing countries theorists like Vandana Shiva argue that ecology movements must recognize that the issues of sustainability and ecology are intimately linked to issues of justice and equity.[13]

Bioregionalism and ecofeminism are both strands of the deep ecology perspective. These perspectives are radical because they go beyond conservation or anti-pollution legislation and seek to challenge the foundations of existing social, political, and economic systems. Bioregionalism challenges the supposed right of human beings to exploit, develop, and own land. Rejecting the delineation of regions along nation-state boundaries, proponents of bio-regionalism advocate the "remapping" of regions and cultures along natural elements of the ecosystem, including rivers, mountain ranges, and forests rather than man-made structures, such as cities and roads. At its core, bioregionalism argues that societies and communities must get in touch with the natural rhythms of the land to ensure social and economic development occurs at a pace that protects and maintains the long-term health of the local ecology. It emphasizes the attachment of distinct regional cultures and identities to their surrounding natural environment.[14] Bioregionalism favours protectionist policies that minimize world trade and encourages the economic self-sufficiency of a region.

As the name suggests, ecofeminism represents the intersection of feminism and environmentalism. Like deep ecology, it seeks to develop a new worldview in an effort to stop the destruction of the environment and transform the relationship between humans and non-humans. However, ecofeminists argue that the root cause of environmental degradation is not anthropocentrism, but rather patriarchy. In a patriarchal society, the domination of nature and the subordination of women are interconnected. Recognizing the historical connection between nature and women, ecofeminists regard industrialization and the notion of technological progress as male projects meant to control both the natural environment and women.[15] Ecofeminists call for a radical transformation of society, which entails dismantling the hierarchal relations of patriarchy and replacing them with a worldview that recognizes the intrinsic value of other peoples, animals, and the physical environment.

ENVIRONMENTALISM IN CONTEMPORARY POLITICS

Environmentalism and the movements it inspired have helped shape our understanding of the relationship between human beings and the natural environment. It has politicized environmental problems and, in so doing, has provided a fundamental critique of contemporary politics and economics. In many countries, influential environmental pressure groups have appeared on the political scene to lobby governments and political parties to adopt ecological ideas. Green parties have also emerged to influence the political agenda through electoral politics. For example, in the 1980s the German Green Party, through coalition governments, was instrumental in the development of environmental policy in that country. In the past decades, international institutions and forums devoted to environmental matters have emerged, such as the United Nations Environmental Program. At the domestic level, environmental principles such as sustainable development have been incorporated in the institutional framework of government. Government agencies and departments such as the Environmental Protection Agency in the United States and Environment Canada have been established to oversee environmental issues in their countries.

Today, environmentalism faces a number of different challenges. Environmentalists argue that economic globalization and the rise of international and regional trade agreements, like the North American Free Trade Agreement, undermine the ability of governments to adequately protect the environment. They predict that environmental standards will diminish as governments strive to harmonize their countries' policies to facilitate trade. Deep ecologists also argue that government policy in the area of the environment has tended to favour economic interests rather than the needs of ecosystems. In recent years, critics of environmentalism and its movement also question the seriousness of environmental problems such as global warming. They dispute the scientific evidence that shows the occurrence of environmental degradation and argue that new technology can reverse any damage done to the environment.

Despite these internal and external challenges, environmentalism continues to influence both the lifestyles of ordinary citizens and government policy. Environmental concerns have become part of the political discourse and have become embedded in domestic and international institutions. The salience of environmentalism as an ideology and political project can only increase in the future as environmental problems become more global in nature.

FEMINISM, ENVIRONMENTALISM, AND THE LEFT–RIGHT DEBATE: CONCLUDING REMARKS

This chapter provided an overview of two recent arrivals to the ideological spectrum: feminism and environmentalism. Both ideologies embody a diversity of perspectives that do not fall neatly on the left–right continuum. For example, some feminist and environmental branches are reformist in nature while others call for a more radical transformation of both political institutions and civil society. Some branches call for greater state involvement in resolving issues related to gender and the environment while others seek to dismantle the state. Indeed, the left–right spectrum is rejected altogether by deep ecologists, who view it as an ideological construct of industrialization. For the most part, however, environmentalism and feminism continue to engage with the ideologies of the past by contributing to the storefront of ideas and introducing new debates in the political discourse.

ENDNOTES

1. Chandra Talpade Mohanty, "Introduction," and "Under Western Eyes," in *Third World Women and the Politics of Feminism*, eds. Chandra Talpade Mohanty, Ann Russo, and Lourdes Torres (Bloomington and Indianapolis: Indiana UP, 1991).
2. Susan Moller Okin, "Gender, the Public and the Private," in *Feminism and Politics*, ed. Anne Phillips (New York: Oxford University Press, 1989).
3. Rosemarie Tong, *Feminist Thought: A Comprehensive Introduction* (Boulder: Westview Press, 1989).
4. Lorraine Code, "Feminist Theory," in *Changing Patterns: Women in Canada*, eds. Sandra Burt, Lorraine Code, and Lindsay Dorney (Toronto: McClelland & Stewart, 1993).
5. Peggy Morton, "Women's Work Is Never Done," in *Women Unite! An Anthology of the Canadian Women's Movement* (Toronto: Canadian Women's Educational Press, 1972).
6. Code, 1993.
7. Kate Millet, *Sexual Politics* (London: Sphere, 1971).
8. Roger Gibbins and Loleen Youngman, *Mindscapes: Political Ideologies Towards the 21st Century* (Toronto: McGraw-Hill Ryerson Limited, 1996).
9. World Commission on Environment and Development, *Our Common Future* (Oxford, U.K.: Oxford University Press, 1987), 43.
10. Rachel Carson, *Silent Spring* (Boston: Houghton Mifflin, 1962).
11. Otherwise known as the Brundtland Commission.
12. Arne Naess, "The Shallow and the Deep, Long-Range Ecology Movement: A Summary," *Inquiry* 16 (1973).
13. Fritjof Capra, *Green Politics* (Santa Fe: Bear, 1986).
14. Vandana Shiva, *Close to Home: Women Reconnect Ecology, Health and Development Worldwide* (Philadelphia: New Society Publishers, 1994).
15. Judith Plant, "Searching for Common Ground," in *Reweaving the World: The Emergence of Ecofeminism* (San Francisco: Sierra Club Books, 1990).

READINGS

As the chapter indicated, feminism encompasses a diversity of perspectives regarding the nature of women's oppression and the appropriate course of action for their emancipation. Liberal feminism emphasizes the autonomy of women as rational beings and calls for equal opportunities in all spheres of life, while Marxist-socialist feminists look to capitalism as the source of women's oppression. Radical feminism views patriarchy as the real culprit and seeks to fundamentally transform culture and social institutions to liberate women from male domination. The diversity of feminist perspectives and the debate that ensues between them are represented in the two selected readings drawn from two different time periods. Mary Wollstonecraft's *A Vindication of the Rights of Woman* (1792) advances the liberal argument that women, being as equally rational as men, should have access to the same educational opportunities. The excerpt from bell hooks' book, *Feminist Theory: From Margin to Center* offers a critique of liberal feminism and calls for a more radical transformation of society.

Written three years after the issuing of the "Declaration of the Rights of Man" by French revolutionaries, Wollstonecraft's *A Vindication of the Rights of Woman* was a protest against the subjection of women. She makes the case for women's equality by appealing to liberal ideals of reason and individual autonomy. She argues that women, relegated to their homes, are denied opportunities to develop and exercise their rational and moral capacities. Women are not naturally submissive or emotional beings; rather, they have been constructed as such by their lack of educational training. Wollstonecraft contends that educated and self-reliant women serve the interests of their families and of society in general.

In "Feminism: A Movement to End Sexist Oppression," hooks discusses the problem of arriving at a universal definition of feminism. She argues that feminism has typically been characterized as a movement striving for social equality between men and women. Its emancipatory project has focused on the liberal ideals of personal freedom and individual autonomy. This definition of feminism, she contends, is problematic for a number of reasons. First, its emphasis on equality speaks to the needs of white, middle-class women and ignores discrimination based on race and class. Second, its emphasis on personal freedoms works to depoliticize the movement. hooks also takes issue with Radical feminism's aim to develop women-centred communities that exclude men, arguing that this vision does not reflect the experiences of all women. Informed by a Socialist feminist perspective, hooks reminds readers that feminism is, above all else, a radical political movement aimed at ending sexist oppression. As such, it should be cognizant of the diversity of women's experience and the importance of class and race in the oppression of women.

This chapter also explored the different branches of environmentalism, including deep ecology and ecofeminism, which makes the link between the protection of ecosystems and social justice and cultural survival, especially as it pertains to women and societies in developing countries. The ecofeminist position is articulated in an excerpt from Vandana Shiva's 1988 book, *Staying Alive*. Shiva argues that the Enlightenment ideal of scientific progress has led to the exploitation of nature, women, and societies in the developing world. Scientific knowledge and economic development are regarded as patriarchal projects, aimed at dominating both nature and women. According to Shiva, the ecofeminist movements in countries like India provide a point of resistance to this project of domination. They have offered an alternative conception of the environment that views it not as a resource to be exploited but as the source of life and survival.

A VINDICATION OF THE RIGHTS OF WOMAN

Mary Wollstonecraft

. . . . Independence I have long considered as the grand blessing of life, the basis of every virtue—and independence I will ever secure by contracting my wants, though I were to live on a barren heath.

It is then an affection for the whole human race that makes my pen dart rapidly along to support what I believe to be the cause of virtue: and the same motive leads me earnestly to wish to see woman placed in a station in which she would advance, instead of retarding, the progress of those glorious principles that give a substance to morality. My opinion, indeed, respecting the rights and duties of woman, seems to flow so

naturally from these simple principles, that I think it scarcely possible, but that some of the enlarged minds who formed your admirable constitution, will coincide with me.[1]

***

Contending for the rights of woman, my main argument is built on this simple principle, that if she be not prepared by education to become the companion of man, she will stop the progress of knowledge and virtue; for truth must be common to all, or it will be inefficacious with respect to its influence on general practice. And how can woman be expected to co-operate unless she know why she ought to be virtuous? unless freedom strengthen her reason till she comprehend her duty, and see in what manner it is connected with her real good? If children are to be educated to understand the true principle of patriotism, their mother must be a patriot; and the love of mankind, from which an orderly train of virtues spring, can only be produced by considering the moral and civil interest of mankind; but the education and situation of woman, at present, shuts her out from such investigations.

In this work I have produced many arguments, which to me were conclusive, to prove that the prevailing notion respecting a sexual character was subversive of morality, and I have contended, that to render the human body and mind more perfect, chastity must more universally prevail, and that chastity will never be respected in the male world till the person of a woman is not, as it were, idolized, when little virtue or sense embellish it with the grand traces of mental beauty, or the interesting simplicity of affection.

Consider, Sir, dispassionately, these observations—for a glimpse of this truth seemed to open before you when you observed, "that to see one half of the human race excluded by the other from all participation of government, was a political phaenomenon that, according to abstract principles, it was impossible to explain."[2] If so, on what does your constitution rest?[3] If the abstract rights of man will bear discussion and explanation, those of woman, by a parity of reasoning, will not shrink from the same test: though a different opinion prevails in this country, built on the very arguments which you use to justify the oppression of woman—prescription.

Consider, I address you as a legislator, whether, when men contend for their freedom, and to be allowed to judge for themselves respecting their own happiness, it be not inconsistent and unjust to subjugate women, even though you firmly believe that you are acting in the manner best calculated to promote their happiness? Who made man the exclusive judge, if woman partake with him the gift of reason?

In this style, argue tyrants of every denomination, from the weak king to the weak father of a family; they are all eager to crush reason; yet always assert that they usurp its throne only to be useful. Do you not act a similar part, when you *force* all women, by denying them civil and political rights, to remain immured in their families groping in the dark? for surely, Sir, you will not assert, that a duty can be binding which is not founded on reason? If indeed this be their destination, arguments may be drawn from reason: and thus augustly supported, the more understanding women acquire, the more they will be attached to their duty—comprehending it—for unless they comprehend it, unless their morals be fixed on the same immutable principle as those of man, no authority can make them discharge it in a virtuous manner. They may be convenient slaves, but slavery will have its constant effect, degrading the master and the abject dependent.

But, if women are to be excluded, without having a voice, from a participation of the natural rights of mankind, prove first, to ward off the charge of injustice and inconsistency, that they want reason—else this flaw in your New Constitution will ever shew that man must, in some shape, act like a tyrant, and tyranny, in whatever part of society it rears its brazen front, will ever undermine morality.

I have repeatedly asserted, and produced what appeared to me irrefragable arguments drawn from matters of fact, to prove my assertion, that women cannot, by force, be confined to domestic concerns; for they will, however ignorant, intermeddle with more weighty affairs, neglecting private duties only to disturb, by cunning tricks, the orderly plans of reason which rise above their comprehension.

***

The education of women has, of late, been more attended to than formerly; yet they are still reckoned a frivolous sex, and ridiculed or pitied by the writers who endeavour by satire or instruction to improve them. It is acknowledged that they spend many of the first years of their lives in acquiring a smattering of accomplishments; meanwhile strength of body and mind are sacrificed to libertine notions of beauty, to the desire of establishing themselves,—the only way women can rise in the world,—by marriage. And this desire making mere animals of them, when they marry they act as such children may be expected to act:—they dress; they paint, and nickname God's creatures.[4]—Surely these weak beings are only fit for a seraglio!—Can they be expected to govern a family with judgment, or take care of the poor babes whom they bring into the world?

***

Women are, in fact, so much degraded by mistaken notions of female excellence, that I do not mean to add a paradox when I assert, that this artificial weakness produces a propensity to tyrannize, and gives birth to cunning, the natural opponent of strength which leads them to play off those contemptible infantine airs that undermine esteem even whilst they excite desire. Let men become more chaste and modest, and if women do not grow wiser in the same ratio, it will be clear that they have weaker understandings. It seems scarcely necessary to say, that I now speak of the sex in general. Many individuals have more sense than their male relatives; and, as nothing preponderates where there is a constant struggle for an equilibrium, without it has[5] naturally more gravity, some women govern their husbands without degrading themselves, because intellect will always govern.

***

In the middle rank of life, to continue the comparison, men, in their youth, are prepared for professions, and marriage is not considered as the grand feature in their lives; whilst women, on the contrary, have no other scheme to sharpen their faculties. It is not business, extensive plans, or any of the excursive flights of ambition, that engross their attention; no, their thoughts are not employed in rearing such noble structures. To rise in the world, and have the liberty of running from pleasure to pleasure, they must marry advantageously, and to this object their time is sacrificed, and their persons often legally prostituted. A man when he enters any profession has his eye steadily fixed on some future advantage (and the mind gains great strength by having all its efforts directed to one point), and, full of his business, pleasure is considered as mere relaxation; whilst women seek for pleasure as the main purpose of existence. In fact, from the education, which they receive from society, the love of pleasure may be said to govern them all; but does this prove that there is a sex in souls? It would be just as rational to declare that the courtiers in France, when a

destructive system of despotism had formed their character, were not men, because liberty, virtue, and humanity, were sacrificed to pleasure and vanity.—Fatal passions, which have ever domineered over the *whole* race!

The same love of pleasure, fostered by the whole tendency of their education, gives a trifling turn to the conduct of women in most circumstances: for instance, they are ever anxious about secondary things; and on the watch for adventures, instead of being occupied by duties.

A man, when he undertakes a journey, has, in general, the end in view; a woman thinks more of the incidental occurrences, the strange things that may possibly occur on the road; the impression that she may make on her fellow-travellers; and, above all, she is anxiously intent on the care of the finery that she carries with her, which is more than ever a part of herself, when going to figure on a new scene; when, to use an apt French turn of expression, she is going to produce a sensation.— Can dignity of mind exist with such trivial cares?

In short, women, in general, as well as the rich of both sexes, have acquired all the follies and vices of civilization, and missed the useful fruit. It is not necessary for me always to premise, that I speak of the condition of the whole sex, leaving exceptions out of the question. Their senses are inflamed, and their understandings neglected, consequently they become the prey of their senses, delicately termed sensibility, and are blown about by every momentary gust of feeling. Civilized women are, therefore, so weakened by false refinement, that, respecting morals, their condition is much below what it would be were they left in a state nearer to nature. Ever restless and anxious, their over exercised sensibility not only renders them uncomfortable themselves, but troublesome, to use a soft phrase, to others. All their thoughts turn on things calculated to excite emotion; and feeling, when they should reason, their conduct is unstable, and their opinions are wavering—not the wavering produced by deliberation or progressive views, but by contradictory emotions. By fits and starts they are warm in many pursuits; yet this warmth, never concentrated into perseverance, soon exhausts itself; exhaled by its own heat, or meeting with some other fleeting passion, to which reason has never given any specific gravity, neutrality ensues. Miserable, indeed, must be that being whose cultivation of mind has only tended to inflame its passions! A distinction should be made between inflaming and strengthening them. The passions thus pampered, whilst the judgment is left unformed, what can be expected to ensue?—Undoubtedly, a mixture of madness and folly!

This observation should not be confined to the *fair* sex; however, at present, I only mean to apply it to them.

Novels, music, poetry, and gallantry, all tend to make women the creatures of sensation, and their character is thus formed in the mould of folly during the time they are acquiring accomplishments, the only improvement they are excited, by their station in society, to acquire. This overstretched sensibility naturally relaxes the other powers of the mind, and prevents intellect from attaining that sovereignty which it ought to attain to render a rational creature useful to others, and content with its own station: for the exercise of the understanding, as life advances, is the only method pointed out by nature to calm the passions.

Satiety has a very different effect, and I have often been forcibly struck by an emphatical description of damnation:—when the spirit is represented as continually hovering with abortive eagerness round the defiled body, unable to enjoy any thing without the organs of sense. Yet, to their senses, are women made slaves, because it is by their sensibility that they obtain present power.

And will moralists pretend to assert, that this is the condition in which one half of the human race should be encouraged to remain with listless inactivity and stupid acquiescence? Kind instructors! what were we created for? To remain, it may be said, innocent; they mean in a state of childhood.—We might as well never have been born, unless it were necessary that we should be created to enable man to acquire the noble privilege of reason, the power of discerning good from evil, whilst we lie down in the dust from whence we were taken, never to rise again.—

***

In the regulation of a family, in the education of children, understanding, in an unsophisticated sense, is particularly required: strength both of body and mind; yet the men who, by their writings, have most earnestly laboured to domesticate women, have endeavoured, by arguments dictated by a gross appetite, which satiety had rendered fastidious, to weaken their bodies and cramp their minds. But, if even by these sinister methods they really *persuaded* women, by working on their feelings, to stay at home, and fulfil the duties of a mother and mistress of a family, I should cautiously oppose opinions that led women to right conduct, by prevailing on them to make the discharge of such important duties the main business of life, though reason were insulted. Yet, and I appeal to experience, if by neglecting the understanding they be as much, nay, more detached from these domestic employments, than they could be by the most serious intellectual pursuit, though it may be observed, that the mass of mankind will never vigorously pursue an intellectual object,[6] I may be allowed to infer that reason is absolutely necessary to enable a woman to perform any duty properly, and I must again repeat, that sensibility is not reason.

***

With respect to women, when they receive a careful education, they are either made fine ladies, brimful of sensibility, and teeming with capricious fancies; or mere notable women.[7] The latter are often friendly, honest creatures, and have a shrewd kind of good sense joined with worldly prudence, that often render them more useful members of society than the fine sentimental lady, though they possess neither greatness of mind nor taste. The intellectual world is shut against them; take them out of their family or neighbourhood, and they stand still; the mind finding no employment, for literature affords a fund of amusement which they have never sought to relish, but frequently to despise. The sentiments and taste of more cultivated minds appear ridiculous, even in those whom chance and family connections have led them to love; but in mere acquaintance they think it all affectation.

A man of sense can only love such a woman on account of her sex, and respect her, because she is a trusty servant. He lets her, to preserve his own peace, scold the servants, and go to church in clothes made of the very best materials. A man of her own size of understanding would, probably, not agree so well with her; for he might wish to encroach on her prerogative, and manage some domestic concerns himself. Yet women, whose minds are not enlarged by cultivation, or the natural selfishness of sensibility expanded by reflection, are very unfit to manage a family; for, by an undue stretch of power, they are always tyrannizing to support a superiority that only rests on the arbitrary distinction of fortune.

***

It is a melancholy truth; yet such is the blessed effect of civilization! the most respectable women are the most oppressed; and, unless they have understandings far superiour to the common run of understandings, taking in both sexes, they must, from being treated like contemptible beings, become contemptible. How many women thus waste life away the prey of discontent, who might have practised as physicians, regulated a farm, managed a shop, and stood erect, supported by their own industry, instead of hanging their heads surcharged with the dew of sensibility, that consumes the beauty to which it at first gave luster.

***

Would men but generously snap our chains, and be content with rational fellowship instead of slavish obedience, they would find us more observant daughters, more affectionate sisters, more faithful wives, more reasonable mothers—in a word, better citizens. We should then love them with true affection, because we should learn to respect ourselves; and the peace of mind of a worthy man would not be interrupted by the idle vanity of his wife, nor the babes sent to nestle in a strange bosom,[8] having never found a home in their mother's.

***

Asserting the rights which women in common with men ought to contend for, I have not attempted to extenuate their faults; but to prove them to be the natural consequence of their education and station in society. If so, it is reasonable to suppose that they will change their character, and correct their vices and follies, when they are allowed to be free in a physical, moral, and civil sense.[9]

Let woman share the rights and she will emulate the virtues of man; for she must grow more perfect when emancipated, or justify the authority that chains such a weak being to her duty.

Reading Notes

1. Parts of the French Constitution of 1791 had been ratified as early as 1789. It had been commissioned as a result of the Tennis Court Oath of June 20, 1789, when the National Assembly vowed not to dissolve until the country had a new constitution.

2. Possibly a liberal translation from Talleyrand's *Rapport*, op. cit., p. 9: "sur quel principe l'un des deux pourroit-il en être désherité par la Société protectrice des droits de tous?"

3. In France's 1791 Constitution only males over twenty-five were citizens. Women were not to get the vote until 1944.

4. Hamlet speaks to Ophelia: "You jig, you amble, and you lisp, and nickname God's creatures, and make your wantonness your ignorance." *Hamlet* III.i.150.

5. We would probably say, "without its having."

6. "The mass of mankind are rather the slaves of their appetites than of their passions" [Wollstonecraft's note].

7. "Notable" women are industrious and energetic housewives.

8. It was common practice for babies to be fed by wet-nurses rather than their own mothers.

9. "I had further enlarged on the advantages which might reasonably be expected to result from an improvement in female manners, towards the general reformation of society; but it appeared to me that such reflections would more properly close the last volume" [Wollstonecraft's note].

FEMINISM: A MOVEMENT TO END SEXIST OPPRESSION

bell hooks

A central problem within feminist discourse has been our inability to either arrive at a consensus of opinion about what feminism is or accept definition(s) that could serve as points of unification. Without agreed upon definition(s) we lack a sound foundation on which to construct theory or engage in overall meaningful praxis. Expressing her frustrations with the absence of clear definitions in a recent essay, "Towards A Revolutionary Ethics," Carmen Vasquez comments:

> We can't even agree on what a "Feminist" is, never mind what she would believe in and how she defines the principles that constitute honor among us. In key with the American capitalist obsession for individualism and anything goes so long as it gets you what you want. Feminism in American has come to mean anything you like, honey. There are as many definitions of Feminism as there are feminists, some of my sisters say, with a chuckle. I don't think it's funny.

It is not funny. It indicates a growing disinterest in feminism as a radical political movement. It is a despairing gesture expressive of the belief that solidarity between women is not possible. It is a sign that the political naïveté which has traditionally characterized woman's lot in male-dominated culture abounds.

Most people in the United States think of feminism or the more commonly used term "women's lib" as a movement that aims to make women the social equals of men. This broad definition, popularized by the media and mainstream segments of the movement, raises problematic questions. Since men are not equals in white supremacist, capitalist, patriarchal class structure, which men do women want to be equal to? Do women share a common vision of what equality means? Implicit in this simplistic definition of women's liberation is a dismissal of race and class as factors that, in conjunction with sexism, determine the extent to which an individual will be discriminated against, exploited, or oppressed. Bourgeois white women interested in women's rights issues have been satisfied with simple definitions for obvious reasons. Rhetorically placing themselves in the same social category as oppressed women, they were not anxious to call attention to race and class privilege.

Women in lower class and poor groups, particularly those who are nonwhite, would not have defined women's liberation as women gaining social equality with men since they are continually reminded in their everyday lives that all women do not share a common social status. Concurrently, they know that many males in their social groups are exploited and oppressed. Knowing that men in their groups do not have social, political, and economic power, they would not deem it liberatory to share their social status. While they are aware that sexism enables men in their respective groups to have privileges denied them, they are more likely to see exaggerated expressions of male chauvinism among their peers as stemming from the male's sense of himself as powerless and ineffectual in relation to ruling male groups, rather than an expression of an overall privileged social status. From the very onset of the women's liberation movement, these women were suspicious of feminism precisely because they recognized the limitations inherent in its definition. They recognized the possibility that feminism defined as social equality with men might easily become a movement that would primarily affect the social standing of white women in middle and upper class groups while affecting only in a very marginal way the social status of working class and poor women. [. . .]

Many women are reluctant to advocate feminism because they are uncertain about the meaning of the term. Other women from exploited and oppressed ethnic groups dismiss the term because they do not wish to be perceived as supporting a racist movement; feminism is often equated with white women's rights effort. Large numbers of women see feminism as synonymous with lesbianism; their homophobia leads them to reject association with any group identified as pro-lesbian. Some women fear the word "feminism" because they shun identification with any political movement, especially one perceived as radical. Of course there are women who do not wish to be associated with women's rights movement in any form so they reject and oppose feminist movement. Most women are more familiar with negative perspectives on "women's lib" than the positive significations of feminism. It is this term's positive political significance and power that we must now struggle to recover and maintain.

Currently feminism seems to be a term without any clear significance. The "anything goes" approach to the definition of the word has rendered it practically meaningless. What is meant by "anything goes" is usually that any woman who wants social equality with men regardless of her political perspective (she can be a conservative right-winger or a nationalist communist) can label herself feminist. Most attempts at defining feminism reflect the class nature of the movement. Definitions are usually liberal in origin and focus on the individual woman's right to freedom and self-determination. In Barbara Berg's *The Remembered Gate: Origins of American Feminism*, she defines feminism as a "broad movement embracing numerous phases of woman's emancipation." However, her emphasis is on women gaining greater individual freedom. Expanding on the above definition, Berg adds:

> It is the freedom to decide her own destiny; freedom from sex-determined role; freedom from society's oppressive restrictions; freedom to express her thoughts fully and to convert them freely into action. Feminism demands the acceptance of woman's right to individual conscience and judgment. It postulates that woman's essential worth stems from her common humanity and does not depend on the other relationships of her life.

This definition of feminism is almost apolitical in tone; yet it is the type of definition many liberal women find appealing. It evokes a very romantic notion of personal freedom which is more acceptable than a definition that emphasizes radical political action.

Many feminist radicals now know that neither a feminism that focuses on woman as an autonomous human being worthy of personal freedom nor one that focuses on the attainment of equality of opportunity with men can rid

society of sexism and male domination. Feminism is a struggle to end sexist oppression. Therefore, it is necessarily a struggle to eradicate the ideology of domination that permeates Western culture on various levels as well as a commitment to reorganizing society so that the self-development of people can take precedence over imperialism, economic expansion, and material desires. Defined in this way, it is unlikely that women would join feminist movement simply because we are biologically the same. A commitment to feminism so defined would demand that each individual participant acquire a critical political consciousness based on ideas and beliefs.

All too often the slogan "the personal is political" (which was first used to stress that woman's everyday reality is informed and shaped by politics and is necessarily political) became a means of encouraging women to think that the experience of discrimination, exploitation, or oppression automatically corresponded with an understanding of the ideological and institutional apparatus shaping one's social status. As a consequence, many women who had not fully examined their situation never developed a sophisticated understanding of their political reality and its relationship to that of women as a collective group. They were encouraged to focus on giving voice to personal experience. Like revolutionaries working to change the lot of colonized people globally, it is necessary for feminist activists to stress that the ability to see and describe one's own reality is a significant step in the long process of self-recovery; but it is only a beginning. When women internalized the idea that describing their own woe was synonymous with developing a critical political consciousness, the progress of feminist movement was stalled. Starting from incomplete perspectives, it is not surprising that theories and strategies developed that were collectively inadequate and misguided. To correct this inadequacy in past analysis, we must now encourage women to develop a comprehensive understanding of women's political reality. Broader perspectives can only emerge as we examine both the personal that is political, the politics of society as a whole, and global revolutionary politics. [. . .]

When feminism is defined in such a way that it calls attention to the diversity of women's social and political reality, it centralizes the experiences all women, especially the women whose social conditions have been least written about, studied, or changed by political movements. When we cease to focus on the simplistic stance "men are the enemy," we are compelled to examine systems of domination and our role in their maintenance and perpetuation. Lack of adequate definition made it easy for bourgeois women, whether liberal or radical in perspective, to maintain their dominance over the leadership of the movement and its direction. This hegemony continues to exist in most feminist organizations. Exploited and oppressed groups of women are usually encouraged by those in power to feel that their situation is hopeless, that they can do nothing to break the pattern of domination. Given such socialization, these women have often felt that our only response to white, bourgeois, hegemonic dominance of feminist movement is to trash, reject, or dismiss feminism. This reaction is in no way threatening to the women who wish to maintain control over the direction of feminist theory and praxis. They prefer us to be silent, passively accepting their ideas. They prefer us speaking against "them" rather than developing our own ideas about feminist movement.

Feminism is the struggle to end sexist oppression. Its aim is not to benefit solely any specific group of women, any particular race or class of women. It does not privilege women over men. It has the power to transform in a meaningful way all our lives. Most importantly, feminism is neither a lifestyle nor a ready-made identity or role one can step into. Diverting energy from feminist movement that aims to change society, many women concentrate on the development of a counter-culture, a woman-centered world wherein participants have little contact with men. Such attempts do not indicate respect or concern for the vast majority of women who are unable to integrate their cultural expressions with the visions offered by alternative woman-centered communities. [. . .]

The willingness to see feminism as a lifestyle choice rather than a political commitment reflects the class nature of the movement. It is not surprising that the vast majority of women who equate feminism with alternative lifestyle are from middle class backgrounds, unmarried, college-educated, often students who are without many of the social and economic responsibilities that working class and poor women who are laborers, parents, homemakers, and wives confront daily. [. . .]

To emphasize that engagement with feminist struggle as political commitment we could avoid using the phrase "I am a feminist" (a linguistic structure designed to refer to some personal aspect of identity and self-definition) and could state "I advocate feminism." Because there has been undue emphasis placed on feminism as an identity or lifestyle, people usually resort to stereotyped perspectives on feminism. Deflecting attention away from stereotypes is necessary if we are to revise our strategy and direction. I have found that saying "I am a feminist" usually means I am plugged into preconceived notions of identity, role, or behaviour. When I say "I advocate feminism" the response is usually "what is feminism?" A phrase like "I advocate" does not imply the kind of absolutism that is suggested by "I am." It does not engage us in the either/or dualistic thinking that is the central ideological component of all systems of domination in Western society. It implies that a choice has been made, that commitment to feminism is an act of will. It does not suggest that by committing oneself to feminism, the possibility of supporting other political movements is negated. [. . .]

The shift in expression from "I am a feminist" to "I advocate feminism" could serve as a useful strategy for eliminating the focus on identity and lifestyle. It could serve as a way women who are concerned about feminism as well as other political movements could express their support while avoiding linguistic structures that give primacy to one particular group. It would also encourage greater exploration in feminist theory.

The shift in definition away from notions of social equality towards an emphasis on ending sexist oppression leads to a shift in attitudes in regard to the development of theory. Given the class nature of feminist movement so far, as well as racial hierarchies, developing theory (the guiding set of beliefs and principles that become the basis for action) has been a task particularly subject to the hegemonic dominance of white academic women. This has led many women outside the privileged race/class group to see the focus on developing theory, even the very use of the term, as a concern that functions only to reinforce the power of the elite group. Such reactions reinforce the sexist/racist/classist notion that developing theory is the domain of the white intellectual. Privileged white women active in feminist movement, whether liberal or radical in perspective, encourage black women to contribute "experiential" work, personal life stories. Personal experiences are important to feminist movement but they cannot take the place of theory. [. . .]

Defining feminism as a movement to end sexist oppression is crucial for the development of theory because it is a starting point indicating the direction of exploration and analysis.

The foundation of future feminist struggle must be solidly based on a recognition of the need to eradicate the underlying cultural basis and causes of sexism and other forms of group oppression. Without challenging and changing these philosophical structures, no feminist reforms will have a long range impact.

STAYING ALIVE

Vandana Shiva

The Age of Enlightenment, and the theory of progress to which it gave rise, was centred on the sacredness of two categories: modern scientific knowledge and economic development. Somewhere along the way, the unbridled pursuit of progress, guided by science and development, began to destroy life without any assessment of how fast and how much of the diversity of life on this planet is disappearing. The act of living and of celebrating and conserving life in all its diversity—in people and in nature—seems to have been sacrificed to progress, and the sanctity of life been substituted by the sanctity of science and development.

Throughout the world, a new questioning is growing, rooted in the experience of those for whom the spread of what was called "Enlightenment" has been the spread of darkness, of the extinction of life and life-enhancing processes. A new awareness is growing that is questioning the sanctity of science and development and revealing that these are not universal categories of progress, but the special projects of modern western patriarchy. This book has grown out of my involvement with women's struggles for survival in India over the last decade. It is informed both by the suffering and insights of those who struggle to sustain and conserve life, and whose struggles question the meaning of a progress, a science, a development which destroys life and threatens survival.

The death of nature is central to this threat to survival. The earth is rapidly dying: her forests are dying, her soils are dying, her waters are dying, her air is dying. Tropical forests, the creators of the world's climate, the cradle of the world's vegetational wealth, are being bulldozed, burnt, ruined or submerged. . . .

With the destruction of forests, water and land, we are losing our life-support systems. This destruction is taking place in the name of "development" and progress, but there must be something seriously wrong with a concept of progress that threatens survival itself. The violence to nature, which seems intrinsic to the dominant development model, is also associated with violence to women who depend on nature for drawing sustenance for themselves, their families, their societies. This violence against nature and women is built into the very mode of perceiving both, and forms the basis of the current development paradigm. This book is an attempt to articulate how rural Indian woman [*sic*], who are still embedded in nature, experience and perceive ecological destruction and its causes, and how they have conceived and initiated processes to arrest the destruction of nature and begin its regeneration. From the diverse and specific grounds of the experience of ecological destruction arises a common identification of its causes in the development process and the view of nature with which it is legitimized. This book focuses on science and development as patriarchal projects not as a denial of other sources of patriarchy, such as religion, but because they are thought to be class, culture and gender neutral.

Seen from the experiences of Third World women, the modes of thinking and action that pass for science and development, respectively, are not universal and humanly inclusive, as they are made out to be; modern science and development are projects of male, western origin, both historically and ideologically. They are the latest and most brutal expression of a patriarchal ideology which is threatening to annihilate nature and the entire human species. The rise of a patriarchal science of nature took place in Europe during the fifteenth and seventeenth centuries as the scientific revolution. During the same period, the closely-related industrial revolution laid the foundations of a patriarchal mode of economic development in industrial capitalism. Contemporary science and development conserve the ideological root and biases of the scientific and industrial revolutions even as they unfold into new areas of activity and new domains of subjugation.

The scientific revolution in Europe transformed nature from *terra mater* into a machine and a source of raw material; with this transformation it removed all ethical and cognitive constraints against its violation and exploitation. The industrial revolution converted economics from the prudent management of resources for sustenance and basic needs satisfaction into a process of commodity production for profit maximization. Industrialism created a limitless appetite for resource exploitation, and modern science provided the ethical and cognitive licence to make such exploitation possible, acceptable—and desirable. The new relationship of man's domination and mastery over nature was thus also associated with new patterns of domination and mastery over women, and their exclusion from participation *as partners* in both science and development.

Contemporary development activity in the Third World superimposes the scientific and economic paradigms created by western, gender-based ideology on communities in other cultures. Ecological destruction and the marginalization of women, we know now, have been the inevitable results of most development programmes and projects based on such paradigms; they violate the integrity of one and destroy the productivity of the other. Women, as victims of the violence of patriarchal forms of development, have risen against it to protect nature and preserve their survival and sustenance. Indian women have been in the forefront of ecological struggles to conserve forests, land and water. They have challenged the western concept of nature as an object of exploitation and have protected her as Prakriti, the living force that supports life. They have challenged the western concept of economics as production of profits and capital accumulation with their own concept of economics as production of sustenance and needs satisfaction. A science that does not respect nature's needs and a development that does not respect people's needs inevitably threaten survival. In their fight to survive the onslaughts of both, women have begun a struggle that challenges the most fundamental categories of western patriarchy—its concepts of nature and women, and of science and development. Their ecological struggle in India is aimed simultaneously at liberating nature from ceaseless exploitation and themselves from limitless marginalization. They are creating a feminist ideology that transcends gender, and a political practice that is humanly inclusive; they are challenging patriarchy's ideological claim to universalism not with another universalizing tendency, but with diversity; and they are challenging the dominant concept of power as violence with the alternative concept of non-violence as power.

***

Inspired by women's struggles for the protection of nature as a condition for human survival, this book goes beyond a statement of women as special victims of the environmental crisis. It attempts to capture and reconstruct those insights and visions that Indian women provide in their struggles for survival, which perceive development and science from outside the categories of modern western patriarchy. These oppositional categories are simultaneously ecological and feminist: they allow the possibility of survival by exposing the parochial basis of science and development and by showing how ecological destruction and the marginalization of women are not inevitable, economically or scientifically.

KEY TERMS

Anthropocentrism   Based on the principle of a human-centred world, where humans are assigned a superior status in their relationship with nature. The natural environment exists to serve the needs of human beings.

Deep Ecology   A branch of environmentalism that views nature and wildlife as worthy of moral consideration, and believes that this principle should govern social, economic, and political relations. It calls for changes in basic economic, technological, and ideological structures in an effort to preserve and restore ecosystems.

Ecocentrism　An organic view of the world that recognizes the interdependence and interconnection between humans and nonhumans.

Environmentalism　An ideology and political project that seeks to protect the quality and continuity of life through the conservation, preservation, or protection of the natural environment and its inhabitants.

Feminism　An ideology and political project based on the belief that men and women are treated unequally socially, politically, and economically. It aims to identify and abolish the sources of women's oppression in all spheres of life.

Gender　As opposed to sex, which refers to physiological differences, gender refers to characteristics of men and women that are socially constructed.

Liberal Feminism　A branch of feminism that seeks equality between men and women. It focuses on equal rights, individualism, liberty, and justice.

Marxist-Socialist Feminism　A branch of feminism that views women's oppression as rooted in both patriarchy and capitalism. Women's emancipation requires the reorganization of institutions found in both the public and private spheres.

Patriarchy　An institutionalized system of male domination and power that subordinates and marginalizes women. Patriarchy is maintained by a number of institutions and processes in society, including motherhood, compulsory sexuality, notions of femininity, and the traditional nuclear family.

Radical Feminism　A branch of feminism that regards patriarchy as the root of all forms of oppression. It focuses on the link between biology and women's status in society. Proponents call for radical social change.

Shallow Ecology　A branch of environmentalism that seeks to achieve short-term environmental objectives within existing institutions and processes.

FURTHER READINGS

Diamond, Irene, and Gloria Feman Orenstein, eds. *Reweaving the World: The Emergence of Ecofeminism.* San Francisco: Sierra Club Books, 1990.

Dobson, Andrew, ed. *The Green Reader.* London: André Deutsch Limited, 1991.

hooks, bell. *Feminist Theory: From Margin to Center.* Cambridge, MA: South End Press, 2000.

Phillips, Anne, ed. *Feminism and Politics.* Oxford: Oxford University Press, 1998.

Tong, Rosemarie. *Feminist Thought: A Comprehensive Introduction.* Boulder and San Francisco: Westview Press, 1989.

Torgerson, Douglas. *The Promise of Green Politics: Environmentalism and the Public Sphere.* Durham: Duke University Press, 1999.

WEB LINKS

Green Party of Canada:
www.green.ca

The United Nations Framework Convention on Climate Change—The Convention and Kyoto
Protocol:
http://unfccc.int/resource/convkp.html

Status of Women Canada:
www.swc-cfc.gc.ca

The Feminist Theory Website:
www.cddc.vt.edu/feminism

Women in Politics site of the Inter-Parliamentary Union:
www.ipu.org/iss-e/women.htm

PART 3

POLITICS AS INSTITUTIONS

An age-old question in the study of politics is whether and how institutions make a difference in political life. The central aim of this section is to introduce the reader to the diversity and consequences of political institutions and state–society relations. Chapter 8 opens with a discussion of the rise of the modern state in the West and compares it with processes of state formation in the non-Western world. Chapters 9 and 10 emphasize that sometimes the same types of institutions may lead to very different outcomes depending on the socio-cultural context in which they are embedded. These chapters address the variations and consequences of three political institutions: federalism, political parties and the electoral system, and presidential versus parliamentary forms of government. The discussion also demonstrates that political scientists do not have a unified vision of what institutions are and how they exert their influence. Chapter 10 on federalism, for instance, emphasizes the view of institutions as products of historical forces, whereas Chapters 9 and 11 on presidential and parliamentary forms, and electoral reforms, present institutions as mere rules of the political game that impose constraints on the players. Here our objective is to make readers aware of two facts: (1) there is a remarkable degree of diversity that characterizes the world of political institutions; and (2) institutional design has specific consequences. Chapter 12 addresses the differing aspects of state–society relations, particularly the role played by political actors such as the elites and interest groups. Here we also examine the role of civil society.

CHAPTER 8

THE STATE

Despite the forces of globalization sweeping through every nook and cranny of our world, states remain very familiar, though sometimes problematic, political organizations. Whether we are travelling or following world events, states—their borders, institutions, symbols, and disputes—preoccupy us in many different ways. This chapter explores the dynamics through which modern states emerged in the West and in the rest of the world. It traces the complex processes that led to the rise of the modern state in the West, underscoring the link inherent in this very process between state making and war making. This is followed by an exploration of the pattern of state formation in the so-called developing world, with particular emphasis placed on the role played by colonialism as an agent of state formation. An appreciation of the impact of colonialism in this latter process allows us to understand the historical causes of the contemporary political instability in many parts of the developing world.

STATE FORMATION IN THE WEST

The modern state is a creature of the Peace of Westphalia (1648). A series of treaties ending the Thirty Years' War, the Peace of Westphalia was signed by the Holy Roman Emperor Ferdinand III, other German princes, France, and Sweden. It established a system of sovereign nation-states, each claiming absolute autonomy in the administration of its domestic affairs. Albeit increasingly challenged by the multiple forces of globalization, the sovereign "Westphalian state" has been the hallmark of the international system for some time now. Although we tend to take the existence of contemporary states as a historical given, the process by which states emerged in the modern world was both protracted and bloody. In his seminal work on this topic, Charles Tilly identifies three main features specific to those areas where national states first emerged in Western Europe in the seventeenth century that, Tilly contends, played a formative role in the emergence of modern states.[1]

The first feature is *cultural homogeneity*. Already in the sixteenth century Western Europe had developed a substantial level of cultural homogeneity among local populations. Well-defined local vernaculars demarcated these populations into linguistic groups unable to communicate with one another. The first nation-states would emerge around these local linguistic groups.

The second feature is that the majority of the population practised a *peasant way of life*. The historical importance of a peasant base to the future emergence of modern states should not be underestimated. It allowed state makers, in this case the rulers, to tax the peasants as they saw fit. In so doing they were able to redirect resources away from the countryside and toward the urban centres. This ability to extract resources from the peasants allowed rulers to use these resources for their own objectives: namely, to finance their growing armies and to wage wars. The existence of a small landlord elite that owned much of the land facilitated this process. It allowed rulers to enter into alliances with these landlords in an effort to subdue and control the peasants.

The third feature is that these areas consisted of *extensive, decentralized, but relatively uniform political structures*. Despite the existence of many different types of authority in these areas—some religious (popes, bishops, abbots, etc.), and others secular (princes, dukes, counts, etc.)—by the fifteenth century all largely came to share a common understanding of what a sovereign state should look like. The acceptance of such uniform political structures facilitated the absorption of smaller political structures into larger ones.

However, centralizing efforts of state makers in Western Europe were almost always resisted in the peripheral areas by the peasantry. This was especially the case in the seventeenth century. Peasants rose in rebellion against the attempts of state makers to extend their control over them and to eliminate them as rival semi-autonomous powers. In the process, the landed peasantry was all but destroyed. The peasant resistance to state makers' centralizing drives was also fuelled by *taxation*. State makers used taxation to raise revenues to finance their expanding armies. They also required armies to extend, control, and defend their frontiers, and thus allow the rulers the ability to use violence effectively within their boundaries. What we have, then, is a very cyclical dynamic that emerges as part and parcel of the process of modern state formation. This dynamic may be represented as follows:

The process of state formation required standing armies, which in turn required

extracting resources from the population through taxation, which led to

the emergence of new bureaucracies and administrative innovations (that is, state institutions to manage the new resources), which also led to

resistance and rebellions by the subject populations. However, these rebellions were crushed by the rulers' armies, thus allowing rulers to

↓

extend their control over more and more areas, and hence extract even more resources, thus increasing the power of their armies and of state institutions.

Naturally, the single most important casualty of this process was the peasantry, who were destroyed as an autonomous force. Consequently, although we tend to take modern states in the developed world as a given, it is more accurate to think of them as the historical product of a bloody and protracted process. Little wonder, then, that attempts to duplicate this process in other parts of the world, and in a telescoped manner, have not led to the desired results. Indeed, the bitter lesson of state formation in the developed world suggests that the formation of modern states is frequently very messy, often bloody, and always a circuitous process.

WAR MAKING AND STATE MAKING

The cyclical dynamic of state formation described above also suggests the existence of a causal relationship between war making and state making, a theme discussed in the selections from Charles Tilly's reading in this chapter. But why is this the case? Mainly because wars require financial resources. Wars cannot be waged without resources to pay the armies who wage them. Yet the extraction of resources from any population requires the establishment of institutions and the training of cadres responsible for the management of these resources. In this very process we can see the emergence of those institutions that serve as the building blocks upon which strong modern states were founded. Indeed, war making has been at the heart of the process of creating strong states possessing strong institutions. Moreover, some political scientists suggest that the weakness of state structures in Africa may be traced to the lack of wars in this continent's history of state formation[2]—a normatively objectionable perspective, to be sure, but one not without supporting empirical evidence.

The modern state's distinguishing characteristic is its sovereignty, i.e., its ability to make decisions without interference from external actors. One can trace back the origins of the concept of the modern state to two parallel developments in sixteenth-century Europe. During this period of history, Europe was in the midst of religious warfare and a constant conflict between the feudal lords and the monarchy. The citizens were constantly conflicted with regard to their loyalties—should one obey the church, the feudal lord, or the king? Both the kings and the lords had their own armies. Both the church and the kings taxed the population. In order to resolve the problems of law and order and to ensure the loyalties of its citizens, the European monarchs established their absolute authority and in the process destroyed the fortresses of the feudal lords. Henry VIII broke away from the Catholic church and proclaimed himself to be the head of the new Anglican church. Meanwhile, the Reformation movement, under the guidance of Luther and Calvin, challenged the authority of the Catholic church. It proclaimed that the scriptures were sovereign and a man stood in direct relationship to God. By undermining the role of the Church as the intermediary between man and God, the Reformation led eventually to the separation of church and state, leading to the rise of a sovereign secular authority. By the seventeenth century, Louis XIV could claim without exaggeration, "L'état, c'est moi!"

Political philosophers of this age, such as Machiavelli, Bodin, and Hobbes, articulated the concept of sovereignty. They stated that sovereignty is indivisible; there can be only a single secular sovereign authority residing in one person, which no other authority, whether moral or secular, can override. Toward the end of the seventeenth century, John Locke began to articulate the concepts of individual rights and a limited government. Once the concept of a secular sovereign state had become entrenched in Europe, the struggle to include individual happiness and the individual rights of life, liberty, and property emerged as rallying points during the American and French revolutions.

THE WELFARE SYSTEM

The **welfare state** took shape mainly between the two world wars.[3] Its ideational origin may be traced back to the work of John Stuart Mill (1806–1873). Unsatisfied by the classical Liberal idea of the equality of rights, Mill advocated an alternative notion, the equality of opportunity to exercise those rights, though he stopped short of advocating an equality of outcomes for all. Mill's ideas would come to form the foundational bases for later welfare state liberals. In practice, the welfare state amounted to an expansion of state duties beyond simply protecting private property to include a more active or interventionist role in promoting distributive justice. This entailed extending an array of social benefits and rights—such as employment insurance, health insurance, collective bargaining rights, and maternity leave—to different sectors of society. Moreover, the political economic logic of the welfare state suggested financing these benefits by taxing private businesses and introducing a system of progressive personal income taxes.

The earliest European experiments with establishing welfare states transpired in post–World War I Germany and in post–World War II Sweden. In the latter case, a corporatist arrangement was negotiated between political parties and interest groups representing labour, agriculture, and big business. The aim was to establish an elaborate welfare system extending benefits to a considerable cross-section of Swedish society, but particularly the middle and lower classes. A similar, but less extensive, experiment was attempted in the United States in the form of Franklin Roosevelt's New Deal. Against considerable opposition from the Supreme Court, Roosevelt's New Deal ushered forth the era of substantial government intervention in the economy of the United States. The objective was to promote equal opportunity for all, and to give individual freedom palpable value. After all, without state intervention, welfare state liberals argued, individuals can neither be free nor equal.

Throughout the twentieth century, welfare state liberalism practically translated into an ever-expanding state apparatus, whose interventionist drive was directed toward satisfying ever-increasing social demands. In the process, the welfare states created what many observers judged to be bloated bureaucracies and inefficient programs. But with the onset of the general global economic crisis of the 1970s as a result of the oil price hikes following the 1973 Arab-Israeli War, the economies of the advanced industrialized countries could no longer sustain the costs of such high levels of state intervention. In the 1980s and 1990s government retrenchment and deregulation became the accepted economic dogma, leaving private business to stimulate growth. Ronald Reagan and Margaret Thatcher championed these policies in the United States and Great Britain, respectively. The World Bank and the International Monetary Fund advocated similar policies for the economies of the least developed countries and those of Eastern Europe.[4] These recommendations have not been implemented without substantial social costs for the lower classes, however. In Latin America, for example, downsizing the public sector has entailed difficult social dislocations. In many parts of the Middle East, state retrenchment has led to the marginalization of the lower and middle classes and their demobilization from one-time inclusive state corporatist organizations. Yet, despite these transformations, the welfare state has yet to be fully discredited, especially in the Scandinavian countries, where it remains a popular socio-economic model.

STATE FORMATION IN THE REST OF THE WORLD

The process of state formation outside Europe has been organically connected to colonialism. Wherever they went, colonial powers created the essential features of a modern state. They demarcated boundaries, planted a modern physical, educational, and health infrastructure, and invested the newly created entities with the symbols of a modern state and a (usually unviable) political system. Crucially important in this process was the delimitation of new political niches in these young entities. After all, the territorial state and its administrative structure now defined the arena, or the political space, in which most of meaningful political life took place.[5] Those who wanted power, access, and resources, or simply self-aggrandizement, namely the commercial and industrial bourgeoisie as well as the urban middle classes, had to organize themselves in a way that made sense in terms of the new political realities; on the other hand, those who did not or could not, namely the rural and the lower urban classes, were soon marginalized and weakened.

It is important to note that states created by colonial powers in the developing world were artificial, not because their borders were indifferent to their ethnic composition, but rather because these new states were many times larger than the political systems, whether tribal or dynastic, that they displaced or encapsulated.[6] Individuals accustomed to smaller avenues of participation and representation had to now redirect their efforts in a manner that made sense in the newly created political entities. Moreover, these new entities were often a mélange of heterogeneous groups, some of whose members had never shared the

After almost two decades of massive devastation of the country during and after the Soviet occupation by the warring tribal factions, Afghanistan is working toward both state building and a reconstruction of its economy. The Bonn Accord of 2002 has set up a framework through which it is intended that the Afghani people create a constitution. In the meanwhile, the transitional authority is setting up the state structures. Here is what the BBC has to say about the establishment of a national army—a significant perquisite for state formation.

NEW AFGHAN ARMY DEVELOPS

By Catherine Davis, BBC correspondent in Kabul

A new national army is emerging in Afghanistan

The first two brigades of the Afghan national army are ready for deployment after completing 10 weeks of training.

At an official ceremony just outside Kabul, the Afghan leader, Hamid Karzai, urged the soldiers to make their contribution to the country's reconstruction.

Plans for a 70,000-strong national army were unveiled by the president late last year.

The challenge is how to create a nationally recognised force in a country long used to private militias and where security remains a daily concern.

The two brigades marched proudly past President Karzai and senior military officials, before standing to attention on a muddy plain flanked by snow-capped mountains.

Symbolic significance

President Karzai paid tribute to those who had already given their lives for Afghanistan, and he thanked the United States and others for helping train and equip the new army.

In his address, the commander of the international forces here said the brigades represented a modern Afghan army, an army standing for all the people of Afghanistan.

The so-called activation of these two brigades has symbolic significance—one observer said it showed the national army was an established organisation within the government and that it had an authoritative presence in the country.

But there is still a long way to go.

Around 2,000 soldiers are said to have been trained so far, while thousands of other Afghans carry arms, and local warlords remain powerful figures.

Attempts to form a national force have been hampered by a lack of non-partisan volunteers, and divisions over how much representation different ethnic factions should have.

Source: From Catherine Davis, "New Afghan Army Develops" *BBC News Online* material (http://news.bbc.co.uk/1hi/south_asia/2853845.stm); reproduced by permission of the BBC.

---

same political sphere in the past. Consequently, it was the expansion of the territorial space and the concentration of politics at the centre of the new states that politicized ethnic identities and created ethnic conflict in many parts of the developing world. However, to understand the root causes of these conflicts we need to focus on the fortunes of the post-independence state in the developing world.

After many newly created states gained independence in the developing world, the state emerged as a target for competing socio-political groups. Those groups wanting to survive politically had to gain access to the state, if not the outright control of state institutions. The logic of this necessity is not difficult to fathom: control over state institutions opened the way for control over state resources, state economic planning, and the state's coercive machinery. All these factors are necessary to enable political elites to gain power and also to retain it. This is the case because political loyalty in these newly created states is based on the ability of politicians to dispense resources to their supporters and to guarantee them access to state institutions and employment. But in states comprising different ethnic, religious, sectarian, or tribal groups, competition over the control of state resources is bound to become a zero-sum game: what is considered a gain by one group is considered a loss by another. Herein lies the origin of different ethnic conflicts in many parts of the developing world. Viewing ethnic conflict from the prism of the post-independence struggles over state institutions and resources allows us to move away from the unconvincing claim that these conflicts are rooted in the political cultural distinctiveness of Third World societies.[7]

DEFINING THE STATE

The most pervasive and influential ideal-type definition of the state is the one advanced by the German sociologist **Max Weber**. According to Weber, the state is a "compulsory political association with continuous organization [whose] administrative staff successfully upholds a claim to the *monopoly* of *legitimate* [emphasis in original] use of force in the enforcement of its order . . . within a given territorial area."[8] Weber's definition is very much an empirical definition. Based on his view, we can empirically judge whether or not a certain political organization merits the label "state." We may do so by looking at the four indicators of statehood that may be drawn from Weber's definition:[9] (1) a continuous administrative staff, (2) a military establishment that successfully monopolizes the legitimate use of violence, (3) a financial and tax collection apparatus that provides the wherewithal to support the administration and the military, and (4) territoriality—does the state have clearly demarcated borders or are its borders fluid and contested?

Interestingly, based on Weber's definition of the state, it is readily evident that there are a number of political organizations in the world, ranging from the international political system to the family, that exist outside the framework of the state. Moreover, there are a number of so-called states in the world today that actually fail to meet Weber's classic definition of the state. For example, in neither Somalia nor Yemen does the state successfully monopolize the legitimate use of violence. In both countries, the tribes claim legitimate use of violence. Also, many African states lack the bureaucratic infrastructure necessary for viable statehood, which would allow central authorities to spread their control over the entire state. In sum, then, the array of contemporary states does not fit Weber's classic definition. Nor are all states composed of a culturally, linguistically, ethnically, or religiously homogeneous population.

The **nation-state** denotes that political organization where the state and the nation tend to overlap. Ireland and the two Koreas are rare examples of such states. In fact, most contemporary states are home to multiple nations or ethnic groups: an advertent (in the case of haphazard colonial map drawing) and sometimes inadvertent (in the case of the immigration of once-colonized peoples to the metropolitan Western centres) consequence of colonialism. Nigeria, Canada, England, Belgium, South Africa, and Iraq are examples of such states. Finally, some nations with active political programs and identities lack the political organizational structure of a state. The Kurds in Iraq and the Basque in Spain are examples of these nations. The Weberian definition of the state is clearly not without limitations when applied to non-Western societies.

Joel Migdal, the author of the third reading for this chapter, suggests an alternative model for understanding state dynamics in developing countries. Migdal retains the ideal-type Weberian definition of the state, but he situates the state within a different social context. He presents a model of state–society relations in the Third World that depicts the state as one among many other social organizations, locked in "an active struggle for social control of the population," in an "existing environment of conflict."[10] In its active struggle with powerful social organizations the state is usually besieged, constrained in its attempt to reorganize society in a manner that allows it considerable social control, an essential condition for state building. Indeed, in the developing world a state's efforts at acquiring a substantial level of control over its citizens through monopolizing the stipulation of social rules governing peoples' social behaviour is actively resisted by existing social organizations—families, clans, tribes, sects, and patron–client dyads. These social organizations control the available material resources and manipulate the imaginative symbols that make up peoples' "strategies of survival," the blueprints that guide people in their actions and beliefs in a contested social environment.[11] In this respect, social organizations offer their own "strategies of survival"—myriad forms of sanctions, rewards, or symbols—to force people to behave according to existing rules and norms. For Migdal, then, the societies in which numerous Third World states exist are "weblike," a "mélange of fairly autonomous social organizations" each vying for social control.[12] Each side attempts to retain or gain the loyalty of the population by offering its own strategies of survival. The state can wrest social control from the different social organizations only by offering people viable "strategies of survival" that can replace those offered by the existing autonomous social organizations.

In this conflict environment, the strength (or weakness) of a state hinges upon its capability to reorganize society and execute state-planned social change in a manner that allows it to enforce its control. The state's capabilities include "the capacities to *penetrate* society, *regulate* social relationships, *extract* resources, and *appropriate* or use resources in determined ways."[13] Examples of these capabilities may include any of the following: penetrating society in a manner that allows the state to reorganize social and class relations; extracting revenue from the population through taxation and using it for social distributive purposes; reorienting people's loyalty away from tribal leaders or ethnic politicians toward state institutions; and finally, spreading state control over professional or voluntary organizations and educational institutions. Strong states can successfully execute these tasks, while weak states possess lesser capabilities to do so. Moreover, the degree of a state's social control and capabilities are closely related: the greater the state's social control, the higher and easier the state's capabilities, and the greater the chances of success for state policies. On the other hand, in strong Third World societies, where the level of state social control is low, the state runs against the tenacious walls of autonomous social organizations whose aim is to disrupt state policies by manipulating incentives and rewards through their own social control networks. In this case, the state is weak. This distinction between strong and weak states is not merely an academic exercise. It goes a long way toward explaining the reasons behind successful and not-so-successful attempts at state building in different parts of the developing world.

STATES AND REGIMES

The labels "state" and "regime" are often used in discussions about states. However, the two terms are not identical. In general, when we talk about the **states** of Europe and North America, that is, democratic states with powerful institutional structures, the governing bodies of these states are called the administration or the government. We thus refer to the Bush administration, the Clinton presidency, the Blair government. It is also assumed that when new elections are held, and consequently these administrations or governments exit their offices, the state does not go with them, nor does the type of political system in place change. For example, until the 1990s the federal government in Canada traditionally alternated between the Liberal Party and the Progressive Conservatives. However, we do not expect Canada's political system to change with every change in government. Alternatively, in many non-democratic states that lack powerful political institutions, we refer to the governing bodies as **regimes**. A regime is defined as "that nexus of alliances within and without the formal bureaucratic and public sectors that the leader forms in order to gain power and to keep it."[14] At its core is the leader, flanked by a coterie of rotating officials who are strategically placed throughout the executive, army, and intelligence establishments. Membership in this coterie is not static. One-time members may be ejected from it, and new elements may be incorporated into it. Nor are regimes monolithic entities. They include liberal and conservative elements, the latter often found in the bureaucracy and the intelligence services. We thus talk about the Iraqi regime, or we used to talk about the regime of Maputo in Zaire. We do so because in these cases a regime change may bring with it either a complete transformation of the political system or the death of the leader, or both.

READINGS

This chapter examined the process of state formation in the developed and developing worlds. It examined the factors that gave rise to the emergence of national states in Western Europe, and compared this process with the legacy of state formation in the rest of the world. This comparison highlighted the different formative factors that ultimately shaped states and their capacities in different parts of the world. The following readings explore this general theme. Charles Tilly's essay highlights the organic link between war making and state making in the creation of strong states in Western Europe. Alternatively, Joel Migdal looks at the historical origins of weak states in the developing world.

In the first reading, Christopher Pierson helps us to isolate nine features of the modern state. These features closely follow Weber's definition of an ideal state. In the second reading, Charles Tilly sums up the results of his seminal and provocative research on the European experience with state formation. His work is essential reading for students of the state. Tilly positions himself against social contract theorists who see the formation of states as a result of the emergence of shared norms and expectations between the ruler and the subject population. Alternatively, Tilly offers a radically different image of the rise of European states. For him, the process of state making is akin to organized crime. He argues that a state's ability to wage war is directly related to its ability to expand its fiscal and extractive capacities. In other words, success in war largely depends on a state's ability to extract from the population the means of war: namely, men, arms, food, and, of course, money. However, enhancing the state's extractive capacities often goes hand in hand with the elimination of local rivals and power seekers. War making shaped the process of state making in other ways as well. Most importantly, it led to the emergence of those state institutions necessary for the waging of a successful war. These include a standing army, war industries, effective bureaucracies, and schools to train state personnel. These institutions, necessary for successful war making outside a given territory, helped central powers check challenges to their authority from local rivals located within this territory. Consequently, war making and its institutional consequences shaped the process of state making in Europe. Tilly's argument is certainly much more complex than the summary offered here. It invites close reading. Students should also ponder the implications of Tilly's argument for other parts of the world. Does his argument fit the North American model of state

TRYING TIMES

Jan 23, 2003
From The Economist Global Agenda

One by one, alleged war criminals from the former Yugoslavia are being brought to justice. And, slowly but surely, democracy is taking root in the new republics.

As a ploy to get the United States on side, the handing-over of Milan Milutinovic, a former Serbian president, appears not to have worked. The United States had threatened to cut financial assistance to what remains of Yugoslavia if it does not arrest war-crimes suspects by the end of March. On January 21st, the day after Mr Milutinovic gave himself up to the international war-crimes tribunal in The Hague, the Americans implied that he was small beer, saying that they were still waiting for three prominent suspects, including General Ratko Mladic, the wartime commander of the Bosnian Serb army, before resuming financial aid.

Mr. Milutinovic, president of Serbia until last December, stands accused, along with his former boss, Slobodan Milosevic, of a "joint criminal enterprise" which led to crimes against humanity in Kosovo and the expulsion of more than 800,000 ethnic Albanians. When he appears before judges next Monday he is expected to plead not guilty on the grounds that he was just a powerless yes-man. His former boss, ex-Yugoslav president Slobodan Milosevic, is already on trial in The Hague, though the hearings have been suspended several times because of his ill health.

In 2001 it was American threats to cut assistance which prompted the new Serbian authorities to hand

over Mr Milosevic. It remains to be seen whether the same tactic will work again. General Mladic, who is believed to be in Serbia, remains a popular figure there

and is said to be well protected by men connected to, if not formally employed by, the Yugoslav military. Also on the run is Radovan Karadzic, the former Bosnian Serb leader, who has evaded capture by NATO troops since they were deployed in the country in 1995.

Although a number of key suspects remain at large, the trials in The Hague are part of a broader return to normality more than a decade after war broke out in the old six-republic Yugoslavia. Those republics, now independent, are being quietly nursed to health with foreign assistance. Even before its secession in 1991, Slovenia saw itself as having closer links to neighbouring Austria than to the rest of Yugoslavia. It is among the group of ten countries poised to enter the European Union (EU) in May next year, well ahead of the other former Yugoslav republics.

Macedonia, too, has managed to achieve independence and international recognition, despite some sniping from neighbouring Greece, which also has a province called Macedonia. The stability of the country was threatened in 2001 when government forces loyal to Macedonia's Slav majority repeatedly clashed with Albanian rebels demanding constitutional reform. A NATO force disarmed the rebels. Last autumn, following a general election, a coalition of moderate-sounding nationalists from both communities took over the reins of government. In March, part of the NATO mission in the country is due to be replaced by an EU force, as part of a strategy to "Europeanise" the Balkans.

Maintaining the peace in Macedonia is also vital to stability across the border in Serbia's disputed province of Kosovo, where the expulsion of ethnic Albanians prompted NATO to wage war on Serbia almost four years ago. The vast majority of those who fled have returned. However, revenge attacks led to the flight of some 230,000 Serbs and other non-Albanians, including Roma gypsies, almost none of whom have since returned to the province, which is now administered by the United Nations.

Michael Steiner, a German, runs Kosovo on behalf of the UN, helped by a band of able foreign administrators. They are slowly devolving power to an elected government and parliament. But there are complications: on January 20th, for instance, a group of ethnic Serb-dominated municipalities, mostly in the north of Kosovo, declared their "union." They are planning their own president, assembly and flag. The UN has declared this illegal but the move is extremely significant. It signals that if overwhelmingly Albanian Kosovo becomes independent, then the Serb-majority areas will attempt to break away so that they can remain part of Serbia. Everyone remembers that a union of Serbian municipalities in Croatia was one of the first steps on the road to war there which lasted from 1991 to 1994. Croatia, run by Franjo Tudjman, an authoritarian nationalist, until his death in 1999, is now in the hands of reformers; its Dalmatian coast is once again attracting western holidaymakers.

In Bosnia, as in Kosovo, refugees have been returning home: more came back last year than at any time since the war there ended in 1995. On January 1st, the EU took over the UN's decade-old police mission, the first operation of this kind by the EU. The NATO-led stabilisation force has fallen in number from nearly 60,000 when the war ended to 12,500 today. NATO feels confident enough about improving prospects for peace that it handed over control of Sarajevo International airport to local authorities at the beginning of the year.

What is left of Yugoslavia—Serbia and the tiny republic of Montenegro—is peaceful but politically hamstrung. The rump federation is having problems electing a president, thanks to low turnouts in recent elections. In Serbia, this is because the two men who came together in 2000 to topple Mr Milosevic had little in common apart from their loathing of the man. Now Vojislav Kostunica, the president of the fragile federation, is trying to become president of Serbia itself. He is opposed by Serbia's prime minister, Zoran Djindjic. Mr Djindjic is seeking to change the constitution to make the presidency irrelevant. He is also trying to prevent Mr Kostunica from winning sufficient parliamentary backing to call a new Serbian general election, as he knows he would probably lose it.

But Mr Djindjic also lacks that most Balkan of qualities: sentimental nationalism. He reasons, persuasively, that Serbia should have no qualms about packing suspects off to The Hague: the fate of a handful of people should not compromise the welfare of millions of Serbs. And, if Montenegro is "lost," what of it? He even favours opening talks on the "final status" of Kosovo now, although he says (but may not mean) that he is against its independence. His goal, above all else, is to get Serbia into the EU—no longer the laughable proposition it was three years ago.

formation? What does it tell us about the process of state making in non-Western regions of the world, especially Africa?

Joel Migdal has played a pivotal role in unpacking the process of state formation in the developing world. The power of his work lies in his ability to reverse previously accepted ideas pertaining to this topic, and, like all profound insights, has consequently opened new avenues for research on this subject. Migdal's main contribution in the following reading is to situate developing countries among the array of competing social organizations challenging the state for social control of the population. As such, Migdal's work allows us to move away from the image of the state as an uncontestable, all-powerful organization. Rather, Migdal sees states in the developing world as political organizations engaged, with other organizations, in a fight to win the minds and loyalty of local populations. This image of the state as one among many social organizations competing for social control goes a long way in explaining the weakness, if not fragility, of many states in the developing world. This weakness is reflected in the failure of many developing countries to penetrate their societies, regulate social relationships within a given territory, extract sufficient resources from the population, and use these resources to achieve specific state policies and objectives. If Migdal's argument strikes you as being too theoretical, think then of the experiences of Lebanon, Afghanistan, Somalia, Sierra Leone, Nigeria, and many other developing countries. Finally, try also to think of the implications of Tilly's argument to Migdal's thesis. In other words, can war help developing countries establish social control over societies composed of competing social organizations or groups? If not, then what other options do developing countries have to do so?

IRAQ: REBUILDING A POSTWAR STATE

Saddam Hussein after his capture

The U.S.–led invasion of Iraq was launched on March 20, 2003. Some twenty-eight days later, on April 9, 2003, Baghdad fell to American troops. Saddam's regime collapsed like a house of cards; his once-feared Republican Guards melted into the population or were destroyed by the firepower of American bombers. On May 1, 2003, George W. Bush declared the end of major combat operations in Iraq. U.S. Marines later captured Saddam on December 13, 2003. The task of rebuilding postwar Iraq now commenced. But waging the peace would prove much more difficult than waging war.

Rebuilding postwar Iraq was bound to be a problematic process. Thirty-five years of ruthless Ba'th rule had thoroughly destroyed the institutions of civil society. In the Shi'a south, this allowed the religious scholars, or "*ulama*," to assume leadership of the community. An autonomous entity had emerged in the Kurdish north in the aftermath of the 1991 U.S.–led war to liberate Kuwait from Iraqi invasion. Iraqi Kurdistan refused to surrender its autonomous status unless the new Iraq was decentralized substantially. The Shi'a and Kurdish communities, systematically persecuted by Saddam's regime, were unwilling to compromise on the distribution of political power and economic resources in the postwar state. In the Sunni triangle—a triangular area connecting the Sunni cities of Baghdad, Ramadi, and Tikrit—a guerilla war exploded in the face of U.S. troops. Foreign terrorists also poured into Iraq via neighboring states to attack U.S. troops. The Iraqi state was being rebuilt in the midst of armed insurrections and terrorist attacks.

Two decisions taken by the civilian administrator of the Coalition Provisional Authority (CPA), L. Paul Bremer III, set the postwar state building process to a false start.[15] Bremer decided to dismantle the Ba'th Party and ban the Iraqi armed forces. This led to an explosion of resentment among Sunni Arabs against the United States. Close to 120,000 Iraqis, many of whom had joined the Ba'th Party for instrumental rather than ideological reasons, lost their jobs overnight as a result of de-Ba'thification. Disbanding the Iraqi Army also turned some 400,000 well-trained Iraqi soldiers unemployed and against the CPA. This also created a security vacuum in the country, a problem compounded by the shortage of coalition military troops deployed in Iraq. The looting and destruction of government institutions immediately after the fall of Baghdad also complicated postwar state building. Institution building was also hampered by postwar corruption and nepotism, and the lack of transparency in the reconstruction effort.

Faced with growing domestic opposition and multiple armed insurgencies, the United States decided to expedite the transfer of power to Iraqis. On June 28, 2004, the CPA transferred power back to Iraqis. This was followed by elections on January 30, 2005, to create a Transitional National Assembly. In turn, a new permanent constitution was passed in a national referendum on October 15, 2005. It established a loose federal structure in Iraq, paving the way for the emergence of autonomous, ethnically based, super-regions in the north and the south. How the provisions of the constitution will be implemented in the future remains to be seen, however. Nevertheless, Sunni Arabs have finally joined the political process underway, and serious efforts are being made to divide the armed opposition in an attempt to isolate the radical terrorist factions. Be that as it may, the road to rebuilding postwar Iraq is bound to be long and difficult.

ENDNOTES

1. See Charles Tilly, ed., *The Formation of National States in Western Europe* (Princeton, NJ: Princeton University Press, 1975).

2. See Jeffrey Herbst, "War and the State in Africa," *International Security* 14, no. 4 (Spring 1990), 117–39.

3. For a general discussion see Christopher Pierson, *Beyond the Welfare State?* (University Park: Pennsylvania State University Press, 1991).

4. See John Williamson, "Democracy and the 'Washington Consensus,' " *World Development* 21, no. 8 (August 1993), 1329–36.

5. See Roger Owen, *State, Power and Politics in the Making of the Modern Middle East* (London: Routledge, 1992), 20–21.

6. See Donald L. Horowitz, *Ethnic Groups in Conflict* (Berkeley: University of California Press, 2000), chapter 1.

7. A good example of this line of argument can be found in Larry Diamond, "Nigeria: The Uncivic Society and the Descent into Praetorianism," in Larry Diamond, Juan J. Linz, and Seymour Martin Lipset, eds., *Politics in Developing Countries: Comparing Experiences with Democracy*, 2nd edition (Boulder: Lynne Rienner Publishers, 1995), 417–91.

8. Max Weber, *The Theory of Social and Economic Organization* (New York: Free Press, 1947), 154.

9. See the discussion in Lisa Anderson, "The State in the Middle East and North Africa," *Comparative Politics*, 20, no. 1 (October 1987), 2.

10. Joel S. Migdal, *Strong Societies and Weak States: State–Society Relations and State Capabilities in the Third World* (Princeton: Princeton University Press, 1988), 30.

11. Ibid., 27. Italics omitted.

12. Ibid., 37. On page 22, Migdal defines state social control as "the successful subordination of people's own inclinations of social behavior or behavior sought by other social organizations in favor of the behavior prescribed by state rules."

13. Ibid., 4–5. Emphasis in original.

14. John Waterbury, *The Egypt of Nasser and Sadat: The Political Economy of Two Regimes* (Princeton: Princeton University Press, 1983), p. xiii.

15. David L. Philips, *Losing Iraq: Inside the Postwar Reconstruction Fiasco* (Boulder: Westview Press, 2005).

MODERN STATES: A MATTER OF DEFINITION

Christopher Pierson

A US Supreme Court judge hearing an obscenity case had to decide what was meant by "pornography." Admitting that he could not define it, the judge insisted nonetheless that "I know it when I see it" (cited in Hawkins and Zimring, 1988, 20). We may feel the same way about the modern state. We might find it difficult to give a precise and comprehensive definition of the state, but we think we recognize it when it flags us down on the motorway, sends us a final tax demand or, of course, arranges for our old age pension to be paid at the nearest post office. From the mandatory certification of our birth (which should have taken place under medical circumstances prescribed by the state) to the compulsory registration of our death, we tend to feel that the state is (nearly) always with us. Even in Anglo-Saxon countries, everyday political discussion is replete with appeals to, condemnations of and murmurings about the state. Rather like the judge, we think that we know the state when we see it, yet it proves extremely difficult to bring it under some brief but generally acceptable definition. "*Everybody* agrees," so Berki argues, that "the modern state . . . is a rather baffling phenomenon" (Berki, 1989, p. 12). At times, it seems that collective bafflement is about as far as the agreement reaches.

A number of commentators, from quite differing political traditions, circumvent this problem by refusing any explanatory value to the category of "the state." More empirically-minded political scientists ask us to focus upon "governments" and the "political system," abandoning the suspiciously metaphysical realm of "the state" for institutions and practices which can be measured with due "operational rigor" (Almond et al., 1988, p. 872; Easton, 1981). Others, who are more critical of the prevailing social order, insist that talk of the state actually serves to *conceal* or *obscure* the exercise of political power. According to Abrams, "the state is not the reality which stands behind the mask of political practice. It is itself the mask which prevents our seeing political practice as it is" (Abrams, 1988, p. 58). Some follow the brilliant and iconoclastic French thinker Foucault in seeking to locate states' activities within a much more complex field of social knowledge/powers. Foucault rejects any clear-cut division between state and society or state and economy. Indeed, he argues that the state may be "no more than a composite reality and a mythicized abstraction." The focus of his attention is not upon the state, but rather upon the much more generic practice of the "art of governing" and the corresponding idea of *governmentality*. "The state" is just one site of the practice of governing (understood as the management of "the conduct of conduct"). State rationality is concerned above all "to develop those elements constitutive of individuals' lives in a way that their development also fosters the strength of the state." "Economy," in Foucault's usage, describes not a separate sphere concerned with the production and distribution of goods and services, but rather the policy ambition of those governors who seek to manage and "dispose of" their populations with maximum efficiency (Foucault, 1979; Foucault, 1991, pp. 91–4, 103).

It is important that we do not lose sight of these rather unorthodox views. Most political scientists, political sociologists, and political economists, however, have felt that there are political structures, institutions, and practices which it makes sense to try to explain under the rubric of the state. While their attempts to do so are very diverse, there has been a surprisingly broad area of agreement about what constitutes the essential elements of the modern state. In this chapter, I will try to establish the most important features of this shared understanding of the modern state.

APPROACHES TO THE MODERN STATE

We can think of analysis of the state characteristically having asked two kinds of questions. The first and more normative or evaluative question is: What should the state be and what should it do? This invites us to consider the proper terms for establishing and maintaining any political authority, for defining the appropriate relationship between the state and its members, and the acceptable limits of state action. This has been the major concern of political philosophers. The second and more "fact-based" or empirical question asks: What are states actually like? This is the question that has most often been addressed by political scientists and political sociologists. In practice, the two approaches cannot be so neatly separated. For many commentators, description and evaluation overlap. For both advocates and opponents, what states are *really* like does imply something about what we can (reasonably) suppose that they *should* be like. Nonetheless, our primary focus here will be upon the second type of question, though with a recognition that more evaluative claims are never far away.

Initially, we may think about these explanations rather crudely in terms of those which focus primarily upon the organizational *means* adopted by the modern state and those which concentrate upon its *functions*. Still the most authoritative source for the first of these approaches is the work of the German political sociologist and economic historian, Max Weber (1864–1920). Active in the early years of the twentieth century, Weber established many of the parameters of statehood which are still common to discussions at the other end of the century. A starting-point for Weber, which contrasted with much earlier thinking, was that the state could not be defined in terms of its goals or functions, but had rather to be understood in terms of its distinctive *means*. Thus, he argued:

> *The state cannot be defined in terms of its ends. There is scarcely any task that some political association has not taken in hand, and there is no task that one could say has always been exclusive and peculiar to those associations which are designated as political ones . . . . Ultimately, one can define the modern state only in terms of the specific means peculiar to it, as to every political association, namely, the use of physical force. (1970a, pp. 77–8; second emphasis added)*

For Weber, *the modern state* was a particular form of *the state* which was, itself, a particular form of a more general category of *political associations*.

> *A compulsory political organization with continuous operations will be called a "state" insofar as its administrative staff successfully upholds the claims to the monopoly of the* legitimate *use of physical force in the enforcement of its order....*
>
> *[The modern state] possesses an administrative and legal order subject to change by legislation, to which the organized activities of the administrative staff, which are also controlled by regulations, are oriented. This system of orders claims binding authority, not only over members of the state, the citizens, most of whom have obtained membership by birth, but also to a very large extent over all action taking place in the area of its jurisdiction. It is thus a compulsory organization with a territorial basis. Furthermore, today, the use of force is regarded as legitimate only so far as it is either permitted by the state or prescribed by it.... The claim of the modern state to monopolize the use of force is as essential to it as its character of compulsory jurisdiction and continuous operation. (1978a, pp. 54–6)*

These economical definitions help us to isolate several of the most important (if contested) features in all subsequent discussions of the mechanisms of the state:

1. (monopoly) control of the means of violence;
2. territoriality;
3. sovereignty;
4. constitutionality;
5. impersonal power;
6. the public bureaucracy;
7. authority/legitimacy; and
8. citizenship.

To these, I shall add a ninth category: taxation. I will discuss each of these in turn.

(MONOPOLY) CONTROL OF THE MEANS OF VIOLENCE

Weber gives great prominence to control over the means of violence as a defining characteristic of the state. Indeed, his very briefest definition sees the state as "a human community that (successfully) claims the monopoly of *the legitimate use of physical force* within a given territory" (Weber, 1970a, p. 78). In fact, control over the means of violence has long been a concern for those whose primary interest is in the "reality" of states' practices. Thus, Thomas Hobbes (1588–1679), the Englishman who many see as the first theorist of the authentically *modern* state, was insistent that, to avoid collapse into civil war, individuals needed to establish over themselves "a Common Power, to keep them in awe, and to direct their actions to the Common Benefit." It seemed to Hobbes that "the only way to erect such a Common Power . . . is to conferre all their power and strength upon one Man, or upon one Assembly of men" and to ensure that the wielder of this "Common Power"—the "great Leviathan"—"hath the use of so much Power and Strength conferred on him, that by terror thereof, he is inabled to forme the wills of them all, to Peace at home, and mutuall ayd against their enemies abroad." Once established, the authority of this "Common Power" proceeds not from consent but from force: "Covenants being but words, and breath, have no force to oblige, contain, constrain, or protect any man, but what it has from the publique Sword" (Hobbes, 1968, pp. 227–31).

Writers in the Marxist tradition have also stressed the importance of the state as organized violence, but for them this is primarily an expression of the intense antagonisms generated by a society divided into classes. Friedrich Engels (1820–1889) articulates the classically Marxist view that the state is an expression of the contradictions of a society divided by irreconcilable class differences. The existence of the state is an admission that "society has become entangled in an insoluble contradiction with itself, that it has split into irreconcilable antagonisms which it is powerless to dispel."

> *But in order that these antagonisms and classes with conflicting economic interests might not consume themselves and society in a fruitless struggle, it became necessary to have a power seemingly standing above society that would alleviate the conflict and keep it within the bounds of "order." This power, arisen out of society but placing itself above it, and alienating more and more from it, is the state. (Engels, 1978, p. 752)*

Of course, as Weber himself was well aware, "the use of physical force is neither the sole, nor even the most usual, method of administration of political organizations" (Weber, 1978a, p. 54). If we look around the contemporary world, we see great variation in the levels of direct physical intimidation that states offer to their citizen-subjects. (Compare, for example, Holland with Indonesia or Sweden with China.) Even the most violent states of modern times (e.g. Stalin's Soviet Union, Hitler's Germany) did not impose their rule by physical force alone. Nor did Weber argue that the state would necessarily reserve to itself all the lawful use of violence. In the USA, for example, citizens have a constitutional right to carry lethal weapons and many states sanction (limited) violence exercised by disciplining parents against their children. Feminist critics have long argued that states frequently fail to uphold their monopoly of violence in restraining the perpetrators of domestic assaults upon women (Dobash and Dobash, 1992). What Weber does see as essential to the state is its status as "the sole source of the 'right' to use violence" (Weber, 1970a, p. 78). Thus, those who exercise violence within the jurisdiction of a state may do so only under the express dispensation of that state. Normally, however, the state will seek to impose its will through the managed consent of its population—an aspect of legitimation to which we return below. Nonetheless, Weber insisted, "the threat of force, and in the case of need its actual use . . . is always the last resort when other [methods] have failed" (Weber, 1978a, p. 54). As Hobbes had it, "command of the Militia, without other Institution, maketh him that hath it Soveraign" (Hobbes, 1968, p. 235). Under many constitutions, the harshest and most lethal remedies are reserved for those who challenge the integrity of the state itself (i.e. those who commit the crime of treason). Yet, even a quite minor breach of the authority of the state (e.g. failure to disclose certain driving documents to the police) may finally result in incarceration. In Berki's irreverent formulation: "Tell the judge, a ridiculous old fogey dressed up in theatrical garb, to bugger off and leave you alone; you see where you will end up" (Berki, 1989, p. 18). As we shall see, states' practice is usually a mixture of (managed) "consent backed by coercion" (see below, pp. 77–8).

In fact, as a number of more recent commentators have suggested (see Mann, 1993a, p. 55; Giddens, 1985, p. 189) the state may never actually attain Weber's monopolization of violence within its jurisdiction, even if we include those forms of violence which are "licensed" by the state. Organized crime and domestic battery are but two forms of chronic violence within contemporary societies which evade effective control by the state. The same commentators point out the extent to which the apparatus of the state's physical violence (above all, the armed forces) is institutionally isolated from many other areas of state activity. There may, nonetheless, be a relationship between the extent of monopolization of violence achieved by the state and actual levels of violence in society. Indeed, the more effectively is the use of force *monopolized* by the state, the less frequent may be the actual resort to violence. This was certainly the supposition of Hobbes and of many of those who have experienced the peculiar horrors of civil war. In Hobbes' view, the individual did a good deal when he [sic] surrendered almost all of his natural liberties to an authoritarian sovereign, since this was the only way of avoiding society descending into a war of all against all in which his life would famously be "solitary, poor, nasty, brutish, and short" (Hobbes, 1968, p. 186).

More important than the actual monopolization of violence may be the inauguration of a unitary order of violence. . . . [W]e shall see that many commentators trace the emergence of the modern state to the historical transition in Europe from forms of feudalism to absolutism. Crudely put, this is a transition from societies built upon multiple sites and sources of power to societies premised on a single legitimating structure. Feudalism is often represented as a pyramidical social formation built upon personal ties of fealty in which the wielders of power at any level depended upon their capacity to mobilise the resources (including armed force) controlled by many lesser power-holders. In such a model, power was not unified in the monarch but diversified among a hierarchy of lesser nobilities. It was also an order in which separate powers and jurisdiction applied to those in religious orders. An important part of the coming of the modern state was the move away from this multi-centred and pluralist structure of powers towards a single (absolutist) centre of power ruling over an undivided social order.

Central to this process of the centralization of state power was the increasing *pacification* of society. To some extent the monopolization of violence within the state was matched by a pacification of relations in society. This was certainly a part of Hobbes' justification for the individual's subjecting himself to "the great Leviathan." Of course, in ways that I have already indicated, this pacification of society was always quite partial. Violence and the threat of violence continued to be a chronic feature of daily life. Yet, there is considerable evidence (in the face of the commonplace claim that our societies are becoming increasingly violent) that the rise of the state coincided with a reduction in the levels of violence in day-to-day life. In part, this had to do with the new forms of surveillance and control that were becoming available to an increasingly powerful state. Pre-modern states could be extraordinarily arbitrary and despotic, but the range of their power was drastically limited. Genghis Khan was a fearful despot, but surely not the equal of Stalin, once famously described as "Jenghiz [sic] Khan with a telephone" (Maclean, 1978, p. 159). As Giddens points out, it was crucial too that the rising economic order (of capitalism) was one in which violence was extruded from the core economic relationship—the sale of labour power (Giddens, 1985, pp. 181–92). Of course, Marx insisted that the *establishment* of capitalism, the process of primitive accumulation, was "written in the annals of mankind in letters of blood and fire" (Marx, 1965, p. 715). Marxists saw the growth of imperialism as a very bloody business and expected that the revolution which would see capitalism replaced by socialism would be a violent one. Yet, the liberal capitalism described in Marx's *Capital* was one in which it was economic necessity, not the threat of violence, that drove workers into an exploitative contract with their capitalist employers.

TERRITORIALITY

A second and seemingly straightforward feature of modern states is that they are geographic or geo-political entities. States occupy an increasingly clearly-defined physical space over which they characteristically claim sole legitimate authority. Once again, this is a feature of statehood which is recognized by a wide range of writers (from Hobbes through Engels and Weber to contemporary theorists such as Mann and Giddens). Indeed, a clearly-defined territoriality is one of the things that marks off the state from earlier political forms, such as pre-modern empires (i.e. those empires which were not the external domain of already-established nation-states). These early empires were extensive and powerful political formations, but their territorial limits tended to be set by ill-defined frontiers rather than by the clearly-demarcated borders with which we are familiar (Giddens, 1985, pp. 49–50). Rule was concentrated at the centre of the empire. The outlying areas tended to be a source of tribute rather than the objects of permanent and tightly-managed administration. Considerable autonomy was allowed to local systems of governance, so long as the expectations of the imperial power could be satisfied.

Modern states defend their territorial integrity with a quite ferocious jealousy. At times, states have been willing to go to war over seemingly valueless tracts of land or uninhabitable islands, apparently unmindful of the considerable costs and the sometimes very limited benefits. As I write, the south-eastern corner of Europe is (yet again) riven by civil war over the competing territorial claims of a number of aspirant states. Among the "restored" states of the "new" Eastern Europe, a number of claims and counter-claims about legitimate borders rumble on. States also lay claim not just to jurisdiction over a particular tract of land, but also to the minerals that lie beneath it, to the waters that surround it (and to their economic product), to the airspace above it and, most importantly, to the people who inhabit it. States have not been an omnipresent form of human organization. Even upon the most expansive definition, the majority of people through most of human history have not lived in states. Nonetheless, we now live on a planet which is almost universally divided into (competing) state jurisdictions. There can hardly be a rocky outcrop anywhere which has not been claimed by at least one (and often by several) jurisdictions.

This raises a number of further points. First, states do not exist in isolation. They are by their very nature part of *a system of competing states*. Frontiers might abut unclaimed territory, but borders are necessarily the dividing line between one state and another. The territoriality of states, their claim to monopolistic powers of adjudication within their boundaries and the existence of an international order premised upon competing nation-states, is definitive of one of the most important general approaches to the state—international relations. The sub-discipline of international relations invites us to focus our studies of the state, first and foremost, upon the *external* and *international* relationships of a series of competing sovereign states operating within an unruly international order. We shall return to this approach. . . .

Second, while the globe is finite and almost every inch of it is now under some state's jurisdiction, this does not mean that particular states are permanent features of the world's landscape. Those of us who live in one of the historically longer-standing states may think of states once having been founded as lasting in perpetuity. But this is not so. Tilly records that "the Europe of 1500 included some five hundred more or less independent political units, the Europe of 1900 about twenty-five" (Tilly, 1975, p. 15). Rather more remarkable is the redrawing of the map of European states between 1980 and 1995. Thirty-three nations competed in football's European Nations' Cup in 1992. In the 1996 competition, there were 48 contestants, including separate teams from Slovakia and the Czech Republic and two national teams from within the borders of the former Yugoslavia! (*The Sunday Times*, 23 January 1994.) Or consider the statehood of one of Europe's central political actors: Germany. Founded little more than a hundred years ago, the country was split into two states for nearly half of that time and resumed its existing borders only in 1991.

Third, as the territory occupied by the state became ever clearer, so did the tendency to identify states with *nations*. The international order is increasingly recognized as one consisting of *nation*-states. This is, both in theory and practice, an extremely contentious and confused area. At this point, it may be useful to try to distinguish between conceptions of the *nation*, *nationalism*, and *the nation-state. The nation* may be taken to describe "a collectivity existing within a clearly demarcated territory, which is subject to a unitary administration" (Giddens, 1985, p. 116). In Greenfeld's usage, the nation is used to describe "a *unique* sovereign people" (Greenfeld, 1992, p. 8). *Nationalism*, by contrast, describes identification within an "imagined community" (Anderson, 1991). According to Giddens, it is "primarily psychological, [expressing] the affiliation of individuals to a set of symbols and beliefs emphasising communality among the members of a political order" (or, we might add, of those *aspiring* to form a distinct political order) (Giddens, 1985, p. 116). In Greenfeld's account:

> National identity in its distinctive modern sense is . . . an identity which derives from membership in a "people," the fundamental characteristic of which

is that it is defined as a "nation." Every member of the "people" thus interpreted partakes in its superior, elite quality, and it is in consequence that a stratified national population is perceived as essentially homogeneous, and the lines of status and class as superficial. This principle lies at the basis of all nationalisms. . . . (1992, p. 7)

We return to the difficult question of the relationship between nations, nationalisms, and the nation-state in Chapter 2. . . .

SOVEREIGNTY

Greenfeld's discussion of the nature of nationalism raises a third core component of the state—its supposed *sovereignty*. Hinsley (1986, pp. 1, 26) defines sovereignty as "the idea that there is a final and absolute authority in the political community," with the proviso that "no final and absolute authority exists elsewhere." The essence of sovereignty is not that the sovereign may do whatever it wishes. After all, even the most unbridled of states cannot make pigs fly. Rather, it is the idea that, within the limits of its jurisdiction (set by the division of the world into a series of similarly sovereign nation-states), no other actor may gainsay the will of the sovereign state. Modern usage is often seen to derive from the French philosopher Jean Bodin (1529–1596), but still the most uncompromising statement of this position is that found in Hobbes' *Leviathan*. For Hobbes, once the members of the commonwealth have come together and agreed to constitute a sovereign power to rule over them, the powers of that sovereign are almost unlimited. The terms of the contract are irrevocable and, since members of the commonwealth have mutually willed the creation of the sovereign, they are deemed to have vicariously willed all of its actions. Since the initial agreement is between the members of the commonwealth (to create a sovereign power) and not between individual subjects and that sovereign power, "there can happen no breach of Covenant on the part of the Soveraigne; and consequently none of his subjects, by any pretence of forfeiture, can be freed from his Subjection." Since "he that doth any thing by authority from another, doth therein no injury to him by whose authority he acteth . . . whatsoever [the Sovereign] doth, it can be no injury to any of his Subjects." It is true "that they that have Soveraigne power, may commit

Iniquity; but not Injustice, or Injury in the proper signification" (Hobbes, 1968, pp. 230–2).

Even for Hobbes, however, there are limitations upon the lawful authority of the Sovereign. "It is manifest," so he argues, "that every Subject has Liberty in all those things, the right whereof cannot by Covenant be transferred." So, "if the Soveraigne command a man (though justly condemned) to kill, wound, or mayme himself; or not to resist those that assault him; or to abstain from the use of food, ayre, medicine, or any other thing without which he cannot live; yet hath that man the Liberty to disobey." And there is one further substantial qualification of the powers of the Sovereign: "The Obligation of Subjects to the Soveraign, is understood to last *as long, and no longer*, that the power lasteth, by which he is able to protect them" (Hobbes, 1968, pp. 268–9, 272; emphasis added).

Subsequent discussion of sovereignty and the state may be seen to have moved in three directions. First, there has been an aspiration, consonant with the brief discussion of nationalism above, to relocate the site of sovereignty not in the state or the government, but rather in *the people*. Although the other great seventeenth-century English political theorist, John Locke (1632–1704), was far from being an untrammelled democrat, he certainly held sovereign power to be much more subject to the will of its citizens. In contrast to Hobbes, he maintained that some form of continuing endorsement of government (however passively expressed) was needed for it to exercise proper and lawful authority. A much more radical position was adopted by Jean Jacques Rousseau (1712–1778) who argued that the principle of sovereignty should be retained, but that it should be relocated in the sovereign people. Certainly, advocates of democratization of the last two centuries have often made their case in terms of *legitimate* sovereignty residing in the people. Those states which are based upon some founding constitutional settlement often posit the sovereignty of the people as their first principle. Thus, the founding authority for the Constitution of the USA rests famously with "We, the people. . . . " (McKay, 1993, p. 305). The location of sovereignty in an unreconstructed constitution, such as we enjoy in Britain, is much more ambiguous.

A second development has been manifest in the attempts not so much to deny as to *apportion* sovereignty. This is, perhaps, clearest in the constitutional principle of the *separation of powers*, under which the functions of government (most usually divided between executive, legislative, and judicial tasks) are allocated to differing institutions and persons. The principle is at its clearest in the US constitutional order, in which the powers of the President, Congress, and the Supreme Court are clearly set out with the intention that no one branch of government should be able to dominate the others. Of course, this may be read as a simple refutation of the Hobbesian idea of sovereignty, i.e. that of all lawful authority residing in one institution or even one person. On the other hand, if the people are held to be sovereign, it may seem that this is but a convenient system for ensuring that the apparatus of government, to which the sovereign devolves its powers for a time, should perform its task effectively without that concentration of power which might pose a threat to the properly sovereign people. Alternatively, we may view such a constitutional order as one in which it is not the particular branches of government but the constitutional order itself which is sovereign.

The third development must be considered rather more unambiguously as a *counter*-movement against the idea of sovereignty. We have seen that democracy may be seen as a way of expressing the wishes of the sovereign people. In a more "realist" tradition, democracy has sometimes been represented as a mechanism for exercising constraint over an apparatus of government in which *de facto* sovereignty is seen to reside. From the advocates of "protective" democracy in the nineteenth century (such as Bentham and J.S. Mill) to the "democratic elite" theorists of the twentieth century (above all, Schumpeter), the democratic process is one through which the people, who are not in fact sovereign, exercise some sort of constraint upon those state actors with whom real sovereignty rests. There is also a longstanding fear of the democratic sovereign. For some, the very real popular legitimacy of the democratic state makes it, if anything, more to be feared than an authoritarian but "illegitimate" state. Liberals and conservatives, in particular, have seen, not very far behind the idea of popular sovereignty, the prospect of "the tyranny of the majority." For conservatives, the principal threat has been to the established order of property; for liberals, it is a challenge to property and individual liberty. For both, the legitimating force of a truly popular democracy is a threat to minorities. We have then, complementing the claims for popular sovereignty expressed through the extension of democratic institutions, a counter-movement stressing the inviolability of certain personal rights and an inviolable private space within which the state should not interfere. Paradoxically, we sometimes find argument and counter-argument voiced by the same individual (as famously in the case of J.S. Mill), as well as calls for a constitutionally self-limiting state, a state which should legislate to constrain its own powers of intervention.

Finally, it is worth stressing that the territoriality and, more especially, the effective sovereignty of modern states were transformed by a series of technical changes which profoundly altered the state's capacity for surveillance and control. New forms of administration, new techniques for record-keeping, new technologies for the transmission and processing of both people and information gave the modern state powers to govern which were simply unavailable to more traditional states. It was one thing for the Pope to assert his authority as the head of all Christendom, but something else for officers of the state to have more or less instantaneous access to the personal details, criminal records and credit status of each of its citizens. According to Giddens, "surveillance as the mobilizing of administrative power—through the storage and control of information—is the primary means of the concentration of authoritative resources involved in the formation of the nation-state" (Giddens, 1985, p. 181). We need to be careful here. Giddens is not saying that changing technology carved the development of modern states. Rather, technological change made available to the modern state forms of surveillance and control which simply had not existed under more traditional state formations.

CONSTITUTIONALITY

In much "official" discourse about modern states, constitutions and the "constitutionality" of the political order enjoy considerable prominence. In this context, constitutions are often taken to describe the basic "rules of the game" of the political process. In many polities, there is a single document or set of documents that lays out and, often at the same time, justifies the state's basic political arrangements. The constitution establishes "the laws about making laws" and may be presented as actually creating or, at least, securing the existence of the state itself. In some states, perhaps in the USA above all, the whole political process is sometimes presented in

"official" explanations as little more than the day-to-day operation of "The Constitution." This narrowly constitutional account of the modern state is what one might expect to hear (in a truncated form) from a tour guide at the House of Commons or on Capitol Hill, or from a practising politician in a particularly pompous mood and with the tapes running.

Political commentators, be they academics, journalists or "ordinary" citizens, have been rather less persuaded that the constitutional model gives a very "realistic" account of what states really do. The severest critics, such as Lenin, have seen claims about constitutional governance as an ideological gloss through which the minority who exercise real power through the state and its monopoly of violence seek to conceal this fact from the subject population (Lenin, 1960). The "realist" school of international relations, inasmuch as it has been at all concerned with constitutionality, has tended to see this as a rather decorous fiction drawing attention away from the "real" business of politics, i.e. a largely non-constitutional clash of powers and interests. Some (perhaps most notoriously, the inter-war German theorist Carl Schmitt) have stressed the importance of establishing who is sovereign in *exceptional* periods, i.e. when constitutional government is suspended. Certainly, there is a reasonable suspicion that the very best of constitutions are no match for the will of a usurping sovereign. The Soviet Constitution of 1936 "guaranteed" extensive liberties to Soviet citizens. But this proved no great impediment to Stalin's reign of terror. Even those who have been willing to give rather greater weight to constitutional accounts (such as the US political scientists Robert Dahl and Charles Lindblom) have doubted that the actual working of constitutional arrangements looks very much like these idealized descriptions.

Nonetheless, "constitutionality" rather more broadly conceived is an extremely important component of the idea of the modern state. We have seen that Weber writes of the modern state possessing "an administrative and legal order subject to change by legislation." The idea that the state constitutes a distinct and rule-governed domain with powers which are (at least formally) distanced from society and the economy is distinctively modern. Most modern states do indeed exercise a form of power which, at least formally, is public, rule-governed, and subject to lawful reform. These characteristics may be as often honoured in the breach as in the observance, but they do nonetheless help to locate the state in modernity. In pre-modern states, social, economic, patriarchal and political powers were largely undifferentiated. Their activities could be justified as *explicitly* arbitrary, absolutist, theocratic, and dynastic in ways which modern states generally cannot. The idea of constitutionality thus points us towards a number of further characteristic features of modern statehood (differentiation from society and economy, "impersonal" power, bureaucratic organization, and so on). But it is an idea that has also done an enormous amount of work in more *normative* accounts of the modern state. It has been an abiding concern of political philosophers to establish what (if anything) justifies the state's claim to the loyalty of its subjects. Is there anything more than "might" that makes the state "right"? This raises questions about the legitimacy of the state, the nature of its authority and the nature of its obligations to its citizens and of its citizens to it.

"THE RULE OF LAW" AND THE EXERCISE OF IMPERSONAL POWER

Of the essence, for those who stress constitutionality, is the idea that a constitutional political order would mean "not the rule of men, but *the rule of law*." There is a very ancient claim in political theory that a good polity is one which is ruled not by the subjective and arbitrary will of particular men [sic], but by the objective determination of general and public laws. According to Kant (1724–1804), "the state is a union of an aggregate of men under rightful law" (cited in Dyson, 1980, p. 107). Especially in the continental European tradition, we find that state activity is often characterized as a special form of (public or administrative) law, an arrangement under which "public law regulates the interrelationships of public authorities with the 'subjects'; private law regulates the relationships of the governed individuals among themselves" (see Dyson, 1980; Weber, 1970b, p. 239). Admittedly, some commentators have always been much more concerned with the state's actual capacity to uphold its own laws than with what would make them "rightful" (e.g. see Kelsen, 1961). But it is widely argued that, within a constitutional order, those who exercise state power must do so in ways which are themselves lawful, constitutional and constrained by publicly-acknowledged procedures. They are generally

seen to act not upon a personal basis, but rather because of their public position as the occupants of particular offices of state.

This aspiration to lawful government should not be conflated with the aspiration to extend democracy. Not only do the calls to make governance constitutional long *precede* any very widespread appeal to make it more democratic, but they have also often been advanced as a way of protecting certain individual or corporate interests *against* the encroachments of democratic governments. However, it is of the essence that, under a law-governed regime, politicians should themselves be subject to the constitutional order and the laws which they have themselves helped to make and enforce. Even under so centralized and sovereign a state as we have in the UK, government ministers may still be arraigned by the courts if they fail to abide by their own rules (however limited may be the effect of such judgments). From this, we may derive the central (if rather idealized) principles of legality and lawfulness as characteristic modes of state activity, of the state as an impersonal power, of politicians and civil servants as the (temporary) occupiers of particular public posts.

THE PUBLIC BUREAUCRACY

For Weber, it was of the essence that the administration of modern states would be *bureaucratic* (Weber, 1978a, pp. 217–26; 1978b, pp. 956–1005). In fact, Weber saw bureaucracy as the generic form of administration in all large-scale organizations of modern society (including, for example, the modern capitalist corporation and the modern army) and this was, in its turn, a particular form of the more general process of rationalization which Weber identified with modernization itself. It established the administration of the modern state as quite distinct from those forms that had preceded it. The public bureaucracy, in Weber's celebrated description, can be isolated around the following features:

1. that bureaucratic administration is conducted according to fixed rules and procedures, within a clearly-established hierarchy and in line with clearly demarcated official responsibilities;
2. that access to employment within the civil service is based upon special examinations and that its effective operation is dependent upon knowledge of its special administrative procedures—a good deal of the power

of the civil service rests upon its specialised knowledge and "expertise";

3. that bureaucratic management is based upon a knowledge of written documents ("the files") and depends upon the impartial application of general rules to particular cases;

4. that the civil servant acts not in a personal capacity, but as the occupier of a particular public office.

Office holding in the civil service is seen as a "vocation," subject to a special sense of public duty, and involves the individual civil servant in a clearly-defined and hierarchical career-path, usually with "a job for life" (Weber, 1978a, pp. 220–1; 1978b, pp. 956–63).

There were great bureaucracies in the pre-modern world (e.g. in ancient Egypt and China), but, for Weber, the modern predominance of bureaucratic organization is a product of the coming of a fully monetized market economy. The reason for its "success" lies in "its purely technical superiority over any other form of organization." Bureaucracy is "formally the most rational known means of exercising authority over human beings . . . the needs of mass administration make it today completely indispensable." According to Weber, "bureaucracy inevitably accompanies modern mass democracy" and "everywhere the modern state is undergoing bureaucratization." He insists that "it is obvious that technically the great modern state is absolutely dependent upon a bureaucratic basis. The larger the state, and the more it is or the more it becomes a great power state, the more unconditionally is this the case." Furthermore, "once fully established, bureaucracy is among those social structures which are the hardest to destroy" (Weber, 1970b, p. 232; 1978a, p. 223; 1978b, pp. 971, 983, 987).

Weber was quite ambivalent about the idea that bureaucracy (along with the more general process of rationalization), characteristic of modernity, represented "progress." He recognized that the treatment of individuals and their particular circumstances as just so many "cases" to be processed according to "the rules" has a cost in terms of the quality of our humanity. He was also fearful that the "routinization" and rule-guidedness which was appropriate to large-scale administration might spill over into the more properly dynamic and value-laden sphere of "politics proper." He was certainly concerned about the consequences of a regime in which

civil servants usurped the proper function of the politician (see Beetham, 1985). The routinized terror of the bureaucratized authoritarian state was to become a prominent theme of twentieth-century fiction (from Kafka to Havel). The dullness and rule-boundedness of public officials has become one of the standing jokes of modernity. Much more at variance with Weber has been the widespread claim that, in practice, bureaucracy is a drastically *inefficient* means of administration. Rather than being grindingly efficient, bureaucracies (in the public sector above all) have been depicted as chronically inefficient. Above all, neo-liberal or "New Right" critics have insisted that bureaucracies are almost universally less efficient as a means of administration than are markets. Bureaucrats are seen as rent-seekers who exploit the monopoly of provision by the state to extract greater material rewards for themselves from a system which tax-paying citizens cannot escape.

AUTHORITY AND LEGITIMACY

Issues of authority and legitimacy are quite central to the appraisal of the modern state. No state can survive for very long exclusively through its power to coerce. Even where power is most unequally distributed and the possibilities for coercion are at their greatest—e.g. in a prisoner-of-war camp—the subordinated can always exercise some level of non-compliance and, across time, the maintenance of social order is "negotiated." How much more is this the case for a state governing many millions of subjects in a comparatively open society? A stable state requires that, for whatever reason, most of the people most of the time will accept its rule.

At this point, it may be useful to turn again to Weber. In *Economy and Society*, he offers the following definitions:

> ***Domination (or "authority")*** *is the probability that a command with a given specific content will be obeyed by a group of persons.*
>
> ***Legitimacy*** *describes "the prestige of being considered binding."*
>
> ***Legitimate authority*** *describes an authority which is obeyed, at least in part, "because it is in some appreciable way regarded by the [subordinate] actor as in some way obligatory or exemplary for him." (1978a, pp. 53, 31)*

Authority and legitimacy imply that, under normal circumstances and for most people, the actions of the state and its demands upon its population will be accepted or, at least, not be actively resisted. Without some level of legitimacy, it is hard to see that any state could be sustained and consequently a great deal of work goes into defending the state's claim to exercise not just effective power, but also legitimate authority.

Virtually all states have sought to make their rule appear legitimate. Sometimes the appeal has been to tradition (to a "natural" order which is said to have governed since time immemorial and/or to have been ordained by God) or to the charismatic qualities of a particular leader (or indeed to both). But what is most characteristic of the modern state is not just the greater weight given to *legal* authority—to the state's embodiment of abstract legal principles enforced through an impartial bureaucratic and judicial apparatus—but, above all, to the idea that the state embodies and expresses the (sovereign) will of the people. In Weber's interpretation, legal authority rests "on a belief in the legality of enacted rules and the right of those elevated to authority under such rules to issue commands" (Weber, 1978a, p. 215). Within such an account, citizens are seen to attribute legitimacy to the modern state on the grounds that it is the appropriate embodiment of "a consistent system of abstract laws" impartially administered by a rule-governed and non-partisan civil service.

Roughly speaking, we can isolate two types of question about legitimate authority. First, there is the question that has dominated much of classical and contemporary political theory: i.e. under what circumstances can the state's actions be considered "valid" and, consequently, under what circumstances should the citizenry obey or, indeed, be made to obey? A second set of questions is more empirical: Why has the state sought to present its actions as legitimate? How do states uphold their claim to legitimacy? Why do people obey?

Since the question of political obligation has been a major problem—in some accounts, *the* major problem for political theorists of the past four centuries (at least)—and since this is not a text in political philosophy, I can give only the briefest indication of where the difficulties lie. Although the problem is older than modernity, it is posed in a peculiarly acute way in the modern period. There was a time when legitimacy might derive from religious authority or simply the custom and practice of a long-established order.

In the post-Enlightenment world, these forms of legitimacy are, at least in principle, very largely rejected (though the attempt to re-establish theocratic states in our own time perhaps challenges this assumption). It seems that the justification of the modern state has normally to be rational and perhaps legal-rational in character. It has also tended, in the West at least, to proceed from certain beliefs about the integrity and autonomy of the human individual. At its simplest, the issue is this: What are the grounds that would justify an agency (such as the state) forcing individuals to do things which they do not wish to do? Of course, one perfectly respectable response (that of most anarchists) is that there are *no* circumstances under which such an imposition could be justified and that, consequently, the state is *never* legitimate. Among those who reject anarchy, probably the most popular response has been to argue that the state is legitimate to the extent that it expresses the authentic will of its population. Thus, the state is not a usurpation of the freedom and autonomy of individuals where it is simply the (collective) representation of our individual wills. In obeying the state, we are simply obeying the dictates of our *own* wills vicariously expressed.

Of course, this rather vulgar formulation hardly does justice to four hundred years of accumulated political wisdom! It raises many more questions than it could possibly answer (not least about how our individual wills may be aggregated and how consent can be maintained across time) and it distracts from the fact that political thinkers have taken a radically different view of the sorts of political institutions to which such a supposition about the state might give rise. It does, however, help to point us towards a ubiquitous feature of arguments about the contemporary state: i.e. that the modern state is widely seen to be legitimate inasmuch as (but no more than) it represents "the will of the people." Of course, in *institutional* terms this carries us no further forward. Hobbes and Rousseau, for example, might be thought to justify the state on the basis of "the will of the people," but to radically different effects. But we might wish to argue that there is here an underlying premise—that we should obey the state because it is an indirect or derived expression of our own wills—that straddles many disparate traditions in modern western political thought.

We should be clear about what this means. It certainly does *not* mean that all modern states are "truly" popular or democratic. Indeed, there is again a perfectly respectable view (held by many Marxists and anarchists among others) that *no* modern state is democratic. If democracy is defined as a political order in which all the people themselves rule and rule themselves directly, no contemporary state can qualify as democratic. We know, too, that many of the most authoritarian regimes of the twentieth century have claimed that their right to rule derived from their being an expression of the "real" will of the people, without or even in defiance of the "empirical" will of the population expressed through duly-constituted electoral procedures. Military regimes across the globe, even those that have held power for many years, characteristically describe themselves as "preparing the way for a restoration of democratic government." The argument is not that states in modernity are genuinely an expression of the will of their peoples, but rather that it is perceived to be important that they should present themselves as such just as the thief, to take Weber's example, acknowledges the legitimacy of laws of property when he seeks to conceal his breach of them, so does the state acknowledge the validity of "popular legitimacy" when, however disingenuously, it commends its own actions as an expression of the popular will.

As we turn to the question of the capacity of states to uphold their claim to exercise legitimate authority, we need further to distinguish two senses of legitimacy. For the most part, political theorists and philosophers have been concerned with establishing the conditions that would make the state's rule justified in terms of some more or less externally-validated rational criteria. For actual states, it is much more important that they should be able to maintain the general population's *belief* in the legitimacy of their claim to rule. Indeed, even this is to claim too much for the state's interest in legitimacy. For states, it will usually be enough that the great majority of the population do not actively regard the existing form of governance as illegitimate—and that they do not act collectively upon this premise. Consider the classification developed by Held:

We may obey or comply [with the instructions of the state] because:

1. *There is no choice in the matter (following orders, or coercion).*

2. *No thought has ever been given to it and we do it as it has always been done (tradition).*

3. *We cannot be bothered one way or another (apathy).*

4. *Although we do not like the situation . . . we cannot imagine things being really different and so we "shrug our shoulders" and accept what seems like fate (pragmatic acquiescence).*

5. *We are dissatisfied with things as they are but nevertheless go along with them in order to secure an end; we acquiesce because it is in the long run to our advantage (instrumental acceptance or conditional agreement/consent).*

6. *In the circumstances before us . . . we conclude that it is "right," "correct," "proper" for us as individuals or members of a collectivity: it is what we genuinely should or ought to do (normative agreement).*

7. *It is what in ideal circumstances . . . we would have agreed to do (ideal normative agreement). (Held, 1989, p. 101).*

All of these constitute reasons for which subjects may obey the state. Only one is unambiguously related to the threat of force, but only a further two rely in any strong sense upon the view that the state's authority is legitimate. Citizens are busy people. They want to hold on to their jobs, to make love, to play football, and to de-flea the cat (though not necessarily in that order). It is enough for the state that they should not spend their time thinking critically about the legitimacy of the state and making this the basis of coordinated political action (see Mann, 1970). It may, of course, be in the state's interests to *encourage* this political indifference, as it always has, by whatever is the contemporary equivalent of the Romans' "bread and circuses" (perhaps organizing a National Lottery).

This said, there is still a residuum of legitimacy which the state must seek to deliver and given the general scepticism that is expressed above, it is worth pointing out that many modern states do have some plausible claim to legitimacy. I have already indicated that there are perfectly respectable grounds for arguing that existing western "democracies" are not really democratic at all. Much more common, though, is the view that, while very imperfect, the sorts of institutions which we associate with western liberal democracy—fixed-term elections, "free" competition between parties, lawful opposition, constitutional arrangements for the scrutiny of government activity, and so on—represent real, if rather limited popular achievements. Democratic élite theorists, for example, argue that while this is still "government by élite," we the people do get to choose by which élite we should be governed and are, from time to time, constitutionally empowered to change our collective mind. They insist that limited as it is, this is about the most democratic order we can hope to achieve in large-scale modern societies. Even those who believe that much more democracy is possible would probably concede that what we have so far is valuable, hard won, and better than the absence of any constitutional constraint upon the activity of the state.

Democracy is a very powerful ideology in contemporary societies. Indeed, some might suppose that in a "post-ideological" world it is the one ideology that remains. Certainly, in many contexts other than the state, we are as individuals willing to accept decisions that go against our own personal will and judgement, if we feel that such decisions have been made by an appropriate community to which we belong with due freedom of discussion and information and through properly-constituted democratic procedures. Acquiescence with the state is an amalgam of indifference, deference, fear, instrumentality, and active consent. For all the inadequacies of liberal democracy, we should not underestimate the extent to which citizens, when they *do* think about the legitimacy of the state's actions (usually in a rather piecemeal way) accept that democratic procedures do give the state some authority to act as it wishes and do place us under some (albeit limited) obligation to obey. But we should remember that states are typically very jealous of their monopoly over the means of violence and no state relies exclusively upon its power to persuade. The characteristic form of state action, as the Italian Marxist Antonio Gramsci observed, is "consent backed by coercion" . . . .

CITIZENSHIP

Citizenship is one of the oldest terms of political discourse, probably as old as the idea of the political community itself. In essence, the citizen is one who is entitled to participate in the life of the political community. Citizen status in the modern world typically denotes a mixture of entitlements or rights of participation and a series of attendant obligations or duties. In Held's helpful summary: "Citizenship is a status which, in principle, bestows upon individuals equal rights and duties, liberties and constraints, powers and responsibilities [within] the political community" (Held, 1995, p. 66). Although the claims of citizenship first articulated in the city-states of the ancient world never quite went away, they burst onto centre stage in the modern world with the events surrounding the French Revolution of 1789. Revolutionary discourse was replete with appeals to citizenship and to the Rights of the Citizen. This republican approach to state and citizenship is neatly caught by Rousseau:

> The public person . . . formed by the union of all other persons was once called the city, and is now known as the republic *or the* body politic. *In its passive role it is called the* state, *when it plays an active role it is the* sovereign; *and when it is compared to others of its own kind, it is a* power. *Those who are associated in it take collectively the name of a people, and call themselves individually* citizens, *in so far as they share in sovereign power, and* subjects, *in so far as they put themselves under the laws of the state. (1968, pp. 61–2)*

This captures the important sense in which modern claims of citizenship concern the transference of sovereignty. According to Turner (1990, p. 211), "the transfer of sovereignty from the body of the king to the body politic of citizens is . . . a major turning point in the history of western democracies." It suggests that even, perhaps above all, in the revolutionary tradition, the entitlements of citizenship are complemented by the duty of the subject to obey the sovereign will. It also points to the association between an expanded citizenship and the shared identity of "a people." In Turner's usage, there are "two parallel movements" in which "a *state* is transformed into a *nation* at the same time that *subjects* are transformed into *citizens*" (Turner 1990, p. 208). Finally, the French revolutionary tradition makes clear that citizenship is a status which is (at least implicitly) *universal*. Thus we have an image of citizenship as empowering, universalistic, rights-based and tied to both democratization and an increasingly active role for the *nation*-state.

Citizenship has certainly been a key term in constituting the relationship of the state to its subject-members, but not always in just the ways that its more uncritical admirers have supposed. Thus, for example, the "universalism" and "participation" identified with citizenship have been extremely ambivalent. First, citizenship rights are not universal in the sense of "natural rights" or "human rights" which are often described as holding good at all times and in all circumstances, placing a general obligation upon those who are capable of satisfying them. Citizenship is normally acquired by the accident of one's place of birth and/or one's parents' citizenship. Not everyone residing within a given state's territory or under its jurisdiction will enjoy the status of a full citizen. Citizenship rights apply only to those who are fortunate enough to enjoy the status of citizen and can generally only be redeemed by the particular state to which such citizenship applies. In the mundane political world, disputes about citizenship have often been about the means of acquiring or the procedures for exclusion from this full citizen status and its attendant rights. At the same time, while citizens' rights imply an entitlement to some form of provision or restraint by the state, they are generally subject to interpretation or even revocation by state authorities. It is often an agency of the state which must decide to whom citizenship is to be attached and what substantively citizenship rights require. Citizenship is also seen to be "exclusive" in at least two further senses. First, various categories of persons may be *formally* excluded from the status of citizen. This was for centuries the experience of women, to whom rights of citizenship (the right to enter into various forms of contract, to vote, to receive welfare benefits) were almost always granted some considerable time after men. Such formal exclusion remains important (especially for immigrant populations, émigré workers, political refugees, and so on). But as formal equality has advanced, so have *substantive* differences of citizenship become more important. This, for example, is at the heart of feminist critiques of existing forms of citizenship (e.g. see Phillips, 1993; Lister, 1993). Men and women may enjoy the same *formal* rights of access to the political process, but actual patterns of social organization—different working lives, provision of child care, the division of domestic labour—mean that men have *systematically* privileged access to the exercise of their citizenship rights. Existing evocations of citizenship are inadequate because of the particular way in which they conceive of the relationship between public life (the domain of citizenship) and the private sphere (which is conceived as politically "off limits"). Citizenship helps to generate a distinctively modern conception of "the public" but it is a public from which certain voices—defined by gender, ethnicity, sexual orientation, or whatever—tend to be excluded.

Finally, since our concern is principally with the relationship of citizenship to the state, it is imperative to record that the strengthening of principles of citizenship may actually furnish *greater* powers to the state. This is not just because an extension of welfare citizenship, for example, puts enormous resources into the hands of the state, enabling it to control the basic life chances of many millions of its subjects. It is also that the rights of citizenship have been powerfully complemented by the *obligations* of citizenship. This was clear in the revolutionary tradition, where the invocation of the state's will as an expression of the collective will of all the citizens was seen to place a mighty obligation upon individual citizens to carry through the will of the state. Therborn (1977) has traced the association between the extension of political citizenship and conscription into the armed forces. Some strands of citizenship thinking—e.g. French republicanism or Soviet constitutional theory—show a strong sense that citizenship entails sometimes onerous duties (including compulsory military service), as well as rights. Citizenship is a double-sided process. In principle, its extension may empower individuals over and against the state. But, at the same time, it implies a strengthening of the authority and the obligation of the state's rule (now presented as the expression of the collective will of all the citizens). . . .

TAXATION

Taxation is mentioned but little discussed in Weber's account of the modern state. Yet the modern state as Weber describes it could not have existed without substantial and regular tax revenues. Indeed, the apparatus it requires, the relationship between tax-state and tax-subject it defines, and the sheer resources it generates, makes the consideration of taxation essential to any explanation of the modern state. We can begin from Braun's definition: "taxes are regularly paid compulsory levies on private units to produce revenues to be spent for public purposes" (Braun, 1975, p. 244). Of course, the extraction of resources from "private units" is very ancient. The church tithe, for example, under which parishioners would pay a tenth of their "income" to the clergy, long pre-dates the modern state and, of course, the ancient and medieval world is full of stories of pillage, piracy, and extortion. What distinguished these early forms of extraction was that they were occasional, sometimes quite random and often justified by little more than brute force or "the right of conquest." Before the eighteenth century, so Mann avers, tax collection was an "expedient in times of emergency and even an abuse which as soon as possible should be replaced by income from public property, particularly domains, and by voluntary contribution" (Mann, 1943, p. 225). Yet, the regime of the "modern tax state," as Schumpeter (1954) calls it, carries all the hallmarks of Weber's modern state. It is systematic, continuous, legal—rational, extensive, regularized, and bureaucratized.

For some commentators, such distinctively modern forms of well-regulated resource extraction become possible only with the emergence of a commercial market- or exchange-based economy. In earlier times, "tax-farming," under which a ruler would sell off or award to a subaltern the right to make an income by extracting what resources he could from the local populace, had been common. Concealment or hoarding were equally common forms of resistance to this exaction. In the modern period, however, we move towards taxation uniformly applied by the state through officials who are responsible for collection, but whose income is not dependent upon these revenues. Modern accounting and banking procedures expose economic activity to state surveillance and expropriation (creating, in turn, the market for offshore tax havens and clever accountants). Indeed, as Giddens argues, the assessment and collection of taxation liabilities is one of the ways in which the state extends its penetrative surveillance of society (Giddens, 1985, pp. 157–9).

In some accounts, taxation (and the apparatus required to collect it) is one of the most basic constituents of the modern state helping to mark if [sic] off from its "feudal" predecessor.

According to Schumpeter, "without financial need the immediate case for the creation of the modern state would have been absent" (Schumpeter, 1954, p. 245). This imperative is especially clear in the work of Tilly. In essence, Tilly's view of the development of the modern European state was this: "War made the state, and the state made war." Making war meant raising taxes.

> *The building of an effective military machine imposed a heavy burden on the population involved: taxes, conscription, requisitions, and more. The very act of building it—when it worked—produced arrangements which could deliver resources to the government for other purposes . . . Thus almost all the major European taxes began as "extraordinary levies" earmarked for particular wars, and became routine sources of governmental revenue. (Tilly, 1975, p. 42)*

None of the ambitions of statemakers could be realized without *extraction*, that is "drawing from its subject population the means of statemaking, warmaking and protection" (Tilly, 1990, p. 96). To simplify a complex historical story, we have a pattern something like this: Proto-states make war. War is costly and requires a systematic and continuous process of extraction of resources. For the successful states, the process of extraction requires a larger state apparatus. The larger state apparatus requires more resources and thus a higher tax revenue and so on. Of course, royal courts could be very extravagant. Mann records that James I spent £15,593 on a bed for the infant Queen Anne! (Mann, 1986, p. 458). But however profligate was the personal expenditure of kings and queens, these costs were generally dwarfed by the expenses of military activity. According to Tilly, "the formation of standing armies provided the largest single incentive to extraction and the largest single means of state coercion over the long run of European statemaking" (Tilly, 1975, p. 73).

As important as the sheer rise in revenue demands was the transformation of public indebtedness. Wars meant not just increased costs to be met in the present but also an increase in the public debt, and this had to be serviced by taxation payments outside times of active warmaking. Mann observes that it was "under Henry VIII that one important and permanent development occurred: Peacetime taxation" (Mann, 1986, p. 57).

Upon Tilly and Mann's account, the development of the modern tax-state is full of unintended consequences. It was not that anyone wished to create a large fiscal state and extractive apparatus. It was rather a necessary by-product of the state's warlike ambitions. Once established "emergency" taxes proved increasingly difficult to remove. (In Britain, income tax started life as a temporary wartime expedient.) Once established, the public debt changed its character (so that by the mid-twentieth century it was seen as an instrument of governments' macroeconomic strategy). The state used taxation not just to raise revenue but also to encourage/dissuade various forms of behaviour (imposing duties on alcohol and tobacco, offering tax relief for preferred family forms and so on).

Again, while the origins of modern taxation regimes may lie in the changing requirements of military activity, there is also some agreement that the pattern of public expenditure shifted in the later nineteenth and twentieth centuries. Despite the colossal costs of warfare in the twentieth century, and the extraordinary impact that the sheer costs of war have had in shaping the world since 1945, we can observe an underlying process of "civilianization" in the changing balance of public expenditures over the last hundred years (Tilly, 1990, pp. 122–3). For most of the eighteenth century, military expenditure accounted for much more than half of all state expenditure in Britain. In the budget for 1992, this figure fell below 10 per cent (CSO, 1995, p. 112). At the same time, however impressive was the growth of state funding in earlier centuries (starting from an extremely low base), in volume terms this has been dwarfed by developments of the last hundred years. The tax take has risen dramatically in the twentieth century from less than 10 per cent in 1890 to something more than 40 per cent by the 1980s (Peacock and Wiseman, 1961, pp. 42–3; *The Economist*, 337, 7943, 1995) and there has been a transformation in the disbursement of these public funds. Of these changes, . . . the most remarkable has been the extraordinary growth of social expenditure—one of the more remarkable, if under-reported, developments of the twentieth century.

Of course, this wholesale transformation in the public finances has had a profound political impact not only upon the state, but also upon its subjects (as well as upon other potential political actors). Few people enjoy paying taxes—"to tax and to please," so Edmund Burke argued, "is not given to men"—and resistance against extraction is very ancient (Burke, 1909). History before the rise of the modern state is littered with "tax revolts" and "peasant's rebellions" against unreasonable forms and levels of taxation. With the rise of the modern state, both the imposition of and the resentment against taxation became more systematic. While both Tilly and Mann, for example, argue that the militarization of the state was essentially turned *outwards* towards other states, the requirement to raise revenue certainly encouraged a more active policing of the *internal* order of nascent states. Control—military, judicial, civil, and fiscal—was a commonplace of the modern tax-state. But, as in other areas of its activity, the modern state could not normally hope to extract resources by force alone, not least because the costs of compliance might make such a regime counterproductive. There was thus an increasing incentive to make the state's taxation regime appear *legitimate*. At the same time, we find a longstanding movement among those who bore the burden of taxation to gain some control over those who extracted their resources. At least in part, the story of the (partial) democratization of the modern state between the eighteenth and twentieth centuries can be understood in terms of the American rebels' fatuous insistence upon "no taxation without representation." For both rulers and ruled, it seemed that taxation might be more bearable if, at least formally, it could be construed as "chosen by the people."

Taxation is still a touchstone of the politics of the modern state. In Britain, the longest-serving Prime Minister of the twentieth century was brought down, at least in part, by her insistence upon reviving a pre-modern form of taxation—the Poll Tax (Butler et al., 1994). Modern British General Elections are sometimes supposed to be won and lost on the basis of the projected headline rate of income tax. It is also widely argued that recent years have seen the growth of an increasing "tax resistance" among democratic publics who feel themselves overburdened by a massive state apparatus. Certainly, the transformation of taxation (who pays and who benefits) has helped to shape the grand contours of the politics of the second half of the twentieth century. Just as important, though a little less remarked upon, are the political constraints imposed by public indebtedness. Those who service the government's debt—and who may, unlike the general citizenry, decline to continue to do so—are in an extremely powerful position to establish the acceptable limits of the state's activity. It is the power that the servicing of the public debt places in the hands of fund-holders, banks and "the markets" (rather than some "bankers' ramp"), which gives internationally-mobile investors such a powerful lever upon the conduct of the state.

Reading References

Abrams, P. (1988) "Notes on the difficulty of studying the state," *Journal of Historical Sociology* 1, 1, 58–89.

Almond, G.A., Nordlinger, E.A., Lowi, T.J. and Fabbrini, S. (1988) "The return to the state," *American Political Science Review* 82, 3, 853–901.

Anderson, B. (1991) *Imagined Communities*, London: Verso.

Beetham, D. (1985) *Max Weber and the Theory of Modern Politics*, Cambridge: Polity.

Berki, R.N. (1989) "Vocabularies of the state," in P. Lassman (ed.) *Politics and Social Theory*, London: Routledge.

Braun, R. (1975) "Taxation, sociopolitical structure, and state-building: Great Britain and Brandenburg–Prussia," in C. Tilly (ed.) *The Formation of National States in Western Europe*, Princeton, NJ: Princeton University Press.

Burke, E. (1909) "On American taxation," in *Speeches*, London: Macmillan.

Butler, D., Adonis, A. and Travis, T. (1994) *Failure in British Government: The Politics of the Poll Tax*, Oxford: Oxford University Press.

CSO (Central Statistical Office), (1995) *Social Trends*, London: HMSO.

Dobash, R.E. and Dobash, R.P. (1992) *Women, Violence and Social Change*, London: Routledge.

Dyson, K. (1980) *The State Tradition in Western Europe*, Oxford: Martin Robertson.

Easton, D. (1981) "The political system besieged by the state," *Political Theory* 9, 3, 303–25.

Engels, F. (1978) "The origin of the family, private property, and the state," in R.C. Tucker (ed.) *The Marx-Engels Reader* (2nd ed.), London: Norton.

Foucault, M. (1979) *'Omnes et Singulatim': Towards a Criticism of 'Political Reason'*, Tanner Lectures.

—— (1991) "Governmentality," in G. Burchell, C. Gordon and P. Miller *The Foucault Effect*, London: Harvester-Wheatsheaf.

Giddens, A. (1981) *A Contemporary Critique of Historical Materialism: Volume 1*, London: Macmillan.

—— (1985) *The Nation-State and Violence*, Cambridge: Polity Press.

Greenfeld, L. (1992) *Nationalism: Five Roads to Modernity*, London: Harvard University Press.

Hawkins, G. and Zimring, F.E. (1988) *Pornography in a Free Society*, Cambridge: Cambridge University Press.

Held, D. (1989) "Power and legitimacy," in *Political Theory and the Modern State*, Cambridge: Polity.

—— (1995) *Democracy and the Global Order*, Cambridge: Polity.

Hinsley, F.H. (1986) *Sovereignty* (2nd ed.), Cambridge: Cambridge University Press.

Hobbes, T. (1968) *Leviathan*, Harmondsworth: Penguin.

Kelsen, H. (1961) *General Theory of Law and State*, New York: Russell & Russell.

Lenin, V.I. (1960) "The state and revolution," in *Collected Works* 25, London: Lawrence & Wishart.

Lister, R. (1993) "Tracing the contours of women's citizenship," *Policy and Politics* 21, 1, 3–16.

Maclean, F. (1978) *Holy Russia*, London: Weidenfeld & Nicolson.

Mann, F.K. (1943) "The sociology of taxation," *Review of Politics* 5, 225–35.

Mann, M. (1970) "The social cohesion of liberal democracy," *American Sociological Review* 35, 3, 423–39.

—— (1986) *The Sources of Social Power: Volume 1: A History of Power from the Beginning to AD 1760*, Cambridge: Cambridge University Press.

—— (1993a) *The Sources of Social Power: Volume II: The Rise of Classes and Nation-state, 1760–1914*, Cambridge: Cambridge University Press.

Marx, K. (1965) *Capital*, Volume One. London: Lawrence & Wishart.

McKay, D. (1993) *American Politics and Society*, (4th ed.), London: Blackwell.

Peacock, A and Wiseman, J. (1961) *The Growth of Public Expenditure in the UK*, Oxford: Oxford University Press.

Phillips, A. (1991) *Engendering Democracy*, Cambridge: Polity.

—— (1993) "Citizenship and feminist theory," in *Democracy and Difference*, Cambridge: Polity.

Rousseau, J.J. (1968) *The Social Contract*, Harmondsworth: Penguin.

Schumpeter, J. (1954) "The crisis of the tax state," *International Economic Papers*, 4, 5–38.

Therborn, G. (1977) "The rule of capital and the rise of democracy," *New Left Review* 103.

Tilly, C. (1975) "Reflections on the history of European state-making," in C. Tilly (ed.) *The Formation of National States in Western Europe*, Princeton, NJ: Princeton University Press.

—— (1990) *Coercion, Capital, and European States, AD 990–1990*, Oxford: Blackwell.

Turner, B.S. (1990) "Outline of a theory of citizenship," *Sociology* 24, 2, 189–217.

Weber, M. (1970a) "Politics as vocation," in H.H. Gerth and C.W. Mills *From Max Weber*, London: Routledge & Kegan Paul.

—— (1970b) "Bureaucracy," in H.H. Gerth and C.W. Mills *From Max Weber*, London: Routledge & Kegan Paul.

—— (1978a) *Economy and Society: Volume I*, New York: Bedminster.

WAR MAKING AND STATE MAKING AS ORGANIZED CRIME

Charles Tilly

WHAT DO STATES DO?

Under the general heading of organized violence, the agents of states characteristically carry on four different activities:

1. War making: Eliminating or neutralizing their own rivals outside the territories in which they have clear and continuous priority as wielders of force
2. State making: Eliminating or neutralizing their rivals inside those territories
3. Protection: Eliminating or neutralizing the enemies of their clients
4. Extraction: Acquiring the means of carrying out the first three activities—war making, state making, and protection

The third item corresponds to protection as analyzed by Lane, but the other three also involve the application of force. They overlap incompletely and to various degrees; for example, war making against the commercial rivals of the local bourgeoisie delivers protection to that bourgeoisie. To the extent that a population is divided into enemy classes and the state extends its favors partially to one class or another, state making actually reduces the protection given some classes.

War making, state making, protection, and extraction each take a number of forms. Extraction, for instance, ranges from outright plunder to regular tribute to bureaucratized taxation. Yet all four depend on the state's tendency to monopolize the concentrated means of coercion. From the perspectives of those who dominate the state, each of them—if carried on effectively—generally reinforces the others. Thus, a state that successfully eradicates its internal rivals strengthens its ability to extract resources, to wage war, and to protect its chief supporters. In the earlier European experience, broadly speaking, those supporters were typically landlords, armed retainers of the monarch, and churchmen.

Each of the major uses of violence produced characteristic forms of organization. War making yielded armies, navies, and supporting services. State making produced durable instruments of surveillance and control within the territory. Protection relied on the organization of war making and state making but added to it an apparatus by which the protected called forth the protection that was their due, notably through courts and representative assemblies. Extraction brought fiscal and accounting structures into being. The organization and deployment of violence themselves account for much of the characteristic structure of European states.

The general rule seems to have operated like this: The more costly the activity, all other things being equal, the greater was the organizational residue. To the extent, for example, that a given government invested in large standing armies—a very costly, if effective, means of war making—the bureaucracy created to service the army was likely to become bulky. Furthermore, a government building a standing army while controlling a small population was likely to incur greater costs, and therefore to build a bulkier structure, than a government within a populous country. Brandenburg–Prussia was the classic case of high cost for available resources. The Prussian effort to build an army matching those of its larger Continental neighbors created an immense structure; it militarized and bureaucratized much of German social life.

In the case of extraction, the smaller the pool of resources and the less commercialized the economy, other things being equal, the more difficult was the work of extracting resources to sustain war and other governmental activities; hence, the more extensive was the fiscal apparatus. England illustrated the corollary of that proposition, with a relatively large and commercialized pool of resources drawn on by a relatively small fiscal apparatus. As Gabriel Ardant has argued, the choice of fiscal strategy probably made an additional difference. On the whole, taxes on land were expensive to collect as compared with taxes on trade, especially large flows of trade past easily controlled checkpoints. Its position astride the entrance to the Baltic gave Denmark an extraordinary opportunity to profit from customs revenues.

With respect to state making (in the narrow sense of eliminating or neutralizing the local rivals of the people who controlled the state), a territory populated by great landlords or by distinct religious groups generally imposed larger costs on a conqueror than one of fragmented power or homogeneous culture. This time, fragmented and homogeneous Sweden, with its relatively small but effective apparatus of control, illustrates the corollary.

Finally, the cost of protection (in the sense of eliminating or neutralizing the enemies of the state makers' clients) mounted with the range over which that protection extended. Portugal's effort to bar the Mediterranean to its merchants' competitors in the spice trade provides a textbook case of an unsuccessful protection effort that nonetheless built up a massive structure.

Thus, the sheer size of the government varied directly with the effort devoted to extraction, state making, protection, and, especially, war making but inversely with the commercialization of the economy and the extent of the resource base. What is more, the relative bulk of different features of the government varied with the cost/resource ratios of extraction, state making, protection, and war making. In Spain we see hypertrophy of Court and courts as the outcome of centuries of effort at subduing internal enemies, whereas in Holland we are amazed to see how small a fiscal apparatus grows up with high taxes within a rich, commercialized economy.

Clearly, war making, extraction, state making, and protection were interdependent. Speaking very, very generally, the classic European state making experience followed [the] causal pattern [illustrated below].

In an idealized sequence, a great lord made war so effectively as to become dominant in a substantial territory, but that war making led to increased extraction of the means of war—men, arms, food, lodging, transportation, supplies, and/or the money to buy them—from the

Figure 8.1

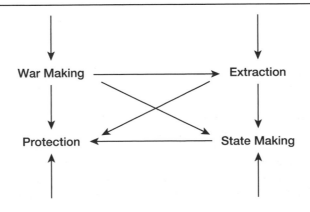

population within that territory. The building up of war-making capacity likewise increased the capacity to extract. The very activity of extraction, if successful, entailed the elimination, neutralization, or cooptation of the great lord's local rivals; thus, it led to state making. As a by-product, it created organization in the form of tax-collection agencies, police forces, courts, exchequers, account keepers; thus it again led to state making. To a lesser extent, war making likewise led to state making through the expansion of military organization itself, as a standing army, war industries, supporting bureaucracies, and (rather later) schools grew up within the state apparatus. All of these structures checked potential rivals and opponents. In the course of making war, extracting resources, and building up the state apparatus, the managers of states formed alliances with specific social classes. The members of those classes loaned resources, provided technical services, or helped ensure the compliance of the rest of the population, all in return for a measure of protection against their own rivals and enemies. As a result of these multiple strategic choices, a distinctive state apparatus grew up within each major section of Europe.

HOW STATES FORMED

This analysis, if correct, has two strong implications for the development of national states. First, popular resistance to war making and state making made a difference. When ordinary people resisted vigorously, authorities made concessions: guarantees of rights, representative institutions, courts of appeal. Those concessions, in their turn, constrained the later paths of war making and state making. To be sure, alliances with fragments of the ruling class greatly increased the effects of popular action; the broad mobilization of gentry against Charles I helped give the English Revolution of 1640 a far greater impact on political institutions than did any of the multiple rebellions during the Tudor era.

Second, the relative balance among war making, protection, extraction, and state making significantly affected the organization of the states that emerged from the four activities. To the extent that war making went on with relatively little extraction, protection, and state making, for example, military forces ended up playing a larger and more autonomous part in

national politics. Spain is perhaps the best European example. To the extent that protection, as in Venice or Holland, prevailed over war making, extraction, and state making, oligarchies of the protected classes tended to dominate subsequent national politics. From the relative predominance of state making sprang the disproportionate elaboration of policing and surveillance; the Papal States illustrate that extreme. Before the twentieth century, the range of viable imbalances was fairly small. Any state that failed to put considerable effort into war making was likely to disappear. As the twentieth century wore on, however, it became increasingly common for one state to lend, give, or sell war-making means to another; in those cases, the recipient state could put a disproportionate effort into extraction, protection, and/or state making and yet survive. In our own time, clients of the United States and the Soviet Union provide numerous examples.

This simplified model, however, neglects the external relations that shaped every national state. Early in the process, the distinction between "internal" and "external" remained as unclear as the distinction between state power and the power accruing to lords allied with the state. Later, three interlocking influences connected any given national state to the European network of states. First, there were the flows of resources in the form of loans and supplies, especially loans and supplies devoted to war making. Second, there was the competition among states for hegemony in disputed territories, which stimulated war making and temporarily erased the distinctions among war making, state making, and extraction. Third, there was the intermittent creation of coalitions of states that temporarily combined their efforts to force a given state into a certain form and position within the international network. The war-making coalition is one example, but the peace-making coalition played an even more crucial part: From 1648, if not before, at the ends of wars all effective European states coalesced temporarily to bargain over the boundaries and rulers of the recent belligerents. From that point on, periods of major reorganization of the European state system came in spurts, at the settlement of widespread wars. From each large war, in general, emerged fewer national states than had entered it.

A MODEL OF STATE–SOCIETY RELATIONS

Joel Migdal

STATES AND WEBLIKE SOCIETIES

In parts of the Third World, the inability of state leaders to achieve predominance in large areas of their countries has been striking. A central argument I elaborate in this book is that the capacity of states (or incapacity, as the case may be), especially the ability to implement social policies and to mobilize the public, relates to the structure of society. The ineffectiveness of state leaders who have faced impenetrable barriers to state predominance has stemmed from the nature of the societies they have confronted—from the resistance posed by chiefs, landlords, bosses, rich peasants, clan leaders, *za'im, effendis, aghas, caciques, kulaks* (for convenience, "strongmen") through their various social organizations.

There can be no understanding of state capabilities in the Third World without first comprehending the social structure of which states are only one part. In those countries where states have faced the greatest obstacles in their leaders' quest for predominance, a social environment continues in which many structures conflict with one another over how social life should be ordered. In fact, this is the environment of conflict. Grindle quoted one Mexican state official's description of such an environment: " 'Going out and meeting with peasants can be a dangerous business in Mexico. It threatens a lot of people.' In some remote areas, the *caciques* were considered to be an unassailable force, even by the party."[1]

Even in these cases, the state's impact should not be underestimated. The image of the strong state is certainly well grounded. In many countries the state still is the most prominent organization in this environment, but its leaders have not established it as predominant, able to govern the details of most people's lives in the society. The leaders have been unable to transform many aspects of the society according to their liking. In Egypt . . . the state undertook a major onslaught in the 1950s and 1960s against wealthy landlords and their rules of the game. State policies did radically alter rural social structure, but President Nasser witnessed the emergence of new patterns, not at all to his liking and not at all what he had expected. The old landed class was gone, but

Nasser's regime was being forced "to rely on the well-to-do peasants as a 'mediator' between the government and the mass of the peasantry. In this the Nasserites resembled every previous administration of rural Egypt, despite the former's very different ideology and social base. Government regulations certainly did little to weaken the strength of the rural middle class."[2] . . . [S]tate actions frequently have brought social changes even when the state has not been predominant and in ways quite different from those set out in official policy.

Many Third World countries have differed from those of both the West and the Socialist bloc, not so much in the amount of social control in the society but in its distribution and its centralization. Both these types of societies, the highly centralized and the more diffused, can be considered "strong" because the overall level of social control is high. They differ because in one the pyramidal structure of society concentrates social control at the apex of the pyramid, in the state, while in the other social control is spread through various fairly autonomous social organizations.[3] Both these sorts differ from "weak" societies in which the overall level of social control is low; the latter have often appeared in the wake of cataclysmic events. Natural disaster, war, and other extraordinary circumstances can greatly decrease the overall level of social control in societies by taking rewards and sanctions out of the hands of leaders of social organizations or by making the strategies of survival they offer irrelevant to the new exigencies people face. Table 8.1 presents a matrix differentiating types of societies by the distribution and overall amount of social control exercised.

Strong Third World societies, then, are not mere putty to be molded by states with sufficient technical resources, managerial abilities, and committed personnel. Although the set of organizations ranging from small kinship groups to large tribes and ethnic groups has been thought as anachronistic as the hand plow, it has often not simply disintegrated under the impact of state policies or even in the wake of increased urbanization and industrialization.[4] The tenacity of these groups and their strongmen leaders can enrage determined state officials.

Table 8.1   **SOCIAL CONTROL OF STATES AND SOCIETIES**

		state	
		strong	**weak**
society	**strong**	—	diffused (Sierra Leone)
	weak	pyramidal (France, Israel)	anarchical (China, 1939–1945; Mexico, 1910–1920)

Prime Minister Indira Gandhi of India experienced such frustration when, as Francine Frankel put it, "the government appeared power-less to carry out its own program of institutional reform," even after her party in 1971 and 1972 had achieved its largest popular mandate in twenty years of electoral politics.[5] Her inability to get people to adopt the state's codes and norms led her to new responses—authoritarianism, harsh methods, including widespread reports of forced sterilization—that still ran headlong into the same brick wall. "Heredity caste groups, each placed in a position of ritual superiority or infe-riority to the others, and all governed in their mutual relationships by customary norms of reciprocal, nonsymmetrical rights and obliga-tions, continued to provide the building blocks of social organization in the hundreds of thou-sands of India's villages."[6]

These castes, and other groups with their own rules in other countries, have continued to exhibit a hard-nosed persistence to survive in many areas and to resist the replacement of their social control by that of a state. It has been far too common in the literature on the Third World to dismiss with a wave of the hand the impor-tance of the local, small organizations with rules different from those of the state. They have seemed so inconsequential, especially to someone who has rarely left the capital city. A book on Sierra Leone demonstrates how easy it is to denigrate local struggles.

Such struggles tend to be largely personal or factional, not based on any broader social divisions. Since the participants tend to be largely in the "residual" sector, *their actions will have little if any impact upon the national arena. And even if their actions do affect the national arena, local leaders have to operate within both legal and financial frameworks set by the national leaders, and are open to fairly drastic coercion if they overtly oppose the national leadership.[7]*

In fact, events and struggles at the local level can have a momentous impact on both the state and the goal of state predominance. . . . For the moment, though, it is worth looking more closely at the nature of social structures in order to understand their relationship to the state.

For each Third World society as a whole, some important commonly shared values and memories provide the bases for the symbolic configuration underpinning social control. Many of these evolved during colonial adminis-tration. Yet these shared experiences have often paled next to the radically different sets of beliefs and recollections dispersed throughout the society. In fact, the very boundaries of these societies may be vague and uncertain.[8] The strength of shared memories and beliefs within various subunits—the clans, tribes, linguistic groups, ethnic groups, and so on—suggests an image for many societies of the Third World quite different from the centralized, pyramidal structure found, say, in many European coun-tries. Numerous Third World societies have been as resilient as an intricate spider's web; one could snip a corner of the web away and the rest of the web would swing majestically between the branches, just as one could snip center strands and have the web continue to exist. Although

Table 8.2   **ETHNIC AND LINGUISTIC FRACTIONALIZATION**

Level of Fractionalization	First World Countries		Second World Countries		Third World Countries	
	No.	%	No.	%	No.	%
Very high	2	7.7	1	11.1	31	30.7
High	6	23.1	2	22.2	26	25.7
Low	7	27.0	2	22.2	25	24.8
Very low	11	42.3	4	44.4	19	18.8
Totals	26	100.0	9	100.0	101	100.0

Note: *Very high* represents the first quartile of the most fractionized thirty four countries; *High* represents the second quartile, and *Low* the third quartile; *Very low* represents the fourth quartile of the least fractionized thirty four countries.

Source: Adapted from Charles Lewis Taylor and Michael G. Hudson, *World Handbook of Political and Social Indicators*, 2d ed. (New Haven: Yale University Press, 1972), pp. 271–74. Copyright © Charles Lewis Taylor and Michael G. Hudson. Reprinted with permission of Yale University Press.

there certainly have been connections between the parts and some parts have been obviously more important than others, often no single part has been totally integral to the existence of the whole.

The difficulties state leaders have had in many Third World countries in achieving social control relate to the state's place in these web-like societies. True, every society, including those of the West, has comingled multiple sets of beliefs and memories. However, the diversity in many Third World societies taken as a whole compared to other societies can be striking. **Weblike societies** host a mélange of fairly autonomous social organizations. Although Table 8.2 by no means covers all types of subunits that have maintained social control in various societies, it does reflect at least the differences in ethnic and linguistic fractionalization between the Third World and elsewhere.

Well over half the Third World countries are either "very high" or "high" in ethnic and linguistic fractionalization, while less than a third of other countries fall into these categories (see Table 8.2). Such statistics have severe limitations; for instance, they camouflage the tremendous differences among Third World societies themselves. Moreover, Table 8.2 does not show how such fragmentation relates to actual social control. Nevertheless, it does convey a warning that Third World societies and states may not fit well into molds shaped on the basis of European or North American experiences.

Our analytic lenses have conditioned us to view *all* modern societies in ways attuned to their centralization of power, rather than in ways suited to weblike structures. We look for cleavages between "social classes," or we look at "national entities." Social change is analyzed in terms of centers conquering peripheries or modern sectors clashing with traditional ones or, perhaps, class conflicting with class. We examine politics in the capital city to see who precisely holds the reins of power; which social class dominates, or who authoritatively allocates values. We have a penchant for seeking out where the ballgame is being played, but our lenses and predilections may have misled us. There may be no one ballgame, no single manager of power. Overarching concepts, such as cohesive social classes or nationalism, may belie the reality of how social control has been exercised and how that has been changing. In many Third World countries, many ballgames may be played simultaneously. In weblike societies, although social control is fragmented and heterogeneous, this does not mean that people are not being governed; they most certainly are. The allocation of values, however, is not centralized. Numerous systems of justice operate simultaneously. The new lenses can give us very different insights into political inertia and political change.

Reading Notes

1. Merilee Serrill Grindle, *Bureaucrats, Politicians, and Peasants in Mexico: A Case Study in Public Policy* (Berkeley: University of California Press, 1977), p. 160.

2. Alan Richards, *Egypt's Agricultural Development, 1800–1980: Technical and Social Change* (Boulder, Colo.: Westview Press, 1982), p. 179.

3. Michael Mann has spoken of the "essentially federal nature of extensive preindustrial societies." *A History of Power from the Beginning to A.D. 1760*, vol. 1 in *The Sources of Social Power* (Cambridge: Cambridge University Press, 1986), p. 10.

4. Suzanne Berger and Michael J. Piore, *Dualism and Discontinuity in Industrial Societies* (Cambridge: Cambridge University Press, 1980).

5. Francine R. Frankel, *India's Political Economy, 1947–1977: The Gradual Revolution* (Princeton, N.J.: Princeton University Press, 1978), p. 4.

6. Ibid., p. 5.

7. John R. Cartwright, *Political Leadership in Sierra Leone* (Toronto: University of Toronto Press, 1978), p. 116.

8. See Anthony Giddens, *The Nation-State and Violence*, vol. 2 of *A Contemporary Critique of Historical Materialism* (Cambridge: Polity Press, 1985), ch. 1. Giddens argues that boundaries are so fuzzy in such cases that one better speaks of frontiers.

KEY TERMS

Max Weber (1864–1920)   German sociologist famous for his definition of the state.

Nation-State   That type of political organization where the territorially defined state overlaps with the idea of a nation.

Regime   The nexus of alliances within and without the formal bureaucratic and public sectors that the leader forms in order to gain power and to keep it.

State   A compulsory political association with continuous organization whose administrative staff successfully upholds a claim to the *monopoly* of *legitimate* use of force in the enforcement of its order within a given territorial area.

Weblike Societies   Developing countries societies composed of competing and autonomous social organizations.

Welfare State   An interventionist state that seeks to promote some measure of social and economic equality among its citizens by redistribution attained through taxation and social programs.

FURTHER READINGS

Diamond, Larry. *Squandered Victory: The American Occupation and the Bungled Effort to Bring Democracy to Iraq.* New York Times Books, 2005.

Englebert, Pierre. "The Contemporary African State: Neither African nor State." *Third World Quarterly* 18, no. 4 (1997): 767–75.

Evans, Peter B., Dietrich Rueschemeyer, and Theda Skocpol,, eds. *Bringing the State Back In.* Cambridge: Cambridge University Press, 1985.

Fukuyama, Francis. *State-Building: Governance and World Order in the 21st Century*. Ithaca: Cornell University Press, 2004.

Migdal, Joel S. "Studying the State." In *Comparative Politics: Rationality, Culture, and Structure*. Edited by Mark Irving Lichbach and Alan S. Zuckerman. Cambridge: Cambridge University Press, 1997.

Pierson, Paul. *Dismantling the Welfare State? Reagan, Thatcher, and the Politics of Retrenchment*. Cambridge: Cambridge University Press, 1994.

Razin, Assaf and Efraim Sadka. *The Decline of the Welfare State: Demography and Globalization*. Cambridge, MA: MIT Press, 2005.

Rubin, Barnett R. *The Fragmentation of Afghanistan: State Formation and Collapse in the International System*. New Haven: Yale University Press, 2002.

Tilly, Charles, ed. *The Formation of National States in Western Europe*. Princeton: Princeton University Press, 1975.

WEB LINKS

The Failed States Index:
www.foreignpolicy.com/story/cms.php?story_id = 3098

Federal Research Division—Country Studies:
http://lcweb2.loc.gov/frd/cs/cshome.html

European Union at a Glance:
http://europa.eu/abc/index_en.htm

Area Studies from Richard Kimber's Political Science Resources:
www.psr.keele.ac.uk

CHAPTER 9

EXECUTIVES AND LEGISLATURES

The three main functions of government are the making, the execution, and the interpretation of laws. These functions are performed by different branches of government: the legislature, the executive, and the judiciary. Political systems differ greatly in their organization of the relationship between these branches. In some cases, the powers of the three branches are separated; elsewhere the lines of separation are not as clear. In such cases, one or another branch may prevail over the others. This chapter will focus on the organization of the relationship between the executive and legislative branches.

THE LEGISLATURE

The central task of the legislature is law production. Depending on the number of their chambers, legislatures may be either unicameral or bicameral. The legislative process can be considerably more complicated in a bicameral than in a unicameral legislature because of the greater number of veto players involved. A **veto player** of a legislative process is defined as an actor whose consent is required for the status-quo bill to be changed and amended. Thus, both chambers of a bicameral legislature may be veto players if the constitution requires that a bill be passed by both in order to become law. Sometimes, one chamber may override a veto of the other chamber if the bill is repassed therein by some specified majority.

In states with bicameral legislatures, the first or lower chamber is elected on the principle of popular representation, while the second or upper chamber is organized on the basis of some other principle. (In Chapter 12 we will be reviewing some of the main types of electoral systems that are used in legislative elections.) For the purposes of electing the first or lower chamber, the entire state is divided into a number of geographically delineated constituencies, each of which is entitled to elect a predefined number of representatives. In some countries, like Canada, each district is entitled to elect one representative, but there are many states around the world with multimember constituencies, for example, Poland. In some states, the entire state is used as a single electoral constituency, as in Slovakia. The actual names of the lower chambers often express this idea of popular representation. Thus, we find first chambers are called the House of Commons (as in Canada or Britain), or the House of Representatives (as in the United States). Similarly, the names of the second chamber usually express the underlying principle of representation on which that legislative body is founded. For example, the British upper chamber is called the House of Lords, which clearly denotes its origins of aristocratic representation; the upper chamber of the Indian Parliament is called the Council of States (Rajya Sabah), suggesting that it provides representation for the subnational units of the federation (the states). Second chambers are often called the Senate (as in Canada or the United States).

An important stage of the legislative process is the scrutiny that a bill receives in the various legislative committees. Members of the legislature receive committee assignments depending on their background, expertise, interests, and seniority. These assignments, especially those on the most powerful committees, are often coveted not only because of the additional financial compensation that legislators receive but also because of the influence that they afford legislators in shaping a bill. Some committees are more prestigious than others because of the nature of their mandate or the area of legislation that they are mandated to scrutinize. For example, standing committees on finance or foreign affairs deal with issue areas of great national significance and, as a result, tend to be more prestigious than others. Legislatures can vary significantly in terms of the strength of their committee system. In some legislatures, however, committees are very weak either because of inadequate resources, facilities, or the large number of assignments per legislator. The more committee assignments a legislator has, the smaller the chances that he or she becomes an expert in any one specific area of legislation. At the same time, it is also important to have a sufficient number of committees to oversee the activities of each government department. Therefore, a good measure of the strength of the committee system in a legislature is the number of permanent legislative committees relative to the number of government departments. All in all, committees are very effective tools in the hands of the legislature to keep a check on the executive (described below).

Legislative committees may be of three major types: permanent or standing, ad hoc, or joint. Standing committees are of a permanent nature; they are mandated to look after bills proposed in clearly defined issue or policy areas. Normally they exercise oversight and scrutiny over the activity of the government department and the civil service in their area of responsibility. The number of standing committees, as well as the restrictions on their activities, provides important information about the power of the legislative branch of government over the executive. The more standing committees there are, the less overburdened committee members will be to deal with bills and issues in their jurisdiction. However, if the number of standing committees is lower, then government departments enjoy greater scope of freedom and autonomy from legislative oversight. In contrast to standing committees, the legislature may decide to form an ad hoc committee in order to examine and investigate a particularly sensitive issue, scandal, or problem of immediate and major concern to the population. Finally, bicameral legislatures may appoint joint committees in order to resolve conflicts that may emerge between the two chambers in the legislative process or simply to ensure that representatives from both chambers are adequately involved in scrutinizing the government.

Legislatures also fulfill an important representative function in a polity. Where the law-making body brings together individuals from various economic classes and cleavage groups (whether ethnic, linguistic, regional or linguistic minorities), it is very likely that the laws passed by the legislature will be both reflective of and responsive to the needs and views of the widest possible range of interests in the political community. As we shall see in the chapter on political parties, the electoral system makes all the difference with regard to the representation of cleavage groups; while the viewpoints of minority groups are better represented under proportional representation in general, they tend to be under-represented under first-past-the-post and majoritarian rules. The first-past-the-post is generally referred to as the plurality electoral system where the eventual winner has to win a only plurality of the votes cast in the constituency. Similarly the majoritarian rules award seats to parties that have received the majority of votes in the electoral district. For details see Chapter 11. This suggests that the nature of the electoral system and the voting rule in a polity has a significant influence on the ability of the legislature to fulfill its representative function!

In non-democratic regimes, the law-making body can still fulfill an important representative function even though its members are not elected in free and fair elections. In such cases, the token representation of diverse social groups in the legislature can be actually used by the political elite to enhance the legitimacy of the non-democratic regime! Since most social groups are represented in the legislature, it is easy to claim that the laws of the land are

Table 9.1 **THE REPRESENTATION OF WOMEN IN SELECTED NATIONAL PARLIAMENTS**

Rank and State	Number of Seats in Parliament or Lower House	# of Female MPs	% of Female MPs
1. Rwanda	80	39	48.8
2. Sweden	349	158	45.3
42. Canada	308	65	21.1
85. Italy	616	71	11.5
101. Hungary	385	35	9.1
107. India	543	45	8.3
138. United Arab Emirates	40	0	0

Source: Adapted from Inter-parliamentary Union, "Women in National Parliaments, as of 31 March 2006", http://www.ipu.org/wmn-e/classif.htm, accessed 30 April, 2006.

reflective of the needs of the general population even though legislators are not elected in contested elections.

Table 9.1 will shed light on one particular aspect of the representative function of legislatures around the world: the representation of women. The Inter-Parliamentary Union, an international association of legislatures, regularly collects and updates a database about the number and percentage of female members of legislative institutions. In 2005, considering all legislatures around the world (both democratically elected and those that are not), only 15.4 percent of parliamentary deputies were female! The representation of women was slightly higher in lower houses and unicameral legislatures than in upper houses: in the former 15.6 percent of all deputies were female while in the latter the corresponding figure is only 14.5 percent!

There are very strong regional differences, however, in terms of the representation of women in parliaments around the world. The highest percentage of female deputies are reported in the Americas (18.6 percent) followed by Europe (18.1 percent), although it is worth mentioning that the Nordic states of Europe (Sweden, Norway, Finland, Denmark, and Iceland) have a much higher average, at 39.7 percent, than the rest of Europe. Next in line is Asia at 15.1 percent followed by sub-Saharan Africa and the Pacific region at 14.6 percent and 11.1 percent, respectively. According to the Inter-Parliamentary Union, Arab states have the smallest number of women deputies at 6 percent on average.

The table shows a very small sample of states and their rank in terms of the rate of the legislative representation of women in all states of the world. Note that the state with the highest percentage is Rwanda! The table also helps us see that there is no significant relationship between the size of the legislature, i.e., the number seats, and the percentage of women deputies. One might expect that as the number of seats increases, so does the opportunity to have more women represented in the legislature. However, the data suggest otherwise: both India and Italy have very large legislatures, yet comparatively speaking, they have very few female deputies.

Finally, let us use the analytical technique we have learnt in Chapter 3 to see whether this relationship is more meaningful on the global scale. Our hypothesis is that the number of female parliamentary deputies will increase as the number of seats in the legislature increases. Our dependent variable is the percentage of all deputies who are female, our

Figure 9.1 **THE SIZE OF LEGISLATURES AND THE REPRESENTATION OF WOMEN**

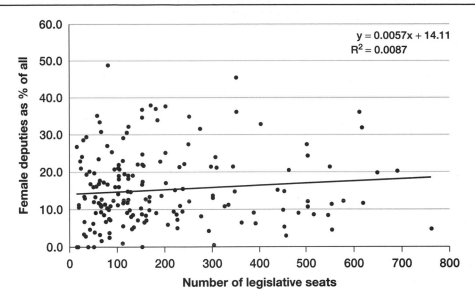

independent variable is the number of seats in the national parliament, or its lower house. As before, we will plot the values of the dependent variable along the vertical axis and those of our independent variable along the horizontal axis. Figure 9.1 shows our findings!

It is striking how weak the relationship between our variables is. The value of the correlation coefficient (R^2) shows that only a very small share of the variance in our dependent variable is explained by changes in the independent variable. We do see, however, that although the relationship is weak it is positive: as the values increases along the x-axis, the values also increase along the y-axis although at a very mild rate of 0.0057. In sum, this short exercise suggests that increasing the overall number of seats in the legislature is not a very effective way of increasing the number of women in national legislatures.

THE EXECUTIVE

Collectively, the executive branch of government is responsible for implementing the laws made by the legislature. At the top of the hierarchy within the executive is the **head of state**, who not only symbolizes the unity of the state but, depending on the constitution, may also have important and effective political powers. In terms of selection, two main types of head of state may be identified: the elected and the hereditary. In countries where the head of state is a non-hereditary office, the head of state is often called the president, as in the United States, India, Germany, Poland, or the Czech Republic, for instance.

Elected heads of state may be further classified according to whether elections are carried out directly by the people or indirectly by the representatives of the people. Examples of directly elected heads of state abound in Latin America. In fact, the constitution of every state in the Southern Cone of the continent (the southernmost areas of South America, including Argentina, Brazil, Chile, Paraguay and Uruguay) provides for a directly elected head of state. In Western Europe, the most important example of a directly elected head of state is France. Heads of state who are indirectly elected can be found in Germany or India.

A number of contemporary democracies still have hereditary monarchs as their chief executive. Some prominent examples are Britain and its former colonies that still belong to the British Commonwealth, Norway, and the Netherlands. In Canada, the governor general represents the British monarch, who technically remains the head of state. Of the three types of head of state, hereditary chief executives tend to have the least amount of political power; their role is primarily ceremonial and titular. Having said this, it must also be acknowledged that the ceremonial function they perform can contribute to enhancing the legitimacy of the standing political and constitutional regime of the state.

Besides the selection process, chief executives may also be distinguished in terms of the number of officeholders. While the overwhelming majority of states have a single person performing the functions of the head of state, some states have a *collegial chief executive*. An important example of the collegial chief executive is found in Switzerland. The seven-member Swiss Federal Council was designed as a *consociational* device to allow the main political and linguistic groups of this deeply divided land to share political power. The Swiss "magic formula," devised in 1959 and followed ever since, requires that the four main political parties (the Social Democrats, the Christian Democrats, the Radical Democrats, and the Swiss Peoples' Party) share the seven seats in the executive in a 2:2:2:1 proportion that roughly reflects the four parties' share of electoral following. Moreover, it is further stipulated by the formula that at least four of the seven members of the Council be German speakers, and that there be at least one French and one Italian speaker on the Council.

Executives can be distinguished in terms of the relationship between the head of state and the head of government. Whereas the former is in charge of representing and maintaining the unity of the state, the latter is responsible for the day-to-day management of the political affairs thereof. Two principal types of executives exist based on the relationship between the heads of state and government: 1) executives in which the two offices are held by the same person, or 2) executive branches in which the two roles are played by different individuals (split executive). The elected president of the United States as well as the directly elected presidents of Southern Cone Latin America and a number of post-Soviet Central Asian states fuse the two functions. In contrast, the directly elected presidents of Western (France) and Eastern Europe (e.g., Poland, Romania, and Bulgaria) do not function as heads of government at the same time.

After the head of state, the **head of government** makes up the next rung in the executive hierarchy. In contrast to the head of state, the duty of the head of government is the day-to-day management of the executive branch. The head of government is assisted by the council of ministers, or **cabinet**. In some political systems, such as Great Britain or Canada, cabinets are collectively responsible to the legislature. This doctrine of *collective cabinet responsibility* encourages both teamwork and consensual decision making in the cabinet. It means that no single member of the cabinet may be censured by the legislature. If the government is defeated in the legislature on a critical bill, then it is considered as the defeat of the entire cabinet, which, depending on the type of bill in question, may be required to resign. Another doctrine to mention with respect to the practice of cabinet government is *individual ministerial responsibility*, which means that each minister is responsible for the affairs of the department, or ministry, that he or she heads. Where individual ministerial responsibility is an established practice, ministers may be compelled to resign their positions as a result of scandal or failure of policy delivery.

The doctrines of collective cabinet and individual ministerial responsibility significantly affect the powers of the head of government. In political systems where these doctrines are practised, the head of government is essentially a *primus inter pares*, meaning that he is the first, or prime, minister among his ministerial colleagues who are technically considered his equals. Despite this seeming equality, prime ministers tend to be more powerful; they can unilaterally decide to call a **vote of confidence** in the legislature. In such political systems, the prime minister can de facto blackmail the cabinet into rallying behind his or her proposed policies or face the legislature on vote of confidence. In contrast, where the cabinet has to make its decisions and resolutions collectively, including the call for a vote of confidence in the legislature, the power of the prime minister is effectively reduced.

In a number of states, the powers of the head of government are much more pronounced than the powers of the cabinet. In Germany, for example, the ministers named by the chancellor (prime minister) are responsible directly to the chancellor, not the legislature. Therefore, the resignation of any one member of the German cabinet can be initiated and demanded by the chancellor only. The chancellor's power over the cabinet stems from the fact that the chancellor is answerable to the legislature. Once elected, the chancellor can be removed only by a *constructive* **vote of no confidence**, which requires that the opposition parties agree on an alternative prime minister.

PRESIDENTIAL AND PARLIAMENTARY FORMS OF GOVERNMENT

Based on the organization and the relationship between the executive and legislative branches of government, there are three types of government: the presidential, the parliamentary, and the semi-presidential ones. The essential characteristics of the presidential government are

1. the direct election of the chief executive (in fact, this executive is called the president);
2. executive and legislative terms that are fixed and independent of one another;
3. the heading of the cabinet by the directly elected chief executive; and
4. some legislative authority in the hands of the directly elected chief executive.[1]

These four characteristics promote a separation of powers between the executive and the legislature. In terms of both their origin and survival, the two branches are essentially independent of one another. Political scientists have debated whether all four characteristics are necessary criteria of presidentialism. For instance, according to Arend Lijphart, the direct popular election of the executive, the non-collegiality of the executive office, and fixed executive term[2] effectively define a presidential form of government.[3]

Whereas presidentialism stresses the separation of powers, the parliamentary form of government is characterized by the fusion of legislative and executive authority. Thus, the parliamentary form of government

1. does not have a directly elected chief executive;
2. has terms of its executive and legislature that are contingent and interconnected; the executive can dismiss the legislature but its own term is dependent on the confidence of the legislature;
3. has a head of state who normally appoints the head of government, who directs the composition of the cabinet; and
4. has a head of state with no legislative authority.

The third or mixed system is the semi-presidential, also called premier-presidential, system of government. This type of government is characterized by

1. the direct election of the chief executive (president);
2. the wide range of powers granted to the directly elected president; and

Table 9.2

Region	Presidential	Parliamentary	Semi-Presidential
North America	United States	Canada	
Central and South America	Argentina, Brazil, Chile, Venezuela	Barbados, Jamaica, Trinidad, Tobago	
Western Europe		United Kingdom, Italy, Germany	France, Austria, Finland
Eastern Europe		Hungary, Czech Republic, Slovakia	Poland, Russia
Asia		India, Malaysia	
Africa	Nigeria, Senegal		

3. the presence of a cabinet and the prime minister who are subject to the confidence of the legislature.

Table 9.2 lists a few examples of each of the three types of government from various regions of the world. Although the table is not exhaustive, it reveals a few interesting patterns with respect to the adoption of the various types of systems.

First, most presidential forms of government are found in Latin America. Following the overthrow of Spanish imperial rule, early Latin American Republicans sought to model their new constitutions on that of the United States. Second, most parliamentary systems of government are found in Western Europe and the former non-European British colonies. Third, among the new democracies of Eastern Europe, the semi-presidential form of government has been the most popular choice.

By virtue of the separate elections of the executive and the legislature in the presidential and the semi-presidential systems, it is possible that different political forces, or **coalitions** of political parties, will come to control the two branches of government. The phenomenon of divided partisan control of the executive and legislative branches is called *divided government*. According to some, a divided government creates deadlock between the two branches of government, reduces the efficiency of policy making, and slows decision making. This view is challenged, however, by David Mayhew,[4] who argues that the disparate political actors in control of the two separate branches can and indeed have learned to cooperate. He found that the number of significant laws passed in the United States was not lower when the government was divided than when it was unified. In a more recent contribution to the debate, George Tsebelis[5] showed that the impact of divided government on law making depends on the ideological position of the players who control the branches. If they are located far apart from one another in the ideological space, then legislative deadlock will most likely characterize their relationship. However, if they are located close to one another, then it will be easy to find a compromise on any particular issue.

This section has reviewed the main functions of government and the principal ways in which the different branches responsible for these functions are organized. We have seen that despite the common functions of modern government, ways of organizing interbranch relations are extremely diverse. Comparative political scientists are interested not only in describing these differences but also in understanding their origins and consequences. As we have seen, the organization of interbranch relations not only impacts policy making but also has implications for other aspects of politics, such as the organization of political parties and pressure groups.

ENDNOTES

1. Shugart and Carey.
2. A fixed executive term means that the length of the term of the executive does not depend on the confidence of the legislature.
3. Note the extent to which Douglas Verney's list of eleven points (beginning on p. 184 of this book) overlaps with these different conceptualizations!
4. David Mayhew, *Divided We Govern: Party Control, Law Making and Investigations, 1946–1990* (New Haven and London: Yale University Press, 1993).
5. George Tsebelis, *Veto Players: How Political Institutions Work* (Princeton University Press, 2002).

READINGS

The relationship between the political executive and the legislature constitutes the most important nexus in any constitutional regime. The effective and efficient functioning of the entire political system rests on a good working relationship between the two branches of government. The first excerpt in this section is a detailed comparative overview of the essential characteristics of the presidential and parliamentary forms of government offered by Douglas Verney. The second reading is an important statement by Juan Linz regarding the dangers of adopting presidential constitutions in new democracies. These articles will help readers gain a clear understanding of the ways in which powers are allocated between the two branches, as well as the consequences that these arrangements have.

Douglas Verney offers a straightforward taxonomy of the main features that characterize the American presidential and the British parliamentary systems. The lists are thorough and comprehensive, although they do not apply to other cases. As we discussed, the powers of the head of state, the head of government, and the legislature vary considerably across the political systems of the world. Whereas the parliamentary–presidential distinction highlights some fundamental differences about institutional choices, it also conceals some important variations. In particular, the taxonomy does not point out where the semi-presidential system fits, although the lists make it possible to identify the various elements of both the parliamentary and presidential systems that make up this hybrid type.

The discussion on constitutional structures is not merely a descriptive exercise. The excerpt by Juan Linz shows the profound consequences that constitutional choices may have on the quality of democratic politics. In particular, Linz provides a strong argument, which has invited a lot of attention and debate, against the use of presidential constitutions in new democracies. He identifies a number of perilous features in presidentialism that new democracies in particular should avoid. These include conflicts emerging from the dual and competing claims to legitimacy between the legislature and the directly elected president; the polarizing impact of the winner-take-all nature of presidential elections on the electorate; the openness of the presidential system to outsiders who can make a sudden breakthrough in politics by abandoning radical populist agendas; and the temporal rigidity of the fixed presidential terms.

PARLIAMENTARY GOVERNMENT AND PRESIDENTIAL GOVERNMENT

Douglas Verney

Parliamentarism is the most widely adopted system of government, and it seems appropriate to refer to British parliamentary experience in particular because it is the British system which has provided an example for a great many other countries. Nowadays when it is fashionable to speak of political systems and theories as "not for export" it is worth bearing in mind the success with which a system adopted piecemeal to suit British constitutional developments has proved feasible in different situations abroad. This is not to imply that the British parliamentary system should be taken as the model and that others are, as it were, deviations from the norm, although generations of Englishmen have been tempted to make this assumption. . . .

Indeed an examination of parliamentarism in various countries indicates that there are two main types of parliamentary procedure, the British and the continental. . . .

This analysis of parliamentarism is concerned less with distinguishing the various forms of parliamentarism than with establishing the highest common factors in different parliamentary systems. . . . It may surprise those who have tended to regard British government as the model as well as the Mother of Parliaments to know that the United Kingdom could abolish the monarchy, adopt a single code of constitutional laws on the pattern of the French or American constitutions, transform the House of Lords into a senate (or even do away with it), introduce a multi-party system based on proportional representation, institute a number of parliamentary committees to deal with specific topics such as finance and foreign affairs, and still possess a parliamentary system.

There would seem to be a number of basic principles applicable to both of the chief varieties of parliamentary government. . . .

1. THE ASSEMBLY BECOMES A PARLIAMENT

Where parliamentary government has evolved rather than been the product of revolution there have often been three phases, though the transition from one to the other has not always been perceptible at the time. First there has been government by a monarch who has been responsible for the whole political system. Then there has arisen an assembly of members who have challenged the hegemony of the king. Finally the assembly has taken over responsibility for government, acting as a parliament, the monarch being deprived of most of his traditional powers.

This has certainly been the pattern in Britain. As late as the seventeenth century King James I could still preach the doctrine of the Divine Right of Kings. . . .

However, by establishing their power over the purse, assemblies were ultimately able to claim their own area of jurisdiction. Henceforth the monarch's role was increasingly that of an executive dependent ultimately on the goodwill of the legislature. Constitutional development entered a second phase in which the term "legislative power" was given to assemblies to distinguish them from the "executive power" of the king. . . .

But even as the theory of the separation of powers was coming into vogue the transition to the third and present phase was under way in Britain. In the eighteenth century the king was already losing his executive power to ministers who came to regard the assembly, not the monarch, as the sovereign to whom they were really responsible. Ministers were increasingly chosen from among members of the assembly and resigned when the assembly withdrew its confidence from them. . . .

In parliamentary monarchies such as Britain, Belgium and Sweden, the monarch has ceased in practice (though not in form) to exercise even the executive power. Government has passed to "his" ministers who are responsible to the legislature. Parliamentary government implies a certain fusion of the executive and legislative functions, the body which has been merely an assembly of representatives being transformed into a parliament. . . .

It is true that for the most part the use of the term "parliament" at one time to include the government and at others to exclude it seems to cause little difficulty, provided some knowledge of the parliamentary system is assumed. In a comparative study of political systems, however, such ambiguity presents certain problems if like is to be compared with like. It therefore becomes necessary to insist on a more precise usage. "Parliament" will at all times signify a body which includes the government. When it is necessary to refer to the legislature excluding members of the government the term "assembly" will be used. . . .

The first characteristic of parliamentarism may now be summarized. It is a political system where the executive, once separate, has been challenged by the assembly which is then transformed into a parliament comprising both government and assembly.

2. THE EXECUTIVE IS DIVIDED INTO TWO PARTS

One important consequence of the transformation of the assembly into a parliament is that the executive is now split in two, a prime minister or chancellor becoming head of the government and the monarch or president acting as head of state. Usually the monarch occupies his throne by hereditary title (though elected monarchies, e.g. in Malaya, are not unknown), while a president is elected by parliament. . . .

3. THE HEAD OF STATE APPOINTS THE HEAD OF GOVERNMENT

The value of a divided executive in constitutional monarchies is fairly obvious. For one thing, the proper business of state can be carried on by a government responsible to the legislature while the mystique of monarchy is preserved. There seems no apparent reason, at first glance, for dividing it in republics. Admittedly it is useful to have someone above the day-to-day political warfare to receive ambassadors and to decorate ceremonial occasions, but this hardly seems to justify the expense of such an office. After all, the president of the United States, who as head of the American government bears the greatest responsibilities of any statesman in the world, manages to combine with his high and lonely eminence the even higher office of head of state.

However, it is in the very nature of the parliamentary system that there shall be two distinct offices, and that the head of the government shall be appointed by the head of state. Were the electorate itself to perform this task, directly or through a special college of electors as in the United States or Finland, the system would become, in this respect at least, presidential in character. . . .

4. THE HEAD OF THE GOVERNMENT APPOINTS THE MINISTRY

An interesting feature of parliamentarism is the distinction made between the prime minister and other ministers. The former is appointed by the head of state; the latter are nominated by the prime minister after his appointment. Usually the selection of various ministers allows a certain amount of personal choice to a head of government, which cannot usually be said of the appointment of a prime minister by the head of state. Ministers are formally appointed by the head of state, who may often no doubt exert an informal influence upon appointments—but so may the state of party alignments and factions in the assembly. . . .

5. THE MINISTRY (OR GOVERNMENT) IS A COLLECTIVE BODY

The transfer from the monarchical executive to a council of ministers has meant that a single person has been replaced by a collective body. Whereas under *anciens régimes* it was the king's pleasure (*le Roi le veult*), under parliamentarism the prime minister is merely first among equals (*primus inter pares*), though no doubt some prime ministers are more forceful than others. . . .

6. MINISTERS ARE USUALLY MEMBERS OF PARLIAMENT

Members of the government have a double role to play in the parliamentary system. They are not only ministers but are at the same time members of parliament, elected (unless they are members of the British House of Lords) like the members of the assembly and equally dependent upon the goodwill of their constituents. . . .

Since, according to the usage adopted in this chapter, parliament comprises both government and assembly, a member of the government is *ipso facto* a member of parliament, but by definition he cannot be a member of the assembly. In fully parliamentary countries such as the United Kingdom where ministers are members of parliament it is difficult to make the distinction between government, parliament and assembly clear. Indeed the attempt to make one seems artificial.

However, not all parliamentary countries have accepted the necessity for ministers to be members of one of the houses of parliament. In Sweden up to a third of the ministry of fifteen members have on occasion in recent years not been members of parliament. In The Netherlands, Norway and Luxembourg ministers are actually forbidden to be members of parliament after their appointment. Here there is a relic of the old doctrine of the separation of powers when ministers were responsible to the monarch. . . .

Generally speaking, nevertheless, it is usual for most if not all ministers to be members of parliament. Where they are not, the system may still be said to be of the parliamentary type if they can take part in parliamentary debates and are truly responsible to the assembly for the conduct of the executive. In Norway, Sweden, The Netherlands and Luxembourg, all parliamentary monarchies, these conditions are fulfilled. In the French Fifth Republic, where the government is not responsible to parliament for the conduct of the president, they are not.

7. THE GOVERNMENT IS POLITICALLY RESPONSIBLE TO THE ASSEMBLY

In parliamentary systems the government is responsible to the assembly which may, if it thinks that the government is acting unwisely or unconstitutionally, refuse to give it support. By a formal vote of censure or by simply not assenting to an important government proposal the assembly can force the government to resign and cause the head of state to appoint a new government. . . .

8. THE HEAD OF GOVERNMENT MAY ADVISE THE HEAD OF STATE TO DISSOLVE PARLIAMENT

In the pre-parliamentary monarchies of Europe the monarch could, if dissatisfied with his assembly, dissolve one or more houses in the hope of securing a more amenable selection of representatives after a new election. Today, when the executive is divided, it is still the head of state who dissolves parliament, but he does so on the request, and only on the request, of the head of government. . . .

Certain states generally regarded as parliamentary severely restrict the right of the executive to dissolve the assembly. In Norway the Storting dissolves itself, the head of state being allowed to dissolve only special sessions, but this is a departure from parliamentarism

inspired by the convention theory of the French Revolution. . . .

9. PARLIAMENT AS A WHOLE IS SUPREME OVER ITS CONSTITUENT PARTS, GOVERNMENT AND ASSEMBLY, NEITHER OF WHICH MAY DOMINATE THE OTHER

The notion of the supremacy of parliament as a whole over its parts is a distinctive characteristic of parliamentary systems. This may seem a glimpse of the obvious to those accustomed to parliamentary government, but it is in fact an important principle, all too often forgotten, that neither of the constituent elements of parliament may completely dominate the other. The government depends upon the support of the assembly if it is to continue in office, but the assembly is not supreme because the government can, if it chooses, dissolve parliament and appeal to the electorate at the polls. Many parliamentary systems have failed because one or other of them has claimed supremacy, and parliament as a whole has not been supreme over both government and assembly.

In practice the nature of parliamentary supremacy varies from country to country. In the United Kingdom and Scandinavia the emphasis is on the government's role in parliament and in Britain the system is actually called "cabinet government." In others, notably the French Third and Fourth Republics, the dominant role in parliament was played by the assembly. . . .

10. THE GOVERNMENT AS A WHOLE IS ONLY INDIRECTLY RESPONSIBLE TO THE ELECTORATE

A parliamentary government, though directly responsible to the assembly, is only indirectly responsible to the electorate. The government as a whole is not directly elected by the voters but is appointed indirectly from amongst the representatives whom they elect to the assembly. The earlier direct relationship of monarch and people whereby persons could petition their sovereign disappeared as parliamentarism was introduced. Today the route to the government lies through elected representatives though in Britain, for example, one may still formally petition the monarch. It is true that members of the government, like other members of parliament, must (unless they are peers) stand before their constituents for election. However, they do so not as members of the government but as candidates for the assembly in the ordinary way. The responsibility for transforming them, once elected, into ministers rests with the prime minister alone (and of course with the monarch in the case of the prime minister). . . .

11. PARLIAMENT IS THE FOCUS OF POWER IN THE POLITICAL SYSTEM

The fusion of the executive and legislative powers in parliament is responsible for the overriding ascendancy of parliament in the political order. It is the stage on which the drama of politics is played out; it is the forum of the nation's ideas; and it is the school where future political leaders are trained. For parliamentarism to succeed, the government must not fret at the constant challenge which the Assembly offers to its programme, nor wince at the criticism made of its administration. The Assembly in turn must resist the temptation to usurp the functions of Government. Here is a delicate balance of powers which check each other without the benefit of separate institutions. . . .

***

Presidential government is often associated with the theory of the separation of powers which was popular in the eighteenth century when the American constitution was framed. Two writers in particular drew attention to this notion. John Locke, writing at the end of the seventeenth century, suggested that the long conflict between the British monarch and the houses of parliament would best be resolved by the separation of the king as executive from the two houses as legislature, each body having its own sphere. In the mid-eighteenth century a French observer of the British political scene, Montesquieu, pronounced himself in favour of the British system of government as one which embodied, in contrast to the despotism of the Bourbons, the separation of the executive, legislative, and judicial powers. Historically the theory as expounded by Locke and more especially Montesquieu is important for an understanding of the climate of opinion in which the American constitution was framed.

However, it is one thing to study this celebrated theory for historical purposes but quite another to trace its contemporary significance for an understanding of presidential government. It was, after all, based on the assumption that a monarch would act as executive and an assembly as legislature. The theory was considered to be an improvement on the absolute monarchies of the continent, which it undoubtedly was, and was praised with them in mind. There was as yet no experience of parliamentarism. Today such constitutional monarchies as still survive are based on the parliamentary principle.

Another offspring and successor of the theory is presidential government, but the substitution of an elected president for a hereditary monarch has, as we have seen, created a system hardly comparable with pre-parliamentary limited monarchies. If presidential government is regarded simply as a direct form or expression of the eighteenth-century doctrine of the separation of powers then (as indeed many people have thought) the Americans may, by adopting their rigid constitution, have artificially prevented their political system from developing into parliamentarism. But if, as it is argued here, the system is a successor to that doctrine then it is not like limited monarchy, the precursor of parliamentary government, but one of its two offsprings, the other being parliamentarism. . . .

It seemed appropriate to begin an analysis of parliamentary government by reference to British political institutions. It is equally valuable to study presidentialism by first examining the American political system. The United States was the first important country to break with the European monarchical tradition and to shake off colonial rule. The break occurred in the eighteenth century when Britain was still a limited monarchy and the theory of the separation of powers was in vogue. The American constitution bears witness to these influences and to the colonial government of governor and legislature, an elected president replacing the king or governor as the executive power. A number of countries—all twenty American republics, Liberia, the Philippines, South Korea and South Vietnam—have followed the example of the United States, though rarely with comparable success. The American political system is therefore the model and prototype of presidential government. Yet the United States, like the United Kingdom, could abolish or transform many of its institutions and remain based on the same theory of government. For example, the framers of the 1787 constitution could have proposed an elective monarch instead of a president, a house of lords rather than a senate, and a unitary political system instead of a federal union of states without destroying the presidential principle—though the name "presidential" would hardly be suitable for a system where the executive was an elective monarch. Presidential, like parliamentary, theory has certain basic characteristics irrespective of any particular political system.

The nature of presidential theory can best be understood by re-stating the eleven propositions [concerning parliamentary government—Ed.] as they apply to presidential government.

1. THE ASSEMBLY REMAINS AN ASSEMBLY ONLY

Parliamentary theory implies that the second phase of constitutional development, in which the assembly and judiciary claim their own areas of jurisdiction alongside the executive, shall give way to a third in which assembly and government are fused in a parliament. Presidential theory on the other hand requires the assembly to remain separate as in the second phase. The American Revolution led to a transfer from colonial rule to the second stage of separate jurisdiction, and there have been some observers who have thought that the rigid constitution has prevented the "natural" development of the American political system towards parliamentarism. This is not so. By abolishing the monarchy and substituting a president for the king and his government, the Americans showed themselves to be truly revolutionary in outlook. The presidential system as established in the USA made parliamentarism both unnecessary and impracticable in that country. The assembly (Congress in the United States) remains an assembly.

2. THE EXECUTIVE IS NOT DIVIDED BUT IS A PRESIDENT ELECTED BY THE PEOPLE FOR A DEFINITE TERM AT THE TIME OF ASSEMBLY ELECTIONS

The retention of a separate executive in the United States was made feasible because the executive remained undivided. It was not, of course, the same institution as the pre-parliamentary monarchical executive. Such a monarch governed by virtue of an ancient tradition into which he was born, and with all the strength and potential weaknesses that this implied. The presidential executive is elected by the people. In an era when governments have had to rely not on some mystique but on popular support the Americans have found a solution which has enabled their separate single executive to withstand criticism. The suggestions that the United States should adopt parliamentarism have proved abortive largely because it cannot be said of the presidency, as it could of hereditary monarchy, that the institution lacked democratic roots. . . .

The president is elected for a definite term of office. This prevents the assembly from forcing his resignation (except by impeachment for a serious misdemeanour) and at the same time requires the president to stand for re-election if he wishes to continue in office. It seems desirable that the chief executive's tenure should be limited to a certain number of terms. . . .

Equally important for the proper operation of the presidential system is the election of the president at the time of the assembly elections. This associates the two branches of government, encourages party unity, and clarifies the issues. Admittedly in the United States simultaneous elections do not prevent the return of a Republican President and a Democratic Congress but the tensions would be even greater if the president was elected for a seven-year term as in France. . . .

3. THE HEAD OF THE GOVERNMENT IS HEAD OF STATE

Whereas in pre-parliamentary monarchies the head of state was also the head of the government, in the presidential system it is the head of the government who becomes at the same time head of state. This is an important distinction because it draws attention to the limited pomp and circumstance surrounding the presidential office. The president is of little consequence until he is elected as political head by the electorate and he ceases to have any powers once his term of office has expired. The ceremonial aspect of his position is but a reflection of his political prestige. . . .

4. THE PRESIDENT APPOINTS HEADS OF DEPARTMENTS WHO ARE HIS SUBORDINATES

In parliamentarism the prime minister appoints his colleagues who together with him form the government. In presidential systems the president appoints secretaries (sometimes called ministers) who are heads of his executive departments. Formally, owing to the rule whereby appointments are subject to the confirmation of the assembly or one of its organs (in the United States the Senate, in the Philippines the Commission on Appointments) his choice may be restricted to persons of whom that body approves. In practice the president has a very wide choice. . . .

5. THE PRESIDENT IS SOLE EXECUTIVE

In contrast to parliamentary government, which is collective, the prime minister being first among equals, presidential government tends to be individual. Admittedly the term "cabinet" is used in the United States to describe the meetings of the president with his secretaries, but it is not a cabinet or ministry in the parliamentary sense. . . .

6. MEMBERS OF THE ASSEMBLY ARE NOT ELIGIBLE FOR OFFICE IN THE ADMINISTRATION AND VICE VERSA

Instead of the parliamentary convention or law whereby the same persons may be part of both the executive and legislative branches of government, it is customary in presidential states for the personnel to be separate. Neither the President nor his aides may sit in the US Congress. Few of the other American republics have copied the complete separation practised in the United States. While ministers may not be members of the assembly (except in Cuba and Peru) they are usually entitled to attend and take part in debates. . . .

7. THE EXECUTIVE IS RESPONSIBLE TO THE CONSTITUTION

The president is not, like parliamentary governments, responsible to the assembly. Instead he is, like pre-parliamentary monarchs, responsible to the constitution. But whereas in the *anciens régimes* this was but a vague notion, in presidential systems it is usually laid down with some precision in a constitutional document. . . .

It is usually the assembly which holds the president ultimately responsible to the constitution by the impeachment process. This does not imply that he is responsible to that body in the parliamentary sense of depending on its confidence in any political capacity. Impeachment enforces *juridical* compliance with the (constitutional) letter of the law and is quite different from the exercise of political control over the president's ordinary conduct of his office. Political responsibility implies a day-to-day relationship between government and assembly; impeachment is the grave and ultimate penalty (only one American President,

Andrew Johnson, was impeached, unsuccessfully) necessary where ordinarily the executive and assembly are not mutually dependent. . . .

8. THE PRESIDENT CANNOT DISSOLVE OR COERCE THE ASSEMBLY

The assembly, as we have just seen, cannot dismiss the president. Likewise, the president may not dissolve the assembly. Neither, therefore, is in a position to coerce the other, and it is not surprising that this system is, *par excellence*, one of checks and balances. In countless ways almost incomprehensible to those accustomed to parliamentarism the presidential system exhibits this mutual independence of the executive and legislative branches of government. . . .

9. THE ASSEMBLY IS ULTIMATELY SUPREME OVER THE OTHER BRANCHES OF GOVERNMENT AND THERE IS NO FUSION OF THE EXECUTIVE AND LEGISLATIVE BRANCHES AS IN A PARLIAMENT

It was remarked of parliamentary systems that neither the government nor the assembly is supreme because both are subordinate parts of the parliamentary institution. In presidential systems such fusion of the executive and legislative powers is replaced by separation, each having its own sphere. As we have just observed, constitutionally the executive cannot interfere in the proceedings of the assembly, still less dissolve it, and the assembly for its part cannot invade the province of the executive. . . .

Since there is no parliament there can be no parliamentary supremacy. Where, then, does supreme power lie in the event of a serious controversy? It has been demonstrated that the assembly cannot force the resignation of the president any more than he can dissolve the assembly. Moreover, both branches of government may find that their actions are declared unconstitutional by yet a third power, the judiciary. In a sense the constitution is supreme. The short answer is that it is intended in presidential government that the different branches shall check and balance one another and that none shall predominate.

Yet in a very real sense it is the assembly which is ultimately supreme. The president may have considerable authority allocated to him in the constitution but he may be powerless unless the assembly grants him the necessary appropriations.

If he acts unconstitutionally the assembly may impeach him. In the event of a serious conflict even the judiciary must bow to the will of the assembly because this body has the right to amend the constitution. The American constitution is not, as is sometimes asserted, simply "what the judges say it is."

It may be suggested that the position does not appear to be altogether different from that in parliamentary states where ultimately the legislature may amend the constitution. This is not so. In parliamentary states the constitution has to be amended by both government and assembly acting as parliament, whereas in presidential systems the assembly may amend the constitution without regard to the president. For example, the American Congress has limited the presidential tenure of office to two terms. . . .

10. THE EXECUTIVE IS DIRECTLY RESPONSIBLE TO THE ELECTORATE

Governments in parliamentary countries are appointed by the head of state; they are not elected. By contrast the presidential executive is dependent on a popular vote and the president alone (and vice-president if there is one), of all the persons in the political system, is elected by the whole body of electors. Whereas the pre-parliamentary monarchies could not in the end withstand the pressure of the people's representatives upon their control of government, a president can say to members of the assembly: "You represent your constituency: I represent the whole people." There is no reply to this argument, and it is perhaps not surprising that in many South American countries and in France at various times the president has been able to go one step further and to assert that he *alone* represented the people. . . .

11. THERE IS NO FOCUS OF POWER IN THE POLITICAL SYSTEM

The political activities of parliamentary systems have their focal point in parliament. Heads of state, governments, elected representatives, political parties, interest groups, and electorates all acknowledge its supremacy.

It is tempting to assume that there must be a similar focal point in presidential systems. This is not so. Instead of concentration there is division; instead of unity, fragmentation. In the design of Washington DC the President's home, the White House, is at the opposite end of Pennsylvania Avenue to the Capitol, where Congress meets. Geographical dispersion symbolizes their political separation. . . .

Those who admire efficient government may be inclined towards the cabinet government form of parliamentarism. Those who prefer more limited government may turn towards presidentialism. It should not be assumed, however, that the presidential form, because it is divided, is necessarily one of weak government. Admittedly, where presidential leadership is lacking the system may even appear to be on the verge of breaking down. But where there is a vigorous executive he may in fact dominate the assembly, as several American Presidents (notably Franklin D. Roosevelt) have succeeded in doing.

Miraculously, in the United States this domination has never gone too far. In much of Central and South America, where there is the form of presidential government but not the substance, the presidential system has been distorted by dictatorship.

It is difficult to explain the failure of presidential government in so many parts of South America and it is perilous to confine such explanation to purely political factors. Historically and culturally South and Central America are utterly different from the United States. However, there are a number of particular political features of these countries' systems which deserve note, not least of which is the multi-party system which characterizes several of them. Where a president is elected by what is in effect a minority vote instead of by the clear majority customary in the United States he lacks that sense of being the people's representative which is so marked a feature of the American presidency. At the very least it adds a complicating factor to the relations of president, assembly, and people, and in all probability contributes to political instability.

Where there is a multi-party system there is the temptation to add to the president's status and independence by giving him a longer term of office than the assembly. Not surprisingly the French Fifth Republic's constitution gives the president a term of seven years compared to the assembly's [five]. Such a long term, while of small moment in a parliamentary system, may make a president in a non-parliamentary system a powerful figure.

Finally, it may be observed that few countries have been able to enjoy the clear distinction between president and assembly so characteristic of the United States. There has been an attempt to introduce something of the "responsibility" common to parliamentary systems. Thus there is a separate "government" in the new French constitution, and this "government" (but not the president) is responsible to the assembly and may be dismissed by it. Yet the history of the Weimar Republic, to say nothing of Latin America, has shown that in practice (as if to confirm political theory) the president (i.e. the real government) may be unaffected by such a procedure and it then becomes an ineffective weapon in the hands of the assembly. If he *is* affected, then the system becomes parliamentary and the attempt to create a separate executive has failed.

For there should be either a separation as in the United States and *no* focus of the political system; or a fusion with parliament as the focus.

PRESIDENTIAL OR PARLIAMENTARY DEMOCRACY: DOES IT MAKE A DIFFERENCE?

Juan Linz

In recent decades renewed efforts have been made to study and understand the variety of political democracies, but most of those analyses have focused on the patterns of political conflict and more specifically on party systems and coalition formation, in contrast to the attention of many classical writers to institutional arrangements.[1] With the exception of the large literature on the impact of electoral systems on the shaping of party systems generated by the early writings of Ferdinand Hermens and the classic work by Maurice Duverger, followed by the writings of Douglas Rae and Giovanni Sartori, Rein Taagepera, and Matthew Shugart among others,[2] political scientists have paid little attention to the role of political institutions, except in the study of particular countries. Debates about monarchy and republic, parliamentary and presidential regimes, the unitary state and federalism have receded into oblivion and not entered the current debates about the functioning of democratic institutions and practices, including their effect on party systems. When a number of countries initiate the process of writing or rewriting constitutions, some of those issues should regain saliency and become part of what Sartori has called political engineering, in an effort to set the basis of democratic consolidation and stability.

Undoubtedly, the constitutional innovations of the postwar period, the German constructive nonconfidence vote, and the constitution of the French Fifth Republic, whose semipresidential regime reinforces the executive to counter the weaknesses of assembly parliamentarism, have attracted imitators and scholarly attention. But we lack a more systematic and behavioral study of the implications for the political process of different institutions on which to base some of the ongoing debates about institutional and constitutional reform. With the notable exception of the book by Kaltefleiter, in which the cases of a bipolar executive like the Weimar Republic and the French Fifth Republic are analyzed; the paper by Stefano Bartolini,[3] on cases of direct election of the head of state to Europe; the writings of Maurice Duverger and the new book by Matthew Soberg Shugart and John M. Carey,[4] the differences between parliamentary, presidential, and semipresidential regimes have not attracted much attention from political scientists. These differences receive only limited attention in the two most recent works comparing contemporary democracies, those of Bingham Powell and Arend Lijphart,[5] who has, however, written an excellent chapter on the implications of presidential regimes for this volume.

The neglect is largely due to the fact that with the outstanding exception of the United States, most of the stable democracies of Europe and the Commonwealth have been parliamentary regimes and a few semipresidential and semiparliamentary, while most of the countries with presidential constitutions have been unstable democracies or authoritarian regimes and therefore have not been included in comparative studies of democracy.[6] Since many social, economic, cultural, and political factors appeared central in the analysis of the crisis and breakdown of democracy in those countries, we find practically no mention of the role of institutional factors in those crises. Only in the case of Chile has there been some reference to the conflict between President Allende and the congress in the analysis of the breakdown of democracy.[7] It might or might not be an accident that so many countries with presidential regimes have encountered great difficulties in establishing stable democracies, but certainly the relationship between the two main types of democratic political institutions and the political process seems to deserve more attention than it has received. It would have been interesting to turn back to earlier debates of constitutionalists and intellectuals, particularly in Latin America, about presidentialism and parliamentarism.[8] But we suspect they would not be particularly helpful for our present concerns because they would reflect, on the one side, admiration for the great American democratic republic and its presidential government, ignoring to some extent what Woodrow Wilson described as congressional government, and on the other, probably bitter criticism of French parliamentarism from the Latin American legal literature.

In my own work on the breakdown of democratic regimes, at the stage of correcting proofs I was struck in rereading O'Donnell's analysis of the impossible game in post-Peronist Argentina by the extraordinary difficulty of integrating or isolating the Peronists in contrast to the Italian communists, which in spite of all the strains in Italian democracy never led to comparable consequences. As a result I wrote a brief excursus on the political implications of presidentialism and parliamentarism that I expanded and that constitutes the basic theme of this essay.[9] The ideas I intend to develop require further research using empirical evidence from different countries, particularly in Latin America but also the Philippines, South Korea, Nigeria, and perhaps Lebanon. . . . Further work on the problem would require research on the perceptions of both political elites and the public of presidents and legislatures in those regimes.

It is striking that most of the discussion of presidential government in classic works on democratic politics is limited to the United States and comparison between that country and the United Kingdom. There is practically no reference to long experience with presidential regimes in Latin America.[10] This gap in the literature inevitably weakens my analysis in this essay. It should be taken as a stimulus for further and more systematic thinking and research.

PRESIDENTIALISM: PRINCIPLES AND REALITIES

It has been argued that the terms *presidentialism* and *parliamentarism* each cover a wide range of political institutional formulas, and that the variety among those formulas is such that it is misleading to generalize about either term. Even two "pure" presidential systems like that of the United States and Argentina, despite the influence of the U.S. Constitution on the constitution Argentina adopted in 1853, are legally quite different—and even more so in practice—so that Carlos Nino contrasts the hyperpresidentialism of his country with a more balanced division of powers in the United States.[11] The same is probably even truer of parliamentary systems when we compare the *gouvernement d'assemblée* of the Third and Fourth Republics in France with the *Kanzlerdemokratie* of the Bundesrepublik.[12] There is the temptation in a debate about the two systems to turn to the extreme—and therefore most questionable—cases for or against the merits of each. As I will show, there are in modern democracies (even leaving aside the so-called semipresidential or semiparliamentary hybrids) some convergencies between the practices of presidentialism in conflictual multiparty systems (like Bolivia's) and parliamentary systems with a personalization of power or leadership similar to presidentialism when one party has an absolute majority or as in Germany with the "rationalized parliamentarism" of the Basic Law (the Bonn Constitution).

However, this should not obscure the fundamental differences between the two systems. All presidential and all parliamentary systems have a common core that allows their differentiation and some systematic comparisons. In addition, most presidential democracies are probably more similar to each other than the larger number of parliamentary democracies are alike, partly because all presidential democracies were inspired by the U.S. model and partly because the societies with such systems (with the outstanding exception of the United States) have some common characteristics. In parliamentary systems the only democratically legitimated institution is the parliament and the government deriving its authority from the confidence of the parliament, either from parliamentary majorities or parliamentary tolerance of minority governments, and only for the time that the legislature is willing to support it between elections and, exceptionally, as long as the parliament is not able to produce an alternative government.

Presidential systems are based on the opposite principle. An executive with considerable powers in the constitution and generally with full control of the composition of his cabinet and the administration is elected by the people (directly or by an electoral college elected for that purpose) for a fixed period of time and is not dependent on a formal vote of confidence by the democratically elected representatives in a parliament; the president is not only the holder of executive power but the symbolic head of state and cannot be dismissed, except in rare cases of impeachment, between elections.

Two features stand out in presidential systems:

1. Both the president, who controls the executive and is elected by the people (or an electoral college elected by the people for that sole purpose), and an elected legislature (unicameral or bicameral) enjoy democratic legitimacy. It is a system of "dual democratic legitimacy."

2. Both the president and the congress are elected for a fixed term, the president's tenure in office is independent of the legislature, and the survival of the legislature is independent of the president. This leads to what we characterize as the "rigidity" of the presidential system.

Most of the characteristics and problems of presidential systems flow from these two essential features. Some other nondefining features of presidentialism are often associated with it and are discussed below, such as term limits or no reelection, automatic succession by a vice president, freedom in appointing and (even more) in dismissing a cabinet, sameness of head of state and head of government. One characteristic so normal that it is often included in the definition is that the presidency is a unipersonal office. There have been only two cases of directly elected pluripersonal "presidencies" the two-person Cypriot administration (1960–63) and the Uruguayan Colegiado (which governed twice—1918–33 and 1952–67).[13]

Dual Democratic Legitimacy

The basic characteristic of presidentialism is the full claim of the president, to democratic legitimacy. Very often the claim has strong plebiscitary components although sometimes it is based on fewer popular votes than are received by many prime ministers in parliamentary systems heading minority cabinets that are perceived by contrast as weakly legitimated by the electorate. To mention just one example: Allende with a 36.2 percent plurality obtained by a heterogeneous coalition (1973) was certainly in a very different position from Adolfo Suárez with 35.1 percent of the vote (1979), as were the opponents Alessandri with 34.9 percent and Felipe González with 30.5 percent, and the less successful contenders Tomic with 27.8 percent and Fraga and Carrillo with respectively 6.1 and 10.8 percent. A presidential system gives the incumbent, who combines the qualities of head of state representing the nation and the powers of the executive, a very different aura and self-image and creates very different popular expectations than those redounding to a prime minister with whatever popularity he might enjoy after receiving the same number of votes.[14]

The most striking fact is that in a presidential system, the legislators, particularly when they represent well-organized, disciplined parties that constitute real ideological and political choices for the voters, also enjoy a democratic legitimacy, and it is possible that the majority of such a legislature might represent a different political choice from that of the voters supporting a president. Under such circumstances, who, on the basis of democratic principles, is better legitimated to speak in the name of the people: the president, or the congressional majority that opposes his policies? Since both derive their power from the vote of the people in a free competition among well-defined alternatives, a conflict is always latent and sometimes likely to erupt dramatically; there is no democratic principle to resolve it, and the mechanisms that might exist in the constitution are generally complex, highly technical, legalistic, and, therefore, of doubtful democratic legitimacy for the electorate. It is therefore no accident that in some of those situations the military intervenes as *"poder moderador."*

It could be argued that such conflicts are normal in the United States and have not led to serious crisis.[15] It would exceed the limits of this essay to explain the uniqueness of American political institutions and practices that have limited the impact of such conflicts, including the unique characteristics of the American political parties that lead many American political scientists to ask for a more responsible, disciplined ideological party system.[16] In my view, the development of modern political parties, in contrast to the American type of parties, particularly in socially or ideologically polarized societies, is likely to make those conflicts especially complex and threatening.

Without going into the complexities of the relationship between the executive and the legislature in different presidential regimes,[17] the relative dangers of predominance of one or the other, and the capacity to veto or stalemate decisions on legislation, there can be no doubt that presidential regimes are based on a dual democratic legitimacy and that no democratic principle can decide who represents the will of the people in principle. In practice, and particularly in developing countries with great regional inequalities in modernization, it is likely that the political and social composition and outlook of the legislature differs from that of the supporters of the president. The territorial principle of representation, sometimes reinforced by inequalities in the districting or the existence of a senate in federal republics, tends to give stronger weight in the legislature to representatives of rural areas and small towns of the provinces than to the metropolises. And it is easy to claim that the democratic credentials of representatives of backward areas are dubious and that these representatives are local oligarchs elected thanks to their clientelistic influences, their social and economic power. Independently of the truth of this claim and of the degree to which a democracy would disqualify voters who, rather than being influenced by trade unions, neighborhood associations, and party machines, are loyal to local notables, tribal leaders, priests, and even bosses, urban progressive elites are tempted to question the representativeness of those elected by them. In such a context, it becomes easy for a president encountering resistance to his program in the legislature to mobilize the people against the oligarchs, to claim true democratic legitimacy, deny it to his opponents, and confront his opponents with his capacity to mobilize his supporters in mass demonstrations.[18]

It is also conceivable that in some societies the president might represent the more traditional or provincial electorates and might use that support to question the right of the more urban and modern segments in a minority to oppose his policies. In the absence of any logical principle to define who really has democratic legitimacy, it is tempting to use ideological formulations to legitimize the presidential component of the system and delegitimize those opposing him, transforming what is an institutional conflict into serious social and political conflicts.

The different "legitimacies" of a popularly elected president and a congress are already well described in this text of 1852:

> *While the votes of France are split up among the seven hundred and fifty members of the National Assembly, they are here, on the contrary, concentrated on a single individual. While each separate representative of the people represents only this or that party, this or that town, this or that bridgehead, or even only the mere necessity of electing some one of the seven hundred and fifty, in which neither the cause nor the man is closely examined, he is the elect of the nation and the act of his election is the trump that the sovereign people plays once every four years. The elected National Assembly stands in a metaphysical relation, but the elected president in a personal relation, to the nation. The National Assembly, indeed, exhibits in its individual representatives the manifold aspects of the national spirit, but in the President this national spirit finds its incarnation. As against the Assembly, he possesses a sort of divine right; he is President by the grace of the people.*

Incidentally this is not the analysis of an institutionalist (or political psychologist) but of the "sociologist" Karl Marx in his "Eighteenth Brumaire of Louis Bonaparte."[19]

Election for a Fixed Term: The "Rigidity" of Presidentialism

The second main institutional characteristic of presidential systems is the fact that presidents are elected for a period of time that, under normal circumstances cannot be modified: not shortened and sometimes, due to provisions preventing reelection, not prolonged. The political process therefore becomes broken into discontinuous, rigidly determined periods without the possibility of continuous readjustments as political, social, and economic events might require. The duration of the mandate of a president becomes an essential political factor to which all actors in the political process have to adjust, and this has many important consequences.

If I had to summarize the basic differences between presidential and parliamentary systems,

I might point to the rigidity that presidentialism introduces into the political process and the much greater flexibility of that process in parliamentary systems. This rigidity might appear to the proponents of presidentialism as an advantage because it reduces some of the incertitudes and unpredictability inherent to parliamentarism, in which a larger number of actors, parties, their leaders, even the rank-and-file legislators, including those changing loyalties, can at any time between elections make basic changes, see to realignments, and above all, change the head of the executive, the prime minister. The search for strong power and predictability would seem to favor presidentialism, but paradoxically, unexpected events from the death of the incumbent to serious errors in judgment, particularly when faced with changing situations, make presidential rule less predictable and often weaker than that of a prime minister, who can always reinforce his authority and democratic legitimacy by asking for a vote of confidence.

The uncertainties of a period of regime transition and consolidation no doubt make the rigidities of a presidential constitution more problematic than a parliamentary system, which permits flexible responses to a changing situation.

One of the presumed advantages of a presidential regime is that it assures the stability of the executive. This has been contrasted with the instability of many parliamentary governments, which undergo frequent crises and changes in the prime ministership, particularly in multiparty European democracies. It would seem that the image of governmental instability in the French Third and Fourth Republics, in Italy today, and more recently in Portugal has contributed to the negative image of parliamentarism held by many scholars, particularly in Latin America, and their preference for presidentialism. In such a comparison it is often forgotten that parliamentary democracies have been able to produce stable governments. Under their apparent instability, the continuity of parties in power, the reshuffling of cabinet members, the continuation of a coalition under the same premier, and the frequent continuity of ministers in key ministries in spite of cabinet crises tend to be forgotten.[20] It is also overlooked that the parliamentary system allows for the removal of the prime minister who has lost control of his party or is involved in a scandal, whose continuation in office might create a serious political crisis. He might be replaced by his party, by the formation of a new coalition, or by the withdrawal of support of parties tolerating the minority government, without a major constitutional crisis. Unless parliamentary alignments make the formation of a democratically based government impossible, parliament with more or less difficulty and with more or less delay should be able to produce a new prime minister. In some cases of more serious crisis, there is always the alternative of calling for new elections, although they often do not resolve the problem but, as in Germany in the early 1930s, compound it.

In contrast, presidents are elected for a fixed term in office. The kind of changes that produce government crises and the substitution of one executive by another are excluded for that time. But this entails a rigidity in the political process that makes adjustment to changing situations extremely difficult; a leader who has lost the confidence of his own party or the parties that acquiesced to his election cannot be replaced. He cannot be substituted with someone abler to compromise with the opposition when polarization has reached an intensity that threatens violence and an illegal overthrow. The extreme measure of impeachment, which is in the constitutional texts, is difficult to use compared to a vote of no confidence. An embattled president is tempted to, and can, use his powers in such a way that his opponents might not be willing to wait until the end of his term to oust him. But there are no mechanisms to remove him without violating the constitution, unless he is willing to resign.[21]

Voluntary resignation under the pressure of party leaders and public opinion would be one way of avoiding the implications of the rigidity of the presidential mandate without the rumbling of tanks or violence in the streets. However, it is an unlikely outcome given the psychology of politicians. Moreover, in a presidential system, particularly one without the possibility of reelection, the incumbent cannot vindicate himself before the electorate. It is difficult for his former supporters to encourage him to such a step, particularly when some consider a vice president, who would automatically succeed him, even less desirable than the incumbent (as in the Fernando Collor crisis in Brazil in mid-1992). After two years and ten months and the complete failure of his administration, President Siles Suazo resigned, preventing another breakdown of civilian rule. Pressure from the opposition parties, the MNR (Movimiento Nacional Revolucionario) and the ADN (Alianza Democrática Nacional), which had the majority in the congress, the hostility of the major business organizations, and rumors of a possible coup had reduced his mandate in a little more than a year. It was exceptional in Bolivian politics because instead of a coup, the crisis led to an election in July 1985 in which ADN gained 28.57 percent of the votes and MNR 26.42 percent (an election in which the trade union movement and the radical left advocated abstention or void voting). Paz Estenssoro of MNR was elected president, and a period of democratic stability was initiated. Suazo's resignation is today widely recognized as a patriotic act.

Even "voluntary" resignation under pressure is likely to generate a serious political crisis because the segment of the electorate that brought the president to power might feel cheated of its choice and rally publicly to the incumbent's support. It is difficult to imagine political leaders resolving the issue without bringing the people into the debate and without using the threat of nondemocratic institutions, like the courts, and, more frequently, of political intervention by the armed forces. The intense conflict underlying such crises cannot be contained within the corridors and smoke-filled rooms of the legislature, as the nonconfidence vote (or more often the threat of it) against a prime minister or a party leader can be.

Identifiability and Accountability

One of the positive characteristics attributed to presidentialism is accountability and identifiability. The voter in casting his ballot knows whom he or she is voting for and who will govern should this candidate win. The person voting for representatives of a party in a parliamentary system presumably does not know who the party will support to be prime minister, and if it is a multiparty system in which the party cannot expect to gain an absolute majority the voter does not know what parties will form a governing coalition.

In reality neither of these statements is true or all the truth the voter would need to know in order to make a "reasonable" choice.

In presidential elections the voter may know much less about who will govern than the voters of a party in most parliamentary systems. The presidential candidates do not need and often do not have any prior record as political leaders. They may not be identified with a party with an ideology or program and record, and there may be little information about the persons likely to serve in a cabinet. The choice is often based on an opinion about *one* individual, a personality, promises, and—let's be honest—an image a candidate projects, which may be an image chosen by advisers (who are not necessarily politicians). This is even more the case in our age of "videopolitics."[22]

It may be argued that the voters of PASOK (Panhellenic Socialist Movement) voted for Papandreou, the British Conservatives voted for Mrs. Thatcher, the PSOE (Partido Socialista Obrero Español) voted for Felipe González, and so forth, although some might have voted for those parties in spite of their leaders or the other way around. Personalization of leadership is not exclusive to presidential politics. There is, however, a difference: leaders in parliamentary systems are not likely to have proposed themselves to the voters without having gained, and sometimes retained over many years, the leadership of their parties, either in power or in the opposition (something far from easy in the competitive world of politics). These leaders represent their parties. In addition, the voter knows that those who will form a cabinet will come from the party and, more often than not, are well-known leaders of the party with an accumulated experience in politics. A prime minister today is quite free in selecting his cabinet but certainly not as free as most presidents.

The argument that in a parliamentary system the voter does not know who will govern is not true in most cases because parties are identified with highly visible leaders. Those leaders appeal directly to the voters, and the campaigns increasingly are focused on the leader who aspires to be prime minister or chancellor. No Conservative voter could ignore that he was voting for Mrs. Thatcher, no PSOE voter that he was casting his ballot for Felipe González, no CDU (Christlich Demokratische Union) voter that Helmut Kohl would form the government. It could be argued that the party's parliamentary group or the notables of the party could remove the chosen leaders, that those who voted for Mrs. Thatcher, for example, had for the remainder of the legislature to accept Major as prime minister. But why would a party change leaders after the investment made in building them up, unless there is a feeling that they have proved inadequate? After all, the parliamentarians and party leaders have much to lose if the voters disapprove; they can be held accountable.

As to the indeterminacy of who will govern when coalitions are necessary in multiparty systems, with some exceptions, this again is not true. Parties commit themselves to an alliance, such as the CDU-CSU-FDP (CSU, Christlich Soziale Union; FDP, Frei Demokratische Partei) before the elections, and the voter for any of those parties knows that a particular person will be chancellor and also that unless one party wins an absolute majority (and even then) the government will include representatives of all the parties in the coalition. This is particularly interesting to those wanting a minor coalition party, such as the FDP, to have an influence. Voters do not know the exact composition of the coalition cabinet—which cabinet posts will go to which parties and leaders—but they know much more than voters for a president in the United States or Brazil know. Parties in parliamentary systems often have a well-known shadow cabinet, while a president-elect starts naming a cabinet only after the election. The identifiability in presidentialism is of *one* person; in parliamentary government most of the time it is of a pool of people and often a number of well-known subleaders.

Let us assume a multiparty system, no absolute majority, no previous coalition agreement. The voter still knows that the prime ministership will go to the leader (or one of the top leaders) of the largest party and knows which are the likely coalition partners of that party. The voter may not like one or the other of the parties, their leaders, or their positions but is likely to know more about the possible cabinets than voters for most presidents know. The voter for a major party hopes that it might govern alone. The voter for a minor party (eligible to enter coalitions) knows it and its leader will not govern alone but hopes that the vote will give it a greater share of power. After all only a limited number of coalitions are possible, and noncontiguous coalitions are exceptional. A Catalan nationalist voter for CiU (Convergéncia i Unió) in a Spanish parliamentary election knows that this party will not form a government but also that if no party has an absolute majority CiU representatives can influence the formation of a government and might even enter it. The voter certainly knows more about who and what to vote for than if he

only had the choice between two presidential candidates. Should his CiU representative enter a coalition he disapproves the party is more accountable than the party of a president who would disappoint Catalanist sentiments to which he might have appealed.

Accountability to the voters for performance is presumably enhanced by the fact that a president is directly and personally responsible for policies—not the cabinet, not a coalition, and not the leaders of the party that might have occupied the prime minister's office in a succession. Only *one* person is clearly identified as governing for the entire period of a mandate. There are no confused or shared responsibilities. So the argument goes.

Let us analyze this argument. First of all there is no way to hold accountable a president who cannot be presented for reelection. Such a president can neither be punished by the voters by defeat nor rewarded for success by reelection with the same or a larger vote than in the previous election. A president who cannot be reelected is "unaccountable."

This is the case in thirteen presidential systems (counting those that provide for one or two interim terms) compared to six systems that have no limit on reelection or a two-term limit. We could add to these the semipresidential (or premier-presidential systems) of France and Finland, which do not limit reelection, and Portugal, which has a two-term limit.[23]

It could be argued that in the case of no reelection the party that supported the election of the president would be held accountable, but in fact that party's new presidential candidate is the person accountable. He would try to identify with his successful predecessor or to disidentify from him in case of failure. In a personalized election this might be easier than when the voter has to support a party that has not changed its leadership or has done so belatedly. Besides, it is partly unfair to punish a party for the actions of a president who, after the election, could govern independently of its confidence.

When reelection is possible, the incumbent president who is perceived negatively paradoxically can try, more or less successfully, to escape blame by shifting it to the congress, particularly if it was dominated by the opposition but even if his own party was in the majority. Just before the election he can propose legislation that the congress rejects and can claim that if his policies had been approved he would have been successful. A prime minister with a majority cannot play such a game. The division of powers can therefore provide an alibi for failure. The congress, even the president's party in the congress, can play a similar game by blaming the executive for not implementing policies it has approved or not submitting the measures necessary to deal with problems.

In conclusion, accountability with separation of powers is not easy to enforce. In a parliamentary system the party with a majority, or even a stable coalition of parties, can easily be made accountable to the voters, as long as the voters do not exclude in principle a vote for parties in the opposition.

The objection that in a parliament, parties, their leaders, and the prime ministers they support cannot be made accountable is valid only under certain conditions: when there are many unstable governments or shifting (and even contradictory) coalitions, and when no party has played a central role in the coalition-making process.

This might have been the case in the Third French Republic and in the "third force" governments of the Fourth Republic. Even in such a fractionalized parliamentary system as the Italian, I surmise that the voters had not much doubt until recently that the Democrazia Cristiana was responsible for governing and could have been made accountable if a sufficient number of voters had considered potential alternative coalitions (which probably were impossible without the participation of the Communists). In addition, in the case of coalitions the minor parties can be and have been held accountable for entering or not entering them, and the major parties for including or not including the minor ones.

However, in many parliamentary systems parties can be made fully accountable. This is true in Westminster-type majoritarian democracies, particularly when a two-party system has emerged, and also in multiparty systems with coalition or minority governments. Voters in such situations often have voted for parties committed to form a particular coalition. The parties campaign with such a commitment although the voters may give more or less weight in the process of policy formation to one or another member of the coalition (checking perhaps the threat of hegemonic rule by one party). This has

been the case in the Federal Republic of Germany. Moreover, the coalition parties can be and have been made accountable in the next election. Obviously one party might break out of the coalition, even change sides for the next election, but voters can reward or punish it for its behavior.

Another problem in presidential systems is not to be ignored: even in the case of possible reelection, the voters have to wait for the end of the presidential term to demand accountability. A prime minister can be made accountable to the parliament and his own party by a vote of no confidence at any time; the party becomes accountable to the voters at the end of the period or even earlier should the leadership crisis in parliament or the governing party lead to anticipated elections.

Winner Take All

In a presidential election whatever the plurality gained the victorious candidate takes over the whole executive branch, while a leader aspiring to be prime minister whose party gains less than 51 percent of the seats might be forced to share power with another party or to constitute a minority government. With some 30 percent of the seats he could not form a noncoalition government, while a president with the same vote could (although he might have a hard time getting the congress to support his policies). The control of the executive in presidential systems is in principle "winner take all."

In addition it is "loser loses all" for defeated presidential candidates, who might end without any public office after the election and, unless they have strong positions as leaders of their party, might have gambled away all their political resources. Where is Michael Dukakis or Vargas Llosa today? The loser often loses all.

Adam Przeworski commenting on this point has written:

> Linz (1984) has developed a number of arguments in favor of parliamentary, as opposed to presidential, systems. I am particularly persuaded by his observation that Presidential systems generate a zero-sum game, whereas parliamentary systems increase total payoffs. The reasons are the following. In presidential systems, the winner takes all: He or she can form a government without including

any losers in the coalition. In fact, the defeated candidate has no political status, as in parliamentary systems, where he or she becomes the leader of the opposition. Hence, in terms of the model developed above, under ceteris paribus conditions (under which W + L = T is the same in both systems), the value of victory, W, is greater and the value of defeat, L, is smaller under presidential than under parliamentary systems. Now, assume that political actors discount the future at the rate of r per annum. Under the presidential system, the term is fixed for some period (t = PRES), and the expected value of the next round is r^{PRES} (pW + (1 − p)L). Under the parliamentary system, the winner governs only as long as he or she can maintain sufficient support in the parliament, say for the period t = PARL, so that the expected value of the next round is r^{PARL} (pW + (1 − p)L).

Elementary algebra will then show that unless the tenure expected under parliamentarism is notably longer than under presidentialism, the loser has a greater incentive to stay in the democratic game under parliamentarism.[24]

My critics, however, are right that with the division of powers a successful presidential candidate might not "take all" because his party might be in the minority in the congress. They are also totally right that when in a parliamentary system a disciplined party gains a majority or more of the seats, it is truly a "winner-take-all" situation. This is likely in a Westminster-type parliamentary system where single-member districts might assure a party a disproportionate number of seats in a culturally homogeneous country. As Mainwaring and Shugart put it, the purest examples of what Lijphart calls majoritarian democracy, in which the winner takes all, are parliamentary rather than presidential democracies.[25] However, this is true only when a party is able to gain an absolute majority of seats, something that does not happen often.

Even when a party in a parliamentary democracy gains an absolute majority of seats— a "winner-take-all" situation, which is likely to happen in a Westminster-type democracy—the party leader or premier may not be in the same position as a president. To stay in office the prime minister has to pay attention to his supporters in the parliamentary party; rebellion of back-benchers or of the barons of the party can terminate his tenure. The fate of a powerful, once popular leader, such as Mrs. Thatcher, is paradigmatic: Mrs. Thatcher's party under the new leadership of John Major could win a subsequent election. Nothing similar could have happened when the failure of Alán García of Peru became apparent, and APRA (Alianza Popular Revolucionaria Americana) had to pay the price in the elections.

One of the possible outcomes of a presidential election is that the defeated candidate loses all. This is likely, and probably desirable, for the "amateur" challenger without party support. But it also is likely in a two-party contest. The defeated candidate, regardless of the number of votes obtained, is not likely to be considered a desirable candidate for the next presidential election and therefore probably will have lost his leadership position in the party. In fact, sometimes the defeated party is left leaderless until a candidate is nominated for the next election. Only in highly ideological and structured parties, or in some multiparty situations, do defeated presidential candidates retain a leadership position. Leaders of parties in parliamentary systems, however, are practically always assigned seats in the legislature and sometimes have the status of "leader of the loyal opposition" (although growing personalization in the campaigns might also lead to their resignation from leadership of the party).

No Reelection and Its Implications

The principle of no reelection or of no immediate reelection is not a defining characteristic of presidentialism, but it is clearly the predominant pattern. Shugart and Carey list eight countries (several of dubious democratic credentials) that allow no reelection, four with no immediate reelection, and one—Venezuela—with two interim terms. Among those allowing immediate reelection, five limit the presidency to two terms and six have no limit (including two semi-presidential or, in their terminology, premier-presidential systems).[26]

The importance assigned to the no-reelection principle is reflected in the fact that the General Treaty of Peace and Amity signed by all Central

American governments at Washington on February 7, 1927, provided that: "The Contracting Parties obligate themselves to maintain in their respective Constitutions the principle of non-reelection to the office of President and Vice President of the Republic, and those of the Contracting Parties whose Constitutions present such reelection, obligate themselves to introduce a constitutional reform to this effect in their next legislative session after the notification of the present Treaty."[27]

The principle of no reelection in many countries has acquired a strong symbolic importance. The memory of lifelong rule by nondemocratic rulers, caudillos and dictators, led to demands of no reelection, like that of Madero against the Porfiriato in Mexico. Attempts to change constitutional provisions barring reelection, efforts to assure what the Latin Americans call *continuismo*, have mobilized public opinion and led to riots and coups not only in Latin America but South Korea.[28] The prospect of reelection of an incumbent to the winner-take-all game often has united presidential hopefuls of quite opposite ideological positions, as some powerful Brazilian governors were united against Goulart.

The continuous support of the electorate for a particular party election after election, which we find to quite a few parliamentary democracies (Scandinavia, the United Kingdom, Italy, India, and Japan) sometimes has assured permanence in the office of prime minister. But it has not led to a demand to limit the term in office and never to violent protest and regime crises comparable to those provoked by efforts of *continuismo*. This tells us something about the different political culture generated by presidentialism and parliamentarism. The stakes in theory are different although in practice parliamentarism might lead to greater continuity in office of highly respected party leaders.

Democracy is by definition a government pro tempore, a government in which the electorate at regular intervals can make those governing accountable and impose a change.[29] The maximum time limit for any government between elections is probably the greatest guarantee against omnipotence and abuse of power, the last hope for those in the minority position. The requirement of periodic elections, however, in principle does not exclude the possibility that those in power might again obtain the confidence of the electorate. A turnover in power

can also have dysfunctional consequences, because no government can be assured the time to implement promises, to carry through between the two elections major programs of social change, to achieve irreversible changes in the society. This is even more true when there is term limitation, as in many presidential systems. And all governments, democratic and nondemocratic, would like to assure themselves continuity over a long period of time.

The concentration of power in a president has led in most presidential regimes to attempts to limit the presidency to one or at most two terms. Those provisions have been frustrating for ambitious leaders, who have been tempted to assure *continuismo* legally. Even in the absence of such ambitions, the consciousness that time to carry out a program associated with one's name is limited must have an impact on political style in presidential regimes. The fear of discontinuity in policies and distrust of a potential successor encourage a sense of urgency, of what Albert Hirschman has called "the wish of *vouloir conclure*,"[30] that might lead to ill-designed policies, rapid implementation, impatience with the opposition, and expenditures that otherwise would be distributed over a longer period of time or policies that might contribute to political tension and sometimes inefficacy. A president wants to be sure that he can inaugurate his Brasilia before leaving office, implement his program of nationalizations, and so forth. A prime minister who can expect his party or the coalition supporting him to win the next election is not likely to be under the same pressure; we have seen prime ministers staying in office over the course of several legislatures without any fear of dictatorship arising because removal could take place anytime without recourse to unconstitutional means. Term limits and the principle of no reelection, whose value cannot be questioned, mean that the political system has to produce a capable and popular leader periodically and that the political capital accumulated by a successful leader cannot be used beyond the leader's term of office.

All political leadership is threatened by the ambitions of second-rank leaders, by their positioning themselves for succession, and sometimes by their intrigues. But inevitably the prospect of a succession at the end of a president's term is likely to foster those tendencies and suspicions of them on the part of the incumbent. The desire for continuity, on the other hand, leads a president to look for a successor who will not challenge him while he is in office. Such a person is not necessarily the most capable and attractive leader. The inevitable succession also creates a distinctive tension between the ex-president and his successor, who will be tempted to assert his independence and his differences with his predecessor, even when both belong to the same party—a process that might become quite threatening to the unity of the party. The person who has been president, with all the power, prestige, and adulation accompanying that office, will always find it difficult to relinquish power and to be excluded from the prospect of regaining it in the case of failure of the successor. That frustration might have important political consequences, such as an attempt to exercise power behind the scenes, to influence the next presidential succession by supporting a candidate different from the one supported by the incumbent, and so forth.

When a president is barred from immediate reelection but can run again after an interim period, as in Venezuela, conflict is likely to develop between the incumbent and his predecessor of the same party. The case of Carlos Andrés Pérez and President Lusinchi . . . comes readily to mind.

Certainly similar problems emerge in parliamentary systems when a prominent leader leaves the premiership but finds himself capable of and willing to return to power. But probably the need to maintain party unity, the deference with which such a leader is likely to be treated by other leaders of his party and by the successor, and the successor's awareness of needing the cooperation of a powerful leader outside of government might facilitate an alternative positioning of the two leaders of the same party. The departing leader knows that he might be called back into office at any time, and his successor also knows that such a possibility exists. The awareness of both leaders that a confrontation between them might be costly to both creates a situation that very often leads to a sharing of power.

Political Style in Presidential and Parliamentary Democracies

The preceeding [*sic*] discussion has focused on the institutional dimensions of our problem. Some of the legal provisions in presidential constitutions and some of the unwritten rules that differentiate the types of democracies have been referred to.

Other aspects that need to be addressed are the way in which political competition is structured in a system in which the people directly elect the president, the style in which authority and power are exercis\ed, the relations among a president, the political class, and the society, and the way in which power is likely to be exercised and conflicts to be resolved. Our assumption is that the institutional characteristics to which we have referred directly or indirectly shape the whole political process and the way of ruling.

Perhaps the most important implication of presidentialism is that it introduces a strong element of zero-sum game into democratic politics with rules that tend toward a "winner-take-all" outcome. A parliamentary election might produce an absolute majority for a particular party, but more normally it gives representation to a number of parties. One perhaps wins a larger plurality than others, and some negotiations and sharing of power become necessary for obtaining majority support for a prime minister or tolerance of a minority government. This means that the prime minister will be much more aware of the demands of different groups and much more concerned about retaining their support. Correspondingly different parties do not lose the expectation of exercising a share of power, an ability to control, and the opportunity to gain benefits for their supporters.

The feeling of having independent power, a mandate from the people, of independence for the period in office from others who might withdraw support, including members of the coalition that elected him, is likely to give a president a sense of power and mission that might be out of proportion to the limited plurality that elected him. This in turn might make resistances he encounters in the political system and the society more frustrating, demoralizing, or irritating than resistances usually are for a prime minister, who knows from the beginning how dependent he is on the support of his party, other parties, other leaders, and the parliament. Unless the prime minister has an absolute majority, the system inevitably includes some of the elements that become institutionalized in what has been called consensus and sometimes consociational democracy.

Certainly there have been and are multiparty coalition governments in presidential systems, based on the need for "national unity," but they are exceptional and often unsatisfactory for the participants. The costs to a party of joining others to save a president in trouble are high. If the endeavor succeeds, the president gets the credit; if it fails, the party is blamed; and the president always has power to dismiss the ministers without being formally accountable for his decision. Those considerations entered into the decision of Fernando Henrique Cardoso not to serve in the cabinet of President Collor in 1992.

In this context it is important to notice that when democracy was reestablished in two Latin American countries with presidential constitutions in difficult circumstances, the political leaders of the major parties turned to consociational types of agreements to obviate some of the implications of giving one party the entire authority associated with the presidency and the zero-sum implications for those not gaining that office. However the difficulty in forming true coalition governments in presidential regimes has led to more formalized and rigid arrangements. The Colombian *Concordancia*, a form of consociationalism, although democratically legitimized after being agreed to by the politicians, established a system that preempted the rights of the voters to choose which party should govern. To prevent the zero-sum implications of presidentialism, which were feared by the politicians, a system of dubious democratic legitimacy was chosen. The Venezuelan *pacto de punto fijo* had the same purpose but not the rigid constitutionalization of the Colombian solution.[31]

The zero-sum character of the political game in presidential regimes is reinforced by the fact that winners and losers are defined for the period of the presidential mandate, a number of years in which there is no hope for shifts in alliances, broadening of the base of support by national unity or emergency grand coalitions, crisis situations that might lead to dissolution and new elections, and so forth.[32] The losers have to wait four or five years without access to executive power and thereby to a share in the formation of cabinets and without access to patronage. The zero-sum game raises the stakes in a presidential election for winners and losers, and inevitably increases the tension and the polarization.

Presidential elections have the advantage of allowing the people to choose directly who will govern them for a period of time. Many multiparty systems with parliamentary institutions leave that decision to the politicians. Presumably, the president has a direct mandate from the people. If a minimal plurality is not required and

a number of candidates compete in a single round, the person elected might have only a small plurality; the difference between the successful candidate and the runner-up might be too small to justify the sense of plebiscitary popular support that the victor and his supporters might sincerely feel. To eliminate this element of chance the electoral laws sometimes require a minimal plurality for the victor and some procedure for choosing when no one reaches that minimum.[33] Those requirements might frustrate the supporters of the most successful candidate. More frequent is the pattern in which the election turns into a confrontation between two leading candidates, either in a first or a second round. Such a bipolar choice under certain conditions is likely to produce considerable polarization. One of the consequences in multiparty systems of the confrontation of two viable candidates is that before the elections, broad coalitions are likely to be formed in which extremist parties with some strength cannot be ignored because success might depend on even the small number of votes they might be able to provide. A party system in which significant numbers of voters identify strongly with such parties gives these voters disproportionate presence among the supporters of the candidates. It is easy for the opponent to point to the dangerous influence of the extremists, and the extremists have a possible blackmail power over a moderate candidate. Unless a strong candidate of the center rallies wide support against those who engage in an alliance with extreme segments of the political spectrum and finds widespread support in the center that cuts into the more clearly defined alternatives, a presidential election can encourage centrifugal and polarizing tendencies in such an electorate.

Where there is great fear of polarization, the politicians may agree on a compromise candidate whom they respect and who does not generate antagonism. Such a candidate may be chosen more for his personal qualities than for the policies he advocates, and he is more likely to be a leader of a small than a large party. Such an option can serve the purpose of making a smooth transition to democracy, with its competition among parties and policies, or of reequilibrating a system in crisis. However, it is very doubtful that such an ad hoc coalition of politicians would want to or could give the president it helped to elect full support to govern, to make difficult decisions that alienate many erstwhile supporters and run counter to their ideological commitments. This problem would be particularly serious in the late years of the mandate. Such a compromise president might therefore provide weak leadership and be left without support in the congress. Many of his former supporters may dissociate themselves from him (without paying the price of a government crisis, as in a parliamentary system) to prepare themselves for legislative elections and the next presidential election.

It can be argued that in a society where the bulk of the electorate places itself at the center of the political spectrum, shares basically moderate positions, agrees on the exclusion of the extremists, and differs only moderately between left of center and right of center, the potentially negative consequences of presidential competition are excluded. With an electorate of overwhelmingly moderate centrist leanings, anyone making an alliance or taking a position that seems to lean toward an extreme is unlikely to win an election, as Goldwater and McGovern discovered on election night. However, most societies facing serious social and economic problems probably do not fit the model of U.S. presidential elections. They are likely instead to be divided in their opinions about an authoritarian regime that had significant support at some point and to have parties that are perceived as extremist with strong organizations and considerable appeal.

In a single-round election, none of the leading candidates in a somewhat polarized society with a volatile electorate can ignore those forces with whom he would otherwise not be ready to collaborate without the very great risk of finding himself short of a plurality. Let us retain for our analysis the potential for polarization and the difficulty of isolating politically extremist alternatives disliked intensely by significant elites or segments of the electorate.

A two-round election with a runoff between leading candidates reduces the uncertainty and thereby might help to produce a more rationally calculated outcome, on the part of both the candidate and the voters. The candidates can point to their own strengths and calculate how much their alliances can contribute to a winning coalition, and those tending more toward the extremes are aware of the limits of their strength. This in some ways would come closer to the process of coalition formation in a parliament in search of a prime minister.

The runoff election would seem, in principle, to be the solution in the case of multiparty presidential systems in which candidates might gain only small pluralities and in which, contrary to "rational" expectations, no broader coalitions are formed to obtain a majority. In a runoff in which only the two leading candidates are allowed to compete, one of them inevitably receives an absolute majority.

However, a number of dysfunctional consequences derive from this method of election:

1. In a highly fragmented system the two leading candidates might enjoy only small pluralities with respect to other candidates and might represent positions on the same segment of the political spectrum.
2. One of the candidates might be an outsider to the party system with no congressional party base.
3. The "majority" generated might not represent a politically more or less homogeneous electorate or a real coalition of parties.
4. The winner, although initially the choice of a small proportion of the electorate, is likely to feel that he represents a "true and plebiscitary" majority.
5. The expectation of a runoff increases the incentive to compete in the first run, either in the hope of placing among the two most favored or of gaining bargaining power for support in the runoff of one of the two leading contenders. Therefore, rather than favoring a coalescence of parties behind a candidate, the system reinforces the existing fragmentation.

Reading Notes

1. My approach would be misunderstood if it were read as strictly institutional and even more as a legal-constitutionalist perspective. I take into account those aspects, although perhaps less than other recent writings such as Matthew Soberg Shugart and John M. Carey, *Presidents and Assemblies: Constitutional Design and Electoral Dynamics* (Cambridge:

Cambridge UP, 1992), which provides for a systematic analysis of the powers of presidents. My focus is on the political logic of presidential systems and some of its likely consequences on the selection of leadership, popular expectations, style of leadership, and articulation of conflicts. Some of the empirical evidence is found in the chapters of this volume, and it is our hope that our analysis will generate more and systematic evidence of those aspects that cannot be found in or directly derived from institutional norms.

2. F.A. Hermens, *Democracy or Anarchy: A Study of Proportional Representation* (Notre Dame, Ind.: Notre Dame UP, 1941); Maurice Duverger, *Political Parties: Their Organization and Activity* (1951; New York: Wiley, 1954); Stein Rokkan, "Elections: Electoral Systems," *International Encyclopedia of the Social Sciences* (New York: Crowell-Collier-Macmillan, 1968); Dieter Nohlen, *Wahlsysteme der Welt* (Munich: Piper, 1978); Douglas Rae, *The Political Consequences of Electoral Laws* (New Haven: Yale UP, 1967); R.S. Katz, *A Theory of Parties and Electoral Systems* (Baltimore: Johns Hopkins UP, 1980); Rein Taagepera and Matthew Soberg Shugart, *Seats and Votes: The Effects and Determinants of Electoral Systems* (New Haven: Yale UP, 1989); B. Grofman and A. Lijphart, eds., *Electoral Laws and Their Political Consequences* (New York: Agathon, 1986); Arend Lijphart and B. Grofman, eds., *Choosing an Electoral System: Issues and Alternatives* (New York: Praeger, 1984); and Giovanni Sartori, "The Influence of Electoral Systems: Faulty Laws or Faulty Method," in Grofman and Lijphart, *Electoral Laws and Their Political Consequences*, pp. 43–68.

3. Werner Kaltefleiter, *Die Funktionen des Staatsoberhauptes in der parlamentarischen Demokratie* (Cologne: Westdeutscher Verlag, 1970); and Stefano Bartolini, "Sistema partitico ed elezione diretta del capo dello stato in Europa," *Rivista italiana di scienza politica* 2 (1984): 209–22.

4. Shugart and Carey, *Presidents and Assemblies;* Waldino Cleto Suárez, "El poder ejecutivo en América Latina. Su capacidad operativa bajo regímenes presidencialistas de gobierno," *Revista de estudios politicos* (nueva época) 29 (Sept.–Oct. 1982): 109–44. Richard Moulin,

Le présidentialisme et la classification des régimes politiques (Paris: Librairie Générale de Droit et de Jurisprudence, 1978), is a work of scholarship in the classical legal tradition, rich in references to the constitutional texts and the academic commentaries with a wealth of information on the variety of presidential systems, the relations between executive and legislature, the role of cabinets, impeachment, party systems and presidentialism, and so forth, in the United States and other presidential regimes, particularly the constitutional history of Chile. It also includes an extensive bibliography. Only the equal treatment of the constitutions of democracies and nondemocratic regimes is disturbing.

5. G. Bingham Powell, Jr., *Contemporary Democracies: Participation, Stability, and Violence* (Cambridge: Harvard UP, 1982), and Arend Lijphart, *Democracies: Pattern of Majoritarian and Consensus Government in Twenty-one Countries* (New Haven: Yale UP, 1984).

6. The neglect until very recently by social scientists of presidentialism outside the United States is reflected in the facts that the *Presidential Studies Quarterly* between 1977 and 1992 (vols. 7 to 22) published only 3 articles on the subject; that the *Legislative Studies Quarterly* between 1976 and 1992 published none; the *International Political Science Abstracts* between 1975 and 1991 lists 141 articles on Latin America, 96 on countries outside the United States and Latin America, and 23 on general topics on the executive or the presidency.

7. Scott Mainwaring, "Presidentialism in Latin America: A Review Essay," *Latin American Research Review* 25, no. 1 (1990): 157–79, is an excellent summary of the literature and debates in Latin America. See also Arturo Valenzuela, *The Breakdown of Democratic Regimes: Chile* (Baltimore: Johns Hopkins UP, 1978). Another important survey article is: Mario D. Serrafero, "Presidencialismo y reforma política en América Latina," *Revista del Centro de Estudios Constitucionales*, Madrid, Jan.–Apr. 1991, pp. 195–233.

8. Mainwaring, "Presidentialism in Latin America."

9. Juan J. Linz, *Crisis Breakdown and Reequilibration*, vol. 1 of *The Breakdown of Democratic Regimes*, edited by J. Linz and

Alfred Stepan (Baltimore: Johns Hopkins UP, 1978); see "Excursus on Presidential and Parliamentary Democracies," pp. 71–74. It would be absurd to argue that presidents need to be elected on a first-past-the-post basis. I agree with Donald L. Horowitz, *A Democratic South Africa? Constitutional Engineering in a Divided Society* (Berkeley: U California P, 1991), that this view is an "untenable assumption about the way presidents are inevitably elected" (p. 20). He attributes such an assumption to me, but all I have done is to discuss the way in which presidents have been and are more often elected—either by a plurality in one round or in a runoff election. He rightly points out that in Nigeria in 1979 and 1983 and in Sri Lanka in 1978 and 1988 a different method of election was used, but it does not seem to me reasonable to base an analysis of presidential politics on those two cases (and a total of four elections at the time of his and my writings) rather than on the cumulative experience in Latin American republics and a few other cases.

10. The important essay by Anthony King, "Executives," in *Handbook of Political Science*, edited by Fred I. Greenstein and Nelson Polsby, vol. 5 of *Governmental Institutions and Processes* (Reading, Mass.: Addison-Wesley, 1975), pp. 173–256, limits itself to a comparison of the United States and the United Kingdom, with no reference to presidentialism outside the United States.

11. In view of the constant clamor for "strong" presidents, the popular hopes linked with "strong" presidents in many countries with presidential regimes, Shugart and Carey's finding that systems rating high in powers of the president in law making and cabinet formation have been more prone to crises is significant.

Ultimately, from its historical origins on, a separation of powers has been conceived to generate "weak" government, "checks and balances" (which can turn into "stalemates," divided responsibility, distrust between powers), just the opposite of "strong" power and leadership. No surprise that the terms of presidents who wanted to be "strong"— Vargas, Allende, Marcos, Goulart, Alán García, Aristide—ended in one or another kind of disaster. We know too little about the role of the presidency in Georgia to tell

if Gamsakhurdia should be in that list, but it would not be surprising if some of the new presidents of former Soviet Union republics might not run the same fate.

See the collection of essays by Carlos S. Nino, Gabriel Banzat, Marcelo Alegre and Marcela Rodríguez, Roberto Gargozelle, Silvino Alvarez and Robert Pablo-Saba, and Jorge Albert Barraguirre, *Presidencialismo y estabilidad democrática en la Argentina* (Buenos Aires: Centro de Estudios Institucionales, 1991) esp. Carlos S. Nino, "El presidencialismo y la justificatión, estabilidad y eficiencia de la demo-cracia," pp. 11–27.

12. Klaus von Beyme, *Die parlamentarischen Regierungssysteme in Europa* (Munich: R. Piper, 1970), is a monumental comparative study of parliamentary regimes.

13. This analysis does not include pluripersonal presidentialism because of its atypical character, the unique circumstances that have led to its establishment, and last but not least its lack of success. For a discussion of plural presidencies, see Shugart and Carey, *Presidents and Assemblies*, pp. 94–105.

Advocates of collegial presidencies should keep in mind the experiences in Roman history and the analysis of George Simmel on the size of groups and decision making in addition to the contemporary failures.

14. The majority runoff has been advocated to avoid election by a small plurality, which is possible in a multiparty election, and to assure election by a majority. The system, however, as Shugart and Carey have noted, has several not so desirable consequences. First it encourages a larger number of candidates in the first run, discouraging the coalescence of opposing forces, so that those who place first and second can attract the support in the runoff of those who failed and those who failed can enhance their bargaining position with one of the two candidates in the runoff. The first candidates in this case obtain a lower percentage of votes compared to election by pure plurality. The second consequence is that the outcome depends on first-round contingencies. Let us remember that in 1989 some Brazilians feared a runoff between Lula and Brizola, the two leftist candidates, if the Right had divided its vote more than it did. To these I would add that in the runoff, the winner might receive a vote out of

proportion to his original electoral appeal that might not, however, represent real support for him but contribute to his sense of being "elected by the people." The presidential majority in this case is as or more "artificial" than a parliamentary majority for a prime minister heading a coalition, but it generates very different expectations.

15. Fred W. Riggs, "The Survival of Presidentialism in America: Para-constitutional Practices," *International Political Science Review* 9, no. 4 (1988): 247–78, is an excellent analysis of "American exceptionalism." For European responses to American presidentialism, see Klaus von Beyme, *America as a Model. The Impact of American Democracy in the World* (Aldershot, U.K.: Gower, 1987), chap. 2, "The Presidential System of Government," pp. 33–76.

16. Committee on Political Parties of the American Political Science Association, *Toward a More Responsible Two-Party System* (New York: Rinehart, 1950).

17. Shugart and Carey, *Presidents and Assemblies*, chap. 6, pp. 106–49.

18. President Fernando Collor of Brazil when, after introducing his stabilization plan on television without previous consultation, he encountered congressional resistance, he threatened congress with mobilizing the masses: "There is no doubt that I have an intimate deep relation with the poor masses" and that congress "must respect me because I am the center of power." Commenting on this, one of his strongest supporters, former finance minister and then senator Roberto Campos lamented: "This is juridical butchery, which lashes confidence in the Collar plan." See *Latin American Regional Reports: Brazil Report* (RB-90-04), 3 May 1990, p. 6, and "Mounting Criticism of Authoritarian Governments Novo Brasil Plan," ibid. (RB-90-05), 7 June 1990, pp. 1–3, Campos quote on p. 31.

President Collor could not, with his electoral constituency, make threats against congress creditable in the way that Goulart (or Allende) could by mobilizing masses in the Petrobras Stadium. For an analysis for the Brazilian crisis in 1964, which was also a crisis of relations between president and congress, and the possible constitutional reform that might have allowed Goulart's

reelection, see Thomas E. Skidmore, *Politics in Brazil, 1930–1964: An Experiment in Democracy* (New York: Oxford UP, 1967).

Alfred Stepan, ed., *Authoritarian Brazil* (New Haven: Yale UP, 1973), and "Political Leadership and Regime Breakdown: Brazil," in Linz and Stepan, *Breakdown of Democratic Regimes*, pp. 119–37, esp. pp. 120–33.

It should be noted that this sense of the "superiority" of the democratic mandate of presidents is found not only in Latin America but in other presidential democracies. For example, de Gaulle on December 17, 1969, in a speech disclosed: that the head of state has his origin in "la confiance profonde de la Nation" and not in "un arrangement momentané entre professionnels de l'astuce" (*Le monde*, 19 Dec. 1965) quoted by Moulin, *Le présidentialisme et la classification des régimes politiques*, p. 27.

19. Karl Marx, "The Eighteenth Brumaire of Louis Bonaparte," in *December 2, 1851. Contemporary Writings on the Coup d'État of Louis Napoleon*, edited by John B. Halsted (Garden City, N.Y.: Doubleday, 1992), pp. 152–53.

20. Mattei Dogan, ed., *Pathways to Power, Selecting Rulers in Pluralist Democracies* (Boulder: Westview, 1989), chap. 10, "Irremovable Leaders and Ministerial Instability in European Democracies," pp. 239–75.

21. The case of María Estela Martínez de Perón, vice president who acceded to the presidency after the death of her husband in July 1974 and was ousted by the March 1976 coup, is a prime example of difficulties caused by the rigidity of presidentialism. Faced with the total failure of her government in November 1975, her opponents wanted to start her impeachment. Then anticipated elections were announced for the end of 1976, but they would not presumably lead to a transfer of power. After a reorganization of the cabinet in August 1975, Christmas brought a mass resignation of cabinet members and December 29 a new demand for impeachment. Mrs. Perón's health was questioned in an effort to apply rules of incapacity. In February 1976 impeachment was again initiated and approved by the lower house but blocked in the senate. After another reorganization of the cabinet, a meeting of party leaders on March 12 was unable to

come to a solution. After a coup on March 29, Mrs. Perón was ousted, imprisoned, and tried by the military regime. For a detailed analysis of this crisis, see Mario Daniel Serrafero, "El presidencialismo en el sistema político argentino" (Ph.D. diss., Universidad Complutense—Instituto Universitario Ortega y Gasset, Madrid, 1992), pp. 265–79. This thesis is an outstanding monograph on the Argentinian presidency. Unfortunately, I have not been able to incorporate many of its findings into my analysis.

At the time of writing, the crises in Venezuela involving President Carlos Andrés Pérez and in Brazil involving President Fernando Collor are further examples of the rigidity of presidentialism.

22. On the vulnerability of a single-person election to the influence of mass media, see the excellent article by Giovanni Sartori, "Video-Power," *Government and Opposition*, Winter 1989, pp. 39–53. See also Thomas E. Skidmore, ed., *Television, Politics, and the Transition to Democracy in Latin America* (Washington, D.C.: Woodrow Wilson Center Press, 1993).

23. Shugart and Carey, *Presidents and Assemblies*, pp. 87–91.

24. Adam Przeworski, *Democracy and the Market. Political and Economic Reforms in Eastern Europe and Latin America* (Cambridge: Cambridge UP, 1991), pp. 34–35.

25. Donald Horowitz, "Comparing Democratic Systems," *Journal of Democracy* 1, no. 4 (1990): 73–79, and my response on pp. 84–91. Scott Mainwaring and Matthew S. Shugart, "Juan Linz, Presidentialism and Democracy: A Critical Appraisal," in *Politics, Society and Democracy: Latin America*, edited by Arturo Valenzuela (Boulder: Westview Press, 1994).

26. Mainwaring, "Presidentialism in Latin America," has dealt extensively with the responses to the tensions between presidents and congresses in Latin America and the immobility derived from it (particularly with multipartism), pp. 167–71.

27. Quoted by Russell H. Fitzgibbon, "Continuismo in Central America and the Caribbean," in *The Evolution of Latin American Government, A Book of Readings*, edited by Asher N. Christensen (New York: Henry Holt, 1951), pp. 430–45, esp. p. 436.

28. Sung-joo Han, "South Korea: Politics in Transition" in *Politics in Developing Countries*, edited by Larry Diamond, Juan J. Linz, and Seymour Martin Lipset (Boulder: Lynne Rienner, 1990), pp. 313–50, esp. p. 321 on the mobilization against the constitutional revision that permitted a third-term presidency of Park Chung Hee in 1969. The constitutional amendment achieved by referendum provoked heavy student agitation and can be considered to have been a turning point in the government's ability to maintain the electoral support necessary to keep the president in office. Many who held a reasonably favorable attitude toward Park and high regard for his achievements were disappointed by the tampering with the constitution (p. 325).

29. Juan J. Linz, "Il fattore tempo nei mutamenti de regime," *Teoría política* 2, no. 1 (1986): 3–47.

30. Albert O. Hirschman, *Journeys toward Progress: Studies of Economic Policy-Making in Latin America* (Garden City, N.Y.: Doubleday, 1965), pp. 313–16 about "la rage de vouloir conclure."

31. Daniel Levine, "Venezuela: The Nature, Sources and Prospects of Democracy," in *Democracy in Developing Countries*, pp. 247–89, esp. pp. 256–60; and *Conflict and Political Change in Venezuela* (Princeton: Princeton UP, 1973). See also Jonathan Hartlyn, *The Politics of Coalition Rule in Colombia* (Cambridge: Cambridge UP, 1988).

32. It is significant that Robert A. Dahl, "A Bipartisan Administration," *New York Times*, 14 Nov. 1973, suggested that, during the period between Nixon's resignation and the election of a new president, a coalition government including Democrats and Republicans be created. Cited by A. Lijphart, *Democracy in Plural Societies* (New Haven: Yale UP, 1977), pp. 28–29.

33. On the method of presidential elections see Shugart and Carey, *Presidents and Assemblies*: pp. 208–25, particularly table 10.1, p. 211, which also gives the median percentage of votes for the two highest-scoring candidates. Dieter Nohlen, ed., *Handbuch der Wahldaten Lateinamerikas und der Karibik* (Opladen: Leske & Budrich, 1993), is the most complete source on election legislation, returns in presidential and congressional elections, names of parties and elected presidents for all the countries south of the Rio Grande and the Caribbean.

KEY TERMS

Cabinet Strictly speaking, the cabinet is the council of ministers, the members of which are responsible for given portfolios or departments of government activity and jurisdiction.

Coalition An alliance of multiple political actors with the express purpose of designing coordinated strategies among its members. For example, a coalition government brings together multiple political parties that harmonize and correlate their ideal policies.

Head of Government The head of the council of ministers.

Head of State The chief executive of a political system.

Veto Player A political actor whose consent is necessary, but not sufficient, to alter the status quo.

Vote of Confidence A legislative vote that is called in order to test whether the executive enjoys the confidence of a working majority in the legislature. Sometimes the head of government may choose to designate the parliamentary vote of a given bill as a matter of confidence. This technique may allow the head of government to rein in potential defectors in the party who may otherwise vote against the party line on the given bill.

Vote of No Confidence Similar to the confidence vote, this is also called to test the ability of the cabinet to enjoy the support of a working majority in the legislature. However, a no-confidence vote is called by the opposition. Some parliamentary systems use the constructive no-confidence vote, which requires that the motion designates an alternative head of government to the one whose removal is sought.

FURTHER READINGS

Laver, Michael and Norman Schofield. *Multiparty Government: The Politics of Coalition in Europe.* New York: Oxford University Press, 1990.

Shugart, Matthew Soberg and John Carey. *Presidents and Assemblies.* New York: Cambridge University Press, 1992.

WEB LINKS

Inter-Parliamentary Union:
www.ipu.org

International Constitutional Law Project of the University of Bern:
www.oefre.unibe.ch/law/icl

CHAPTER 10

FEDERALISM AND FEDERATIONS

"Federalism" is one of the most commonly used political terms in Canada. Canadian citizens have a "federal government" and, by and large, are aware they live in a federation. They have heard from several different political actors about "reforming federalism." In Quebec, politics is permeated by references to "federalists" and "sovereignists." Yet despite the fact that "federalism" is a central term in Canadian political discourse, it remains mysterious for most Canadians. How does federalism work? What purpose does it serve? What is a federation? Although dominant in North America (Canada, the United States, and Mexico are all federations), this model is not used very much elsewhere. There are five federations in Latin America/the Caribbean (Venezuela, Argentina, Brazil, and St. Kitts and Nevis); four in Western Europe (Germany, Austria, Belgium, Switzerland); three in Asia (India, Pakistan, and Malaysia); three in Africa (Ethiopia, Nigeria, the Comoros); two in Eastern Europe (Russia and Serbia and Montenegro), two in the Pacific (Australia and Micronesia); and one in the Middle East (the United Arab Emirates).[1] All other states, although they may exhibit federal features (Spain, for example), are technically unitary states.

This chapter tackles questions relating to the nature, structure, and workings of federalism and federations. After an introduction, it is divided into four sections. The first section defines the two concepts of federalism and federation (or federal states). It specifies the features of federations and distinguishes them from other types of states, such as the unitary state or the confederation. The second section explores intergovernmental relations and fiscal arrangements in federations. The third section examines the different faces federalism can take (centralized/decentralized, symmetrical/asymmetrical). The fourth section looks at selected federal models around the world.

CONCEPTUAL DISTINCTIONS

We saw in the previous chapter on parliamentary and presidential systems different systems of government have different ways of organizing the relationship between the legislative and executive branches. This type of division of power is *functional* because it involves the question of roles: who does what in the political process. Federalism and federations are also about structuring and organizing political power, but they refer to the *territorial* division of power: which unit is empowered to act in which policy area (education, social services, the environment, and so on). Federalism and federation are often used interchangeably in everyday language, but political scientists tend to make a distinction between them. **Federalism** is understood as a *principle* of government that seeks to reconcile unity and diversity through the exercise of political power along multiple autonomous levels. **Federation** refers to political systems where two or more levels of government are sovereign within their own specified jurisdiction. We will now elaborate on these concepts.

As we just mentioned, federalism refers to a principle or even a philosophy of government. The crux of this principle is the idea of combining self-rule and shared rule. Through federalism, different political units can live together yet apart since they share a government while at the same time having their own. In this context, these units coexist within a common political framework but also enjoy political autonomy. Therefore, federalism attempts to maintain the delicate balance between the federal government's tendency to favour centralization and the will of the units to preserve and/or expand their own powers. This definition suggests two observations about federalism. The first observation is that it is not a new idea. The historic "confederations" of Native bands in North America, the "leagues" of Ancient Greece and the Swiss "confederation" (from the thirteenth to the nineteenth century) are all examples of political arrangements that are coherent with the idea of federalism.[2] The second observation is that federalism can be found in states that do not explicitly call themselves federations. Spain, for example, is not formally a federation but clearly finds inspiration in federalism as its constitution specifies the existence of seventeen "autonomous communities" with their own powers.

Federalism as a principle has two main political uses. The first, which is closely tied to the liberal ideology discussed earlier in the book, is the fragmentation of political power and the creation of checks and balances in the political system. In dividing power between two or more levels of government, federalism offers a protection against absolutism and authoritarianism in two ways: it limits the power that one individual, group, or government can have, and features two poles of political power that can monitor and check each other's actions. This political use of federalism was at the centre of the creation of the first modern federation, the United States. The main preoccupation of the American founding fathers was avoiding the tyranny that they thought derived from the British monarchy. It is in this context that they created a republican regime with a presidential and federal system. Federalism is therefore a liberal idea, which raises the question of authoritarian regimes, such as the former U.S.S.R., that are said to exercise political power following the federal principle. In truth, federalism and authoritarianism are antithetical because territorial self-rule cannot exist in any meaningful manner in an authoritarian regime. In the Soviet Union, for example, the territorial division of power allowed for no real autonomy of the republics because their political leaders were effectively controlled by the Communist party.

The second political usage of federalism is managing ethnic, linguistic, or religious diversity. The idea is that conflicts in multi-ethnic, multi-lingual, or multi-confessional states can be avoided, or at least lessened, by devolving power over language, culture, and other fields such as education that traditionally create tensions between the various communities. Typically, when federalism is used for this purpose there is one or more ethnic, linguistic, or religious groups that are minorities within a state but majorities inside federated units (Canadian provinces, Swiss cantons, etc.). In these countries, sensitive policy areas are made the prerogative of these units so that minority groups can decide them for themselves rather than struggle with the majority group and therefore strain intergroup relationships. In some cases, federalism is presented by the minority group as an essential condition for political union because it views autonomy as a safeguard against cultural domination and assimilation. This was the case in Canada, where French-Canadian leaders pushed for federalism while John A. Macdonald and other English-Canadian elites preferred the model of the unitary state that we will discuss shortly. Switzerland is, along with Canada, a good illustration of the use of federalism for the purpose of managing ethnic, linguistic, and religious diversity. Swiss federalism presents a framework of autonomy for four language groups (German, French, Italian, Romansch) and two religions (Protestantism and Catholicism). Swiss federalism is often hailed as the key ingredient for the peaceful coexistence of these various groups and the presence of a strong Swiss national identity, although it must be said that there are other aspects of the Swiss political system (the use of referenda, political neutrality, the collegial executive) that contribute to this unique outcome.[3]

The second key concept of this chapter is federation. As already mentioned, federalism is a principle of territorial government whereas "federation" is a more descriptive concept referring to types of political system, more specifically, to the way territory is structured politically. A federation is a *state where two or more levels of government are sovereign (autonomous) within their own given jurisdiction.* In this sense, it is a practical application of the idea of self-rule and shared rule. Therefore, a federation comprises a federal level of political authority and *constituent* (or federated) units whose names vary: provinces in Canada; states in Australia, India, and the United States; Länder in Germany; cantons in Switzerland; regions and communities in Belgium, and so on. It should also be noted that some federations have also formally recognized the existence of local government. This is the case for Switzerland and also for India, which in 1992 constitutionally created local government as the third layer of the federation, investing it with significant powers and a compulsory representation (33 percent) of women in all elected bodies. In addition to the sharing of sovereignty between levels of government, federations generally present three other features.

The first of these features is a formal division of power between central and regional governments. In some federal states, such as Canada, Australia, and the United States, the level of government that has executive responsibility in a certain field also has legislative responsibility for this same field. In others, such as Germany and Austria, the federal government tends to have most of the legislative responsibility while the constituent units are given authority over the implementation of the legislation. Powers of federal governments almost always include citizenship and immigration, defence, foreign policy, international trade and commerce, and the currency. Constituent units usually have power in the areas of language, culture, health, education, social services, and municipal affairs. Some federations also specify the powers of local governments. In practice, even sometimes in theory, the division of power between federal government and constituent units is rarely clear and neat. For example, most federations specify concurrent powers, that is, powers that should be exercised by both levels of governments.

The pattern followed in dividing up powers affects the extent to which each level of government acts autonomously in different spheres. On the one hand, federations in which powers are primarily exclusive (Canada, Switzerland, and, to a greater extent, Belgium), that is, specified to either the federal government or the constituent units, favour a greater independence between the two levels of government. On the other hand, federations with many concurrent powers necessarily involve greater interaction. The fiscal capabilities of the constituent units are also a factor affecting their degree of autonomy within their fields. Health, education, and social services, which in most federations are predominantly the responsibility of constituent units, are very expensive to fund. In this context, a weak fiscal basis would necessarily hamper the real autonomy of constituent units. This is an issue in most federations because federal governments tend to have the greater fiscal powers. As a consequence of the greater resources of federal governments, most federations recognize, albeit almost never formally, a *spending power* that is typically used to establish programs in education, health, and social services. This is a source of considerable tension in Canada, where some provinces, most notably Quebec, resent its use by the federal government to get involved in provincial jurisdictions. Above and beyond these political parameters, it can be said that the complexity of modern politics almost inevitably involves cooperation between federal governments and constituent units, thereby further blurring the division of powers.

The second feature of federations is that the division of powers is specified in a constitution. A constitution is the supreme law of a land; it is the law to which all other laws must

Table 10.1 **FEDERAL GOVERNMENT REVENUES BEFORE INTERGOVERNMENTAL TRANSFERS AS A PERCENTAGE OF TOTAL (FEDERAL-STATE-LOCAL) GOVERNMENT REVENUES**

	1986	1996
Malaysia	87.2	89.9
Spain	87.9	84.0*
Austria	71.6	72.8...
Australia	74.4	69.1
United States	64.7	65.8
India	68.2	64.6*
Germany	64.5	64.5
Canada	48.4	47.7......
Switzerland	48.1	44.7......
European Union	0.9	1.2

* These figures are for 1994.

... These figures are for 1995.

...... These figures are for 1993.

Source: Ronald L. Watts, *The Spending Power in Federal Systems: A Comparative Study* (Kingston: Institute of Intergovernmental Relations, Queen's University, 1999), p. 52. Reprinted with permission.

conform. Consequently, procedures for amending constitutions are more complex than for ordinary laws. For example, a 50 + 1 majority in a representative assembly cannot change constitutions. In federations, the amending procedure typically involves constituent units. This is consistent with the logic of federalism whereby each level of government is sovereign within its own jurisdiction, since it means that federal governments cannot unilaterally change the distribution of powers. The exact procedure for amending the constitution of federations varies from case to case, and within federations there are typically different procedures for different types of change. In Canada, constitutional change requires the direct approval of provinces: unanimity is needed for the most substantial changes (to central institutions, for example) while seven provinces totalling more than 50 percent of the population is the requirement for most other transformations. A change affecting only one province can be implemented with the joint approval of this province and the federal government. The unanimity rule makes the Canadian constitution quite rigid; therefore, bringing about formal changes in Canadian federalism is difficult.

In most federations, constitutional change in the division of powers requires a qualified majority in the two federal legislatures, one of which represents the constituent units, and the support of a majority (regular or qualified) of the constituent units themselves.[4] This is the case in the United States, where constitutional change necessitates a two-thirds majority in the House of Representatives and the Senate in addition to the support of three-quarters of the states. In Switzerland and Australia, the requirement is a qualified majority in the federal legislatures and popular support as demonstrated by a referendum where the change is approved by an overall majority and a majority of constituent units. In Germany, only qualified majorities in both legislatures are necessary. However, constituent units are still consulted because one of the legislatures, the Bundesrat, is composed of members appointed by the Länder. Belgium is an exception, since its formula involves the calling of elections and the subsequent approval by a qualified majority in the newly formed legislatures.

The third feature of federations is the representation of constituent units within central institutions. Federalism and federations attempt to strike a delicate balance between unity and diversity, self-rule and shared rule, independence and interdependence. The act of dividing power in a way that provides autonomy for constituent units reflects the preoccupation of respecting diversity, establishing self-rule, and guaranteeing independence. The idea of having constituent units participating in decision making and policy making at the federal level embodies the concern with unity, shared rule, and interdependence. Indeed, federations need to offer formal points of contact between the levels of governments in order to ensure some measure of unity. This is often said to be a problem in Canada because the body that was originally designed to offer a representation of the provinces within the federal institutions, the Senate, cannot effectively play this role because its members are unelected. Contrary to the Canadian Senate, the Senate of the United States provides meaningful representation for its constituent units because it combines formal power with the democratic legitimacy provided by the election of two senators per state. A different model is the German federation where, as we have already mentioned, the members of the Bundesrat are not elected by the population of the various Länder, but appointed by their already elected executives.

UNITARY STATE AND CONFEDERATION

This portrait of the federal model should be put in perspective since there is an alternate way of organizing politics territorially. This alternative is the unitary state. **Unitary states** are generally more centralized than federations, although they may have, like federations, more than one level of government. In fact, they usually do. All states, for example, have local (or municipal) governments. Some unitary states have "regions," which are typically given powers in such fields as transportation, regional economic and urban development, and policing. Therefore, there is an important caveat when contrasting federations with unitary states. Just as federations cannot simply be defined as states that have two or more levels of government (we saw that there is much more to a federation), unitary states should not be defined as states where there is only one level of government. The crucial feature of a unitary state is that whatever powers regions or other governments have, they are delegated only by the central state, which means they can be "brought back" at any time without the approval of regional governments. In other words, the division of power can be changed unilaterally by the central government. This is due to the fact that the division of power is not written into the constitution; rather, it is specified in an ordinary law that can be changed with a majority in parliament. France, for example, is a unitary state, despite the fact that in 1982 it enacted a law on regionalization. The law created regional governments with elected representatives and a set of powers, but the whole system can be changed or eliminated by the central state. Therefore, France is not a federation, nor does it espouse the federalist principles of unity in diversity and shared-rule/self-rule. On the contrary, the French state rests on the ideas of indivisibility and centralization.

A third model of territorial organization must be mentioned, although it is much more rare than either federations or unitary states: confederations. A **confederation** is a political unit composed of *independent* states that accept to cede some of their sovereignty to common institutions. Each state remains independent, and decisions typically require unanimity. Confederations are therefore more decentralized than federations. They are often transitory arrangements that represent a stage in either a process of federalization or the dismantling of a state, whether it be federal or unitary. The longest-lived confederation was most probably the Swiss confederation, which existed from 1291 to 1847 when it transformed itself into a federation. Contemporary examples are harder to find. The Community of Independent States (CIS), which was the immediate successor to the Soviet Union, is one, but it rapidly dissolved into 15 sovereign states with no common political institutions. The European Union could be said to be another, as member states have accepted to cede some sovereignty to a common set of political institutions while retaining their status as independent states. Finally, the Parti Québécois (PQ) project of "sovereignty-association" or "sovereignty with partnership" seems to describe a confederal model.

INTERGOVERNMENTAL RELATIONS AND FISCAL ARRANGEMENTS

As stated, the division of power in federations, even when it appears to be clear in the constitution, almost never translates into a situation where the two levels of government can act without having to interact with one another. It is this need for interaction that explains why federations have developed mechanisms of consultation, coordination, and conflict solving. These mechanisms are rarely specified in the constitution. In Canada, for example, the only discernable constitutional provision for linking provincial and federal governments for the purpose of coordination is the existence of the lieutenant governor, an appointee of the federal government serving in the provinces. Indeed, the practice of *intergovernmental relations* has developed outside the formal constitutional framework in response to the need for mutual consultation resulting from the increasing role of the state in society. In contrast, India has set up a National Development Council that includes federal and state governments and serves the function of coordination and policy planning.

At the broadest level, the most common strategy adopted for conducting intergovernmental relations is known as *executive federalism*. The main actors of executive federalism are members of government as well as high-level civil servants. Executive federalism generally features meetings of cabinet ministers on issues relevant to their portfolio. For example, environment ministers may meet to discuss penalties for corporate polluters in the hope of harmonizing their positions, or health ministers can gather to examine the state of the health care system so as to share information and discuss policy alternatives. Much less frequent, but more highly publicized, are first ministers' meetings, where all the heads of government in the federation get together to set the broader direction of federalism. Some federations have opted for a more formalized executive federalism. For example, in 1992 Australia created a forum for intergovernmental relations, the Council of Australian Governments.

In Canada, executive federalism is generally defined in opposition to *cooperative federalism*, which was the predominant framework for intergovernmental relations before the 1960s. Cooperative federalism did not involve elected politicians as much as executive federalism. Rather, coordination and information sharing was done through the different levels of bureaucracy. Intergovernmental relations were therefore less visible, subtler, and also less competitive because elected officials, who have political stakes in the way federalism evolves, were less involved.

Table 10.2 **CONDITIONAL TRANSFERS AS A PERCENTAGE OF FEDERAL TRANSFERS***

United States	100.0
European Union	100.0
Switzerland	73.1...
Malaysia	67.9
Germany	64.5
Australia	53.0
India	38.0
Spain	23.5......
Canada §	4.3

* Comparable data for Austria and Belgium are not available.

... These figures are for 1995.

...... The Autonomous Communities with "high level" policy responsibilities were used to calculate this figure.

§ EPF and CHST transfers are considered as unconditional. If treated as conditional, the percentage for Canada would be 43.6 percent.

Source: Ronald L. Watts, *The Spending Power in Federal Systems: A Comparative Study* (Kingston: Institute of Intergovernmental Relations, Queen's University, 1999), p. 52. Reprinted with permission.

We saw in the last section that federalism tends to give policy areas such as health care and education, which are expensive to fund, to constituents that have less revenue than the federal governments. For this reason, federations have also developed mechanisms for financial transfers. There are two types of financial transfers in federations: conditional and unconditional. Conditional transfers are transfers for which the federal government stipulates how the funds should be spent. Unconditional transfers come with no strings attached. In the United States, virtually all transfers are conditional, whereas in Canada most are unconditional.

In giving autonomy to constituent units, federations may unwillingly accentuate uneven economic development. In other words, rich regions can benefit from their comparative advantage (greater population, better technology, more natural resources, etc.) to really prosper, while poorer regions might be left to struggle. Political leaders of federations have recognized this issue, which raises concerns for the principles of equality and justice while at the same time posing the question of the long-term survival of the federal system. In this context, most federations (the United States being the notable exception) have "solidarity transfers" or "equalization payments" (as they are called in Canada), which are unconditional. The idea behind equalization payments is of course to reduce socio-economic disparities between constituent units and, more specifically, to prevent disparities in the levels of social services among those units. These issues are particularly significant for developing countries that use these mechanisms to create equity. These types of payments generally stem from the federal government and are based on an agreed-upon formula. The exception is Germany, where the federal government is bypassed as there is a "money pool" into which rich Länder pay and from which poor Länder receive.

CENTRALIZATION/DECENTRALIZATION, SYMMETRY/ASYMMETRY

Federations can take on different appearances. Two pairs of concepts are frequently used to describe or characterize federations. The first is centralization/decentralization. This conceptual dichotomy refers to the relative power of the federal government and the constituent units. At the broadest level, a centralized federation is a federation in which the powers of the federal government are relatively greater than those of the constituent units. A decentralized federation is a federation in which the powers of the constituent units are relatively greater than those of the federal government. Centralization and decentralization are best seen as two ends of a continuum that can serve to shed light not only on federations, but also on all other types of states. At the centralization end, we would find traditional unitary states, such as France, followed by states with federal trends (Spain, South Africa) and centralized federations (Austria, Mexico). At the decentralization end, we would find confederations followed by decentralized federations (Belgium, Canada, the United Arab Emirates).

Characterizing, as we just did, the degree of centralization/decentralization of federations is tricky because it is unclear which criterion should be used. Indeed, at least three different criteria can be taken into consideration when evaluating the balance of power between the levels of government.[5] A fair assessment of the centralized or decentralized character of a federation most likely demands a consideration of all three of these criteria.

The first criterion is the written constitution. Which level of government is given more powers? Who has power over the most important fields? Who is given residual powers, that is,

Table 10.3 **FEDERAL GOVERNMENT EXPENDITURES AFTER INTERGOVERNMENTAL TRANSFERS AS A PERCENTAGE OF TOTAL (FEDERAL-STATE-LOCAL) GOVERNMENT EXPENDITURES**

	1986	1996
Malaysia	82.4	85.6
Austria	70.5	68.8...
Spain	79.4	68.5*
United States	56.0	61.2
India	47.3	54.8*
Australia	52.7	53.0
Germany	35.7	41.2
Canada	41.4	40.6......
Switzerland	35.0	36.7...
European Union	2.1	2.5

* These figures are for 1995.

... These figures are for 1994.

...... These figures are for 1993.

Source: Ronald L. Watts, *The Spending Power in Federal Systems: A Comparative Study* (Kingston: Institute of Intergovernmental Relations, Queen's University, 1999), p. 52. Reprinted with permission.

power over all fields that are not specified in the constitution? Is there any other clause that indicates that one level of government is favoured over the other? This is seemingly a straightforward approach for assessing the degree of centralization/decentralization of a federation. However, it is often misleading because federalism is a dynamic process. In other words, federations change, sometimes becoming quite different from their original forms as specified in the constitution. For example, most political scientists agree that Canada is, comparatively speaking, a decentralized federation despite the fact that the written constitution suggests otherwise. The 1867 Canadian constitution gave the most important powers of the time, as well as residual powers, to the federal government; on concurrent powers such as agriculture and immigration, the priority in case of conflict goes to the federal legislation; the federal government, through the lieutenant governors, can suspend or void provincial legislation through the powers of reservation and disallowance respectively; it can also, using a declaratory power, take over local works if it considers them to be of national interest.

A second criterion that can be used to assess the degree of centralization/decentralization of a federation is government expenditures. Here, the idea is to compare the relative importance of public spending by the different levels of government. The argument is that federations with the highest percentage of public spending for constituent units are the more decentralized since their units are the most able to use their powers to effectively provide public services. From this perspective, federations such as Malaysia and Austria are centralized, while Switzerland, Canada, and Germany are decentralized.

A third criterion involves looking at the federal institutions. From this angle, the formal division of power between levels of government and the relative importance of their public expenditures is not overly relevant. Rather, the focus is primarily on the representation of the constituent units in these institutions, and on their capacity to shape federal policy making. From this perspective, Canada, with its nearly irrelevant Senate, appears more centralized than the United States or Germany, which provide for more effective representation of the constituent units in the federal institutions. Among these institutions, courts of justice are also noteworthy. Federations need to have in place some type of court, tribunal, or council to arbitrate the unavoidable disputes between levels of government over who is empowered to do what. In this context, the process of appointing judges, or any other persons who rule on these disputes, is relevant to the centralization/decentralization debate. Typically, federations tend to involve constituent units in the appointment of judges to the highest courts. In Canada, however, the appointment of judges to the Supreme Court, as well as those of the federal and higher-level provincial courts, is the prerogative of the federal government. The nature of this process adds to the rather weak presence and limited input of Canadian provinces in federal institutions.

In addition to being centralized or decentralized, federations can be symmetrical or asymmetrical. Symmetry/asymmetry is the second pair of concepts frequently used to qualify federations. Of course, federations are rarely completely symmetrical or asymmetrical, just as they usually present features of both centralization and decentralization. Symmetry in federations means that all constituent units have a similar status and similar powers. In contrast, asymmetry involves one or more constituent units having a distinct status and different powers. Asymmetry tends to be a response to constituent units being different with respect to such things as economic development, population, and culture/language. Asymmetry can be constitutionally specified. The Belgian constitution, for example, recognizes the existence of two different types of constituent units, regions and communities, each with different sets of powers. In Canada, Quebec leaders have advocated constitutionally specified asymmetry since the Quiet Revolution, but it has proven quite controversial in other provinces. The failed Meech Lake and Charlottetown accords, which recognized Quebec as a distinct society within Canada, would have introduced a significant element of asymmetry in the Canadian federation. However, through Quebec the Canadian federation exhibits signs of political asymmetry, which refers to constituent units developing a de facto distinct status or acquiring additional powers through informal arrangements. Quebec has its own pension plan, collects its own taxes, and has greater powers than other provinces in the fields of immigration and human resources training.

FEDERALISM AND FEDERATION IN CONTEMPORARY POLITICS

Despite the apparent advantages that federalism presents for limiting political power and managing ethnic, linguistic, or religious diversity, there are only twenty-two federations among currently existing states.[6] The small number of federations can partly be explained by the dilemmas posed by its political uses. As already stated, federalism coexists very uneasily with authoritarianism because it divides political power. In this context, regimes that are not liberal-democratic are unlikely to choose a federal model. Also, many are skeptical of federalism's capacity to manage ethnic diversity, arguing instead that it only encourages secession. From this perspective, the unitary state is argued to be better suited for the purpose of national cohesion and integration. In fact, federations are often perceived as being fragile states because they divide sovereignty internally and have to maintain a delicate balance between centralization and decentralization. This is quite ironic, since the world's superpower is a federation, but is nonetheless in line with much of the contemporary Western political tradition, which tends to see the centralized unitary state as the symbol of modernity, unity, and efficiency.

Canada is a good case in which to examine contemporary issues on federalism. A common debate about Canadian federalism concerns the extent of its centralization/decentralization. Most political scientists agree that Canada was originally a very centralized federation that underwent a decentralization period early on (1867–1914) as provinces struggled to establish a balance with the federal government. The wars and 1933 financial crisis are generally said to have corresponded with a new wave of centralization, while the 1960s, in the context of Quebec's Quiet Revolution, are associated with decentralization. There is less agreement on the period that follows. It is probably fair to say that the Trudeau years featured a centralized *vision* of Canadian federalism in which a strong federal government was responsible for redistributing wealth and designing national social programs in the hope of forging a "just society." However, provinces, most importantly Alberta and Quebec, proved combative in challenging the scope of action of the federal government, which means that the actual evolution of federalism during this period is open to debate. Similarly, the Mulroney governments (1984–1993) embarked on projects for constitutional reforms that favoured decentralization, but these reforms never materialized, and the fundamental structures of Canadian federalism remained unchanged. Today, political scientists are split on the centralized/decentralized nature of the Canadian federation. Those who argue it is decentralized point to the activity of the provinces in many different fields or, from a more technical perspective, to the high percentage of provincial expenditures in relation to total public expenditures. Political scientists suggesting that Canada is a rather centralized federation tend to focus on the fact that the federal government often uses its spending power to intervene in fields seemingly reserved for provinces, and that it sometimes links financial transfers to national standards and guidelines.

Another debate associated with Canadian federalism involves asymmetry. Quebec governments since the Quiet Revolution have expressed a preference for asymmetrical federalism in which Quebec would have, as specified in the constitution, a distinct status and more powers. The argument is that as the only province with a French-speaking majority, Quebec needs powers that the other provinces are comfortable leaving with the federal government as well as the recognition that it forms a distinct society within Canada. The Meech Lake and Charlottetown accords failed, in part, because the asymmetrical dimension they carried was opposed by many Canadian political actors and citizens.[7] In large part, Canada's national unity problem is the result of two different conceptions of federalism: a first, which sees the country made up of two (or three, to take into account Native communities) national/linguistic groups whose formal recognition should be the basis for federalism; and a second, where Canada is composed of ten equal provinces with a similar constitutional status.

Quebec nationalism represents the greatest challenge to Canadian federalism because it seeks both asymmetry and decentralization while threatening secession. This type of situation is not unique to Canada but is shared by many other federations (Belgium, India, Nigeria, St. Kitts and Nevis, and Russia). We have said that a purpose of federalism is accommodating diversity, but it should be specified that this task is never achieved; rather, it represents an ongoing and unending process. In other words, federalism does not "solve" issues of ethnic, linguistic, and religious diversity, but simply provides a framework for their peaceful management. A second challenge to the Canadian federation, which is also experienced by many other federal states, involves the current process of globalization. What are the consequences of free trade, regional economic and/or political integration, and the renewed importance of global financial institutions (WTO, World Bank, etc.) on federalism? There is no consensus here. Some political scientists argue that in taking power away from the state, globalization favours decentralization. The idea is that as the ability of federal governments to ensure national cohesion, economic and otherwise, declines because of commitments to free trade, deregulation, deficit elimination, and debt reduction, they are likely to transfer responsibilities to their constituent units, thereby empowering them. Other political scientists are skeptical toward this scenario, suggesting instead that the proliferation of international agreements and forums legitimize states, therefore strengthening federal governments that are their only recognized voice.

In Western Europe, federalism seems to be on the upswing. Belgium, which formally became a federation in 1993, represents an original model that tends to highlight the flexibility of federalism as a device for managing ethnic/linguistic diversity.[8] Belgium is divided into two language groups: Dutch speakers (Flemings) and French speakers (Francophones). Flemings inhabit primarily the northern part of the country (Flanders) but are also present in the capital, Brussels. Francophones are found both in Brussels and in the southern part of the country (Wallonia). Flemings living in both Flanders and Brussels generally feel like they belong to a single community and have traditionally been concerned primarily with cultural and linguistic promotion. Among Francophones, identification is a bit different because those living in Wallonia have a Walloon identity, while those living in Brussels often identify themselves as Brusselers. In addition, Walloons are mainly preoccupied with economic development, as they are comparatively poorer than Flemings and Brusselers. To accommodate these different identities and interests, the Belgian federation has been built to involve two different types of constituent units. There are communities, whose membership is defined by language, not territory, that are empowered to act in fields involving culture and language. The creation of communities, of which there are three (Flemish, Francophone, and German speaking for the smallest language group in the country), responds to the Flemish identity and its preoccupation with protecting and promoting the Dutch language. There are also regions, whose more conventional membership is linked to territory, which have power over economic development and related areas. The establishment of regions, of which there are also three (Flanders, Wallonia, and Brussels), addressed the Walloon identity and its focus on socio-economic conditions.

SPANISH NATIONALITIES AND REGIONS

Federalism has also inspired the architects of Spain's democratic constitution.[9] Spain does not call itself a federation, but its constitution provides autonomy for seventeen "autonomous communities," therefore following federalism as a principle. The logic of federalism in Spain follows the two political uses that we discussed earlier. First, the creation of autonomous communities constituted a response to distinct identities in Catalonia, the Basque Country, and Galicia. In fact, these three autonomous communities have a distinct status, since the constitution recognizes them as "historical nationalities" while the others are simply "regions." There is therefore asymmetry in the Spanish use of federalism. Second, federalism provides a safeguard against authoritarianism. Spain was a dictatorship for nearly forty years before it began its democratic transition in the late 1970s, and it generally lacked a democratic tradition. In this context, dividing political power between a

SPANISH NATIONALITIES AND REGIONS (*Communidades Autónomas*)

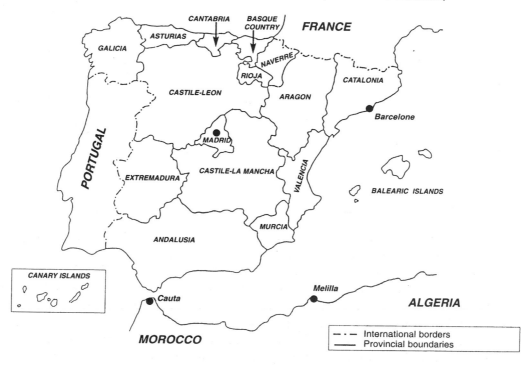

central state and autonomous communities was designed to strengthen the young Spanish democracy.

The influence of federalism is also visible in the process of European integration. As we already mentioned, the European Union (EU) currently resembles a confederation since member states remain independent and consensus is required in making important decisions. However, many political scientists see the European Union as evolving toward the federal model or, at least, as being permeated by federalism. They point to the apparent willingness of forging "an ever closer union," and at current efforts at drafting a European constitution, giving meaning to European citizenship and improving the quality of democracy and representation in EU institutions. Through constitutionalism, citizenship, and democracy, all concepts usually associated with states, it is often argued that the EU is inching closer to a federal model. Supporting this argument is the fact that the view of a federal EU has supporters in many member states (most notably Belgium, Italy, Luxembourg, the Netherlands, France, and Germany). However, in other member states such as Great Britain, Sweden, and Denmark, the federal model is strongly opposed because it is seen as being a threat to these states' cultures, democratic traditions, international presence, social policies, and so on. Many political scientists see in this reluctance of some member states to significantly increase political integration a sign that the EU is best described by the concept of *intergovernmentalism*, that is, simply as an association of independent states.

ENDNOTES

1. Ronald L. Watts, *Comparing Federal Systems, 2nd ed.* (Kingston, Institute of Intergovernmental Relations: McGill-Queen's University Press, 1999), 10.
2. Ibid., 2.
3. Wolf Linder, *Swiss Democracy: Possible Solutions to Conflict in Multicultural Societies* (London: MacMillan, 1998).
4. For more, see Note 1, Ronald L. Watts, *Comparing Federal Systems*, 101–04.
5. Watts presents a discussion of this issue with slightly different sets of criteria. See ibid., 71–80.
6. Ibid., 10.
7. Ken McRoberts, *Misconceiving Canada* (Toronto: Oxford University Press, 1997).
8. Rolf Falter, "Belgium's Peculiar Way to Federalism," in *Nationalism in Belgium: Shifting Identities, 1780–1995*, eds. Kas Deprez and Louis Vos (New York: St. Martin's Press, 1998), 177–97.
9. Luis Moreno, *The Federalization of Spain* (London: Frank Cass, 2001).

READINGS

This chapter has explored the nature and workings of federal political systems. It has made a distinction between federalism as a principle of government and federations as a particular structure of the territorial division of power. At the broadest level, it is important to remember the great diversity in the forms federalism can take and the crucial political functions it can serve. The two readings selected for this chapter emphasize these points. On the one hand, Daniel Elazar elaborates on the various political arrangements that are derived from federalism. On the other, Richard Simeon and Daniel-Patrick Conway discuss the usefulness of federalism as a strategy for the accommodation of sub-state nationalism.

The first reading is by Daniel Elazar, a prominent scholar of federalism. In this piece, Elazar develops the argument that "federalism" needs to be understood more broadly than "federations." Indeed, one of Elazar's main contributions to the study of federalism is the idea that it is much more than a set of institutions. Rather, Elazar views federalism as a political principle that stresses the idea of partnership and therefore can take many forms. In this context, he sees federalism at work in many contemporary political arrangements beyond federations and even states with federal features such as Spain. He describes several forms: *federacies*, a political relationship between a larger and smaller political unit (United States and Puerto Rico); *associated state arrangements*, a looser partnership between states usually specified by treaty (Switzerland–Liechtenstein); *condominiums*, the joint rule of a political unit by two external states in a way that provides this unit with autonomy (Andorra was a condominium of France and Spain until 1993); *common markets* and *unions* such as the EU; and *leagues*, a grouping of independent states with common historical, cultural, or economic ties (the Arab league). Elazar saw, when writing his book (1987), a "federalist revolution" in the growing numbers of states and other political arrangements with federal trends. His observation seems to have been confirmed considering the new federal models that have emerged, or are currently emerging: Belgium, South Africa, the EU, and so on. He concludes by saying that federalism is a key resource in meeting the challenges of stability and peace in a culturally diverse world.

In the second excerpt, Richard Simeon and Daniel-Patrick Conway explain how some political scientists are enthusiastic about the capacity of federalism to successfully manage multinational states while others see it as intensifying intergroup conflicts, or even as representing a "slippery slope" toward secession. The two authors argue that it is difficult to make this type of generalization about federalism because federal models vary so much; most importantly, they have different divisions of power, intergovernmental relations, and modes of representation for constituent units at the centre. From this angle, the authors are critical of Canadian federalism for its lack of integrative features in comparison with other models such as Germany's. Simeon and Conway also make the crucial point that federal structures cannot be the only answer or solution to managing cultural diversity, but that other elements are equally important and condition the success of federalism to generate peace and stability: civil society, party systems, Charters of Rights, and other institutional features such as system of government. The idea that federalism should never be studied in isolation from social and other institutional elements may be the larger lesson to draw from this contribution.

EXPLORING FEDERALISM

Daniel Elazar

THE FEDERAL IDEA

As many philosophers, theologians, and political theorists in the Western world have noted, the federal idea has its roots in the Bible.[1] Indeed, the first usage of the term was for theological purposes, to define the partnership between man and God described in the Bible, which, in turn, gave form to the idea of a covenantal (or federal) relationship between individuals and families leading to the formation of a body politic and between bodies politic leading to the creation of compound politics. The political applications of the theological usage gave rise to the transformation of the term "federal" into an explicitly political concept.[2]

The term "federal" is derived from the Latin *foedus*, which, like the Hebrew term *brit*, means covenant. In essence, a federal arrangement is one of partnership, established and regulated by a covenant, whose internal relationships reflect the special kind of sharing that must prevail among the partners, based on a mutual recognition of the integrity of each partner and the attempt to foster a special unity among them. Significantly, *shalom*, the Hebrew term for peace, is a cognate of *brit*, having to do with the creation of the covenantal wholeness that is true peace.[3]

Federal principles are concerned with the combination of self-rule and shared rule. In the broadest sense, federalism involves the linking of individuals, groups, and polities in lasting but limited union in such a way as to provide for the energetic pursuit of common ends while maintaining the respective integrities of all parties. As a political principle, federalism has to do with the constitutional diffusion of power so that the constituting elements in a federal arrangement share in the processes of common policy making and administration by right, while the activities of the common government are conducted in such a way as to maintain their respective integrities. Federal systems do this by constitutionally distributing power among general and constituent governing bodies in a manner designed to protect the existence and authority of all. In a federal system, basic policies are made and implemented through negotiation in some form so that all can share in the system's decision-making and executing processes.

THE FEDERALIST REVOLUTION

The federalist revolution is among the most widespread—if one of the most unnoticed—of the various revolutions that are changing the face of the globe in our time. In the modern and postmodern epochs federalism has emerged as a major means of accommodating the spreading desire of people to preserve or revive the advantages of small societies with the growing necessity for larger combinations to employ common resources or to maintain or strengthen their cultural distinctiveness within more extensive polities. Consequently, federal arrangements have been widely applied, on one hand, to integrate new polities while preserving legitimate internal diversities and, on the other, to link established polities for economic advantage and greater security. Nearly 40 percent of the world's population now lives within polities that are formally federal; another third live in polities that apply federal arrangements in some way.[4]

The term "federal arrangements" suggest [*sic*] that there is more than one way to apply federal principles. Indeed, to use a biological analogy, federalism can be considered a genus of political organization of which there are several species. Europe knew of only one federal arrangement, *confederation*, whereby several pre-existing polities joined together to form a common government for strictly limited purposes, usually foreign affairs and defense, which remained dependent upon its constituent polities. Two centuries ago, the United States invented modern federalism and added *federation* as a second form, one that was widely emulated in the nineteenth century. A federation is a polity compounded of strong constituent entities and a strong general government, each possessing powers delegated to it by the people and empowered to deal directly with the citizenry in the exercise of those powers.

In the twentieth century, especially since World War II, new federal arrangements have been developed, or federal elements have been recognized in older ones previously not well understood. *Federacies*, *associated state arrangements*, and *common markets* are postmodern applications of the federal principle. In a federacy arrangement, a larger power and a smaller polity are linked asymmetrically in a federal relationship whereby the latter has greater autonomy than other segments of the former and, in return, has a smaller role in the governance of the larger power. The relationship between them is more like that of a federation than a confederation and can be dissolved only by mutual agreement. Associated state arrangements are equally asymmetrical but are like confederations in that they can be dissolved unilaterally by either of the parties. Consequently, the associated states have even less of a role in the governance of the associated power. Common markets are forms of confederation emphasizing shared economic rather than political functions.

Political scientists have rediscovered the federal characteristics present in *consociational polities*, *unions*, and *leagues*. Consociational polities are nonterritorial federations in which polities divided into transgenerational religious, cultural, ethnic, or ideological groupings are constituted as federations of "camps," "sectors," or "pillars" and jointly governed by coalitions of the leaders of each. Unions are polities compounded in such a way that their constituent entities preserve their respective integrities primarily or exclusively through the common organs of the general government rather than through dual government structures. Leagues, on the other hand, are linkages of politically independent polities for specific purposes, which function through a common secretariat rather than a government and from which members may unilaterally withdraw. Although neither is a species of federalism, properly speaking, both use federal principles in their constitution and governance. New regional arrangements, which are essentially leagues that emphasize regional development, represent more limited applications of federal mechanisms. There is every reason to expect that in the postmodern world new applications of the federal principle will be developed in addition to the arrangements we already know, including *functional authorities* for the joint implementation of particular tasks and *condominiums* involving joint rule by two powers over a shared territory in such a way that the inhabitants of the latter have substantial self-rule. Thus reality is coming to reflect the various faces of federalism.

A major reason for this evolution lies in the reassertion of ethnic and regional identities, now worldwide in scope, which promises to be one of the major political issues of this generation and the next century. There are some 3,000 ethnic or tribal groups in the world conscious of their respective identities. Of the more than 160 politically "sovereign" states now in existence, more than 141 are multiethnic in composition. More than one-third of those states, 58 to be exact, are involved in formal arrangements using federal principles in some way to accommodate demands for self-rule or shared rule within their boundaries or in partnership with other polities. In sum, although the ideology of the nation-state—a single state embracing a single nation—remains strong, the nation-state itself is rare.[5]

The federalist revolution in Western Europe is taking on two forms. On one hand, Western Europe is moving toward a new-style confederation of old states through the European Community and, on the other, there is a revival of even older ethnic and regional identities in the political arena. As a result, Belgium, Italy, and Spain have constitutionally regionalized themselves or are in the process of doing so, and even France is being forced to move in that direction, at least in the case of Corsica. Portugal has devolved power to its island provinces—as the Netherlands and Denmark have long since done. Switzerland, Germany, and Austria, already federal systems, are undergoing an intensification of their federalist dimensions in one way or another. The issue remains alive, if unresolved, in Britain. The idea of a Europe of ethnic regions is a potent force on that continent.[6]

Most of the new states of Asia and Africa must come to grips with the multiethnic issue. It is an issue that can be accommodated peacefully only through the application of federal principles that will combine kinship (the basis of ethnicity) and consent (the basis of democratic government) into politically viable, constitutionally protected arrangements involving territorial and nonterritorial polities. Although only a few of those states have formally federal systems, as in India, Malaysia, Nigeria, and Pakistan, a number of others have adopted other federal arrangements internally and are combining in multinational arrangements on a regional basis.[7]

Western Asia and the eastern Mediterranean region, known collectively as the Middle East, are no exceptions to this problem of ethnic diversity. Indeed, many of that region's current problems can be traced to the breakdown of the Ottoman Empire, which had succeeded in accommodating communal diversity within a universal state for several centuries. The intercommunal wars in Cyprus, Iraq, Lebanon, and Sudan, not to speak of the minority problems in Egypt, Iran, and Syria and the Israel–Arab conflict, offer headline testimony to this reality. Federal solutions are no less relevant in the Middle East than elsewhere, but especially in the Middle East is the need great for a postmodern federalism that is not simply based upon territorial boundaries but recognizes the existence of long-enduring peoples as well.[8]

On the other hand, in the older, more established federal systems of North America, the reemphasis of ethnic and cultural differences has challenged accepted federal arrangements. In Canada, this challenge has taken the form of a provincial secessionist movement and in the United States, an emphasis on nonterritorial as against territorial-based subnational loyalties on one hand and a revival of Native American (Indian) tribal aspirations on the other.[9] Latin America, the first cultural area outside of the

United States to adopt federal solutions to encourage political liberty, continues to struggle with the problems of reconciling the republican dimensions of federalism with its penchant for autocratic leadership.[10]

In sum, federal forms have been applied to a widening variety of relationships ranging from federalism in support of group pluralism and individual liberties in the United States, to federalism in support of local liberties in Switzerland and federalism on a linguistic basis in India, to federalism as a means of gaining mild decentralization in Venezuela. Federal arrangements to accommodate ethnic differences are becoming more widespread than ever in Canada, Belgium, Spain, and the United Kingdom (under other names), Malaysia, and Nigeria. In every case, these developments have emerged as practical responses to real situations.

In most if not all of these cases, whether they know it or not, the various parties have arrived at the point which the late Martin Diamond described as the classic position of federalism—the position expressed by the song that Jimmy Durante, the American comedian, belted out in the film, *The Man Who Came to Dinner*: "Did you ever have the feeling that you want to go, and the feeling that you want to stay?" That is the classic problem for which federalism, as a technology, was invented.

FEDERALISM, CONFLICT RESOLUTION, AND POLITICAL INTEGRATION

In its quest for a stable and peaceful world, humanity today finds itself confronted with a number of political problems, many of which are seemingly intransigent, whose sources lie in conflicting national, ethnic, linguistic, and racial claims arising out of historical experiences. Some of these problems are headline material almost daily, others are less visible but consistently aggravating, and still others have been temporarily submerged but only await the appropriate moment to reappear further to disturb the worldwide quest for peace. The just resolution of these problems is essential if local and world peace is to be attained on the basis of some approximation of justice, yet in none of these cases is justice a simple matter; hence the conflicting claims of the parties involved have not proved amenable to the usual forms of political compromise. New forms for resolving those problems are desperately needed, for the sake of

the parties involved at least as much as for the sake of the world as a whole.

The federal principle offers one possible resource for resolving these problems. As suggested above, using the federal principle does not necessarily mean establishing a federal system in the conventional sense of a modern federal state. The essence of federalism is not to be found in a particular set of institutions but in the institutionalization of particular relationships among the participants in political life. Consequently, federalism is a phenomenon that provides many options for the organization of political authority and power; as long as the proper relations are created, a wide variety of political structures can be developed that are consistent with federal principles.

It is useful to reiterate what is meant by federalism in this context. The simplest possible definition is *self-rule plus shared rule*. Federalism thus defined involves some kind of contractual linkage of a presumably permanent character that (1) provides for power sharing, (2) cuts around the issue of sovereignty, and (3) supplements but does not seek to replace or diminish prior organic ties where they exist.

One cautionary note is necessary: despite all these opportunities for using federalism to resolve problems of political organization and integration, the record of attempting federal solutions has been mixed at best. In some cases, the attempts have been so successful that the polities established have become models of their kind—Switzerland and the United States, for example. In others, federal structures have been introduced but are recognized by objective observers to be essentially window dressing—the USSR and Czechoslovakia, for example. In still others, efforts to introduce federal solutions have simply failed—Ethiopia and Ghana, for example. We will have occasion to examine the cultural, social, economic, and political conditions that influence the success or failure of federal experiments.

There also is the serious problem of "thinking federal," that is, of approaching the problem of organizing political relationships from a federalist rather than a monist or centralist perspective. I would suggest that we can see in the formation of any federal polity some conception of the federal *idea*, some persuasion or ideology that endorsed federal solutions, some particular application of the federal *principle*, and some particular federal *framework.* That leads us to the question of federalism and political integration as presently conceptualized.

The study of political integration has been high on the agenda of contemporary political science. Curiously, however, the relationship between the federal principle and political integration has been almost totally ignored, not only in theory but even in studies of political integration in federal polities. On one level, this curious neglect may reflect the current tendency in political science circles to treat terms like federalism as either too legalistic and hence unsuitable for the behavioral science of politics or too vague for proper scientific definition. On another, the neglect may reflect the currently widespread political science doctrine that every political system has a center and a periphery, "by nature," as it were; that only what happens in the center is politically significant; and that federalism is merely a form of decentralization, perhaps less efficient than other forms because of the various constitutional barriers characteristic of federal systems. Under such terms, political integration becomes a matter of building a strong center and tying the periphery closer to it, hence federal arrangements are either unimportant or represent a way station toward full integration.

Federalism, understood on its own terms, offers an alternative to the center–periphery model, for political integration as for other things political. The matrix model of federalism is policentric by design. The essence of the federal matrix is conveyed both in the original meaning of the term—a womb that frames and embraces in contrast with a single focal point, or center, that concentrates—and in its contemporary meaning—a communications network that establishes the linkages that create the whole.

Political integration on the matrix model is very different from integration around a common center. In the first place, the measure of political integration is not the strength of the center as opposed to the peripheries; rather, it is the strength of the framework. Thus both the whole and the parts can gain in strength simultaneously and, indeed, must do so on an interdependent basis. Furthermore, political integration on a federal basis offers possibilities for linkages beyond the limits of the conventional nation-state.

Reading Notes

1. See Delbert Hillers, *Covenant: The History of the Biblical Idea* (Baltimore: Johns Hopkins University Press, 1969); George E. Mendenhall, *Law and Covenant in Israel and the Ancient Near East* (Pittsburgh: University of Pittsburgh Press, 1955); and Moshe Weinfeld, "Covenant," in *Encyclopedia Judaica* (Jerusalem: Keter Books, 1973), 5:1012–22.

2. See, for example, G.H. Dodge, *The Political Theory of the Huguenots of Dispersion* (New York: Octagon Books, 1947); E.J. Shirley, *Richard Hooker and Contemporary Political Ideas* (Naperville, Ill.: Allenson, 1949); R.H. Murray, *The Political Consequences of the Reformation* (New York: Russell and Russell, 1960); and Christopher Hill, *Intellectual Origins of the English Revolution* (New York: Oxford University Press, 1965).

3. "Peace" in *Encyclopedia Judaica*, 13:194–99; Daniel J. Elazar, *The Vocabulary of Covenant* (Philadelphia: Center for the Study of Federalism, 1983).

4. See Daniel J. Elazar, ed., *Federalism and Political Integration* (Ramat Gan, Israel: Turtledove Publishing, 1979), *Self Rule/Shared Rule* (Ramat Gan, Israel: Turtledove Publishing, 1979), and *Handbook of Federal and Autonomy Arrangements* (Jerusalem: Jerusalem Center for Public Affairs, forthcoming). What follows is a summary of the varieties of federal arrangements. The following chapters deal with them more elaborately.

5. Ivo D. Duchacek elaborates on this theme in "Antagonistic Cooperation: Territorial and Ethnic Communities," *Publius* 7, no. 4 (1977): 3–31.

6. Martin O. Heisler, ed., *Politics in Europe* (New York: David McKay, 1974); Leon N. Lindberg and Stuart A. Scheingold, *Europe's Would-Be Polity: Patterns of Change in the European Community* (Englewood Cliffs, N.J.: Prentice-Hall, 1970); Guy Heraud, *L'Europe des ethnics* (Nice: Presses de Europe, 1963).

7. See Benjamin Akzin, *States and Nations* (Garden City, N.Y.: Doubleday, Anchor Books, 1966); Cynthia Enloe, "Internal Colonialism, Federalism and Alternative State Development Strategies," *Publius* 7, no. 4 (1977): 145–61; and "The Neglected Strata: States in the City-Federal Politics of Malaysia," *Publius* 5, no. 2 (1975): 151–71; and Ivo D. Duchacek, ed., *Federalism and Ethnicity*, a special issue of *Publius* 7, no. 4 (1977).

8. Myron Weiner, "Matching Peoples, Territories and States: Post Ottoman Irredentism in the Balkans and in the Middle East," in Daniel J. Elazar, ed., *Governing Peoples and Territories* (Philadelphia: Institute for the Study of Human Issues, 1983), pp. 101–46.

9. See Filippo Sabetti and Harold M. Waller, eds., *Crisis and Continuity in Canadian Federalism*, special issue of *Publius* 14, no. 1 (1984); Murray Friedman, "Religion and Politics in an Age of Pluralism, 1945–1976: An Ethnocultural View," *Publius* 10, no. 3 (1980): 45–77; Russell L. Barsh and James Y. Henderson, *The Road: Indian Tribes and Political Liberty* (Berkeley and Los Angeles: University of California Press, 1980); and Wilcomb E. Washburn, *Red Man's Law and White Man's Law: A Study of the Past and Present Status of the American Indian* (New York: Charles Scribner's Sons, 1971).

10. See Howard Penniman, ed., *Venezuela at the Polls: The National Elections of 1978* (Washington, D.C.: American Enterprise Institute for Public Policy Research, 1980).

FEDERALISM AND THE MANAGEMENT OF CONFLICT IN MULTINATIONAL SOCIETIES

Richard Simeon and Daniel-Patrick Conway

THE LOGIC OF FEDERALISM

The logic in support of federalism is simple: conflict will be reduced by a measure of disengagement, of separation. Harmony will be increased in a system in which territorially concentrated minorities are able to exercise autonomy or self-determination on matters crucial to their identity and continued existence, without the fear of being overridden or vetoed by the majority group. Similarly, a federal system will limit the ability of the majority to impose its will on the minorities. Hence they will be reconciled to the system—realizing both the advantages of autonomy and the benefits—economic, social and otherwise—of participation in a larger political entity. Thus, "In a federal system, a national state majority cannot prevail over a minority that happens to constitute a majority in one of the local communities that is constitutionally privileged" (Dahl, in Linz 1997). Federalism provides protection against domination by the majority, an opportunity for self-fulfillment and self-development for the minority, through institutions that it controls, while maintaining the ability of both groups to pursue common goals.

But another line of argument suggests that federalism is Janus-faced. It asserts that federalism can perpetuate and intensify the very conflicts it is designed to manage. This is because they are institutionalized and entrenched in the very design of the political system. Federalism empowers minority elites who are likely to have a vested interest in sustaining and perhaps exacerbating the conflict. At the extreme, federalism can provide the institutional tools and resources for nation building; a base that can make a move towards secession plausible and viable in the future (Dion 1992). As we will see, this "slippery slope" argument is one that has been prominent in debates in several of our countries.

So the question is: which analysis is right? Or, more specifically, under what conditions is federalism more likely to constitute a stable accommodation within a divided society; and under what conditions will it be more likely to prove ineffective and unstable, leading to dissolution or secession?

DIFFICULTIES IN MAKING GENERALIZATIONS

There are enormous difficulties about making any sort of generalization about federal systems. First, with respect to democratic, multinational federations, such as we are considering here, there is a very small number of cases, each with widely varying history and circumstances.

Second, the causal arrows run both ways. On the one hand federalism is a response to, and is shaped by, the underlying divisions; on the other, federalism can powerfully influence societal divisions and the ways in which they are mobilized and expressed. It privileges some, and undercuts others (Cairns 1977).

Third, there is the question of what do we mean by "success" in managing conflict? Avoidance of violence, chaos and stalemate are criteria that all sides can accept. But beyond that, success or failure depends on the perspective one brings. Minorities are likely to judge "success" primarily by the extent to which federalism maximizes their group's freedom and autonomy. Majorities are likely to judge it in terms of whether it limits their freedom of action. Minorities are likely to judge it a failure if autonomy is decreased or aspirations for greater autonomy are not met. Majorities are likely to see failure in the loss of power to those minorities, or if they see them as receiving special privileges. Secession may be the ultimate success for at least some members of national groups in the federation; for many members of the majority, it is the essential failure. However, if it comes to secession, it is interesting to ask whether that is more likely to occur in a peaceful and orderly way when it occurs under a federal system. Perhaps so, because partial institutional disengagement has already taken place. The newly independent state already has a government.

Yet another difficulty in generalizing about the effectiveness of federalism in managing ethnonational conflicts is that federal institutions themselves vary so much. There is no single model: federations differ along a great many dimensions, and each is in some sense *sui generis*. There are as many adjectives attached to the term federalism as there are federal countries, hence William Riker's famous observation that federalism does not exist; and no generalizations can be made about it (1975). This suggests that an exploration of our question requires two levels of analysis. We can ask whether federalism makes a difference as a generic system of governance; or we can look at variations within federations to assess whether some federal designs may be more effective than others.

Federations also vary in their underlying political dynamics. Perhaps most important here

is what we call building or disbuilding; or what Linz calls "bringing together" or "holding together" (1997, p. 12), to which could be added "coming apart." Carl Friedrich (1968) describes federalism not as a single static form of government, but as a process. If so, we need to ask in what direction the process is going. Is it a matter of previously separate units coming together for whatever reason? The best recent example of this, perhaps, is the European Union. Or is the dynamic one in which previously unitary or relatively centralized regimes are coming apart, with powers devolving to provincial units at an accelerating rate, with no logical stopping place short of secession? Once either dynamic has become established, it will be very difficult to reverse. Finally, the effects of federal institutions will be greatly affected by their interaction with other aspects of the institutional structure such as the electoral system and the design of legislatures and executives. Especially pertinent are the mechanisms of intrastate federalism, or representation of states and provinces at the centre. The key issue here is whether national institutions serve to ensure full participation of the minorities in national as well as regional politics, and the extent to which they bind federal and provincial governments into relationships of trust and mutual dependence. With these observations in mind, let us examine some cases.

***

CONDITIONS UNDER WHICH FEDERALISM IS LIKELY TO PROVE SUCCESSFUL

This discussion raises the question: are there conditions under which federalism is likely to be more or less successful in the management of ethnocultural conflict?

First, does the design of the federal system itself matter—in terms of how powers are distributed, the strength of intrastate mechanisms and the mechanisms of intergovernmental relations? As argued above, I think it probably does. (See also Meadwell 1998.) The separated or divided Canadian model, with its watertight, compartmentalized mode of dividing powers, a Senate that represents neither citizens nor governments of the constituent units, and a form of intergovernmental relations that consists of diplomatic interactions among executives as if they were international actors seems less able to establish a stable accommodation. It does provide Quebec with a high degree of autonomy, but does not offset the integration of Quebecers into the federal system. The logic of watertight compartments—as distinct from concurrent powers—is a recipe for a zero-sum approach to overlapping responsibilities, and a politics of fighting for turf. Executive-dominated intergovernmental relations reinforce this tendency, focusing conflicts on the strategic goals of premiers and prime ministers, and undercutting more cooperative "functional" cooperation at lower levels. At least in recent years, the logic of Canadian intergovernmental relations has suggested a move towards a confederal model. In addition, the decentralized and divided model of Canadian federalism—making Quebec, in Dion's terms, the most powerful subnational government in the world—equips Quebec with the tools and resources that make a move towards secession both plausible and viable (1992).

This contrasts sharply with the German model of federalism which emphasizes interdependence, partnership, cooperation and consensus (Simeon 1998). Under such conditions, the two orders of government are much more tightly bound. Secession or confederalism thus becomes less likely. One should not exaggerate this argument however. Germany is not a multinational federation. It is possible that if the German *Länder* did represent strong ethnic or linguistic populations, the interdependencies and resulting need for cooperation would generate conflict and paralysis.

This suggests that "federalism is not enough" (Cairns 1995). By themselves, federal institutions are no guarantee of either success or failure. They need to be reinforced by other factors, both societal and institutional. Given that federalism is a process of "building out" it needs to be balanced by a process of "building in." In other words, the success of federalism depends, to a large extent, on the "integrative counterweights" to the process.

At the societal level it seems clear that in addition to strong national or community loyalties and identities, federalism can only survive if these are paralleled by significant elements of shared or overarching identities and values. Federalism is predicated on the existence of "nested identities" (see Smith 1995), the ability to maintain dual loyalties, a sense of simultaneous difference and of commonality. Miller argues that nested nationalities "think of themselves as belonging both to the smaller community and to the larger one, and they do not experience this as schizophrenic, because their two identities fit together reasonably well["] (Miller 1998). Once this symbiosis erodes, then federalism is indeed likely to give way to secession. Such feelings of common interest and mutual respect are critical conditions for the success of federalism, whether expressed as the *vouloir vivre ensemble* in Canada or Belgium, *Ubuntu* in South Africa, or *Bundestreue* in Germany.

The values of both the minority and the majority are important here. For the minority group it is a question of whether they retain some identity and loyalty to the larger entity. For the majority, the willingness to temper the commitment to simple majority rule and to accept the institutionalization of difference are critical. Majoritarianism, Lijphart says, is both undemocratic and dangerous in heterogeneous societies (1977, p. 3). Nordlinger (1972) goes further, arguing that the majority must be prepared to make the major concessions. (These observations are highly relevant to the current Canadian debate, where there is on the one hand the growth of sovereigntist sentiment, and on the other a declining willingness outside Quebec to make concessions, or to temper concepts like majoritarianism and the equality of citizens and provinces with the recognition of Quebec as a "distinct society").

Institutions may affect whether such dual values and loyalties are sustained. Mutually advantageous economic linkages, and the presence of other divisions in the society that cross-cut or overlap the ethnic/linguistic divide are also required.

Even more important, is the evolution of civil society, below the level of institutions and constitutional debate. Institutions cannot keep a country together if there is no other social cohesion. Hence it is critical to assess the dynamic of societal networks and their associational linkages. Is there a trend towards increasingly separated societies in which intragroup dynamics dominate? Are groups that once were able to bridge across groups finding accommodation more difficult, and are they dividing themselves into the social equivalents of confederalism, "sovereignty-association" or secession? If so, the capacity of federal institutions to manage accommodation at the political level will dramatically decline. More research on this dimension of social capital in divided societies is greatly needed. Again, we need to consider the causal arrows here: does fragmentation or division at the institutional level drive division at the societal level; or does disengagement at the societal level precede political-institutional change?

Institutional factors other than federalism are also likely to affect the capacity to manage ethnic conflict. We have already mentioned the importance of intrastate elements in central institutions, especially but not limited to second chambers. Electoral systems are also important, primarily because of the extent to which they can distort or exaggerate regional and linguistic differences or create incentives for exclusionary rather than inclusive electoral strategies. Executive dominance and simple majoritarianism in the parliamentary institutions of each level of government also shapes the conflict. The effect of Canada's institutional makeup is to structure the relationship between French-speaking and English-speaking Canadians as a Quebec–Canada relationship, as a partnership between two powerful, centralized governments, each of which includes or excludes minority political views. Thus they sharpen and polarize the debate. Additionally, the existence of nine other provinces, endowed with the same powers as Quebec, has other effects. Other provinces and regions have an incentive to emulate Quebec, and assert their own status as "distinct societies." It should come as little surprise therefore, that they powerfully support arguments for the "equality of the provinces" model, as distinct from the "partnership of two nations" model.

Party systems exist at the boundary between institutions and societies. If federalism is to be a device for integration and accommodation, then it needs to be supported by integrative party systems. This includes both the existence of at least some parties able to attain cross-regional and national support as well as linkages between the party systems that exist at central and regional levels. In Canada of course, we have seen long periods when the major national parties have been unable to win support in one or more major regions; and in recent years explicitly regional and "national" parties (the Reform and the Bloc Québécois) have grown stronger. In addition, especially in Quebec there are sharp differences between provincial and central party systems, and even between parties of the same name but at different levels. Indeed, the political incentives facing federalist leaders at the central level (to win Canada-wide support) and at the provincial level (to combat the sovereigntists) virtually guarantees conflict between them. In Spain, the role played by regional parties in national coalitions is an important factor. In Belgium the virtually total linguistic division among the political parties removes an important vehicle for integration. Again, there is the dilemma: integrative parties are needed to bridge the ethnolinguistic divide; but that divide (along with regional cleavages) means that integrative parties will face major hurdles, especially in divided federal systems.

A final institutional factor is the existence of Charters of Rights. They can help provide overarching common values and can provide assurance to the "minorities within the minorities," thus helping reconcile them to the power that a decentralized federation gives to the minority national group. The boundaries of ethnicity seldom coincide perfectly with the political boundaries of states. Without guarantees for their status, the options for these "minorities within the minority" become far less attractive—either "ethnic cleansing" to bring political and cultural boundaries into line, or "partition."

Thus, federalism is not the only institutional factor affecting how ethnonational politics are played out; and the effects of federalism depend greatly on the role of federalism within the larger institutional and social structure. As well, in all the cases studied here, the international environment—the EU for Belgium, Spain and Scotland; North American economic integration for Canada—will continue to have an important influence on the relations between national and subnational governments.

Reading Notes

Cairns, Alan. (1977). "The Governments and Societies of Canadian Federalism," *Canadian Journal of Political Science* 10: 695–725.

Cairns, Alan C. (1995). "Constitutional Government and the Two Faces of Ethnicity: Federalism Is Not Enough," in Karen Knop et al. (eds.), *Rethinking Federalism: Citizens, Markets, and Governments in a Changing World.* Vancouver: UBC Press, pp. 15–39.

Dion, Stéphane. (1992). "Explaining Quebec Nationalism," in R. Kent Weaver (ed.), *The Collapse of Canada?* Washington, DC: Brooking Institution, pp. 77–121.

Friedrich, Carl. (1968). *Trends of Federalism in Theory and Practice.* New York: Praeger.

Lijphart, Arend. (1977). *Democracy in Plural Societies: A Comparative Exploration.* New Haven: Yale University Press.

Linz, Juan. (1997). "Some Thoughts on the Victory and Future of Democracy," in Axel Hadenius (ed.), *Democracy's Victory and Crisis.* New York: Cambridge University Press, pp. 404–26.

Meadwell, Hudson. (1998). "Nations, States and Unions: Institutional Design and State Breaking," paper presented to the American Political Science Association, Boston.

Miller, David. (1998). "Secession and the Principle of Nationality," in Jocelyne Couture, Kai Nielsen and Michel Seymour (eds.), *Rethinking Nationalism.* Calgary: University of Calgary Press, pp. 261–82 and in Margaret Moore (ed.), *National Self-Determination and Secession.* Oxford: Oxford University Press, pp. 62–78.

Nordlinger, Eric A. (1972). *Conflict Regulation in Divided Societies.* Occasional Papers in International Affairs, no. 29. Cambridge, MA: Harvard University.

Riker, William. (1975). "Federalism," in Fred Greenstein and Nelson Polsby (eds.), *Handbook of Political Science*, vol. 5. Reading, MA; Don Mills, Ont.: Addison-Wesley, pp. 93–172.

Simeon, Richard. (1998). "Considerations on the Design of Federations: The South African Constitution in Comparative Perspective," *SA Public Law* 13: 42–71.

Smith, Graham (ed.). (1995). *Federalism: The Multiethnic Challenge.* London: Longman.

KEY TERMS

Confederation   A political unit composed of independent states that accept to cede some of their sovereignty to common institutions. In this system, a set of sovereign states decide to create a union for the realization of specific goals (e.g., economic, military, etc.). The sovereign states delegate a certain number of powers to the government of the union. The state reserves the power to secede from the confederal system.

Federalism   A principle of government that seeks to reconcile unity and diversity through the exercise of political power along multiple autonomous levels.

Federation   A state in which two or more levels of government are sovereign within their own constitutionally specified jurisdictions.

Unitary State   A state in which any powers exercised by subnational governments are delegated only by the centre. In other words, subnational governments are not sovereign in prescribed fields and the central state can change the territorial division of power without the consent of the subnational units.

FURTHER READINGS

Burgess, Michael, and Alain-G. Gagnon, eds. *Comparative Federalism and Federations: Competing Trends and Future Directions.* Hemel Hempstead, UK: Harvester Wheatsheaf, 1993.

Duchacek, Ivo. *Comparative Federalism: The Territorial Dimension of Politics.* Lanham, MD: University Press of America, revised edition, 1987.

Elazar, Daniel. *Federalism and the Way to Peace.* Kingston, ON: Institute of Intergovernmental Relations, Queen's University, 1994.

Forsyth, Murray. *Federalism and Nationalism.* Leicester, UK: Leicester University Press, 1989.

Griffiths, Ann L., ed. *Handbook of Federal Countries 2002.* Montreal: Forum of Federations, McGill-Queen's University Press, 2002.

Simeon, Richard, and Ian Robinson. *State, Society and the Development of Canadian Federalism.* Toronto: University of Toronto Press, 1990.

Smiley, Donald. *The Federal Condition in Canada.* Toronto: McGraw-Hill Ryerson, 1987.

WEB LINKS

Institute of Intergovernmental Relations, Queen's University:
www.iigr.ca/iigr.php

Forum of Federations:
www.forumoffederations.org

Institute of Federalism, University of Fribourg:
www.federalism.ch/index.php?page=448&lang=0

CHAPTER 11

POLITICAL PARTIES AND ELECTORAL SYSTEMS

DEFINING POLITICAL PARTIES

A classic definition of **political party** is offered by Anthony Downs in his seminal work *An Economic Theory of Democracy*. Downs defines a political party as a team of individuals who are united for the purpose of capturing political power. Although, as the title of his book suggests, Downs primarily examined political parties in democratic contexts, the definition lends itself to studying political parties in both democratic and non-democratic regimes. The key words in the Downsian definition of a political party are "individuals" and "power." The advantage of this definition is that it reminds us that even though political parties often claim to represent and speak for the interest of particular social, economic, national, linguistic, and other groups, ultimately they remain a collection of individuals who decided to unite their efforts and form an organization in order to advance their chances of obtaining political power.

The notion of power is important because it is ultimately the pursuit of this goal that distinguishes political parties from any other kind of organization, political or not. Of course, it is possible, and history provides us with plenty of examples, that power-seeking individual leaders press their agendas and pursue their goals by engaging the support of organizations other than a political party. For instance, frustration with the inability of the civil political elite to deal with the pressing social and economic crises of the nation led General Pervez Musharraf of Pakistan to enlist the support of the military in overthrowing the duly elected democratic government and installing himself as president. This case showed that an organization, the military, may in particular circumstances be called upon by a political entrepreneur to assist him or her in the pursuit of power, that is, play a function other than what it was mandated to perform by its original design. However, a political party is unique in that its sole purpose is to assist the entrepreneur to both capture and hold onto political power.

THE ORIGIN OF POLITICAL PARTIES

The emergence of modern political parties is the result of the extension of the franchise to increasingly larger segments of the population. As the number of people involved in electing the government has increased, so has the necessity to aggregate their interests and preferences into coalitions that would bring their representatives to power at election time. However, political parties also existed much earlier, and, in fact, it is difficult to think about the history of politics anywhere without also thinking about the fights and struggles among the different factions and organizations that supported different individuals, programs, or leaders. For instance, the politics of the early medieval Italian city-state of Florence was structured by the struggle between the Guelph and Guibbelin factions, who differed in their views about the division of power between the Pope and the Holy Roman Emperor. We could even go further back in history to find an instance of factions being very important in the deliberation of the Imperial Roman Senate.

TYPES OF POLITICAL PARTIES

Maurice Duverger showed that, in terms of their origin and organization, modern political parties may be divided into two types: the cadre party and the mass party. The cadre party emerged at the dawn of modern democratization out of the perceived need by aristocratic parliamentarians to establish a political machine or organization that would ensure their continued re-election to the legislature. As such, the cadre party is characterized both by originating inside the established legislature and by having a loose organization, since the sole purpose of such a party is to provide a prominent individual, or a local notable, to get into a position of power. In contrast, the mass party was organized by political outsiders, mainly the working class as well as members of the politically disenfranchised or lately enfranchised segments of the population, in order to demand concessions that would make their participation in formal parliamentary politics possible. In stark contrast to cadre parties, mass parties needed to mobilize large numbers of followers in order to be influential and successful, while the purpose of the cadre party was to ensure that sufficient following was mobilized to help the particular notable retain his position of authority. The British Conservative Party, or Canada's Liberal and Conservative parties are examples of Duverger's cadre parties, while workers' parties in both states (the Labour Party in Britain and the NDP in Canada) are examples of mass parties.

COMPONENTS OF A MODERN POLITICAL PARTY

At the core of every party are the leaders, or elite, who occupy the highest decision-making offices of the organization. The elite of the party includes both the elected and the non-elected officials of the organization. For example, in parliamentary democracies successful candidates of political parties sit in the national legislature deliberating about laws. These elected representatives of the party comprise the party elite no less and no more than the leaders of the organizational apparatus of the party, which consists of individuals who do not occupy an elected public post. Of course, there can be, and often are, overlaps between the organizational and the elected elite. Further removed from the decision-making locus of the party are the activists, such as volunteer party workers. Volunteers engage in a number of activities ranging from the organization of meetings between the public and the party's candidate or office holder to soliciting input from the public that may help the party refine its program. By definition, volunteers do not get paid for the work they do; however, they may be motivated by a number of factors to offer their services to the party. For example, there may be a family tradition of volunteering for political work; individuals may feel so passionate about the outcome of a political competition that they may want to do whatever they can to ensure that their preferred political party will win political power; or they may be interested in learning more about how the nation's political process works.

Finally, those furthest removed from the decision-making centre of the party are members of the public, who constitute a passive reservoir of the party's actual strength. In a democracy, a party's success is measured by the number of votes it secures in any given election (and, consequently, by the number of seats that it wins). The important task that a party faces is to convince voters, who may otherwise not be interested in joining the party and partaking of the various benefits of membership, to give it their support at election time. This is why the party activists' job of gauging the mood of public opinion in an inter-election period is so important. If a political party "reads" the public right, it can put together a program that appeals to a large enough segment to guarantee the party victory. Similarly, in non-democratic settings the role of the public remains extremely powerful, although parties are used by a power-seeking elite in very different ways, such as co-optation and the demobilization of political support that might otherwise benefit alternative forces.

PARTIES AND IDEOLOGIES

Political parties also differ in terms of the ideology according to which they seek to use political power once they have captured it. While some political parties limit their appeal to the specific values of a single ideology, others seek to build large electoral coalitions by transcending the ideational confines that any single ideology would impose on them. Such **catch-all** parties may bring together individuals of widely different value predisposition. Examples of catch-all parties include the Canadian Liberal Party, which has tried to broker the regional and linguistic differences among its supporters, or the Indian National Congress party, which for four decades governed post-colonial India by having successfully built and maintained an electoral coalition that cut across the centrifugal line of fissure that threatened to rip the nation apart upon independence.

In his seminal work, Klaus von Beyme identified a number of ideological families, the so-called *familles spirituelles*, in the west European party systems. These families are the socialist, social-democratic, conservative, Christian-democratic, nationalist, religious, ethnic, liberal, agrarian, and radical-populist. Political parties that belong to these families are also called **cleavage-based parties** because they mobilize voters along particular, clearly identifiable lines of political cleavage, such as religion, ethnicity, language, etc. Clearly, catch-all parties by definition cannot be cleavage based. By identifying the electoral strength of parties that belong to these families, we can understand a lot about the nature of political discourse and conflict in a country.

PARTY SYSTEMS

The discussion so far has centred on what political parties are, how they function, and how we can distinguish among different types of parties in terms of different variables. Let us now turn to an examination of the different ways in which political parties are related to each other, i.e., the party system. In a very general sense a system, any system, consists of a set of patterned interactions among its individual units. Thus, a **party system** may be defined as the set of patterned interactions among political parties. While this definition suggests that the basic units of a party system are political parties, other non-party, within-party, and supra-partisan actors may also play an important role in shaping the dynamics of the party system. For example, a number of social democratic parties in the Western world have developed intimate ties to the organized labour movement. This relationship not only allows the trade union movement to have an effective political voice, but also helps the party to have an organization at its disposal that it can use to mobilize electoral support or public support in inter-election periods. Although the organized labour movement is not a partisan actor in the strict sense of the word, it clearly impacts the dynamics of the party system. The more organized the labour movement is and the more resources it can garner, the more advantages it bestows on its affiliated party. In the non-Western world, Argentina provides an excellent illustration of a non-party movement that constitutes the backbone of a political party: the electoral and popular support of the Peronist Party.

In a similar way, corporations and business groups also contribute to the shaping of the party system. Corporate donations are made in an effort to ensure that the political party that assumes power will implement policies and laws that favour and cater to the donor's interests. Economic organizations, however, are far from being the only entities involved in party politics. In India, the Vishwa Hindu Parishad, an umbrella organization dedicated to the cause of promoting and conserving Hindu identity and interest, has made significant contributions to the advancement and rise of the Bharatiya Janata Party, which emerged from being a small party to become the one with the largest number of seats in the Indian legislature by the late 1990s.

Besides non-party actors, within-party and supra-partisan groups may also play an extremely important role in the party system. The former refers to factions, tendencies, and platforms within political parties. As discussed earlier, sub-party groups are held together by strong bonds in some, but certainly not all, parties. When these bonds are weak, sub-party groups may threaten to exit the parent organization. By so doing, they may contribute not only to the fragmentation of the party system but also to its ideological polarization, depending on the values they would embrace. Intra-party clashes among these groups may also have effects beyond the party itself. Internal frictions and factional disputes may make the party subject to claims about its unsuitability to govern. Moreover, such events may also lead to public disenchantment not only with the party itself but also with party politics in general. As far as supra-partisan actors are concerned, political parties often find it in their interest to form alliances (cartels) and coalitions with other parties. Normally, the reason for the formation of such alliances lies in the power-seeking motivation of political parties. In other words, a party will seek the formation of an alliance when the probability of capturing power is greater than it would be if the party sought power on its own. As shown later in the chapter, particular **electoral systems** may provide political parties with strong incentives to form such supra-partisan entities.

TYPES OF PARTY SYSTEMS

Students of political party systems have long debated the most important properties that define a party system. Perhaps the single most influential argument in this debate has been put forward by Giovanni Sartori. He claims that the two most important variables by which party systems can be distinguished are (1) the number of parties in the system and (2) the degree of ideological polarization among them. Sartori argues that these two variables are important not only because they capture the most important aspect of party competition, but also because the dynamics that emerge from different configurations of these variables have an impact on the broader political system as well. Let us look at Sartori's model in some depth.

With regard to the number of political parties, Sartori considers and counts only those parties that are relevant. Relevance, in this context, is defined by a party having either coalition or blackmail potential. A party has coalition potential if it has either participated in government or is always available as a coalition partner. In contrast, a party has blackmail potential if it has the demonstrated ability to bring down and terminate governments. Relevance, however, is not the only way to count political parties. Political scientists have also measured the fragmentation of the party system by using somewhat more sophisticated mathematical indices.

The second variable in Sartori's framework is ideological polarization. According to this variable, Sartori identifies two classes of party systems: those in which the ideological stretch among the relevant parties of the system is low, and those in which this stretch is high. Figure 11.1 on the next page shows the different possible combinations of party systems

Figure 11.1   **EXTENT OF POLARIZATION**

		LOW	HIGH
Number of parties	1	predominant party system	polarized predominance
	2	bipartism	polarized bipartism
	3–5	moderate pluralism	limited but polarized pluralism
	>5	extreme but moderate pluralism	polarized pluralism

based on these variables. Sartori notes that democratic party competition is difficult to sustain in a party system of polarized pluralism. He found that a party system of this type severely destabilized Italy's post–World War II democracy.

In an important study, Scott Mainwaring and Timothy Scully have shown that these party system types may take a long time to emerge and constitute an equilibrium in new democracies. Therefore, they argue that in the new democracies of the Third Wave, Sartori's typology of party systems may not be as relevant or adequate because party competition in these nations has not yet become patterned. (Remember that patterned recurrence is a fundamental part of the definition of a system. Thus, in nations where party competition has not become patterned, it is impossible to even speak of a party system!) Mainwaring and Scully have proposed an alternative framework that is specifically designed to analyze party competition in emerging democracies. This framework distinguishes **political party systems** according to a single variable—the degree of institutionalization. According to this framework, party system institutionalization is defined by four characteristics:

1. the stability of the pattern of inter-party competition;
2. the stability of parties; roots in society;
3. the consensus that political parties are the legitimate vehicles through which elections are conducted and government power is acquired; and
4. the existence of parties with stable internal rules and procedures.

ELECTORAL SYSTEMS AND PARTY SYSTEMS

A central question in the party system literature concerns what accounts for cross-system differences in the number of political parties. The most famous argument in this regard is Duverger's law, which establishes a direct causal relationship between the number of parties and the electoral system, i.e., the set of rules and regulations that governs the process by which votes that are cast by the electorate are translated into political representation (which may be either a seat in a legislature, or a presidential victory, etc. Note that Duverger's law extends only to democracies!). Duverger's law stipulates that in equilibrium,

1. plurality or first-past-the-post electoral systems lead to the creation of a two-party system; and
2. proportional representation electoral systems lead to multi-party systems.

The general insight behind the law is that the more permissive the electoral system, i.e., the more proportional it is, the easier it will be for even smaller political parties to survive the electoral race and obtain legislative representation. In contrast, the non-permissive nature of **plurality and majority** electoral rules penalizes small parties and their candidates, who, over time, will find it too costly to enter a competition in which they have little chance, if any, of success. Therefore, only large parties will survive over time as non-viable parties will either refrain from running candidates or will simply be deserted by strategically minded voters. In order to understand the mechanics of various electoral rules, let us examine them a little more closely.

The Plurality System and Its Variants

The plurality electoral system is also often referred to as the first-past-the-post (FPTP) or single-member-simple-plurality rule. This formula has been used by most ex-colonies of Britain. This electoral system divides the states into a number of constituencies, each of which elects one representative to the national legislature. Normally, constituencies tend to be of the same population size in order to ensure that each representative in the legislature will represent the same number of people. (The number of representatives that a constituency is entitled to is called the district magnitude. Thus, the district magnitude in FPTP is 1.) In each constituency, the candidate who receives the highest number of votes will be the winner and will enter the national legislature as the representative of the people residing in that constituency. The reason this electoral system is called plurality is that the eventual winner has to win only a plurality of the votes cast in the constituency. In fact, it tends to be very rare that a winning candidate would garner a majority of the votes cast, which is an important shortcoming of this electoral system in terms of the quality of democracy.

This problem is somewhat remedied by the so-called majority run-off system, used, among others, in French presidential elections. In the majority run-off system, if no candidate wins a majority of the votes cast, a second round is held between the top two candidates. Obviously, a lot hinges on the alliances and coalitions that the two candidates can form before the second round.

Another interesting variation of the pure FPTP system is the single nontransferable vote (SNTV), which is used, among others, in Japan and Taiwan. The main difference between SNTV and FPTP is in the magnitude of the districts. Whereas district magnitude in FPTP is 1, in SNTV it is greater than one; each constituency elects multiple representatives. This electoral system has been noted to present political parties with a coordination problem. If candidates of the same political party enter the same district, they may in fact be stealing votes away from each other rather than from their opponents!

Let us illustrate some of the problems associated with the use of the FPTP electoral system in the Canadian context. On June 28, 2004, general elections were held to the lower house of Canada's national parliament, the House of Commons. The elections produced a hung parliament, one in which no political party had a majority of the legislative seats. In theory, such a situation can make it very difficult for any one political party to form a government since in the absence of a coalition (see definition in Chapter 9) the opposition parties will have a majority and can vote the government out of office by passing a vote of no-confidence (again, if you are not sure of what these terms mean, revisit Chapter 9!). Following parliamentary convention, the leader of the party with the most seats, in this case the Liberal party of Canada, formed the new government. The election results are shown in Table 11.1.

Table 11.1 **THE RESULTS OF THE 2004 CANADIAN GENERAL ELECTION**

Party	% of Popular Vote	% of Parliamentary Seats	Seat Bonus
Liberal Party	36.7%	43.81%	+7.11
Conservative Party	29.6%	32.1%	+2.5%
Bloc Québécois	12.4%	17.5%	+5.1%
New Democratic Party	15.7%	6.2%	−9.5%

We need to make a number of important observations on the basis of the table. First, clearly Duverger's law does not work very neatly in the case of this Canadian election. Although the FPTP electoral system was used, the party system clearly consisted of more than two political parties. But how many parties were there exactly in Canada in this parliament? One answer might be that there were four, which is true given the actual number of parties that won seats in the House of Commons. However, this measure does not help us discriminate among parties in terms of their size: if we say that there were four parties then we actually count the largest party to be equal with the smallest party even though the former had more than twice as many votes and more than seven times as many seats!

One scientific way of calculating the number of parties in a parliament is a famous method first proposed by Marku Laakso and Rein Taagepera in 1979. This method calculates the effective number of parties (ENP) in the legislature by dividing into unity the sum of the squared percentages of seats, expressed in decimal form that each party won. Similarly, the effective number of electoral parties works by inserting the votes share of each party into the formula, which looks as follows:

$$ENP = 1/\sum^{t=1} P_n{}^2$$

where P is the percentage of either the total national vote polled by party n in a given election, $t = 1$, or the percentage of the total legislative seats that the party won in the given election examined. We will do the calculation for you using the numbers in Table 11.1; however, you should check it on your own to practise using this important quantitative indicator of party systems. The effective number of electoral parties in the 2004 Canadian election was 3.81 and the effective number of parliamentary parties was 3.03. This might look odd given that there were actually four political parties winning seats in the House of Commons. Yet, as we have said earlier, when we weigh parties in terms of their share of the votes, or seats, we can get much more nuanced and precise information about the degree of multipartism than the impressionistic evidence based on the actual number of parties allows.

Why did Duverger's law not work in the Canadian case? Was this an exceptional election? The answer is no. In fact, Canada has always deviated from the prediction that Duverger made for one very important reason: the country has a number of regionally based political cleavages that has made it possible for smaller regional protest parties to survive and do very well in the party system due to the advantages conferred upon them by the mechanical dynamics of the electoral system. In order to see what this statement really means, we need to take a closer look at how votes and seats are counted under this electoral system.

Imagine that our four political parties were competing in three electoral districts (we will call them West, Centre and East) and they receive the following share of the votes in each:

Table 11.2 **A HYPOTHETICAL DISTRIBUTION OF VOTES BY PARTY USING THE FIRST-PAST-THE-POST SYSTEM**

	West	Centre	East	Total
Liberal	34 (wins)	36 (wins)	20	90 votes, 2 seats
Conservative	33	34	19	86 votes, 0 seats
New Democratic Party	33	30	10	73 votes, 0 seats
Bloc Québécois	0	0	51 (wins)	51 votes, 1 seat

In this example, the party with the fewest votes across the three districts, the Bloc, actually emerges with the second highest number of seats! This can happen because this electoral system does not reward parties at all for votes that they receive in those districts where they do not actually win. For this reason, FPTP is often called a winner-take-all electoral system: if a party's vote share is a thousand miles wide but only an inch deep, then it will not win many seats in the legislature! For a famous study on this phenomenon in the Canadian context, read Alan Cairns (1968).

Now, we can turn back to Table 11.1. Notice that there are considerable differences between the percentage of the vote and the percentage of seats that the four national political parties won in that Canadian election. The last column identifies the so-called "seat bonus" of each party, which is calculated by subtracting the percentage of votes that a party received from its percentage of seats: the larger the difference the greater the values of the seat bonus, while smaller values (especially negative ones) indicate that a party is underrepresented in the legislature. The seat bonus of the Liberal Party is the largest, which is not very surprising given that this was the largest party in electoral terms anyway. However, notice that although the Conservative Party received more than twice as many votes across the country as the Bloc Québécois, its seat bonus was only half of this smaller party! Moreover, even though the New Democratic Party won actually more votes in the country than the Bloc Québécois did, it received only about a third of the seats that the Bloc was entitled to! In contrast to the Conservatives and the New Democratic Party, the Bloc focused its electoral activities in a single province of the country, Quebec. As we see, this was quite profitable in electoral terms.

Before we turn to the next family of electoral systems (PR), note that there is another country using the FPTP electoral rule without producing a two-party system: India. Figure 11.2 shows how the effective number of electoral parties has changed in India over time, from 1952 to 2004. It is striking to notice how the fragmentation of the party system has increased since 1989. Similar to the Canadian case, Indian politics have become increasingly more regionalized in the 1990s as a result of the transfer of significant policy authority from the central to the state (Chhibber and Kollman 2004, 1998). Therefore, we have seen an exponential growth in the number of regional parties in the Indian party system, providing yet another exception to Duverger's famous dictum!

Proportional Representation (PR)

As its name suggests, **proportional representation**, the second family of electoral systems seeks to strike a proportional balance between the electoral support of a political party and its share of political office. A perfectly proportional system would be one that allocates to

Figure 11.2 **THE EFFECTIVE NUMBER OF NATIONAL PARTIES IN INDIA, 1952–2004**

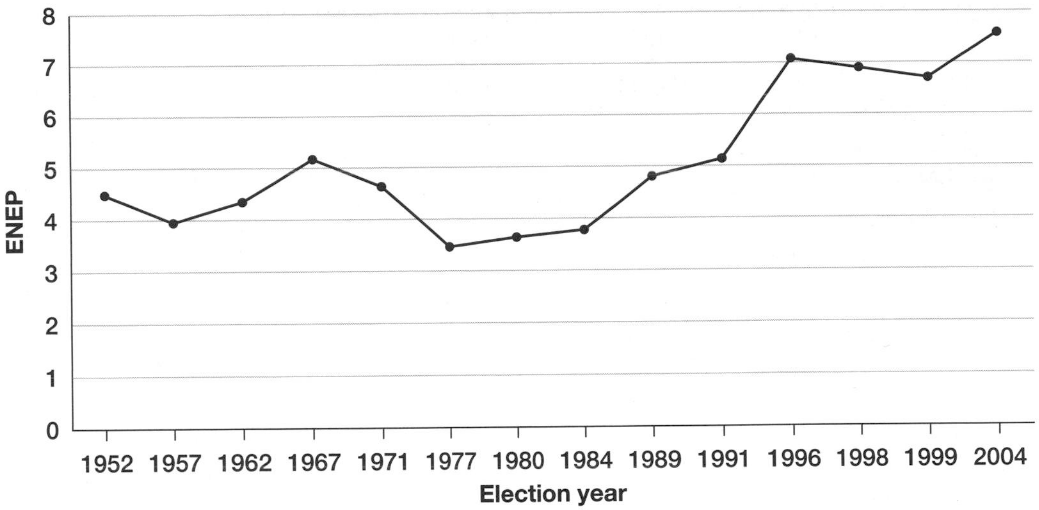

each political party the same percentage of legislative seats as the percentage of the votes that it has secured. However, no state uses a perfectly proportional rule; proportionality may be restricted in a variety of ways. The most important tools that are used to this effect are

- threshold;
- highest average versus quota-based formula; and
- magnitude of electoral districts.

The threshold is a set percentage of the total votes cast that any given political party must receive in order to qualify for representation in the legislature. Clearly, the threshold does limit the proportionality of the system, since votes that have been cast for parties that do not meet the threshold are wasted. Legal thresholds range widely from one nation to another. PR systems also differ in terms of the mathematical formulae that they use to convert votes into seats. The two main kinds of rules used are the highest average and the quota (or largest remainder) rules. Overall, highest average rules tend to favour larger parties, while quota-based systems are more favourable toward smaller political parties. Finally, the magnitude of the electoral district refers to the number of representatives that each constituency, or electoral district, can elect and delegate to the national legislature. As a rule of thumb, the smaller the district magnitude, the smaller the chances for small parties to succeed in winning seats. Therefore, highly proportional electoral systems tend to have high magnitude districts. For instance, in post-communist Slovakia the entire country is considered one electoral district with a magnitude of 150, which is the total number of legislative seats in the country's parliament. Clearly, small political parties fare better in Slovakia than in the neighbouring Czech Republic, where the magnitude of the average electoral district is 25.

Political scientists have long debated the relative merits and demerits of these different types of electoral systems. On the one hand, advocates of the plurality/majority rules argue that a legislature with few parties tends to be much more effective in terms of legislation and policy making than a fragmented parliament. On the other hand, advocates of PR argue that providing adequate representation to the widest possible range of political views is much more important in a democracy than governmental effectiveness. PR, in their view, is a "better" electoral system because it forces the composition of the legislature to reflect much more closely the distribution of popular preferences than a plurality/majority system. In sum, these differences highlight the tradeoff that crafters of electoral rules have to make between effectiveness and representativeness.

Let us examine how proportional representation works in practice by taking a close look at what is generally considered one of the most proportional systems in the world, the Israeli electoral regime. Similarly to Slovakia, the entire country in Israel also functions as one large electoral district, electing the 120 members of the unicameral legislature, the Knesset. Political parties present lists of candidates to the voters, who have to check the list of the party that they like the most. At the end of the day, those party lists that received less than 1.5 percent of the total votes cast across the country are disqualified from winning seats; in other words, a party must have more than 1.5 percent of the national vote in order to win some parliamentary representation in Israel. This threshold is one of the lowest in those countries that use different version of PR.

The conversion of votes into seats is carried out by using the d'Hondt highest average formula, which favours larger parties, as we will see below. Once it has been determined how many seats each political party is entitled to, on the basis of the votes that their list has received, candidates are automatically selected from their list in the order in which they were listed. Thus, a if a particular party has a list of 120 names (the maximum number that could be elected by any party given the number of seats) but the votes that the party received allowed it to win only 35 seats, then the first 35 candidates on the list will enter the legislature. It is not surprising that leaders of political parties want to be at the top of the list of their party.

The general elections that were held in Israel on January 28, 2002, produced a very fragmented Knesset. Similar to our earlier Canadian example, no political party won a majority of the seats, making the process of government formation quite difficult. However, while such election results are very unusual in Canada, they are much more frequent in Israel. The first important observation we can make pertains to Duverger's law: as we can see, the use of a proportional representation system produced a multi-party system with twelve political parties in the parliament. We can confirm this further by calculating the effective number of parties based on parties' votes and seats. The results are 7.05 and 5.8 respectively. Clearly, Duverger's prediction is confirmed because the use of a much more proportional electoral system in Israel led to a much higher number of parties there than in Canada, where the FPTP electoral rule is used.

Our second observation pertains to the distortion between parties/vote and seat shares. Notice that while in our Canadian example the largest party had a seat bonus of +7.11, in our Israeli example the largest party had a seat bonus of only +3.9 percent! Moreover, while the most underrepresented party in Canada, the NDP, had a "seat deficit" of −9.5 percent, the most underrepresented party in Israel, Ra'am, had a "seat deficit" of only −0.4 percent. It is very clear that there is a much closer correspondence between votes and seats in Israel than in Canada. Of course, not all PR systems work in such a fair manner. The use of different formulae by which votes are converted into seats, the level of the minimum threshold that parties must receive before they can qualify for seats, and the total number of seats that electoral districts fill can all make a substantial difference in how proportional the system will be.

Mixed-Member Systems

A third type of electoral system seeks to combine elements of both the majoritarian and proportional electoral rules. These are the so-called **mixed-member systems**, which combine elements of the two different electoral systems. Whereas some members of parliament

Table 11.3 **VOTES AND SEATS IN THE ISRAELI KNESSET, 2002**

Party	% of Votes	% of Seats	Seat Bonus
Likud	29.4	33.3	+3.9
Labour	14.5	15.8	+1.3
Shimi	12.3	12.5	+0.2
Shas	8.2	9.2	+1
National Union	5.9	5.8	−0.1
Meretz	5.2	5	−0.2
National Religious Party	4.1	4.2	+0.1
Torah Judaism	4.3	4.2	−0.1
Hadash	3	3.3	+0.3
One Nation	2.8	3.3	+0.5
Balad	2.3	2.5	+0.2
Ra'am	2.1	1.7	−0.4

Table 11.4 **THE DISTRIBUTION OF PR AND NON-PR SEATS IN SELECTED MIXED-MEMBER SYSTEMS**

State	% of Seats Elected by PR	% of Seats Elected by Plurality-Majority
Germany	51.3% (variable)	48.7%
Hungary	54.4%	45.6%
Japan	37.5%	62.5%
Lithuania	49.6%	50.4%
Russia	50.0%	50.0%

are elected on the basis of a majoritarian rule, others are elected on the basis of some form of PR. Table 11.4 shows some examples of how PR and non-PR elements are combined to elect national parliaments under mixed electoral systems.

How do mixed systems work? Let us examine it by looking at the Lithuanian legislature, Seimas, which is divided into two almost equal portions: 70 of the total 141 seats are filled through a PR election that takes place among party lists, as discussed in the previous section, while the remaining 71 seat are filled by the winners of the single-member district contests, similar to Canada. Thus, voters have two votes to cast. The first vote must be cast for the list of the party the voter likes while the other vote must to be cast for a local candidate. A voter, of course, can choose to vote for a candidate who belongs to a party other than the list he or she supports. Such a phenomenon is called **split-ticket voting**.

A party list needs to win at least 5 percent of the nation-wide list vote in order to qualify for seats, so the threshold is much higher than in Israel. In contrast to the FPTP electoral

Table 11.5 **SEATS AND VOTES IN THE LITHUANIAN SEIMAS, 2004**

Party	% of Votes	% of Seats	Seat Bonus
Labour Party	28.4%	27.6%	−0.8%
Working for Lithuania	20.6%	22%	+1.4%
Homeland	14.8%	17.7%	+2.9%
Order and Justice	11.4%	7.1%	−4.3%
Liberal and Centre Union	9.2%	12.8%	+3.6%
Farmers' Party and New Democracy	6.6%	7.1%	+0.5%
Lithuanian Poles' Electoral Action	3.8%	1.4%	−2.4%

rule, however, the Lithuanian single-member district races are decided by a top-two majority run-off rule rather than ordinary plurality. This means that if no candidate won a majority of the votes in a district, then the top two finishers compete against each other one more time in a run-off election held two weeks later. Table 11.5 shows the results of the 2004 Lithuanian election.

Now let us compare the Lithuanian results with our earlier Canadian and Israeli examples. The Lithuanian party system occupies an intermediate position in terms of the effective number of parties: in terms of votes it is 5.8, and in terms of seats it is 5.5. Thus the mixed system creates a more fragmented party system than FPTP but a less fragmented one than PR. The seat bonuses reinforce that. While we do not see the kind of extreme over- and underrepresentation of parties that we saw in the Canadian example, the conversion of votes into seats is clearly more distorted here than in the pure PR case of Israel.

The Representational Consequences of Electoral Systems: Women in Parliament

On balance, it seems that the closer an electoral system is to the case of pure PR, like Israel, the wider the range of political views that can be represented in parliament through the presence of multiple political parties. If so, then the choice of an electoral system should also have a strong impact on the ability of the legislature to fulfill its representative function as discussed in Chapter 9. We'll take a closer look by examining the relationship between the choice of an electoral system choice and the representation of women in legislature.

According to a study by the International Institute for Democracy and Electoral Assistance, legislatures that are elected via proportional representation rules have a significantly higher percentage of female deputies than legislatures that are elected by non-PR rules. Based on the post–World War II electoral history of twenty-four industrialized democracies, Figure 11.3 provides empirical evidence for this difference. Throughout the second half of the twentieth century, PR systems consistently provided female parliamentarians than non-PR systems did. Although there has been an increase in the overall rate of female representation even in non-PR systems since the 1970s, the difference across the two systems has increased exponentially over time. By the late 1990s, PR systems have led to more than twice as many female deputies in democratic legislatures than non-PR systems!

Figure 11.3 **ELECTORAL SYSTEMS AND FEMALE REPRESENTATION**

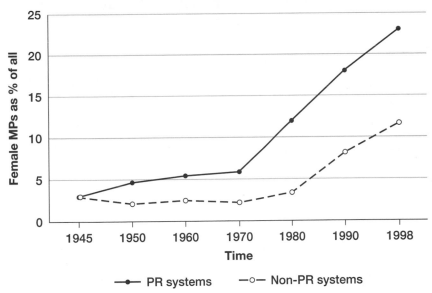

Source: www.idea.int/gender/wip-handbook and www.ipu.org/wmn-e/world.htm

In this chapter, we have seen how diverse and fascinating the world of political parties and party system is. As we continue our exploration of other political institutions, it is important to remember the critical role that political parties play in the functioning and maintaining of electoral democracies. Despite this functional commonality, however, even democratic parties and party systems are as different as the contexts in which they are established. Through methodologically rigorous positive comparative analysis, we can gain a better understanding of both the causes and consequences of this diversity.

READINGS

The following selection of readings provides a combination of theoretical and historical perspectives on some of the issues addressed in this chapter. The first reading is the classic statement by Maurice Duverger about the relationship between the electoral and party systems. The significance of Duverger's law for the scientific development of political science cannot be emphasized enough: few other statements and theories in the discipline have received as much attention and have been subjected to as many tests. In fact, in a famous article about the history of political science, William Riker shows that even though the content of Duverger's law has been contested and debated, it has generated a very significant body of cumulative knowledge and, as such, has helped make political science a genuine science.

The second reading by Andrew McLaren Carstairs takes us back in time to show the emergence of alternative electoral rules in France and the United Kingdom. These readings will help you see that the choice of electoral system is always the result of often long-drawn-out political battles. As you read through the pages that follow, note the logical reasons that compelled British and French political actors to advance their arguments regarding particular voting systems. In the end, what led to the consolidation of the electoral systems that these countries currently use?

POLITICAL PARTIES: THEIR ORGANIZATION AND ACTIVITY IN THE MODERN STATE

Maurice Duverger

THE TWO-PARTY SYSTEM AND THE ELECTORAL REGIME

If we accept the idea that the two-party system is natural we still have to explain why nature should have flourished so freely in the Anglo-Saxon countries and their few imitators and why nature should have been thwarted in the countries on the continent of Europe. As a matter of form we may mention the explanations based upon the 'genius of the Anglo-Saxon peoples' (frequent with American authors) and upon the 'temperament of the Latin races' (though the multi-party system exists in Scandinavia, in the Netherlands, and in Germany); not that they are entirely false but they belong to a realm of generalizations too vague and too approximate to allow of the formulation of valid conclusions; it is pointless to repeat the work of Gustave Le Bon. In passing we may glance as well at the explanation furnished by Salvador de Madariaga, who connects the two-party system with the sporting instincts of the British people, which lead them to view political campaigns as a match between rival teams: the sporting instincts must have disappeared between 1910 and 1945, when the three-party system was in operation. Nor can we take more seriously the picturesque comments of André Maurois, who contrasted the rectangular arrangement of the House of Commons and its two rows of facing benches leading naturally to the two-party system with the French semi-circle in which the absence of any clear line of demarcation encouraged the multiplication of groups. It is an amusing comment but it works both ways: is the seating arrangement in parliament the cause or the consequence of the number of parties? Which came first, the semi-circle or the multiplicity of parties, the rectangle or the two-party system? The reply is disillusioning: in England the shape of the chamber is anterior to the two-party system but in France the topography of parliament is posterior to the tendency towards the multi-party system; moreover the Americans have adopted the semi-circular chamber and their two parties are none the worse.

The historical explanation is more worthy of consideration. The age-long habit of dualism in England and America is obviously a factor in its present strength. It remains to be discovered why this habit has taken such firm root: otherwise the problem is simply referred back in time. Only individual investigation of the circumstances in each country can determine the real origins of the two-party system. The influence of such national factors is certainly very considerable; but we must not in their favour underestimate the importance of one general factor of a technical kind, the electoral system. Its effect can be expressed in the following formula: *the simple-majority single-ballot system favours the two-party system*. Of all the hypotheses that have been defined in this book, this approaches the most nearly perhaps to a true sociological law. An almost complete correlation is observable between the simple-majority single-ballot system and the two-party system: dualist countries use the simple-majority vote and simple-majority vote countries are dualist. The exceptions are very rare and can generally be explained as the result of special conditions.

We must give a few details about this coexistence of the simple majority and the two-party systems. First let us cite the example of Great Britain and the dominions: the simple-majority system with a single ballot is in operation in all; the two-party system operates in all, with a Conservative-Labour antagonism tending to replace the Conservative-Liberal antagonism. It will be seen later that Canada, which appears to present an exception, in fact conforms to the general rule.[1] Although it is more recent and more restricted in time the case of Turkey is perhaps more impressive. In this country, which had been subjected for twenty years to the rule of a single party, divergent tendencies were manifest as early as 1946; the secession of the Nationalist party, which broke away from the opposition Democratic party in 1948, might have been expected to give rise to a multi-party system. On the contrary, at the 1950 elections the simple-majority single-ballot system, based on the British pattern (and intensified by list-voting), gave birth to a two-party system: of 487 deputies in the Great National Assembly only ten (i.e. 2.07%) did not belong to one or other of the two major parties,

Democrats and Popular Republicans. Nine were Independents and one belonged to the Nationalist party. In the United States the traditional two-party system also coexists with the simple-majority single-ballot system. The American electoral system is, of course, very special, and the present-day development of primaries introduces into it a kind of double poll, but the attempt sometimes made to identify this technique with the 'second ballot' is quite mistaken. The nomination of candidates by an internal vote inside each party is quite a different thing from the real election. The fact that the nomination is open makes no difference: the primaries are a feature of party organization and not of the electoral system.

The American procedure corresponds to the usual machinery of the simple-majority single-ballot system. The absence of a second ballot and of further polls, particularly in the presidential election, constitutes in fact one of the historical reasons for the emergence and the maintenance of the two-party system. In the few local elections in which proportional representation has from time to time been tried it shattered the two-party system: for example in New York between 1936 and 1947, where there were represented on the City Council 5 parties in 1937

(13 Democrats, 3 Republicans, 5 American Labor, 3 City Fusionists, 2 dissident Democrats) 6 parties in 1941 (by the addition of 1 Communist), and 7 parties in 1947 (as a result of an internal split in the American Labor party supported by the Garment Trade unions). The same influence of the simple-majority single-ballot system is also to be noted in the sphere of the primary; Key has observed that in primaries in the South where the nomination is conducted at a single ballot the Democratic party generally divides into two factions; on the other hand, in the system with two successive primaries which correspond to the second-ballot system—the second or run-off primary operating in the event of no candidate securing an absolute majority at the first primary—the factions tend to increase in number of statistics comparing the number of candidates for nomination before and after the adoption of the run-off primary seem to confirm its multiplying effect (Fig. 11.4).

Not counting Latin-America, which may be neglected because the frequent and effective interference of the government in both polls and parties denatures the whole system, four countries provide exceptions to the rule: on the one hand pre-1894 Belgium, where the

Figure 11.4 **EFFECT OF SECOND BALLOT ON NUMBER OF CONTENDERS IN TEXAS DEMOCRATIC PARTY PRIMARIES**

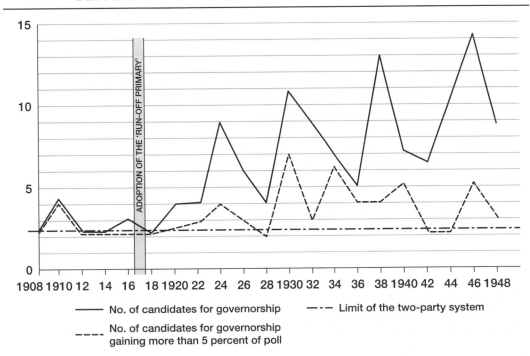

two-party system coexisted with the second ballot, on the other, pre-1911 Sweden, pre-1920 Denmark, and present-day Canada, in which the simple-majority single-ballot system is to be found alongside the multi-party system.

In the first case the exception is more apparent than real: the second ballot was provided for in the Belgian electoral law, but in practice it scarcely ever operated before the introduction of universal suffrage. In 1892, for example, in 41 constituencies there were no more than four *second* ballots, of which three (at Nivelles, Charleroi, and Tournal) were the result of cross-voting and incomplete voting, only two lists being presented at the first ballot; in fact, only in a single arrondissement, at Mons, did the second ballot truly operate as a result of votes being shared amongst three rival lists. After the introduction of universal suffrage the appearance of the Socialist party brought the full legal machinery into play: the three-cornered fight caused twelve *second* ballots in 1894 and fifteen in 1894–8. But during the period of dualism the elections took place in practice after the pattern of the single-ballot system. It remains to be determined why practice was not in conformity with the letter of the law, why the possibility of a second ballot did not produce three-cornered fights, party splits, and the break-up of the two-party system: we shall attempt an answer below.

The case of Sweden before 1909, when proportional representation was introduced, is scarcely less exceptional. In reality, under the complicated system of limited suffrage then in operation (direct election in the towns and indirect in the countryside, voting for single candidates or several candidates according to the constituency) the lines of demarcation between the parties long remained fluid and vague. There were scarcely any true organized parties in the country; there were not even any clearly delimited parliamentary groups; it is impossible to arrive at any precise electoral statistics giving the political complexion of candidates for the pre–1911 period. The system can be called neither two-party nor multi-party. Rather was there an absence of parties. Furthermore certain special political or social problems (secession from Norway, opposition between town and country, growth of a rural left-wing movement) here modified the natural duality of opinion. However, within each constituency the struggle was often limited to two candidates, which

restored the two-party system at the local level. On the national level we can also discern below the surface variations among the short-lived and fluid groups a fairly marked tendency towards two parties. From 1867 to 1888 there were two opposing parties: the Conservatives, drawing their support from the towns, and the *Lantmannapartiet*, whose strength lay in the rural areas. As from 1888 the Lantmanna split into two groups, the 'Old Lantmanna' standing for Free Trade, and the "New Lantmanna' which was protectionist: but the two groups reunited in 1895. In 1906 a new split divided the National Progressives from the Lantmanna but the two factions worked in close agreement: they were much more like two tendencies within the same party than two different parties. The coagulating effect of the simple-majority ballot is noticeable. Meanwhile the old Right was gradually disappearing and a Liberal party based upon the urban middle class was taking shape; at the end of the nineteenth century, therefore, there was to be found in Sweden the classic two-party system: Conservatives (Lantmanna) *v.* Liberals, modified however in 1896 by the appearance of the Socialist party. In fact, at the beginning of the twentieth century, the political divisions in the Riksdag, in so far as lines of demarcation between the parties can be drawn, resembled those in the British Parliament, the presence of Socialists making a breach in the Conservative *v.* Liberal dualism.

Denmark is a much clearer exception to the general tendency. In spite of the simple-majority single-ballot system there were four major parties just before the reform of the electoral system: Right, Liberals (*Venstre*), Radicals, Socialists. But in fact this four-party division at the national level often masked a two-party division at the local level: in very many constituencies only two candidates fought the campaign; thus, in 1910, out of 114 constituencies, 89 were in this position, compared with 24 constituencies having 3 candidates only and 1 with 4; the reduction in the number of candidates was moreover very marked in comparison with previous years (254 candidates in 1910, 296 in 1909, 309 in 1906). In 1913 there was a sudden rise to 314 candidates with only 41 constituencies in which there was a straight fight, 55 with 3 rival candidates, 15 with 4 and 1 with 5. This increase can however be largely explained by the desperate effort made by the Right to avert the decline with which it was seriously threatened: compared with 47 candidates in 1910 it managed to put up 88 in 1913; however, in spite of this considerable effort, its seats fell in number from 13 to 7 (although the total vote it polled increased from 64,900 to 81,400, and the 17,000 extra votes, chiefly won over from the Liberals, cost the latter party 13 seats). In 1910, furthermore, there was a close electoral understanding between the Radicals and the Socialists, since in no case did these two parties put up candidates against one another; this agreement would appear to have broken down in 1913, however, when we find that 17 Socialists were put up against Radicals, and also 7 Radicals against Socialists. Finally, if a comparison be made of the situation of the parties in 1913 with their earlier position, a definite concentration is apparent. Indeed, in 1906 there were five parties (as a result of the creation of the Radical party); in 1909 the fusion of the Agrarian party (moderate) with the Liberals reduced this number to four; lastly, we must take into account the fact that from the beginning of the century onwards there was a growing process of elimination of the Right which seems to have been accelerating, for the disparity between the percentage of the poll and the percentage of parliamentary seats continually increased. In 1913 the Conservative Right, with its seven deputies, had only 6.14% of all the seats in parliament. In reality the situation was undoubtedly tending towards a tripartism analogous to that in England at the same period where the Socialist party was for the first time taking up a position alongside the two 'bourgeois' parties. The majority ballot was in fact exercising its normal reducing effect, and the agreement between Radicals and Socialists made it possible even to anticipate the coming of a new form of bipartism, resultant upon a fusion of the two left-wing groups. It was proportional representation that put a stop to this development.

Of the four political parties in Canada only two have national status, the Liberals on the one hand and the Conservatives on the other. It is only in certain provinces that the other parties (Labour and Social-Credit) have any real power, so that they may be said to be local parties. This example, in common with the examples provided by Sweden and Denmark, makes it possible to define the limits of the influence of the simple-majority single-ballot system: it tends to the creation of a two-party system inside the individual constituency;[2] but the parties opposed may be different in different areas of the country. 'The simple-majority system therefore makes possible the creation of local parties or the retreat of national parties to local positions. Even in Great Britain there existed from 1874 to 1918 an Irish party that was remarkably stable. The British Liberal party too shows a distinct tendency to become a Welsh party. None the less, the increased centralization of organization within the parties and the consequent tendency to see political problems from the wider, national standpoint tend of themselves to project on to the entire country the localized two-party system brought about by the ballot procedure: however, the true effect of the simple-majority system is limited to local bipartism.

The effect is produced in a very simple way. Take for example a British constituency in which the Conservatives have 35,000 votes, Labour 40,000, and Liberal 15,000: it is obvious that the success of Labour is entirely dependent on the presence of the Liberal party; if the Liberal party should withdraw its candidate it can be assumed that a majority of the voters supporting him will transfer to the Conservative, the minority being divided between Labour and abstention. Two alternatives are therefore possible: either the Liberal party may reach agreement with the Conservatives to withdraw its candidate (in exchange for some form of compensation in other constituencies), in which case the two-party system is restored as a result of fusion or of an alliance very like fusion; or else the Liberal party may persist in its independent line, the electors will gradually desert it, and the two-party system will be restored by elimination.

The first alternative has already taken place in its weaker form (alliance akin to fusion) in Great Britain with the Conservatives and National Liberals as well as in Germany with the Christian Democrats (C.D.U.) and the Liberals (F.D.P.) in the simple-majority district elections in some *Länder*, e.g. Westphalia, N. Rhineland, Schleswig-Holstein. Frequently it is but the prelude to the extreme form, total fusion, which is the normal term of the development and is often attended by schism, some members of the former Centre party preferring to join the opposition party. In Australia Liberals and Conservatives coalesced as early as 1909 in face of the growth of Labour. In New Zealand they waited until 1935 to do so: from 1913 to 1928 the Liberal party had pursued a progressively declining path which threatened its natural extinction; in 1928 a sudden renaissance put it on equal terms with the Conservatives; but as from 1931 it began to decline again and once again became the third party; faced with the Labour threat, increased by the economic crisis, it resolved on fusion after the 1935 elections. In South Africa the secession of the Nationalists in 1913, coupled with the growth of the Labour party, had produced by 1918 four parties of almost equal strength; in face of the danger of such a situation in a simple-majority single-ballot system the old Unionist party fused with General Smuts' South African party, while General Hertzog's Nationalist party signed an electoral pact with Labour which proved fatal to the latter: the two-party system was restored by both fusion and elimination.

Elimination in this sense (the second way in which bipartism is restored) is itself the result of two factors working together: a mechanical and a psychological factor. The mechanical factor consists in the 'under-representation' of the third, i.e. the weakest party, its percentage of seats being inferior to its percentage of the poll. Of course in a simple-majority system with two parties the vanquished is always under-represented by comparison with the victor, as we shall see below, but in cases where there is a third party it is under-represented to an even greater extent than the less favoured of the other two. The example of Britain is very striking: before 1922, the Labour party was under-represented by comparison with the Liberal party; thereafter the converse regularly occurred (with the one exception of 1931, which can be explained by the serious internal crisis in the Labour party and the crushing victory of the Conservatives); in this way the third party finds the electoral system mechanically unfair to it (Fig. 11.5). So long as a new party which aims at competing with the two old parties still remains weak the system works against it, raising a barrier against its progress. If, however, it succeeds in outstripping one of its forerunners, then the latter takes its place as third party and the process of elimination is transferred.

The psychological factor is ambiguous in the same way. In cases where there are three parties operating under the simple-majority single-ballot system the electors soon realize that their votes are wasted if they continue to give them to the third party; whence their natural tendency to transfer their vote to the less evil of its two adversaries in order to prevent the success of the greater evil. This 'polarization' effect works to the detriment of a new party so long as it is the weakest party but is turned against the less favoured of its older rivals as soon as the new party outstrips it. It operates in fact in the same way as 'under-representation'. The reversal of the two effects does not always occur at the same moment, under-representation generally being the earlier, for a certain lapse of time is required before the electors become aware of the decline of a party and transfer their votes to another. The natural consequence is a fairly long period of confusion during which the hesitation of the electors combines with the transposition of the 'under-representation' effect to give an entirely false picture of the balance of power amongst the parties: England experienced such drawbacks between 1923 and 1935. The impulse of the electoral system towards the creation of bipartism is therefore only a long-term effect.

The simple-majority single-ballot system appears then to be capable of maintaining an established dualism in spite of schisms in old parties and the birth of new parties. For a new party to succeed in establishing itself firmly it must have at its disposal strong backing locally or great and powerful organization nationally. In the first case, moreover, it will remain circumscribed within the geographical area of its origin and will only emerge from it slowly and painfully, as the example of Canada demonstrates. Only in the second case can it hope for a speedy development which will raise it to the position of second party, in which it will be favoured by the polarization and under-representation effects. Here perhaps we touch upon one of the deep-seated reasons which have led all Anglo-Saxon Socialist parties to organize themselves on a Trade Union basis; it alone could put at their disposal sufficient strength for the 'take-off', small parties being eliminated or driven back into the field of local campaigns. The simple-majority system seems equally capable of re-establishing dualism when it has been destroyed by the appearance of a third party. The comparison between Great Britain and Belgium offers a striking contrast: in both countries a traditional two-party system was broken up at the beginning of the century by the emergence of Socialism. Fifty years later the majority system restored bipartism in Great Britain by the

Figure 11.5 **DISPARITY BETWEEN PERCENTAGE OF VOTES AND PERCENTAGE OF SEATS IN GREAT BRITAIN**

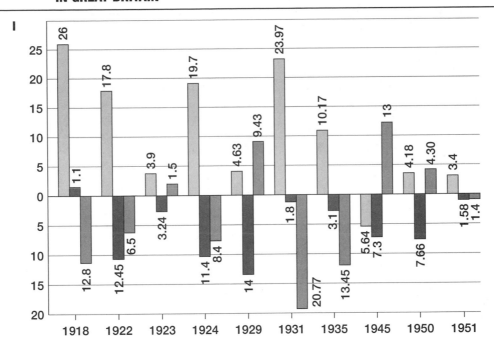

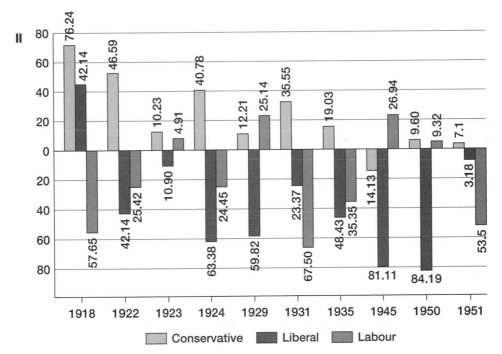

Conservative   Liberal   Labour

elimination of the Liberals (Fig. 11.6), whereas in Belgium proportional representation saved the Liberal party and later made possible the birth of the Communist party, without counting a few other parties between the wars.

Can we go further and say that the simple-majority system is capable of producing bipartism in countries where it has never existed? If they already show a fairly clear tendency towards two parties, the answer would unquestionably be

Figure 11.6 **ELIMINATION OF LIBERAL PARTY IN GREAT BRITAIN**

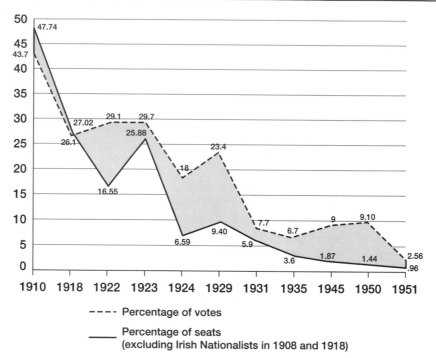

- - - - Percentage of votes

——— Percentage of seats
(excluding Irish Nationalists in 1908 and 1918)

in the affirmative. The establishment of the simple-majority single-ballot system in Western Germany would undoubtedly have the effect of gradually destroying the small and medium-sized parties, leaving the Socialists and Christian Democrats face to face; there is undoubtedly no country in which the technical conditions more nearly approach those required for the establishment of a parliamentary system after the British pattern. In Italy an electoral reform of the same kind would have the same results—with the sole difference that the Communists would be one of the two parties, which would greatly imperil the future of the democratic system. However, the brutal application of the single-ballot system in a country in which multipartism has taken deep root, as in France, would not produce the same results, except after a very long delay. The electoral system works in the direction of bipartism; it does not necessarily and absolutely lead to it in spite of all obstacles. The basic tendency combines with many others which attenuate it, check it, or arrest it. With these reserves we can nevertheless consider that dualism of parties is the 'brazen law' (as Marx would have said) of the simple-majority single-ballot electoral system.

Reading Notes

1. Australia too offers an exception since the development of the *Country party*. But the system of preferential voting in operation there profoundly modifies the machinery of the simple-majority poll and makes it more like a two-ballot system by allowing a regrouping of the scattered votes. It is moreover a striking fact that the appearance of the Country party coincided with the introduction of the preferential vote.

2. Note that in Canada this tendency to have only two parties within each constituency is by no means absolute, especially since the 1957 elections, which put an end to Liberal supremacy. In several constituencies there are, in fact, three or four parties, and this is an obstacle to true representation. The situation is rather like that in Great Britain between 1920 and 1935, when there was temporarily a three-party system. The situation in Canada today seems to have the same transitory character.

A SHORT HISTORY OF ELECTORAL SYSTEMS IN WESTERN EUROPE

Andrew McLaren Carstairs

FRANCE

The French revolution spread throughout Europe the notion that political sovereignty lies with the people, and that liberty consists in the opportunity to exercise that sovereignty. France was much less successful, however, in indicating by precept or example the practical methods by which these principles might be implemented. The fact that since 1789 there have been five republics, two monarchies, two empires and about fifteen constitutions (depending on what magnitude of change is regarded as a new constitution) is an indication of the numerous changes which took place.

Between 1848, when universal manhood suffrage was adopted for assembly elections, and 1958, when the Fifth Republic was established, these changes included fourteen major changes of the electoral law. The electoral system was rarely based on proportional representation, and indeed it was only between 1945 and 1951 that a true form of PR was adopted. There were, however, many other changes in the electoral system, though France has never adopted the one which has prevailed in Britain since 1885, that is to say, the relative majority system in single-member constituencies.

Elections for the national assembly from 1789 to 1817 were indirect, but in 1817 direct elections were established, and also an electoral system based on multi-member constituencies. Under this system, an absolute majority was required for election in the first two out of three possible ballots, and also a number of votes equal to at least a quarter of the registered electorate. In 1830 the system was changed to single-member constituencies, and for election in either of the first two ballots votes equivalent to one-third of the registered electorate were not required. From 1831 onwards the system of single-member constituencies was continued, but candidates could now, and for more than half a century thereafter, stand for election in more than one constituency (though of course taking a seat in only one of them). It was in this period that deputies began to organise themselves into party groups, and that socialist ideas spread, culminating in the revolution of February 1848, the end of the July monarchy and the accession of the House of Orleans.

Many different electoral systems have existed since 1848, but the second-ballot system in single-member constituencies, with an absolute majority required in the first ballot, existed in all but the following periods:

1848–52 and 1871–3 multi-member constituencies, with a relative majority sufficing for election, but a second ballot required if a sufficient number of candidates did not achieve a stipulated number of votes;

1873–5 and 1885–9 multi-member constituencies, with an absolute majority required at a first ballot, but a relative majority sufficing at a second ballot;

1919–27 and 1951–8 mixed majority and proportional systems;

1945–51 a proportional system.

From 1789 onwards elections were based on a means-tested suffrage. Universal manhood suffrage was introduced in 1848, but it was not until after the establishment of the Third Republic in 1870 that elections were able to function freely and fairly. Between 1815 and 1848 the assembly had frequently been dissolved by the monarch if members were recalcitrant in opposition to government policy, and elections were highly corrupt. Under the Second Empire, from 1852 to 1869, elections were systematically manipulated by the government to secure the return of a compliant body of members. Even after 1870 means were sometimes found by one faction or another to manipulate the electoral system to their own advantage. Also, although the commonest election system was the absolute majority in a first ballot in a single-member constituency, it was at first unusual for more than two candidates to stand for election in a constituency, and only one ballot was commonly needed. Since most constituency elections were won at the first ballot the system was much the same in practice, though not in form, as the relative majority or 'first past the post' system. Later in the nineteenth century and before the First World War the number of second ballots varied considerably, but in 1927 they reached 70 percent of all constituency elections, and remained at a high level thereafter.

One of the prominent features of the electoral systems in France was the addiction of French governments to what is commonly referred to as 'electoral engineering'. A government in power has on many occasions passed an electoral law with a bias introduced in its own favour, in the hope, which was however often disappointed, that the out-going representatives might be returned to office. From the period since 1848 some examples of this may be selected.

After the 1848 revolution electoral systems based on multi-member constituencies were adopted, but when Napoleon III gained power in 1851 he introduced in their place, in 1852, the system of single-member constituencies, and elections based on an absolute majority in a first ballot. A significant feature of the particular system adopted was that candidatures at the second ballot were open to any candidate, and not confined to those who had participated in the first. This made it easier for the government to manipulate the results of an election by introducing a candidate of its own at the second stage. Elections were so extensively manipulated during the period of the Second Empire that free elections could hardly be said to have existed at that time.

After the war of 1870 and the establishment of the Third Republic the electoral system reverted to the law of 1849 which provided for elections in multi-member constituencies. In the election of 1871 the members returned were mainly Conservatives and Monarchists. At that time, however, and until 1889, it was possible for candidates to stand in more than one constituency (though to occupy only one seat), so that in July 1871 numerous by-elections had to be held for seats remaining unfilled, and in these it was mainly Republicans who were successful. The Conservatives and Monarchists still had a majority after the by-elections, but their failure in these was due to disagreements within the parties and their division into Legitimists, Orleanists and Bonapartists, who were less successful in forming electoral agreements than the Republicans. Through an electoral law of 1875 the Conservative majority restored single-member constituencies, in the hope that this would enable local magnates and the clergy to exert greater influence on the electorate; and the second-ballot system, reintroduced in 1873, was retained. The disunity of the Conservatives was such, however, that at the second ballot the Republicans obtained 70 percent of the seats with 58 percent of the votes, so that the attempt to manipulate the electoral system to the advantage of the Conservatives proved to be a failure.

Meanwhile Marshal McMahon had been elected president by a Conservative majority, but in 1877 he caused outrage by dissolving the assembly, and in the ensuing election in the same year the Republicans were returned with a substantial majority of both votes and seats. In spite of their successive victories in single-member constituencies the Republicans considered that multi-member constituencies were to their greater advantage. After a further Republican victory in 1881 a Bill was at last passed in 1885, restoring multi-member constituencies with second ballots. The election of 1885 was the only one held under this new Electoral Act, and the first ballot falsified the expectations of the Republicans, since with 56 percent of the votes they gained only 127 seats as against 177 for the Conservatives. It was only through superior organisation at the second ballot that they succeeded in the end in gaining a substantial overall majority.

During the period from 1885 to 1889 the Republicans were discredited by scandals, and General Boulanger entered the field as an advocate of reform. He became an exponent of a particular type of electoral manipulation in that he himself stood as a candidate in several constituencies, so as to propagate his cause as widely as possible, at the cost of making it necessary to hold numerous by-elections. In 1889 multiple candidatures were prohibited, and the electoral system was changed back to single-member constituencies and two ballots. At this time members of the assembly had largely changed their views about the merits of the various electoral systems, single-member constituencies now being favoured by the Republicans, and multi-member constituencies by the Conservatives. The election of 1889 inflicted another decisive defeat upon the Conservatives, and from this time onwards the Republican form of government came to be generally accepted, and support for the monarchist cause dwindled. During the period up to 1914 it was the Radicals who gained most seats under the then existing electoral system, and both Conservatives and Socialists now increasingly advocated proportional representation.

The electoral law of 1919 was a compromise between the Radicals and the Socialists, and was an attempt to combine the merits of proportional representation with those of the majority system. Under this law elections were held in multi-member constituencies, and electors were given as many votes as there were seats to be filled. *Panachage* was permitted, but not cumulative voting. Seats in each constituency were allocated to parties and candidates in three stages. (1) Any candidate supported by an absolute majority of voters was elected. (2) A Hare quota was calculated by dividing the number of voters by the number of seats to be filled. For each party list the average vote for candidates was calculated by dividing the number of votes for the list by the number of candidates. Each party obtained as many seats as the number of times the constituency quota was contained in the party's average of votes per candidate. (3) If any seats remained vacant, they *all* went to the party with the highest average of votes per candidate. At the second and third stages of the election seats were allocated to those individual candidates on the party lists who had most votes.

This electoral system was intended to promote the establishment of a party in parliament with a majority of seats, or at least with a strong enough support to be able effectively to maintain a government in power, but it had certain defects. It was highly unproportional, especially in the third stage of allocation of seats to parties. Also it could result in the election of some candidates who had fewer votes than others not elected, since a list might have a high average of votes per candidate through attracting many votes for one or two popular candidates, and this might gain seats for other party candidates with relatively few votes, and fewer than some candidates in less successful parties.

Having largely surrendered their demand for PR, the Socialists suffered a disadvantage from the system they had helped to introduce, gaining only 11 percent of the seats for 23 percent of the votes. In 1924, however, the Alliance of the Left (Cartel des Gauches) gained 47 percent of the seats for 38 percent of the votes. In 1927 the Radicals persuaded the Socialists to support the reintroduction of single-member constituencies and two ballots, but once again the results were miscalculated. In 1928 it was the right and the right-centre who were better organised, and they gained sixty-seven of the

seats which the left might have won if the electoral system had not been changed.

It was next the turn of the right to seek to manipulate the electoral system by establishing a relative majority system on British lines (one of the few occasions on which this was seriously considered), but a Bill to achieve this was rejected by the senate. Under the same electoral system as in 1928 it was the Socialists who were better organised in 1932, and they gained a majority through a shift of Radical voters to the left. Finally there was a victory for the left-wing Popular Front in the election of 1936, the last of the elections of the Third Republic.

Unlike most of the countries in Western Europe, France did not, either before or soon after the First World War, establish a system of proportional representation, and it was only in 1945 that a true form of PR was introduced for the first time. The municipal elections of that year showed that the Socialist and Communist parties were now much stronger than they had been before the war, and much stronger also than any party of the centre or right. There has for a long time been a demand within the Socialist and Communist parties and in the labour movement generally for the establishment of PR, on grounds of both principles and expediency. The provisional government formed at the end of the war sought to encourage the creation of a few large, stable and well-disciplined parties which would act responsibly and sustain an effective government in power, but also to achieve a fair and accurate representation of political opinion in parliament, which would be a source of strength to any government which reflected that opinion, and confer 'legitimacy' on the new regime. This last consideration provided an inducement for parties of the centre and right as well as of the left to accept a proportional system for the election of a constituent assembly.

The electoral law of 1945 provided for a rigid party-list system of PR. The distribution of seats took place at that constituency level only, most of the constituencies being individual departments, and it took place in two stages in accordance with the D'Hondt/Hagenbach-Bischoff system. The Hare quota was used at the first stage of the count, and the D'Hondt divisor method at the second. This system favoured the larger parties, which were the parties of the left, and it was particularly favourable to those parties in the smaller constituencies.

In April 1946 the Socialists proposed that in addition to the seats won in the constituencies each eligible party should be entitled to the allocation of additional seats on the basis of proportionality as the national level. This was to be achieved by the application of the D'Hondt/Hagenbach-Bischoff method (with Hare quota) to the votes and seats of the parties in the nation as a whole. However, the proposed electoral system was defeated in a referendum in May 1946. It was a provision in the proposals which confined candidatures to party nominees, offering no choice between individual candidates, which aroused most opposition from the centre and the right.

The Radicals and parties on the left now agreed on a new formula which was accepted. Electors were still permitted to vote for any one list (that is, no *panachage* was permitted), but they could vote for candidates on the list in order of preference. However, the preferences were not to be taken into account unless half the electors in the constituency had varied the order on the list, and this was so seldom the case that electors had virtually no influence on the order of the candidates on the lists. The attempt to achieve proportionality at the national as well as the constituency level was abandoned. Only one election was held under this system, that of 1 November 1946, when a reasonably good correspondence between votes and seats was achieved.

In 1947 General de Gaulle formed a party of his supporters, the Rassemblement du Peuple Francais, and politicians of the centre became alarmed at the prospect of advances being made by this party on the right and the Communists on the left, both regarded as hostile to the parliamentary system of government. An electoral system was therefore devised to operate to the disadvantage of these two parties. This involved, in effect, the application of two separate electoral systems, one for the Paris region where the Gaullists and Communists were strong, and one for the provinces where they were weaker. In the Paris region there was applied one of the electoral systems which favours the smallest parties to the greatest extent, which was the hare quota system with remaining seats allocated on the basis of the 'largest remainders'. For the provinces, the proportional system previously in existence was partly retained, but subject to certain far-reaching modifications. First it was provided that if any party list, or any alliance of party lists, succeeded in gaining an absolute majority of votes in a constituency, then the list or alliance should be awarded *all* the seats in that constituency. Secondly, the right to form alliances was restricted to 'national' parties, which were defined as those which submitted lists in at least thirty constituencies. Thirdly, each list must contain as many candidates as there were seats to be filled in the constituency. Fourthly, if no party or alliance had an absolute majority of votes in a constituency, then the seats were to be allocated to party lists and alliances by application of the D'Hondt system; and the allocation of seats to lists within an alliance was also to be by the D'Hondt system.

This electoral system gave a great advantage to those parties which formed alliances, or in other words to those parties of the centre who had collaborated to devise it, and which intended to collaborate in the formation of alliances. It was easier for an alliance than for a single party to achieve an absolute majority of votes in a constituency and thus gain all the seats; and even where there was no absolute majority the D'Hondt system gave an advantage to larger parties and alliances.

In the elections of June 1951, the results in the Paris area were reasonably proportional, which meant that the strength of the Gaullists and Communists in that area gave neither of those parties an advantage over the rest. In the provinces, however, the electoral system discriminated against the Communists and the Gaullists, and how it did so may be demonstrated by certain examples (cited by Cotteret and Emeri) in Tables 11.6 and 11.7.

Table 11.6 ELECTION IN ARIÈGE, JUNE 1951

	Percentage of Votes	Number of Seats
Allied lists		
Socialists	30.0	2
Radical Socialists	25.0	1
MRP	8.6	—
Total	63.6	3
Separate lists		
Communists	30.0	—
Gaullists	6.4	—

In Table 11.6 the allied lists gained together an absolute majority of votes, and were therefore allocated all the seats. By application of the D'Hondt method to the parties within the alliance, the Socialists were allocated two of the seats, and the Radical Socialists were allocated one. Although the Communists had about as many votes as the Socialists and more than the Radical Socialists, they obtained no seat.

To show how the system worked when there was no absolute majority for a list or an alliance, an example is provided in Table 11.6 from Bouchés-du-Rhône, in a constituency where four seats were to be allocated. By application of the D'Hondt system, two seats were allocated to the allied lists, and two to the Communists. Within the allied lists, the D'Hondt system allocated one seat to the Socialists and one to the Radical Socialists. Thus the Radical Socialists gained a seat with fewer votes than the Gaullists, who gained none.

There were many other anomalous results in this election, which worked out according to the plans of the centre parties but could hardly be regarded as other than fraudulent. If the 1946 electoral system had been retained, and if the voting pattern had been the same as in 1951, the Communists would have gained 169 seats and the Gaullists 133, but instead they gained only 97 and 107 respectively. Only in one constituency did a single party list gain an absolute majority of votes, and therefore receive all the seats, but alliances (of centre parties) achieved this result in thirty-nine constituencies. Parties of the centre gained 51 percent of the votes, but 62.5 percent of the seats.

Although the electoral system was designed to protect parliament from 'anti-system' parties,

its manifest unfairness had the effect of reducing confidence in parliament and the politicians, and even the beneficiaries of the system became alarmed at the results. Further electoral reform was therefore in the air, but it was not achieved before the government, as a result of successive defeats in parliament, exercised its right to dissolve parliament and hold another general election. For this election the same electoral system had to be used again. This time it was the *Poujadistes* who succeeded in exploiting the system to the greatest extent, by fielding notionally separate parties of shopkeepers, peasants and consumers respectively, spreading the net to catch as many votes as possible, and filling party lists with straw candidates to ensure that the parties would be represented in at least thirty constituencies to gain recognition as 'national' parties entitled to form alliances among themselves. The lists then formed alliances in about half the constituencies.

General de Gaulle had hitherto taken an unfavourable view of majority electoral systems in single-member constituencies. He did not consider that in the interwar period they had provided the clear-cut results of which they were supposed to be capable. In 1950 he declared in a press conference that the only types of election which were 'frank and honest' were those achieved by means of party lists and all the other types were fakes or swindles (*truquages*). Yet when he was returned to power in 1958 the electoral system which he established by a decree in October of that year was the same as that which was established by Louis-Napoleon after his *coup d'etat* in December 1851; and for the next ten years this system served de Gaulle's purpose very well. This was the two-ballot system in single-member constituencies. A modification introduced by de Gaulle, in order to discourage frivolous candidatures, was that candidates who failed to secure 5 percent of the votes were disqualified from standing at a second ballot, forfeited their deposit, and had to reimburse certain election expenses to the state. No new candidates were permitted at the second ballot.

At the election of 1958, under the new electoral system, only 9 percent of the seats were filled at the first ballot, which was much fewer than in any election during the Third Republic. The most striking result was that the Gaullists, with 20 percent of the votes, gained more than 40 percent of

Table 11.7 ELECTION UN BOUCHÉS-DU-RHÔNE, JUNE 1951

	Number of Votes	Number of Seats
Allied lists		
Socialists	31,819	1
Radical Socialists	17,617	1
MRP	13,533	—
Total	62,969	2
Separate lists		
Communists	47,235	2
Gaullists	18,985	—

the seats, while the Communists, with 19 percent of the votes, gained only 2 percent of the seats. This was the consequence of votes being transferred at the second ballot, which left the Communists isolated without support. In 1962, after de Gaulle had won a referendum on the issue that the president of the Republic should be elected directly by the people, the Gaullists won an even greater victory in the election of that year, with the Communists again the chief party to suffer. The trend in favour of the Gaullists continued in the elections of 1967 and 1968. In 1968 the Communists gained 20 percent of the votes but only 7 percent of the seats, while the Gaullists achieved 70 percent of the seats with only 44 percent of the votes.

The advantage for the Gaullists under this electoral system lay in the close collaboration which now existed between the parties which supported de Gaulle, so that collectively they benefited much more than other parties at the second ballot. It was the operation of the system in practice, rather than the nature of the regulations, which was significantly to the advantage of the Gaullists. The allied parties commonly agreed upon a single candidate to represent them in each constituency.

However, by 1973, other new alliances and alignments were also emerging, particularly an electoral agreement, for the first time since 1934, between the Socialists and the Communists. The representation of the Gaullists and their supporters fell from over 72 percent of the seats in 1968 to less than 55 percent in 1973. The Communists, with 14.9 percent of the votes, succeeded in obtaining exactly the same share of the seats, and the left-wing alliance as a whole gained about 36 percent of the seats from 46 percent of the votes. Events were beginning to suggest that the Gaullists might not continue to enjoy the main benefits of the existing electoral system, nor remain much longer in office.

In 1966 Etienne Weill-Raynal, a member of the executive committee of the Socialist Party, had put forward proposals for proportional representation based on single-member constituencies, with the allocation of additional seats to achieve proportionality at the national level. This was different from the PR system which had existed between 1945 and 1951, when party lists were submitted and proportionality determined at the constituency level only. Weill-Raynal pointed out that his proposals were similar to those made by

Léon Blum as early as 1926, and they were in the main adopted by a convention of the Socialist Party which was held at Suresnes in March 1972.

It was proposed that to compensate for disproportionality arising out of elections by relative majority in single-member constituencies, proportionality should be achieved successively at the levels of the regions and the nation as a whole. There were to be 321 single-member constituency seats, 152 additional regional seats, and 70 additional national seats; the additional seats to be allocated to parties by means of a quota and the method of the largest remainder. The additional seats were to be allocated to constituencies in accordance with the percentage share of the total vote which each party had gained in its constituencies. Since departments and constituencies varied considerably in size, it was provided that small constituencies should be assured of a minimum number of constituency seats. Since, on the other hand, large departments would then be liable to have relatively fewer seats in terms of population, it was also provided that there should be a limit on the number of additional seats which each department might be awarded. These provisions were a departure from true proportionality, and so also was another provision that to share in the allocation of additional seats a party must have gained at least 5 percent of the national vote.

At least as early as 1966 the Communist Party had also adopted PR as part of their own party programme, and as an element of any joint programme which parties of the left might agree to support. This did in fact become part of the common programme when the electoral agreement was formed between the Socialists and the Communists for the election of 1973.

The left were not, however, the only advocates of PR. This had traditionally been a policy of the radical Mouvement Républicain Populaire until the establishment of the Fifth Republic. In 1957 Valéry Giscard d'Estaing had supported a Bill to establish PR on the lines of the German system, and in October 1972 a union of parties of the centre approved a report by Senator Barrachin which recommended the adoption of such a system. The parties of the centre had a common interest in preventing the unduly inflated representation which the majority system was liable to give to major parties, including those of the extreme right or the extreme left. The Communist Party, for their part, appeared to have surrendered, for the time being at least, their more remote prospects of achieving the totality of power, and had opted instead for a better prospect of achieving a share of it. For the attainment of electoral reform, however, it was necessary first that the left or centre should be able, under the existing electoral system, to achieve a victory over the Gaullists and their allies, and this they did not succeed in doing in 1973 or 1978.

France is a conspicuous example of a country in which the possibilities of 'electoral engineering' have been fully realised, and in which the electoral system has been especially prone to manipulation by parties in power. This has sometimes been done in the supposed interest of safeguarding the parliamentary system against anti-democratic or 'anti-system' parties, but the constant manipulation of the electoral system has itself been liable to bring discredit upon parliament as a body which purports to the representative.

There is little evidence on the other hand that it is the electoral system which has mainly determined the nature of the party and political system. During the period between 1831 and 1881 the two-ballot system worked very much as if it were a one-ballot system, with only a small minority of results decided at a second ballot, so that for half a century it functioned in the manner of a relative majority system. But there was no tendency then for a two-party system to

emerge. When universal manhood suffrage increased the electorate from a quarter of a million to 8 million voters there was no party in existence which could at that time cope with the task of organization which the new mass electorate required. After the establishment of the Third Republic the various conservative and republican parties were much divided among themselves, and it was only about the turn of the century that mass party organisation began to emerge.

Moreover there was a strong element of localism in French politics which had a long tradition behind it and which even in the twentieth century remained an abiding characteristic. The concentration of power, wealth and administration in Paris had been, and continued to be, counteracted by particularism in the provinces. Parties still tended to be groups of deputies in the assembly rather than cohesive national organisations. There was much mobility of membership between parties as deputies decided their alignment on constantly changing issues of current politics.

Since in France there is no 'stable' two-party system which might be sacrificed by electoral reform, the case is all the stronger for establishing a 'stable' electoral system. The most stable system is likely to be one which is manifestly fair and achieves a high degree of correspondence between votes and seats. There appears in recent years to have been growing support from several political parities for an electoral system of this kind.

Reading References

Successive changes in the French electoral system are fully described by Peter Campbell in *French Electoral Systems and Elections since 1789,* and particular attention is given to the French experience by Jean-Marie Cotteret and Claude Emeri in *Les systèmes électoraux.* Developments during the last twenty years or so are examined by J. R. Fears in *Political Parties and Elections in the French Fifth*

Republic. Recent movements in favour of proportional representation in France were discussed by Etienne Weill-Raynal in the *Revue politique et parlementaire,* in articles entitled "La représentation nationale proportionnelle avec scrutin individuel" (1966), and "La réforme electorate, enjeu des prochaines élections?" (1973).

THE UNITED KINGDOM AND IRELAND

THE UNITED KINGDOM

In the United Kingdom, unlike all other countries in Western Europe apart from the Swiss Republic, the constitutional balance of power between Crown and parliament had already by the begin-

ning of the nineteenth century been settled decisively in favour of parliament. However, the French revolution and the Napoleonic wars and their aftermath were periods in which far-reaching economic changes were taking place in

Britain, and these were accompanied by social upheaval and political unrest. At this time existing political institutions came under criticism and attack, and although there was little support for sweeping and radical measures there was a mounting demand for parliamentary reform. It was in response to this popular demand that a Whig government introduced the Reform Bill which was passed in 1832.

What this Act chiefly accomplished was to remove some notorious abuses and anomalies by abolishing a number of 'rotten boroughs' in which members of parliament were nominated by some landed magnate, and a start was made at the same time with several other parliamentary reforms. Of the changes made in the 'age of reform' between 1832 and 1885 there were four of particular importance: an extension of the franchise by stages in 1832, 1867 and 1884; the registration from 1832 onwards of those who were entitled to vote; changes in the designation of constituencies and the distribution of seats, to correspond more closely with the distribution of population; and measures to check the corruption in elections which tended to nullify the representative character of parliament. It took more than fifty years to complete the transformation of parliament from a body which was largely under the control of aristocrats and wealthy landowners into one which represented most of the adult male population. It is in the light of these changes that one should consider the nature and effects of the electoral system which was used.

In many respects, the legislation of 1883 to 1885 marked a turning point in the electoral history of the United Kingdom. After this, representation was placed on a much fairer basis, and the outcome of elections was much more a reflection of the will of the electorate, and much less the result of influence and manipulation by the powerful few. The boroughs and the southern counties were no longer grossly overrepresented; the urban and industrial areas were no longer grossly underrepresented; corruption in elections was at last brought under control; and the influence of landed magnates on the election of members was greatly reduced. Until this time the electoral system, in the sense of how seats were allocated to votes, was of relatively minor importance, since the votes themselves could scarcely be regarded as a true expression of the opinions of the electorate.

The first extension of the franchise in 1832 increased the electorate by 49 percent in both boroughs and counties. In the counties the chief qualification continued to be the possession of a 40-shilling freehold, but as a concession to the landed interest the franchise was extended also to certain categories of copyholders, leaseholders and tenants. In the boroughs, the qualifications for the franchise had varied considerably from one borough to another. Ancient franchises were continued (except in the case of freemen, only for the lifetime of those who possessed them), but a new franchise applicable to all boroughs was introduced in the form of a £10 household franchise, that is, a voting right for all those who occupied a building to the value of £10 per annum.

In 1867 the suffrage was extended to citizens in boroughs who were householders, regardless of the value of the house, and this for the first time enfranchised the working classes in the boroughs, but while the electorate was increased by 88 percent overall, it was increased by 134 percent in the boroughs and only 45 percent in the counties.

In 1884 there was at last introduced a uniform qualification in the form of the household suffrage, which removed the great anomalies which had often existed on either side of a boundary between borough and county. This measure increased the electorate by 162 percent in the counties, 11 percent in the boroughs and 67 percent overall. The increases in the electorate which resulted from each successive extension of the franchise were as indicated by the figures in Table 11.8.

The representation introduced in Simon de Montfort's parliament in 1265 was based on two-member constituencies in counties and boroughs, and in England in 1831 the two-member constituencies were still almost universal. There were some exceptions, since four members each were returned by London, Yorkshire and the borough of Weymouth and Morecombe Regis, and only one member each from the boroughs of Abingdon, Banbury, Bewdley, Higham Ferrers

Table 11.8 UK ELECTORATE AS A PERCENTAGE OF THE POPULATION, 1831–86

1831	1.8%
1833	2.7%
1869	6.4%
1886	12.1%

and Monmouth; but these seventeen seats accounted for less than 4 percent of those in England, and all the rest were from two-member constituencies. It was quite otherwise in the counties of the 'Celtic fringe'. In Ireland, all the boroughs except Dublin and Cork had each since 1800 been represented by one member only, making thirty-two single-member seats out of one hundred. In Wales, all counties and boroughs alike had throughout the eighteenth century been represented by only one member since 1707, but some shires did not even have one, since three pairs of shires each shared one member between them, alternating from one shire to the other in successive elections. However, in the United Kingdom as a whole in 1831 single-member constituencies accounted for only 107 out of 758 seats, or little more than 16 percent of all seats. Elections were by relative majority, and in the multi-member constituencies this was the 'block vote' system.

In the redistribution of 1831 the number of single-member constituencies in Ireland and Wales was slightly reduced, but those in England were increased by fifty-one, and those in Scotland were also increased. However, single-member constituencies, now 145 in number in the United Kingdom, still accounted for only 22 percent of the total number of seats. On the other hand some *county* constituencies with large populations were allocated more than two seats in multi-member constituencies—Yorkshire received two more seats, and between 1832 and 1885 there were seven counties with three seats each, including Berkshire, Buckinghamshire, Cambridgeshire, Dorsetshire, Herefordshire, Hertfordshire and Oxfordshire.

In the redistribution of 1867–8 there was a net addition of twenty-six single-member constituencies in the United Kingdom, but this still did not greatly alter the balance in favour of such seats—they still accounted for little more than a quarter of the total number of 660 seats at that time. In the same redistribution, the number of three-member constituencies was increased by allocating one additional seat each to the heavily populated *cities* of Birmingham, Leeds, Liverpool, Manchester and Glasgow.

It was only in 1885 that a great and decisive change was made in favour of single-member constituencies. After the redistribution of that year there survived (apart from the universities) only twenty-four constituencies which had two members each, and none which had more than two members. (Only twelve of these twenty-four constituencies continued to have two members between 1918 and 1948.) With the exception of these two-member constituencies, all counties and boroughs were in 1885 split up into as many divisions as they had been allotted seats, and each division returned one member of parliament.

The conservative (Whig and Tory) sentiment had hitherto been in favour of representation of communities and interests rather than a numerically determined fraction of the population, yet in 1885 it was the Conservatives who favoured single-member constituencies as a system from which they could hope to secure greater representation for minorities than was likely under the 'block vote' system in two-member or multi-member constituencies. The great extension of the suffrage in 1884 had made it seem urgent to secure some safeguard against the mass vote of the working class; the best safeguard appeared to the Tories at the time to be the adoption of numerous single-member constituencies; and it was on the understanding that redistribution would be based on such constituencies that the Tories in the House of Lords had withdrawn their opposition to the Reform Bill of 1884.

The preference for single-member constituencies in order that minorities might be better represented was well founded in view of the existing majority system of election. The majority system had itself, however, come under criticism. In 1831 a Tory member, W. M. Praed, protested that, while parliament had been trying to reconstruct the framework of representative government, that particular part of its machinery which regulated how the opinions of all classes of the community might be fairly represented in parliament had passed wholly unnoticed in the parliamentary debates. He proposed that in the seven counties which were to have three members each an elector should have only two votes. Lord Althorp opposed Praed's amendment on the grounds that past evidence did not suggest that minorities were inadequately represented in parliament which had majority systems of election. Nevertheless, proposals in favour of the limited vote were later renewed by Lord John Russell in 1854 and 1860. He sought to counterbalance an extension of the franchise by this system of election so as to ensure representation for minorities in the three-member constituencies.

When the household suffrage was adopted for the boroughs in 1867, the limited vote system was introduced for all constituencies which had more than two members. This meant that in the five cities and seven counties which had three-member constituencies electors would be entitled to case not more than two votes each; and in London, which had four seats, they could not cast more than three. But all these constituencies together accounted for only 40 out of 660 seats in parliament in 1868.

The limited vote did not, moreover, *guarantee* representation for a minority, or even for a majority, since the result depended on how many candidates stood on behalf of a party or group, and how the votes were distributed between them. A party could promote their own interest by accurately assessing the maximum number of candidates they should nominate, and by organising the votes of their supporters in such a way as to secure for each candidate the minimum number of votes necessary for his election. The Liberal Party 'caucus' in Birmingham were most successful in organising their elections in this manner, and no Conservative was elected from Birmingham between 1867 and 1885.

So far as electoral results are concerned, a scrutiny of the voting in the three-member constituencies other than Birmingham does not suggest that party organisation was often effective, or even consistently used to influence elections. In most of the three-member elections seats were fairly divided between the parties and manipulation was not much in evidence. Nevertheless, by 1885 the limited vote had a poor reputation, largely as a result of the Birmingham experience, and it now had few supporters. At this time there was more debate on proposals for proportional representation which had been the subject of much discussion after the publication, in 1859, of Thomas Hare's treatise on *The Election of Representatives, Parliamentary and Municipal*, and the whole-hearted support given to his proposals by John Stuart Mill, who said that they were 'among the very greatest improvements yet made in the theory and practice of government'.

To safeguard the representation of minorities Lord John Russell had proposed a redistribution of constituency seats and the limited vote, but Hare proposed the abolition of all constituency boundaries, and the use of the single transferable vote for the election of all members of parliament in a single constituency. The proposal of a single national constituency was one aspect of the proposal of the single transferable vote which came under the strongest attack from its critics, including Walter Bagehot, who regarded this as its fundamental defect, regardless of other details. However, as the idea of the single constituency was soon discarded, it is other criticisms by Bagehot which have had more enduring influence. Of these the most fundamental was that representation was only one of the functions of parliament, and that in Bagehot's view a more important function, indeed the most important of all, was the choice of a government and its maintenance in power. Bagehot himself was undogmatic in his opinion that in this respect the existing system was satisfactory—he said that the best government was that which people thought was the best, and 'tried by this rule, the House of Commons does its appointing business well. It chooses rules as we wish rulers to be chosen. If it did not, in a speaking and writing age, we should soon know.'

For both Hare and Mill the chief sum of the electoral system was that voters should be able to elect not merely mediocre party 'hacks', but members of the uneducated and intellectual 'elite' (a term which Mill used freely, but not of course in its modern pejorative sense); and their chief fear was that through the extension of the franchise irresistible power should pass to the uneducated masses and lead to disastrous class legislation. They saw the single transferable vote as a means of ensuring the representation of minorities, but the one minority whose representation they thought was vital was the minority of the educated elite. Hare would have been content to leave the franchise as it was at the time, which would have restricted the electorate to about one-sixth of the adult male population. Mill, on the other hand, favoured the extension of the franchise, but feared the consequences of working-class votes. He found a solution to this dilemma in Hare's electoral system, since it provided a vital safeguard for the educated minority, whose influence in parliament he expected to be greater than its numbers.

Both Mill and Hare took a highly unfavourable view of the role and influence of political parties, and for this reason the single transferable vote had for them a particular attraction in being a personal and not a party system of voting. Mill believed that electors should not vote for a candidate because of his party membership, or even the particular views which he held, but because of his superior capacity for making independent judgments based on knowledge and wisdom. Nevertheless, Mill foresaw the possibility that even with the single transferable vote electors might seek the election of members who would act in their own particular interest, and in parliament a majority of such members might exercise their power in an oppressive manner. He therefore advocated a system of plural voting in which extra votes would be given to electors with educational qualifications and attainments.

Bagehot agreed with Mill on the need for a governing elite, but for him, in the 'deferential society' which existed in England, this object was already attained, since electors habitually voted for their social superiors. Bagehot also took an opposite view about parties. Assuming that the main function of parliament was maintaining a government in power, he said 'we at once perceive that party is of its essence. There never was an election without a party . . . The House of Commons lies in a state of perpetual potential choice: at any moment it can choose a ruler and dismiss a ruler. And therefore party is inherent in it, it is bone of its bone, and breath of its breath.'

When Mill agreed to stand as a candidate for Westminster in the general election of 1865, he stood as an independent, and refused to commit himself to support any party or local interest, or any policies except those which he had himself publicly advocated. In parliament he proposed an amendment to the Reform Bill of 1867 which would have introduced STV, but withdrew it in the interest of ensuring that the Bill as a whole should be passed.

When the next Reform Bill was debated the movement in favour of STV was revived, and in 1884 the Proportional Representation Society was established under the chairmanship of Sir John Lubbock. However, in the face of the reluctance of the Tories in the House of Lords to accept the extension of the franchise, an understanding was reached between the Liberal and Tory leaders that seats should be redistributed in such a way as to separate the urban from the rural parts of county constituencies, so that rural Tory votes should not be swamped by urban Liberals. As already related, the means of achieving this involved the division of existing constituencies, and resulted in single-member representation in all except twenty-four of the constituencies. This excluded the possibility of the single transferable vote in multi-member constituencies, and in consequence Sir Robert Courtney, who was a strong supporter of STV, resigned from the Liberal government. For the next twenty years the movement for a reform of the electoral system made little headway.

After the turn of the century the advocacy of electoral reform was revived, partly through public interest in the adoption of PR in Belgium and subsequently in some other countries. A Royal Commission on Electoral Systems, appointed in 1909, submitted a report which rejected PR, including the single transferable vote, but recommended the adoption of the alternative vote. At this time, however, parliament and the nation were preoccupied with the constitutional crisis between the Commons and the Lords, and the Royal Commission's report was not even debated in the House of Commons. Neither its evidence nor its conclusions appear to have had much influence on public opinion.

During the First World War there was an accumulation of problems which made it necessary to consider some electoral changes, not only women's suffrage but also votes for servicemen, the state of the electoral register, and the unresolved issue of proportional representation. In August 1916, when Asquith was still prime minister, the speaker of the House of Commons, J. W. Lowther, agreed to convene a conference of members of both houses of parliament to make recommendations on electoral reforms. Among its numerous recommendations was one unanimously in favour of the single transferable vote system of election in all boroughs which elected three or more members, and the alternative vote system in single-member constituencies.

A Bill based on the recommendations of the speaker's conference was introduced, but Lloyd George, who was now prime minister, insisted that a decision not only on women's suffrage but also, in spite of the unanimous recommendations of the speaker's conference, on the electoral system, should be left to a free vote in the House of Commons. It seems that the leaders of both the Liberal and Conservative parties were at this time hostile to the conference's proposals on this subject. In view of the unanimous recommendation of the all-party conference some members of parliament, including F. E. Smith on the Conservative side and Ramsay Macdonald and Philip Snowden among Labour members, criticised the decision to leave the choice of electoral system to a free vote, and controversy on this point weakened confidence in the speaker's conferences as a means of achieving agreement on such issues.

In the Commons, at the committee stage of the Bill, the single transferable vote was rejected, and the alternative vote was accepted by a majority of one vote. The Lords subsequently rejected the alternative vote in favour of STV, and finally a compromise was reached when it was agreed to instruct the boundary commissioners to prepare a limited scheme which would apply STV for the election of 100 members. When the scheme was prepared it was opposed by practically every member who would have been personally affected by it, and this contributed largely to its rejection.

In succeeding years a campaign for the single transferable vote was continued, but in 1920 a Bill for its adoption was rejected in the Commons by 211 votes to 112. On this occasion more than 80 percent of the Independent Liberals and labour members voted in favour, and more than 80 percent of the Conservatives against, but more than one-third of the Coalition Liberals were also against the measure. The Liberals had always been divided on the issue, and it was only in the general election of 1922 that proportional representation became for the first time part of the official policy of the Independent Liberal Party.

In May 1924, during the minority Labour government, a Bill for proportional representation was put forward by the Liberals, but Labour backbenchers resented a suggestion that Liberal support for the government might be reconsidered if they did not support this measure. Labour members refused to accept a recommendation by their own government that they should facilitate the passing of the Bill, and it was rejected by a majority of nearly two to one. On this occasion nearly three-quarters of the Labour vote was against the Bill, as well as 95 percent of the Conservative vote. It seems that it was from about the time of the 1923 election that a majority of Labour members turned against proportional representation. Success at the polls, and the prospect of outright victory under the existing electoral system, were powerful reasons for changing their minds.

The next serious attempt to achieve electoral reform was made during the next minority Labour government of 1929 to 1931. Once again

an objective of the Liberals was to secure electoral reform in return for their support of the Labour government, and once again there was resentment on the Labour side at having to pay this price for Liberal support. However, an all-party conference was convened, with the former speaker, Lowther, now Viscount Ullswater, as chairman, not the current speaker, Captain Fitzroy, but still commonly referred to as a speaker's conference. This conference found it impossible to reconcile divergent aims and opinions, and it ended without making any agreed recommendations.

The Ullswater Conference having terminated in the summer of 1930, the Liberals through Lloyd George still offered to maintain the government in power in return for a measure of electoral reform. However, the government would propose only the alternative vote and would not support PR, although the National Liberal Federation had just declared in favour of PR and had rejected the alternative vote even as a second-best solution. A Bill which included the alternative vote was passed in the Commons, only to be drastically altered by amendments in the Lords. Before any further consideration of the measure had taken place in the Commons the government had fallen, and that was the end of the Bill.

During the Second World War an accumulation of problems which affected the organisation of elections resulted in the establishment in 1943 of another speaker's conference. In the conference, proportional representation was rejected by 25 votes to 4, and the alternative vote by 20 votes to 5.

In 1945 the Labour Party received 62 percent of the seats in parliament with 48 percent of the votes, whereas in 1931, with 30 percent of the votes, they had received fewer than 9 percent of the seats. Their confidence that the electoral system would eventually operate to their advantage now proved to be justified. On other electoral matters measures were taken by the Labour government which aroused some controversy. During the recent speaker's conference it had been agreed that while a spouse should no longer be permitted to exercise an additional vote by virtue of any business vote for which her husband was qualified, neither the business vote itself nor the university vote should be abolished. Nevertheless, in the Representation of the People Bill of 1948, plural voting was abolished, and both the business vote and the university vote were swept aside. These and other alleged breaches of interparty agreements raised again, as in 1918, the question whether the speaker's conferences could be relied upon to resolve disagreements between parties on matters relating to electoral reform.

In 1948 single-member constituencies, which had become the norm since 1885, at last became the sole type of constituency. The problem of redistribution of constituencies had also become urgent in view of past population changes, and in 1944 the solution was to establish permanent boundary commissions. At first the commissions were under instruction to review the constituency boundaries every three to seven years, but in time it was felt that frequent changes in constituencies caused confusion, prevented continuity of representation and made it necessary both to rearrange party political organisations at constituency level, and to alter the local administration of elections. By an Act of 1958 the maximum time-limit between reviews of boundaries was extended to fifteen years, but this raised other difficulties. Shifts in population, especially out of city centres into suburban or largely rural areas, worked at this time to the disadvantage of the Conservatives, and the longer the delay between each redistribution the greater was their disadvantage likely to be.

In 1884–5 the Conservatives had favoured single-member constituencies for the sake of fairer representation under the relative majority system, but over the years since 1884 there were many occasions on which considerable discrepancies had appeared in the election results between the votes obtained by the parties and the seats they had won. In many elections, both before the First World War and in the interwar period, so many seats were uncontested that it is difficult to assess what the electoral support for each party was. Since the Second World War, however, when uncontested seats have been negligible in number, there have clearly been great discrepancies between votes and seats. The most conspicuous anomalies arose in 1974, when in the two elections of that year the Liberals obtained 19.3 percent of the votes but only 2.2 and 2.0 percent respectively of the seats.

In view of the obvious discrepancies between votes and seats, greater emphasis has been placed by supporters of the existing electoral system on the fact that single-member constituencies make possible an intimate and valuable relationship between a member and his constituents, since it makes the member responsible for finding remedies for their grievances and protecting their interests whatever their views or political affiliations may be. There is little doubt that for members themselves this is a salutary function, though it may make excessive demands on their time and energy. Whether the monopoly enjoyed in this respect by a single member in each constituency is equally to the advantage of the constituents themselves is more open to question. Also, the view of a member as essentially a servant of his constituents is at variance with the view, expounded much earlier by Edmund Burke, that he should be essentially a servant of the nation as a whole, regardless of local interests. On an empirical level, it may be questioned whether the aggregate results achieved by members through their action on behalf of individual constituents can bear comparison with the results they achieve by the way they vote in parliament, and whether the benefits of the personal relationship can justify the misrepresentation in parliament of the views of the electorate.

However, the chief argument in favour of the relative majority system has been that while anomalies in representation may be deplored, the system performs the vital function of returning a party with a solid majority of seats in parliament, and therefore promoted strong and stable government. Against this it may be pointed out that on no occasion after 1905 has any party, other than a coalition, secured a majority of the *votes* which were cast, and on many occasions solid party majorities did not emerge. The minority Labour governments of the interwar years are cases in point. Since the Second World War, in five general elections out of eleven (1950, 1951, 1964 and February and October 1974) the governing party held fewer than 51 percent of the seats in parliament, and on one occasion (February 1974) fewer than 48 percent. On two occasions (1951 and February 1974) the party which formed the government had more seats but fewer votes than the main opposition party. On two occasions (February and October 1974) the governing party had fewer than 40 percent of the votes cast.

Apart from the failure of the electoral system to achieve its intended purpose, it has recently been maintained that the two-party system, with each party alternating in power, has led in recent years in the United Kingdom to 'adversary politics' which threaten the stability and continuity of government. Consensus on major issues of policy no longer exists, governments tend increasingly to reverse the policies of their predecessors, and policies and reforms requiring long periods for their fulfilment are neglected in favour of short-term expedients.

In spite of earlier unsuccessful attempts to introduce a reform of the electoral system, a speaker's conference had once more been appointed in 1965 to consider, among other things, the 'methods of election, with particular reference to preferential voting'. In 1968 the conference recommended by 19 votes to 1 against any change in the existing system. In 1975, concern over the more recent working of the electoral system led to the convening by the Hansard Society of a Commission on Electoral Reform, whose report advocated the adoption of an 'additional member system', or else the single transferable vote. This report was followed by the formation of the national Committee for Electoral Reform under the chairmanship of Lord Hartech. Pressure groups favouring electoral reform were also established within each of the main political parties. The proposal of the 'additional member system' was intended to combine the merits of personal relationships in single-member constituencies with those of proportional representation of parties.

Britain's membership of the European Community has raised questions of electoral systems in a different form. For elections to the European assembly, after the first direct elections in 1979, it has been agreed in the assembly that a common system of election should be adopted by all member nations for subsequent elections. If this is accomplished, it does not seem likely that the simple majority system which, among the EEC nations, is used only in the United Kingdom, will be the one which will be adopted. The introduction of a different system for the European assembly could eventually reinforce demands for the adoption of a different system in the United Kingdom itself.

Reading References

A standard work on electoral reforms in Britain in the nineteenth century is Charles Seymour, *Electoral Reform in England and Wales*. The extent and significance of the earlier changes are examined by Norman Gash in *Politics in the Age of Peel*. The reforms proposed and those achieved after the return of a Liberal government in 1906 are the subject of *Electoral Reform in War and Peace, 1906–1918*, by Martin Pugh. For developments after the First World War the authority is David Butler, in *The Electoral System in Britain, 1918–1951*. The consequences of the electoral system are discussed by Peter Pulzer in *Political Representation and Elections in Britain*. For information on the structure of constituencies and election results before the Reform Acts one may consult Henry Stooke Smith's *The Parliament of England from 1715 to 1847*; and for the period after 1832 the series of *British Parliamentary Election Results*, edited by F. W. S. Craig.

KEY TERMS

Catch-All Party   The type of political party that appeals to voters across the boundaries of ideological and social cleavages. In order to retain their support base, catch-all parties have to broker the manifold differences that divide their followers. Examples of catch-all parties include the Liberal Party of Canada, the Indian National Congress Party, or the Liberal Democratic Party of Japan.

Cleavage-based Party   The type of political party that seeks to appeal to specific groups along particular political cleavages. Examples of such parties include workers' parties or religious confessional parties.

Electoral System   The set of rules and regulations according to which the electoral process is organized. Its most important components include rules on eligibility to vote; the number of votes that each voter can cast; the electoral formula according to which votes are converted into seats; the number of seats that can be won in each electoral district; and, in cases where voters have multiple votes, regulations about whether voters can cumulate the votes they are entitled to and whether they must use all votes or can abstain partially.

Mixed-Member Electoral System   The type of electoral system that combines elements of PR and majority-plurality systems.

Plurality and Majority Electoral Systems   Types of electoral system that award seats to parties that have received either the plurality or the majority of votes in the electoral district. In contrast to proportional representation, the share of legislative seats that political parties receive under these electoral systems is not in proportion with their share of electoral votes.

Political Party   A team of individuals united for the common purpose of capturing government power and implementing a commonly agreed-upon policy agenda.

Political Party System   A set of patterned relationships among political parties. The most important properties of a party system are its fragmentation, polarization, and institutionalization. The first refers to the number of parties in the system, the second to the degree of ideological difference among them, and the third stands for stability in both the identity of individual parties and the properties of the party system.

Proportional Representation (PR)   The type of electoral system that provides a close correspondence between the percentage of votes and seats that political parties receive in a general election. PR systems normally have large electoral districts in terms of the number of seats that can be won. The most commonly used formulae that PR systems use are the highest average (for example, d'Hondt) and the largest remainder (such as Hare or Hagenbach-Bischoff) rules.

Split-Ticket Voting   Some electoral systems provide voters with multiple votes to cast. If voters cast these multiple votes for candidates of different political parties, then they cast a split vote.

FURTHER READINGS

Blais, Andre, and R.K. Carty. "The Impact of the Electoral Formulae on the Creation of Majority Governments." *Electoral Studies* 6 (1987): 99–110.

Cairns, Alan. "The Electoral System and the Party System in Canada, 1921–1965." *Canadian Journal of Political Science* 1(1968): 55–80.

Chhibber, Pradeep and Kenneth Kollman. "Party Aggregation and the Number of Parties in India and the United States." *American Political Science Review* 92 (1998): 329–42.

Chhibber, Pradeep and Kenneth Kollman. *The Formation of National Party Systems*. Princeton: Princeton University Press, 2004.

Cox, Gary W. *Making Votes Count: Strategic Coordination in the World's Electoral Systems*. Cambridge: Cambridge University Press, 1997.

Katz, Richard. *Democracy and Elections*. New York: Oxford University Press, 1997.

Lijphart, Arend. *Electoral Systems and Party Systems: A Study of Twenty-Seven Democracies, 1945–1990*. Oxford: Oxford University Press, 1994.

Rae, Douglas. *The Political Consequences of Electoral Laws.* New Haven: Yale University Press, 1971.

Rule, Wilma. 1987. "Electoral Systems, Contextual Factors, and Women's Opportunity for Election to Parliament in Twenty-Three Democracies." *Western Political Quarterly* 40.

WEB LINKS

International Institute for Democracy and Electoral Assistance:
www.idea.int

Information and Statistics about the Latest Elections in Every Country of the World:
www.electionworld.org

Liberal Party of Canada:
www.liberal.ca

CHAPTER 12

STATE–SOCIETY RELATIONS

What kinds of relations exist between the state and society in democratic and non-democratic political systems? This chapter explores the theme commonly labelled by political science scholars as state–society relations. An examination of this important theme allows students to appreciate the different ways in which the state impinges on the daily lives of its citizens, and how social groups organize and articulate their interests under different types of state–society relations, first in democratic and then non-democratic political systems. Each system is examined theoretically; then, practical examples are offered. The chapter closes with a discussion of civil society.

STATE–SOCIETY RELATIONS IN DEMOCRATIC POLITICAL SYSTEMS

There are three ways of organizing state–society relations in democratic political systems: pluralism, societal corporatism (neo-corporatism), and consociational democracy. Each form is distinguished in two ways: first, by the level of competition permitted in the political arena and, second, by how interest groups are founded and organized to represent the interests of their constituencies.

Pluralism

The main premise of **pluralism** is that power in society is not monopolized by a single group or an alliance of groups that collectively may form the power elite. Rather, pluralism assumes that there is a dispersion of power among government agencies and among a plurality of social groups and interests. Pluralism, as a theory of state–society relations, derives its inspiration from James Madison, who wrote in the *Federalist Papers* (1788) that it is natural for individuals to have interests. Consequently, there are clashes of judgment, conflicts of interest, and dissent, which lead to the formation of factions. Factions are thus inevitable. In order to prevent the tyranny of a majority (when one faction forms a majority), constitutional arrangements and political institutions must be designed to protect individual freedoms and check the inducements on the part of the stronger factions to sacrifice the weaker sections of society. Arthur Bentley (1908) and David Truman (1958) popularized the concept of pluralism in the early twentieth century. For them, unlike Madison, the existence of diverse and competitive interests is a source of stability in a democratic society. A robust pluralist system corrects its own mistakes.

Pluralism is based on the assumption that the society is associational. Individuals who have multiple interests join groups in order to pursue their common interests. In a democratic polity, groups interact and counteract, and public policy is a product of these group interactions. Political power is diffused as it is not concentrated in the hands of one single group or a set of groups. Pluralism also assumes that meaningful political competition among social and interest groups is unconstrained, provided such activity is legal. Interest groups are thus allowed to organize as they wish and to compete freely as each seeks to shape public (or government) policies. From this perspective (albeit the state as an institutional structure plays a regulatory role), bargaining and competition take place *between* different interest groups, each representing particular interests. The state is not a constituent part of interest competition; under this scenario, the state acts like an impartial referee. Its involvement is limited to converting the victories of the groups into statutes. Although adhering to the basic premises of the naturalness of interests and the formation of groups conducive to the functioning of democracy, neopluralists such as Robert Dahl recognize the unequal involvement of groups in politics. Due to an unequal distribution of socio-economic resources, all interest groups do not have the same access to the policy-making process. Groups with a poor resource base are unable to participate equally in the political process. The neopluralists also point out that the state and its various institutions forge alliances with interest groups to advance their own particular interests.

Examples of interest group competition can usually be found in liberal democracies, which are best represented in the United States, where powerful lobbies—the National Rifle Association (NRA), the Health Insurance Association of America (HIAA), the tobacco lobby, etc.—have been successful in influencing legislation on important topics: gun laws, health care reform, cigarette taxes, etc. They have done so by investing millions of dollars in television commercials to mobilize supporters and shape public opinion. Moreover, they are especially effective in shaping congressional attitudes toward bills presented by the president to specialized congressional committees. They do so mainly through generous financial contributions to the election campaigns of strategically placed congressional members.

Societal Corporatism

Societal corporatism is another form of state–society relations in a democratic political system. However, before we can discuss it, it is important to look at the term corporatism in general, as corporatism exists in non-democratic state–society relations in the form of state corporatism, which is discussed later in the chapter. Philippe Schmitter provided one of the earliest and often-cited generic definitions of corporatism:

> *Corporatism can be defined as a system of interest representation in which the constituent units are organized into a limited number of singular, compulsory, noncompetitive, hierarchically ordered and functionally differentiated categories, recognized or licensed (if not created) by the state and granted a deliberate representational monopoly within their respective categories in exchange for observing certain controls on their selection of leaders and articulation of demands and support.*[1]

According to this definition, corporatism may be used to study state–society relations in democratic and authoritarian contexts. Indeed, different types of corporatist arrangements have been employed by the fascist dictatorships of Mussolini and Hitler, the authoritarian regimes of Latin America and the Middle East, and the modern democracies of Germany, Sweden, and Austria. Schmitter distinguishes between *societal corporatism* (or corporatism from below) and *state corporatism* (or corporatism from above), reserving the former label for the analysis of different patterns of governability and interest group representation in advanced capitalist states.[2] In contrast to pluralism, both subtypes of corporatism favour order over unrestrained conflict between different social interests and groups. Moreover, both subtypes are based not on interest competition, but on interest representation. Indeed, as Schmitter's definition suggests, the notion of interest representation is crucial to corporatism as a way of organizing state–society relations. Another crucial feature of corporatism is the leading role played by the state either in licensing or, in some cases, creating the representative bodies of the main active sectors of society: the labour movement, the business chambers, professionals, peasants, women, and so on.

Societal corporatism (also called "neo-corporatism") is a form of interest group representation in modern democracies. In this case, the state recognizes one formal leading organization (or what is labelled a "peak association"), such as a labour union, a trade organization, or a chamber of industry, to represent the interests of the respective functional groups—workers, traders, industrialists. These singular peak associations are organized in a hierarchical manner. For example, the peak association for workers represents the majority of individuals in society belonging to this functional category. Moreover, the national leadership of these peak associations tend to wield considerable influence over their members.

Under societal corporatism, direct negotiations between representatives of the different functional groups (organized in peak associations) and the executive branch of the state are regularly held to reach agreement on the country's economic, trade, labour, or welfare policies. The objective is to achieve some form of coordination and cooperation between the state and strategic sectors of society in the formulation of important economic and social policies. More often than not, the members of these peak associations accept the agreements reached between their representatives and the executive branch. If they do not, these agreements are then renegotiated. Once the members of the peak associations accept the agreements negotiated by their leaders, the executive branch uses its majority status in the legislature to translate these agreements into binding laws.

This neo-corporatist pattern of state–society relations has explicit consequences for public policy deliberations. These deliberations tend to be more regularized and less competitive than under pluralism because under pluralism multiple interest groups can organize and compete with one another and with the different branches of the state—for example, with the executive and the legislature—to influence public policy. In contrast, under neo-corporatism the functional groups are singular, and the state grants them "deliberate representational monopoly within their respective categories," as Schmitter's definition on the previous page suggests. Moreover, these groups are organized vertically in relation to the executive branch of the state.

Post–World War II Germany provides a good example of neo-corporatism in practice. Social and economic policies in post-war Germany have been subject to a consensus reached through tripartite negotiations among the government and representatives of business associations and the trade unions. In these negotiations, decisions are made on a host of socio-economic matters, including welfare benefits, vacation policies, and working conditions. Labour interests are represented by the powerful German Federation of Labour, while big business is represented by the Federation of German Industry, the Federation of German Employer Associations, and the German Industrial and Trade Conference, all examples of peak associations. In Germany, the consequence of adopting neo-corporatism has been socio-economic stability, a highly productive workforce, and a relatively predictable economy.

Consociational Democracy

Consociational democracy is the third form of state–society relations in democratic political systems. It is a model for organizing state–society relations in **plural societies**. Consociational democracy is found in those societies where the population is divided along religious, linguistic, regional, racial, ethnic, or cultural lines.

Arend Lijphart is chiefly responsible for popularizing the consociational democracy model. Lijphart posed a deceptively simple question: What explains political stability in a number of small European countries with plural societies? Belgium, the Netherlands,

Switzerland, and Austria (from 1946–1966) were some of the countries Lijphart studied. All these countries have plural societies divided along what Lijphart calls segmental (or vertical) cleavages. For example, by the twentieth century, Dutch society was divided into four tight and relatively isolated "camps": Catholics, Protestants, liberals, and socialists. Political parties and passions, cultural associations, and even marriage patterns mirrored and overlapped with these vertical divisions. In the case of Belgium, the population is divided into linguistically distinct and regionally concentrated Walloons and Flemings, a situation that has historically served to harden political differences between these two segments. What then explains the political stability of these otherwise deeply divided plural societies?

For Lijphart a peculiar political system, labelled "consociational democracy," and its concomitant organization of state–society relations, best explains the political stability of these countries, despite their deeply divided societies. Consociational democracy is based on cooperation and accommodation among the elites of the different segments of society. The objective is to overcome divisions and conflicts at the mass level through elite accommodation (or cooperation). Only by channelling conflict in deeply divided societies away from the streets and toward the leaders of the different segments can disagreements be contained and resolved peacefully. At the same time, minimal trespassing is allowed among the different segments of society. The cultural, religious, and personal affairs of the different segments are protected, to minimize friction and the resultant political instability.

As a way of organizing state–society relations, consociational democracy is defined by four basic characteristics. These four characteristics are all deviations from the parliamentary democracies of the British Westminster majority-rule style of politics.

GOVERNMENT BY GRAND COALITION

This is the basic principle of consociational democracy. The essential characteristic of the grand coalition is the participation by the leaders of all the significant segments (religious, ethnic, or linguistic groups) of society in ruling a plural society. Although it can take different institutional forms—a cabinet or a (Swiss) federal council, etc.—the grand coalition provides a forum where segmental elites can resolve political problems through compromise and intersegmental bargaining. In fact, Lijphart contends that participation in this grand coalition by all the elites of the different segments is in and of itself a cause for accommodation and compromise and thus an important guarantee for political stability in deeply divided societies.

MUTUAL VETO

By giving the leaders of every segment the right to veto political decisions, the mutual veto aims at ensuring that the interest of each segment is taken into consideration in the decision-making process. In turn, the mutual veto mechanism is meant to guarantee unanimity in decision making and, more importantly, adherence to political decisions by all the different segments, particularly their leaders.

PROPORTIONALITY

All the segments of the population should be represented (through their elites) not only in the decision-making bodies of the state, but also in a manner proportional to their numerical strength in society. Thus proportionality regulates the division of the political, civil service, ambassadorial, and other government posts among the different segments of the society in a way reflective of their numerical weight. Consequently, each segment is allocated a number of ministers in cabinet, and a number of ambassadors, judges, and directors roughly proportional to their demographic (and sometimes economic) weight in the state. Proportionality is also adhered to in the allocation of public funds to the different segments and regions. The latter is the case when linguistic or ethnic or religious divisions overlap with regional ones.

SEGMENTAL AUTONOMY

Every segment of society has autonomy in administering its exclusive social and personal spheres, especially those of a cultural, linguistic, or religious nature. The objective is to provide minority groups with a level of autonomy that enables them to protect their distinct identity and cultural practices against assimilationist pressures from the culturally and demographically dominant segment(s). Consequently, each segment runs its own schools, teaches its own history, and administers its own religious and cultural affairs.

Lijphart argues that consociational democracy not only is an empirical explanation of the political stability of a number of deeply divided Western societies, but also may serve as a normative example for plural societies in the so-called developing world. From this perspective, political engineering can go a long way in defusing ethnic, sectarian, or communal conflict in different parts of the developing world, such as Lebanon, Nigeria, Malaysia, India, and Afghanistan. However, this optimistic view has its critics. In Lebanon, for example, debate has raged among students of Lebanese politics regarding the applicability of Lijphart's model to Lebanese politics. Some contend that consociational democracy was never properly applied in Lebanon, a predicament that led to the 1975–1990 civil war. Others suggest that the model was applied despite the presence of some political deviations from Lijphart's ideal form. At best, consociational democracy was not very instrumental in promoting political stability in Lebanon, a deeply divided country. At worst, consociational democracy, with its emphasis on consensual decision making and elite accommodation, may have actually exacerbated sectarian divisions and contributed to Lebanon's collapse.[3]

Another critique focuses on the differences in the nature of the segmental cleavages in the developing world. Donald Horowitz suggests that in the European context hostility toward members of other segments is less intense than in the deeply divided societies of the developing world. This is not due to cultural factors, however. Rather, it is so because in most European states with deeply divided societies, and especially in Switzerland and Belgium, there are greater **cross-cutting cleavages**, namely class cleavages, that tend to ameliorate segmental hostility. Moreover, the longer history of state formation in Europe seems to have engendered the kind of supra-segmental national sentiments that are often lacking in many developing countries.[4]

There are at least three dilemmas that confront the successful application of consociational democracy:

- *Immobilism*—Because decision making has to be consensual and has to include the leaders of all the different segments of society, it is thus necessarily slow and vulnerable to deadlocks.
- *Administrative Corruption*—Because the allocation of posts in state institutions tends to be governed by the logic of proportionality and political appointments rather than by merit, these institutions are vulnerable to corruption. Moreover, reforming these institutions in the long run becomes a source of conflict among the different segments. Interestingly, this negative feature of consociational democracy is especially pronounced among societies in the developing world, where the state has yet to be firmly institutionalized.

- *The Elite's Dilemma*—Consociational democracy's gravest dilemma is the challenge faced by the different segmental elites to continuously reach accommodation with and make concessions to one another while maintaining the confidence and control of the members of their own segments. Indeed, it is this dilemma that often proves to be the Achilles' heel of consociational democracy in the developing world, impeding elite accommodation and causing the breakup of the political system. Lebanon in the late 1960s and early 1970s is an instructive example of the pitfalls of this dilemma.

STATE–SOCIETY RELATIONS IN NON-DEMOCRATIC POLITICAL SYSTEMS

State Corporatism

Experiments with **state corporatism** have historically assumed different forms. They run a wide gamut, including the fascist experiments in Mussolini's Italy and Hitler's Germany, the totalitarianism of Saddam Hussein's Iraq, the bureaucratic authoritarianism of military regimes in Latin America, and the single-party authoritarian regimes of many states in the Middle East and Africa, as well as pre–Vicente Fox Mexico. These different manifestations of state corporatism share a common element: the attempt by the leadership of the state, whether military or not, to organize the active components of society into, following Schmitter's definition, "a limited number of singular, compulsory, noncompetitive, hierarchically ordered, and functionally differentiated categories." The objective of this mode of organizing state–society relations is to penetrate every component of society, and thus allow the leadership of the state substantial control over the active sectors of the population.

The earliest experiments with state corporatism were fascism in Italy under Mussolini and national socialism in Germany under Hitler.[5] These experiments were based on the idea of establishing a hierarchical state structure, with a clear chain of command running from the leader to the masses, and passing through the party. The leader led the party, the party led the state, and the party penetrated society and organized the different social groups into front organizations divided along functional lines. Front groups included organizations for youth, women, students, workers, and officers.

The corporate state established by Mussolini in 1927 also sought to organize the economic sphere. To eliminate class conflict in the Italian state, Mussolini created twenty-two "corporations" to represent the different sectors of the economy—chemical trades, credit and insurance, building trades, fruits, lumber and woods, etc. Each corporation included all the relevant economic actors—workers, employers, managers, owners, and government representatives. The function of these corporations was to coordinate activities and resolve conflict among the different economic groups, set prices and wages, regulate jobs, and monitor work conditions. Although this corporatist arrangement was meant to resolve conflict between the different classes of society for the benefit of the larger Italian nation, it also allowed the fascist Italian state considerable supervision over the economy and, more importantly, the reorganization of the economy for war purposes.

Not all experiments with state corporatism followed the fascist model, however. In the 1930s and 1940s Latin American regimes turned to controlled inclusionary state corporatist modes of interest representation to contain the social and political fallouts of a specific development model: import-substituting industrialization.[6] In other parts of the developing

An Example of a Corporatist Organization: The General Peasants' Union in Syria

After assuming power in 1963, the Ba'th regime in Syria sought to mobilize peasants into a Ba'th-controlled national corporatist institution. Toward this end, Legislative Decree 127 of 14 December 1964 founded the General Peasants' Union (GPU), an overarching national institution explicitly concerned with mobilizing peasants along corporatist patterns. The corporatist structure of the GPU is pyramidal: the base is composed of village-level peasant committees formed in any village whose population exceeds 400. These peasant committees are grouped into district-level leagues, which are in turn gathered into thirteen province-level federations that combine into the GPU at the national level. In an effort to deny peasants organizational autonomy, Article 69 of Decree 127 banned the formation of independent peasant or agricultural syndicates. To maintain tight Ba'th control over the GPU, it is linked to the Ba'th Party through a special bureau of the Regional Command, the Peasants' Regional Bureau. This Bureau is headed by a member of the Ba'th Party's Regional Command, and is responsible for setting GPU policy and supervising GPU leaders—who are also party members—at both the national and local levels. Moreover, the president of the GPU is a member of the Peasants' Regional Bureau, and sits on the Ba'th's central committee. These intertwined party-GPU channels ensure that the GPU is tightly controlled from above by the Ba'th Party. On October 20, 1969, Legislative Decree 253 was promulgated replacing Decree 127. Ostensibly intended to deepen the socialist transformation of rural society, it aimed to streamline the peasant population along even tighter corporatist channels and democratic–centralist patterns. Thus every peasant gathering of more than thirty members was now compelled to form a peasant syndicate. These syndicates were in turn incorporated into the GPU's hierarchy of corporatist structures at the administrative, provincial, and national level. The aim of this organizational innovation was to narrow the base structure of the GPU and facilitate peasant control.[7]

Societal and State Corporatism Contrasted

One way of contrasting societal corporatism with state corporatism is to look at the power relationship that exists between the different interest/functional groups and the state. In societal corporatism the interest groups wield substantially more bargaining power than the state. This is so because, given the democratic nature of the political system, decisions pertaining to the different economic and social policies are reached after careful deliberations between representatives of workers, business, and the state. Moreover, these deliberations aim to achieve a workable consensus. Consequently, under societal corporatism the state cannot simply ignore the demands of the different interest groups. This is not the case under state corporatism. Given the authoritarian nature of the state, the different functional corporatist organizations wield much less negotiating power vis-à-vis the state than their counterparts do under societal corporatism. Thus, the state can dictate its demands on the different organizations.

world, state corporatism was used strictly politically to allow authoritarian regimes substantial control over the active sectors of society. In Syria, for example, the Ba'th regime that came to power in 1963 created a complex corporatist ensemble. This ensemble was based on mobilizing the different components of society into Ba'th-controlled, functionally differentiated, compulsory or quasi-compulsory, non-competitive corporatist "popular organizations" for peasants, workers, students, women, youth, artisans, and professionals. By linking each of these corporatist organizations to a specialized Regional Command Bureau in the ruling party headed by a member of the Regional Command, and by ensuring that the national and local leaders of these organizations were party members appointed to leadership positions by the party, the Ba'th Party was able to maintain control over this ensemble of corporatist institutions.[8] The cumulative impact of these measures was a high level of regime control over the active components of Syrian society.

CIVIL SOCIETY

The concept of civil society has had a recent renaissance among students of political science. It has generated useful insights for the debates on democracy and democratization, a theme discussed in Part Four of this book. In this chapter, readers will be introduced to the main contemporary variations of this concept.

Scholars of political science have employed the concept of civil society in two ways.[9] In the first variation, civil society is understood in organizational terms as that ensemble of private institutions and social organizations, beyond state control, that tends to check the predatory power of the state, create a buffer between the state and citizens, and consequently empower the latter. Civil society institutions thus include trade unions, professional syndicates, guilds, parties, chambers of commerce and industry, popular and charitable organizations, and nongovernmental organizations (NGOs). From this point of view, civil society plays a pivotal role as a counterweight to the ever-expanding power of an intrusive state. It also plays, and has played, an instrumental role in struggles for democratization throughout Eastern Europe, Latin America, Africa, and the Middle East, mainly by mobilizing social groups and agents against authoritarian regimes. In North America and Western Europe, civil society organizations have been at the forefront of struggles against the detrimental effects of globalization and environmental degradation, and in defence of minority rights and welfare services.

The second variation on the concept of civil society traces the historical emergence and consolidation of ideas of pluralism and tolerance within (mainly Western) societies. Often associated with the name of Alexis de Tocqueville (1805–1859), it considers civil society in terms of attitudes and ideas. Moreover, this approach underscores the historical role played by civil society in fostering a pluralistic, tolerant, and participant civic culture. This culture is assumed to be rooted in the dense fabric of civic engagement and manifested in terms of social trust among citizens of the same region or community. In turn, this "civility" of civil society is considered a crucial cultural condition for the emergence and sustenance of a participatory citizenship, for government efficiency, and, hence, for an effective democracy as well as economic well-being. Robert Putnam's reading in this chapter exemplifies this approach to the concept of civil society.

Although civil society has become an extremely popular concept and has gained virtually global currency, both the academic community and civil society activists have begun to question some of the assumptions underlying the normative considerations of civil society. Those studying the democratization process in newly democratic countries, while agreeing with the strong relationship between a vibrant civil society and the success of a democracy, suggest that the newly created political institutions can themselves generate a culture of participation, tolerance, and cooperation. In this respect, civil society can be generated. To assume that one needs a pluralistic and participatory culture, deeply rooted in the dense fabric of civic engagements, in order to generate a successful democracy is to impose a Western experience of democratization on the non-Western developing world. Others point out that some of the civil society organizations that have emerged in the non-Western world do not necessarily pursue the virtues of tolerance and cooperation.

More recently, but especially after the battle in Seattle in 1999,[10] attention has focused on the emergence of a global civil society as a significant social force struggling to limit the excesses of multinational corporations and great industrial powers.[11] Composed of a complex network of civil society organizations spread across the world, and connected through

SCOTT LONDON'S INTERVIEW WITH BENJAMIN BARBER

Barber: The great danger in any democratic republic is the danger that people think democracy is an automaton—that is to say, an engine that goes of itself without any effort and that like the battery in the advertisement, it just keeps going and going and going. But, in fact, democracy doesn't keep going and going and going. It requires the fuel of active citizenship. America's been at it for a long time. There is a sense on the part of some Americans of being burned out, of apathy, of not caring. . . . So there is always that sense that democracy doesn't have to be worked at, when the fact is that in a democracy, like a good marriage, a good relationship, a good job, you've got to work at it all the time and the minute you stop working, no matter how good it's been, it starts going downhill. . . .

London: What kind of work?

Barber: Civic work. Civic activity. And that means much more than just voting, maybe doing jury duty once in a while. Citizenship is in a certain sense a full-time occupation. Which is why it is hard, because Americans also have other jobs—they've got families, they've got to earn a living. Citizenship is, at its best, a full-time job. It means taking ongoing responsibility for all of the communities in which you live: your family, your neighborhood, your church, your school, your synagogue, the town, the state, the nation, and of course increasingly now we talk about a genuine responsibility to the whole globe environmentally as well. Those are tremendous responsibilities and they do exact a real price. People get tired out, they don't want to have the time for it, so it takes *that* kind of civic work. It's a work that is not discharged by voting—people think somehow "Now I've been a good citizen, I voted, now I can go home again." But voting is the *first* step towards citizenship, not the last step. . . .

London: . . . You say that our lives are inextricably linked with our communities. What do you mean by this?

Barber: Well, I mean by this that individualism, separation, the idea that we live lonely, solitary lives, is to start with simply a myth. It doesn't capture how almost everyone around the globe, certainly everybody in America, lives. We live in families, we live in neighborhoods, we live in churches, synagogues, mosques, we live in work places, where we hold jobs and interact with other people. We are embedded, in other words, in groups of people whose lives and whose fates impinge on ours, and ours impinges on theirs. To pretend that we are the solitary clients or consumers or individuals that market economics or legal personhood has to impose on us is really to misunderstand the starting place for how we live. We live in communities, whether or not people prefer to or not. We live in communities, we are embedded in them, and democratic citizenship is a way of trying to make our relationships to the communities we live in equitable, fair, judicious, and equal.

Democracy is a form of community. There are other forms too: hegemonic, patriarchal, boss-relations where someone tells someone else what to do. Democratic communities are ones in which we make decisions together. But I want to say that we need to start with a simple acknowledgement that the reality is that whether we like it or not we are embedded beings, are communal beings, which means nothing more than saying that we all live in families, we live in neighborhoods, we go to churches, we go to schools, with other people. The old saying, "no man is an island" is not some kind of an aphorism of the ideal, it's a way simply of describing reality for all of our lives.

Source: Reprinted with permission of Scott London.

the Internet, global civil society seeks to limit the powers of transnational organizations (TNCs), protect the environment and endangered species, and punish multinational corporations that privilege profit over minimal standards of human dignity and democracy. At the outset, global civil society targeted the World Bank, the International Monetary Fund (IMF), and the World Trade Organization (WTO) as the main institutions lobbying for the implementation of a thoroughly neoliberal economic platform that included deregulation, the elimination of economic borders and social safety nets, and the privatization of public sectors. In the next phase of its struggle, global civil society targeted global corporations and financial markets.

Global civil society has exploded into the scene in massive anti-globalization demonstrations in countries across the world, culminating in the World Social Forum in Porto Alegre, Brazil, in 2001. This gathering, attended by some 18,000 citizens from almost every nationality, class, religion, and race, established a complex web of alliances between groups committed to a fairer, more inclusive world. Global civil society has also been proactive in advancing positive alternatives to the socio-economic and political ideas that structure the current rules of global domination.

ENDNOTES

1. Philippe C. Schmitter, "Still the Century of Corporatism?" in *The Review of Politics* 36, no. 1 (January 1974), 93–94.

2. See Philippe C. Schmitter, "Interest Intermediation and Regime Governability in Contemporary Western Europe and North America," in *Organizing Interests in Western Europe: Pluralism, Corporatism, and the Transformation of Politics*, ed. Suzanne Berger (Cambridge, MA: Cambridge University Press, 1981), 285–327.

3. See Michael Hudson, "The Problem of Authoritative Power in Lebanese Politics: Why Consociationalism Failed," in *Lebanon: A History of Conflict and Consensus*, eds. Nadim Shehadi and Danna Haffar Mills (London: I.B. Tauris, 1988), 224–39.

4. See Donald L. Horowitz, *Ethnic Groups in Conflict* (Berkeley: University of California Press, 2000), 568–76.

5. See Nicos Poulantzas, *Fascism and Dictatorship: The Third International and the Problem of Fascism* (London: NLB, 1974).

6. Schmitter argued in his 1974 essay that state corporatism was imposed due to the imperatives of capitalist accumulation. See the corrective to Schmitter's original formulation in Philip D. Oxhorn, "Is the Century of Corporatism Over? Neoliberalism and the Rise of Neopluralism," in *What Kind of Democracy? What Kind of Market? Latin America in the Age of Neoliberalism*, eds. Philip D. Oxhorn and Graciela Ducatenzeiler, (University Park, PA: Pennsylvania State University Press, 1998), 197–200. For a detailed analysis of the "controlled inclusion" facet of state corporatism see Philip D. Oxhorn, "From Controlled Inclusion to Reactionary Exclusion: The Struggle for Civil Society in Latin America," in *Civil Society: Theory, History, Comparison*, ed. John Hall (Cambridge, MA: Polity Press, 1995), 250–77.

7. For the organization of the GPU see Syrian Arab Republic, *Le Syndicalisme Paysan en Republique Arabe Syrienne: Historique et Realisations* (Damas: Office Arabe de Presse et de Documentation, n.d.); and Raymond A. Hinnebusch, *Peasant and Bureaucracy in Ba'thist Syria: The Political Economy of Rural Development* (Boulder: Westview Press, 1989), 64–68.

8. See Ameen Asber, *Tatawwur al-Nudhum al-Siyasiyya wa-l-Dusturiyya fi Suriyya: 1946–1973* [The Development of Political and Constitutional Systems in Syria] (Beirut: Dar al-Nahar lil-Nashr, 1979), 64–65.

9. For an excellent discussion see Rex Brynen, "Introduction," in *Political Liberalization and Democratization in the Arab World: Theoretical Perspectives*, eds. Rex Brynen, Bahgat Korany, and Paul Noble (Boulder: Lynne Rienner, 1995), 10–12.

10. During the WTO ministerial conference, a massive street protest was held by various groups opposed to free trade and market-oriented economic policies favoured by the World Bank and other international financial institutions perceived by the protesters as anti-labour, anti-poor, and anti-sustainable environment.

11. See David C. Korten, Nicanor Perlas, and Vandana Shiva, "Global Civil Society: The Path Ahead," at: www.pcdf.org/civilsociety/path.htm (December 8, 2005).

READINGS

This chapter traced the different ways of organizing state–society relations in democratic contexts (pluralism, societal corporatism, consociational democracy) and in the non-democratic context (state corporatism). The chapter closed with an examination of two contrasting perspectives of civil society. The following excerpts explore these variations within the state–society theme. Douglas Chalmers examines the various meanings of corporatism and compares corporatism with pluralism. Arend Lijphart explains the main features of consociational democracy in comparative perspective. Finally, Robert Putnam's lecture voices a warning against the future implications of the decline in social trust in America.

In the first excerpt, Chalmers compares pluralism and corporatism. Students should pay special attention to the differences highlighted by the reading between these two types of state–society relations, especially vis-à-vis their different conceptions of the role of the state in society, a theme discussed at length in this chapter. Chalmers also offers a succinct discussion of the varied meanings of corporatism in its different contexts. Finally, his reading, though somewhat outdated, provides a flavour of the contemporary debates surrounding pluralism as a concept and as a tool for analysis when the chapter was first written in 1985. As such, it provides a narrow window to the history of the broader discipline.

The excerpts by Arend Lijphart are selected from his influential book *Democracy in Plural Societies*. Lijphart's excerpts offer introductory students a direct encounter with the ideas of a political scientist whose work has become essential reading for students of comparative politics. Undoubtedly, Lijphart's conclusions continue to elicit both praise and criticism. This reading summarizes Lijphart's conclusions about the viability of a particular type of democracy, consociational democracy, in plural societies; it also enumerates the main characteristics of this type of democracy. As you read, keep in mind Lijphart's central empirical question: what explains the political stability enjoyed by a number of small European states with plural societies? And, as an exercise in comparative analysis, ask yourself whether the Canadian political system manifests any of the consociational elements discussed by Lijphart. If so, which ones? Finally, building on the discussion in the chapter about the problems of exporting the consociational model to developing countries, think of arguments you would use to defend the viability of consociational democracy in these countries.

The third excerpt is taken from a lively lecture presented by Robert Putnam. Putnam made his mark in political science some years ago with the 1993 publication of a co-authored book entitled *Making Democracy Work*. The book sought to explain why some Italian regions were more successful than others in providing stable local governments and basic services to the local population. The answer lay in the varying levels of civic trust among the populations of the different regions. In those regions where democratic values, in this case high levels of civic trust, prevailed, local institutions functioned efficiently; where they failed to do so, the local population tended to be distrustful and divided. In his lecture, Putnam applies the same argument to the decline in civic trust and connectedness in North America in order to determine its cause and implications. Interestingly, Putnam blames this growing trend on television, naming the comedy *Friends* as a chief culprit. It is an interesting argument well worth considering. Upon reading his lecture, ask yourself whether or not you agree with his diagnosis and conclusions. If not, then why? Is TV the source for the decline in social trust? What about the role of the Internet?

CORPORATISM AND COMPARATIVE POLITICS

Douglas Chalmers

THE MEANINGS OF CORPORATISM

"Corporatism" is an ambiguous term. This is to be expected because it serves many purposes. It provides guidance for research, plays a part in political discourse, and contributes to theory. In each one of those contexts it picks up diverse meanings. Ambiguity, however, is not always a drawback. If we were constructing a tightly wrought proposition or theory, it would be, but corporatism is far from doing that. In pointing a way or suggesting approaches, ambiguity can be positive. The corporatist concept is a frame through which we may tentatively enter a new domain. It is not a precise template for drawing conclusions, but a rough map that guides scholars in exploring the major features of the new terrain.

Like many terms in political science, corporatism is used by political movements and activists to rally support and define a political position. As such it is the object of scrutiny by political scientists as a symbol that plays a role in political affairs independent of the scholar. Corporatism also has an analytical role as an instrument used by scholars in understanding politics. This double level of symbolism is the normal state of affairs for political scientists, but it complicates the job of theory construction.

The concept's twofold character is particularly relevant because "corporatism" as a political symbol is much more highly charged (negatively so) than, say, "pluralism." Many scholars writing on the subject find it necessary to open their analysis with a disclaimer. Because of corporatism's association with fascism in most readers' minds, a scholar's first task is to establish his or her detachment. Corporatism may never play a very strong role in "pure" analysis because it is so negatively charged. Many U.S. scholars have similar problems with using "communism" as an analytical concept. The associations of the term "corporatism" gave it a certain shock value in the 1960s that made its use vivid and interesting, but if it is to play an important analytical role, the concept may need a new name.

State–Group Relationships

Probably the most commonly assumed meaning of corporatism concerns the relationship between interests and the governing apparatus.

The image of a corporatist relationship that comes most readily to mind is that of a formal organization representing a major economic or professional interest before state officials within the framework of an official institution. Take, for example, a business association in an official government consultative council. The group is *corporate,* and is *incorporated* into the state.[1]

> *Corporatism can be defined as a system of interest representation in which the constituent units are organized into a limited number of singular compulsory, noncompetitive, hierarchically ordered and functionally differentiated categories, recognized or licensed (if not created) by the state and granted a deliberate representational monopoly within their respective categories in exchange for observing certain controls on their selection of leaders and articulation of demands and supports.*[2]

Although Schmitter does, in this definition, refer to a "system of representation" all of the distinguishing characteristics of this definition of corporatism concern the way individual groups relate to the state.

A central aspect of Schmitter's definition is the definite legal (or conventional) form that corporatist relationships take. These forms set the general terms of an exchange relationship that defines the interdependence of the interest organization and the government officials. The content of the exchange specifies the relative power of the group and the state and defines the degree of mutual autonomy. The legal quality of this relationship is crucial to corporatism. This is not to say that corporatism dwells on mere legal formalities, laws on paper that are often ignored in practice. It also includes customary and informal patterns as well. But it insists on drawing attention to whatever specifies rights and obligations and norms of behavior. More than pluralism and Marxism, corporatism emphasizes the direct connection between law and power and between law and interest.

As compared to the pluralist view, the distinctive quality of corporatist studies is their attention to the state. Pluralism places the bargaining and confrontation between groups at the center of its analysis, but corporatism does not see interest groups mainly in terms of their relationship to other interest groups. Those relations (conflictual or cooperative) are controlled by the formal requirements of the law, and the group's life is shaped by its exchange relationship with the state. This relationship determines the power of the state over the group and, conversely, the ability of the group to exploit its privileged position vis-à-vis state authorities to its own advantage. The pluralist view conceives of the state in essentially regulatory terms. Few pluralists would limit the state's actual behavior to the watchdog role posited by early liberals, and most recognize the importance and extent of regulation. But in a pluralist model the state is not a constituent part of interests, as it is in corporatism. Rather, it remains external to those interests, setting boundaries, rules, and incentives.

The Marxian, or class model does place more emphasis on the importance of the relationships between the state and societal groups. Class analysis pays close attention to the exchange or power relationship, which determines whether the state is being used to control one group on behalf of another.[3] However, it considers formal relationships to be merely changeable forms for establishing domination. Corporatism, on the other hand, makes those formal relationships a topic of central concern, for they are seen as the building blocks of the whole structure.

One of the qualities of a state–group relationship that gives it a corporatist character is suggested by Schmitter's use of the term "monopoly." Only one group is given the right to speak for a specified category of people. Schmitter is referring most particularly to the identification of a single organization to represent that category on various councils of state, such as an official trade organization or a labor union.

The "monopoly" associated with corporatism also can refer to the exclusive authority from the state to regulate a specified sphere of social activity. For example, in most societies the state gives doctors the exclusive right to practice medicine and gives their professional association the right to determine who can be a doctor and what standards they should uphold. In some contemporary authoritarian states, official labor organizations have a different, but related form of status, in that only one labor union organization is tolerated and all workers must belong to

it. The union organization acquires the power to determine who can work, and who shall benefit from state services related to the members' status as workers.

"Monopoly" may be an unfortunate choice of words, however, to describe either the representational or social regulating function of corporatist organizations. It suggests broad control over a relatively stable set of people. In modern societies diverse and rapidly changing social structures imply that the boundaries of any particular occupational category are overlapping and constantly shifting. Courts and legislatures are constantly arbitrating between them and redrawing their boundaries. Sometimes college professors are workers and sometimes they constitute a separate profession. Farmers are sometimes considered part of the business community and sometimes a sort of self-employed working class. Even in one of the best defined spheres, the practice of medicine has its boundary problems. Legally, chiropractors are partly in and partly out of the practice of medicine.

The shifting boundaries mean that monopoly status in the sense of exclusive control over a fixed group is always problematical.[4] For corporatism the most relevant sense of the phrase "granting a monopoly," however, is rather the active state role in defining and redefining both the powers of these organizations and the group they control and represent. The state creates "official" or "legally recognized" organizations. In a highly authoritarian corporatist society, the government may carry out this active role one step further by actively suppressing any competing claimants, but even in nonrepressive corporatist societies, the notion conveyed by the term "monopoly" lies in the official grant of rights and privileges, rather than the total control of a fixed social category.

The most important subdivision of corporatism is based on variations in the power relationship between interest groups and the state. There are state-dominated groups and group-dominated states. Schmitter refers to "societal" and "state" corporatism. The state-dominated version is associated with authoritarianism and dependent developing countries.[5] The "societal" form is more an evolution—perhaps a corruption—of liberalism.

Sometimes, unfortunately, this distinction is ignored. On the one hand, the association of corporatism with fascism has encouraged many to write about corporatist relationships as if their defining characteristic was the dominance of the state. On the other, one can also find "corporatism" used to emphasize—reasonably enough—the importance and dominance of corporations. As with all typologies based on power relationships, it is questionable how clear and stable these types are in practice. Societal groups have different degrees of power over different dimensions of their relationship to the state, and this balance varies with time.

Corporatism as a Regime

"Corporatism" is also used to refer to a comprehensive organization of political society beyond state–group relationships. This is the conventional application of the term for, say, Italian Fascism, which sought to replace the system of parties and parliament with a system of corporatist bodies, in which "all" interests would have a firm and fixed role in the political decisionmaking process. In fact, although much of the legal apparatus for this was constructed, corporatism was never completely implemented in Italy. This is not unusual. Incomplete implementation is a major finding in almost every study about almost every corporatist experiment.[6] On these grounds, it would be easy to dismiss all corporatist pretensions to describe regimes, especially if one assumes that the only form that corporatist relationships may take is that of constitutionally established councils of corporations. This was how constitutional theorists of the nineteenth and early twentieth centuries spoke of corporatism.

This vision of corporatism as a regime is unduly restrictive, however. It is more useful to apply "corporatism" to any comprehensive set of relationships in which the major interests in society have been brought into a formal, specified set of exchange relationships with the state.

Almost no modern state has a council of corporations, yet several qualities are central as criteria for labeling some of them "corporatist." The first two are extensions to the entire system of relations that hold between one corporatist group and the state. One may say that a corporatist regime exists when most major groups in society are corporatist, that is, defined in legal terms with specific sets of rights and duties. The regime would not be corporatist if there was a constant redefinition of groups based, say, on

negotiating power. To be corporatist, a regime must also have a relatively fixed pattern of representation, in which some definition of the important interests in society is established, maintained, and changed only with deliberation. If the groups relevant to policymaking were redefined on every issue, the system could not be considered corporatist.

Although these two criteria are clearly satisfied by a council of corporations or by other traditional corporatist deliberative bodies, they would also be satisfied by a stable but more informal pattern of comprehensive consultations, indicative planning bodies, and the like.[7] The regularity of ties, resting on a certain explicitness and stability, distinguishes them from pluralist arrangements. Obviously, this is a matter of degree. If regulatory agencies develop fixed clienteles, with—by custom or by law—privileged status for some groups, this is a move toward corporatism. Similarly, if corporatist institutions become more fluid in ways that bypass administrative decision, they are becoming pluralist.

On another level, corporatism implies something about how a system handles conflicts between groups. In the pluralist model, the primary form of interaction between groups is negotiation or bargaining. The class model of politics assumes either solidarity (between similarly placed groups) or irreconcilable conflict, with the first case represented by the marketplace, and the latter by war. In the corporatist model, the interaction between groups is carefully regulated by the instrumentalities of the state, and some planned, rational outcome is to be expected. If bargaining is the model for pluralism, and military conflict the model for class theory, then bureaucratic planning seems to be the model for corporatism. Like liberalism, corporatism assumes that interest groups do not stand in hostile contradiction, but rather postulates a regulated framework in which groups resolve conflicts guided by representatives of the community, the servants of the state. Corporatism has much in common with socialism's understanding of society after the end of class conflict. In that utopia, a fundamental harmony of groups within the state would presumably be achieved. Corporatist theory holds that this harmony is possible in the short run, and need not wait for the transformation of society.[8]

The need for methods to reconcile the bitter conflicts of the early twentieth century was one of the main impulses for the ideology of corporatism. Because corporatism has often been formulated as an explicit alternative both to the "chaos" and "greed" seen as products of the liberal model and to the bitter struggle foreseen by theorists of class conflict, it is not surprising that the controlled, nondestructive character of corporatist relationships is emphasized by corporatist theorists, particularly conservative ones.

Two problems remain with these definitions: (1) specifying what interests are representable and (2) determining whether there is any implied equality in the representations of various groups.

What sorts of interests are represented in a corporatist regime? Corporatism, like pluralism and Marxism, makes "interest" a central concept, but like them, never succeeds in defining it operationally. Thus, a definitive listing of legitimate interests to be represented in a corporatist regime is not available. In root versions of corporatism, these interests were associated with specific functional roles, prominently including the army, the church, and commercial and artisans' guilds. These versions apply to pre-absolutist days in Europe and to the colonial period in Latin America, when (at least in retrospect) the organizations in question were well developed and the boundaries between them clearly defined.

In contemporary societies the application is more difficult. Pluralists and Marxists begin with interest groups that are generated in society and explore their interaction. Pluralists assume no fixed definitions of interests; Marxists build primary definitions of interests around relationships to material production processes. In corporatism, however, interests are assumed to be limited and given—in contrast to pluralism—and are assumed to be determined by their function for the community as a whole, not by their dialectical confrontation around production or any other process. There is, however, no widely agreed-upon set of functions, and therefore no established set of corporatist interest groups. Most self-consciously implemented schemes in this century (for example, in Portugal and Italy) appear to begin with a quasi-Marxist definition of classes, broaden the definition to include all major economic interests, and add the professions.

There seem to be no specifically corporatist interests. The lack of precision here is a real problem for corporatism, and I shall return to it in our evaluation.

Does a regime qualify as corporatist if restrictions are sharply imposed on some segments of the population and privileged access granted to others? In many states—Latin American bureaucratic-authoritarian regimes, for example—no broad-based councils exist, yet labor is caught in a state-dominated legal structure and certain economic interests have privileged legal status. Should these be denied the label "corporatist"? It has been argued with much justification that corporatist language was used in these cases as a smokescreen for the implementation of strong governmental controls over labor and dissident political groups.[9]

Evenhandedness does not seem to be part of a definition of corporatism. Rather, the very diversity and specificity of ways in which different groups establish links with the state and are treated by the state is the hallmark of corporatism. In many cases that have concerned scholars in the 1970s and 1980s—the imposition of authoritarian controls in military takeovers in Latin America and elsewhere in the Third World—the imposition of unequal controls was clearly the product of a particular historical situation. With whatever justice, the military could claim that their unequal treatment of various groups in society was to correct the imbalances of the prior regime. In other words, the contrast in treatment accorded different segments of the population under corporatism is not only possible, but expected. There must, however, be some criteria of "appropriate inequalities," presumably based on the quality of a group's contribution to the community good. The nature of the interests represented would, one imagines, dictate the sort of link (including the power and exchange relationship) that the group has with the state. And since the specification of the appropriate interests is already problematic in corporatism, there is not much to help us in dealing with this question.

Clearly the concept of a corporatist regime is highly normative—more a matter of ideals than ideal types. The good things that would result from a successful corporatist regime substitute for a concrete description of just what that society would entail. One is left with a utopian picture in which there is a place for everything and everything is in its place. In this imagined regime, all important groups are represented in the formal structures of the state, and the state monitors and guides their interactions to avoid violent or otherwise illegitimate conflict and to secure stability and peace, appropriate rewards, and collective effectiveness. This is an image of an organic state.[10]

In the corporatist utopia, there is a formal structure that (in specific contrast to an ideal of equality) accords recognition to members of society based on the quality of their contributions, mediated through groups and institutions. Political interaction is regulated by a notion of the common good, and institutions enforce that notion. The spheres of life are carefully delimited.

Reading Notes

1. One sees references to the "corporate state" or the "corporate society" referring to the prominence of business corporations in political affairs, or, perhaps, the similarity of the state apparatus to a business corporation. This is not the meaning here. It may be a peculiarly American usage, in fact, to identify "corporations" only with business corporations.

2. Philippe Schmitter, "Still the Century of Corporatism?" in Frederick B. Pike and Thomas Stritch, eds., *The New Corporatism: Social and Political Structures in the Iberian World* (Notre Dame, IN: University of Notre Dame Press, 1974), pp. 93–94.

3. For this reason, class analysis and corporatist approaches both seem more relevant than pluralism to areas such as Latin America and the Third World in general, where the state is called upon to play a central role.

4. The more common meaning of "monopoly" remains applicable, of course. Firms still get monopoly profits by a variety of techniques ranging from a clever use of patents to coercion. Even this seems to be more difficult, however, with so many marginally different products. In any case, monopolies of representation are far more difficult to maintain.

5. See Schmitter, "Still the Century of Corporatism?" Note the association of corporatism with authoritarianism in the studies of the phenomenon in Latin America, as in James Malloy, ed., *Authoritarianism and Corporatism in Latin America* (Pittsburgh: Pittsburgh University Press, 1977).

6. For Italy see A. Aquarone, *L'organizzazione dello stato totalitario* (Turin: Guilio Einaudi, 1965).

7. Charles W. Anderson argues that parliaments are the typical institutional form of corporatism, and he is clearly right in that the ancient corporations met in bodies that evolved into modern parliaments. The modern typical form of corporatism would be, however, the administrative/ consultative committee. Parliaments are too much the loci of bargaining among individuals (at least in the United States) or groups representing party factions that are not clearly interest linked to be significant as corporatist institutions. See his comments in Charles W. Anderson, "Political Design and the Representation of Interests," in P. Schmitter and G. Lehmbruch, eds., *Trends Towards Corporatist Intermediation* (Beverly Hills, CA: Sage, 1979), pp. 271–98.

8. Alfred Stepan, in *The State and Society: Peru in Comparative Perspective* (Princeton, NJ: Princeton University Press, 1978), discusses the "organic state" tradition, which emphasizes the integral nature of the community. He distinguishes this tradition sharply from corporatism generally on the grounds that the latter refers only to the institutions that relate individual interest groups with the state. This may be clarifying, but the two concepts have been used together, and depend on each other too much to make the separation permanent.

9. See Guillermo O'Donnell, "Corporatism and the Question of the State," in Malloy, *Authoritarianism and Corporatism.*

10. The term is central to Stepan's analysis in *The State and Society.*

CONSOCIATION: THE MODEL AND ITS APPLICATIONS IN DIVIDED SOCIETIES

Arend Lijphart

THE CONSOCIATIONAL MODEL

It is widely—and correctly—assumed that it is difficult to maintain a democratic regime and domestic peace in a society that is deeply divided by religious, ideological, linguistic, regional, cultural, racial, or ethnic divisions. Consociation is a model of political co-operation which is more likely to achieve both democracy and peaceful coexistence in divided societies than the alternative models, in particular the majoritarian or Westminster model of democracy.

The consociational model is characterised by four principles. The two most important principles are grand coalition government or power-sharing and a high degree of autonomy for the different groups into which the society is divided. (These groups will henceforth be referred to as the *segments* of the divided society.) Two secondary principles are the minority veto and proportionality.

First, a grand coalition or power-sharing government is an executive in which the political leaders of all significant segments participate. Power-sharing may take various institutional forms. The most straightforward form is that of a grand coalition cabinet in a parliamentary system. In presidential systems, power-sharing may be accomplished by distributing the presidency and other high offices among the different segments. These power-sharing arrangements may be strengthened by broadly constituted councils or committees with important co-ordinating and advisory functions.

Secondly, consociational democracy delegates as much decision-making as possible to the separate segments. This segmental autonomy complements the grand coalition principle: on all issues of common interest, the decisions should be made jointly by the segments; on all other issues, decision-making should be left to each segment. A special form of segmental autonomy that is particularly suitable for divided societies with geographically concentrated segments is federalism. If the segments are geographically interspersed, segmental autonomy will have to take a mainly non-territorial form.

Thirdly, proportionality is the basic standard of political representation, civil service appointments, and allocation of public funds. The great advantage of the proportionality rule is that it is widely recognised as an eminently fair standard of distribution. Moreover, it facilitates the decision-making process because it is a ready-made method which makes it unnecessary to spend time on the consideration of other methods of distribution. As a principle of political representation, proportionality is especially important as a guarantee for the fair representation of minority segments. There are two extensions of the proportionality rule that entail even greater minority protection: the over-representation of small segments and parity of representation. Parity is attained when the minority or minorities are over-represented to such an extent that they reach a level of equality with the majority or the largest group. Minority overrepresentation and parity are especially useful alternatives to proportionality when a divided society consists of groups of highly unequal size. In federal states, these two principles are often applied to the composition of the upper house.

Fourthly, the minority veto is the ultimate weapon that minorities need to protect their vital interests. Even when a minority segment participates in a power-sharing executive, it may be overruled or outvoted by the majority. This may not present a problem when only minor issues are being decided, but when a minority's vital interests are at stake, the veto provides essential protection. The minority veto is synonymous with John C. Calhoun's "concurrent majority" principle: that is, for a proposal to be adopted, it needs not only an overall majority in favour of it, but also a concurrent majority in each segment.

***

CONSOCIATION VERSUS MAJORITARIANISM

The four principles of consociational democracy can be clarified further by contrasting them with the characteristics of majoritarian democracy, exemplified most clearly by the Westminster model. The essence of the Westminster model is the concentration of political power in the hands of the majority. Instead of *concentrating* power, the consociational model's basic approach is to *share, diffuse, separate, divide, decentralise, and limit* power.

Grand coalition or power-sharing stands in sharp contrast with the concentration of power in a one-party, bare-majority, non-coalition cabinet which is typical of the Westminster model. In the Westminster model, the cabinet is composed of members of the majority party—which, in a divided society, is likely to be the party representing the majority segment—and the minority is completely excluded. In parliament there is a confrontation between government and opposition, but the government has majority support and can get its proposals enacted even against strenuous objections by the minority. Instead of this majoritarian government versus opposition pattern, the consociational model prescribes shared, joint, and consensual decision-making.

In the Westminster model, the system of government is unitary and centralised; there are no restricted geographical or functional areas from which the parliamentary majority is barred. Instead of centralised government, the consociational model prescribes the decentralisation of power to regional and local governments and/or to non-territorial groups. In contrast to the unitary and centralised characteristics of the majoritarian model, segmental autonomy entails minority rule over the minority itself in a specified area—either a geographical or functional area—that is the minority segment's exclusive concern.

The basic electoral rule of the Westminster model is the winner-take-all principle; in the single-member district plurality or "first past the post" system, the candidate with the majority vote (or, if there is no majority, with the largest minority vote) wins, and all other candidates are excluded. The consociational principle of proportionality abolishes this sharp distinction between winners and losers: both majorities and minorities can be "winners" in the sense of being able to elect their candidates to office in proportion to each group's relative electoral support. In practice, the effect of the plurality method of election is to exaggerate the representation and power of the majority. It may be called "*dis*proportional representation" in favour of the majority. Proportional representation treats majorities and minorities equally, and does not discriminate against either small or large parties. The two extensions of the proportionality principle discussed above—minority over-representation and parity—are also methods of *dis*proportional representation, but here the disproportionality is not in favour of the majority, as in the Westminster model, but in favour of minorities and small groups.

Finally, a typical feature of the Westminster model is an "unwritten" constitution which can be amended by a normal majority vote. This means that the majority has the right to change even the most fundamental rules of government—a right without restrictions except morality and common sense. The minority veto of the consociational model limits the power of the majority to disregard the interests and preferences of the minority when constitutional or other vitally important issues are at stake.

THE DECLINE OF CIVIL SOCIETY: HOW COME? SO WHAT?

Robert Putnam

It is a great pleasure to be here and an honour to be asked to deliver the 1996 John L. Manion Lecture.[1] This evening I want to share a mystery with you, a detective story that I have been working on for the last several years. Please forgive me, though, if I begin with a brief autobiographical note which will help to explain how I came to this evening's topic.

Several years ago I was engaged in a very academic study of a very obscure topic—the

character, quality, and performance of local government in Italy. Over a twenty-year period, with a number of colleagues, I measured the effectiveness of different regional governments. As a political scientist I am interested in why some governments work better than others. If you are a botanist and want to study plant development, you might take genetically identical seeds and plant them in different pots of soil, then water them differently to see how they grow and how their growth is a function of their physical environment. If you are a political scientist and you want to study the development of public institutions, you would take the same paper organization and set it in different social, economic and cultural contexts to see how the institution is influenced by its environment. Normally, political science is not an experimental science, so it is not possible for political scientists to do this kind of research.

***

For twenty years my colleagues and I very carefully explored the performance of these governments. We examined their budgets; we explored their administrative arrangements and administrative efficiency; we counted the number of day-care centres or irrigation projects they produced; we measured their "street-level" responsiveness to citizen inquiries.

We discovered that some of these regional governments were, and are, quite efficient and effective, but others were, and are, clear disasters. I have never had the pleasure of experiencing the efficiency of Canadian government, but I do have experience of the government of the Commonwealth of Massachusetts, and I can assure you that many of these Italian regional governments are much more efficient, much more effective, creative and innovative than the government of Massachusetts. Still others are disasters—corrupt, inefficient, never answer their mail. So the questions were: Why is this so? Why do some governments work better than others? What were the secret ingredients, the secret elements, in the soil?

We had lots of ideas. We thought it might be that richer, more economically advanced regions could afford better governments. We thought it might be related to education. (It's a conceit of educators to think that maybe we make a difference.) We thought it might be related to the political party system. We had lots of ideas, many hypotheses. We did not, however, guess what turned out to be the best predictors of government performance—choral societies and football clubs! And rotary clubs, and reading groups, and hiking clubs, and so on! That is, some of these communities had dense networks of civic engagement. People were connected with one another and with their government. It wasn't simply that they were more apt to vote in regions with high-performance governments, but that they were connected horizontally with one another in a dense fabric of civic life.

A norm of reciprocity had evolved in these regions, the type of reciprocity that makes a community work and, of course, also makes governments work much more effectively and efficiently. These regions had this dense civic fabric, this tradition, this habit of connecting with one's neighbours and with community institutions. These regions were also wealthier, more economically advanced. For a long time we thought this was so because *wealth* produced choral societies. We conjectured that people in economically advanced, more affluent places could afford to take the time to become engaged in community affairs, while the poor sickly peasants didn't have much opportunity to join a choral society. We thought wealth produced choral societies.

We had it, however, exactly backwards. It was not wealth that had produced choral societies, it was—at least in the Italian case—the choral societies that had produced wealth. That is, two identical regions one hundred years ago were equally backward, but one happened to have a tradition of civic engagement and it became wealthier and wealthier. We discovered to our amazement that this pattern of civic connectedness was a crucial ingredient, not only in explaining why some institutions work better than others, but also, at least partly, in explaining levels of economic well-being.

SOCIAL CAPITAL

I want to introduce here some social science jargon, for which I apologize but which may be helpful in our subsequent discussion—*social capital.* We all know what *physical* capital is—it is some physical object that makes you more productive than you would be if you didn't have it. A screwdriver, for instance. You save up your nickels and dimes and you invest in a screwdriver so that you can repair more bicycles more quickly than you could without the screwdriver. That is physical capital. Then, about twenty years ago, economists began talking about *human* capital to refer to an analogy between a screwdriver and a degree from the University of Toronto. If you save up your money and go to college or to auto mechanics school, you can be more productive and more efficient than you would be if you lacked that training. That is human capital.

Now we are talking about *social* capital to refer to the features in our community life that make us more productive—a high level of engagement, trust, and reciprocity. If you are fortunate enough to live or work in a community or an organization like that, you can be more productive than you would be in a different context. This kind of social capital turned out to be crucial, at least in part, in explaining economic development, institutional performance, and so on. And that is the end of my preface. The question was why some governments work better than others, and the answer was choral societies—that is, social capital.

THE DECLINE IN TRUST

When I finished the research in Italy several years ago and came back to the United States, I began to worry, as a citizen, about a problem that concerns most people in the United States now—a sense that our institutions are not working as well as they once did. There are many metrics of this, many measures. One convenient measure is the answer to the pollsters' question that has been asked for thirty or forty years: Do you trust the government in Washington to do what is right most of the time?

When I was growing up in the fifties and sixties, if you asked Americans if they trust the government to do what is right most of the time, 75 percent would have said yes. That answer now seems antique. Last year, to the same question, about 20 percent of Americans said that they trust the government to do what is right most of the time. And that reflects a steady thirty-year decline, not linked to any particular administration or any particular party.

Trust has been down under Democrats and under Republicans, in periods of prosperity as well as in periods of economic hard times. And it is not only distrust of government that has grown, and certainly not just the federal government. It is also a distrust of state and local government, a distrust and lack of appreciation, lack of approval, of the performance of most of the institutions in our society. Trust in business is down, trust in churches is down, trust in medicine is down. Trust in—I am sorry to have to say this—trust in universities is down. We have this feeling that none of our institutions is working as well as it did twenty or thirty years ago.

The degree of this decline in confidence in public institutions is greater in the United States than in any of the advanced industrial democracies, at least to my knowledge. And the length of time during which this decline has occurred is greatest in the United States, but there are many other advanced industrial countries with similar trends. Everyone in the room is more expert on Canadian politics and government than I am, but I have the impression that there has been a similar decline, not so deep, more modest (that is the Canadian way of doing things)—but still the trend is here. I am not talking about this particular government, but about a general sense that civic institutions are no longer working as well. The trends are down in Sweden, in Japan, in Italy, in Britain, and in many of the advanced industrial countries.

THE DECLINE IN CIVIC ENGAGEMENT

This evening I will focus on the United States because this is the case I know best, and it is where I have done my research. I began to wonder whether there could be a connection between this problem that worries me as a citizen—the performance of our institutions—and what I have been studying as a scholar, namely social capital. So several years ago I began investigating trends in social capital, trends in civic engagement in the United States over the past twenty or thirty years. What I found at first surprised me and then, increasingly, distressed me—and now, frankly, it has become a matter of grave concern to me.

What I found is that over this period there has been a substantial decline in many forms of civic engagement in the United States. The simplest example, and the one most familiar to Americans, is that we are voting less, about 25 percent less, than we were a generation ago. But this decline turns out to be relatively more modest than some of the other metrics of civic engagement, and it is certainly not the most important one. I mention it only because it is the most visible. There are other examples within the domain of politics and government. Pollsters, for instance, have been asking Americans every year for the last twenty or twenty-five years if they have been to any meeting within the last year at which there has been a discussion of town or school affairs. The results show a decline in this type of civic engagement of nearly 40 percent over the last twenty years. And there are similar declines in other measures of civic deliberation. We are not just voting less, we are exchanging ideas with one another less about public affairs.

What I want to emphasize most is that this decline is not only true of politics—we Americans are connecting with one another and with our communities much less in many other spheres. Consider, for a moment, participation in community organizations. In the United States, the most common and most important of these are religious organizations. Since roughly half of all community activity in America is religious—roughly half of all memberships are religious, roughly half of all philanthropy is religious, and roughly half of all volunteering is in a religious context—the trends in American religious activity and religious behaviour can tell us a great deal. Depending to some extent on what measures are used, there is evidence of a decline of about 20 percent, perhaps even 25 percent, in the number of Americans, for example, who say that they went to church last Sunday.

I want to pause here for just a second to report on a rather unkind recent sociological study in which pollsters asked people the standard question, Did you go to church last Sunday? and then went to see whether those who said yes were actually in the pews. I have two unfortunate things to report. First of all, we fib a lot about whether we went to church. Roughly twice as many of us say we were there as actually were. And there is also some evidence that we are fibbing more than our parents did. So these poll numbers, if anything, underestimate the degree to which there has been a decline in attendance at church, but not in every single congregation or in every denomination. Some have been gaining, some have been declining. Evangelical religion has been growing over this period, but not enough to offset the really catastrophic collapse in attendance at the mainline religious organizations—Methodist, Lutheran, Episcopal, and Catholic as well. The decline in participation in religious organizations has been significant.

This is true also of trade unions. A generation ago the most important kind of affiliation for many working-class Americans, especially working-class men, was membership in trade unions. However, membership in trade unions is off by about 50 percent, or perhaps close to 60 percent, over this period. Thus, we are not going to church or the union lodge as often as we did in the past.

There are similar trends in many other kinds of civic organizations. Take, for example, what I have come to call the "animal" clubs— men's organizations. This is not a slur; it reflects the fact that I have discovered in the course of doing this research that most American men's clubs are named for animals—the Lions Club, the Moose Club, the Elks Club and the Eagles Club—and, of course, there are a few others like the Masons. All of these groups have experienced a decline of between 20 and 50 percent in membership over this period. In fact, the trend over this whole century is quite interesting. Over most of the century, it appears, rising numbers of American men belonged to such organizations (and the same pattern applies to women's organizations). More American men, proportionately, apparently belonged to "animal" clubs in 1960 than in 1950, and more in 1950 than in 1940. This was the trend over the whole of this century until suddenly, silently, inexplicably, all of them began to experience plateauing, followed by a steadily and then more rapidly declining membership over the last 20 to 25 years. There are other examples as well: volunteering for the Red Cross is off by more than 50 percent over this same period, and there are similar declines in adult volunteers for Boy Scouts and other community organizations.

BOWLING ALONE: THE DECLINE IN "CONNECTEDNESS"

In many ways, therefore, we are connecting less. This does not mean, of course, that every single organization in America has lost members. That is not true. To take one example, membership in professional organizations has risen substantially, though hardly more than the number of Americans in professional and higher managerial jobs, so the "density" of such membership in the relevant portion of the population has not grown. On the other hand, some organizations have boomed. I happen to belong to the most rapidly expanding organization in America, one that has gone, over the same period, from about 300 thousand to 34 million members. This organization is called the AARP, the American Association of Retired Persons. I belong to this organization because when you turn fifty in America, and if you have a driver's licence, you get a letter in the mail asking you if would you like to join the AARP. Thinking that I might get a discount at motels or something, I signed up for the AARP, and I am an active member in good standing. My total membership activity each year consists in the 36 seconds that it takes to write a cheque for eight dollars, and then I flip through the pages of *Modern Maturity* magazine! This is the general rule. Organizations in which membership means moving a pen, writing a cheque, are exploding. Organizations in which membership means being there, knowing another member, are stagnant or declining. (I don't know any other member of the AARP even though there are 34 million of us. Actuarially, I must know another member, of course, but I wouldn't know that I know another member because we never meet.) It is not that there are no lobbies—there are important big lobbies that have grown during this period. But the organizations in which you commit with other people are the ones that have experienced a decline in connectedness.

Here is some evidence that I hope will knock your socks off—membership in bowling leagues has dropped! (I can see that it didn't. Well, that is because you don't realize how important bowling is in America.) Bowling is big in America. More Americans bowled last year than voted last year. And bowling is up, up by 10 percent over this last decade or so. But bowling leagues, bowling with teams, is off by 40 percent over the same period. You will wonder how a professor knows such strange facts. The answer is that I happened to run into the man who owns one of the largest chains of bowling alleys in America who said, "You know, Professor Putnam, you happened on a major economic problem in our industry." It turns out that if you bowl in a league, a team, you drink four times as much beer and you eat four times as many pretzels—the money in bowling is made in beer and pretzels, not in balls and shoes. So this man is very much worried about the decline in league bowling, even though the numbers of people coming in the door are the same, or actually up. He is worried about the decline in league bowling because of the bottom line.

I, also, am worried about the decline in league bowling, and to explain why, I need to describe how team bowling works. If you bowl in a league in the United States, there are two teams with five people in a team—ten people. At any given time, two people are at the lane bowling

and the other eight are sitting in a semicircle of benches at the back of the lanes drinking their beer, eating their pretzels, and talking. They are mainly talking about whether O.J. did it, but occasionally they talk about bond issues, or whether the garbage is being picked up properly, or how the local schools are performing. What I mean—and this is why I use bowling teams as a serious example—is that this is yet another occasion that we once had, but no longer have, for sustained conversation with other people we know well about shared interests and community affairs.

This is not to say that we are not talking about politics in America. We are *shouting* about politics in America! We have this talk radio plague (I hope it hasn't arrived in Canada) in which a caller says, "Hi, I'm Ted from Toledo . . ." and then he goes on. I don't know Ted, I don't even know whether Ted is Ted, and I don't know if he is taking responsibility for his views in the way that my bowling league partner is. If you and I see each other every two weeks at the bowling alley and you say something crazy, you are taking responsibility for your views because you have to come back and face me again next week. This is fundamentally what has been happening to American democracy: we are less and less able to have serious discussions with people we know well. I don't mean high-brow academic discussions, I just mean having conversations with your neighbours about how things are going. I mean taking responsibility for your views. This is what this decline in social capital means. It is not just in a formal context, and it is not just in bowling leagues, or churches, or unions. It is a decline in informal connections.

This absence of civic conversation is characteristic not only of formal organizations but also of informal ties. For example, over the last thirty years American sociologists have asked people to keep a time budget of how they spend every minute of a particular day (so many minutes brushing their teeth, and so on). Therefore, we know how Americans have been spending their time over these thirty years and how this has been changing. In fact, the pattern has remained pretty constant. We spend about exactly the same number of minutes on most of our activities, such as commuting, as people did thirty years ago. This is somewhat surprising, but despite all the gains in technology, the number of hours spent commuting seems to have been constant for most of the century.

Against this pattern of basic consistency over time in how we spend our day is the fact that we are spending about 25 percent less time in ordinary conversation with other people and about 50 percent less time than we did thirty years ago in organizational meetings. And we know our neighbours less well. Over the past twenty or twenty-five years the number of people who say they never spend a social evening with a neighbour has doubled. It is not only in voting, it is not only in politics, it is not even only in a formal organizational context. It is in many different ways that we are no longer connecting with one another.

Furthermore—and this is in some sense the crux of the matter—we trust one another less. A generation ago if you asked Americans if they trust other people, nearly two thirds would have said yes. Today, if you asked that same question of Americans, nearly two thirds would say no. We are losing those habits of reciprocity and trust that are characteristic of communities with high levels of social capital.

***

THE PRIME SUSPECT

Then what has caused this decline in social trust, in civic engagement, in "connectedness"? In general, this is a case, like the Agatha Christie novel *Murder on the Orient Express*, in which there are multiple culprits. The most reasonable conclusion from the available evidence, however, is that *a prime suspect is television.*

The timing is right. Television has hit America like a lightning bolt—the fastest infusion of any technological innovation in history. In 1949 less than ten percent of American homes had television; by 1959 more than ninety percent of American homes had television. It came like a lightning bolt and has had a continuing reverberation, so that by now the data say that the average American spends four hours a day watching television. That is not counting the hours that the set is on in the other room, but only the hours spent in front of it. There are some things you can do while you are watching television, but you cannot bowl and you cannot go to the PTA.

The main effect of the introduction of television—and this, by the way, is not unique to the United States—has been to make us more homebodies and more isolated. And whereas in the very first period all the family was sitting around the hearth watching television together, now, with the number of multi-set homes skyrocketing, we are just watching alone. And what we are watching is simulated social capital. We are watching the most popular television show in America, a show called *Friends*. Well, *Friends* is about social capital, but it is not *real* social capital. Like the program set in a Boston bar called *Cheers*, where "everybody knows your name," a lot of what you watch on television is designed to make you think that you actually have these good buddies you see every week—but they don't see you.

The statistical evidence is that for every hour you spend reading a newspaper you are substantially more likely to vote, more likely to trust other people, more likely to join a group. For every hour you spend in front of the television you are statistically substantially less likely to vote, less likely to join a group, and less likely to trust other people. So, although television is not the only part of the story, I think that it is a large part of the problem.

What about the Internet and "computer-mediated communication"? The net effect of the electronic revolution has been to make our communities, or what we experience as our communities, much wider geographically, and much thinner sociologically. Every day I can easily communicate with people in Germany and Japan, but I don't know the person across the street, and the fact that I don't know the person across the street would astonish my father more than the fact that I am talking to people across the globe every day. Place-based social capital is being replaced by function-based social capital. That is what the electronic revolution does.

For some purposes, function-based social capital is just as good, but for some purposes it is not. My friends abroad are great, and perhaps it is less likely there will be a war because I talk to them every day—but that does not do any good for the crime rate in my neighbourhood. I doubt that electronic communication has caused civic disengagement, for the computer came two or three decades into the change. On the other hand, we have to find ways in which we can use this electronic network structure to create *real* communities with *real* face-to-face interaction, not just phosphorous-to-phosphorous interaction.

Reading Note

1. This lecture draws on material first reported in the following articles by Dr. Putnam: "Bowling Alone: America's Declining Social Capital," *Journal of Democracy,* vol. 6, no. 1 (January 1995), pp. 65–78; and "Tuning In, Tuning Out: The Strange Disappearance of Social Capital in America," in *P.S.: Political Science and Politics,* vol. 28, no. 4 (December 1995), pp. 1–20.

KEY TERMS

Consociational Democracy   A type of democracy characterized by a grand coalition, proportional representation, mutual veto, and segmental autonomy.

Cross-Cutting Cleavages   When horizontal and vertical divisions intersect in a society.

Pluralism   A form of state–society relations that assumes a dispersion of power among the state and different social interests.

Plural Society   A society in which the population is divided along different ethnic, linguistic, religious, regional, and/or cultural lines.

Societal Corporatism   A way of organizing state–society relations in democratic, capitalist societies whereby compulsory, single, functional, hierarchical interest groups emerge from below. This system replaces mature pluralistic state–society relations.

State Corporatism   A way of organizing state–society relations in authoritarian states whereby the state creates compulsory, single, functional, hierarchical interest groups.

FURTHER READINGS

Bratton, Michael. "Beyond the State: Civil Society and Associational Life in Africa." *World Politics* 41, no. 3 (April 1989): 407–30.

Cohen, Joshua, and Joel Rogers. *Associations and Democracy.* London: Verso, 1995.

Collier, David. "Trajectory of a Concept: Corporatism in the Study of Latin American Politics." In *Latin America in Comparative Perspective: New Approaches to Methods and Analysis,* edited by Peter H. Smith. Boulder: Westview Press, 1995.

Gellner, Ernest. "Civil Society in Historical Context." *International Social Science Journal* 43, no. 3 (August 1991): 495–510.

Lijphart, Arend. *Democracy in Plural Societies.* New Haven: Yale University Press, 1977.

Lijphart, Arend, and Markus M. Crepaz. "Corporatism and Consensus Democracy in Eighteen Countries: Conceptual and Empirical Linkages." *British Journal of Political Science* 21, no. 2 (April 1991): 235–56.

Putnam, Robert D., with Robert Leonardi and Raffaella Y. Nanetti. *Making Democracy Work.* Princeton: Princeton University Press, 1993.

Reynolds, Andrew, ed. *The Architecture of Democracy: Constitutional Design, Conflict Management, and Democracy.* New York: Oxford University Press, 2002.

Sabetti, Filippo. *The Search for Good Government: Understanding the Paradox of Italian Democracy.* Montreal & Kingston: McGill-Queen's University Press, 2000.

Seligman, Adam B. *The Idea of Civil Society.* New York: Free Press, 1992.

Wiarda, Howard J. *Civil Society: The American Model and Third World Development.* Boulder: Westview Press, 2003.

WEB LINKS

Links to American Interest Groups from the University of California:
www.library.ucsb.edu/subj/politica.html#interest

LSE Centre for Civil Society:
www.lse.ac.uk/collections/CCS

Civicus: World Alliance for Citizen Participation:
www.civicus.org

People-Centered Development Forum:
www.pcdf.org

The United Nations:
www.un.org/partners/civil_society/home.html

Democracy in America—Alexis De Tocqueville:
http://xroads.virginia.edu/~HYPER/DETOC/home.html

Yearbook of International Organizations:
www.uia.org/organizations/pub.php

PART 4

POLITICS AS CHANGE

The main objective of this section is to introduce readers to issues and events that are challenging or redefining our understandings of politics and political life. While the previous sections provide an overview of traditional areas of study in political science, such as methodology, ideologies, and institutions, this section examines some of the issues that are at the forefront of contemporary debates. Chapter 13 examines the issue of democracy and democratization. The discussion centres on opportunities for further democratization and dangers for democratic stability in the new millennium. Chapter 14 explores the impact of globalization on the state, citizenship, and governance, as well as the challenges it poses for countries in the developing world. Chapter 15 explores the theme of nations and nationalism. The discussion includes an introduction to different conceptions and theoretical approaches to nationalism and an exploration of the contemporary significance and consequences of nationalism, such as self-determination and secession. Chapter 16 explores the relationship between religion and politics and the rise of fundamentalist religious movements in various parts of the world. It examines the socio-economic and political conditions that give rise to these groups and ends with a discussion of Islamic fundamentalism. Chapter 17 provides a general discussion on the concept of citizenship, which highlights how the term has traditionally been defined in the context of the state. It then explores two alternatives to the formal-legal conceptualization of democratic citizenship—citizenship as political activity and citizenship as identity. The chapter ends with a discussion on the possibility of a "post-national" citizenship in this era of globalization.

CHAPTER 13

DEMOCRACY AND DEMOCRATIZATION

Since the beginning of what Samuel Huntington[1] calls the First Wave of democratization (1828), states around the world have been converging on the adoption of democratic political regimes. Although the convergence has been characterized by ebb and flow rather than a continuous trend, the number of democracies has been gradually increasing. This chapter will explore some of the ways in which democracy has been defined as well as alternative theories that have been proposed to account for its emergence.

WHAT IS DEMOCRACY?

Political scientists and thinkers have classified political regimes in a variety of ways. As a result, the exact definition of democracy has also shifted depending on the analytical framework used. In one of the first attempts at a comprehensive classification of political constitutions, Aristotle distinguished political regimes on the basis of the number of rulers and whether their rule was aimed at serving their own selfish or the general public's interests. Table 13.1 shows that democracy in Aristotle's framework is identified as the political regime defined by the selfish rule of the many. In contrast to the best or ideal type of political regime, the polity, the Aristotelian definition of democracy clearly carries a pejorative connotation.

Perhaps the most influential contemporary definition of democracy is the one offered by Robert Dahl[2] who classifies political regimes according to two criteria: the degree of contestation of political power and the extent of popular participation in such contestation. The ideal type of political system for Dahl, what he calls **polyarchy**, is one that is characterized by free competition and full participation. The two-dimensional framework proposed by Dahl has become widely adopted by political scientists to measure the extent to which various states approximate the democratic ideal. Indeed, the framework helps us appreciate the rich variety of alternative political regimes.

Another parsimonious definition of democracy captures the important notion of the uncertainty of political competition. Adam Przeworski[3] argues that democracy is quintessentially characterized by the fact that the winners of political competition do not have a guaranteed control over the power that they have won. Therefore, if the losers of the political game know that they have a reasonable chance to win in the future then they have an incentive to stay within the rules of the game and accept their losing status. When losers think this way then democracy becomes an equilibrium because neither the winning nor the losing side of

Table 13.1

Number of Rulers	Selfish Rule	Rule in the General Interest
one	tyranny	kingship
few	oligarchy	aristocracy
many	democracy	polity

the competition has an incentive to depart from it unilaterally. If, however, for some reason, the losers believe that they may acquire greater power by not accepting their loss but by subverting the regime, then democracy is not in equilibrium. In short, according to this perspective, democracy is organized uncertainty. It becomes an equilibrium when the losers of a political competition estimate that the anticipated cost of subverting the democratic order is greater than the expected costs of staying within the regimes and accepting their loss.

THE HISTORY OF DEMOCRATIZATION

The history of the global spread of democracy has been circuitous; the number of states adopting democratic forms of government has continually risen and fallen. Samuel Huntington calls the periods of democratic spread the waves of democracy, and has identified three of them in the history of the modern world.[4] The first two waves were followed by reverse waves, that is, the collapse of democratic systems and their replacement by alternative non-democratic forms of government. However, thus far no reverse wave has followed the most recent **wave of democracy**.

Lasting from 1828 to 1926, the first of the three waves was considerably longer than either the second or the third. The expansion in the number of democracies in this period, however, was followed by the collapse of a number of new democracies in the inter-war period, mainly in Europe, for instance, in Germany and Italy. The second wave of democratization was the shortest of the three; it lasted from the end of the Second World War until 1962. Democratization during the period was the result of both the reconstruction of the post-war European order and the general move toward decolonization. A number of former European colonies in Asia and Africa, for instance Kenya, Nigeria, and India, became independent states adopting democratic constitutions. However, very few of the new democracies established in the ex-colonies survived. The collapse of these democracies, together with the rise of military dictatorships in Latin America, accounted for the second reverse wave that lasted until 1975.

The Portuguese Revolution of 1974, with the overthrow of the fascist dictatorship of Antonio Salazar and his successor Caetano, marks the beginning of the third wave in the global resurgence of democracy. In the wake of the Portuguese Revolution, the authoritarian dictatorship in neighbouring Spain, which had been established as early as 1936 by General Franco, also crumbled. The third wave saw the redemocratization of a large number of states in Latin America, Asia, and Africa. The single largest ripple in the third wave was the democratization of the formerly communist states of Eastern and Central Europe. In fact, by the mid-1990s, only one-quarter of the world's states could be classified as authoritarian, with the remaining three-quarters being either fully democratic (one-half) or semi-democratic (one-quarter). The regional distribution of these regime types is instructive. Today, the single largest regional bloc of authoritarian regimes remains the Middle East and the Persian Gulf, followed by sub-Saharan Africa and Asia. The most democratic regions are Western Europe, North America, and Australia, followed by sub-Saharan Africa and Latin America. Besides sub-Saharan Africa, the former Eastern bloc of communist states remains the region with the highest number of semi-democracies.

TYPES OF DEMOCRACY: MAJORITARIAN AND CONSENSUS DEMOCRACIES

In his famous address at the battlefield of Gettysburg in the midst of the American Civil War, Abraham Lincoln spoke of democracy as government of the people by the people and for the people. According to Arend Lijphart, a contemporary political scientist, however, this

Table 13.2

Institutional Variable	Majoritarian	Consensual
1. executive power	single party majority	multiparty coalitions
2. executive–legislative relationship	executive dominance	balance of power
3. party system	two-party system	multiparty system
4. electoral system	majoritarian or plurality	PR
5. interest group system	pluralist	corporatism
6. levels of government	unitary	federalism
7. legislative chambers	unicameralism	bicameralism
8. constitutional amendment	by simple majority	by special majority
9. judicial review	no	yes
10. central banks	executive dependent	independent

Source: Arend Lijphart, *Patterns of Democracy—Government Forms and Performance in Thirty-Six Countries* (New Haven and London: Yale University Press, 1999).

definition of democracy raises the question, who exactly should be engaged in the business of governing?[5] In his research, he has found that there are two basic models of modern democracies, each based on a different answer to this question. The first model is the **majoritarian** one, based on the assumption that the majority of the people should be responsible for governing. The second model is the consensual one, which, in contrast, rests on the assumption that government belongs to and must be practised by as many people as possible. These differences are reflected in the institutional design of modern democracies. Whereas the institutional design of majoritarian democracies concentrates political power in the hands of a political majority, that of consensual democracies divides political power among various political groups, encouraging them to practice power sharing. The ten specific institutional differences that Lijphart found to define the two models of democracy are summarized in Table 13.2.

THEORIES OF DEMOCRATIZATION AND DEMOCRATIC CONSOLIDATION

One of the central questions examined by students of democracy concerns the emergence and stabilization of democratic regimes. In this section we will review theories representing three contending perspectives on democratization: the modernization, the rational choice, and the structural schools.

In what has become the classic piece on democratization in the modernization school, Seymour Martin Lipset argued that "the more well-to-do a nation, the greater the chances that it will sustain democracy."[6] Lipset's finding was based on the correlations that he had established between various indices measuring the socio-economic development of states and the stability of their democracies. The indices that he used to measure the degree of modernization were per capita income, the number of telephones per 1000 individuals, the percentage of the male population employed in agriculture, percentage of the population

DEMOCRACY AND ITS VARIANTS

While Lijphart categorizes democracies on the basis of their institutional differences, political scientists have also identified a number of other differences among democratic regimes. The following list provides a quick overview of the different kinds of democracies:

Consensus democracy   Type of democracy that emphasizes the dispersal of political power.

Delegative democracy   A type of democracy in which those elected to office enjoy unconstrained abilities to govern without regard to their electoral promises or popular needs and demands.

Deliberative democracy   An ideal type of democracy in which collectively rational outcomes emerge as the consensus of free, independent, and self-enforcing exchange of ideas among rational individuals.

Direct democracy   A type of democracy in which political decisions are made by the direct participation of the people. On occasion, even **representative democracies** resort to methods of direct democracy. For instance, a plebiscite is an example of the use of direct democracy.

Procedural view of democracy   The view according to which the establishment of particular institutions is sufficient for a regime to be classified as a democracy. At a minimum these institutions are multiparty competition, universal franchise, and constitutional guarantees of social and political rights and liberties.

Social democracy   The type of democracy that emphasizes the importance of collective as opposed to individual rights and development.

---

living in metropolitan areas, and the percentage of literate people. Except for the agricultural male labour force, higher values in each of these indices were taken as a reflection of a greater degree of modernization.

Lipset found that the stable democracies of Europe, as well as the English-speaking world, including Canada, Australia, and the United States, were all highly modernized, while a sample of unstable European democracies and dictatorships showed much lower degrees of modernization. Lipset also extended his analysis to Latin American states and found a strong correlation between the decline in the level of modernization and the stability of the dictatorships in the region.

In contrast to the modernization school, the structural approach has emphasized the importance of long-term historical developments in the domestic and transitional structures of power in accounting for democratization. In a classic work of this school of thought, Barrington Moore argued that "the route to modernity" has proceeded via three historical routes of political development: a bourgeois *revolution* leading to democracy; a *revolution from above* leading to authoritarian dictatorship; and a *peasant revolution* leading to state socialism and communism.[7] Moore's model identifies three variables that affect which of the three routes the state would follow: the economic positions of the landed aristocracy and its attributes and responses to the commercialization of agriculture; the political strength of the bourgeoisie; and the fate of the peasantry.

The historical route to democracy was characterized by a strong and well-organized bourgeoisie, the commercial and industrial middle class, which managed to break the political power of the landed elites via bourgeois revolution. An important condition of the success of the bourgeois revolution was the adaptation of the landed aristocracy to the market incentives created by the commercialization of agriculture. Therefore, the aristocracy would form a coalition with the rising and successful bourgeoisie. According to Barrington Moore, this was the general story that explained the historical development of democracy in England, France, and even the United States. However, in states where the commercialization of agriculture failed to result in the appropriate changes in the attitude and strategy of the landed aristocracy, and where the bourgeoisie remained weak and under-organized, the route to democracy was blocked in favour of more authoritarian solutions. In such cases the aristocracy was not interested in transforming the peasantry into commodified labour. Instead, it relied on the coercive apparatus of the state to extract more revenue from them. The ruling social coalition that emerged in these states was that between the conservative aristocracy and the bourgeoisie against the peasants and workers. Due to its weakness, the bourgeoisie also relied on the coercion of the state to oppress workers in order to increase its own revenue extraction. Germany in the nineteenth century is an example of this scenario of class coalitions preventing the development of stable democracy.

A more recent structural explanation of democratization has been provided by Rueschmeyer et al.[8] Like Barrington Moore, they identify changes in the dynamics of class struggle and class power as the critical variables promoting or hindering democratization. However, unlike Moore, Rueschmeyer et al. identify five classes with different interests and attitudes toward democracy. According to their explanation, democratization is the result of the formation of a winning coalition, or alliance, among the pro-democracy classes.

According to Rueschmeyer et al. the class most hostile to democracy has been the landed aristocracy, or the landlord class, because of its dependence on cheap labour. The landlord class has traditionally feared democratization because democracy implied an improvement in the bargaining position of rural workers and labourers. For precisely the opposite reasons, the peasantry and small farmers have been in favour of democratization; however, except for rural labourers on large plantations and haciendas, they were traditionally poorly organized. Rueschmeyer et al. identify the urban working class as the pivotal actor in the struggle for democracy. The industrial proletariat has been traditionally interested in the expansion of political and civil rights and freedoms in order to increase its bargaining position vis-à-vis its employers. Unlike the peasantry, the urban working classes were well organized due to their concentration at the factory site. The authors also note the importance of two other classes, each of which is characterized by ambiguous positions toward democratization: the urban bourgeoisie and the salaried middle class.

Besides domestic class coalitions, Rueschmeyer et al. also emphasize the importance of state power and the impact of transnational developments. With regard to the former, they find that a state that is too autonomous and independent of society, or one that is captured by any particular class coalition, slows democratization. In the first case, the state itself may become too oppressive and may develop a vested interest in restricting the growth of democratic freedoms. In the latter scenario, a given coalition may use the state apparatus to restrict expansion of democratic rights to other classes in order to maintain its own dominant position.

Among transitional influences, Rueschmeyer et al. draw particular attention to the patterns of geopolitical dependence, war, and ideational flows across boundaries. Geopolitical dependence may hinder democratization by strengthening and militarizing the state, while economic dependence may hinder democratization by delaying industrialization. War may have a positive impact on democratization through both the domestic mobilization of hitherto repressed classes, who are assumed to be interested in the expansion of democratic rights, and the foreign imposition of democratic regimes by the winners of the war. Indeed, due to both reasons, substantial democratization took place in continental Europe following both world wars.

The rational choice approach to democratization has explored how the strategic choices by leaders of the opposition and the incumbent authoritarian regime equilibrate to produce a transition to democracy. In contrast to both previous approaches, the rational choice approach seeks to understand how an agreement on democracy becomes an equilibrium in the interaction between the authoritarian leader and the reformers. Drawing on the general insight of game theory, the rational choice perspective on democratization has identified the importance of the leaders in charge of the incumbent elite and the opposition elite, their preferences, and the payoffs they associate with the particular outcomes that their chosen strategies yield.

In this section, we have reviewed alternative definitions of democracy and various approaches to understanding the process of democratization. However, it is important to note that the emphasis has been on understanding democracy as a particular way of organizing politics and not on defining it by the political and policy outcomes it produces. The central lesson of the chapter is to remind us of the diversity of ways in which democracy has emerged as an equilibrium at different times and in different parts of the world.

DEMOCRACY AROUND THE WORLD TODAY

Freedom House, a major think-tank devoted to the cross-national and inter-temporal study of democracy around the world, has built a large database about the degree of democratic rights in all states in the world. Every year the organization ranks states in terms of how free and fair their electoral and political processes are as well as the general state of tolerance toward citizens' use of their civil rights and freedoms, such as free speech, freedoms of association etc. The ranking is done on a 7-point scale, with 1 indicating maximum the freest and 7 the least-free conditions in both the political and civil freedoms categories. Based on the country scores for 2005, we can compare the state of democratic freedoms across the major regions of the world today, as Table 13.3 shows.

Clearly, political and civil rights are closely correlated: those regions where political freedoms flourish are also characterized by high degrees of freedoms in terms of civil rights. Conversely, where political freedoms are limited, civil rights are also curtailed. Nonetheless, you should notice that even though the states of post-communist Eastern Europe and the former Soviet Union have a lower degree of political freedoms than Sub-Saharan Africa, they do provide a slightly greater extent of civil rights to their citizens. Overall, the most extensive freedoms are found in Western Europe, followed by the Americas, while the Middle East is the least-free region in the world today.

Table 13.3 **POLITICAL FREEDOMS AND CIVIL RIGHTS AROUND THE WORLD**

Regions	Political Rights	Civil Liberties
Western Europe	1.06	1.10
Americas	2.56	2.72
Asia	4.08	4.04
Sub-Saharan Africa	4.43	4.14
Post-Soviet and Eastern Europe	4.65	4.06
Middle East	5.54	5.18

Of course, the regional figures are only averages that conceal a tremendous amount of variation with each geographically defined area. In order to provide a more detailed snapshot view of the distribution of freedoms around the world in 2005, take look at Table 13.4, which sorts all states of the world in three categories: free, partly free, and not free, based on the combined average score that the state gets on both the political freedoms and the civil rights measure.

Table 13.4   POLITICAL AND CIVIL RIGHTS AND FREEDOMS IN THE STATES OF THE WORLD, 2005

Free	Partly Free	Not Free
Andorra	Albania	Afghanistan
Australia	Bolivia	Algeria
Austria	East Timor	Angola
Bahamas	Ecuador	Azerbaijan
Barbados	Honduras	Bhutan
Belgium	Kenya	Brunei
Canada	Macedonia	Cambodia
Cape Verde	Madagascar	Central African Republic
Chile	Nicaragua	Chad
Costa Rica	Niger	Egypt
Cyprus (Greek)	Papua New Guinea	Guinea
Czech Republic	Paraguay	Kazakhstan
Denmark	Seychelles	Kyrgyzstan
Dominica	Solomon Islands	Lebanon
Estonia	Sri Lanka	Maldives
Finland	Trinidad & Tobago	Mauritania
France	Turkey	Oman
Germany	Georgia	Pakistan
Hungary	Indonesia	Qatar
Iceland	Moldova	Russia
Ireland	Mozambique	Rwanda
Italy	Venezuela	Tajikistan
Kiribati	Bosnia-Herzegovina	Togo
Liechtenstein	Fiji	Tunisia
Luxembourg	Sierra Leone	Cameroon
Malta	Tanzania	Congo (Kinshasa)
Marshall Islands	Ukraine	Cote d'Ivoire

Table 13.4 **continued**

Free	Partly Free	Not Free
Mauritius	Bangladesh	Iran
Micronesia	Colombia	United Arab Emirates
Nauru	Comoros	Somalia
Netherlands	Gambia, The	Iraq
New Zealand	Guatemala	Swaziland
Norway	Guinea-Bissau	Belarus
Palau	Malawi	China
Poland	Malaysia	Equatorial Guinea
Portugal	Nigeria	Eritrea
San Marino	Zambia	Haiti
Slovakia	Kuwait	Laos
Slovenia	Tonga	Uzbekistan
Spain	Armenia	Vietnam
Sweden	Burkina Faso	Zimbabwe
Switzerland	Congo (Brazzaville)	Burma
Tuvalu	Gabon	Cuba
United Kingdom	Jordan	Libya
United States	Liberia	North Korea
Uruguay	Morocco	Saudi Arabia
Belize	Singapore	Sudan
Bulgaria	Uganda	Syria
Greece	Bahrain	Turkmenistan
Grenada	Burundi	
Japan	Djibouti	
Latvia	Ethiopia	
Panama	Nepal	
South Africa	Yemen	
South Korea		
St. Kitts & Nevis		
St. Lucia		
Suriname		
Israel		

continued

Table 13.4   **continued**

Free	Partly Free	Not Free
Monaco		
St. Vincent & Grenadines		
Taiwan		
Antigua & Barbuda		
Argentina		
Benin		
Botswana		
Croatia		
Dominican Republic		
Ghana		
Guyana		
Lithuania		
Mali		
Mexico		
Mongolia		
Samoa		
Sao Tome & Principe		
Vanuatu		
Brazil		
El Salvador		
India		
Jamaica		
Lesotho		
Namibia		
Peru		
Philippines		
Senegal		
Thailand		
Romania		
Serbia & Montenegro		

ENDNOTES

1. Samuel Huntington, *The Third Wave: Democratization in the Late Twentieth Century* (Norman: University of Oklahoma Press, 1991).
2. Robert Dahl, *Polyarchy: Participation and Opposition* (New Haven: Yale University Press, 1971).
3. Adam Przeworski, *Democracy and the Market: Political and Economic Reforms in Eastern Europe and Latin America* (Cambridge, MA: Cambridge University Press, 1991).
4. Huntington, *The Third Wave*.
5. Arend Lijphart, *Democracy in Plural Societies: A Comparative Exploration* (Greensboro, NC: Empire Books, 1977).
6. Seymour Martin Lipset, "Some Social Requisites of Democracy: Economic Development and Political Legitimacy," *American Political Science Review*, Vol. 53, No. 1 (March 1959), pp. 69–105.
7. Barrington Moore, *Social Origins of Dictatorship and Democracy: Lord and Peasant in the Making of the Modern World* (Boston: Beacon Press, 1966).
8. Dietrich Rueschemeyer, Marilyn Rueschemeyer, and Bjorn Wittrock (eds.), *Participation and Democracy East and West* (Armonk, NY: M.E. Sharpe, 1998).

READINGS

We have examined the different ways and historical routes in which democracy has been established in the modern world. We have noted, in particular, that the Third Wave has resulted in an unprecedented increase in the number of democratic regimes in the world. The following readings provide two arguments about democratization and the future of democracy in the current era. The readings are complementary, in that both define democracy as **liberal democracy**; however, they are different in their respective theoretical and analytical foci. In the first excerpt, Francis Fukuyama presents a much-debated argument that the political victory of democracy over its ideological rivals in the twentieth century marks the last stage of the political evolution of mankind—in fact, the end of history. Similarly, Samuel Huntington also views democratization as progress in the second excerpt. In contrast to Fukuyama's philosophical approach, Huntington looks at the root causes of democratization at the level of individual political actors and factions.

Fukuyama adopts a Hegelian view of history in arguing that changes in the material conditions of mankind reflect and are themselves the causes of ideational processes. This suggests that the material progress of the Western world is itself the reflection of an ideational progress, specifically the emergence and triumph of liberal democracy over other ideological contenders, specifically communism and fascism. Fukuyama is conscious of the possible future challenges that religious fundamentalism and nationalism may pose to liberal democracy; however, he does not see much in these challenges that liberalism cannot deal with and resolve. Since liberal democracy marks the end of the evolution of mankind in terms of political ideology, it also marks the end of history in terms of Hegelian philosophy. Fukuyama ends his piece on a bitter note, predicting that the "end of history will be a very sad time" for art and philosophy as narrow economic calculations and technical problem solving will be mankind's primary concerns.

In the second reading, Huntington argues that the transition to democracy in the Third Wave took place in different ways in different countries, depending on the strategies of the actors that were involved in and led the process. In particular, he distinguishes five different groups of actors that have played a role in democratization: the standpatters, the liberal reformers, and the democratic reformers on the part of the ruling elite; and the democratic moderates and revolutionary extremists on the part of the opposition. Depending on which of these actors led the process, Huntington identifies three types of transition in the Third Wave: transformation, replacement, and transplacement. This reading helps us understand how the preferences of and strategic interactions among political actors shape the outcome of democratization. In contrast to structural theories of democratization, this perspective emphasizes the important role of human agency. Huntington's analysis rests on the assumption that individual political actors seek to advance their own political gains; the different types of transitions represent different equilibria of the strategic choices that the respective actors have made.

THE END OF HISTORY?

Francis Fukuyama

In watching the flow of events over the past decade or so, it is hard to avoid the feeling that something very fundamental has happened in world history. The past year has seen a flood of articles commemorating the end of the Cold War, and the fact that "peace" seems to be breaking out in many regions of the world. Most of these analyses lack any larger conceptual framework for distinguishing between what is essential and what is contingent or accidental in world history, and are predictably superficial. If Mr. Gorbachev were ousted from the Kremlin or a new Ayatollah proclaimed the millennium for a desolate Middle Eastern capital, these same commentators would scramble to announce the rebirth of a new era of conflict.

And yet, all of these people sense dimly that there is some larger process at work, a process that gives coherence and order to the daily headlines. The twentieth century saw the developed world descend into a paroxysm of ideological violence, as liberalism contended first with the remnants of absolutism, then bolshevism and fascism, and finally an updated Marxism that threatened to lead to the ultimate apocalypse of nuclear war. But the century that began full of self-confidence in the ultimate triumph of Western liberal democracy seems at its close to be returning full circle to where it started: not to an "end of ideology" or a convergence between capitalism and socialism, as earlier predicted, but to an unabashed victory of economic and political liberalism.

The triumph of the West, of the Western *idea*, is evident first of all in the total exhaustion of viable systematic alternatives to Western liberalism. In the past decade, there have been unmistakable changes in the intellectual climate of the world's two largest communist countries, and the beginnings of significant reform movements in both. But this phenomenon extends beyond high politics and it can be seen also in the ineluctable spread of consumerist Western culture in such diverse contexts as the peasants' markets and color television sets now omnipresent throughout China, the cooperative restaurants and clothing stores opened in the past year in Moscow, the Beethoven piped into Japanese department stores, and the rock music enjoyed alike in Prague, Rangoon, and Tehran.

What we may be witnessing is not just the end of the Cold War, or the passing of a particular period of postwar history, but the end of history as such: that is, the end point of mankind's ideological evolution and the universalization of Western liberal democracy as the final form of human government. This is not to say that there will no longer be events to fill the pages of *Foreign Affairs*'s yearly summaries of international relations, for the victory of liberalism has occurred primarily in the realm of ideas or consciousness and is as yet incomplete in the real or material world. But there are powerful reasons for believing that it is the ideal that will govern the material world *in the long run*. To understand how this is so, we must first consider some theoretical issues concerning the nature of historical change.

I

The notion of the end of history is not an original one. Its best known propagator was Karl Marx, who believed that the direction of historical development was a purposeful one determined by the interplay of material forces, and would come to an end only with the achievement of a communist utopia that would finally resolve all prior contradictions. But the concept of history as a dialectical process with a beginning, a middle, and an end was borrowed by Marx from his great German predecessor Georg Wilhelm Friedrich Hegel.

For better or worse, much of Hegel's historicism has become part of our contemporary intellectual baggage. The notion that mankind has progressed through a series of primitive stages of consciousness on his path to the present, and that these stages corresponded to concrete forms of social organization such as tribal, slave-owning, theocratic, and finally democratic-egalitarian societies, has become inseparable from the modern understanding of man. Hegel was the first philosopher to speak the language of modern social science, insofar as man for him was the product of his concrete historical and social environment and not, as earlier natural right theorists would have it, a collection of more or less fixed "natural" attributes. The mastery and transformation of man's natural environment through the application of science and technology was originally not a Marxist concept, but a Hegelian one. Unlike later historicists whose historical relativism degenerated into relativism *tout court*, however, Hegel believed that history culminated in an absolute moment—a moment in which a final, rational form of society and state became victorious.

It is Hegel's misfortune to be known now primarily as Marx's precursor, and it is our misfortune that few of us are familiar with Hegel's work from direct study, but only as it has been filtered through the distorting lens of Marxism. In France, however, there has been an effort to save Hegel from his Marxist interpreters and to resurrect him as the philosopher who most correctly speaks to our time. Among those modern French interpreters of Hegel, the greatest was certainly Alexandre Kojève, a brilliant Russian emigre who taught a highly influential series of seminars in Paris in the 1930s at the *Ecole Practique des Hautes Etudes*.[1] While largely unknown in the United States, Kojève had a major impact on the intellectual life of the continent. Among his students ranged such future

luminaries as Jean-Paul Sartre on the Left and Raymond Aron on the Right; postwar existentialism borrowed many of its basic categories from Hegel via Kojève.

Kojève sought to resurrect the Hegel of the *Phenomenology of Mind*, the Hegel who proclaimed history to be at an end in 1806. For as early as this Hegel saw in Napoleon's defeat of the Prussian monarchy at the Battle of Jena the victory of the ideals of the French Revolution, and the imminent universalization of the state incorporating the principles of liberty and equality. Kojève, far from rejecting Hegel in light of the turbulent events of the next century and a half, insisted that the latter had been essentially correct.[2] The Battle of Jena marked the end of history because it was at that point that the *vanguard* of humanity (a term quite familiar to Marxists) actualized the *principles* of the French Revolution. While there was considerable work to be done after 1806—abolishing slavery and the slave trade, extending the franchise to workers, women, blacks, and other racial minorities, etc.— the basic *principles* of the liberal democratic state could not be improved upon. The two world wars in this century and their attendant revolutions and upheavals simply had the effect of extending those principles spatially, such that the various provinces of human civilization were brought up to the level of its most advanced outposts, and of forcing those societies in Europe and North America at the vanguard of civilization to implement their liberalism more fully.

The state that emerges at the end of history is liberal insofar as it recognizes and protects through a system of law man's universal right to freedom, and democratic insofar as it exists only with the consent of the governed. For Kojève, this so-called "universal homogenous state" found real-life embodiment in the countries of postwar Western Europe—precisely those flabby, prosperous, self-satisfied, inward-looking, weak-willed states whose grandest project was nothing more heroic than the creation of the Common Market.[3] But this was only to be expected. For human history and the conflict that characterized it was based on the existence of "contradictions": primitive man's quest for mutual recognition, the dialectic of the master and slave, the transformation and mastery of nature, the struggle of the universal recognition of rights, and the dichotomy between proletarian and capitalist. But in the universal homogenous state, all prior contradictions are resolved and all human needs are satisfied. There is no struggle or conflict over "large" issues, and consequently no need for generals or statesmen; what remains is primarily economic activity. And indeed, Kojève's life was consistent with his teaching. Believing that there was no more work for philosophers as well, since Hegel (correctly understood) had already achieved absolute knowledge, Kojève left teaching after the war and spent the remainder of his life working as a bureaucrat in the European Economic Community, until his death in 1968.

To his contemporaries at mid-century, Kojève's proclamation of the end of history must have seemed like the typical eccentric solipsism of a French intellectual, coming as it did on the heels of World War II and at the very height of the Cold War. To comprehend how Kojève could have been so audacious as to assert that history has ended, we must first of all understand the meaning of Hegelian idealism.

II

For Hegel, the contradictions that drive history exist first of all in the realm of human consciousness, i.e. on the level of ideas[4]—not the trivial election year proposals of American politicians, but ideas in the sense of large unifying world views that might best be understood under the rubric of ideology. Ideology in this sense is not restricted to the secular and explicit political doctrines we usually associate with the term, but can include religion, culture, and the complex of moral values underlying any society as well.

Hegel's view of the relationship between the ideal and the real or material worlds was an extremely complicated one, beginning with the fact that for him the distinction between the two was only apparent.[5] He did not believe that the real world conformed or could be made to conform to ideological preconceptions of philosophy professors in any simpleminded way, or that the "material" world could not impinge on the ideal. Indeed, Hegel the professor was temporarily thrown out of work as a result of a very material event, the Battle of Jena. But while Hegel's writing and thinking could be stopped by a bullet from the material world, the hand on the trigger of the gun was motivated in turn by the ideas of liberty and equality that had driven the French Revolution.

For Hegel, all human behavior in the material world, and hence all human history, is rooted in a prior state of consciousness—an idea similar to the one expressed by John Maynard Keynes when he said that the views of men of affairs were usually derived from defunct economists and academic scribblers of earlier generations. This consciousness may not be explicit and self-aware, as are modern political doctrines, but may rather take the form of religion or simple cultural or moral habits. And yet this realm of consciousness *in the long run* necessarily becomes manifest in the material world, indeed creates the material world in its own image. Consciousness is cause and not effect, and can develop autonomously from the material world; hence the real subtext underlying the apparent jumble of current events is the history of ideology.

Hegel's idealism has fared poorly at the hands of later thinkers. Marx reversed the priority of the real and the ideal completely, relegating the entire realm of consciousness—religion, art, culture, philosophy itself—to a "superstructure" that was determined entirely by the prevailing material mode of production. Yet another unfortunate legacy of Marxism is our tendency to retreat into materialist or utilitarian explanations of political or historical phenomena, and our disinclination to believe in the autonomous power of ideas. A recent example of this is Paul Kennedy's hugely successful *The Rise and Fall of the Great Powers*, which ascribes the decline of great powers to simple economic overextension. Obviously, this is true on some level: an empire whose economy is barely above the level of subsistence cannot bankrupt its treasury indefinitely. But whether a highly productive modern industrial society chooses to spend 3 or 7 percent of its GNP on defense rather than consumption is entirely a matter of that society's political priorities, which are in turn determined in the realm of consciousness.

The materialist bias of modern thought is characteristic not only of people on the Left who may be sympathetic to Marxism, but of many passionate anti-Marxists as well. Indeed, there is on the Right what one might label the *Wall Street Journal* school of deterministic materialism that discounts the importance of ideology and culture and sees man as essentially a rational, profit-maximizing individual. It is precisely this kind of individual and his pursuit of material incentives that is posited as the basis for economic life as such in economic textbooks.[6] One small example will illustrate the problematic character of such materialist views.

Max Weber begins his famous book, *The Protestant Ethic and the Spirit of Capitalism,* by noting the different economic performance of Protestant and Catholic communities throughout Europe and America, summed up in the proverb that Protestants eat well while Catholics sleep well. Weber notes that according to any economic theory that posited man as a rational profit-maximizer, raising the piece-work rate should increase labor productivity. But in fact, in many traditional peasant communities, raising the piece-work rate actually had the opposite effect of *lowering* labor productivity: at the higher rate, a peasant accustomed to earning two and one-half marks per day found he could earn the same amount by working less, and did so because he valued leisure more than income. The choices of leisure over income, or of the militaristic life of the Spartan hoplite over the wealth of the Athenian trader, or even the ascetic life of the early capitalist entrepreneur over that of a traditional leisured aristocrat, cannot possibly be explained by the impersonal working of material forces, but come preeminently out of the sphere of consciousness—what we have labeled here broadly as ideology. And indeed, a central theme of Weber's work was to prove that contrary to Marx, the material mode of production, far from being the "base," was itself a "superstructure" with roots in religion and culture, and that to understand the emergence of modern capitalism and the profit motive one had to study their antecedents in the realm of the spirit.

As we look around the contemporary world, the poverty of materialist theories of economic development is all too apparent. The *Wall Street Journal* school of deterministic materialism habitually points to the stunning economic success of Asia in the past few decades as evidence of the viability of free market economics, with the implication that all societies would see similar development were they simply to allow their populations to pursue their material self-interest freely. Surely free markets and stable political systems are a necessary precondition to capitalist economic growth. But just as surely the cultural heritage of those Far Eastern societies, the ethic of work and saving and family, a religious heritage that does not, like Islam, place restrictions on certain forms of economic behavior, and other deeply ingrained moral qualities, are equally important in explaining their economic performance.[7] And yet the intellectual weight of

materialism is such that not a single respectable contemporary theory of economic development addresses consciousness and culture seriously as the matrix within which economic behavior is formed.

Failure to understand that the roots of economic behavior lie in the realm of consciousness and culture leads to the common mistake of attributing material causes to phenomena that are essentially ideal in nature. For example, it is commonplace in the West to interpret the reform movements first in China and most recently in the Soviet Union as the victory of the material over the ideal—that is, a recognition that ideological incentives could not replace material ones in stimulating a highly productive modern economy, and that if one wanted to prosper one had to appeal to baser forms of self-interest. But the deep defects of socialist economies were evident thirty or forty years ago to anyone who chose to look. Why was it that these countries moved away from central planning in the 1980s? The answer must be found in the consciousness of the elites and leaders ruling them, who decided to opt for the "Protestant" life of wealth and risk over the "Catholic" path of poverty and security.[8] That change was in no way made inevitable by the material conditions in which either country found itself on the eve of the reform, but instead came about as the result of the victory of one idea over another.[9]

For Kojève, as for all good Hegelians, understanding the underlying processes of history requires understanding developments in the realm of consciousness or ideas, since consciousness will ultimately remake the material world in its own image. To say that history ended in 1806 meant that mankind's ideological evolution ended in the ideals of the French or American Revolutions: while particular regimes in the real world might not implement these ideals fully, their theoretical truth is absolute and could not be improved upon. Hence it did not matter to Kojève that the consciousness of the postwar generation of Europeans had not been universalized throughout the world; if ideological development had in fact ended, the homogenous state would eventually become victorious throughout the material world.

I have neither the space nor, frankly, the ability to defend in depth Hegel's radical idealist perspective. The issue is not whether Hegel's system was right, but whether his perspective might uncover the problematic nature of many materialist explanations we often take for granted. This is not to deny the role of material factors as such. To a literal-minded idealist, human society can be built around any arbitrary set of principles regardless of their relationship to the material world. And in fact men have proven themselves able to endure the most extreme material hardships in the name of ideas that exist in the realm of the spirit alone, be it the divinity of cows or the nature of the Holy Trinity.[10]

But while man's very perception of the material world is shaped by his historical consciousness of it, the material world can clearly affect in return the viability of a particular state of consciousness. In particular, the spectacular abundance of advanced liberal economies and the infinitely diverse consumer culture made possible by them seem to both foster and preserve liberalism in the political sphere. I want to avoid the materialist determinism that says that liberal economics inevitably produces liberal politics, because I believe that both economics and politics presuppose an autonomous prior state of consciousness that makes them possible. But that state of consciousness that permits the growth of liberalism seems to stabilize in the way one would expect at the end of history if it is underwritten by the abundance of a modern free market economy. We might summarize the content of the universal homogenous state as liberal democracy in the political sphere combined with easy access to VCRs and stereos in the economic.

III

Have we in fact reached the end of history? Are there, in other words, any fundamental "contradictions" in human life that cannot be resolved in the context of modern liberalism, that would be resolvable by an alternative political-economic structure? If we accept the idealist premises laid out above, we must seek an answer to this question in the realm of ideology and consciousness. Our task is not to answer exhaustively the challenges to liberalism promoted by every crackpot messiah around the world, but only those that are embodied in important social or political forces and movements, and which are therefore part of world history. For our purposes, it matters very little what strange thoughts occur to people in Albania or Burkina Faso, for we are interested in what one could in some sense call the common ideological heritage of mankind.

In the past century, there have been two major challenges to liberalism, those of fascism and of communism. The former[11] saw the political weakness, materialism, anomie, and lack of community of the West as fundamental contradictions in liberal societies that could only be resolved by a strong state that forged a new "people" on the basis of national exclusiveness. Fascism was destroyed as a living ideology by World War II. This was a defeat, of course, on a very material level, but it amounted to a defeat of the idea as well. What destroyed fascism as an idea was not universal moral revulsion against it, since plenty of people were willing to endorse the idea as long as it seemed the wave of the future, but its lack of success. After the war, it seemed to most people that German fascism as well as its other European and Asian variants were bound to self-destruct. There was no material reason why new fascist movements could not have sprung up again after the war in other locales, but for the fact that expansionist ultranationalism, with its promise of unending conflict leading to disastrous military defeat, had completely lost its appeal. The ruins of the Reich chancellory as well as the atomic bombs dropped on Hiroshima and Nagasaki killed this ideology on the level of consciousness as well as materially, and all of the proto-fascist movements spawned by the German and Japanese examples like the Peronist movement in Argentina or Subhas Chandra Bose's Indian National Army withered after the war.

The ideological challenge mounted by the other great alternative to liberalism, communism, was far more serious. Marx, speaking Hegel's language, asserted that liberal society contained a fundamental contradiction that could not be resolved within its context, that between capital and labor, and this contradiction has constituted the chief accusation against liberalism ever since. But surely, the class issue has actually been successfully resolved in the West. As Kojève (among others) noted, the egalitarianism of modern America represents the essential achievement of the classless society envisioned by Marx. This is not to say that there are not rich people and poor people in the United States, or that the gap between them has not grown in recent years. But the root causes of economic inequality do not have to do with the underlying legal and social structure of our society, which remains fundamentally egalitarian and moderately redistributionist, so much as with the cultural and social characteristics of the groups that make it up, which are in turn the historical legacy of premodern conditions. Thus black poverty in the United States is not the inherent product of liberalism, but is rather the "legacy of slavery and racism" which persisted long after the formal abolition of slavery.

As a result of the receding of the class issue, the appeal of communism in the developed Western world, it is safe to say, is lower today than any time since the end of the First World War. This can be measured in any number of ways: in the declining membership and electoral pull of the major European communist parties, and their overtly revisionist programs; in the corresponding electoral success of conservative parties from Britain and Germany to the United States and Japan, which are unabashedly pro-market and anti-statist; and in an intellectual climate whose most "advanced" members no longer believe that bourgeois society is something that ultimately needs to be overcome. This is not to say that the opinions of progressive intellectuals in Western countries are not deeply pathological in any number of ways. But those who believe that the future must inevitably be socialist tend to be very old, or very marginal to the real political discourse of their societies.

One may argue that the socialist alternative was never terribly plausible for the North Atlantic world, and was sustained for the last several decades primarily by its success outside of this region. But it is precisely in the non-European world that one is most struck by the occurrence of major ideological transformations. Surely the most remarkable changes have occurred in Asia. Due to the strength and adaptability of the indigenous cultures there, Asia became a battleground for a variety of imported Western ideologies early in this century. Liberalism in Asia was a very weak reed in the period after World War I; it is easy today to forget how gloomy Asia's political future looked as recently as ten or fifteen years ago. It is easy to forget as well how momentous the outcome of Asian ideological struggles seemed for world political development as a whole.

The first Asian alternative to liberalism to be decisively defeated was the fascist one represented by Imperial Japan. Japanese fascism (like its German version) was defeated by the force of American arms in the Pacific war, and liberal democracy was imposed on Japan by a victorious United States. Western capitalism and political liberalism when transplanted to Japan were adapted and transformed by the Japanese in such a way as to be scarcely recognizable.[12] Many Americans are now aware that Japanese industrial organization is very different from that prevailing in the United States or Europe, and it is questionable what relationship the factional maneuvering that takes place with the governing Liberal Democratic Party bears to democracy. Nonetheless, the very fact that the essential elements of economic and political liberalism have been so successfully grafted onto uniquely Japanese traditions and institutions guarantees their survival in the long run. More important is the contribution that Japan has made in turn to world history by following in the footsteps of the United States to create a truly universal consumer culture that has become both a symbol and an underpinning of the universal homogenous state. V.S. Naipaul travelling in Khomeini's Iran shortly after the revolution noted the omnipresent signs advertising the products of Sony, Hitachi, and JVC, whose appeal remained virtually irresistible and gave the lie to the regime's pretensions of restoring a state based on the rule of the *Shariah*. Desire for access to the consumer culture, created in large measure by Japan, has played a crucial role in fostering the spread of economic liberalism throughout Asia, and hence in promoting political liberalism as well.

The economic success of the other newly industrializing countries (NICs) in Asia following on the example of Japan is by now a familiar story. What is important from a Hegelian standpoint is that political liberalism has been following economic liberalism, more slowly than many had hoped but with seeming inevitability. Here again we see the victory of the idea of the universal homogenous state. South Korea had developed into a modern, urbanized society with an increasingly large and well-educated middle class that could not possibly be isolated from the larger democratic trends around them. Under these circumstances it seemed intolerable to a large part of this population that it should be ruled by an anachronistic military regime while Japan, only a decade or so ahead in economic terms, had parliamentary institutions for over forty years. Even the former socialist regime in Burma, which for so many decades existed in dismal isolation from the larger trends dominating Asia, was buffeted in the past year by pressures to liberalize both its economy and political system. It is said that unhappiness with strongman Ne Win began when a senior Burmese officer went to Singapore for medical treatment and broke down crying when he saw how far socialist Burma had been left behind by its ASEAN neighbors.

But the power of the liberal idea would seem much less impressive if it had not infected the largest and oldest culture in Asia, China. The simple existence of communist China created an alternative pole of ideological attraction, and as such constituted a threat to liberalism. But the past fifteen years have seen an almost total discrediting of Marxism-Leninism as an economic system. Beginning with the famous third plenum of the Tenth Central Committee in 1978, the Chinese Communist party set about decollectivizing agriculture for the 800 million Chinese who still lived in the countryside. The role of the state in agriculture was reduced to that of a tax collector, while production of consumer goods was sharply increased in order to give peasants a taste of the universal homogenous state and thereby an incentive to work. The reform doubled Chinese grain output in only five years, and in the process created for Deng Xiao-ping a solid political base from which he was able to extend the reform to other parts of the economy. Economic statistics do not begin to describe the dynamism, initiative, and openness evident in China since the reform began.

China could not now be described in any way as a liberal democracy. At present, no more than 20 percent of its economy has been marketized, and most importantly it continues to be ruled by a self-appointed Communist party which has given no hint of wanting to devolve power. Deng has made none of Gorbachev's promises regarding democratization of the political system and there is no Chinese equivalent of *glasnost*. The Chinese leadership has in fact been much more circumspect in criticizing Mao and Maoism than Gorbachev with respect to Brezhnev and Stalin, and the regime continues to pay lip service to Marxism-Leninism as its ideological underpinning. But anyone familiar with the outlook and behavior of the new technocratic elite now governing China knows that Marxism and ideological principles have become virtually irrelevant as guides to policy, and that bourgeois consumerism has a real meaning in that country for the first time since the revolution. The various slowdowns in the pace of

reform, the campaigns against "spiritual pollution" and crackdowns on political dissent are more properly seen as tactical adjustments made in the process of managing what is an extraordinarily difficult political transition. By ducking the question of political reform while putting the economy on a new footing, Deng has managed to avoid the breakdown of authority that has accompanied Gorbachev's *perestroika*. Yet the pull of the liberal idea continues to be very strong as economic power devolves and the economy becomes more open to the outside world. There are currently over 20,000 Chinese students studying in the U.S. and other Western countries, almost all of them children of the Chinese elite. It is hard to believe that when they return home to run the country they will be content for China to be the only country in Asia unaffected by the larger democratizing trend. The student demonstrations in Beijing that broke out first in December 1986 and recurred recently on the occasion of Hu Yao-bang's death were only the beginning of what will inevitably be mounting pressure for change in the political system as well.

What is important about China from the standpoint of world history is not the present state of the reform or even its future prospects. The central issue is the fact that the People's Republic of China can no longer act as a beacon for illiberal forces around the world, whether they be guerrillas in some Asian jungle or middle class students in Paris. Maoism, rather than being the pattern for Asia's future, became an anachronism, and it was the mainland Chinese who in fact were decisively influenced by the prosperity and dynamism of their overseas co-ethnics—the ironic ultimate victory of Taiwan.

Important as these changes in China have been, however, it is developments in the Soviet Union—the original "homeland of the world proletariat"—that have put the final nail in the coffin of the Marxist-Leninist alternative to liberal democracy. It should be clear that in terms of formal institutions, not much has changed in the four years since Gorbachev has come to power: free markets and the cooperative movement represent only a small part of the Soviet economy, which remains centrally planned; the political system is still dominated by the Communist party, which has only begun to democratize internally and to share power with other groups; the regime continues to assert that it is seeking only to modernize socialism and that its ideological basis remains Marxism-Leninism; and, finally, Gorbachev faces a potentially powerful conservative opposition that could undo many of the changes that have taken place to date. Moreover, it is hard to be too sanguine about the chances for success of Gorbachev's proposed reforms, either in the sphere of economics or politics. But my purpose here is not to analyze events in the short-term, or to make predictions for policy purposes, but to look at underlying trends in the sphere of ideology and consciousness. And in that respect, it is clear that an astounding transformation has occurred.

Emigres from the Soviet Union have been reporting for at least the last generation now that virtually nobody in that country truly believes in Marxism-Leninism any longer, and that this was nowhere more true than in the Soviet elite, which continued to mouth Marxist slogans out of sheer cynicism. The corruption and decadence of the late Brezhnev-era Soviet state seemed to matter little, however, for as long as the state itself refused to throw into question any of the fundamental principles underlying Soviet society, the system was capable of functioning adequately out of sheer inertia and could even muster some dynamism in the realm of foreign and defense policy. Marxism-Leninism was like a magical incantation which, however absurd and devoid of meaning, was the only common basis on which the elite could agree to rule Soviet society.

What has happened in the four years since Gorbachev's coming to power is a revolutionary assault on the most fundamental institutions and principles of Stalinism, and their replacement by other principles which do not amount to liberalism *per se* but whose only connecting thread is liberalism. This is most evident in the economic sphere, where the reform economists around Gorbachev have become steadily more radical in their support for free markets, to the point where some like Nikolai Shmelev do not mind being compared in public to Milton Friedman. There is a virtual consensus among the currently dominant school of Soviet economists now that central planning and the command system of allocation are the root cause of economic inefficiency, and that if the Soviet system is ever to heal itself, it must permit free and decentralized decision-making with respect to investment, labor, and prices. After a couple of initial years of ideological confusion, these principles have finally been incorporated into policy with the promulgation of new laws on enterprise autonomy, cooperatives, and finally in 1988 on lease arrangements and family farming. There are, of course, a number of fatal flaws in the current implementation of the reform, most notably the absence of a thorough-going price reform. But the problem is no longer a *conceptual* one: Gorbachev and his lieutenants seem to understand the economic logic of marketization well enough, but like the leaders of a Third World country facing the IMF, are afraid of the social consequences of ending consumer subsidies and other forms of dependence on the state sector.

In the political sphere, the proposed changes to the Soviet constitution, legal system, and party rules amount to much less than the establishment of a liberal state. Gorbachev has spoken of democratization primarily in the sphere of internal party affairs, and has shown little intention of ending the Communist party's monopoly of power; indeed, the political reform seeks to legitimize and therefore strengthen the CPSU's rule.[13] Nonetheless, the general principles underlying many of the reforms—that the "people" should be truly responsible for their own affairs, that higher political bodies should be answerable to lower ones, and not vice versa, that the rule of law should prevail over arbitrary police actions, with separation of powers and an independent judiciary, that there should be legal protection for property rights, the need for open discussion of public issues and the right of public dissent, the empowering of the Soviets as a forum in which the whole Soviet people can participate, and of a political culture that is more tolerant and pluralistic—come from a source fundamentally alien to the USSR's Marxist-Leninist tradition, even if they are incompletely articulated and poorly implemented in practice.

Gorbachev's repeated assertions that he is doing no more than trying to restore the original meaning of Leninism are themselves a kind of Orwellian doublespeak. Gorbachev and his allies have consistently maintained that intraparty democracy was somehow the essence of Leninism, and that the various liberal practices of open debate, secret ballot elections, and rule of law were all part of the Leninist heritage, corrupted only later by Stalin. While almost anyone would look good compared to Stalin, drawing so sharp a line between Lenin and his successor is questionable. The essence of Lenin's democratic centralism was centralism, not democracy; that is, the absolutely rigid, monolithic, and disciplined dictatorship of a hierarchically organized vanguard Communist party, speaking in the name of the *demos*. All of Lenin's vicious polemics against Karl Kautsky, Rosa Luxemburg, and various other Menshevik and Social Democratic rivals, not to mention his contempt for "bourgeois legality" and freedoms, centered around his profound conviction that a revolution could not be successfully made by a democratically run organization.

Gorbachev's claim that he is seeking to return to the true Lenin is perfectly easy to understand: having fostered a thorough denunciation of Stalinism and Brezhnevism as the root of the USSR's present predicament, he needs some point in Soviet history on which to anchor the legitimacy of the CPSU's continued rule. But Gorbachev's tactical requirements should not blind us to the fact that the democratizing and decentralizing principles which he has enunciated in both the economic and political spheres are highly subversive of some of the most fundamental precepts of both Marxism and Leninism. Indeed, if the bulk of the present economic reform proposals were put into effect, it is hard to know how the Soviet economy would be more socialist than those of other Western countries with large public sectors.

The Soviet Union could in no way be described as a liberal or democratic country now, nor do I think that it is terribly likely that *perestroika* will succeed such that the label will be thinkable any time in the near future. But at the end of history it is not necessary that all societies become successful liberal societies, merely that they end their ideological pretensions of representing different and higher forms of human society. And in this respect I believe that something very important has happened in the Soviet Union in the past few years: the criticisms of the Soviet system sanctioned by Gorbachev have been so thorough and devastating that there is very little chance of going back to either Stalinism or Brezhnevism in any simple way. Gorbachev has finally permitted people to say what they had privately understood for many years, namely, that the magical incantations of Marxism-Leninism were nonsense, that Soviet socialism was not superior to the West in any respect but was in fact a monumental failure. The conservative opposition in

the USSR, consisting both of simple workers afraid of unemployment and inflation and of party officials fearful of losing their jobs and privileges, is outspoken and may be strong enough to force Gorbachev's ouster in the next few years. But what both groups desire is tradition, order, and authority; they manifest no deep commitment to Marxism-Leninism, except insofar as they have invested much of their own lives in it.[14] For authority to be restored in the Soviet Union after Gorbachev's demolition work, it must be on the basis of some new and vigorous ideology which has not yet appeared on the horizon.

If we admit for the moment that the fascist and communist challenges to liberalism are dead, are there any other ideological competitors left? Or put another way, are there contradictions in liberal society beyond that of class that are not resolvable? Two possibilities suggest themselves, those of religion and nationalism.

The rise of religious fundamentalism in recent years within the Christian, Jewish, and Muslim traditions has been widely noted. One is inclined to say that the revival of religion in some way attests to a broad unhappiness with the impersonality and spiritual vacuity of liberal consumerist societies. Yet while the emptiness at the core of liberalism is most certainly a defect in the ideology—indeed, a flaw that one does not need the perspective of religion to recognize[15]—it is not at all clear that it is remediable through politics. Modern liberalism itself was historically a consequence of the weakness of religiously-based societies which, failing to agree on the nature of the good life, could not provide even the minimal preconditions of peace and stability. In the contemporary world only Islam has offered a theocratic state as a political alternative to both liberalism and communism. But the doctrine has little appeal for non-Muslims, and it is hard to believe that the movement will take on any universal significance. Other less organized religious impulses have been successfully satisfied within the sphere of personal life that is permitted in liberal societies.

The other major "contradiction" potentially unresolvable by liberalism is the one posed by nationalism and other forms of racial and ethnic consciousness. It is certainly true that a very large degree of conflict since the Battle of Jena has had its roots in nationalism. Two cataclysmic world wars in this century have been spawned by the nationalism of the developed world in various guises, and if those passions have been muted to a certain extent in postwar Europe, they are still extremely powerful in the Third World. Nationalism has been a threat to liberalism historically in Germany, and continues to be one in isolated parts of "post-historical" Europe like Northern Ireland.

But it is not clear that nationalism represents an irreconcilable contradiction in the heart of liberalism. In the first place, nationalism is not one single phenomenon but several, ranging from mild cultural nostalgia to the highly organized and elaborately articulated doctrine of National Socialism. Only systematic nationalism of the latter sort can qualify as a formal ideology on the level of liberalism or communism. The vast majority of the world's nationalist movements do not have a political program beyond the negative desire of independence *from* some other group or people, and do not offer anything like a comprehensive agenda for socio-economic organization. As such, they are compatible with doctrines and ideologies that do offer such agendas. While they may constitute a source of conflict for liberal societies, this conflict does not arise from liberalism itself so much as from the fact that the liberalism in question is incomplete. Certainly a great deal of the world's ethnic and nationalist tension can be explained in terms of peoples who are forced to live in unrepresentative political systems that they have not chosen.

While it is impossible to rule out the sudden appearance of new ideologies or previously unrecognized contradictions in liberal societies, then, the present world seems to confirm that the fundamental principles of socio-political organization have not advanced terribly far since 1806. Many of the wars and revolutions fought since that time have been undertaken in the name of ideologies which claimed to be more advanced than liberalism, but whose pretensions were ultimately unmasked by history. In the meantime, they have helped to spread the universal homogenous state to the point where it could have a significant effect on the overall character of international relations.

IV

What are the implications of the end of history for international relations? Clearly, the vast bulk of the Third World remains very much mired in history, and will be a terrain of conflict for many years to come. But let us focus for the time being on the larger and more developed states of the world who after all account for the greater part of world politics. Russia and China are not likely to join the developed nations of the West as liberal societies any time in the foreseeable future, but suppose for a moment that Marxism-Leninism ceases to be a factor driving the foreign policies of these states—a prospect which, if not yet here, the last few years have made a real possibility. How will the overall characteristics of a de-ideologized world differ from those of the one with which we are familiar at such a hypothetical juncture?

The most common answer is—not very much. For there is a very widespread belief among many observers of international relations that underneath the skin of ideology is a hard core of great power national interest that guarantees a fairly high level of competition and conflict between nations. Indeed, according to one academically popular school of international relations theory, conflict inheres in the international system as such, and to understand the prospects for conflict one must look at the shape of the system—for example, whether it is bipolar or multipolar—rather than at the specific character of the nations and regimes that constitute it. This school in effect applies a Hobbesian view of politics to international relations, and assumes that aggression and insecurity are universal characteristics of human societies rather than the product of specific historical circumstances.

Believers in this line of thought take the relations that existed between the participants in the classical nineteenth-century European balance of power as a model for what a de-ideologized contemporary world would look like. Charles Krauthammer, for example, recently explained that if as a result of Gorbachev's reforms the USSR is shorn of Marxist-Leninist ideology, its behavior will revert to that of nineteenth century imperial Russia.[16] While he finds this more reassuring than the threat posed by a communist Russia, he implies that there will still be a substantial degree of competition and conflict in the international system, just as there was say between Russia and Britain or Wilhelmine Germany in the last century. This is, of course, a convenient point of view for people who want to admit that something major is changing in the Soviet Union, but do not want to accept responsibility for recommending the radical policy redirection implicit in such a view. But is it true?

In fact, the notion that ideology is a super-structure imposed on a substratum of permanent great power interest is a highly questionable proposition. For the way in which any state defines its national interest is not universal but rests on some kind of prior ideological basis, just as we saw that economic behavior is determined by a prior state of consciousness. In this century, states have adopted highly articulated doctrines with explicit foreign policy agendas legitimizing expansionism, like Marxism-Leninism or National Socialism.

The expansionist and competitive behavior of nineteenth-century European states rested on no less ideal a basis; it just so happened that the ideology driving it was less explicit than the doctrines of the twentieth century. For one thing, most "liberal" European societies were illiberal insofar as they believed in the legitimacy of imperialism, that is, the right of one nation to rule over other nations without regard for the wishes of the ruled. The justifications for imperialism varied from nation to nation, from a crude belief in the legitimacy of force, particularly when applied to non-Europeans, to the White Man's Burden and Europe's Christianizing mission, to the desire to give people of color access to the culture of Rabelais and Molière. But whatever the particular ideological basis, every "developed" country believed in the acceptability of higher civilizations ruling lower ones—including, incidentally, the United States with regard to the Philippines. This led to a drive for pure territorial aggrandizement in the latter half of the century and played no small role in causing the Great War.

The radical and deformed outgrowth of nineteenth-century imperialism was German fascism, an ideology which justified Germany's right not only to rule over non-European peoples, but over *all* non-German ones. But in retrospect it seems that Hitler represented a diseased bypath in the general course of European development, and since his fiery defeat, the legitimacy of any kind of territorial aggrandizement has been thoroughly discredited.[17] Since the Second World War, European nationalism has been defanged and shorn of any real relevance to foreign policy, with the consequence that the nineteenth-century model of great power behavior has become a serious anachronism. The most extreme form of nationalism that any Western European state has mustered since 1945 has been Gaullism, whose self-assertion has been confined largely to the realm of nuisance politics and culture. International life for the part of the world that has reached the end of history is far more preoccupied with economics than with politics or strategy.

The developed states of the West do maintain defense establishments and in the postwar period have competed vigorously for influence to meet a worldwide communist threat. This behavior has been driven, however, by an external threat from states that possess overtly expansionist ideologies, and would not exist in their absence. To take the "neo-realist" theory seriously, one would have to believe that "natural" competitive behavior would reassert itself among the OECD states were Russia and China to disappear from the face of the earth. That is, West Germany and France would arm themselves against each other as they did in the 1930s, Australia and New Zealand would send military advisers to block each other's advances in Africa, and the U.S.-Canadian border would become fortified. Such a prospect is, of course, ludicrous: minus Marxist-Leninist ideology, we are far more likely to see the "Common Marketization" of world politics than the disintegration of the EEC into nineteenth-century competitiveness. Indeed, as our experience in dealing with Europe on matters such as terrorism or Libya prove, they are much further gone than we down the road that denies the legitimacy of the use of force in international politics, even in self-defense.

The automatic assumption that Russia shorn of its expansionist communist ideology should pick up where the czars left off just prior to the Bolshevik Revolution is therefore a curious one. It assumes that the evolution of human consciousness has stood still in the meantime, and that the Soviets, while picking up currently fashionable ideas in the realm of economics, will return to foreign policy views a century out of date in the rest of Europe. This is certainly not what happened to China after it began its reform process. Chinese competitiveness and expansionism on the world scene have virtually disappeared: Beijing no longer sponsors Maoist insurgencies or tries to cultivate influence in distant African countries as it did in the 1960s. This is not to say that there are no troublesome aspects to contemporary Chinese foreign policy, such as the reckless sale of ballistic missile technology in the Middle East; and the PRC continues to manifest traditional great power behavior in its sponsorship of the Khmer Rouge against Vietnam. But the former is explained by commercial motives and the latter is a vestige of earlier ideologically-based rivalries. The new China far more resembles Gaullist France than pre-World War I Germany.

The real question for the future, however, is the degree to which Soviet elites have assimilated the consciousness of the universal homogenous state that is post-Hitler Europe. From their writings and from my own personal contacts with them, there is no question in my mind that the liberal Soviet intelligentsia rallying around Gorbachev has arrived at the end-of-history view in a remarkably short time, due in no small measure to the contacts they have had since the Brezhnev era with the larger European civilization around them. "New political thinking," the general rubric for their views, describes a world dominated by economic concerns, in which there are no ideological grounds for major conflict between nations, and in which, consequently, the use of military force becomes less legitimate. As Foreign Minister Shevardnadze put it in mid-1988:

> The struggle between two opposing systems is no longer a determining tendency of the present-day era. At the modern stage, the ability to build up material wealth at an accelerated rate on the basis of front-ranking science and high-level techniques and technology, and to distribute it fairly, and through joint efforts to restore and protect the resources necessary for mankind's survival acquires decisive importance.[18]

The post-historical consciousness represented by "new thinking" is only one possible future for the Soviet Union, however. There has always been a very strong current of great Russian chauvinism in the Soviet Union, which has found freer expression since the advent of *glasnost*. It may be possible to return to traditional Marxism-Leninism for a while as a simple rallying point for those who want to restore the authority that Gorbachev has dissipated. But as in Poland, Marxism-Leninism is dead as a mobilizing ideology: under its banner people cannot be made to work harder, and its adherents have lost confidence in themselves. Unlike the propagators of traditional Marxism-Leninism, however, ultranationalists in the USSR believe in their Slavophile cause passionately, and one gets

the sense that the fascist alternative is not one that has played itself out entirely there.

The Soviet Union, then, is at a fork in the road: it can start down the path that was staked out by Western Europe forty-five years ago, a path that most of Asia has followed, or it can realize its own uniqueness and remain stuck in history. The choice it makes will be highly important for us, given the Soviet Union's size and military strength, for that power will continue to preoccupy us and slow our realization that we have already emerged on the other side of history.

V

The passing of Marxism-Leninism first from China and then from the Soviet Union will mean its death as a living ideology of world historical significance. For while there may be some isolated true believers left in places like Managua, Pyongyang, or Cambridge, Massachusetts, the fact that there is not a single large state in which it is a going concern undermines completely its pretensions to being in the vanguard of human history. And the death of this ideology means the growing "Common Marketization" of international relations, and the diminution of the likelihood of large-scale conflict between states.

This does not by any means imply the end of international conflict *per se*. For the world at that point would be divided between a part that was historical and a part that was post-historical. Conflict between states still in history, and between those states and those at the end of history, would still be possible. There would still be a high and perhaps rising level of ethnic and nationalist violence, since those are impulses incompletely played out, even in parts of the post-historical world. Palestinians and Kurds, Sikhs and Tamils, Irish Catholics and Walloons, Armenians and Azeris, will continue to have their unresolved grievances. This implies that terrorism and wars of national liberation will continue to be an important item on the international agenda. But large-scale conflict must involve large states still caught in the grip of history, and they are what appear to be passing from the scene.

The end of history will be a very sad time. The struggle for recognition, the willingness to risk one's life for a purely abstract goal, the worldwide ideological struggle that called forth daring, courage, imagination, and idealism, will be replaced by economic calculation, the endless solving of technical problems, environmental concerns, and the satisfaction of sophisticated consumer demands. In the post-historical period there will be neither art nor philosophy, just the perpetual caretaking of the museum of human history. I can feel in myself, and see in others around me, a powerful nostalgia for the time when history existed. Such nostalgia, in fact, will continue to fuel competition and conflict even in the post-historical world for some time to come. Even though I recognize its inevitability, I have the most ambivalent feelings for the civilization that has been created in Europe since 1945, with its north Atlantic and Asian offshoots. Perhaps this very prospect of centuries of boredom at the end of history will serve to get history started once again.

Reading Notes

1. Kojève's best-known work is his *Introduction à la lecture de Hegel* (Paris: Editions Gallimard, 1947), which is a transcript of the *Ecole Practique* lectures from the 1930s. This book is available in English entitled *Introduction to the Reading of Hegel* arranged by Raymond Queneau, edited by Allan Bloom, and translated by James Nichols (New York: Basic Books, 1969).

2. In this respect Kojève stands in sharp contrast to contemporary German interpreters of Hegel like Herbert Marcuse who, being more sympathetic to Marx, regarded Hegel ultimately as an historically bound and incomplete philosopher.

3. Kojève alternatively identified the end of history with the postwar "American way of life," toward which he thought the Soviet Union was moving as well.

4. This notion was expressed in the famous aphorism from the preface to the *Philosophy of History* to the effect that "everything that is rational is real, and everything that is real is rational."

5. Indeed, for Hegel the very dichotomy between the ideal and material worlds was itself only an apparent one that was ultimately overcome by the self-conscious subject; in his system, the material world is itself only an aspect of mind.

6. In fact, modern economists, recognizing that man does not always behave as a *profit*-maximizer, posit a "utility" function, utility being either income or some other good that can be maximized: leisure, sexual satisfaction, or the pleasure of philosophizing. That profit must be replaced with a value like utility indicates the cogency of the idealist perspective.

7. One need look no further than the recent performance of Vietnamese immigrants in the U.S. school system when compared to their black or Hispanic classmates to realize that culture and consciousness are absolutely crucial to explain not only economic behavior but virtually every other important aspect of life as well.

8. I understand that a full explanation of the origins of the reform movements in China and Russia is a good deal more complicated than this simple formula would suggest. The Soviet reform, for example, was motivated in good measure by Moscow's sense of *insecurity* in the technological-military realm. Nonetheless, neither country on the eve of its reforms was in such a state of *material* crisis that one could have predicted the surprising reform paths ultimately taken.

9. It is still not clear whether the Soviet people are as "Protestant" as Gorbachev and will follow him down that path.

10. The internal politics of the Byzantine Empire at the time of Justinian revolved around a conflict between the so-called monophysites and monothelites, who believed that the unity of the Holy Trinity was alternatively one of nature or of will. This conflict corresponded to some extent to one between proponents of different racing teams in the Hippodrome in Byzantium and led to a not insignificant level of political violence. Modern historians would tend to seek the roots of such conflicts in antagonisms between social classes or some other modern economic category, being unwilling to believe that men would kill each other over the nature of the Trinity.

11. I am not using the term "fascism" here in its most precise sense, fully aware of the frequent misuse of this term to denounce anyone to the right of the user. "Fascism" here denotes any organized ultra-nationalist movement with universalistic pretensions—not universalistic with regard to its nationalism, of course, since the latter is exclusive by definition, but with regard to the movement's belief in its right to rule other people. Hence Imperial Japan would qualify as fascist while former strongman Stoessner's Paraguay or Pinochet's Chile would not. Obviously fascist ideologies cannot be universalistic in the sense of Marxism or liberalism, but the structure of the doctrine can be transferred from country to country.

12. I use the example of Japan with some caution, since Kojève late in his life came to conclude that Japan, with its culture based on purely formal arts, proved that the universal homogenous state was not victorious and that history had perhaps not ended. See the long note at the end of the second edition of *Introduction à la Lecture de Hegel*, 462–3.

13. This is not true in Poland and Hungary, however, whose Communist parties have taken moves toward true power-sharing and pluralism.

14. This is particularly true of the leading Soviet conservative, former Second Secretary Yegor Ligachev, who has publicly recognized many of the deep defects of the Brezhnev period.

15. I am thinking particularly of Rousseau and the Western philosophical tradition that flows from him that was highly critical of Lockean or Hobbesian liberalism, though one could criticize liberalism from the standpoint of classical political philosophy as well.

16. See his article, "Beyond the Cold War," *New Republic*, December 19, 1988.

17. It took European colonial powers like France several years after the war to admit the illegitimacy of their empires, but decolonialization was an inevitable consequence of the Allied victory which had been based on the promise of a restoration of democratic freedoms.

18. *Vestnik Ministerstva Inostrannikh Del SSSR* no. 15 (August 1988), 27–46. "New thinking" does of course serve a propagandistic purpose in persuading Western audiences of Soviet good intentions. But the fact that it is good propaganda does not mean that its formulators do not take many of its ideas seriously.

THE THIRD WAVE: DEMOCRATIZATION IN THE LATE TWENTIETH CENTURY

Samuel Huntington

TRANSITION PROCESSES

The third wave transitions were complex political processes involving a variety of groups struggling for power and for and against democracy and other goals. In terms of their attitudes toward democratization, the crucial participants in the processes were the standpatters, liberal reformers, and democratic reformers in the governing coalition, and democratic moderates and revolutionary extremists in the opposition. In noncommunist authoritarian systems, the standpatters within the government were normally perceived as right-wing, fascist, and nationalist. The opponents of democratization in the opposition were normally left-wing, revolutionary, and Marxist-Leninist. Supporters of democracy in both government and opposition could be conceived as occupying middle positions on the left–right continuum. In communist systems left and right were less clear. Standpatters were normally thought of as Stalinist or Brezhnevite. Within the opposition, the extremist opponents of democracy were not revolutionary left-wingers but often nationalist groups thought of as right-wing.

Within the governing coalition some groups often came to favor democratization, while others opposed it, and others supported limited reform or liberalization (see Figure 13.1). Opposition attitudes toward democracy were also usually

Figure 13.1 **POLITICAL GROUPS INVOLVED IN DEMOCRATIZATION**

	Attitudes Toward Democracy		
	Against	For	Against
		Reformers	
Government		Democratizers Liberals	Standpatters
Opposition	Radical Extremists	Democratic Moderates	

divided. Supporters of the existing dictatorship always opposed democracy; opponents of the existing dictatorship often opposed democracy. Almost invariably, however, they used the rhetoric of democracy in their efforts to replace the existing authoritarian regime with one of their own. The groups involved in the politics of democratization thus had both conflicting and common objectives. Reformers and standpatters divided over liberalization and democratization but presumably had a common interest in constraining the power of opposition groups. Moderates and radicals had a common interest in bringing down the existing regime and getting into power but disagreed about what sort of new regime should be created. Reformers and moderates had a common interest in creating democracy but often divided over how the costs of creating it should be borne and how power within it should be apportioned. Standpatters and radicals were totally opposed on the issue of who should rule but had a common interest in weakening the democratic groups in the center and in polarizing politics in the society.

The attitudes and goals of particular individuals and groups at times changed in the democratization process. If democratization did not produce the dangers they feared, people who had been liberal reformers or even standpatters might come to accept democracy. Similarly, participation in the processes of democratization could lead members of extremist opposition groups to moderate their revolutionary propensities and accept the constraints and opportunities democracy offered.

The relative power of the groups shaped the nature of the democratization process and often changed during that process. If standpatters dominated the government and extremists the

opposition, democratization was impossible, as, for example, where a right-wing personal dictator determined to hang on to power confronted an opposition dominated by Marxist-Leninists. Transition to democracy was, of course, facilitated if prodemocratic groups were dominant in both the government and opposition. The differences in power between reformers and moderates, however, shaped how the process occurred. In 1976, for instance, the Spanish opposition urged a complete "democratic break" or *ruptura* with the Franco legacy and creation of a provisional government and a constituent assembly to formulate a new constitutional order. Adolfo Suárez was powerful enough, however, to fend this off and produce democratization working through the Franco constitutional mechanism.[1] If democratic groups were strong in the opposition but not in the government, democratization depended on events undermining the government and bringing the opposition to power. If democratic groups were dominant in the governing coalition, but not in the opposition, the effort at democratization could be threatened by insurgent violence and by a backlash increase in power of standpatter groups possibly leading to a coup d'etat.

The three crucial interactions in democratization processes were those between government and opposition, between reformers and standpatters in the governing coalition, and between moderates and extremists in the opposition. In all transitions these three central interactions played some role. The relative importance and the conflictual or cooperative character of these interactions, however, varied with the overall nature of the transition process. In transformations, the interaction between reformers and standpatters within the governing coalition was of central importance; and the transformation only occurred if reformers were stronger than standpatters, if the government was stronger than the opposition, and if the moderates were stronger than the extremists. As the transformation went on, opposition moderates were often coopted into the governing coalition while standpatter groups opposing democratization defected from it. In replacements, the interactions between government and opposition and between moderates and extremists were important; the opposition eventually had to be stronger than the government, and the moderates had to be stronger than the extremists. A successive defection of groups often led to the downfall of the regime and inauguration of the democratic system. In transplacements, the central interaction was between reformers and moderates not widely unequal in power, with each being able to dominate the antidemocratic groups on its side of the line between the government and the opposition. In some transplacements, government and former opposition groups agreed on at least a temporary sharing of power.

TRANSFORMATIONS

In transformations those in power in the authoritarian regime take the lead and play the decisive role in ending that regime and changing it into a democratic system. The line between transformations and transplacements is fuzzy, and some cases might be legitimately classified in either category. Overall, however, transformations accounted for approximately sixteen out of thirty-five third wave transitions that had occurred or that appeared to be underway by the end of the 1980s. These sixteen cases of liberalization or democratization included changes from five one-party systems, three personal dictatorships, and eight military regimes. Transformation requires the government to be stronger than the opposition. Consequently, it occurred in well-established military regimes where governments clearly controlled the ultimate means of coercion vis-à-vis the opposition and/or vis-à-vis authoritarian systems that had been successful economically, such as Spain, Brazil, Taiwan, Mexico, and, compared to other communist states, Hungary. The leaders of these countries had the power to move their countries toward democracy if they wanted to. In every case the opposition was, at least at the beginning

of the process, markedly weaker than the government. In Brazil, for example, as Stepan points out, when "liberalization began, there was no significant political opposition, no economic crisis, and no collapse of the coercive apparatus due to defeat in war."[2] In Brazil and elsewhere the people best situated to end the authoritarian regime were the leaders of the regime—and they did.

The prototypical cases of transformation were Spain, Brazil, and, among communist regimes, Hungary. The most important case, if it materializes, will be the Soviet Union. The Brazilian transition was "liberation from above" or "regime-initiated liberalization." In Spain "it was a question of reformist elements associated with the incumbent dictatorship, initiating processes of political change from within the established regime."[3] The two transitions differed significantly, however, in their duration. In Spain in less than three and a half years after the death of Franco, a democratizing prime minister had replaced a liberalizing one, the Franco legislature had voted the end of the regime, political reform had been endorsed in a referendum, political parties (including the Communist party) were legalized, a new assembly was elected, a democratic constitution was drafted and approved in a referendum, the major political actors reached agreement on economic policy, and parliamentary elections were held under the new constitution. Suárez reportedly told his cabinet that "his strategy would be based on speed. He would keep ahead of the game by introducing specific measures faster than the *continuistas* of the Francoist establishment could respond to them." While the reforms were compressed within a short period of time, however, they were also undertaken sequentially. Hence, it has also been argued that "By staggering the reforms, Suárez avoided antagonizing too many sectors of the franquist regime simultaneously. The last set of democratic reforms provoked open hostility from the military and other franquist hardliners, but the President [Suárez] had greatly gained considerable momentum and support." In effect, then, Suárez followed a highly compressed version of the Kemalist "Fabian strategy, blitzkrieg tactics" pattern of reform.[4]

In Brazil, in contrast, President Geisel determined that political change was to be "gradual, slow, and sure." The process began at the end of the Médici administration in 1973, continued through the Geisel and Figueiredo administrations, jumped forward with the installation of a civilian president in 1985, and culminated in the adoption of a new constitution in 1988 and the popular election of a president in 1989. The regime-decreed movements toward democratization were interspersed with actions taken to reassure hardliners in the military and elsewhere. In effect, Presidents Geisel and Figueiredo followed a two-step forward, one-step backward policy. The result was a creeping democratization in which the control of the government over the process was never seriously challenged. In 1973 Brazil had a repressive military dictatorship; in 1989 it was a full-scale democracy. It is customary to date the arrival of democracy in Brazil in January 1985, when the electoral college chose a civilian president. In fact, however, there was no clear break; the genius of the Brazilian transformation is that it is virtually impossible to say at what point Brazil stopped being a dictatorship and became a democracy.

Spain and Brazil were the prototypical cases of change from above, and the Spanish case in particular became the model for subsequent democratizations in Latin America and Eastern Europe. In 1988 and 1989, for instance, Hungarian leaders consulted extensively with Spanish leaders on how to introduce democracy and in April 1989 a Spanish delegation went to Budapest to offer advice. Six months later one commentator pointed to the similarities in the two transitions:

> *The last years of the Kadar era did bear some resemblance to the benign authoritarianism of Franco's decaying dictatorship. Imre Pozsgay plays the part of Prince Juan Carlos in this comparison. He is a reassuring symbol of continuity in the midst of radical change. Liberal-minded economic experts with links to the old establishment and the new entrepreneurial class provide a technocratic elite for the transition, much as the new bourgeois elites associated with Opus Dei did in Spain. The opposition parties also figure in this analogy, emerging from underground in much the same way the Spanish exiles did once it was safe to come out. And as in Spain, the Hungarian oppositionists—moderate in style, radically democratic in substance—are playing a vital role in the reinvention of democracy.*[5]

Third wave transformations usually evolved through five major phases, four of which occurred within the authoritarian system.

Emergence of Reformers

The first step was the emergence of a group of leaders or potential leaders within the authoritarian regime who believed that movement in the direction of democracy was desirable or necessary. Why did they conclude this? The reasons why people became democratic reformers varied greatly from country to country and seldom were clear. They can, however, be grouped into five categories. First, reformers often concluded that the costs of staying in power—such as politicizing their armed forces, dividing the coalition that had supported them, grappling with seemingly unsolvable problems (usually economic), and increasing repression—had reached the point where a graceful exit from power was desirable. The leaders of military regimes were particularly sensitive to the corrosive effects of political involvement on the integrity, professionalism, coherence, and command structure of the military. "We all directly or indirectly," Gen. Morales Bermudez observed as he led Peru toward democracy, "had been witnesses to what was happening to this institution fundamental to our fatherland, and in the same vein, to the other institutions. And we don't want that." In a similar vein, Gen. Fernando Matthei, head of the Chilean air force, warned, "If the transition toward democracy is not initiated promptly, we shall ruin the armed forces in a way no Marxist infiltration could."[6]

Second, in some cases reformers wished to reduce the risks they faced if they held on to power and then eventually lost it. If the opposition seemed to be gaining strength, arranging for a democratic transition was one way of achieving this. It is, after all, preferable to risk losing office than to risk losing life.

Third, in some cases, including India, Chile, and Turkey, authoritarian leaders believed that they or their associates would not lose office. Having made commitments to restore democratic institutions and being faced with declining legitimacy and support these rulers could see the desirability of attempting to renew their legitimacy by organizing elections in anticipation that the voters would continue them in power. This anticipation was usually wrong. . . .

Fourth, reformers often believed that democratizing would produce benefits for their country: increase its international legitimacy, reduce U.S. or other sanctions against their regime, and open the door to economic and military assistance, International Monetary Fund (IMF) loans, invitations to Washington, and inclusion in international gatherings dominated by the leaders of the Western alliance.

Finally, in many cases, including Spain, Brazil, Hungary, and Turkey and some other military regimes, reformers believed that democracy was the "right" form of government and that their country had evolved to the point where, like other developed and respected countries, it too should have a democratic political system.

Liberal reformers tended to see liberalization as a way of defusing opposition to their regime without fully democratizing the regime. They would ease up on repression, restore some civil liberties, reduce censorship, permit broader discussion of public issues, and allow civil society—associations, churches, unions, business organizations—greater scope to conduct their affairs. Liberalizers did not, however, wish to introduce fully participatory competitive elections that could cause current leaders to lose power. They wanted to create a kinder, gentler, more secure and stable authoritarianism without altering fundamentally the nature of their system. Some reformers were undoubtedly unsure themselves how far they wished to go in opening up the politics of their country. They also at times undoubtedly felt the need to veil their intentions: democratizers tended to reassure standpatters by giving the impression that they were only liberalizing; liberalizers attempted to win broader popular support by creating the impression they were democratizing. Debates consequently raged over how far Geisel, Botha, Gorbachev, and others "really" wanted to go.

The emergence of liberalizers and democratizers within an authoritarian system creates a first-order force for political change. It also, however, can have a second-order effect. In military regimes in particular it divides the ruling group, further politicizes the military, and hence leads more officers to believe that "the military as government" must be ended in order to preserve "the military as institution." The debate over whether or not to withdraw from government in itself becomes an argument to withdraw from government.

Acquiring Power

Democratic reformers not only had to exist within the authoritarian regime, they also had to be in power in that regime. How did this come about? In three cases leaders who created the authoritarian regime presided over its transition to democracy. In India and Turkey, authoritarian regimes were defined from the start as interruptions in the formal pattern of democracy. The regimes were short-lived, ending with elections organized by the authoritarian leaders in the false anticipation that they or the candidates they supported would win those elections. In Chile General Pinochet created the regime, remained in power for seventeen years, established a lengthy schedule for the transition to democracy, implemented that schedule in anticipation that the voters would extend him in office for eight more years, and exited grudgingly from power when they did not. Otherwise those who created authoritarian regimes or who led such regimes for prolonged periods of time did not take the lead in ending those regimes. In all these cases, transformation occurred because reformers replaced standpatters in power.

Reformers came to power in authoritarian regimes in three ways. First, in Spain and Taiwan, the founding and long-ruling authoritarian leaders, Franco and Chiang Kai-shek died. Their designated successors, Juan Carlos and Chiang Ching-kuo, succeeded to the mantle, responded to the momentous social and economic changes that had occurred in their countries, and began the process of democratization. In the Soviet Union, the deaths in the course of three years of Brezhnev, Andropov, and Chernenko allowed Gorbachev to come to power. In a sense, Franco, Chiang, and Brezhnev died in time; Deng Xiaoping did not.

In Brazil and in Mexico, the authoritarian system itself provided for regular change in leadership. This made the acquisition of power by reformers possible but not necessary. In Brazil, as was pointed out previously, two factions existed in the military. Repression reached its peak between 1969 and 1972 during the presidency of General Médici, a hard-liner. In a major struggle within the military establishment at the end of his term, the soft-line Sorbonne group was able to secure the nomination of General Ernesto Geisel for president, in part because his brother was minister of war. Guided by his chief associate, General Golbery do Couto e Silva, Geisel began the process of democratization and acted decisively to ensure that he would, in turn, be succeeded in 1978 by another member of the Sorbonne group, General João Batista Figueiredo. In Mexico, outgoing President José Lopez Portillo in 1981 followed standard practice in selecting his minister of planning and budgets, Miguel de la Madrid, as his successor. De la Madrid was an economic and political liberalizer and, rejecting more traditional and old-guard candidates, chose a young reforming technocrat, Carlos Salinas, to continue the opening up process.

Where authoritarian leaders did not die and were not regularly changed, democratic reformers had to oust the ruler and install prodemocratic leadership. In military governments, other than Brazil, this meant the replacement by coup d'etat of one military leader by another: Morales Bermudez replaced Velasco in Peru; Poveda replaced Rodríguez Lara in Ecuador; Mejía replaced Rios Montt in Guatemala; Murtala Muhammed replaced Gowon in Nigeria.[7] In the one-party system in Hungary, reformers mobilized their strength and deposed the long-ruling Janos Kadar at a special party conference in May 1988, replacing him as secretary general with Karoly Grosz. Grosz, however, was only a semireformer, and a year later the Central Committee replaced him with a four-person presidium dominated by reformers. In October 1989 one of them, Rezso Nyers, became party president. In Bulgaria in the fall of 1989, reform-minded Communist party leaders ousted Todor Zhivkov from the dominant position he had occupied for thirty-five years. The leadership changes associated with some liberalizing and democratizing reforms are summarized in Table 13.5.

The Failure of Liberalization

A critical issue in the third wave concerned the role of liberal reformers and the stability of a liberalized authoritarian polity. Liberal reformers who succeeded standpatter leaders usually turned out to be transition figures with brief stays in power. In Taiwan, Hungary, and Mexico, liberalizers were quickly succeeded by more democratically oriented reformers. In Brazil, although some analysts are dubious, it seems reasonably clear that Geisel and Golbery were committed to meaningful democratization from the start.[8] Even if they did just intend to liberalize the authoritarian system rather than replace it,

Figueiredo extended the process to democratization. "I have to make this country into a democracy," he said in 1978 before taking office, and he did.[9]

In Spain the hard-line prime minister, Admiral Luis Carrero Blanco, was assassinated in December 1973, and Franco appointed Carlos Arias Navarro to succeed him. Arias was the classic liberal reformer. He wished to modify the Franco regime in order to preserve it. In a famous speech on February 12, 1974, he proposed an opening (*apertura*) and recommended a number of modest reforms including, for instance, permitting political associations to function but not political parties. He "was too much of a conservative and Francoist at heart to carry out a true democratization of the regime." His reform proposals were torpedoed by the standpatters of the "bunker," including Franco; at the same time the proposals stimulated the opposition to demand a more extensive opening. In the end, Arias "discredited *aperturismo* just as Carrero had discredited immobilism."[10] In November 1975 Franco died and Juan Carlos succeeded him as chief of state. Juan Carlos was committed to transforming Spain into a true, European-style parliamentary democracy, Arias resisted this change, and in July 1976 Juan Carlos replaced him with Adolfo Suárez, who moved quickly to introduce democracy.

The transition from liberalized authoritarianism, however, could move backward as well as forward. A limited opening could raise expectations of further change that could lead to instability, upheaval, and even violence; these, in turn, could provoke an antidemocratic reaction and replacement of the liberalizing leadership with standpatter leaders. In Greece, Papadopoulos attempted to shift from a standpatter to a liberalizing stance; this led to the Polytechnic student demonstration and its bloody suppression; a reaction followed and the liberalizing Papadopoulos was replaced by the hard-line Ioannidis. In Argentina General Roberto Viola succeeded the hard-line General Jorge Videla as president and began to liberalize. This produced a reaction in the military, Viola's ouster, and his replacement by hard-line General Leopoldo Galtieri. In China ultimate power presumably rested with Deng Xiao-ping. In 1987, however Zhao Ziyang became general secretary of the Communist party and began to open up the political system. This led to the massive student

Table 13.5 **LEADERSHIP CHANGE AND REFORM, 1973–90**

Country	Standpat Leader	Change	Reform Leader I	Change	Reform Leader II	First Democratic Election
Nigeria	Gowon	July 1975 coup	Murtala Mohammed	February 1976 death	Obasanjo	August 1979
Ecuador	Rodriguez Lara	January 1976 coup	Poveda	—	—	April 1979
Peru	Velasco	August 1975 coup	Morales Bermudez	—	—	May 1980
Brazil	Medici	March 1974 succession	Geisel	March 1979 succession	Figueiredo	January 1985
Guatemala	Rios Montt	August 1983 coup	Mejia	—	—	December 1985
Spain	Franco	November 1975 death	Juan Carlos	—	Juan Carlos	March 1979
	Carrero Blanco	December 1973 death	Arias	July 1976 ouster	Suárez	
Taiwan	Chiang Kai-shek	April 1975 death	Chiang Ching-kuo	January 1988 death	Lee Teng-hui	
Hungary	Kadar	May 1988 ouster	Grosz	May–October 1989 ouster	Nyers-Pozsgay	March 1990
Mexico	Portillo	December 1982 succession	De la Madrid	December 1988 succession	Salinas	
South Africa	Vorster	September 1978 ouster	Botha	September 1989 ouster	de Klerk	
USSR	Chernenko	March 1985 death	Gorbachev			
Bulgaria	Zhivkov	November 1989 ouster	Mladenov	—	—	June 1990

demonstrations in Tiananmen Square in the spring of 1989, which, in turn, provoked a hard-line reaction, the crushing of the student movement, the ouster of Zhao, and his replacement by Li Peng. In Burma, Gen. Ne Win, who had ruled Burma for twenty-six years, ostensibly retired from office in July 1988 and was replaced by Gen. Sein Lwin, another hard-liner. Mounting protests and violence forced Sein Lwin out within three weeks. He was succeeded by a civilian and presumed moderate, Maung Maung, who proposed elections and attempted to negotiate with opposition groups. Protests continued, however, and in September the army deposed Maung Maung, took control of the government, bloodily suppressed the demonstrations, and ended the movement toward liberalization.

The dilemmas of the liberalizer were reflected in the experiences of P.W. Botha and Mikhail Gorbachev. Both leaders introduced major liberalizing reforms in their societies. Botha came to power in 1978 with the slogan

"Adapt or die" and legalized black trade unions, repealed the marriage laws, established mixed trading zones, granted citizenship to urban blacks, permitted blacks to acquire freehold title, substantially reduced petty apartheid, increased significantly investment in black education, abolished the pass laws, provided for elected black township councils, and created houses of parliament representing coloureds and Asians, although not blacks. Gorbachev opened up public discussion, greatly reduced censorship, dramatically challenged the power of the Communist party apparat, and introduced at least modest forms of government responsibility to an elected legislature. Both leaders gave their societies new constitutions incorporating many reforms and also creating new and very powerful posts of president, which they then assumed. It seems probable that neither Botha nor Gorbachev, however, wanted fundamental change in their political systems. Their reforms were designed to improve and to moderate, but also to bolster the existing system and make it more acceptable to their societies. They themselves said as much repeatedly. Botha did not intend to end white power; Gorbachev did not intend to end communist power. As liberal reformers they wanted to change but also to preserve the systems that they led and in whose bureaucracies they had spent their careers.

Botha's liberalizing but not democratizing reforms stimulated intensified demands from South African blacks for their full incorporation into the political system. In September 1984 black townships erupted with protests that led to violence, repression, and the deployment of military forces into the townships. The efforts at reform simultaneously ended, and Botha the reformer was widely viewed as having become Botha the repressor. The reform process only got underway again in 1989 when Botha was replaced by F.W. de Klerk, whose more extensive reforms led to criticisms from Botha and his resignation from the National party. In 1989 and 1990 Gorbachev's liberalizing but not democratizing reforms appeared to be stimulating comparable upheaval, protests, and violence in the Soviet Union. As in South Africa, communal groups fought each other and the central authorities. The dilemma for Gorbachev was clear. Moving forward toward fullscale democratization would mean not only the end of communist power in the Soviet Union but very probably the

end of the Soviet Union. Leading a hard-line reaction to the upheavals would mean the end of his efforts at economic reform, his greatly improved relations with the West, and his global image as a creative and humane leader. Andrei Sakharov put the choices squarely to Gorbachev in 1989: "A middle course in situations like these is almost impossible. The country and you personally are at a crossroads—either increase the process of change maximally or try to retain the administrative command system with all its qualities."[11]

Where it was tried, liberalization stimulated the desire for democratization in some groups and the desire for repression in others. The experience of the third wave strongly suggests that liberalized authoritarianism is not a stable equilibrium; the halfway house does not stand.

Backward Legitimacy: Subduing the Standpatters

The achievement of power enabled the reformers to start democratizing but it did not eliminate the ability of the standpatters to challenge the reformers. The standpatter elements of what had been the governing coalition—the Francoist "bunker" in Spain, the military hard-liners in Brazil and other Latin American countries, the Stalinists in Hungary, the mainlander old guard in the KMT, the party bosses and bureaucracy in the PRI, the *Verkrampte* wing of the National party—did not give up easily. In the government, military, and party bureaucracies standpatters worked to stop or slow down the processes of change. In the non-one-party systems—Brazil, Ecuador, Peru, Guatemala, Nigeria, and Spain—standpatter groups in the military attempted coups d'etat and made other efforts to dislodge the reformers from power. In South Africa and in Hungary, standpatter factions broke away from the dominant parties, charging them with betraying the basic principles on which the parties were based.

Reform governments attempted to neutralize standpatter opposition by weakening, reassuring, and converting the standpatters. Countering standpatter resistance often required a concentration of power in the reform chief executive. Geisel asserted himself as "dictator of the *abertura*" in order to force the Brazilian military out of politics.[12] Juan Carlos exercised his power and prerogatives to the full in moving Spain toward democracy, not least in the surprise selection of Suárez as prime minister. Botha and Gorbachev, as we have seen, created powerful new presidential offices for themselves. Salinas dramatically asserted his powers during his first years as Mexico's president.

The first requirement for reform leaders was to purge the governmental, military, and, where appropriate, party bureaucracies, replacing standpatters in top offices with supporters of reform. This was typically done in selective fashion so as not to provoke a strong reaction and so as to promote fissions within the standpatter ranks. In addition to weakening standpatters, reform leaders also tried to reassure and convert them. In military regimes, the reformers argued that it was time to go back, after a necessary but limited authoritarian interlude, to the democratic principles that were the basis of their country's political system. In this sense, they appealed for a "return to legitimacy." In the nonmilitary authoritarian systems, reformers invoked "backward legitimacy" and stressed elements of continuity with the past.[13] In Spain, for instance, the monarchy was reestablished and Suárez adhered to the provisions of the Franco constitution in abolishing that constitution: no Francoist could claim that there were procedural irregularities. In Mexico and South Africa the reformers in the PRI and National party cast themselves in the traditions of those parties. On Taiwan the KMT reformers appealed to Sun Yat-Sen's three principles.

Backward legitimacy had two appeals and two effects: it legitimated the new order because it was a product of the old, and it retrospectively legitimated the old order because it had produced the new. It elicited consensus from all except opposition extremists who had no use for either the old authoritarian regime or the new democratic one. Reformers also appealed to standpatters on the grounds that they were preempting the radical opposition and hence minimizing instability and violence. Suárez, for instance, asked the Spanish army to support him for these reasons and the dominant elements in the army accepted the transition because there "was no illegitimacy, no disorder in the streets, no significant threat of breakdown and subversion." Inevitably, the reformers also found that, as Geisel put it, they could "not advance without some retreats" and that hence, on occasion, as in the 1977 "April package" in Brazil, they had to make concessions to the standpatters.[14]

Coopting the Opposition

Once in power the democratic reformers usually moved quickly to begin the process of democratization. This normally involved consultations with leaders of the opposition, the political parties, and major social groups and institutions. In some instances relatively formal negotiations occurred and quite explicit agreements or pacts were reached. In other cases, the consultations and negotiations were more informal. In Ecuador and Nigeria the government appointed commissions to develop plans and policies for the new system. In Spain, Peru, Nigeria, and eventually in Brazil elected assemblies drafted new constitutions. In several instances referenda were held to approve the new constitutional arrangements.

As the reformers alienated standpatters within the governing coalition, they had to reinforce themselves by developing support within the opposition and by expanding the political arena and appealing to the new groups that were becoming politically active as a result of the opening. Skillful reformers used the increased pressure from these groups for democratization to weaken the standpatters, and used the threat of a standpatter coup as well as the attractions of a share in power to strengthen moderate groups in the opposition.

To these ends, reformers in government negotiated with the principal opposition groups and arrived at explicit or tacit agreements with them. In Spain, for instance, the Communist party recognized that it was too weak to follow a "radical *rupturista* policy" and instead went along with a "*ruptura pactada*" even though the pact was "purely tacit." In October 1977 Suárez won the agreement of the Communist and Socialist parties to the *Pactos de la Moncloa* comprising a mixture of fairly severe economic austerity measures and some social reforms. Secret negotiations with Santiago Carrillo, the principal Communist leader, "played on the PCE [Partido Comunista de España] leader's anxiety to be near the levers of power and secured his backing for an austerity package."[15] In Hungary explicit negotiations occurred in the fall of 1989 between the Communist party and the Opposition Round Table representing the principal other parties and groups. In Brazil informal understandings developed between the government and the opposition parties, the Movimento Democrático Brasileiro (MDB) and the Partido Movimento Democrático Brasileiro

(PMDB). On Taiwan in 1986 the government and the opposition arrived at an understanding on the parameters within which political change would take place and, in a week-long conference in July 1990, agreed on a full schedule of democratization.

Moderation and cooperation by the democratic opposition—their involvement in the process as junior partners—were essential to successful transformation. In almost all countries, the principal opposition parties—the MDB-PMDB in Brazil, the Socialists and Communists in Spain, the Democratic Progressive Party (DPP) in Taiwan, the Civic Forum in Hungary, the Alianza Popular Revolucionaria Americana (APRA) in Peru, the Christian Democrats in Chile—were led by moderates and followed moderate policies, at times in the face of considerable provocation by standpatter groups in the government.

Skidmore's summary of what occurred in Brazil neatly catches the central relationships involved in transformation processes:

> In the end, liberalization was the product of an intense dialectical relationship between the government and the opposition. The military who favored abertura had to proceed cautiously, for fear of arousing the hardliners. Their overtures to the opposition were designed to draw out the "responsible" elements, thereby showing there were moderates ready to cooperate with the government. At the same time, the opposition constantly pressed the government to end its arbitrary excesses, thereby reminding the military that their rule lacked legitimacy. Meanwhile, the opposition moderates had to remind the radicals that they would play into the hands of the hardliners if they pushed too hard. This intricate political relationship functioned successfully because there was a consensus among both military and civilians in favor of a return to an (almost) open political system.[16]

Guidelines for Democratizers 1: Reforming Authoritarian Systems

The principal lessons of the Spanish, Brazilian, and other transformations for democratic reformers in authoritarian governments include the following:

1. Secure your political base. As quickly as possible place supporters of democratization in key power positions in the government, the party, and the military.
2. Maintain backward legitimacy, that is, make changes through the established procedures of the nondemocratic regime and reassure standpatter groups with symbolic concessions, following a course of two steps forward, one step backward.
3. Gradually shift your own constituency so as to reduce your dependence on government groups opposing change and to broaden your constituency in the direction of opposition groups supporting democracy.
4. Be prepared for the standpatters to take some extreme action to stop change (e.g., a coup attempt)—possibly even stimulate them to do so—and then crack down on them ruthlessly, isolating and discrediting the more extreme opponents of change.
5. Seize and keep control of the initiative in the democratization process. Only lead from strength and never introduce democratization measures in response to obvious pressure from more extreme radical opposition groups.
6. Keep expectations low as to how far change can go; talk in terms of maintaining an ongoing process rather than achieving some fully elaborated democratic utopia.
7. Encourage development of a responsible, moderate opposition party, which the key groups in society (including the military) will accept as a plausible nonthreatening alternative government.
8. Create a sense of inevitability about the process of democratization so that it becomes widely accepted as a necessary and natural course of development even if to some people it remains an undesirable one.

REPLACEMENTS

Replacements involve a very different process from transformations. Reformers within the regime are weak or nonexistent. The dominant elements in government are standpatters staunchly opposed to regime change. Democratization consequently results from the opposition gaining strength and the government losing strength until the government collapses or is overthrown. The former opposition groups come to power and the conflict then often enters a new phase as groups in the new government struggle among themselves over the nature of the regime they should institute. Replacement, in short, involves three distinct phases: the struggle to produce the fall, the fall, and the struggle after the fall.

Most third wave democratizations required some cooperation from those in power. Only six replacements had occurred by 1990. Replacements were rare in transitions from one-party systems (one out of eleven) and military regimes (two out of sixteen) and more common in transitions from personal dictatorships (three out of seven). As we have pointed out, with some exceptions (Gandhi, Evren, Pinochet), leaders who created authoritarian regimes did not end those regimes. Changes of leadership within authoritarian systems were much more likely in military regimes through "second phase" coups or, in one-party systems, through regular succession or the action of constituted party bodies. Personal dictators, however, seldom retired voluntarily, and the nature of their power—personal rather than military or organizational—made it difficult for opponents within the regime to oust them and, indeed, made it unlikely that such opponents would exist in any significant numbers or strength. The personal dictator was thus likely to hang on until he died or until the regime itself came to an end. The life of the regime became the life of the dictator. Politically and at times literally (e.g., Franco, Ceausescu) the deaths of the dictator and the regime coincided.

Democratic reformers were notably weak in or missing from the authoritarian regimes that disappeared in replacements. In Argentina and Greece, the liberalizing leaders Viola and Papadopoulos were forced out of power and succeeded by military hard-liners. In Portugal Caetano initiated some liberalizing reforms and then backed away from them. In the Philippines, Romania, and East Germany, the entourages of Marcos, Ceausescu, and Honecker contained few if any democrats or even liberals. In all six cases standpatters monopolized power, and the possibility of initiating reform from within was almost totally absent.

An authoritarian system exists because the government is politically stronger than the opposition. It is replaced when the government becomes weaker than the opposition. Hence replacement requires the opposition to wear down the government and shift the balance of power in its favor. When they were initiated, the authoritarian regimes involved in the third wave were almost always popular and widely supported. They usually had the backing of a broad coalition of groups. Over time, however, as with any government, their strength deteriorated. The Greek and Argentine military regimes suffered the humiliation of military defeat. The Portuguese and Philippine regimes were unable to win counterinsurgency wars, and the Philippine regime created a martyr and stole an election. The Romanian regime followed policies that deeply antagonized its people and isolated itself from them; hence it was vulnerable to the cumulative snowballing of the antiauthoritarian movement throughout Eastern Europe. The case of East Germany was more ambiguous. Although the regime was relatively successful in some respects, the inevitable comparison with West Germany was an inherent weakness, and the opening of the transit corridor through Hungary dramatically undermined the regime's authority. The party leadership resigned in early December 1989, and a caretaker government took over. The regime's authority, however, evaporated, and with it the reasons for the East German state.

The erosion of support for the regime sometimes occurred openly, but, given the repressive character of authoritarian regimes, it was more likely to occur covertly. Authoritarian leaders were often unaware of how unpopular they were. Covert disaffection then manifested itself when some triggering event exposed the weakness of the regime. In Greece and Argentina it was military defeat. In Portugal and East Germany it was the explicit turning against the regime of its ultimate source of power—the army in Portugal, the Soviet Union in East Germany. The actions of the Turks, the British, the Portuguese military, and Gorbachev galvanized and brought into the open the disaffection from the regime of other groups in those societies. In all these cases, only a few weak groups rallied to the support of the regime. Many people had become disaffected from the regime but, because it was an authoritarian regime, a triggering event was required to crystalize the disaffection.

Students are the universal opposition; they oppose whatever regime exists in their society. By themselves, however, students do not bring down regimes. Lacking substantial support from other groups in the population, they were gunned down by the military and police in Greece in November 1973, Burma in September 1988, and China in June 1989. The military are the ultimate support of regimes. If they withdraw their support, if they carry out a coup against the regime, or if they refuse to use force against those who threaten to overthrow the regime, the regime falls. In between the perpetual opposition of the students and the necessary support of the military are other groups whose support for or opposition to the regime depends on circumstances. In noncommunist authoritarian systems, such as the Philippines, these groups tended to disaffect in sequence. The disaffection of the students was followed by that of intellectuals in general and then by the leaders of previously existing political parties, many of whom may have supported or acquiesced in the authoritarian takeover. Typically the broader reaches of the middle class—white-collar workers, professionals, small business proprietors—became alienated. In a Catholic country, Church leaders also were early and effective opponents of the regime. If labor unions existed and were not totally controlled by the government, at some point they joined the opposition. So also, and most important, did larger business groups and the bourgeoisie. In due course, the United States or other foreign sources of support became disaffected. Finally and conclusively, the military decided not to support the government or actively to side with the opposition against the government.

In five out of six replacements, consequently, the exception being Argentina, military disaffection was essential to bringing down the regime. In the personal dictatorships in Portugal, the Philippines, and Romania, this military disaffection was promoted by the dictator's policies weakening military professionalism, politicizing and corrupting the officer corps, and creating competing paramilitary and security forces. Opposition to the government normally (Portugal was the only exception) had to be widespread before the military deserted the government. If disaffection was not widespread, it was either because the most probable sources of opposition—the middle class, bourgeoisie, religious groups—were small and weak or because the regime had the support of these groups, usually as a result of successful policies for economic development. In Burma and China the armed forces brutally suppressed protests that were largely student-led. In societies that were more highly developed economically, opposition to authoritarianism commanded a wider range of

support. When this opposition took to the streets in the Philippines, East Germany, and Romania, military units did not fire on broadly representative groups of their fellow citizens.

A popular image of democratic transitions is that repressive governments are brought down by "people power," the mass mobilization of outraged citizens demanding and eventually forcing a change of regime. Some form of mass action did take place in almost every third wave regime change. Mass demonstrations, protests, and strikes played central roles, however, in only about six transitions completed or underway at the end of the 1980s. These included the replacements in the Philippines, East Germany, and Romania, and the transplacements in Korea, Poland, and Czechoslovakia. In Chile frequent mass actions attempted, without success, to alter Pinochet's plan for transformation. In East Germany, uniquely, both "exit" and "voice," in Hirschman's terms, played major roles, with protest taking the form first of massive departure of citizens from the country and then of massive street demonstrations in Leipzig and Berlin.

In the Philippines, Portugal, Romania, and Greece, when the regime collapsed, it collapsed quickly. One day the authoritarian government was in power, the next day it was not. In Argentina and East Germany, the authoritarian regimes were quickly delegitimated but clung to power while attempting to negotiate terms for the change in regime. In Argentina, the successor military government of General Reynaldo Bignone, which took over in July 1982 immediately after the Falklands defeat, was "relatively successful" in maintaining some regime control over the transition for six months. In December 1982, however, mounting public opposition and the development of opposition organizations led to mass protests, a general strike, Bignone's scheduling of elections, and the rejection by the united opposition parties of the terms proposed by the military for the transfer of power. The authority of the lame-duck military regime continued to deteriorate until it was replaced by the Alfonsín government elected in October 1983. "The military government collapsed," one author observed; "it had no influence over the choice of candidates or the election itself, it excluded no one, and reserved neither powers nor veto prerogatives for itself in the future. In addition, it was unable to guarantee either its autonomy in relation to the future constitutional government or the promise of a future military policy, and, even less—given the winning candidate—the basis for an agreement on the ongoing struggle against the guerrillas."[17] In East Germany in early 1990 a somewhat similar situation existed, with a weak and discredited communist government clinging to power, and its prime minister, Hans Modrow, playing the role of Bignone.

The emphasis in transformations on procedural continuity and backward legitimacy was absent from replacements. The institutions, procedures, ideas, and individuals connected with the previous regime were instead considered tainted and the emphasis was on a sharp, clean break with the past. Those who succeeded the authoritarian rulers based their rule on "forward legitimacy," what they would bring about in the future and their lack of involvement in or connection with the previous regime.

In transformations and transplacements the leaders of the authoritarian regimes usually left politics and went back to the barracks or private life quietly and with some respect and dignity. Authoritarian leaders who lost power through replacements, in contrast, suffered unhappy fates. Marcos and Caetano were forced into exile. Ceausescu was summarily executed. The military officers who ran Greece and Argentina were tried and imprisoned. In East Germany punishments were threatened against Honecker and other former leaders in notable contrast to the absence of such action in Poland, Hungary, and Czechoslovakia. The dictators removed by foreign intervention in Grenada and Panama were similarly subjected to prosecution and punishment.

The peaceful collapse of an authoritarian regime usually produced a glorious if brief moment of public euphoria, of carnations and champagne, absent from transformations. The collapse also created a potential vacuum of authority absent from transformations. In Greece and the Philippines, the vacuum was quickly filled by the accession to power of Karamanlis and Aquino, popular political leaders who guided their countries to democracy. In Iran the authority vacuum was filled by the ayatollah, who guided Iran elsewhere. In Argentina and East Germany the Bignone and Modrow governments weakly filled the interim between the collapse of the authoritarian regimes and the election of democratic governments.

Before the fall, opposition groups are united by their desire to bring about the fall. After the fall, divisions appear among them and they struggle over the distribution of power and the nature of the new regime that must be established. The fate of democracy was determined by the relative power of democratic moderates and antidemocratic radicals. In Argentina and Greece, the authoritarian regimes had not been in power for long, political parties quickly reappeared, and an overwhelming consensus existed among political leaders and groups on the need quickly to reestablish democratic institutions. In the Philippines overt opposition to democracy, apart from the NPA insurgency, also was minimal.

In Nicaragua, Iran, Portugal, and Romania the abrupt collapse of the dictatorships led to struggles among the former opposition groups and parties as to who would exercise power and what sort of regime would be created. In Nicaragua and Iran the democratic moderates lost out. In Portugal . . . a state of revolutionary ferment existed between April 1974 and November 1975. A consolidation of power by the antidemocratic Marxist-Leninist coalition of the Communist party and left-wing military officers was entirely possible. In the end, after intense struggles between military factions, mass mobilizations, demonstrations, and strikes, the military action by Eanes settled Portugal on a democratic course. "What started as a coup," as Robert Harvey observed, "became a revolution which was stopped by a reaction before it became an anarchy. Out of the tumult a democracy was born."[18]

The choices in Portugal were between bourgeois democracy and Marxist-Leninist dictatorship. The choices in Romania in 1990 were less clear, but democracy also was not inevitable. The lack of effectively organized opposition parties and groups, the absence of previous experience with democracy, the violence involved in the overthrow of Ceausescu, the deep desire for revenge against people associated with the dictatorship combined with the widespread involvement of much of the population with the dictatorship, the many leaders of the new government who had been part of the old regime— all did not augur well for the emergence of democracy. At the end of 1989 some Romanians enthusiastically compared what was happening in their country to what had happened two hundred years earlier in France. They might also have noted that the French Revolution ended in a military dictatorship.

Guidelines for Democratizers 2: Overthrowing Authoritarian Regimes

The history of replacements suggests the following guidelines for opposition democratic moderates attempting to overthrow an authoritarian regime:[19]

1. Focus attention on the illegitimacy or dubious legitimacy of the authoritarian regime; that is its most vulnerable point. Attack the regime on general issues that are of widespread concern, such as corruption and brutality. If the regime is performing successfully (particularly economically) these attacks will not be effective. Once its performance falters (as it must), highlighting its illegitimacy becomes the single most important lever for dislodging it from power.

2. Like democratic rulers, authoritarian rulers over time alienate erstwhile supporters. Encourage these disaffected groups to support democracy as the necessary alternative to the current system. Make particular efforts to enlist business leaders, middle-class professionals, religious figures, and political party leaders, most of whom probably supported creation of the authoritarian system. The more "respectable" and "responsible" the opposition appears, the easier it is to win more supporters.

3. Cultivate generals. In the last analysis, whether the regime collapses or not depends on whether they support the regime, join you in opposition to it, or stand by on the sidelines. Support from the military could be helpful when the crisis comes, but all you really need is military unwillingness to defend the regime.

4. Practice and preach nonviolence. . . . Among other things, this will make it easier for you to win over the security forces: soldiers do not tend to be sympathetic to people who have been hurling Molotov cocktails at them.

5. Seize every opportunity to express opposition to the regime, including participation in elections it organizes. . . .

6. Develop contacts with the global media, foreign human rights organizations, and transnational organizations such as churches. In particular, mobilize supporters in the United States. American congressmembers are always looking for moral causes to get publicity for themselves and to use against the American administration. Dramatize your cause to them and provide them with material for TV photo opportunities and headline-making speeches.

7. Promote unity among opposition groups. Attempt to create comprehensive umbrella organizations that will facilitate cooperation among such groups. This will be difficult and, as the examples of the Philippines, Chile, Korea, and South Africa show, authoritarian rulers are often expert in promoting opposition disunity. One test of your qualifications to become a democratic leader of your country is your ability to overcome these obstacles and secure some measure of opposition unity. Remember Gabriel Almond's truth: "Great leaders are great coalition builders."[20]

8. When the authoritarian regime falls, be prepared quickly to fill the vacuum of authority that results. This can be done by: pushing to the fore a popular, charismatic, democratically inclined leader; promptly organizing elections to provide popular legitimacy to a new government; and building international legitimacy by getting support of foreign and transnational actors (international organizations, the United States, the European Community, the Catholic Church). Recognize that some of your former coalition partners will want to establish a new dictatorship of their own and quietly organize the supporters of democracy to counter this effort if it materializes.

TRANSPLACEMENTS

In transplacements democratization is produced by the combined actions of government and opposition. Within the government the balance between standpatters and reformers is such that the government is willing to negotiate a change of regime—unlike the situation of standpatter dominance that leads to replacement—but it is unwilling to initiate a change of regime. It has to be pushed and or pulled into formal or informal negotiations with the opposition. Within the opposition democratic moderates are strong enough to prevail over antidemocratic radicals, but they are not strong enough to overthrow the government. Hence they too see virtues in negotiation.

Approximately eleven of thirty-five liberalizations and democratizations that occurred or began in the 1970s and 1980s approximated the transplacement model. The most notable ones were in Poland, Czechoslovakia, Uruguay, and Korea; the regime changes in Bolivia, Honduras, El Salvador, and Nicaragua also involved significant elements of transplacement. In El Salvador and Honduras the negotiations were in part with the United States government, acting as a surrogate for democratic moderates. In 1989 and 1990, South Africa began a transplacement process, and Mongolia and Nepal appeared to be moving in that direction. Some features of transplacement were also present in Chile. The Pinochet regime was strong enough, however, to resist opposition pressure to negotiate democratization and stubbornly adhered to the schedule for regime change that it laid down in 1980.

In successful transplacements, the dominant groups in both government and opposition recognized that they were incapable of unilaterally determining the nature of the future political system in their society. Government and opposition leaders often developed these views after testing each other's strength and resolve in a political dialectic. Initially, the opposition usually believed that it would be able to bring about the downfall of the government at some point in the not too distant future. This belief was on occasion wildly unrealistic, but so long as opposition leaders held to it, serious negotiations with the government were impossible. In contrast, the government usually initially believed that it could effectively contain and suppress the opposition without incurring unacceptable costs. Transplacements occurred when the beliefs of both changed. The opposition realized that it was not strong enough to overthrow the government. The government realized that the opposition was strong enough to increase significantly the costs of nonnegotiation in terms of increased repression leading to further alienation of groups from the government, intensified divisions within the ruling coalition, increased possibility of a hardline takeover of the government, and significant losses in international legitimacy.

The transplacement dialectic often involved a distinct sequence of steps. First, the government engaged in some liberalization and began to lose power and authority. Second, the opposition exploited this loosening by and weakening of the government to expand its support and intensify its activities with the hope and expectation it would shortly be able to bring down the government. Third, the government reacted forcefully to contain and suppress the mobilization of political power by the opposition. Fourth, government and opposition leaders perceived a standoff emerging and began to explore the possibilities of a negotiated transition. This fourth step was not, however, inevitable. Conceivably, the government, perhaps after a change of leadership, could brutally use its military and police forces to restore its power, at least temporarily. Or the opposition could continue to develop its strength, further eroding the power of the government and eventually bringing about its downfall. Transplacements thus required some rough equality of strength between government and opposition as well as uncertainty on each side as to who would prevail in a major test of strength. In these circumstances, the risks of negotiation and compromise appeared less than the risks of confrontation and catastrophe.

The political process leading to transplacement was thus often marked by a seesawing back and forth of strikes, protests, and demonstrations, on the one hand, and repression, jailings, police violence, states of siege, and martial law, on the other. Cycles of protest and repression in Poland, Czechoslovakia, Uruguay, Korea, and Chile eventually led to negotiated agreements between government and opposition in all cases except that of Chile.

In Uruguay, for instance, mounting protests and demonstrations in the fall of 1983 stimulated the negotiations leading to the military withdrawal from power. In Bolivia in 1978 "a series of conflicts and protest movements" preceded the military's agreeing to a timetable for elections.[21] In Korea as in Uruguay, the military regime had earlier forcefully suppressed protests. In the spring of 1987, however, the demonstrations became more massive and broad-based and increasingly involved the middle class. The government first reacted in its usual fashion but then shifted, agreed to negotiate, and accepted the central demands of the opposition. In Poland the 1988 strikes had a similar impact. As one commentator explained, "The strikes made the round table not only possible, but necessary—for both sides. Paradoxically, the strikes were strong enough to compel the communists to go to the round table, yet too weak to allow Solidarity's leaders to refuse negotiations. That's why the round table talks took place."[22]

In transplacements, the eyeball-to-eyeball confrontation in the central square of the capital between massed protesters and serried ranks of police revealed each side's strengths and weaknesses. The opposition could mobilize massive support; the government could contain and withstand opposition pressure.

Politics in South Africa in the 1980s also evolved along the lines of the four-step model. In the late 1970s P.W. Botha began the process of liberalizing reform, arousing black expectations and then frustrating them when the 1983 constitution denied blacks a national political role. This led to uprisings in the black townships in 1984 and 1985, which stimulated black hopes that the collapse of the Afrikaner-dominated regime was imminent. The government's forceful and effective suppression of black and white dissent then compelled the opposition drastically to revise their hopes. At the same time, the uprisings attracted international attention, stimulated condemnation of both the apartheid system and the government's tactics, and led the United States and European governments to intensify economic sanctions against South Africa. As the hopes for revolution of the African National Congress (ANC) radicals declined, the worries of the National party government about international legitimacy and the economic future increased. In the mid-1970s, Joe Slovo, head of the South African Communist party and the ANC's military organization, argued that the ANC could overthrow the government and win power through sustained guerrilla warfare and revolution. In the late 1980s he remained committed to the use of violence, but saw negotiations as the more likely route for achieving ANC goals. After becoming president of South Africa in 1989, F.W. de Klerk also emphasized the importance of negotiations. The lesson of Rhodesia, he said, was that "When the opportunity was there for real, constructive negotiation, it was not grasped. . . . It went wrong because in the reality of their circumstances they waited too long before engaging in fundamental negotiation and dialogue. We must not make that mistake, and we are determined not to repeat that mistake."[23] The two political leaders were learning from their own experience and that of others.

In Chile, in contrast, the government was willing and able to avoid negotiation. Major strikes erupted in the spring of 1983, but a national general strike was suppressed by the government. Beginning in May 1983 the opposition organized massive monthly demonstrations on "Days of National Protest." These were broken up by the police, usually with several people being killed. Economic problems and the opposition protests forced the Pinochet government to initiate a dialogue with the opposition. The economy then began to recover, however, and the middle classes became alarmed at the breakdown of law and order. A national strike in October 1984 was put down with considerable bloodshed. Shortly thereafter the government reimposed the state of siege that had been cancelled in 1979. The opposition efforts thus failed to overthrow the government or to induce it to engage in meaningful negotiations. The opposition had "overestimated its strength and underestimated the government's."[24] It had also underestimated Pinochet's tenacity and political skill and the willingness of Chilean security forces to shoot unarmed civilian demonstrators.

Transplacements required leaders on both sides willing to risk negotiations. Divisions of opinion over negotiations usually existed within governing elites. At times, the top leaders had to be pressured by their colleagues and by circumstances to negotiate with the opposition. In 1989, for instance, Adam Michnik argued that Poland, like Hungary, was following "the Spanish way to democracy." At one level, he was right in that both the Spanish and Polish transitions were basically peaceful. At a more particular level, however, the Spanish analogy did not hold for Poland because Jaruzelski was not a Juan Carlos or Suárez (whereas Imre Pozsgay in Hungary in considerable measure was). Jaruzelski was a reluctant democrat who had to be pushed by the deterioration of his country and his regime into negotiations with Solidarity.[25] In Uruguay the president, General Gregorio Alvarez, wanted to prolong his power and postpone democratization and had to be forced by the other members of the military junta to move ahead with the regime change. In Chile, General Pinochet was somewhat similarly under pressure from other junta members, especially the air force commander, General Fernando Matthei, to be more forthcoming in dealing with the opposition, but Pinochet successfully resisted this pressure.

In other countries changes occurred in the top leadership before serious negotiations with the opposition began. In Korea the government of General Chun Doo Hwan followed a staunch standpatter policy of stonewalling opposition demands and suppressing opposition activity. In 1987, however, the governing party designated Roh Tae Woo as its candidate to succeed Chun. Roh dramatically reversed Chun's policies, announced a political opening, and entered into negotiations with the opposition leader.[26] In Czechoslovakia the long-in-power standpatter Communist party general secretary, Gustav Husak, was succeeded by the mildly reformist Milos Jakes in December 1987. Once the opposition became mobilized in the fall of 1989, however, Jakes was replaced by the reformer Karel Urbanek. Urbanek and the reformist prime minister, Ladislav Adamec, then negotiated arrangements for the transition to democracy with Vaclav Havel and the other leaders of the opposition Civic Forum. In South Africa, de Klerk moved beyond his predecessor's aborted transformation process from above to transplacement-type negotiations with black opposition leaders. Uncertainty, ambiguity, and division of opinion over democratization thus tended to characterize the ruling circles in transplacement situations. These regimes were not overwhelmingly committed either to holding on to power ruthlessly or to moving decisively toward democracy.

Disagreement and uncertainty existed not only on the government side in transplacements. In fact, the one group more likely to be divided against itself than the leaders of a decaying authoritarian government are the opposition leaders who aspire to replace them. In replacement situations the government suppresses the opposition and the opposition has an overriding common interest in bringing down the government. As the Philippine and Nicaraguan examples indicate, even under these conditions securing unity among opposition leaders and parties may be extremely difficult, and the unity achieved is often tenuous and fragile. In transplacements, where it is a question not of overthrowing the government but of negotiating with it, opposition unity is even more difficult to achieve. It was not achieved in Korea, and hence the governmental candidate, Roh Tae Woo, was elected president with a minority of the vote, as the two opposition candidates split the antigovernment majority by opposing each other. In Uruguay, because its leader was still imprisoned, one opposition

party—the National party—rejected the agreement reached between the two other parties and the military. In South Africa a major obstacle to democratic reform was the many divisions within the opposition between parliamentary and nonparliamentary groups, Afrikaner and English, black and white, and among black ideological and tribal groups. At no time before the 1990s did the South African government confront anything but a bewildering multiplicity of opposition groups whose differences among themselves were often as great as their differences with the government.

In Chile the opposition was seriously divided into a large number of parties, factions, and coalitions. In 1983, the moderate centrist opposition parties were able to join together in the Democratic Alliance. In August 1985 a broader group of a dozen parties joined in the National Accord calling for a transition to democracy. Yet conflicts over leadership and tactics continued. In 1986 the Chilean opposition mobilized massive protests, hoping to duplicate in Santiago what had just happened in Manila. The opposition, however, was divided and its militancy frightened conservatives. The problem, as one observer put it at the time, was that "the general is not being challenged by a moderate opposition movement that has got itself together under the leadership of a respected figure. There is no Chilean Cory."[27] In Poland, on the other hand, things were different. Lech Walesa was a Polish Cory, and Solidarity dominated the opposition for most of a decade. In Czechoslovakia the transplacement occurred so quickly that differences among opposition political groups did not have time to materialize.

In transplacements democratic moderates have to be sufficiently strong within the opposition to be credible negotiating partners with the government. Almost always some groups within the opposition reject negotiations with the government. They fear that negotiations will produce undesirable compromises and they hope that continued opposition pressure will bring about the collapse or the overthrow of the government. In Poland in 1988–89, right-wing opposition groups urged a boycott of the Round Table talks. In Chile left-wing opposition groups carried out terrorist attacks that undermined the efforts of the moderate opposition to negotiate with the government. Similarly, in Korea radicals rejected the agreement on elections reached by the government and the leading opposition groups. In Uruguay, the opposition was dominated by leaders of moderate political parties and extremists were less of a problem.

For negotiations to occur each party had to concede some degree of legitimacy to the other. The opposition had to recognize the government as a worthy partner in change and implicitly if not explicitly acquiesce in its current right to rule. The government, in turn, had to accept the opposition groups as legitimate representatives of significant segments of society. The government could do this more easily if the opposition groups had not engaged in violence. Negotiations were also easier if the opposition groups, such as political parties under a military regime, had previously been legitimate participants in the political process. It was easier for the opposition to negotiate if the government had used only limited violence against it and if there were some democratic reformers in the government whom it had reason to believe shared its goals.

In transplacements, unlike transformations and replacements, government leaders often negotiated the basic terms of the regime change with opposition leaders they had previously had under arrest: Lech Walesa, Vaclav Havel, Jorge Batlle Ibanez, Kim Dae Jung and Kim Young Sam, Walter Sisulu and Nelson Mandela. There were good reasons for this. Opposition leaders who have been in prison have not been fighting the government, violently or nonviolently; they have been living with it. They have also experienced the reality of government power. Governmental leaders who released their captives were usually interested in reform, and those released were usually moderate enough to be willing to negotiate with their former captors. Imprisonment also enhanced the moral authority of the former prisoners. This helped them to unite the opposition groups, at least temporarily, and to hold out the prospect to the government that they could secure the acquiescence of their followers to whatever agreement was reached.

At one point in the Brazilian transition, General Golbery reportedly told an opposition leader, "You get your radicals under control and we will control ours."[28] Getting radicals under control often requires the cooperation of the other side. In transplacement negotiations, each party has an interest in strengthening the other party so that he can deal more effectively with the extremists on his side. In June 1990, for

instance, Nelson Mandela commented on the problems F.W. de Klerk was having with white hard-liners and said that the ANC had appealed "to whites to assist de Klerk. We are also trying to address the problems of white opposition to him. Discussions have already been started with influential sectors in the right wing." At the same time, Mandela said that his own desire to meet with Chief Mengosuthu Buthelezi had been vetoed by militants within the ANC and that he had to accept that decision because he was "a loyal and disciplined member of the A.N.C."[29] De Klerk obviously had an interest in strengthening Mandela and helping him deal with his militant left-wing opposition.

Negotiations for regime change were at times preceded by "prenegotiations" about the conditions for entering into negotiations. In South Africa, the government precondition was that the ANC renounce violence. ANC preconditions were that the government urban opposition groups [sic] and release political prisoners. In some cases prenegotiations concerned which opposition individuals and groups would be involved in the negotiations.

Negotiations were sometimes lengthy and sometimes brief. They often were interrupted as one party or the other broke them off. As the negotiations continued, however, the political future of each of the parties became more engaged with their success. If the negotiations failed, standpatters within the governing coalition and radicals in the opposition stood ready to capitalize on that failure and to bring down the leaders who had engaged in negotiations. A common interest emerged and the sense of a common fate. "[I]n a way," Nelson Mandela observed in August 1990, "there is an alliance now" between the ANC and the National party. "We are on one boat, one ship," agreed National Party leader R.F. Botha, "and the sharks to the left and the sharks to the right are not going to distinguish between us when we fall overboard."[30] Consequently, as negotiations continued, the parties became more willing to compromise in order to reach an agreement.

The agreements they reached often generated attacks from others in government and opposition who thought the negotiators had conceded too much. The specific agreements reflected, of course, issues peculiar to their countries. Of central importance in almost all negotiations, however, was the exchange of guarantees.

In transformations former officials of the authoritarian regime were almost never punished; in replacements they almost always were. In transplacements this was often an issue to be negotiated; the military leaders in Uruguay and Korea, for instance, demanded guarantees against prosecution and punishment for any human rights violations. In other situations, negotiated guarantees involved arrangements for the sharing of power or for changes in power through elections. In Poland each side was guaranteed an explicit share of the seats in the legislature. In Czechoslovakia positions in the cabinet were divided between the two parties. In both these countries coalition governments reassured communists and the opposition that their interests would be protected during the transition. In Korea the governing party agreed to a direct, open election for the presidency on the assumption, and possibly the understanding, that at least two major opposition candidates would run, thereby making highly probable victory for the government party's candidate.

The risks of confrontation and of losing thus impel government and opposition to negotiate with each other; and guarantees that neither will lose everything become the basis for agreement. Both get the opportunity to share in power or to compete for power. Opposition leaders know they will not be sent back to prison; government leaders know they will not have to flee into exile. Mutual reduction in risk prompts reformers and moderates to cooperate in establishing democracy.

Guidelines for Democratizers 3: Negotiating Regime Changes

For democratic reformers in government:

1. Following the guidelines for transforming authoritarian systems . . . first isolate and weaken your standpatter opposition and consolidate your hold on the government and political machinery.
2. Also following those guidelines, seize the initiative and surprise both opposition and standpatters with the concessions you are willing to make, but never make concessions under obvious opposition pressure.
3. Secure endorsement of the concept of negotiations from leading generals or other top officials in the security establishment.

4. Do what you can to enhance the stature, authority, and moderation of your principal opposition negotiating partner.
5. Establish confidential and reliable back-channels for negotiating key central questions with opposition leaders.
6. If the negotiation succeeds, you very probably will be in the opposition. Your prime concern, consequently, should be securing guarantees and safeguards for the rights of the opposition and of groups that have been associated with your government (e.g., the military). Everything else is negotiable.

For democratic moderates in the opposition:

1. Be prepared to mobilize your supporters for demonstrations when these will weaken the standpatters in the government. Too many marches and protests, however, are likely to strengthen them, weaken your negotiating partner, and arouse middle-class concern about law and order.
2. Be moderate; appear statesmanlike.
3. Be prepared to negotiate and, if necessary, make concessions on all issues except the holding of free and fair elections.
4. Recognize the high probability that you will win those elections and do not take actions that will seriously complicate your governing your country.

For both government and opposition democratizers:

1. The political conditions favorable to a negotiated transition will not last indefinitely. Seize the opportunity they present and move quickly to resolve the central issues.
2. Recognize that your political future and that of your partner depend on your success in reaching agreement on the transition to democracy.
3. Resist the demands of leaders and groups on your side that either delay the negotiating process or threaten the core interest of your negotiating partner.
4. Recognize that the agreement you reach will be the only alternative; radicals and standpatters may denounce it, but they will not be able to produce an alternative that commands broad support.
5. When in doubt, compromise.

Reading Notes

1. See Raymond Carr, "Introduction: The Spanish Transition to Democracy in Historical Perspective," in *Spain in the 1980s: The Democratic Transition and a New International Role*, ed. Robert P. Clark and Michael H. Haltzel (Cambridge: Ballinger, 1987), pp. 3–4.

2. Alfred Stepan, "Introduction," in *Democratizing Brazil: Problems of Transition and Consolidation*, ed. Stepan (New York: Oxford University Press, 1989), p. ix.

3. Ibid.; Scott Mainwaring, "The Transition to Democracy in Brazil," *Journal of Interamerican Studies and World Affairs* 28 (Spring 1986), p. 149; Kenneth Medhurst, "Spain's Evolutionary Pathway from Dictatorship to Democracy," in *New Mediterranean Democracies*, ed. Pridham, p. 30.

4. Paul Preston, *The Triumph of Democracy in Spain* (London: Methuen, 1986), p. 93; Donald Share and Scott Mainwaring, "Transitions Through Transaction: Democratization in Brazil and Spain," in *Political Liberalization in Brazil: Dynamics, Dilemmas, and Future Prospects*, ed. Wayne A. Selcher (Boulder Colo.: Westview Press, 1986), p. 179; Samuel P. Huntington, *Political Order in Changing Societies* (New Haven: Yale University Press, 1968), pp. 344–57.

5. Jacques Rupnik, "Hungary's Quiet Revolution," *New Republic*, November 20, 1989, p. 20; *New York Times*, April 16, 1989, p. E3.

6. Quoted by Abugattas in *Authoritarians and Democrats*, ed. Malloy and Seligson, p. 129, and by Sylvia T. Borzutzky, "The Pinochet Regime: Crisis and Consolidation," in *Authoritarians and Democrats*, ed. Malloy and Seligson, p. 85.

7. See Needler, "The Military Withdrawal," pp. 621–23 on "second phase" coups and the observation that "the military government that returns power to civilian hands is not the same one that seized power from the constitutional government in the first place."

8. Stepan, *Rethinking Military Politics*, pp. 32–40 and Thomas E. Skidmore, "Brazil's Slow Road to Democratization: 1974–1985," in *Democratizing Brazil*, ed.

Stepan, p. 33. The interpretation coincides with my own impression of Golbery's intentions that I formed in 1974 working with him on plans for Brazil's democratization. For a contrary argument, see Silvio R. Duncan Baretta and John Markoff, "Brazil's *Abertura*: A Transition from What to What?" in *Authoritarians and Democrats*, ed. Malloy and Seligson, pp. 45–46.

9. Quoted in Francisco Weffort, "Why Democracy?" in *Democratizing Brazil*, ed. Stepan, p. 332.

10. Raymond Carr and Juan Pablo Fusi Aizpurua, *Spain: Dictatorship to Democracy*, 2nd ed. (London: Allen & Unwin, 1981), pp. 198–206.

11. Quoted in David Remnick, "The Struggle for Light," *New York Review of Books*, August 16, 1990, p. 6.

12. See Stepan, *Rethinking Military Politics*, pp. 42–43.

13. Giuseppe Di Palma highlighted the significance of backward legitimacy in "Founding Coalitions in Southern Europe: Legitimacy and Hegemony," *Government and Opposition* 15 (Spring 1980), p. 170. See also Nancy Bermeo, "Redemocratization and Transition Elections: A Comparison of Spain and Portugal," *Comparative Politics* 19 (January 1987), p. 218.

14. Stanley G. Payne, "The Role of the Armed Forces in the Spanish Transition," in *Spain in the 1980s*, ed. Clark and Haltzel, p. 86; Stepan, *Rethinking Military Politics*, p. 36.

15. Theses presented by the Central Committee, Ninth Congress, Communist Party of Spain, April 5–9, 1978, quoted in Juan J. Linz, "Some Comparative Thoughts on the Transition to Democracy in Portugal and Spain," in Jorge Braga de Macedo and Simon Serfaty, eds., *Portugal Since the Revolution: Economic and Political Perspectives* (Boulder, Colo.: Westview Press, 1981), p. 44; Preston, *Triumph of Democracy in Spain*, p. 137.

16. Skidmore, "Brazil's Slow Road," in *Democratizing Brazil*, ed. Stepan, p. 34.

17. Virgilio R. Beltran, "Political Transition in Argentina: 1982 to 1985," *Armed Forces and Society* 13 (Winter 1987), p. 217; Scott Mainwaring and Eduardo J. Viola, "Brazil and Argentina in the 1980s," *Journal of*

International Affairs 38 (Winter 1985), pp. 206–9.

18. Robert Harvey, Portugal: Birth of a Democracy (London: Macmillan, 1978), p. 2.

19. Myron Weiner has formulated a similar and more concise set of recommendations: "For those who seek democratization the lessons are these: mobilize large-scale nonviolent opposition to the regime, seek support from the center and, if necessary, from the conservative right, restrain the left and keep them from dominating the agenda of the movement, woo sections of the military, seek sympathetic coverage from the western media, and press the United States for support." "Empirical Democratic Theory and the Transition from Authoritarianism to Democracy," PS 20 (Fall 1987), p. 866.

20. Gabriel A. Almond, "Approaches to Developmental Causation," in Crisis, Choice, and Change: Historical Studies of Political Development, ed. Gabriel A. Almond, Scott C. Flanagan, and Robert J. Mundt (Boston: Little, Brown, 1973), p. 32.

21. Washington Post, October 7, 1983, p. A3; Laurence Whitehead, "Bolivia's Failed Democratization, 1977–1980," in Transitions from Authoritarian Rule: Latin America, ed. Guillermo O'Donnell, Philippe C. Schmitter, and Laurence Whitehead (Baltimore: Johns Hopkins University Press, 1986), p. 59.

22. "Leoplitax" (identified as a "political commentator in the Polish underground press"), Uncaptive Minds 2 (May–June–July 1989), p. 5.

23. Steve Mufson, "Uncle Joe," New Republic, September 28, 1987, pp. 22–23; Washington

Post National Weekly, February 19–25, 1990, p. 7.

24. Edgardo Boeniger, "The Chilean Road to Democracy," Foreign Affairs 64 (Spring 1986), p. 821.

25. Anna Husarska, "A Talk with Adam Michnik," New Leader, April 3–17, 1989, p. 10; Marcin Sulkowski, "The Dispute About the General," Uncaptive Minds 3 (March–April 1990), pp. 7–9.

26. See James Cotton, "From Authoritarianism to Democracy in South Korea," Political Studies 37 (June 1989), pp. 252–53.

27. Economist, May 10, 1986, p. 39; Alfred Stepan, "The Last Days of Pinochet?" New York Review of Books, June 2, 1988, p. 34.

28. Quoted by Weffort, "Why Democracy," in Democratizing Brazil, ed. Stepan, p. 345, and by Thomas G. Sanders, "Decompression," in Military Government and the Movement Toward Democracy in South America, ed. Howard Handelman and Thomas G. Sanders (Bloomington: Indiana University Press, 1981), p. 157. As Weffort points out, this advice was somewhat beside the point in Brazil. Before starting its transformation process the Brazilian military regime had physically eliminated most of the serious radicals. The aide's advice is much more relevant in transplacement situations.

29. Time, June 25, 1990, p. 21.

30. Mandela quoted in Pauline H. Baker, "Turbulent Transitions," Journal of Democracy 1 (Fall 1990), p. 17; Botha quoted in Washington Post National Weekly Edition, May 14–20, 1990, p. 17.

KEY TERMS

Liberal Democracy   The type of democracy that emphasizes the protection and unhindered practice of the political and civil rights and liberties of individual citizens.

Majoritarian Democracy   Type of democracy that concentrates political power in the hands of an electoral majority.

Polyarchy   An ideal political system, which, according to Robert Dahl, is characterized by the full participation of the population in the electoral process, and full contestability of government. Democracy approximates this ideal type very closely.

Representative Democracy A type of democracy in which the political will of the people is exercised through the decisions and choices of the agents whom they select to represent them. Representative democracy provides for indirect rule by the people. A parliamentary democracy is a form of indirect and representative democracy.

Wave of Democracy Sudden increase in the number of democratic regimes.

FURTHER READINGS

Colomer, Josep. *Strategic Transitions: Game Theory and Democratization*. Baltimore: Johns Hopkins University Press, 2000.

Dahl, Robert. *Polyarchy: Participation and Opposition*. New Haven: Yale University Press, 1971.

Held, David. *Models of Democracy*. Cambridge, MA: Polity Press, 1996.

Przeworski, Adam. *Democracy and the Market: Political and Economic Reforms in Eastern Europe and Latin America*. Cambridge MA: Cambridge University Press, 1991.

WEB LINKS

Freedom House:
www.freedomhouse.org

Human Development Reports:
http://hdr.undp.org

US Federal Research Division—Country Studies:
http://lcweb2.loc.gov/frd/cs/cshome.html

CHAPTER 14

GLOBALIZATION

What is globalization? While the term "globalization" is frequently invoked in the political and economic discourses of the West, it often remains undefined. Some authors use globalization to describe increases in international economic integration, spurred on by the rapid international flows of trade, investments, and information. Others adopt a broader definition of globalization that encompasses the forces that are transforming political and cultural landscapes, both at the national and international levels. The emergence of transnational issues, such as environmental pollution, terrorism, and AIDS, and the social movements that have rallied around them, have underscored the interdependence and interconnection of people and events across the globe. This chapter examines the various dimensions of globalization and their implications for politics, governance, and civil society.

ECONOMIC DIMENSIONS OF GLOBALIZATION

"**Globalization**" is often used to describe the increased integration and internationalization of economic affairs facilitated by rapid technological changes in information gathering and communications. While some argue that the phenomenon described as globalization is nothing new, given that international connectedness has always existed, others distinguish today's era of globalization by the intensity and scope of worldwide economic integration.[1] National economies have become integrated by way of increased trade linkages, growth in cross-border financial flows, increased international production, and lastly through treaties and supranational institutions. A distinguishing feature of globalization is the emergence of supranational decision-making bodies dealing with economic issues such as monetary policy and trade. International organizations such as the World Trade Organization (WTO), the International Monetary Fund (IMF), and the World Bank have become the most important institutions in economic affairs. They have facilitated the proliferation of cross-border exchanges by reducing barriers to trade and finance between countries.

Another important feature of today's global economy is the phenomenon of multinational or transnational corporations. These corporations are major actors in global trade and especially in global production. Companies are increasingly looking beyond their national markets, and enjoying the comparative advantage of alternative production sites in other countries. For example, in an effort to increase profits, a Canadian company can move its production process to Mexico where labour is cheaper. Due to the direct investment they provide to the host countries' economies, multinational firms are often exempt from domestic economic policies, such as minimum wage laws.

The implications of economic globalization for developed and developing countries have been a subject of much debate. Proponents of globalization argue that everyone benefits in a global economy. Increased economic integration provides developed countries with larger markets for their goods, while developing countries reap the economic benefits of sharing in the global production process via multinational corporations. This neoliberal economic perspective, often referred to as the "Washington consensus," is reflected in the IMF–led structural adjustment programs aimed at promoting capital liberalization in the developing world. Others, however, argue that economic globalization, and the international governance regime that accompanies it, is skewed in favour of wealthier countries. Rejecting standard neoliberal economic theory, researchers studying the developing countries contend that the globalization of production actually impedes long-term economic growth in those countries by preventing them from investing in industries that contribute to long-term economic growth. Due to the low cost of labour, developing countries are usually given the labour-intensive parts of the global production process. This prevents these countries from investing in industries that drive economic development in the long term. Rather than promoting economic self-sufficiency and prosperity, globalization helps maintain the economic dependency of developing countries in the global economic system. Globalization therefore leads to greater wealth disparity between the developed and developing worlds. For this reason, many critics argue that globalization constitutes a modern form of colonization.[2]

The international division of labour and production also has implications for workers in advanced industrial societies. Critics of globalization argue that as labour-intensive production gets shifted to more attractive (i.e., cheaper) sites in developing countries, income disparities between high-skilled and low-skilled workers in advanced societies will rise. For example, low-skilled workers in manufacturing, many of whom are women and minorities, are most vulnerable in this global economy. Moreover, the political influence of labour is also significantly hampered by globalization. The capacity of unions to organize and demand better wages in collective bargaining is severely limited because firms can decide to "set up shop" elsewhere. For these reasons, the gap between rich and poor and skilled and unskilled labourers will only increase in industrialized societies.

GLOBALIZATION AND STATE SOVEREIGNTY

The impact of globalization on **state sovereignty** has become an important issue of debate among scholars. Held and McGrew identify three perspectives on this issue that have emerged in the scholarly literature: the "hyperglobalists," the "skeptics," and the "transformationalists." Hyperglobalists believe economic globalization is bringing about revolutionary change to prevailing political institutions and processes. The emergence of a single global economy and the growing influence of international decision-making bodies like the World Trade Organization and the World Bank are shifting the locus of political authority from the nation-state to global finance and corporate capital. As Held and McGrew explain, "the hyperglobalists hold, the autonomy and sovereignty of nation-states have been eclipsed by contemporary processes of economic globalization."[3] Strange argues that globalization has eroded the power of the state in three important areas: defence, finance, and welfare. In the area of defence, war has become less rational and therefore less likely as countries become more "interconnected" through trade. As Strange explains, " . . . people recognize that success in gaining world market shares has replaced territorial acquisition as the means to survival."[4] The increased mobility of capital has also diminished the state's authority in the area of finance. With the notable exception of the United States, most states no longer have the power to control their own currencies. Moreover, states are constrained by global market forces when setting interest rates and inflation rates. For example, higher interest rates lead to higher exchange rates, which in turn, diminish the international competitiveness of export-oriented industries. Globalization has therefore limited the state's scope of action in the area of monetary policy. The final area in which the state's authority is diminished is welfare. Programs and services typically associated with the **welfare state** are in jeopardy as states strive to create a favourable investment climate in their countries. Taxation, the major source of funding of welfare programs, discourages multinational companies from investing in the domestic economy. These global economic forces, many argue, compel states to cut back on social services and programs.

The state's authority to act in these areas has been significantly constrained by supranational institutions like the IMF, the World Bank, and the WTO. As mentioned earlier, the IMF is responsible for undertaking detailed reviews of the monetary policies of member states. The IMF's and World Bank's influence on monetary and fiscal policy is especially pronounced in countries participating in the agencies' structural adjustment programs. State sovereignty is also constrained by the WTO, which requires member governments to abide by its regulations governing international trade. As Scholte explains, "the WTO charter commits member states to alter their statutes and procedures to conform with transworld trade law, and in trade disputes a WTO ruling against *a* state is binding unless *every* member of the organization votes to overturn the judgment. In these ways and others, many decisions concerning the regulatory environment for capitalism now come to rather than from the state."[5]

The "skeptics," on the other hand, reject the idea of a unified global economy and dismiss the view that globalization constitutes a new or revolutionary phenomenon. Influenced by Marxist-Leninist thought, the skeptical position contends that economic globalization has been propelled by the most powerful capitalist states to secure their global dominance. It represents the latest mode of development of contemporary capitalism.[6] Globalization is another term for global capitalism and imperialism and is therefore condemned by skeptics for propagating liberal market principles to more regions of the world. Globalization therefore is not undermining state autonomy and sovereignty; rather, it is a manifestation of the nation-state's continuing role in the organization of capitalism. As Scholte explains,

> *Indeed, states have played an indispensable enabling role in the globalization of capital. Contrary to liberalist presumptions, every market requires a framework of rules, and states have created much of the regulatory environment in which transborder capital has thrived. For example, governments have facilitated global firms' operations and profits with suitably constructed property guarantees, investment codes, currency regulations, tax regimes, labor laws, and police protection.[7]*

The transformationalist perspective adopts a more neutral stance in its analysis, recognizing both positive and negative transformations brought about by emerging global forces. It neither celebrates nor condemns globalization; rather, it focuses on the way globalization is transforming social values, practices, and institutions in societies around the world. This position views globalization as a multidimensional and uneven process that is reorganizing political, economic, and cultural power.[8] The impact of globalization is contradictory; it can simultaneously unleash both divisive and unifying forces. Unlike the hyperglobalists, who argue that the state is in decline, transformationalists do not agree that state sovereignty is eroding; rather, they contend that the roles and functions of the state are being reconfigured within this new global system. Weiss refers to the state's "transformative capacities," that is, its ability "to adapt to external shocks and pressures by generating ever-new means of governing the process of industrial change."[9] Tranformationalists contend that we must move beyond the globalization versus state sovereignty debate as a zero-sum game. Instead, it is appropriate to view the state as transforming, as well as being transformed by, globalization. As Held explains, "Economic globalization by no means necessarily translates into a diminution of state power; rather, it is transforming the conditions under which state power is exercised."[10]

GLOBALIZATION AND THE WELFARE STATE

The impact of globalization on the welfare state and citizenship rights is another important area of debate. The main objectives of the modern welfare state were and continue to be to reduce poverty, to redistribute wealth among its citizens, and to provide a social safety net against various risks, including unemployment and ill health. Many argue that globalization has constrained the ability of nation-states to achieve these objectives, arguing that global economic forces undermine the fiscal basis of the welfare state. The drive toward economic integration has put pressure on national governments to cut their public expenditures on welfare programs in order to satisfy international competitive imperatives. National governments are pressured to lower taxes and cut social spending in an effort to encourage economic development. Moreover, social policies become increasingly aligned with the needs of the market rather than the needs of citizens. In the long run, these pressures will lead to the dismantling of welfare states and increasing inequalities in society.

Much of the discussion and research on the impact of globalization on welfare states centres on the case of the European Union (EU). Countries in Western Europe have joined together to form an economic and political union that, among other things, would eradicate trade barriers among member countries. Some argue that in an effort to facilitate economic integration, member countries have cut public spending in social welfare and income support programs. Open borders, they argue, have led to a "race to the bottom" in terms of the level of social provision. This is also the case in environmental policy, where national governments are feeling the pressure to relax their environmental standards and laws in order to attract foreign investment in their countries. Member states have adapted their national standards and regulations to be in line with those of other states in order to remain competitive in regional and global markets.

Paradoxically, the same global forces that are undermining the economic viability of the welfare state also contribute to greater reliance on its social safety net. As explained earlier, the international division of labour and production has led to greater income insecurity in advanced industrialized countries. As firms move their operations to underdeveloped countries where labour is cheap, low-skilled workers in developed countries experience greater unemployment and lower wages. The increased vulnerability of workers in the global economy creates internal pressures for national governments to continue providing social programs. The welfare state, therefore, is far from being dismantled; rather, as Pierson explains, it is being restructured and renegotiated as new political demands emerge within individual states.[11]

GLOBALIZATION AND CULTURE

The debate on globalization and culture centres on whether global dynamics will lead to a universal culture or to greater cultural fragmentation in the world. The universalization perspective claims that globalization is contributing to a united world culture, with all societies converging to a similar point under the rubric of a single "global civilization." Globalization, through information technologies like the Internet and international commerce, is affecting many components of culture, including language, religion, and lifestyles. As existing communities and cultures become increasingly interconnected, their values and ways of life are being redefined and homogenized, especially in urban centres. For example, it is becoming increasingly difficult to distinguish large urban centres in China, such as Shanghai, from those found in North America. There is growing optimism that globalization will gradually erode cultural barriers that have traditionally divided peoples around the world and that homogenization of local cultures will ultimately lead to a more peaceful world. Proponents of globalization argue that economic interdependence will lead to the adoption of democratic values around the world.

Other scholars are less optimistic of the democratic potential of cultural homogenization. Benjamin Barber argues that globalization is unleashing homogenizing and divisive forces that threaten democratic values and practices. Barber conceptualizes these paradoxical forces as the strife between McWorld forces, which represent the homogenizing global consumer culture, and Jihad forces, which fragment people along tribal, racial, and religious lines. McWorld represents the forces of economic integration that are drawing nations into one homogenous global network. While McWorld emphasizes peace, order, and stability, it also contradicts democracy by privileging market imperatives over political rights and civic liberties. Jihad also represents positive values such as solidarity and community; however, it brings with it undemocratic regimes such as theocracy, military rule, and dictatorships. Barber argues that the contradictory forces of McWorld and Jihad ultimately undermine democracy and its guardian, the nation-state.[12]

Critics of cultural globalization bemoan the loss of cultural diversity, arguing that globalization constitutes the imposition of American "consumer" culture on the entire world. The United States is regarded as the "cultural imperialist," exporting liberal-capitalist values to different regions of the world through cultural products, i.e., films, music, and television shows. For those critics, globalization is synonymous with Americanization, that is, the imperialistic worldwide expansion of Western consumer values at the expense of the world-views of other cultures. Through cultural imperialism, developing countries are pressured to alter their social institutions according to the values and practices of the West. The hegemony of American culture has been facilitated by the concentration of media ownership around the globe.

The homogenization of culture, however, is not inevitable. World culture theorists contend that while a world culture is indeed emerging, it does not require cultural sameness. As Ulf Hannerz explains, "There is now a world culture but we had better make sure we understand what this means: not a replication of uniformity but an organization of diversity, an increasing interconnectedness of varied local cultures as well as a development of cultures without a clear anchorage in any one territory."[13] Cultural globalization values and fosters cultural diversity in several ways. Interaction across national borders and the mixing of cultures in particular places encourages cultural pluralization. Moreover, the push for integration leads to resistance in various parts of the world as local cultures contest and resist adaptation to "foreign" or "Western" ideas. This leads to the preservation of traditional and local cultures. The state as well can be a point of resistance to cultural globalization. Governments in communist and fundamentalist Islamic countries, for example, strive to limit the influence of "Western" values and ideas by placing controls on their dissemination within their borders. Globalization also leads to "hybridization" or "glocalization" processes, whereby local cultures interpret global practices and norms in different ways according to their own traditions and value systems. Finally, globalization has led to the institutionalization of cultural diversity as a value in various international organizations like the UN and within individual countries. For example, Canada's multicultural policy reflects and reinforces the value of a culturally diverse society.

GLOBALIZATION AND CIVIL SOCIETY

The ability of nation-states to administer the economic and social affairs of their citizens has been challenged by globalization and the emergence of supranational decision-making bodies. International economic pressures are increasingly challenging the capacity of national governments to maintain and protect citizenship rights long associated with welfare provision and entitlements. The decline of the nation-state's authority to act in many areas of life has led to the re-emergence of civil society, or the third sector, as a significant player in global governance. While international and supranational institutions like the WTO and World Bank govern the economic dimension of globalization, civil society has taken up the cause of safeguarding democratic ideals and principles at the global level.

Civil society, or the third sector, refers to a domain or sphere that is parallel to but separate from the state. It comprises a broad range of organizations and associations that are found outside that state and the market, from advocacy groups to trade unions and professional associations.[14] At the centre of civil society are non-governmental organizations (NGOs)—advocacy groups dedicated to public interest causes such as environmental protection, women's issues, and human rights. While these organizations have always existed, their numbers and scope of action have broadened significantly with the advent of globalization. Their social and political agendas, once circumscribed to national boundaries, have become global in perspective, goals, and strategies. Many of these groups "think globally and act locally"; that is, they adopt a global perspective while directing their activism at the grass-roots level.

Other NGOs specifically address transnational problems and pursue their agendas by working with "like-minded" groups in other parts of the world. Communications technology like the Internet has facilitated the emergence of transnational networks addressing a diversity of issues from HIV/AIDS to aboriginal issues. Often, these networks have been successful in shaping policies at both the domestic and the international levels and have been able to put international pressure on governments that have transgressed in the area of human rights. For example, civil society organizations concerned with human rights and women's issues have been instrumental in bringing greater international attention to human rights violations in many parts of the world. They have appealed to international laws and decision-making bodies to influence the policies of individual governments. Today, many international conferences on global issues such as environment and development and human rights provide forums for NGOs to participate in the deliberations.

For many, the emerging global civil society is quickly replacing the nation-state as the defender of democratic values and principles. As the ability of national governments to influence decisions at the international and national levels diminishes, so does their capacity to protect political and civil rights of their citizens. Falk points to the emancipatory potential of the global civil society, arguing that NGOs have been responsible for the development of international humanitarian laws by which individual governments must abide.[15] Moreover, these groups, through protest movements, have drawn our attention to a number of issues, including environmental degradation. In recent years, NGOs have protested against what they perceive to be undemocratic decision-making processes of international institutions like the WTO and Group of Eight conferences. These protest movements have pressed for greater participation on the part of civil society in international decision-making bodies in order to influence decisions and policies that impact the lives of ordinary citizens.

Non-governmental organizations challenge traditional state-based notions of political community and citizenship, and advance the idea of a **cosmopolitan democracy** in which

PRIVATE WATER, PUBLIC GOOD

Globalization's next big brawl could well be about water. Across the world, the push is on to privatize cities' water services. Extreme caution is warranted before letting private companies provide something so essential. But there are cases where privatizing has helped hundreds of thousands of the poorest. The key is strong public regulation and rate increases for those who can afford them.

Water privatizations have caused widespread protests. Nearly 200 people were hurt and one boy was shot dead in protests in 2000 in Cochabamba, Bolivia, where a subsidiary of Bechtel substantially raised water rates.

In the view of many, water is a kind of natural right that no one should control. But while water may have come from God, it came without pipes. The cities of the developing world are ringed by slums that have no access to the water system and either use unclean river water or buy water from private sellers at exorbitant prices.

A top priority of every city should be getting water to those outside the water system. This means hooking up poor areas and providing the destitute with subsidies. But that requires money. American water systems are heavily subsidized by taxpayers. This is unrealistic in the developing world, where tax collection is very low. The only realistic solution is to subsidize the poor by charging industrial, wealthy, and middle-class users much higher rates.

Private systems, common in Europe, are still fairly rare in the developing world. When well managed, they can work well. Unfortunately, the rush to privatize has greatly outstripped the public interest. This is in part because of pressure from the water industry, which is largely European. At the behest of these companies, Europe is asking for rules at the World Trade Organization that would make it harder for governments to keep public control of services, including drinking water—a bald industry-protection measure that has no business in a trade agreement. The World Bank has also conditioned loans for water reform on private-sector participation.

If allowed, private water companies will favor richer customers, shift risks back to the government and invest as little as possible. In too many cases, companies have repeatedly renegotiated their original contract to increase rates or get out of requirements to connect poor neighborhoods. Governments that turn to privatization will need a lot of help from international institutions if they are to play the strong regulatory role required to make a privately run system a success.

Source: "Private Water, Public Good." Originally Published in *The New York Times*, March 11, 2003. Reprinted with permission.

members of different societies come together as world citizens in a global political community. Advocates of cosmopolitan democracy argue that as the state's capacity to influence the global forces that affect it diminishes, a transnational political order would have to emerge to protect democratic rights around the world. David Held, a strong proponent of cosmopolitan democracy, argues that democratic theory has to be reformulated in light of the erosion of state autonomy and calls for the conceptualization of a new political order.[16] He describes cosmopolitan democracy as a system of governance emerging from the diverse conditions and interconnections between different peoples and nations. He argues that while the economic dimension of globalization, that is, the internationalization of trade and finance and multinational corporations, undermines democracy, emerging forms of political governance containing transnational NGOs and social movements, as well as institutions like the EU and the UN, allow democracy to thrive at the global level. A cosmopolitan democratic community would consist of "an international community of democratic states and societies committed to upholding democratic public law both within and across their boundaries."[17] Others, however, view the possibility of a global citizenship and a global democratic community with skepticism, arguing that individuals will continue to identify themselves with their national political community. As Ignatieff argues, only the nation-state can continue to provide security and protection as well as recognition to citizens.[18]

NATIONAL AND REGIONAL RESPONSES TO GLOBALIZATION

The impact of globalization and the manner in which it is construed varies across countries and societies. In the Arab world, resistance to globalization is expressed mainly in the political-cultural spheres. Anti-American sentiments and terrorist attacks against U.S. regional allies and interests are in large measure expressions of opposition to Washington's increased political, military, economic, and cultural intrusion into Arab states and societies. This reflects the anger and disillusionment felt by dispossessed sectors of Arab society who have found themselves locked out of the political, social, and economic benefits of globalization. The conservative sectors of Arab societies have rejected post-9/11 American calls for social and educational reforms to counter the appeal of radical ideas, labelling them a camouflaged attempt to remake Arab societies and cultures away from their pristine Muslim identity. The more liberal social sectors express support for thorough cultural and political reform in the Arab world. They desire to see governments held accountable and citizens empowered through genuine and meaningful political participation. They also call for greater dialogue and tolerance not only between ethnic and cultural minorities in the Arab world, but also among the world's different religions and cultures. Increased globalization in the Arab world is bound to intensify this debate inside Arab states and societies in the short term. Most Arabs remain skeptical of George W. Bush's discourse about the necessity to spread democracy in the Arab world. They suspect that such American declarations are at best tactical, deployed to elicit sympathy for America at its moment of crisis in Iraq, and to force Arab regimes to adopt the American geopolitical regional agenda, but especially vis-à-vis Iraq, terrorism, weapons of mass destruction, and Israel. Yet Western consumer and cultural products remain popular among the middle and upper-middle urban classes of the Arab world. Indeed, English has emerged as the lingua franca of a young generation of Westernized Arabs who care much more about Beyonce than bin Laden.

The impact of globalization on countries like China and India has also been contradictory. In today's globalized world, India and China are two economic giants in Asia. With forty percent of the world's population residing in these two countries, their economies have outperformed those of the industrial developed world. Although the two countries have divergent patterns of growth with two different regime types—India a democracy and China a closed communist political system—they have pushed for extensive liberalization reforms by privatizing their economies. Both countries have emerged as attractive sources for foreign investment due to their prevailing low wages and a huge domestic market of middle-class consumers. China has overwhelmingly become the location for global manufacturing. India is fast becoming the preferred place for production and software and the handling of outsourced business services. While globalization has brought prosperity to these nations, it has not been without costs. The gap between the rich and poor has been increasing in both these countries. The marginalized sectors of the society—the rural poor, the working class poor in the urban centres, women—have become the major victims of globalization. Their lot, instead of improving, has become worse. In other words, the poor have become poorer. More than one-third of their populations live below the poverty line. India still lags in literacy. In both these countries, certain segments of the population, particularly women, do not enjoy the same privileges and rights as others. While globalization, via the Internet and international NGOs, has heightened the world's awareness of the social inequalities that exist in this part of the world, the economic benefits of globalization have not ameliorated the political and economic status of the poor in these societies.

***

The preceding discussion has highlighted a number of key issues and debates raised by globalization. While some would argue that globalization is not a unique phenomenon, others have emphasized the numerous ways in which global forces are transforming the political and economic landscape both at the national and international levels. Globalization not only entails greater economic integration but also denotes greater interconnectedness among people and places. It is a multi-dimensional process that is transforming notions of identity, governance, and civil society. Real or imagined, global economic pressures are influencing policies pursued by individual governments, as well as altering the relationship between citizen and state. An important point made in this chapter is that globalization is neither good nor bad, given its uneven and often contradictory effects. Understanding and assigning meaning to these effects continues to be a challenging and important task in the study of politics.

ENDNOTES

1. Leslie Pal, *Beyond Policy Analysis: Public Issues Management in Turbulent Times* (Scarborough: Nelson, 2000).
2. Martin Khor, *Views from the South: The Effects of Globalization and the WTO on Third World Countries* (Food First Books/International Forum on Globalization, 2000).
3. David Held and Anthony McGrew, "Globalization," *Oxford Companion to Politics*, 2001.
4. Susan Strange, "The Erosion of the State," *Current History* 96, no. 613 (November 1997): 366–69.
5. Jan Aart Scholte, "Global Capitalism and the State," *International Affairs* 73, no. 3 (July 1997): 427–52.
6. M. Castells, *The Rise of Network Society*, 2nd ed. (London: Blackwell Publishers, 2000).
7. Scholte, 1999.
8. D. Held, and A. McGrew, D. Goldblatt, and J. Perraton, *Global Transformations: Politics, Economics and Culture* (Cambridge, UK: Polity Press, 1999).
9. Linda Weiss, *The Myth of the Powerless State: Governing the Economy in a Global Era* (Cambridge, MA: Polity Press, 1998), 4.
10. Held, 2000.
11. Paul Pierson, "The New Politics of the Welfare State," *World Politics* 48, no. 2 (1996): 143–79.
12. Benjamin Barber, "Jihad vs. McWorld," *The Atlantic Monthly* (March 1992), 53–63.
13. Ulf Hannerz, *Transnational Connections: Culture, People, Places* (London: Routledge Press, 1996), 102.
14. Thomas Carothers, "Think Again: Civil Society," *Foreign Policy* (Winter 1999–2000). Accessed online at http://www.globalpolicy.org/ngos/civsoc.htm.
15. Robert Falk, *Predatory Globalization: A Critique* (Cambridge, UK: Polity Press, 1999).
16. David Held, *Democracy and the Global Order: From the Modern State to Cosmopolitan Governance* (Cambridge, UK: Polity Press, 1995).
17. Ibid., 229.
18. Michael Ignatieff, *Blood and Belonging: Journeys into the New Nationalism* (Toronto: Viking, 1993).

READINGS

The readings for this chapter are Benjamin Barber's "Jihad vs. McWorld" and an excerpt from Saskia Sassen's *Losing Control: Sovereignty in an Age of Globalization*. Barber's article provides an insightful analysis of the universalizing and tribalizing forces that accompany globalization and their consequences for democracy. He argues that both globalism and tribalism are detrimental to democratic ideals and values. The McWorld forces of globalism, which emphasize laissez-faire market imperatives and economic efficiency, undermine democratic principles of social justice and equality. While these universalizing forces encourage political and economic stability, they do so at the expense of community and cultural identity. This universalizing trend, however, also gives rise to the Jihad forces of tribalism in the form of religious fundamentalism and ethnic separatist movements. Minority groups, Barber asserts, struggle to resist integration and cultural imperialism by reasserting religious and ethnic identities and group conflicts. Both McWorld and Jihad forces work to undermine the sovereignty of the nation-state, thus undermining citizenship, democratic institutions, and rights. Barber contends that democratic values and institutions in the era of globalization can best be safeguarded through a confederal system of representation in which quasi-independent groups and communities come together in an economic and political union while still maintaining autonomy in local jurisdictional matters.

The second reading is from Saskia Sassen's book *Losing Control: Sovereignty in an Age of Globalization.* She discusses how globalization is impacting territoriality and sovereignty, two fundamental principles of the nation-state. She argues that sovereignty no longer resides within nation-states, but is located in transnational legal regimes and supranational institutions that govern the global economy. Governments are now held accountable for their policies by these new international organizations and agreements. Territoriality is also being partially denationalized with the geographical distribution of economic activities across state boundaries. Labour-intensive production is offshored to developing countries while highly competitive industries are disproportionately located in the "global cities" of highly developed countries. Sassen argues that territorial denationalizing of economic activities and new supranational legal regimes are not diminishing the significance of the state but instead reconfiguring its role in the economic arena. States, she argues, are not victims of globalization; rather, they have actively taken part in the negotiation and implementation of new legal regimes for global capital.

JIHAD VS. MCWORLD

Benjamin Barber

The two axial principles of our age— tribalism and globalism—clash at every point except one: they may both be threatening to democracy.

Just beyond the horizon of current events lie two possible political futures—both bleak, neither democratic. The first is a retribalization of large swaths of humankind by war and bloodshed: a threatened Lebanonization of national states in which culture is pitted against culture, people against people, tribe against tribe—a Jihad in the name of a hundred narrowly conceived faiths against every kind of interdependence, every kind of artificial social cooperation and civic mutuality. The second is being borne in on us by the onrush of economic and ecological forces that demand integration and uniformity and that mesmerize the world with fast music, fast computers, and fast food—with MTV, Macintosh, and McDonald's, pressing nations into one commercially homogenous global network: one McWorld tied together by technology, ecology, communications, and commerce. The planet is falling precipitly apart *and* coming reluctantly together at the very same moment.

These two tendencies are sometimes visible in the same countries at the same instant: thus Yugoslavia, clamoring just recently to join the

New Europe, is exploding into fragments; India is trying to live up to its reputation as the world's largest integral democracy while powerful new fundamentalist parties like the Hindu nationalist Bharatiya Janata Party, along with nationalist assassins, are imperiling its hard-won unity. States are breaking up or joining up: the Soviet Union has disappeared almost overnight, its parts forming new unions with one another or with like-minded nationalities in neighboring states. The old interwar national state based on territory and political sovereignty looks to be a mere transitional development.

The tendencies of what I am here calling the forces of Jihad and the forces of McWorld operate with equal strength in opposite directions, the one driven by parochial hatreds, the other by universalizing markets, the one re-creating ancient subnational and ethnic borders from within, the other making national borders porous from without. They have one thing in common: neither offers much hope to citizens looking for practical ways to govern themselves democratically. If the global future is to pit Jihad's centrifugal whirlwind against McWorld's centripetal black hole, the outcome is unlikely to be democratic—or so I will argue.

MCWORLD, OR THE GLOBALIZATION OF POLITICS

Four imperatives make up the dynamic of McWorld: a market imperative, a resource imperative, an information-technology imperative, and an ecological imperative. By shrinking the world and diminishing the salience of national borders, these imperatives have in combination achieved a considerable victory over factiousness and particularism, and not least of all over their most virulent traditional form—nationalism. It is the realists who are now Europeans, the utopians who dream nostalgically of a resurgent England or Germany, perhaps even a resurgent Wales or Saxony. Yesterday's wishful cry for one world has yielded to the reality of McWorld.

The Market Imperative

Marxist and Leninist theories of imperialism assumed that the quest for ever-expanding markets would in time compel nation-based capitalist economies to push against national boundaries in search of an international economic imperium. Whatever else has happened to

the scientistic predictions of Marxism, in this domain they have proved farsighted. All national economies are now vulnerable to the inroads of larger, transnational markets within which trade is free, currencies are convertible, access to banking is open, and contracts are enforceable under law. In Europe, Asia, Africa, the South Pacific, and the Americas such markets are eroding national sovereignty and giving rise to entities—international banks, trade associations, transnational lobbies like OPEC and Greenpeace, world news services like CNN and the BBC, and multinational corporations that increasingly lack a meaningful national identity—that neither reflect nor respect nationhood as an organizing or regulative principle.

The market imperative has also reinforced the quest for international peace and stability, requisites of an efficient international economy. Markets are enemies of parochialism, isolation, fractiousness, war. Market psychology attenuates the psychology of ideological and religious cleavages and assumes a concord among producers and consumers—categories that ill fit narrowly conceived national or religious cultures. Shopping has little tolerance for blue laws, whether dictated by pub-closing British paternalism, Sabbath-observing Jewish Orthodox fundamentalism, or no-Sunday-liquor-sales Massachusetts puritanism. In the context of common markets, international law ceases to be a vision of justice and becomes a workaday framework for getting things done—enforcing contracts, ensuring that governments abide by deals, regulating trade and currency relations, and so forth.

Common markets demand a common language, as well as a common currency, and they produce common behaviors of the kind bred by cosmopolitan city life everywhere. Commercial pilots, computer programmers, international bankers, media specialists, oil riggers, entertainment celebrities, ecology experts, demographers, accountants, professors, athletes—these compose a new breed of men and women for whom religion, culture, and nationality can seem only marginal elements in a working identity. Although sociologists of everyday life will no doubt continue to distinguish a Japanese from an American mode, shopping has a common signature throughout the world. Cynics might even say that some of the recent revolutions in Eastern Europe have had as their true goal not liberty and the right to vote but well-paying jobs and the right to shop (although the vote is proving easier to acquire than consumer goods). The market imperative is, then, plenty powerful; but, notwithstanding some of the claims made for "democratic capitalism," it is not identical with the democratic imperative.

The Resource Imperative

Democrats once dreamed of societies whose political autonomy rested firmly on economic independence. The Athenians idealized what they called autarky, and tried for a while to create a way of life simple and austere enough to make the polis genuinely self-sufficient. To be free meant to be independent of any other community or polis. Not even the Athenians were able to achieve autarky, however: human nature, it turns out, is dependency. By the time of Pericles, Athenian politics was inextricably bound up with a flowering empire held together by naval power and commerce—an empire that, even as it appeared to enhance Athenian might, ate away at Athenian independence and autarky. Master and slave, it turned out, were bound together by mutual insufficiency.

The dream of autarky briefly engrossed nineteenth-century America as well, for the underpopulated, endlessly bountiful land, the cornucopia of natural resources, and the natural barriers of a continent walled in by two great seas led many to believe that America could be a world unto itself. Given this past, it has been harder for Americans than for most to accept the inevitability of interdependence. But the rapid depletion of resources even in a country like ours, where they once seemed inexhaustible, and the maldistribution of arable soil and mineral resources on the planet, leave even the wealthiest societies ever more resource-dependent and many other nations in permanently desperate straits.

Every nation, it turns out, needs something another nation has; some nations have almost nothing they need.

The Information-Technology Imperative

Enlightenment science and the technologies derived from it are inherently universalizing. They entail a quest for descriptive principles of general application, a search for universal solutions to particular problems, and an unswerving embrace of objectivity and impartiality.

Scientific progress embodies and depends on open communication, a common discourse rooted in rationality, collaboration, and an easy and regular flow and exchange of information. Such ideals can be hypocritical covers for power-mongering by elites, and they may be shown to be wanting in many other ways, but they are entailed by the very idea of science and they make science and globalization practical allies.

Business, banking, and commerce all depend on information flow and are facilitated by new communication technologies. The hardware of these technologies tends to be systemic and integrated—computer, television, cable, satellite, laser, fiber-optic, and microchip technologies combining to create a vast interactive communications and information network that can potentially give every person on earth access to every other person, and make every datum, every byte, available to every set of eyes. If the automobile was, as George Ball once said (when he gave his blessing to a Fiat factory in the Soviet Union during the Cold War), "an ideology on four wheels," then electronic telecommunication and information systems are an ideology at 186,000 miles per second—which makes for a very small planet in a very big hurry. Individual cultures speak particular languages; commerce and science increasingly speak English; the whole world speaks logarithms and binary mathematics.

Moreover, the pursuit of science and technology asks for, even compels, open societies. Satellite footprints do not respect national borders; telephone wires penetrate the most closed societies. With photocopying and then fax machines having infiltrated Soviet universities and *samizdat* literary circles in the eighties, and computer modems having multiplied like rabbits in communism's bureaucratic warrens thereafter, *glasnost* could not be far behind. In their social requisites, secrecy and science are enemies.

The new technology's software is perhaps even more globalizing than its hardware. The information arm of international commerce's sprawling body reaches out and touches distinct nations and parochial cultures, and gives them a common face chiseled in Hollywood, on Madison Avenue, and in Silicon Valley. Throughout the 1980s one of the most-watched television programs in South Africa was *The Cosby Show*. The demise of apartheid was already in production. Exhibitors at the 1991 Cannes film festival expressed growing anxiety over the "homogenization" and "Americanization" of the global film industry when, for the third year running, American films dominated the awards ceremonies. America has dominated the world's popular culture for much longer, and much more decisively. In November of 1991 Switzerland's once insular culture boasted best-seller lists featuring *Terminator 2* as the No. 1 movie, *Scarlett* as the No. 1 book, and Prince's *Diamonds and Pearls* as the No. 1 record album. No wonder the Japanese are buying Hollywood film studios even faster than Americans are buying Japanese television sets. This kind of software supremacy may in the long term be far more important than hardware superiority, because culture has become more potent than armaments. What is the power of the Pentagon compared with Disneyland? Can the Sixth Fleet keep up with CNN? McDonald's in Moscow and Coke in China will do more to create a global culture than military colonization ever could. It is less the goods than the brand names that do the work, for they convey life-style images that alter perception and challenge behavior. They make up the seductive software of McWorld's common (at times much too common) soul.

Yet in all this high-tech commercial world there is nothing that looks particularly democratic. It lends itself to surveillance as well as liberty, to new forms of manipulation and covert control as well as new kinds of participation, to skewed, unjust market outcomes as well as greater productivity. The consumer society and the open society are not quite synonymous. Capitalism and democracy have a relationship, but it is something less than a marriage. An efficient free market after all requires that consumers be free to vote their dollars on competing goods, not that citizens be free to vote their values and beliefs on competing political candidates and programs. The free market flourished in junta-run Chile, in military-governed Taiwan and Korea, and, earlier, in a variety of autocratic European empires as well as their colonial possessions.

The Ecological Imperative

The impact of globalization on ecology is a cliche even to world leaders who ignore it. We know well enough that the German forests can be destroyed by Swiss and Italians driving gas-guzzlers fueled by leaded gas. We also know that the planet can be asphyxiated by greenhouse gases because Brazilian farmers want to be part of the twentieth century and are burning down tropical rain forests to clear a little land to plough, and because Indonesians make a living out of converting their lush jungle into toothpicks for fastidious Japanese diners, upsetting the delicate oxygen balance and in effect puncturing our global lungs. Yet this ecological consciousness has meant not only greater awareness but also greater inequality, as modernized nations try to slam the door behind them, saying to developing nations, "The world cannot afford your modernization; ours has wrung it dry!"

Each of the four imperatives just cited is transnational, transideological, and transcultural. Each applies impartially to Catholics, Jews, Muslims, Hindus, and Buddhists; to democrats and totalitarians; to capitalists and socialists. The Enlightenment dream of a universal rational society has to a remarkable degree been realized—but in a form that is commercialized, homogenized, depoliticized, bureaucratized, and, of course, radically incomplete, for the movement toward McWorld is in competition with forces of global breakdown, national dissolution, and centrifugal corruption. These forces, working in the opposite direction, are the essence of what I call Jihad.

JIHAD, OR THE LEBANONIZATION OF THE WORLD

OPEC, the World Bank, the United Nations, the International Red Cross, the multinational corporation . . . there are scores of institutions that reflect globalization. But they often appear as ineffective reactors to the world's real actors: national states and, to an ever greater degree, subnational factions in permanent rebellion against uniformity and integration—even the kind represented by universal law and justice. The headlines feature these players regularly: they are cultures, not countries; parts, not wholes; sects, not religions; rebellious factions and dissenting minorities at war not just with globalism but with the traditional nation-state. Kurds, Basques, Puerto Ricans, Ossetians, East Timoreans, Quebecois, the Catholics of Northern Ireland, Abkhasians, Kurile Islander Japanese, the Zulus of Inkatha, Catalonians, Tamils, and, of course, Palestinians—people without countries, inhabiting nations not their own, seeking smaller worlds within borders that will seal them off from modernity.

A powerful irony is at work here. Nationalism was once a force of integration and unification, a movement aimed at bringing together disparate clans, tribes, and cultural fragments under new, assimilationist flags. But as Ortega y Gasset noted more than sixty years ago, having won its victories, nationalism changed its strategy. In the 1920s, and again today, it is more often a reactionary and divisive force, pulverizing the very nations it once helped cement together. The force that creates nations is "inclusive," Ortega wrote in *The Revolt of the Masses*. "In periods of consolidation, nationalism has a positive value, and is a lofty standard. But in Europe everything is more than consolidated, and nationalism is nothing but a mania . . ."

This mania has left the post–Cold War world smoldering with hot wars; the international scene is little more unified than it was at the end of the Great War, in Ortega's own time. There were more than thirty wars in progress last year, most of them ethnic, racial, tribal, or religious in character, and the list of unsafe regions doesn't seem to be getting any shorter. Some new world order!

The aim of many of these small-scale wars is to redraw boundaries, to implode states and resecure parochial identities: to escape McWorld's dully insistent imperatives. The mood is that of Jihad: war not as an instrument of policy but as an emblem of identity, an expression of community, an end in itself. Even where there is no shooting war, there is fractiousness, secession, and the quest for ever smaller communities. Add to the list of dangerous countries those at risk: In Switzerland and Spain, Jurassian and Basque separatists still argue the virtues of ancient identities, sometimes in the language of bombs. Hyperdisintegration in the former Soviet Union may well continue unabated—not just a Ukraine independent from the Soviet Union but a Bessarabian Ukraine independent from the Ukrainian republic; not just Russia severed from the defunct union but Tatarstan severed from Russia. Yugoslavia makes even the disunited, ex-Soviet, nonsocialist republics that were once the Soviet Union look integrated, its sectarian fatherlands springing up within factional motherlands like weeds within weeds within weeds. Kurdish independence would threaten the territorial integrity of four Middle Eastern nations. Well before the current cataclysm Soviet Georgia made a claim for autonomy from the Soviet Union, only to be faced with its Ossetians (164,000 in a republic of 5.5 million) demanding their own self-determination within Georgia. The Abkhasian minority in Georgia has followed suit. Even the good will established by Canada's once promising Meech Lake protocols is in danger, with Francophone Quebec again threatening the dissolution of the federation. In South Africa the emergence from apartheid was hardly achieved when friction between Inkatha's Zulus and the African National Congress's tribally identified members threatened to replace Europeans' racism with an indigenous tribal war. After thirty years of attempted integration using the colonial language (English) as a unifier, Nigeria is now playing with the idea of linguistic multiculturalism—which could mean the cultural breakup of the nation into hundreds of tribal fragments. Even Saddam Hussein has benefited from the threat of internal Jihad, having used renewed tribal and religious warfare to turn last season's mortal enemies into reluctant allies of an Iraqi nationhood that he nearly destroyed.

The passing of communism has torn away the thin veneer of internationalism (workers of the world unite!) to reveal ethnic prejudices that are not only ugly and deep-seated but increasingly murderous. Europe's old scourge, anti-Semitism, is back with a vengeance, but it is only one of many antagonisms. It appears all too easy to throw the historical gears into reverse and pass from a Communist dictatorship back into a tribal state.

Among the tribes, religion is also a battlefield. ("Jihad" is a rich word whose generic meaning is "struggle"—usually the struggle of the soul to avert evil. Strictly applied to religious war, it is used only in reference to battles where the faith is under assault, or battles against a government that denies the practice of Islam. My use here is rhetorical, but does follow both journalistic practice and history.) Remember the Thirty Years War? Whatever forms of Enlightenment universalism might once have come to grace such historically related forms of monotheism as Judaism, Christianity, and Islam, in many of their modern incarnations they are parochial rather than cosmopolitan, angry rather than loving, proselytizing rather than ecumenical, zealous rather than rationalist, sectarian rather than deistic, ethnocentric rather than universalizing. As a result, like the new forms of hypernationalism, the new expressions of religious fundamentalism are fractious and pulverizing, never integrating. This is religion as the Crusaders knew it: a battle to the death for souls that if not saved will be forever lost.

The atmospherics of Jihad have resulted in a breakdown of civility in the name of identity, of comity in the name of community. International relations have sometimes taken on the aspect of gang war—cultural turf battles featuring tribal factions that were supposed to be sublimated as integral parts of large national, economic, post-colonial, and constitutional entities.

THE DARKENING FUTURE OF DEMOCRACY

These rather melodramatic tableaux vivants do not tell the whole story, however. For all their defects, Jihad and McWorld have their attractions. Yet, to repeat and insist, the attractions are unrelated to democracy. Neither McWorld nor Jihad is remotely democratic in impulse. Neither needs democracy; neither promotes democracy.

McWorld does manage to look pretty seductive in a world obsessed with Jihad. It delivers peace, prosperity, and relative unity—if at the cost of independence, community, and identity (which is generally based on difference). The primary political values required by the global market are order and tranquillity, and freedom—as in the phrases "free trade," "free press," and "free love." Human rights are needed to a degree, but not citizenship or participation—and no more social justice and equality than are necessary to promote efficient economic production and consumption. Multi-national corporations sometimes seem to prefer doing business with local oligarchs, inasmuch as they can take confidence from dealing with the boss on all crucial matters. Despots who slaughter their own populations are no problem, so long as they leave markets in place and refrain from making war on their neighbors (Saddam Hussein's fatal mistake). In trading partners, predictability is of more value than justice.

The Eastern European revolutions that seemed to arise out of concern for global democratic values quickly deteriorated into a stampede in the general direction of free markets and their ubiquitous, television-promoted shopping malls. East Germany's Neues Forum, that courageous gathering of intellectuals, students, and workers which overturned the Stalinist regime in Berlin in 1989, lasted only six months in Germany's mini-version of McWorld. Then it gave way to money and markets and monopolies from the West. By the time of the first all-German elections, it could scarcely manage to secure three percent of the vote. Elsewhere there is growing evidence that glasnost will go and perestroika—defined as privatization and an opening of markets to Western bidders—will stay. So understandably anxious are the new rulers of Eastern Europe and whatever entities are forged from the residues of the Soviet Union to gain access to credit and markets and technology—McWorld's flourishing new currencies—that they have shown themselves willing to trade away democratic prospects in pursuit of them: not just old totalitarian ideologies and command-economy production models but some possible indigenous experiments with a third way between capitalism and socialism, such as economic cooperatives and employee stock-ownership plans, both of which have their ardent supporters in the East.

Jihad delivers a different set of virtues: a vibrant local identity, a sense of community, solidarity among kinsmen, neighbors, and countrymen, narrowly conceived. But it also guarantees parochialism and is grounded in exclusion. Solidarity is secured through war against outsiders. And solidarity often means obedience to a hierarchy in governance, fanaticism in beliefs, and the obliteration of individual selves in the name of the group. Deference to leaders and intolerance toward outsiders (and toward "enemies within") are hallmarks of tribalism—hardly the attitudes required for the cultivation of new democratic women and men capable of governing themselves. Where new democratic experiments have been conducted in retribalizing societies, in both Europe and the Third World, the result has often been anarchy, repression, persecution, and the coming of new, noncommunist forms of very old kinds of despotism. During the past year, Havel's velvet revolution in Czechoslovakia was imperiled by partisans of "Czechland" and of Slovakia as independent entities. India seemed little less rent by Sikh, Hindu, Muslim, and Tamil infighting than it was immediately after the British pulled out, more than forty years ago.

To the extent that either McWorld or Jihad has a *natural* politics, it has turned out to be more of an antipolitics. For McWorld, it is the antipolitics of globalism: bureaucratic, technocratic, and meritocratic, focused (as Marx predicted it would be) on the administration of things—with people, however, among the chief things to be administered. In its politico-economic imperatives McWorld has been guided by laissez-faire market principles that privilege efficiency, productivity, and benefi-cence at the expense of civic liberty and self-government.

For Jihad, the antipolitics of tribalization has been explicitly antidemocratic: one-party dictatorship, government by military junta, theo-cratic fundamentalism—often associated with a version of the *Fuhrerprinzip* that empowers an individual to rule on behalf of a people. Even the government of India, struggling for decades to model democracy for a people who will soon number a billion, longs for great leaders; and for every Mahatma Gandhi, Indira Gandhi, or Rajiv Gandhi taken from them by zealous assassins, the Indians appear to seek a replacement who will deliver them from the lengthy travail of their freedom.

THE CONFEDERAL OPTION

How can democracy be secured and spread in a world whose primary tendencies are at best indifferent to it (McWorld) and at worst deeply antithetical to it (Jihad)? My guess is that global-ization will eventually vanquish retribalization. The ethos of material "civilization" has not yet encountered an obstacle it has been unable to thrust aside. Ortega may have grasped in the 1920s a clue to our own future in the coming millennium.

> *Everyone sees the need of a new principle of life. But as always happens in similar crises—some people attempt to save the situation by an artificial intensifica-tion of the very principle which has led to decay. This is the meaning of the "nationalist" outburst of recent years. . . . things have always gone that way. The last flare, the longest; the last sigh, the deepest. On the very eve of their disap-pearance there is an intensification of frontiers—military and economic.*

Jihad may be a last deep sigh before the eternal yawn of McWorld. On the other hand, Ortega was not exactly prescient; his prophecy of peace and internationalism came just before blitzkrieg, world war, and the Holocaust tore the old order to bits. Yet democracy is how we remonstrate with reality, the rebuke our aspira-tions offer to history. And if retribalization is inhospitable to democracy, there is nonetheless a form of democratic government that can accom-modate parochialism and communitarianism, one that can even save them from their defects

and make them more tolerant and participatory: decentralized participatory democracy. And if McWorld is indifferent to democracy, there is nonetheless a form of democratic government that suits global markets passably well—representative government in its federal or, better still, confederal variation.

With its concern for accountability, the protection of minorities, and the universal rule of law, a confederalized representative system would serve the political needs of McWorld as well as oligarchic bureaucratism or meritocratic elitism is currently doing. As we are already beginning to see, many nations may survive in the long term only as confederations that afford local regions smaller than "nations" extensive jurisdiction. Recommended reading for democ-rats of the twenty-first century is not the U.S. Constitution or the French Declaration of Rights of Man and Citizen but the Articles of Confederation, that suddenly pertinent docu-ment that stitched together the thirteen American colonies into what then seemed a too loose confederation of independent states but now appears a new form of political realism, as veterans of Yeltsin's new Russia and the new Europe created at Maastricht will attest.

By the same token, the participatory and direct form of democracy that engages citizens in civic activity and civic judgment and goes well beyond just voting and accountability—the system I have called "strong democracy"—suits the political needs of decentralized communities as well as theocratic and nationalist party dicta-torships have done. Local neighborhoods need not be democratic, but they can be. Real democ-racy has flourished in diminutive settings: the spirit of liberty, Tocqueville said, is local. Participatory democracy, if not naturally appo-site to tribalism, has an undeniable attractiveness under conditions of parochialism.

Democracy in any of these variations will, however, continue to be obstructed by the unde-mocratic and antidemocratic trends toward uniformitarian globalism and intolerant retrib-alization which I have portrayed here. For democracy to persist in our brave new McWorld, we will have to commit acts of conscious political will—a possibility, but hardly a probability, under these conditions. Political will requires much more than the quick fix of the transfer of institutions. Like technology transfer, institution transfer rests on foolish assumptions about a uniform world of the kind that once fired the imagination of colonial administrators. Spread English justice to the colonies by exporting wigs. Let an East Indian trading company act as the vanguard to Britain's free parliamentary institutions. Today's well-intentioned quick-fixers in the National Endowment for Democracy and the Kennedy School of Government, in the unions and foundations and universities zealously nurturing contacts in Eastern Europe and the Third World, are hoping to democratize by long distance. Post Bulgaria a parliament by first-class mail. Fed Ex the Bill of Rights to Sri Lanka. Cable Cambodia some common law.

Yet Eastern Europe has already demonstrated that importing free political parties, parliaments, and presses cannot establish a democratic civil society; imposing a free market may even have the opposite effect. Democracy grows from the bottom up and cannot be imposed from the top down. Civil society has to be built from the inside out. The institutional superstructure comes last. Poland may become democratic, but then again it may heed the Pope, and prefer to found its politics on its Catholicism, with uncertain consequences for democracy. Bulgaria may become democratic, but it may prefer tribal war. The former Soviet Union may become a democratic confederation, or it may just grow into an anarchic and weak conglomeration of markets for other nations' goods and services.

Democrats need to seek out indigenous democratic impulses. There is always a desire for self-government, always some expression of participation, accountability, consent, and representation, even in traditional hierarchical societies. These need to be identified, tapped, modified, and incorporated into new democratic practices with an indigenous flavor. The tortoises among the democratizers may ultimately outlive or outpace the hares, for they will have the time and patience to explore conditions along the way, and to adapt their gait to changing circumstances. Tragically, democracy in a hurry often looks something like France in 1794 or China in 1989.

It certainly seems possible that the most attractive democratic ideal in the face of the brutal realities of Jihad and the dull realities of McWorld will be a confederal union of semi-autonomous communities smaller than nation-states, tied together into regional economic associations and markets larger than nation-states—participatory and self-determining in local matters at the bottom, representative and accountable at the top. The nation-state would play a diminished role, and sovereignty would lose some of its political potency. The Green movement adage "Think globally, act locally" would actually come to describe the conduct of politics.

This vision reflects only an ideal, however— one that is not terribly likely to be realized. Freedom, Jean-Jacques Rousseau once wrote, is a food easy to eat but hard to digest. Still, democracy has always played itself out against the odds. And democracy remains both a form of coherence as binding as McWorld and a secular faith potentially as inspiriting as Jihad.

THE STATE AND THE NEW GEOGRAPHY OF POWER

Saskia Sassen

Economic globalization represents a major transformation in the territorial organization of economic activity and politico-economic power. How does it reconfigure the territorial exclusivity of sovereign states, and what does this do to both sovereignty and a system of rule based on sovereign states? Has economic globalization over the last ten or fifteen years contributed to a major institutional discontinuity in the history of the modern state, the modern interstate system, and, particularly, the system of rule?

The term *sovereignty* has a long history, beginning with Aristotle, running through Bodin and Hobbes and the American and French revolutions, and arriving today at yet another major transformation. From being the sovereignty of the ruler, it became the will of the people as contained in the nation-state, that is, popular sovereignty. It was for a long time centered in a concern with internal order, a notion that influenced international law and politics for many centuries. Sovereignty often was "an attribute of a powerful individual whose legitimacy over territory . . . rested on a purportedly direct or delegated divine or historic authority."[1] The international legal system did not necessarily register these changes as they were happening. But by the end of World War II the notion of sovereignty based on the will of the people had become established as one of the conditions of political legitimacy for a government.[2] Article 1 of the UN Charter established as one of the purposes of the UN the development of friendly relations among states "based on respect for the principles of equal rights and self-determination of peoples"; the Universal Declaration of Human Rights of 1948, Article 21 (3), provided that ["]the will of the people shall be the basis of authority of government . . . through elections. . . ."[3] What is significant here is that this was now expressed in a fundamental international constitutive legal document. "In international law, the sovereign had finally been dethroned."[4]

The sovereignty of the modern state was constituted in mutually exclusive territories and the concentration of sovereignty in nations. There are other systems of rule, particularly those centered in supranational organizations and emergent private transnational legal regimes, and earlier forms of such supranational powers reigned on occasion over single states, as when the League of Nations gave itself the right of intervention for the purpose of protecting minority rights. Systems of rule need not be territorial, as in certain kinds of kinship-based systems; they may not be territorially fixed, as in nomadic societies; or, while territorially fixed, they need not be exclusive.[5] In the main, however, rule in the modern world flows from the absolute sovereignty of the state over its national territory.

Achieving exclusive territoriality was no easy task. It took centuries of struggle, wars, treaties made and treaties broken, to nationalize territories along mutually exclusive lines and secure the distinctive concentration of power and system of rule that is the sovereign state. Multiple systems of rule coexisted during the transition from the medieval system of rule to the modern state: there were centralizing monarchies in Western Europe, city-states in Italy, and city-leagues in Germany.[6] Even when nation-states with exclusive territoriality and sovereignty were beginning to emerge, other forms might have become effective alternatives—for example, the Italian city-states and the Hanseatic League in northern Europe—and the formation of and claims by central states were widely

contested.[7] Even now, there continue to be other forms of concentration of power and other systems of rule, for instance, nonterritorial or nonexclusive systems such as the Catholic Church and the so-called Arab nation.

There have long been problems with the exclusive territoriality of the modern state. Inevitably, one thinks of Garrett Mattingly's account of the right of embassy in medieval Europe. After succeeding brilliantly at creating mutually exclusive territories, states found there was no space left for the protected conduct of diplomacy; indeed, diplomats often felt—and indeed were—threatened, as well as pelted with vegetables. Moreover, for activities not covered by specific immunities, diplomats could be tried in the courts of the host state, just like any other subject.[8] There were various intermediate forms granting specific immunities. For example, the right of embassy could often be granted without reference to a specific sovereign, allowing subject cities to negotiate directly with one another. This form of the right of embassy became increasingly problematic when the right to embassy became a matter of sovereign recognition. As Mattingly notes, having achieved absolute sovereignty, the new states found they could only communicate with each other "by tolerating within themselves little islands of alien sovereignty."[9] The doctrine of extraterritoriality was thus the answer, and its consequences are still evident today, as when a diplomat parks anywhere in the city with impunity, de jure.[10] In the long history of securing and legitimating exclusive territoriality, particularly in this century, a variety of extraterritorial regimes have accumulated. And then there is, of course, Hugo Grotius's doctrine of mare liberum, which remains with us today.[11]

It is not enough simply to posit, as is so often done, that economic globalization has brought with it declining significance for the national state. Today, the major dynamics at work in the global economy carry the capacity to undo the particular form of the intersection of sovereignty and territory embedded in the modern state and the modern state system. But does this mean that sovereignty or territoriality are less important features in the international system?

Addressing these questions requires an examination of the major aspects of economic globalization that contribute to what I think of as a new geography of power. One much-noted fact is that firms can now operate across borders with ease; indeed, for many, this is what globalization is about. But I wish to examine three other components in the new geography of power.

The first of these components concerns the actual territories where much globalization materializes in specific institutions and processes. What kind of territoriality does this represent? The second component concerns the ascendance of a new legal regime for governing cross-border economic transactions, a trend not sufficiently recognized in the social science literature. A rather peculiar passion for legality (and lawyers) drives the globalization of the corporate economy, and there has been a massive amount of legal innovation around the growth of globalization. The third component I wish to address is the growing number of economic activities taking place in electronic space. Electronic space overrides all existing territorial jurisdiction. Further, this growing virtualization of economic activity, particularly in the leading information industries such as finance and specialized corporate services, may be contributing to a crisis in control that transcends the capacities of both the state and the institutional apparatus of the economy. The speed made possible by the new technologies is creating orders of magnitude—in, for instance, the foreign currency markets—that escape the governing capacities of private and government overseers.

Adding these three components of the new geography of power to the global footlooseness of corporate capital reveals aspects of the relation between global economy and national state that the prevalent notion of a global–national duality does not adequately or usefully capture. This duality is conceived as a mutually exclusive set of terrains where the national economy or state loses what the global economy gains. Dualization has fed the proposition that the national state must decline in a globalized economy.

TERRITORIALITY IN A GLOBAL ECONOMY

To elaborate on these three components of the new geography of power, I will begin with the question of the spaces of the global economy. What is the strategic geography of globalization or, more conceptually, the particular form of territoriality that is taking shape in the global economy today?

My starting point is a set of practices and institutions: global financial markets; the ascendance of Anglo-American law firms in international business transactions; the Uruguay Round of the GATT and the formation of the World Trade Organization (WTO); the role of credit-rating agencies and other such delightful entities in international capital markets; the provisions in the GATT and NAFTA for the circulation of service workers as part of the international trade and investment in services; and immigration, particularly the cross-border circulation of low-wage workers. In my earlier research I did not think about these subjects in terms of governance and accountability; here, I seek to understand the spatial configuration and legal/regulatory regimes that specify them.

An aspect of economic globalization that has received the most attention from general and specialized commentators is the geographic dispersal of firms' factories, offices, service outlets, and markets. One of many versions of this is the global assembly line in manufacturing, perhaps most famously dramatized by the infamous case of IBM's personal computer carrying the label Made in the USA when more than 70 percent of its component parts were manufactured overseas, typically in low-wage countries.[12] Yet another version is the export-processing zone— a special tariff and taxation regime that allows firms, mostly from high-wage countries, to export semiprocessed components for further processing in low-wage countries and then to reimport them back to the country of origin without tariffs on the value added through processing. There are now hundreds of such zones; the best-known instance is the Northern Industrialization Program in Mexico, the so-called *maquiladoras*. In Mexico, there are plants from many different countries, including Japanese plants making auto parts and electronic components shipped to Japanese plants in the United States. Another common example is the offshoring of clerical work. So-called clerical factories are growing rapidly in both numbers and types of locations: they can now be found in China even though workers do not necessarily know English. The clerical work that is offshored involves largely routine data entering and is, in many ways, an extension of the common practice in the highly developed countries of locating back offices in suburban areas or shipping clerical work to private households. There are several other variations of this trend toward worldwide geographic dispersal and internationalization. Indeed, national governments have reason to know this well: they are forever struggling to capture the elusive taxes of corporations operating in more than one country.

From the perspective of the national state, specifically the state in highly developed countries, offshoring creates a space economy that goes beyond the regulatory umbrella of the state. And in this regard, the significance of the state is in decline. Here we can point only to the different ways in which globalization brings about this partial denationalizing in developing and highly developed countries. In much of the developing world, it has assumed the form of free trade zones and export manufacturing zones where firms can locate production facilities without being subject to local taxes and various other regulations; such zones exist in many Latin American and Asian countries. In these cases, an actual piece of land becomes denationalized; with financial operations, the process assumes a more institutional and functional meaning.

Conceivably, the geographic dispersal of factories and offices could have gone along with a dispersal in control and profits, a democratizing, if you will, of the corporate structure. Instead, it takes place as part of highly integrated corporate structures with strong tendencies toward concentration in control and profit appropriation. Large corporations log many of these operations as "overseas sales," and it is well known that a very high share, about 40 percent, of international trade actually occurs intrafirm, and, according to some sources, the proportion is even higher than that.[13]

There are two major implications here for the question of territoriality and sovereignty in the context of a global economy. First, when there is geographic dispersal of factories, offices, and service outlets in an integrated corporate system, particularly one with centralized top-level control, there is also a growth in central functions. Put simply, the more globalized firms become, the more their central functions grow: in importance, in complexity, and in number of transactions.[14] The sometimes staggering figures involved in this worldwide dispersal demand extensive coordination and management at parent headquarters. For instance, in the early 1990s U.S. firms had more than 18,000 affiliates

overseas; less known is the fact that German firms had even more, 19,000, up from 14,000 in the early 1980s or that well over 50 percent of the workforces of firms such as Ford Motors, GM, IBM, and Exxon are overseas.[15] A lot of this dispersal has been going on for a long time, and it does not proceed under a single organizational form: behind these general figures lie many types of establishments, hierarchies of control, and degrees of autonomy.[16]

The second implication in terms of territoriality and sovereignty in a global economy is that these central functions are disproportionately concentrated in the national territories of the highly developed countries. This means that an interpretation of the impact of globalization as creating a space economy that extends beyond the regulatory capacity of a single state is only half the story. It is important to clarify here that central functions involve not only top-level headquarters but also all the top-level financial, legal, accounting, managerial, executive, and planning functions necessary to run a corporate organization operating in more than one and now often several countries. These central functions partly take place at corporate headquarters, but many have become so specialized and complex that headquarters increasingly buy them from specialized firms rather than producing them in-house. This has led to the creation of what has been called the corporate services complex, that is, the network of financial, legal, accounting, advertising, and other corporate service firms that handle the difficulties of operating in more than one national legal system, national accounting system, advertising culture, etc., and do so under conditions of rapid innovations in all these fields.[17]

As a rule, firms in more routinized lines of activity, with predominantly regional or national markets, appear to be increasingly free to move or install their headquarters outside cities, while those in highly competitive and innovative lines of activity and/or with a strong world market orientation appear to benefit from being located at the heart of major international business centers, no matter how high the costs. Both types of firms need some kind of corporate services complex, and the more specialized complexes are most likely to be in cities rather than, say, suburban office parks. Thus the agglomerations of firms carrying out central functions for the management and coordination of global economic systems are disproportionately concentrated in the highly developed countries, particularly, though not exclusively, in the kinds of cities I call global cities, such as New York, Paris, and Amsterdam.[18]

Another instance today of this negotiation between a transnational process or dynamic and a national territory is that of the global financial markets. The orders of magnitude in these markets have risen sharply, as illustrated by the estimated 75 trillion U.S. dollars in turnover in the global capital market, a major component of the global economy. These transactions are partly dependent on telecommunications systems that make possible the instantaneous transmission of money and information around the globe. Much attention has gone to the new technologies' capacity for instantaneous transmission. But equally important is the extent to which the global financial markets are located in particular cities in the highly developed countries. The degrees of concentration are unexpectedly high. For instance, international bank lending by countries increased from 1.9 trillion dollars in 1980 to 6.2 trillion dollars in 1991; seven countries accounted for 65 percent of this total in both 1980 and 1991. What countries? Yes, the usual suspects: the United States, the U.K., Japan, Switzerland, France, Germany, and Luxembourg.[19]

Stock markets worldwide have become globally integrated. Besides deregulation in the 1980s in all the major European and North American markets, the late 1980s and early 1990s saw the addition of such markets as Buenos Aires, São Paulo, Bangkok, Taipei, etc. The integration of a growing number of stock markets has contributed to raise the capital that can be mobilized through them. Worldwide market value reached 13 trillion dollars in 1995. This globally integrated stock market, which makes possible the circulation of publicly listed shares around the globe in seconds, functions within a grid of very material, physical, strategic places: that is, cities belonging to national territories.

NEW LEGAL REGIMES

The operation of worldwide networks of factories, offices, and service outlets and the deregulation and global integration of stock markets have involved a variety of major and minor legal innovations. Earlier, I discussed the struggle to nationalize territory and form mutually exclusive sovereign territories, in particular the question of the right of embassy, which evolved into a form of extraterritoriality through which to resolve the tension between exclusive territoriality and the need for transactions among states. The impact of economic globalization on national territory and state sovereignty could be yet another form of such extraterritoriality, only on a much larger scale. My discussion about territory in the global economy posits that much that we describe as global, including some of the most strategic functions necessary for globalization, is grounded in national territories. Is this a form of extraterritoriality that leaves the sovereignty of the state fundamentally unaltered? Or is it a development of a different sort, one that affects the sovereignty of the state and partially transforms the notions of both territoriality and sovereignty?

To address these questions, it is necessary to examine the particular forms of legal innovation that have been produced and within which much of globalization is encased and further to consider how they interact with the state or, more specifically, with the sovereignty of the state. These legal innovations and changes are often characterized as "deregulation" and taken as somewhat of a given (though not by legal scholars). In much social science, *deregulation* is another name for the declining significance of the state. But, it seems to me, these legal changes contain a more specific process, one that along with the reconfiguration of space may signal a more fundamental transformation in the matter of sovereignty, pointing to new contents and new locations for the particular systemic property that we call sovereignty. As with the discussion of territory in the global economy, my beginning point is a set of practices and minor legal forms, microhistories, that can, however, accumulate into major trends or regimes—and I am afraid are about to do so.

Firms operating transnationally need to ensure the functions traditionally exercised by the state in the national realm of the economy, such as guaranteeing property rights and contracts.[20] Yet insofar as economic globalization extends the economy—but not the sovereignty—of the nation-state beyond its boundaries, this guarantee would appear to be threatened.

In fact, globalization has been accompanied by the creation of new legal regimes and practices and the expansion and renovation of some older firms that bypass national legal systems.

Globalization and governmental deregulation have not meant the absence of regulatory regimes and institutions for the governance of international economic relations. Among the most important in the private sector today are international commercial arbitration and the variety of institutions that fulfill the rating and advisory functions that have become essential for the operation of the global economy.

Over the past twenty years, international commercial arbitration has been transformed and institutionalized as the leading contractual method for the resolution of transnational commercial disputes.[21] Again, a few figures tell a quick and dirty story. There has been an enormous growth in arbitration centers. Excluding those concerned with maritime and commodity disputes—an older tradition—there were 120 centers by 1991, with another 7 established by 1993; among the more recent are those of Bahrain, Singapore, Sydney, and Vietnam. There were about a thousand arbitrators by 1990, a number that had doubled by 1992.[22] In a major study on international commercial arbitration, Yves Dezalay and Bryant Garth find that it is a delocalized and decentralized market for the administration of international commercial disputes, connected by more or less powerful institutions and individuals who are both competitive and complementary.[23] It is in this regard a far from unitary system of justice, perhaps organized, as Dezalay and Garth put it, around one great lex mercatoria, which might have been envisioned by some of the pioneering idealists of law.[24]

Another private regulatory system is represented by the debt security or bond-rating agencies that have come to play an increasingly important role in the global economy. Two agencies dominate the market in ratings, with listings of 3 trillion U.S. dollars each: Moody's Investors Service, usually referred to as Moody's, and Standard and Poor's Ratings Group, usually referred to as Standard and Poor.[25] Ten years ago Moody's and Standard and Poor had no analysts outside the United States; by 1993 they each had about a hundred in Europe, Japan, and Australia. In his study of credit-rating processes, Sinclair found that they have leverage because of their distinct gate-keeping functions for investment funds sought by corporations and governments.[26] In this regard they can be seen as a significant force in the operation and expansion of the global economy.[27] And as with business law, the U.S. agencies have expanded their influence overseas; to some extent, their growing clout can be seen as both a function and a promoter of U.S. financial orthodoxy, particularly its short-term perspective.

Americanization

Transnational institutions and regimes raise questions about the relation between state sovereignty and the governance of global economic processes. International commercial arbitration is basically a private justice system, and credit-rating agencies are private gate-keeping systems. With other institutions, they have emerged as important governance mechanisms whose authority is not centered in the state. The current relocation of authority has transformed the capacities of governments and can be thought of as an instance of Rosenau's "governance without government."[28] . . . It has also spurred the formation of transnational legal regimes, which have penetrated into national fields hitherto closed.[29] In their turn, national legal fields are becoming more internationalized in some of the major developed economies. Some of the old divisions between the national and the global are becoming weaker and, to some extent, have been neutralized. The new transnational regimes could, in principle, have assumed various forms and contents; but, in fact, they are assuming a specific form, one wherein the states of the highly developed countries play a strategic geopolitical role. The hegemony of neoliberal concepts of economic relations, with its strong emphasis on markets, deregulation, and free international trade, influenced policy in the USA and the U.K. in the 1980s and now increasingly does so in continental Europe as well. This has contributed to the formation of transnational legal regimes that are centered in Western economic concepts.[30]

Dezalay and Garth note that the "international" is itself constituted largely from a competition among national approaches. There is no global law. Martin Shapiro, too, notes that there is not much of a regime of international law, either through the establishment of a single global lawgiver and enforcer or through a nation-state consensus. He also posits that if there were, it would be an international rather than a global law; in fact, it is not even certain that the concept of law itself has become universal, that is, that human relations everywhere in the world will be governed by some, though perhaps not the same, law. The globalization of law refers to a very limited, specialized set of legal phenomena, and Shapiro argues that it will almost always refer to North America and Europe and only sometimes to Japan and some other Asian countries.[31]

The international thus emerges as a site for regulatory competition among essentially national approaches, whatever the issue: environmental protection, constitutionalism, human rights.[32] From this perspective "international" or "transnational" has become in the most recent period a form of Americanization, though the process has hardly been smooth. Contestation crops up everywhere, some of it highly visible and formalized, some of it not. In some countries, especially in Europe, there is resistance to what is perceived as the Americanization of the global capital market's standards for the regulation of financial systems and standards for reporting financial information. Sinclair notes that the internationalization of ratings by the two leading U.S. agencies could be seen as another step toward global financial integration or as fulfilling an American agenda. Resentment against U.S. agencies is clearly on the rise in Europe, as became evident when Credit Suisse was downgraded in 1991 and, in early 1992, the Swiss Bank Corporation met the same fate. Conflict is also evident in the difficulty with which foreign agencies gain SEC standing as Nationally Recognized Statistical Rating Organizations in the USA. The *Financial Times*—to mention one example—has reported on private discussions in London, Paris, and Frankfurt concerning the possibility of setting up a Europe-wide agency to compete with the major U.S.–based agencies.[33]

The most widely recognized instance of Americanization is seen, of course, in the profound influence U.S. popular culture exerts on global culture.[34] But, though less widely recognized and more difficult to specify, it has also become very clear in the legal forms ascendant in international business transactions.[35] Through the IMF and the International Bank for Reconstruction and Development (IBRD) as well as the GATT, the U.S. vision has spread to—some would say been imposed on—the developing world.[36]

The competition among national legal systems or approaches is particularly evident in business law, where the Anglo-American model of the business enterprise and competition is beginning to replace the Continental model of legal artisans and corporatist control over the profession.[37] More generally, U.S. dominance in the global economy over the last few decades has meant that the globalization of law through private corporate lawmaking has assumed the form of the Americanization of commercial law.[38] Certain U.S. legal practices are being diffused throughout the world—for instance, the legal device of franchising. Shapiro notes that this may not stem only from U.S. dominance but also from common law's receptivity to contract and other commercial law innovations. For example, it is widely believed in Europe that EC legal business goes to London because lawyers there are better at legal innovations to facilitate new and evolving transnational business relations. "For whatever reasons, it is now possible to argue that American business law has become a kind of global *jus commune* incorporated explicitly or implicitly into transnational contracts and beginning to be incorporated into the case law and even the statutes of many other nations."[39]

All the reasons for this Americanization are somewhat interrelated: the rationalization of arbitration know-how, the ascendance of large Anglo-American transnational legal services firms, and the emergence of a new specialty in conflict resolution.[40] The large Anglo-American law firms that dominate the international market of business law include arbitration as one of the array of services they offer. Specialists in conflict are practitioners formed from the two great groups that have dominated legal practice in the United States: corporate lawyers, known for their competence as negotiators in the creation of contracts, and trial lawyers, whose talent lies in jury trials. The growing importance in the 1980s of such transactions as mergers and acquisitions, as well as antitrust and other litigation, contributed to a new specialization: knowing how to combine judicial attacks and behind-the-scenes negotiations to reach the optimum outcome for the client. Dezalay and Garth note that under these conditions judicial recourse becomes a weapon in a struggle that will almost certainly end before trial. Notwithstanding its deep roots in the Continental tradition, especially the French and Swiss traditions, this system of private justice is becoming increasingly Americanized.

THE VIRTUALIZATION OF ECONOMIC ACTIVITY

The third component in the new geography of power is the growing importance of electronic space. There is much to be said on this issue. Here, I can isolate one particular matter: the distinctive challenge that the virtualization of a growing number of economic activities presents not only to the existing state regulatory apparatus but also to private-sector institutions increasingly dependent on the new technologies. Taken to its extreme, this may signal a control crisis in the making, one for which we lack an analytical vocabulary.

The questions of control here have to do not with the extension of the economy beyond the territory of the state but with digitalization—that is, electronic markets—and orders of magnitude such as those that can be achieved in the financial markets, thanks to the transaction speeds made possible by the new technologies. The best example is probably the foreign currency market, which operates largely in electronic space and has achieved volumes—a trillion dollars a day—that leave the central banks incapable of exercising the influence on exchange rates they are expected to wield (though may, in fact, not always have had). The growing virtualization of economic activities raises questions of control that also go beyond the notions of non-state-centered systems of coordination prevalent in the literature on governance.

The State Reconfigured

In many ways, the state is involved in this emerging transnational governance system. But it is a state that has itself undergone transformation and participated in legitimating a new doctrine about its role in the economy. Central to this new doctrine is a growing consensus among states to further the growth and strength of the global economy. This combination of elements is illustrated by some of the aspects of the December 1994 crisis in Mexico.

Mexico's crisis was defined rather generally in international political and business circles, as well as in much of the press, as the result of the global financial markets' loss of confidence in the Mexican economy and the government's

leadership of it. The U.S. government defined the crisis as a global economic security issue with direct impact on the U.S. economy and pushed hard to get the U.S. legislature and the governments of other highly developed countries to come to Mexico's aid. It opted for a financial "solution," an aid package that would allow the Mexican government to pay its obligations to foreign investors and thereby restore foreign (and national) investors' confidence in the Mexican economy. This financial response was but one of several potential choices. For instance, there could conceivably have been an emphasis on promoting manufacturing growth and protecting small businesses and homeowners from the bankruptcies faced by many in Mexico. And the U.S. government could also have exhorted the Mexican government to give up on restoring confidence in the global financial market and focus instead on the production of real value added in the Mexican economy. To complicate matters further, this crisis, which was largely presented as a global economic security issue, was handled not by the secretary of state—as it would have been twenty years ago—but by the secretary of the treasury, Robert Rubin, someone who had been the so-called dean of Wall Street. There are two rather important novel elements here: first, that Treasury should handle this international crisis, and, second, that the secretary of that agency was a former top partner at Goldman, Sachs & Co. on Wall Street, one of the leading global financial firms. My aim here is not to point to even the slightest potential for corruption but rather to raise the question of what is desirable economically, and how we define problems and their best solutions.

The shift in responsibility from the State Department to Treasury signals the extent to which the state itself has been transformed by its participation in the implementation of globalization and by the pressures of globalization. Many governments now see their responsibilities as going beyond traditional foreign policy and extending to world trade, the global environment, and global economic stability.[41] This participation of the state in the international arena is an extremely multifaceted and complex matter, and one in which some states participate much more than others. In some cases, it *can* be seen as benevolent—for example, in certain matters concerning the global environment—and in others less so—as when the governments of the highly developed countries, particularly the United States, push for worldwide market reform and privatization in developing countries.

I confine the analysis here to the economic arena, where the international role of the state has been read in rather diverse, though not necessarily mutually exclusive, ways. For instance, according to some, much of this new role of states in the global economy is dominated by the furthering of a broad neoliberal conception, to the point where it represents a constitutionalizing of this project.[42] Others emphasize that effective international participation by national governments can contribute to the strengthening of the rule of law at the global level.[43]

Yet others see the participation of the state in international systems as contributing to the loss of sovereignty. One can see this in recent debates over the World Trade Organization, fueled by concerns that it imposes restrictions on the political autonomy of the national state by placing the principle of free trade above all other considerations. For example, some fear that it will be used to enforce the GATT trade regulations to the point of overturning federal, state, and local laws. This is then seen as jeopardizing a nation's right to enact its own consumer, labor, and environmental laws. It is worth noting here that many in the United States who supported the GATT did not like the role of the WTO because they did not like the idea of binding the nation to an international dispute-resolution tribunal not fully controlled by the United States.

An important question running through these different interpretations is whether the new transnational regimes and institutions are creating systems that strengthen the claims of certain actors (corporations, the large multinational legal firms) and correspondingly weaken the positions of states and smaller players. John Ruggie has pointed out that "global markets and transnationalized corporate structures . . . are not in the business of replacing states," yet they can have the potential for producing fundamental changes in the system of states.[44]

What matters here is that global capital has made claims on national states, which have responded through the production of new forms of legality. The new geography of global economic processes, the strategic territories for economic globalization, have to be defined in terms of both the practices of corporate actors, including the requisite infrastructure, and the work of the state

in producing or legitimating new legal regimes. Views that characterize the national state as simply losing significance fail to capture this very important fact and reduce what is happening to a function of the global–national duality: what one wins, the other loses. By contrast, I view deregulation not simply as a loss of control by the state but as a crucial mechanism for handling the juxtaposition of the interstate consensus to pursue globalization and the fact that national legal systems remain as the major, or crucial, instantiation through which guarantees of contract and property rights are enforced.

There are two distinct issues here. One is the formation of new legal regimes that negotiate between national sovereignty and the transnational practices of corporate economic actors. The second is the particular content of these new regimes, one that strengthens the advantages of certain types of economic actors and weakens those of others. Concerning governance, these two aspects translate into two different agendas. One is centered on the effort to create viable systems of coordination and order among the powerful economic actors now operating globally (to ensure, one could say, that the big boys at the top don't kill each other). International commercial arbitration and credit-rating agencies can be seen as contributing to this type of order. The second is focused less on how to create order at the top than on equity and distributive questions in the context of a globally integrated economic system with immense inequalities in the profit-making capacities of firms and the earnings capacities of households.

This second, equity-oriented agenda is further constrained by some of the order-creating governance issues arising from a global economic system increasingly dominated by finance. For now, I want to raise two larger questions of principle and politics: What actors gain legitimacy to govern the global economy and take over rules and authorities previously controlled by the national state? Do the new systems for governance that are emerging and the confinement of the role of national states in the global economy to promoting deregulation, markets, and privatization indicate a decline of international public law?[45]

I see an important parallel here. Certain components of the state's authority to protect rights are being displaced onto so-called universal human rights codes. . . . While the national state was and remains in many ways the guarantor of the social, political, and civil rights of a nation's people, from the 1970s on we see a significant transformation in this area. Human rights codes have become a somewhat autonomous source of authority that can delegitimize a state's particular actions if it violates such codes. Thus both the global capital market and human rights codes can extract accountability from the state, but they do so with very different agendas. Both have gained a kind of legitimacy.

It is clear that defining the nation-state and the global economy as mutually exclusive operations is, in my analysis, highly problematic. The strategic spaces where many global processes take place are often national; the mechanisms through which the new legal forms necessary for globalization are implemented are often part of state institutions; the infrastructure that makes possible the hypermobility of financial capital at the global scale is situated in various national territories. The condition of the nation-state, in my view, cannot be reduced to one of declining significance. The shrinking capacity of the state to regulate many of its industries cannot be explained simply by the fact that firms now operate in a global rather than in a national economy. The state itself has been a key agent in the implementation of global processes, and it has emerged quite altered by this participation. The form and content of participation varies between highly developed and developing countries and within each of these groupings.

Sovereignty and territory, then, remain key features of the international system. But they have been reconstituted and partly displaced onto other institutional arenas outside the state and outside the framework of nationalized territory. I argue that sovereignty has been decentered and territory partly denationalized. From a longer historical perspective, this would represent a transformation in the articulation of sovereignty and territory as they have marked the formation of the modern state and interstate system. And it would entail a need to expand the analytic terrain within which the social sciences examine some of these processes, that is to say, the explicit or implicit tendency to use the nation-state as the container of social, political, and economic processes.

The denationalization of territory occurs through both corporate practices and the as yet fragmentary ascendant new legal regime. This process does not unfold within the geographic conception of territory shared by the generals who fought the wars for nationalizing territory in earlier centuries. It is instead a denationalizing of specific institutional arenas. (Manhattan is the equivalent of a free trade zone when it comes to finance, but it is not Manhattan the geographic entity, with all its layers of activity, functions, and regulations that is a free trade zone; it is a highly specialized functional or institutional realm that has become denationalized.)

Sovereignty remains a feature of the system, but it is now located in a multiplicity of institutional arenas: the new emergent transnational private legal regimes, new supranational organizations (such as the WTO and the institutions of the European Union), and the various international human rights codes. All these institutions constrain the autonomy of national states; states operating under the rule of law are caught in a web of obligations they cannot disregard easily (though they clearly can to some extent, as is illustrated by the United States' unpaid duties to the United Nations: if this were a personal credit card debt, you or I would be in jail).

What I see is the beginning of an unbundling of sovereignty as we have known it for many centuries—but not always. Scholars examining changes in mentalities or social epistemologies have remarked that significant, epochal change frequently could not be grasped by contemporaries: the vocabularies, categories, master images available to them were unable to capture fundamental change. Suffering from the same limitations, all we see is the collapse of sovereignty as we know it. But it seems to me that rather than sovereignty eroding as a consequence of globalization and supranational organizations, it is being transformed. There is plenty of it around, but the sites for its concentration have changed over the last two decades—and economic globalization has certainly been a key factor in all this. Over the last ten or fifteen years, that process has reconfigured the intersection of territoriality and sovereignty as it had been constituted over the last century, after struggles lasting many more. This reconfiguration is partial, selective, and above all strategic. Some of its repercussions for distributive justice and equity are profoundly disturbing. And even in the domain of immigration policy, where the state is still considered as absolutely sovereign, the new web of obligations and rights that states need to take into account under the rule of law in the making of policy has caused conditions to change.

Reading Notes

1. Reisman 1990, 867.
2. Franck 1992; Jacobson 1996.
3. Reisman 1990; McDougal and Reisman 1981.
4. Reisman 1990, 868.
5. See the classification of different types of relationships between a system of rule and territoriality in Ruggie 1993.
6. See Anderson 1974; Wallerstein 1974; Giddens 1987.
7. See Tilly 1990. On the Italian city-states and the Hanseatic League in northern Europe, see the analysis in Spruyt 1994.
8. See Mattingly's (1988) account of the right of embassy in medieval times as a specific, formal right with only partial immunities.
9. Mattingly 1988, 244. See also Kratochwil 1986.
10. In this case, the site for extraterritoriality is the individual holding diplomatic status.
11. Grotius's doctrine was a response to the Dutch East Indies Company's effort to monopolize access to the oceans; it resolved the vacuum left by the failure of Spain and Portugal to agree on a division of the maritime trade routes.
12. There is a vast literature on this subject. See, e.g., Bonacich et al. 1994; Morales 1994; Ward 1990.
13. See United Nations Centre for Transnational Corporations 1993, 1995. The center was an autonomous entity until 1994, when it became part of UNCTAD, the United Nations Conference on Trade and Development.
14. I elaborated these issues in Sassen 1991. This process of corporate integration should not be confused with vertical integration as conventionally defined. See also Gereffi, Korzeniewicz, and Korzeniewicz 1994 on commodity chains and Porter's (1990) value-added chains, two constructs that also illustrate the difference between corporate integration on a world scale and vertical integration as conventionally defined.
15. More detailed accounts of these figures and sources can be found in Sassen 1994a.
16. See, e.g., Harrison 1994.
17. See Sassen 1991, 1994a; Knox and Taylor 1995; Brotchie et al. 1995; *Le Débat*, 1994.
18. It is important to unbundle analytically the fact of strategic functions for the global economy or for global operation from the overall corporate economy of a country. Traditional economic complexes have valorization dynamics that tend to be far more articulated with the public economic functions of the state, the quintessential example being Fordist manufacturing. Global markets in finance and advanced services, however, partly operate under a regulatory umbrella that is market centered. This raises questions of control, especially in view of the currently inadequate capacities to govern transactions in electronic space. Global control and command functions are partly handled within national corporate structures but also constitute a distinct corporate subsector, which can be conceived of as part of a network that connects global cities across the globe. In this sense, global cities are different from the old capitals of erstwhile empires, in that they are a function of cross-border networks rather than simply the most powerful city of an empire. There is, in my conceptualization, no such entity as a single global city akin to the single capital of an empire; the category "global city" only makes sense as a component of a global network of strategic sites. See Sassen 1991. For the purposes of certain kinds of inquiry, this distinction may not matter; for the purposes of understanding the global economy, it does.
19. These data come from the Bank for International Settlements, the so-called central bankers' bank.
20. See Mittelman 1996; Panitch 1996; Cox 1987.
21. There are, of course, other mechanisms for resolving business disputes. The larger system includes arbitration controlled by courts, arbitration that is parallel to courts, and various court and out-of-court mechanisms such as mediation. The following description of international commercial arbitration is taken from Dezalay and Garth 1995. For these authors, international commercial arbitration means something different today from what it did twenty years ago. Increasingly formal, it has come to resemble U.S.–style litigation as it has become

more successful and institutionalized. Today, international business contracts for the sale of goods, joint ventures, construction projects, distributorships, and the like typically call for arbitration in the event of a dispute arising from the contractual arrangement. The main reason given for this choice is that arbitration allows each party to avoid being forced to submit to the courts of the other. Also important is the secrecy of the process. Such arbitration can be institutional, following the rules of institutions such as the International Chamber of Commerce in Paris, the American Arbitration Association, the London Court of International Commercial Arbitration, or many others, or it can be ad hoc, often following the rules of the UN Commission on International Trade Law (UNCITRAL). The arbitrators, usually three private individuals selected by the parties, act as private judges, holding hearings and issuing judgments. There are few grounds for appeal to courts, and the final decision of the arbitrators is more easily enforced among signatory countries than would be a court judgment (under the terms of a widely adopted 1958 New York Convention).

22. Dezalay and Garth 1995; Aksen, 1990. Despite this increase in size, there is a kind of international arbitration community, a club of sorts, with relatively few important institutions and limited numbers of individuals in each country who are the key players both as counsel and arbitrators. But the enormous growth of arbitration over the last decade has led to sharp competition in the business; indeed, it has become big legal business (Salacuse 1991). Dezalay and Garth found that multinational legal firms sharpen the competition further because they have the capacity to forum shop among institutions, sets of rules, laws, and arbitrators. The large English and U.S. law firms have used their power in the international business world to impose their conception of arbitration and more largely of the practice of law. This is well illustrated by the case of France. Although French firms rank among the top providers of information services and industrial engineering services in Europe and have a strong though not

outstanding position in financial and insurance services, they are at an increasing disadvantage in legal and accounting services. French law firms are at a particular disadvantage because of their legal system (the Napoleonic Code): Anglo-American law tends to govern international transactions. Foreign firms with offices in Paris dominate the servicing of the legal needs of firms in France, both French and foreign, that operate internationally (Carrez 1991) (see *Le Débat* 1994).

23. Summarized in Dezalay and Garth 1995; see also Dezalay 1992.

24. Dezalay and Garth 1995. The so-called lex mercatoria was conceived by many as a return to an international law of business independent of national laws (Carbonneau 1990). Anglo-American practitioners tend not to support this Continental, highly academic notion (see Carbonneau 1990), and insofar as they are "Americanizing" the field, they are moving it farther away from academic law and lex mercatoria.

25. There are several rating agencies in other countries, but they are oriented to the domestic markets. The possibility of a European-based rating agency has been discussed, particularly with the merger of a London-based agency (IBCA) with a French one (Euronotation).

26. As the demand for ratings grows, so does the authoritativeness of the notion behind them. Sinclair (1994) considers this to be ill founded given the judgments that are central to it. The processes intrinsic to ratings are tied to certain assumptions, which are in turn tied to dominant interests, notably narrow theories of market efficiency. They aim for undistorted price signals and little if any government intervention. Sinclair notes that transition costs such as unemployment are usually not factored into evaluations and considered to be outweighed by the new environment created (143).

27. Their power has grown in good part because of disintermediation and the globalization of the capital market. Some functions fulfilled by banks (i.e., intermediation) have lost considerable weight in the running of capital markets. Thus, insofar as banks are subject to considerable government regulation and

their successors are not, government regulation over the capital markets has declined. Ratings agencies, which are private entities, have taken over some of the functions of banks in organizing information for suppliers and borrowers of capital. An important question is whether the new agencies and the larger complex of entities represented by Wall Street have indeed formed a new intermediary sector (see Thrift 1987).

28. Rosenau and Czempiel 1992.

29. See Trubek et al. 1993.

30. This hegemony has not passed unnoticed and is engendering considerable debate. For instance, a familiar issue that is emerging as significant in view of the spread of Western legal concepts involves a critical examination of the philosophical premises of authorship and property that define the legal arena in the West (e.g., Coombe 1993).

31. See Shapiro 1993. There have been a few particular common developments and many particular parallel developments in law across the world. Thus, as a concomitant of the globalization of markets and the organization of transnational corporations, there has been a move toward relatively uniform global contract and commercial law. This can be seen as a private lawmaking system wherein two or more parties create a set of rules to govern their future relations. Such a system of private lawmaking can exist transnationally even when there is no transnational court or sovereign to resolve disputes and secure enforcement. The case of international commercial arbitration discussed earlier illustrates this well. See also Shapiro 1979.

32. Charny 1991; Trachtman 1993. Two other categories that may also partly overlap with internationalization are important to distinguish, at least analytically: multilateralism and what Ruggie (1993) has called multiperspectival institutions.

33. See Sinclair 1994.

34. For a discussion of the concept of cultural globalization, see King 1991 and Robertson 1991, especially Robertson's notion of the world as a single place, what he calls the "global human condition." I would say that globalization is also a process that produces differentiation, but of a character very different from that associated with such differentiating notions as national character, national culture, and national society. For example, the corporate world today has a global geography, but it isn't everywhere in the world: in fact, it has highly defined and structured spaces; it is also increasingly sharply differentiated from noncorporate segments in the economies of the particular locations (such as New York City) or countries where it operates.

35. Shapiro 1993 finds that law and the political structures that produce and sustain it are far more national and far less international than are trade and politics as such (63). He argues that the U.S. domestic legal regime may have to respond to global changes in law. For the most part, he claims, national regimes of law and lawyering will remain self-generating, though in response to globally perceived needs. In my reading, it is this last point that may well be emerging as a growing factor in shaping legal form and legal practice.

36. The best-known instance of this is probably the austerity policy imposed on many developing countries. Such policies also point up the participation of states in furthering the goals of globalization, because they have to be run through national governments and reprocessed as national policies. It is clearer here than in other cases that the global is not simply the non-national, that global processes materialize in national territories and institutions. There is a distinction here to be made—and to be specified theoretically and empirically—between international law (whether public or private), which is always implemented through national governments, and these policies, which are part of the effort to foster globalization.

37. Dezalay 1992. See also Carrez 1991; and Sinclair 1994.

38. Shapiro 1993.

39. Shapiro 1993, 39; Wiegand 1991.

40. Dezalay 1992.

41. Aman 1995, 437.

42. See Panitch 1996; Cox 1987; Mittelman 1996.

43. Aman, 1995; Young 1989; Rosenau 1992.

44. Ruggie 1993, 143.

45. See Kennedy 1988; Negri 1995.

Reading References

Aksen, Gerald. 1990. "Arbitration and Other Means of Dispute Settlement." In D. Goldsweig and R. Cummings, eds., *International Joint Ventures: A Practical Approach to Working with Foreign Investors in the U.S. and Abroad*, pp. 287–94. Chicago: American Bar Association.

Aman, Alfred C., Jr. 1995. "A Global Perspective on Current Regulatory Reform: Rejection, Relocation, or Reinvention?" *Indiana Journal of Global Legal Studies* 2: 429–64.

Anderson, Perry. 1974. *Lineages of the Absolutist State*. London: New Left Books.

Bonacich, Edna, Lucie Cheng, Norma Chinchilla, Nora Hamilton, and Paul Ong, eds. 1994. *Global Production: The Apparel Industry in the Pacific Rim*. Philadelphia: Temple University Press.

Brotchie, John, Mike Batty, Ed Blakely, Peter Hall, and Peter Newton, eds. 1995. *Cities in Competition: Productive and Sustainable Cities for the Twenty-first Century*. Melbourne: Longman Australia.

Carbonneau, Thomas, ed. 1990. *Lex Mercatoria and Arbitration*. Dobbs Ferry, N.Y.: Transnational Juris Publications.

Carrez, Jean-François. 1991. *Le développement des fonctions tertiares internationales à Paris et dans les métropoles régionales: Rapport au premier ministre*. Paris: La Documentation française.

Charny, David. 1991. "Competition among Jurisdictions in Formulating Corporate Law Rules: An American Perspective on the 'Race to the Bottom' in the European Communities." *Harvard International Law Journal* 32, no. 2: 423–56.

Coombe, Rosemary J. 1993. "The Properties of Culture and the Politics of Possessing Identity: Native Claims in the Cultural Appropriation Controversy." *Canadian Journal of Law and Jurisprudence* 6, no. 2 (July): 249–85.

Cox, Robert. 1987. *Production, Power, and World Order: Social Forces in the Making of History*. New York: Columbia University Press.

Le Débat. 1994. *Le Nouveau Paris* (special issue) (summer).

Dezalay, Yves. 1992. *Marchands de droit*. Paris: Fayard.

Dezalay, Yves, and Bryant Garth. 1995. "Merchants of Law as Moral Entrepreneurs: Constructing International Justice from the Competition for Transnational Business Disputes." *Law and Society Review* 29, no. 1: 27–64.

Franck, Thomas M. 1992. "The Emerging Right to Democratic Governance." *American Journal of International Law* 86, no. 1: 46–91.

Gereffi, G., M. Korzeniewicz, and R.P. Korzeniewicz. 1994. (eds), *Commodity Chains and Global Capitalism*. Westport, CT.: Greenwood Press.

Giddens, Anthony. 1987. *The Nation-State and Violence*. Berkeley: University of California Press.

Harrison, Bennett. 1994. *Lean and Mean: The Changing Landscape of Corporate Power in the Age of Flexibility*. New York: Basic Books.

Jacobson, David. 1996. *Rights Across Borders: Immigration and the Decline of Citizenship*. Baltimore: Johns Hopkins University Press.

Kennedy, David. 1988. "A New Stream of International Law Scholarship." *Wisconsin International Law Journal* 7, no. 1: 1–49.

King, Anthony D., ed. 1991. *Culture, Globalization, and the World-System: Contemporary Conditions for the Representation of Identity*. Current Debates in Art History 3. Binghamton: Department of Art and Art History, State University of New York at Binghamton.

Knox, Paul L., and Peter J. Taylor, eds. 1995. *World Cities in a World-System*. Cambridge: Cambridge University Press.

Kratochwil, Friedrich. 1986. "Of Systems, Boundaries and Territoriality." *World Politics* 34 (October): 27–52.

Mattingly, Garrett. 1988. *Renaissance Diplomacy*. New York: Dover.

McDougal, M.S., and W.M. Reisman. 1981. *International Law Essays: A Supplement to International Law in Contemporary Perspective*. Mineola, N.Y.: Foundation Press.

Mittelman, James H., ed. 1996. *Globalization: Critical Reflections. International Political Economy Yearbook*, vol. 9. Boulder, Colo.: Lynne Riener.

Morales, Rebecca. 1994. *Flexible Production: Restructuring of the International Automobile Industry*. Cambridge: Polity Press.

Negri, Toni. 1995. "A quoi sert encore l'Etat?" *Pouvoirs Pouvoir. Futur Antérieur* (special issue) 25–26: 135–52.

Panitch, Leo. 1996. "Rethinking the Role of the State in an Era of Globalization." In James H. Mittelman, ed., *Globalization: Critical Reflections, International Political Economy Yearbook*, vol. 9. Boulder, Colo.: Lynne Riener.

Porter, Michael, E. 1990. *The Competitive Advantage of Nations*. New York: Free Press.

Reisman, W. Michael. 1990. "Sovereignty and Human Rights in Contemporary International Law." *American Journal of International Law* 84, no. 4 (October): 866–76.

Robertson, R. 1991. "Social Theory, Cultural Relativity, and the Problem of Globality." In Anthony D. King, ed., *Culture, Globalization, and the World-System: Contemporary Conditions for the Representation of Identity*, pp. 69–90. Current Debates in Art History 3. Binghamton: Department of Art and Art History, State University of New York at Binghamton.

Rosenau, J.N. 1992. "Governance, Order, and Change in World Politics." In J.N. Rosenau and E.O. Czempiel, eds., *Governance Without Government: Order and Change in World Politics*, pp. 1–29. Cambridge: Cambridge University Press.

Rosenau, J.N., and E.O. Czempiel, eds. 1992. *Governance Without Government: Order and Change in World Politics*. Cambridge: Cambridge University Press.

Ruggie, John Gerard. 1993. "Territoriality and Beyond: Problematizing Modernity in International Relations." *International Organization* 47, no. 1 (winter): 139–74.

Salacuse, Jeswald. 1991. *Making Global Deals: Negotiating in the International Marketplace*. Boston: Houghton Mifflin.

Sassen, Saskia. 1994a. *Cities in a World Economy*. Thousand Oaks, Calif.: Pine Forge/Sage.

———. 1991. *The Global City: New York, London, Tokyo*. Princeton, N.J.: Princeton University Press.

Shapiro, Martin. 1993. "The Globalization of Law." *Indiana Journal of Global Legal Studies* 1 (fall): 37–64.

———. 1979. "Judicial Activism." In S.M. Lipset, ed., *The Third Century: America as a Post-industrial Society*. Stanford, Calif.: Hoover Institution Press–Stanford University.

Sinclair, Timothy J. 1994. "Passing Judgement: Credit Rating Processes as Regulatory Mechanisms of Governance in the Emerging World Order." *Review of International Political Economy* 1, no. 1 (spring): 133–59.

Spruyt, Hendrik. 1994. *The Sovereign State and Its Competitors: An Analysis of Systems Change*. Princeton, N.J.: Princeton University Press.

Thrift, N. 1987. "The Fixers: The Urban Geography of International Commercial Capital." In J. Henderson and M. Castells, eds., *Global Restructuring and Territorial Development*. London: Sage.

Tilly, Charles. 1990. *Coercion, Capital, and European States, A.D. 990–1990*. Oxford: Blackwell.

Trachtman, Joel. 1993. "International Regulatory Competition, Externalization, and Jurisdiction." *Harvard International Law Journal* 34, no. 1: 47–104.

Trubek, David M., Yves Dezalay, Ruth Buchanan, and John R. Davis. 1993. "Global Restructuring and the Law: The Internationalization of Legal Fields and Creation of Transnational Arenas." Working Paper Series on the Political Economy of Legal Change. No. 1. Madison: Global Studies Research Program, University of Wisconsin.

United Nations Conference on Trade and Development (UNCTAD). 1995. *1995 World Investment Report: Transnational Corporations and Competitiveness*. New York: UNCTAD, Division on Transnational Corporations and Investment.

———. 1993. *1993 World Investment Report: Transnational Corporations and Integrated International Production*. New York: UNCTAD, Programme on Transnational Corporations of the United Nations.

Wallerstein, Immanuel. 1974. *The Modern World System*. Vol. 1. New York: Academic Press.

Ward, Kathryn B., ed. 1990. *Women Workers and Global Restructuring*. Ithaca, N.Y.: ILR Press.

Wiegand, Wolfgang. 1991. "The Reception of American Law in Europe." *American Journal of Comparative Law* 39, no. 2: 229–48.

Young, O.R. 1989. *International Cooperation: Building Regimes for Natural Resources and the Environment*. Ithaca, N.Y.: Cornell University Press.

KEY TERMS

Civil Society   A set of groups, institutions, and interactions located between the state, the market, and the private sphere.

Cosmopolitan Democracy   A transnational governance regime comprising international institutions, democratic states, and civil societies committed to protecting human rights and democratic public law both within national borders and at the regional and international levels.

Globalization   A set of processes that are transforming and reorganizing social relations and intensifying economic, social, and political interconnections among people across territorial boundaries.

State Sovereignty   The absolute and final authority of a country to regulate internal matters without being subject to any power outside itself.

Welfare State   An interventionist state that seeks to promote some measure of social and economic equality among its citizens by redistribution attained through taxation and social programs.

FURTHER READINGS

Falk, Robert. *Predatory Globalization: A Critique.* Cambridge, UK: Polity Press, 1999.

Held, David. *Democracy and the Global Order: From the Modern State to Cosmopolitan Governance.* Cambridge, UK: Polity Press, 1995.

Strange, Susan. "The Erosion of the State." In *Current History* (November 1997): 365–69.

Weiss, Linda. "The Myth of the Powerless State." *New Left Review* 225 (September/October 1997): 3–27.

WEB LINKS

World Trade Organization:
www.wto.org

CorpWatch—Holding Corporations Accountable:
www.corpwatch.org

Links to Articles and Reviews Examining Issues Related to Globalization:
http://globalpolicy.igc.org/globaliz

Organisation for Economic Co-operation and Development:
www.oecd.org

CHAPTER 15

NATIONS AND NATIONALISM

What is a nation? What is nationalism? Where do nations and nationalism come from? These are questions that have perplexed political scientists for years and for which there is really no consensus regarding answers. This chapter presents the central debates in the area of nationalism studies, highlighting the strengths and weaknesses of the different positions. It first provides some definitions while introducing some distinctions between types of nations and nationalism. It then discusses various theoretical approaches to these phenomena and assesses their future relevance as political forces. The chapter concludes with an overview of nationalism in contemporary politics.

DEFINITIONS AND CONCEPTUAL DISTINCTIONS

The meaning of the concepts of nation and nationalism is a hotly debated issue in political science, which means that defining nations and nationalism can be a perilous exercise. In fact, political scientists often use the concept of **nation** interchangeably with other concepts such as state and ethnic group while ethnicity, and even tribalism, sometimes substitute for **nationalism**.[1] Three distinctions are needed to eliminate, or at least reduce, this terminological confusion. The first is that a nation is not a state. The tendency to assume that nation and state are one and the same is in large part the product of the political discourse. Political leaders speak of nations when referring to states. The most visible international organization is called the United Nations, although its membership is determined by statehood. International relations is a sub-field of political science that traditionally has been about inter-*state* relations. The state is a legal concept, determined by sovereignty and international recognition, while the nation is sociological in nature and represents therefore a more subjective concept characterized by identity. Consequently, a state may harbour more than one nation. An example here is Spain, where Catalonia and the Basque Country may be considered nations distinct from the Spanish one. A nation may also be spread out in several different states. The case of the Kurds is a commonly cited example of this situation, since as a group they exhibit a sense of solidarity that does not conform to formal citizenship, be it Turkish, Syrian, Iranian, or Iraqi. Of course, the state (legal concept) sometimes corresponds to the nation (sociological one). This is the case for the United States and some other countries, most of which—Norway, Portugal, Korea, and Japan—are ethnically and linguistically homogeneous.

The second distinction, which is less clear and more controversial, is between nation and ethnic group. Typically, the literature on nationalism uses the label "ethnic group" when discussing developing countries and, to a lesser extent, Eastern Europe (the Yorubas of Nigeria, the Serbs, etc.) and "nation" in reference to industrialized democracies (Quebec, Scotland, Catalonia). What does this mean? The concepts of "nation" and "ethnic group" have been attributed different normative connotations by political scientists: nations are generally portrayed as modern, developed, and democratic, while ethnic groups tend to be depicted as backward, exclusive, and a source of violence. From this perspective, the usage of the two sets of concepts simply reflects the assumption that group identity takes different forms and has different consequences in the Western and non-Western worlds. But is there something more substantial differentiating nation and ethnic group? The key here is that the nation has an inherent political dimension.[2] Both nations and ethnic groups are *human communities united by a special sense of solidarity deriving from shared features, most importantly, language, religion, ancestry (real or imagined), history, myths, and symbols.* However, a definition of the nation also needs to highlight that this human community *seeks, in the name of this solidarity, to gain or maintain a distinct political situation, usually autonomy or independence.* A last distinction between the use of the concepts of ethnic group and nation is that only the former sometimes refers to immigrant communities within established states (for example, the Italians of Toronto).

Above and beyond these squabbles over definition in the strictest sense, political scientists also disagree on what constitutes the nation. The debate here involves *objective* and *subjective* conceptualizations of the nation. The objective conceptualization suggests that nations are products of shared objective criteria. Former Soviet leader Joseph Stalin, not otherwise known as a political theorist(!), has produced a definition of nation that exemplifies the objective perspective. Stalin argued that the nation was a "stable community of people formed on the basis of a common language, territory, economic life, and psychological make-up manifested in a common culture."[3] From this angle, one can locate a nation, and indeed decide if a particular group forms a nation, by searching for these specific criteria. The subjective conceptualization suggests that nations exist first and foremost as a result of a collective act of will and a voluntary decision to belong. This view is best illustrated by French scholar Ernest Renan's metaphor of the nation as an everyday plebiscite.[4] From this perspective, a nation is not readily identifiable to the external observer since its existence is a matter of choice. It is an "imagined community."[5] Therefore, a nation is whatever group says it constitutes a nation. The objective and subjective conceptualizations of the nation are better seen as ideal types, that is, categories that do not exist as such in reality. Indeed, there is some consensus among political scientists that nations cannot be reduced to one or the other category, but rather that they have both objective and subjective components.

Let us now turn to nationalism. Four sets of distinctions permeate discussions on this concept. The first is the terminological use of nationalism and the related concept of ethnicity. The second involves the views of nationalism as an ideology or idea, and as a movement or political process. The third is between state and sub-state nationalism. The fourth features the concepts of "ethnic" and "civic" nationalism.

At the level of terminology, scholars tend to make a similar distinction between nationalism and ethnicity as they do between nation and ethnic group. They use "nationalism" to speak of developed societies. This term has more positive connotations than "ethnicity," which tends to be reserved for developing countries and linked with conditions of backwardness, ethnocentrism, and violence. However, as was the case for the distinction between nation and ethnic group, there is one substantial difference between nationalism and ethnicity: nationalism is inherently political while ethnicity can be strictly cultural.

The academic study of nationalism, usually said to have been launched in the 1940s by historians Hans Kohn and Carleton B. Hayes, was initially permeated by the perspective of nationalism as an ideology. For example, the nationalist independence movement of African and Asian colonies in the 1960s and 1970s tended to be viewed as driven by a particular ideology, namely, anti-colonialism. In the context of the ideological conception of nationalism, the definition put forward by Ernest Gellner is particularly appropriate: *nationalism is the idea that the political and cultural units should be congruent.*[6] However, this definition is quite general and abstract as is the premise that nationalism is an ideology. For this reason, political scientists tend to speak much more of nationalism as a concrete political process, usually linked to modernization, that involves identity and mobilization. From this perspective nationalism is a *movement that makes political claims on behalf of a nation and on the basis of a national identity.*

Another distinction found in the literature on nationalism is between *state* and *sub-state nationalism.* State nationalism refers to the nationalism of existing states, that is, to German nationalism, American nationalism, Japanese nationalism, and so on. Just like sub-state nationalism, it is characterized by a sense of solidarity that underpins a collective identity, but its aim is obviously not the creation of a new political entity. Rather, it involves the defence of that state's sovereignty, or the nation's identity, in the face of real or perceived threats, military, political, economic, or cultural. French nationalism, for example, was a central force in World War I, where it was stimulated by Germany's political and military ambitions. It is still a powerful force today but reacts primarily to globalization and American influence, which are perceived as economic and cultural menaces. State nationalism is not necessarily a defensive movement; it can embody a show of force, represent a statement about power, prestige, or status, or even correspond to outright aggression. The German nationalism that led to World War II, blending notions of racial superiority with goals of expansion and domination, is an extreme example of the latter instance.

More controversial is the suggestion that some nationalisms are "ethnic" while others are "civic." This distinction essentially refers to the criteria used to determine membership in a nation. In the case of ethnic (or cultural) nationalism, these criteria are ascriptive, which means one is born with them and they cannot be readily acquired. In other words, inclusion in the nation is a matter of meeting specific criteria that are either totally or mostly objective. Race and ancestry are the two most rigid criteria for determining membership in a nation. Religion can be changed, but most likely not without considerable emotional turmoil. Cultural practices can be altered, but here again such a change is often demanding and can be painful. A language can be acquired, which makes it arguably the most flexible of objective criteria, although some societies might exclude those individuals who are not considered to have a sufficient mastery of the tongue. The classic historical example of an **ethnic nationalism** is Germany. In its territorial dispute with France over the region of Alsace-Lorraine in the late nineteenth and early twentieth centuries, the German position was that this population was part of the German nation because it spoke German and had German ancestry; its preference on citizenship, that is, which state it wanted to belong to, did not matter. Of course, Nazi Germany serves as an extreme example of a nationalism where inclusion and exclusion is determined by factors beyond an individual's control. Today, Germany is a liberal-democratic state. However, it still emphasizes descent in the definition of the nation. For example, children born in Germany of foreign parents were, as recently as 2000, not automatically granted German citizenship.

Since ethnic nationalism distinguishes between insiders and outsiders on the basis of features that, at the very least, are difficult to acquire, it is generally viewed negatively by political scientists. Ethnic nationalism is said to be illiberal, often associated with authoritarian regimes, and conducive to violence. Indeed, there is much in the way of logical reasoning and empirical evidence to substantiate these claims. Ethnic nationalism puts minorities in a precarious position because it involves political power being exercised in the name of a particular group and works on a logic of homogeneity and homogenization. Ethnic nationalist movements, which arose in Eastern Europe after the end of the Cold War, most notably Serb nationalism, exhibited these features of authoritarianism and violence toward other groups. It is therefore not surprising that ethnic nationalism is typically characterized as backward, unenlightened, and dangerous. Political scientists have suggested that two situations make ethnic nationalism more likely. The first is a social, political, economic, and ideological context that does not correspond to Western modernity. In other words, secular industrialized societies with liberal-democratic traditions and high levels of economic development would not be good candidates for the development of ethnic nationalism. This has led scholars to simply suggest that ethnic nationalism was the type of nationalism associated with Eastern Europe and developing countries.[7] The second situation considered favourable to ethnic nationalism is when a nationalist movement seeks the creation of an independent state. The general idea is that sub-state nationalism needs, much more than state nationalism, to refer to objective markers in order to generate enough political mobilization to realize its objectives.

Civic nationalism refers to a type of nationalism that emphasizes choice as opposed to objective criteria. In practical terms, this means that the only condition required to be included in a nation is to live within its territorial borders and accept its laws. This type of nationalism takes elements of citizenship, such as the rights and responsibilities that link individuals to the state, as the cement for national cohesion. The traditional examples here are France and the United States. In France, the conception of the nation has its roots in the 1789 Revolution, which framed the political community in the language of freedom and equality of rights. In its later conflict with Germany over Alsace-Lorraine, France took the position that citizenship should be determined by the will of the region's inhabitants. American nationalism (often called patriotism) has successfully integrated different cultural groups through a focus on liberal-democratic values, capitalist principles, and a sense of exceptionalism forged in reference to the outside world.

Civic nationalism is generally considered to be the "good" nationalism. Its inclusive character makes it more conducive to liberalism, democracy, and civil peace. It is also said to be forward looking, progressive, and enlightened, and to generally foster a positive sense of solidarity in societies. It is argued that, while ethnic nationalism is linked to pre-modern and developing societies, civic nationalism is an offshoot of modernity. In this context, it is very much a Western phenomenon. Finally, nationalism is said to have more chance of being civic when it supports an already existing state because it is less likely to engage as heavily in nationalist mobilization as a movement seeking state creation.

This distinction between civic and ethnic nationalism is increasingly questioned by political scientists. Three main problems have been identified. First, few nationalisms seem to be either purely civic or ethnic. Even France and the United States, generally considered to be the classic cases of civic nationalism, are not without cultural components. In France, citizens of North African backgrounds are not that well accepted by some segments of French society. This is demonstrated most clearly by the presence of a far right-wing party, the Front National (FN), which shocked all observers by advancing to the second round of the 2002 presidential election with more than 16 percent of popular support. The FN decries immigration as a threat to the coherence of the French nation and targets populations of North African origins who, despite the fact they speak French, are still considered outsiders because of their religion (they tend to be Muslims) and the colour of their skin. In the United States, Blacks were, until the 1960s, second-class citizens who were only imperfectly integrated into the American nation. In the 1950s, in the context of acute Cold War tensions, Senator Joseph McCarthy spearheaded a political movement that accused suspected Communist sympathizers of being "un-American." This category, though not ethnic or cultural per se, still reflected an exclusion that was not the product of an individual's free will. The second problem is that sub-state nationalism can be mostly civic while state nationalism can be mostly ethnic. Scottish nationalism is a sub-state nationalism that seeks either increased autonomy within the United Kingdom or outright independence. Its definition of the nation is very much territorial, which means that it includes everyone living in Scotland and excludes everyone living outside (even those with a Scottish background). It is much more civic than many state nationalisms in Eastern Europe, such as Romanian or Ukrainian, where the nation is defined in terms of the majority group. Finally, some political scientists have argued that the civic–ethnic distinction suffers from a Western bias because it suggests that the "good" civic nationalism is primarily associated with the developed West while the "bad" ethnic nationalism is primarily associated with Eastern Europe and developing countries. However, there are empirical problems with these connections: ethnic nationalism can certainly be found in Northern Ireland and Spain's Basque Country, two Western developed societies. Also, the foundations of the civic–ethnic distinction rest on the controversial moral assumption of the supremacy of the Western social and political model, and on the idea that only Western-style modernization can trigger the transition from ethnic to civic nationalism.

MODERNISM AND PRIMORDIALISM

The foregoing discussion on the dual character of nationalism is arguably one of two crucial debates in this field of study. The other, which has permeated the field even more, is on the origins and nature of nations and nationalism. It pits *modernists* against *primordialists*. The fundamental argument of modernists is threefold. First, nations and nationalism are modern rather than ancient.[8] Nations are constructed. They have no significant pre-modern roots, and their emergence can be understood strictly in the context of a transition from traditional to modern societies that occurred at the earliest in late seventeenth-century Europe. Typically, **modernists** argue that the breakdown of the feudal society, state centralization corresponding to the territorial consolidation of political authority, the introduction of liberal ideas, and the advent of capitalism and industrialization rendered necessary the congruence between the political and cultural units. In other words, modernization demands cultural homogenization for the sake of social unity and economic effectiveness. Differently put, modern societies need fluid channels of communication and, therefore, cultural homogeneity. As a consequence, modernists suggest that for the first time in human history, political authority governed in the name of one population, not several, that occupied a well-circumscribed territory and was thought to form a social and cultural whole. Some modernists, looking at more recent historical periods, put less emphasis on modernization processes and more on political elites in the construction of nations.[9] These scholars suggest that the large-scale mobilization inherent to modern politics serves as the motor for nationalism. In other words, political competition in the context of the modern state produces references to territory and culture that spur the construction of nations. Whichever specific perspective is used, the modernist argument is that nationalism creates nations, and not the other way around.

The second modernist argument is that the origins of nations and nationalism are European. More specifically, nations and nationalism are said to originate from the French Revolution. Indeed, there was something peculiar to this historical event in that it vested sovereignty upon the people instead of the monarch. Subjects became citizens with rights and responsibility linking them with the political community as whole. Political power was to be exercised, and wars fought, in the name of this political community, the nation, which rested on the principles of liberty, equality, and solidarity. Modernists argue that the idea of the nation developed in the context of the French Revolution spread through Europe as a consequence of both the influence of France's political and intellectual elites and the military adventures of the Napoleonic regime. The modernist perspective also has clear implications for the grounding of nations and nationalism outside Europe, particularly in the developing world. It suggests that these concepts are alien to non-European societies, that they did not exist there prior to their "exportation" by European countries. Indeed, modernists explain nationalism in the developing world by colonization, arguing that the concept of nation was brought over to, and indeed forced upon, Asian, African, Latin American, and Middle Eastern societies by colonial powers.

The third argument of the modernist perspective is that culture is not that important in the constitution of nations. Modernists oppose the idea that there is any kind of naturalness to nations that would have its roots in the sharing of a common culture. They argue that nations and nationalism are socially and politically constructed rather than culturally determined. Consequently, modernists suggest that nations are sometimes created from scratch. They are often without any tangible cultural basis or, at least, almost always deprived of any straightforward continuous cultural history. Even when the sociopolitical processes that are at the heart of the formation of nations sometimes shape pre-existing cultural conditions in a way that gives them political and subjective meaning, it is social, political, and/or economic variables that are deemed crucial, not cultural ones. What is important about cultural markers such as language, modernists suggest, is that they serve as a resource for the creation of symbols and myths that are central to nationalism and its popular appeal. Indeed, the modernist perspective greatly stresses the idea that nationalism is about the re-invention of tradition and the re-interpretation of history for purposes of mobilizing the masses and achieving political power. This is consistent with the argument that nations are fabricated, therefore fluid and malleable.

The primordialist perspective brings different views on the origins of nations and nationalism. **Primordialists** are skeptical towards the modernist position that nations are constructed. Instead, they suggest there is a certain naturalness to nations. They argue that belonging to a cultural community is a fundamental need of the human condition, and that, as a consequence, nations are a permanent feature of human history. In this context, nations cannot be purely modern phenomena.[10] At a minimum, their roots are much older. They lie in ancient cultural forms that, although shaped by historical processes such as those connected to modernization, have a logic of their own that is manifested in a common identity and the belief in a common destiny. In other words, nations have direct ancestors; they have a genealogy. For example, this view suggests that contemporary Basque or Scottish nationalism is only the most recent expression of a cultural community that has consistently expressed its personality, if not necessarily politically, then at least through poetry, the arts, and so on. A stronger primordialist position suggests that nations as such, and not only their roots, existed in the pre-modern period. From this perspective, there exist "ancient nations," and primordialists point to Egypt, Ethiopia, Armenia, Greece, and Israel as examples. According to the primordialist view, nations are naturally present in humanity, and nationalism is their logical consequence. In sum, nations create nationalism.

Primordialists also disagree with the modernist argument that nations and nationalism are a European invention. They argue that nations represent the most fundamental form of collective sociopolitical organization and that, as a consequence, their existence is independent of any specific historical period and regional context. In other words, primordialists suggest that, while the term "nation" may have European origins, the reality of the nation is, and has always been, universal. Primordialists would, for example, point at Aboriginal populations in the Americas, Australia, and New Zealand as clear cases of non-Western nations that existed long before the arrival of European settlers. They would argue that Aboriginal groups such as Canada's Cree or Ojibway exhibit all the criteria of the nation: a cultural unity and identity permeating a political system strongly connected to territory. Modernists would oppose this position by suggesting that the *absence* of a fully developed state with clear territorial boundaries, which hosts a population whose members, at least for the most part, never have face-to-face relations, represents a significant qualitative difference from the form of political organization that emerged in eighteenth-century Europe and that was subsequently spread around the world.

Finally, primordialism considers that culture is the most important constitutive element of the nation and the foremost force behind nationalism. It suggests that cultural cleavages are more fundamental, and indeed more primordial, than any other type of cleavage such as class or gender, and that they generate identities that are also more important and more powerful than any others.[11] Primordialists argue that culture, and more specifically language, has a natural symbolic meaning, and that it creates bonds that, because they are deeply intertwined with feelings and emotions, touch the very core of human beings. They also suggest that culture is not only an extremely powerful force in producing identity and shaping social relations, but also has natural political consequences. Groups with a distinct culture, the argument goes, will want to be governed by people and institutions reflecting this same culture. In other words, they will seek political independence, or at least autonomy. From this primordialist perspective, nations are natural and coherent entities. They pre-exist social interactions and politics. Indeed, their existence is primarily the result of the overwhelming power of culture.

Both the modernist and the primordialist perspectives enhance, albeit in different ways, our understanding of nationalism. They also both have drawbacks. Modernism has the merit of confronting the crudest and most simplistic aspects of primordialism: the portrayal of nations as natural, almost eternal entities, and cultural essentialism. Modernists do not view nations as "givens" of social existence but rather as the result of socio-political processes of identity construction and political mobilization. The modernist view that nations are socially and politically constructed makes nationalism more intelligible for the social sciences. Where primordialism is stronger is in its ability to tackle the emotional and a-rational (not irrational) dimension of nationalism.[12] At least it provides a framework to comprehend the attraction of nationalism, including the role of religion in shaping many nationalist movements (for example, Islam in Iran and Central Asia). Modernism, because it emphasizes factors other than culture, has more difficulty in accounting for the power of nationalism as a political force. The modernist perspective can explain how and why myths are fabricated and symbols generated, but it does not say why these myths and symbols resonate within a population.

In addition to this disagreement on the broad question of the nature of nations and nationalism, there also exist contending theories of nationalism, each with its strengths and weaknesses. Indeed, political scientists have favoured different types of explanation for the workings of nationalism. A first type of explanation, which derives from the previously discussed primordialist position, is **cultural**. From primordialism, this explanation takes the idea that culture is a powerful force and that it fulfills the natural need for human beings to have a cultural identity and to belong to cultural, national groups. It says that the cultural diversity of human societies inevitably leads to group identities and claims for political recognition, autonomy, or independence. In other words, nations are objective realities; they exist naturally, and nationalism simply corresponds to their awakening, which can be triggered by various social, political, economic, or ideological factors. As was the case for primordialism, the cultural explanation for nationalism seems well equipped to tackle the emotional component of nationalism or, in other words, to explain why followers follow. However, it does not really explain why and how identities are formed and mobilized because it assumes this process to be natural and almost spontaneous. Also, it is hard pressed to explain why some cultural groups never develop a strong identity, or at least, never articulate political claims, and why some are willing to sacrifice their lives for the nation but others are not. Indeed, it has difficulty accounting for the fact that not all groups united by a common culture (for example, India's multiple linguistic communities) develop nationalism, while there exist nations, such as Switzerland, that include several different historical cultural groups.

A second type of explanation for nationalism is **economic** in nature. It holds that nationalism is ultimately the product of the uneven development of the capitalist economy. Its roots are not primarily in culture but rather in material conditions. There are at least two versions of this explanation. The first version, often dubbed "internal colonialism," tackles nationalism from a neo-Marxist perspective and suggests that it is the consequence of the deliberate exploitation and oppression of peripheral regions by a central state.[13] Therefore, underdevelopment produced by economic exploitation is what fuels nationalism. This thesis has been shown to be problematic empirically since nationalist movements have emerged in richer regions such as Catalonia. The second version of the economic explanation makes room for nationalism to emerge in these more wealthy regions since it does not make nationalism the result of patterns of oppression but rather the consequence of the territorial discrepancies in capitalist development. However, the emphasis here is really on psychological dispositions rather than on developmental conditions per se. Indeed, from this perspective, nationalism in richer regions stems from feelings of frustration and resentment resulting from the belief that the region is being "held back" by, or subsidizes, the rest of the country. Still from this perspective, nationalism in poorer areas has its roots in similar sentiments deriving from the view that the region is being deprived of money and other resources, or simply that not enough is done by the central state to rectify the situation. These economic explanations seem to capture a dimension of nationalism, since many nationalist claims and grievances are about the central state's territorial distribution of resources and economic development policies. However, the causality between uneven development and nationalism is not always clear. As one scholar of nationalism has said, "defining ethnonational conflicts in terms of economic equality is a bit like defining them in terms of oxygen: where you find the one, you can be reasonably certain of finding the other."[14]

Finally, there is also the **political approach** to nationalism, which holds that it is a *political* phenomenon or, in other words, a specific form of politics. From this perspective, nationalism is about power and features elites most prominently. The idea is that nationalist mobilization is a consequence of political elites struggling for power. More specifically, the relationship between elites and nationalism is conceptualized in one of two ways. The first views nationalism as an almost accidental by-product of elite competition: struggles for power between leaders of linguistic groups, for example, would be more likely to structure politics around language and trigger processes of identity construction and nationalist mobilization. The second insists more on the usefulness of nationalism for political elites trying to gain an advantage in their power struggles: elites make a strategic decision to mobilize, politicize, and even create identities to further their own immediate political objectives. Whatever its specific version, the political explanation suggests that political elites are instrumental in creating and using myths and symbols for the purpose of stimulating nationalist mobilization and constructing identities. It represents a modernist and "top–down" view of nationalism. This approach has the advantage of focusing on the actual manifestation of nationalism. After all, nationalism is most visible in the political sphere. It is a political outcome that tends to come in the form of a movement, with leaders and followers. The weakness of the political explanation is that it has difficulty explaining why elite competition and power struggles do not always lead to nationalism, even in conditions of cultural diversity.

NATIONALISM AND GLOBALIZATION

How important will nationalism be as a political force in the future? This question, which is hotly debated by political scientists, tends to be linked to the current processes of globalization. In other words, does globalization stimulate or marginalize nationalism? There is no agreement on this question, which is further complicated by the fact that state and sub-state nationalism are often said to be differently affected by globalization. On state nationalism, the dominant thinking is that it is weakened by globalization. The argument is that economic interdependence, as well as transnational modes of communication and political activism resulting in large part from technological advancements, works to marginalize the importance of national communities and identities. Economic interdependence, and free trade in particular, lessens the role of the state in governing the economy and, as a consequence, in implementing social policies. This weakened state finds it therefore more difficult to generate the symbols necessary to maintain the cohesion of the national community. At the same time, global communications, through the Internet and/or social movements, opens up new channels of political action and identification. In Western Europe, where globalization has involved political integration in the form of the European Union (EU), the transfer of power from states to supranational institutions is one additional process that diminishes the power and scope of action of the state, thereby further decreasing its ability to effectively promote and protect national identity. This idea that globalization undermines state nationalism is not shared by all political scientists. There are some who suggest that the forces of globalization will trigger a backlash from national communities seeking to preserve their identities. This position also holds that states are much more resilient than often assumed and are only marginally affected by globalization, which means that they still represent a significant force in sustaining these communities.

The relationship between globalization and sub-state nationalism is also the subject of debate. One view suggests that globalization represents a trend that is contrary to sub-state nationalism. It holds that globalization involves the construction of continental blocs, economic and/or political, and is therefore antithetical to the objective of political independence put forward by many nationalist movements. In other words, the trend is toward association and integration rather than dissociation and disintegration. The opposite view, which is increasingly popular, believes that nationalist movements are spurred by globalization. The argument here is that globalization, because it makes state intervention less apparent and less decisive, puts the onus on regional governments to take charge of such issues as economic development and removes many of the benefits these same regions could find in remaining part of the state. Also, free-trade agreements and economic interdependence, which make it possible for small economies to thrive, diminish the risks of economic difficulties and isolation traditionally associated with secession.

NATIONALISM IN CONTEMPORARY POLITICS

Canada is a particularly interesting case for studying nationalism. Perhaps most striking is the fact that Quebec nationalism is the nationalist movement that, among others in Western societies, is closest to achieving secession. Quebec nationalism grew out of the 1960s' Quiet Revolution, which represents an important period of social, political, and economic modernization in the province's history. The Quiet Revolution marks a turning point for nationalism in Quebec. Before the 1960s, the idea of a French-Canadian nation was defined heavily by the Catholic religion and the rural-traditional lifestyle and economy. It was not associated with a particular territory, as there were French-Canadians not only in Quebec but also across Canada. French-Canadian nationalism was strongly ethnic, as membership was defined by a combination of religion, language, and descent. The Quiet Revolution, because it was driven by the Quebec state and featured a new political elite of liberal bent, transformed nationalism in two ways. First, the nation was now termed "Québécois" rather than French-Canadian, and it was circumscribed by territorial provincial borders. Second, religion and descent were evacuated as defining elements in favour of language, which made this new nationalism more civic. The Québécois nationalist movement also became articulated by two different parties: the Parti libéral du Québec (PLQ) and the Parti Québécois (PQ). The PLQ puts forward two political claims, distinct status and increased political autonomy, both of which are couched in terms of the linguistic peculiarity of the province. In others words, recognition and extensive autonomy are said to be necessary since the Quebec government is in the special situation of having to protect the French language and culture in Canada. The PQ pushes this logic further and seeks independence. Quebec nationalism presents the Canadian federation with serious challenges. Through the PQ, it raises the issue of secession in the form of referendums on independence (or "sovereignty"). Two of these referendums were held: the first in 1980, in which the option of "sovereignty-association" was defeated 60 percent to 40 percent, and the second in 1995, which yielded the close result of 50.5 percent to 49.5 percent. The PLQ seeks constitutional change as a way of guaranteeing formal recognition and additional autonomy. The Meech Lake (1987) and Charlottetown (1992) accords represented two attempts at meeting these demands, but their failures leave the PLQ's claims unanswered.

Nationalism in Canada is not limited to Quebec; it can also be found within Aboriginal populations. There are three formal categories of Aboriginals in Canada, which correspond to three broad historical/cultural groups: Indians, Metis, and Inuits. Nationalism is most important in the case of Indians, more specifically for status Indians, a legal sub-category referring to Indians who are formally registered with the federal government and administered by the 1876 Indian Act. This act represents the background for nationalism within this group of Aboriginals because its subjugating and controlling character, as exemplified by the many restrictions on individual liberties, left the Indian population with terrible socio-economic conditions and serious cultural dislocations. In order to improve this situation, Indian leaders have put forward two main claims: self-government, which was included in the failed Charlottetown accord but has not been the focus of comprehensive negotiations since then, and ownership of and access to land, which is the subject of an ongoing judicial process. These claims are explicitly based on the argument that Aboriginals are nations, and that they are therefore entitled to the political autonomy necessary to preserve their culture and identity. The fact that the political organization representing status Indians is called the Assembly of First Nations (AFN) reveals the importance of the idea of the nation for Canada's Aboriginals. The Inuit population, living in the North, also articulated demands for autonomy on the basis of a distinct culture, history, and national identity. The creation in 1999 of the territory of Nunavut represented a response to these claims.

Quebec and, to a lesser degree, Aboriginal nationalism presents significant challenges to the Canadian national identity. Quebec nationalism, for example, questions the very existence of a Canadian nation. Moreover, if the PQ were ever to succeed in its objective of secession, the contours of this nation would be seriously altered. There are also external forces that could, if not now then sometime in the future, pose equally serious challenges to the Canadian identity. Of foremost significance here is continental integration through free trade, which raises the issue of the political and cultural consequences of closer economic links with the United States. More generally, the presence of a neighbour with such political, economic, and cultural weight is often seen as a threat to Canada's autonomy and distinctiveness. In this context, it is hardly surprising that Canadian nationalism tends to surface most forcefully when its relationship with the United States seems to grow closer.

Nationalist movements in Western Europe have arguably not been as successful as Quebec's, but they represent strong political forces in at least three countries. In Spain, Catalan and Basque nationalism was crucial in shaping the institutional arrangements of the post-dictatorship era, which began in the late 1970s. Victims of brutal political and cultural repression during the nearly forty-year dictatorship of General Francisco Franco, Catalans and Basques were determined to see that democracy in Spain came with regional autonomy, a position that led to the creation of a system of autonomous communities (*Communidades Autónomas*) that includes Catalonia and the Basque Country. The Catalan and Basque nationalist movements are quite different. Catalan nationalism seeks greater autonomy within Spain but not independence. Its crucial cultural marker is the distinct Catalan language. It is mostly civic and non-violent. Basque nationalism generally seeks independence from Spain rather than only autonomy. It emphasizes the ideas of descent and "blood" much more than its Catalan counterpart. The distinct Basque language, spoken by only about half of the population of the Basque Country, does not feature as prominently in the definition of the nation as does the Catalan language in Catalonia. Basque nationalism also includes a stream that advocates violence to achieve its objective of independence. The terrorist organization ETA (*Euzkadi ta Askatasuna*, Basque Land and Freedom) is increasingly criticized in the Basque Country but retains support that is non-negligible. As a consequence, Basque nationalism advocating violence is one of the most problematic issues in Spanish politics today. In Belgium, Flemings, who inhabit Flanders in the northern half of the country and are Dutch speakers, succeeded in transforming the state into a federation in 1993 and have since been pushing for further decentralization. Flemish nationalism was historically fed, if not created, by a Belgian state that functioned almost exclusively in French from its creation in 1830 until the early twentieth century, and that was dominated by French speakers until thirty years ago. Flemings see extensive autonomy as a necessity for the preservation of their language and culture, and also for the health of their economy, which they see as being handicapped by the poorer Walloon region in the South. Flemish nationalists do speak of independence for Flanders. However, there are serious obstacles for such a project. Brussels, Belgium's capital, is located in historical Flemish territories but is now a predominantly French-speaking city. This means that an independent Flanders would have to either exclude Brussels or absorb a very significant number of Francophones, two options that are problematic for Flemish nationalists. Also, political turmoil in the country that hosts the capital of Europe could be viewed negatively by the European Union and its member states. In the United Kingdom, Scottish and, to a lesser degree, Welsh nationalism has gathered considerable steam over the last twenty years. In fact, the decision by the U.K.'s Labour government to implement "devolution," that is, to grant political autonomy to Scotland and Wales, was in large part the result of pressures from Scottish nationalism. As is the case for most other nationalist movements, Scottish nationalism is Janus-faced in its objective, as autonomy within the United Kingdom and outright independence are both considered. For the Scottish National Party (SNP), independence is the preferred choice in part because it sees the EU as a political and economic safety net that would soften the shock of secession.

In Western Europe, the unique process of political integration presents considerable implications for the nationalism of states. At the most general level, the transfer of powers from states to the supranational institutions of the European Union involves the relinquishing of sovereignty, which has historically acted as a central pivot of nationhood and national identity. In this context, the fact that all Western European states, with the exception of Switzerland and Norway, have joined the EU indicates that state nationalism in the region is either waning or being redefined in a way that makes it less exclusive and more accommodating toward other political loyalties. Another indication that state nationalism in Western Europe is undergoing change is that most member states accept that political integration involves, at least to some degree, the construction of a common identity and even a European citizenship. This is particularly significant, since notions of identity and citizenship are also closely tied to nationalism in these states. The resistance of some countries, most notably the United Kingdom, and of political forces, such as right-wing parties, to these ambitious projects of common identity and citizenship further suggests that the EU is at least *seen* as posing a fundamental challenge to the nation.

The area where nationalism has been a particularly significant political force in the last fifteen years is Eastern Europe. The weakening of the Soviet Union, especially as it became exposed by the loss of satellite regimes such as Poland and Czechoslovakia, opened the way for nationalist politics in many of its republics, most importantly the Baltic states and Ukraine. In this context, nationalism contributed to the ultimate downfall of the Soviet Union and was the motor for the creation of fifteen new states. The end of the Soviet Union also opened up different avenues for politics in Eastern Europe, one of which was nationalism. Nationalism in post-communist Eastern Europe took both peaceful and violent forms. On the one hand, Czechoslovakia was dissolved into two independent states in 1993, the Czech Republic and Slovakia, primarily as a result of Slovak nationalism. This event is quite significant for scholars of nationalism because it was one of the few peaceful secessions in modern history. On the other hand, the disintegration of Yugoslavia is one of the bloodiest events of the post–Cold War era. Politics in Yugoslavia after the fall of the Soviet Union quickly became nationalist politics. By most accounts, the trigger for the bloodshed was the desire of Serb leaders to hang onto political power and, in this context, to seek the creation of a "Great Serbia" through the "ethnic cleansing" of Croats, Bosnian Muslims, and Kosovar Albanians. As a consequence of Serb nationalism, many regions of Yugoslavia have become independent states: Slovenia, Croatia, Bosnia-Herzegovina, and Macedonia. The current republic of Yugoslavia is overwhelmingly Serb. Nationalism in post-communist Eastern Europe has also come in the form of state nationalism, many of which are more ethnic than civic and pose the question of minority rights. The Baltic states of Latvia, Estonia, and Lithuania have generally been not very accommodating, even threatening, toward their Russian minorities. Romania and Slovakia have conceptualized their nation in terms that tend to exclude their Hungarian and Roma (Gypsy) populations.

If violent nationalist conflicts have been part of politics in Eastern Europe since the end of the Cold War, the same can be said for Africa. The most dramatic case here is Rwanda, where Hutus and Tutsis were involved in a bloody conflict that saw, by most accounts, the former perpetrate the genocide of the latter, that is, attempt to eliminate the entire Tutsi population. Although less discussed than the conflicts in the former Yugoslavia, the violence in Rwanda rose to unbelievable proportions with close to one million people killed. Africa presents many other cases of nationalist or, as they are usually called when it comes to this continent, ethnic conflicts. In Nigeria, for example, tensions between Hausas, Yorubas, and Ibos—three groups with distinct languages and histories, which are also divided along religious lines (Hausas are predominantly Muslim while Christianity and indigenous practices are important among Yorubas and Ibos)—create political instability and threaten civil peace. Overall, it is estimated that more than forty groups have been involved in violent nationalist conflicts in Africa since most states gained independence in the 1960s.[15] One reason often invoked for this large number of violent nationalist conflicts in Africa is the arbitrary character of the borders, which were drawn and imposed by colonial powers. The very recent origin of these borders also explains why the nationalism of states is weak in Africa. These borders have generally not been seriously challenged: the Organization for African Unity has made the preservation of borders a fundamental principle so as to avoid nationalist violence. Some elites, however, have questioned these borders in the name of pan-Africanism, which is the idea of the political unification of Africa. Pan-Africanism was strongest in the 1960s when it was articulated by Ghana's Kwame Nkrumah and has been recently championed by Libya's Mouammar Qadhafi. This type of unification movement can also be found in the Middle East, where political borders, also imposed by colonial powers, have been questioned on the grounds that they artificially divide an Arab nation. Arab nationalism, as is the case for pan-Africanism, had its heyday a few decades ago, when it was galvanized by the wars with Israel, particularly the Suez crisis of 1956, and spearheaded by Egyptian leader Gamal Abdel Nasser. The Middle East also has at least one significant sub-state nationalism stemming from the Kurdish population, which is found in Iran, Iraq, Syria, and Turkey and seeks the creation of an independent state.

South Asia provides good examples of both sub-state and state nationalism. In 1947 India, a British colony, was divided into two states—India and Pakistan—each with its own brand of nationalism. The partition of the former India caused large-scale migration of Hindus and Muslims across the new border and triggered widespread nationalist violence. The Indian National Congress Party, under the leadership of Mahatma Gandhi, envisioned a secular India with its majority Hindu population living in a democratic society with other religious minorities such as Muslims, Sikhs, Jains, and Christians. This view has only partially been translated into practice, as India has a secular constitution but sporadically experiences bursts of religion (Hinduism)-driven nationalism. Meanwhile, Pakistan was formed as a separate homeland for Muslims, and Pakistan has ever since struggled to define itself and the role of Islam within a democratic society. This problem is rendered more acute by the presence of many ethnic/linguistic minorities (Punjabis, Baluchis, Pathans, and Sindhis).

EUROPE: NO TRUCK WITH TERRORISM; SPAIN AND ITS BASQUES

The Central Government Is Determined to Smash ETA by War, not Jaw.

"Everything to do with the banning [of Batasuna] is aimed at taking away the vote from so many thousands of people who have a legitimate political choice. They can count on our moral support." That was the pledge last weekend to the supporters of ETA's now-banned political wing from Xabier Arzalluz, leader of the non-violent Basque Nationalist Party (PNV). To many it sounded like an appeal for votes. To Spain's prime minister, Jose Mara Aznar, it confirmed his conviction that Mr Arzalluz and his party are hand-in-glove with ETA's gunmen. With views so wide apart, can the central government ever reach agreement on the future of the Basque region with the PNV government that runs it? And does Mr Aznar have any long-term policy for it other than smashing ETA and demonising the PNV?

The short answer to both questions is most probably no. Local elections, the first since Batasuna was banned last summer, are due in the region in May. The PNV regional premier, Juan Jose Ibarretxe, has said that this year he will put his plan for a referendum on whether the region should become a "free state associated with Spain" (and perhaps sharing the Spanish king) to the Basque assembly. He claims this would lead to an ETA ceasefire and the prize of greater autonomy. Mr Aznar sees the idea as a threat to Spain's territorial integrity and a sop to ETA.

Yet for all the climate of fear created by the terrorists, for the past month the steep green hills and narrow industrialised valleys of the Basque country have been free of ETA's bombs and bullets. The last murder was in December, when a police officer trying to spot-check a car that was, in fact, carrying explosives to Madrid, was shot dead. French and Spanish police, who last year arrested about 190 real or alleged etarras, 60 of them in France, have grabbed another dozen more this year. Politicians are yet again speculating, albeit cautiously, on the prospect of eliminating ETA.

That is unlikely: the serpent's head has proved itself in the past capable of quick regrowth. Mr Aznar, [who] pledged to step down early next year, is determined to try to cut it off for good. After the breakdown of a 14-month ceasefire in 1998–99, he ruled out any further attempts at dialogue with ETA. Many doubt that his iron-fisted policy can resolve the long-term Basque problem, but it is popular in a country that has grown sick of ETA's violence.

He is backing tough police action with tougher laws: a new one has just raised the minimum prison term for ETA terrorists from 30 to 40 years. And in a further show of determination, Mr Aznar recently said he would stand as a councilor for his People's Party in the Basque city of Bilbao. It's a gesture, he admits, "a symbol of solidarity" with local councilors who work under threat of death, as indeed they do. But, he said, he wants to show that the region must become like any other part of Spain. Just as Mr Arzalluz's firebrand nationalism reflects the Basque experience of oppression under General Franco, Mr Aznar to some extent reflects the old right wing that believed zealously in the integrity of a Catholic Spain and the use of mano dura, the firm hand, to ensure it.

On the political front, some form of protest from the banned Batasuna is likely before the local elections. A new radical Basque-nationalist political formation is to be unveiled on February 16th, though no one knows whether it intends to compete in the elections. But Mr Aznar said last week that he feared the PNV more than ex-Batasuna. He suspects it may try some shock tactic, spurred both by the hope of mopping up ex-Batasuna votes and by the failure of Mr Ibarretxe's efforts to sell his idea of "association" with Spain to the region's thoroughly sceptical businessmen (and indeed even in a tour abroad).

Mr. Aznar must hope that, even after its likely successes in the local elections, the PNV will not dare to call for a referendum on its association idea. But if it does? As with the rest of the prime minister's uncompromising Basque policy, says a former aide, "there is no plan B."

As a consequence, both state and sub-state nationalism are central to Pakistan's struggle to define a national identity. Post-independence India has undergone a process of nation-building that presented a different type of challenge, namely the presence of fourteen territorial/linguistic groups, more than three thousand caste groups, and a large Muslim minority. The chosen strategy was a type of federalism that gave autonomy to linguistic groups. Indian federalism had important consequences for nationalism. At the broadest level, it bolstered regional identity and stimulated claims for autonomy or independence. There are currently autonomist movements in Assam and Maharashtra and secessionist ones in the Punjab and Jammu and Kashmir. Federalism also created new linguistic minorities (within states), which in some cases have been victims of discriminatory policies.

ENDNOTES

1. Walker Connor, "A Nation Is a Nation, Is a State, Is an Ethnic Group, Is a . . . ," *Ethnic and Racial Studies* 1 (1978): 377–400.
2. The following definitions draw from Jean-Pierre Derriennic, *Nationalisme et démocratie: Réflexion sur les illusions des indépendantistes québécois* (Quebec: Boréal, 1995), 17.
3. See Joseph Stalin, "The Nation," in *Nationalism*, ed. John Hutchinson and Anthony D. Smith (Oxford: Oxford University Press, 1994), 20. Taken from "The Nation," in *Marxism and the Natural Question*, from *The Essential Stalin: Major Theoretical Writings 1905–1952*, ed. Bruce Franklin (London: Croom Helm, 1973), 57–61.
4. See Ernest Renan, "Qu'est-ce qu'une nation?" in *Nationalism*, ed. John Hutchinson and Anthony D. Smith (Oxford: Oxford University Press, 1994), 17. Taken from *Qu'est-ce qu'une nation?* trans. Ida Mae Snyder (Paris: Calmann-Levy, 1882), 26–29.
5. Benedict Anderson, *Imagined Communities*, 2nd ed. (London: Verso, 1991).
6. See Ernest Gellner, "Culture and Organisation, State and Nationalism," in *Nationalism* (London: Weidenfeld & Nicolson, 1997), 5–13.
7. Hans Kohn, *The Idea of Nationalism: A Study in Its Origins and Background* (New York: Macmillan, 1944).
8. Ernest Gellner, *Nations and Nationalism* (London: Blackwell, 1983); John Breuilly, *Nationalism and the State* (New York: St. Martin's Press, 1982).
9. Paul Brass, *Ethnicity and Nationalism: Theory and Comparison* (London: Sage, 1991).
10. Anthony D. Smith, *The Ethnic Origins of Nations* (New York: Blackwell, 1986).
11. Edward Shils, "Primordial, Personal, Sacred and Civil Ties," in *British Journal of Sociology* 8 (1957): 130–45; Clifford Geertz, ed., *Old Societies, New States: The Quest for Modernity in Asia and Africa* (London: The Free Press, 1963); Harold Isaacs, *Idols of the Tribe: Group Identity and Political Change* (Cambridge: Harvard University Press, 1975).
12. Jack Eller and Reed Coughlan, "The Poverty of Primordialism: The Demystification of Ethnic Attachments," in *Ethnic and Racial Studies* 16 (1993): 183–202.
13. Michael Hechter, *Internal Colonialism: The Celtic Fringe in British National Development, 1536–1966* (Berkeley: University of California Press, 1975).
14. Walker Connor, "The Seductive Lure of Economic Explanations," in *Ethnonationalism: The Quest for Understanding* (Princeton: Princeton University Press, 1994), 147.
15. Shaheen Mozaffar and James R. Scarritt, "Why Autonomy Is Not a Viable Option for Managing Ethnic Conflict in African Plural Societies," *Nationalism and Ethnic Politics* 5, no. 3 and 4 (1999): 245.

READINGS

As this chapter has shown, nationalism is a key force in contemporary politics, despite or perhaps as a result of the current context of globalization. It is also a multidimensional phenomenon (civic and ethnic nationalism, nationalism as an idea and a movement, state and sub-state nationalism) that is the subject of different understandings on the part of academics. The readings selected for this chapter illustrate some of these positions. The first is a classic account of nationalism as a modern phenomenon. The second is a critical appraisal of the implication of the civic–ethnic dichotomy.

The first excerpt is drawn from Eric Hobsbawm's *Nations and Nationalism since 1780*. This book is, along with Ernest Gellner's *Nations and Nationalism* and Benedict Anderson's *Imagined Communities*, one of the most often cited, and arguably most important, works on nationalism in the last twenty years. Hobsbawm, like Gellner and Anderson, is a modernist. The objective behind his writing is therefore to show that nations are modern phenomena that are constructed through social and political interactions. In *Nations and Nationalism since 1780*, he takes aim at primordialism and states the basic arguments of the modernist perspective. Hobsbawm argues that the nation is connected to a specific historical period that broadly corresponds to the rise of the modern state, as well as technological advances and a particularly significant stage in economic development. While he believes that nations and nationalism are constructed from "above" (i.e., by the state and political elites), he also insists that attention needs to be paid to "the view from below" (i.e., the masses). This position distinguishes him from other modernists, such as Gellner, whose analytical focus is strictly on processes of state construction. Hobsbawm suggests that a focus on civil society is necessary to understand the processes of identity formation and transformation, and that it is these issues of national identification that are in most need of research.

In the next excerpt, David Brown asks a fundamental analytical and normative question about nationalism: are there good and bad ones? This question is usually framed in terms of the ethnic–civic dichotomy in which civic nationalism is good and ethnic nationalism is bad. Brown is critical of the idea that the ethnic–civic nationalism distinction necessarily determines the character of nationalism (liberal or not). Instead, he argues that civic nationalism is not always liberal, while ethnic, or cultural, nationalism need not be illiberal. This criticism has been discussed previously in this chapter and put forward by other authors. Where Brown's argument is most original is in the suggestion that the liberal or illiberal nature of nationalism has nothing to do with the way the nation is defined (i.e., in civic or ethnic/cultural terms) but rather depends on who defines it and in what context. Indeed, Brown holds that nationalism is most likely to be liberal if it is spearheaded by confident elites who do not view the outside world as a menace and tends to be illiberal if it is articulated by insecure elites and as a reaction against perceived external threats. From this perspective, the question of whether a nationalist movement is liberal or not becomes unrelated to its characterization as ethnic or civic. Rather, it is an issue of power (who has it?) and political context.

NATIONS AND NATIONALISM SINCE 1780: INTRODUCTION

Eric Hobsbawm

Nevertheless, in approaching "the national question" "it is more profitable to begin with the concept of 'the nation' (i.e. with 'nationalism') than with the reality it represents." For "[t]he 'nation' as conceived by nationalism, can be recognized prospectively; the real 'nation' can only be recognized *a posteriori*."[1] This is the approach of the present book. It pays particular attention to the changes and transformations of the concept, particularly towards the end of the nineteenth century. Concepts, of course, are not part of free-floating philosophical discourse, but socially, historically and locally rooted, and must be explained in terms of these realities.

For the rest, the position of the writer may be summarized as follows.

(1) I use the term "nationalism" in the sense defined by Gellner, namely to mean "primarily a principle which holds that the political and national unit should be congruent."[2] I would add that this principle also implies that the political duty of Ruritanians to the polity which encompasses and represents the Ruritanian nation, overrides all other public obligations, and in extreme cases (such as wars) all other obligations of whatever kind. This implication distinguishes modern nationalism from other and less demanding forms of national or group identification which we shall also encounter.

(2) Like most serious students, I do not regard the "nation" as a primary nor as an unchanging social entity. It belongs exclusively to a particular, and historically recent, period. It is a social entity only insofar as it relates to a certain kind of modern territorial state, the "nation-state," and it is pointless to discuss nation and nationality except insofar as both relate to it. Moreover, with Gellner I would stress the element of artefact, invention and social engineering which enters into the making of nations. "Nations as a natural, God-given way of classifying men, as an inherent . . . political destiny, are a myth; nationalism, which sometimes takes pre-existing cultures and turns them into nations, sometimes invents them, and often obliterates pre-existing cultures: *that* is a reality."[3] In short, for the purposes of analysis nationalism comes before nations. Nations do not make states and nationalisms but the other way round.

(3) The "national question," as the old Marxists called it, is situated at the point of intersection of politics, technology and social transformation. Nations exist not only as functions of a particular kind of territorial state or the aspiration to establish one—broadly speaking, the citizen state of the French Revolution—but also in the context of a particular stage of technological and economic development. Most students today will agree that standard national languages, spoken or written, cannot emerge as such before printing, mass literacy and hence, mass schooling. It has even been argued that popular spoken Italian as an idiom capable of expressing the full range of what a twentieth-century language needs outside the domestic and face-to-face sphere of communication, is only being constructed today as a function of the needs of national television programming.[4] Nations and their associated phenomena must therefore be analysed in terms of political, technical, administrative, economic and other conditions and requirements.

(4) For this reason they are, in my view, dual phenomena, constructed essentially from above, but which cannot be understood unless also analysed from below, that is in terms of the assumptions, hopes, needs, longings and interests of ordinary people, which are not necessarily national and still less nationalist. If I have a major criticism of Gellner's work it is that his preferred perspective of modernization from above makes it difficult to pay adequate attention to the view from below.

That view from below, i.e. the nation as seen not by governments and the spokesmen and activists of nationalist (or non-nationalist) movements, but by the ordinary persons who are the objects of their action and propaganda, is exceedingly difficult to discover. Fortunately social historians have learned how to investigate the history of ideas, opinions and feelings at the sub-literary level, so that we are today less likely to confuse, as historians once habitually did, editorials in select newspapers with public opinion. We do not know much for certain. However, three things are clear.

First, official ideologies of states and movements are not guides to what it is in the minds of even the most loyal citizens or supporters. Second, and more specifically, we cannot assume that for most people national identification—when it exists—excludes or is always or ever superior to, the remainder of the set of identifications which constitute the social being. In fact, it is always combined with identifications of another kind, even when it is felt to be superior to them. Thirdly, national identification and what it is believed to imply, can change and shift in time, even in the course of quite short periods. In my judgment this is the area of national studies in which thinking and research are most urgently needed today.

(5) The development of nations and nationalism within old established states such as Britain and France has not been studied very intensively, though it is now attracting attention.[5] The existence of this gap is illustrated by the neglect, in Britain, of any problems connected with English nationalism—a term which in itself sounds odd to many ears—compared to the attention paid to

Scots, Welsh, not to mention Irish nationalism. On the other hand there have in recent years been major advances in the study of national movements aspiring to be states, mainly following Hroch's pathbreaking comparative studies of small European national movements. Two points in this excellent writer's analysis are embodied in my own. First, "national consciousness" develops unevenly among the social groupings and *regions* of a country; this regional diversity and its reasons have in the past been notably neglected. Most students would, incidentally, agree that, whatever the nature of the social groups first captured by "national consciousness," the popular masses—workers, servants, peasants—are the last to be affected by it. Second, and in consequence, I follow his useful division of the history of national movements into three phases. In nineteenth-century Europe, for which it was developed, phase A was purely cultural, literary and folkloric, and had no particular political or even national implications, any more than the researches (by non-Romanies) of the Gypsy Lore Society have for the subjects of these enquiries. In phase B we find a body of pioneers and militants of "the national idea" and the beginnings of political campaigning for this idea. The bulk of Hroch's work is concerned with this phase and the analysis of the origins, composition and distribution of this *minorité agissante*. My own concern in this book is more with phase C when—and not before—nationalist programmes acquire mass support, or at least some of the mass support that nationalists always

claim they represent. The transition from phase B to phase C is evidently a crucial moment in the chronology of national movements. Sometimes, as in Ireland, it occurs before the creation of a national state; probably very much more often it occurs afterwards, as a consequence of that creation. Sometimes, as in the so-called Third World, it does not happen even then.

Finally, I cannot but add that no serious historian of nations and nationalism can be a committed political nationalist, except in the sense in which believers in the literal truth of the Scriptures, while unable to make contributions to evolutionary theory, are not precluded from making contributions to archaeology and Semitic philology. Nationalism requires too much belief in what is patently not so. As Renan said: "Getting its history wrong is part of being a nation."[6] Historians are professionally obliged not to get it wrong, or at least to make an effort not to. To be Irish and proudly attached to Ireland—even to be proudly Catholic-Irish or Ulster-Protestant Irish—is not in itself incompatible with the serious study of Irish history. To be a Fenian or an Orangeman, I would judge, is not so compatible, any more than being a Zionist is compatible with writing a genuinely serious history of the Jews; unless the historian leaves his or her convictions behind when entering the library or the study. Some nationalist historians have been unable to do so. Fortunately, in setting out to write the present book I have not needed to leave my non-historical convictions behind.

Reading Notes

1. E.J. Hobsbawm, "Some reflections on nationalism," p. 387.
2. Ernest Gellner, *Nations and Nationalism*, p. 1. This basically political definition is also accepted by some other writers, e.g., John Breuilly, *Nationalism and the State*, p. 3.
3. Gellner, *Nations and Nationalism*, pp. 48–9.
4. Antonio Sorella, "La televisione e la lingua italiana (*Trimestre. Periodico di Cultura*, 14, 2–4 (1982), pp. 291–300.
5. For the range of such work, see Raphael Samuel (ed.), *Patriotism. The Making and Unmaking of British National Identity* (3 vols., London 1989). I have found the work of Linda Colley particularly stimulating, e.g. "Whose nation? Class and national consciousness in Britain 1750–1830" (*Past & Present*, 113, 1986), pp. 96–117.
6. Ernest Renan, "Qu'est-ce qu'une nation?" in *Nationalism*, ed. John Hutchinson and Anthony D. Smith (Oxford: Oxford University Press, 1994), pp. 7–8, "L'oubli et je dirai même l'erreur historique, sont un facteur essentiel de la formation d'une nation et c'est ainsi que le progrès des études historiques est souvent pour la nationalité un danger."

ARE THERE GOOD AND BAD NATIONALISMS?

David Brown

A REFORMATION

It might be possible to explain more effectively the difference between the liberal and illiberal versions of nationalism if we make a connection between Kohn's distinction between nationalisms which arise out of an "inferiority complex" in relation to an "alien" other (Kohn 1944: 330) and those which arise out of optimistic "faith . . . in the virtues of life and liberty in the new and unfettered world" (p. 293), and Greenfeld's distinction between those nationalisms which are articulated by classes or status groups feeling marginalised, and those articulated by an upwardly mobile class or status group imbued with self confidence and pride. Such a connection is sometimes implied by Greenfeld,[1] but is more clearly indicated by Peter Alter in his distinction between what he termed "Risorgimento" nationalism, and "Integral" nationalism. Alter explains the rise of Fascist (integral) nationalism in Germany as being based both on the insecurities of the "old and the new middle classes . . . [who] felt their material existence and social status to be under threat" (Alter 1989: 46); and also on the "crisis of national self-confidence, the putative looming of extraordinary perils from outside, real or perceived threats to the continued existence of the nation" (46). Liberal (Risorgimento) nationalism similarly began as a "protest movement" (p. 29) but developed in a liberal direction first because it "accompanie[d] the liberation . . . of new social strata" (p. 28), and second, because it articulated an intrinsically self-confident mood of awakening and resurrection which saw a process of emancipation from oppression as already underway or imminent.

Thus instead of arguing as hitherto that cultural nationalisms are intrinsically illiberal, it may be useful to reformulate the argument. Perhaps it is those nationalisms, whether civic or cultural, which are articulated by insecure elites and which constitute *ressentiment*-based reactions against others who are perceived as threatening, which consequently become illiberal. By the same token, perhaps civic and cultural nationalisms which begin as protest movements but do not develop their identity primarily in relation to threatening others, and which are articulated by self-confident elites, are most likely to take a liberal form. Feelings of insecurity on the part both of the articulators of nationalist ideologies, and of their mass audiences, have the potentiality to transform all nationalisms in collectivist and illiberal directions, irrespective of their civic and cultural mix, depending upon how "the other" and thence "the self" are depicted.

This reformulation of the argument builds upon the insights of Kohn and Meinecke, but involves a shift of focus. Instead of looking to the character of the community or the incidence of middle classes for the explanation of whether nationalism is liberal or authoritarian, we are led to look both at the ways in which political elites depict the nationalist goals, and the insecurities, threats or enemies which inhibit their attainment; and also at the receptivity of the wider populace to these nationalist visions and threats.

Illiberal nationalism is thus most likely when it is articulated by an insecure class or stratum, and where the wider populace is also experiencing insecurities which make it receptive to the collectivist solutions offered by propagators of nationalism. Political leaders may, in differing circumstances, portray contemporary threats as coming from oppositionist activists or from class unrest, and may thereby be led, as in the case of Singapore, in the direction of depicting ideas of individual rights and liberties as the primary threat to the nationalist vision. They can then assert that the survival and development of the predominantly civic nation depends upon ensuring that the national "general will" is not weakened or subverted by the partial vested interests of dissident individuals. In those cases where opposition is clustered in particular regions of the country, or amongst particular cultural groups, then political elites may choose to demonise such opposition, as in contemporary Kenya, by depicting it as ethnic in origin, and denigrating it as sectarianism, communalism or racism. Elsewhere, it may be that political leaders can convince the populace that the threat comes from outside—from other nation-states whose territorial, economic or political claims can be shown to impinge on the national destiny—so that such nationalisms will be "illiberal" in the sense that they assert the superiority of the national "us" over the alien "other," either in xenophobic attacks on specific nation-states, or in more generalised denigrations of foreign influences as communist, western values, Asian menace, etc. Political elites who wish to close off their society against external influences or employ scapegoat strategies against minorities might, as previously noted, find it useful to depict the threats in racial terms, and to popularise their own myths of common history in racial terms. The influence of such depictions upon national consciousness partly depends, no doubt, both on the culture of the society, and on the actual situational challenges, and thence the types of insecurities facing the society; but political elites do have flexibility in the portrayal of enemies, and this gives a fluidity to the character of nationalism, and in particular to the liberalism or illiberalism of nationalist politics.

Thus civic nationalism may develop in either liberal or illiberal directions depending upon how effectively its visions of civic community are employed by the mobilising elites to resolve societal aspirations or fears. And cultural nationalism should be seen as neither intrinsically the "progressive" engine of minority and indigenous ethnic rights, nor intrinsically "regressive" and oppressive of the individual, as its recent manifestations in the Balkans might seem to indicate. As John Hutchinson showed in his study of cultural nationalism, the character of Irish nationalism changed remarkably in three different "revivals," from Anglo-Irish and liberal to Gaelic and populist, depending upon which intellectuals were mobilising it; which threats and dangers they stressed; and which symbols—religious or secular—they employed (Hutchinson 1987).

CONCLUSIONS

The distinction between the two ideal-type models of nationalism, civic and cultural, is indeed a significant one, distinguishing visions of community which are rooted in perceptions of common ancestry, from those which focus on perceptions of the continuous integration of individuals of diverse backgrounds into one new family home, with its distinctive institutions and common destiny. This distinction is central to an understanding of the political tensions and dynamics of modern nationalisms, and, in particular, to the debate as to how states should be managing their ethnic minorities. But the focus here has been upon unpacking the sets of assumptions which have been associated with the two terms in relation to their allegedly intrinsic liberalism or illiberalism. The view that civic nationalism is liberal because it refers to a voluntaristic society, while cultural nationalism is illiberal because it refers to an ascriptive community, has been criticised, since both forms of nationalism seek to tie the component individuals into communities of obligation which are depicted as persisting through time, and both have the capacity to prioritise either the collectivity or the individual. The view that civic nationalism is liberal because of the presence of a strong middle class was also criticised, on the ground that illiberal middle classes are not unusual. Finally, the view that cultural nationalism tends to be illiberal because its origins are reactive, was criticised on the grounds that the link between cultural nationalism and reactive nationalism seems more likely to be a contingent one. It was then argued, however, that nationalisms which are both articulated by a marginalised or insecure class or status group, and which appeal to a widespread *ressentiment*-based reaction to a threatening other, are indeed more likely to be illiberal than are nationalisms which are internally generated and articulated by secure elites. But the nature and extent of this illiberalism should be seen as a political variable. The conclusion is that the difference between liberal and illiberal manifestations of nationalism cannot be explained by reference to the distinction between its civic and cultural forms. Nationalism does have two ideological faces, civic and cultural; but its political character is surely protean rather than Janus-faced.

Reading Note

1. She uses the term consistently to refer to reaction to other nationalisms, but locates that reaction primarily in the groups who articulate the national consciousness. She never uses the term to refer to the frustrated status expectations of elite groups in the absence of any externally directed resentments (Greenfeld 1992).

Reading References

Alter, P. 1989. *Nationalism.* London: Edward Arnold.

Breuilly, J. 1993. *Nationalism and the State.* Chicago: University of Chicago Press.

Colley, L. 1986. "Whose Nation? Class and National Consciousness in Britain 1750–1830" (*Past & Present,* 113).

Gellner, E. 1983. *Nations and Nationalism.* Ithaca, NY: Cornell University Press.

Greenfeld, L. 1992. *Nationalism: Five Roads to Modernity.* Cambridge, MA: Harvard University Press.

Hobsbawm, E.J. 1972. "Some Reflections on Nationalism," in T.J. Nossiter, A.H. Hanson, Stein Rokkan, eds., *Imagination and Precision in the Social Sciences: Essays in Memory of Peter Nettl.* London: Faber & Faber.

Hutchinson, J. 1987. *The Dynamics of Cultural Nationalism: The Gaelic Revival and the Creation of the Irish Nation State.* London: Allen and Unwin.

Kohn, H. 1944. *The Idea of Nationalism.* New York: Macmillan.

Raphael, S. (ed.). 1989. *Patriotism. The Making and Unmaking of British National Identity* (3 vols.). London and New York: Routledge.

Renan, E. *Qu est que c'est une nation?*

Sorella, Antonio. 1982. "La televisione e la lingua italiana (*Trimestre. Periodico di Cultura*), Vol. 14, 2–4 .

KEY TERMS

Civic Nationalism   Nationalism where inclusion in the nation is a matter of choice.

Cultural Approach to Nationalism   Nationalism is explained by the overwhelming power of culture (especially language) and the identity it naturally fosters.

Economic Approach to Nationalism   Nationalism is a consequence of the uneven development of capitalism.

Ethnic Nationalism   Nationalism where inclusion in the nation is determined on the basis of objective criteria such as race and ancestry.

Modernism   The view that nations are constructed entities whose origins are European and rooted in the rise of the modern state.

Nation   A human community united by a special sense of solidarity deriving from shared features, most importantly language, religion, ancestry (real or imagined), history, myths, and symbols, and that seeks, in the name of this solidarity, to gain or maintain a distinct political situation, usually autonomy or independence.

Nationalism   A movement that makes political claims on behalf of a nation and on the basis of a national identity.

Political Approach to Nationalism   Nationalism is the product of manipulative elites and/or processes of state construction.

Primordialism   The view that nations are natural entities whose existence pre-dates modernity and that respond to the fundamental need of humans to belong to a cultural community.

FURTHER READINGS

Anderson, Benedict. *Imagined Communities.* 2nd ed. New York: Verso, 1991.

Chatterjee, Partha. *Nationalist Thought and the Colonial World: A Derivative Discourse.* 2nd ed. Minneapolis: University of Minnesota Press, 1986.

Esman, Milton. *Ethnic Politics.* Ithaca: Cornell University Press, 1994.

Gellner, Ernest. *Nations and Nationalism.* Ithaca: Cornell University Press, 1983.

Greenfeld, Liah. *Nationalism: Five Roads to Modernity.* Cambridge, MA: Harvard University Press, 1992.

Guibernau, Montserrat, and John Hutchinson, eds. *Understanding Nationalism.* Cambridge, MA: Polity Press, 2001.

Horowitz, Donald. *Ethnic Groups in Conflicts.* Berkeley: University of California Press, 1985.

Keating, Michael. *Nations against the State: The New Politics of Nationalism in Québec, Catalonia and Scotland.* New York: St. Martin's Press, 1996.

Kellas, James. *The Politics of Nationalism and Ethnicity.* 2nd ed. New York: St. Martin's Press, 1998.

Yuval-Davis, Nira. *Gender and Nation.* London: Sage, 1997.

WEB LINKS

The Association for the Study of Ethnicity and Nationalism:
www.lse.ac.uk/collections/ASEN/

The WWW Virtual Library on Migration and Ethnic Relations:
www.ercomer.org/wwwvl/index.html

Minorities at Risk Project:
www.cidcm.umd.edu/inscr/mar

CHAPTER 16

RELIGION AND POLITICS

The world has witnessed a number of great transformations in recent decades. These include the different waves of democratization in Latin America and Eastern Europe; the fall of the Soviet Union and the subsequent end of the Cold War; the growing trend toward continental cooperation and convergence, whether in Europe, the Americas, or Africa; and certainly the multifaceted forces of and reactions to globalization. Yet perhaps the past decades will also long be remembered for yet another great transformation: the explosion of religious movements and ideas in both national and transnational political arenas. Indeed, the convergence of religion and politics is probably the single most important legacy of the past three decades, one whose ramifications will resonate for some time to come. This chapter explores the relationship between religion and politics, focusing on the rise of fundamentalist religious movements in recent decades, and attempts to locate these movements in their varying socio-economic and political contexts. In so doing, it shows that what has been euphemistically labelled religious **fundamentalism** is a universal phenomenon, not unique to only one part of the world, and that religious groups are diverse, spanning a very broad spectrum of types, from those that preach spiritual rebirth to those that deploy violent means to achieve their ends.

THE ORIGINS OF FUNDAMENTALISM

No term has captured news headlines more than "fundamentalism." Although it is contemporaneously associated with Muslim religious groups, by origins the term dates back to an American religious movement of the early twentieth century.[1] This movement took its name from a collection of twelve booklets entitled *The Fundamentals: A Testimony of the Truth*, published between 1910 and 1915 by Milton and Lyman Steward. Concerned with what they diagnosed as the spiritual and moral decline spreading throughout Protestantism, these wealthy oil businessmen from California circulated millions of copies of *The Fundamentals* in the hope of revitalizing the faith. In many ways the Steward brothers and others who shared their views, labelled fundamentalists, were reacting to a number of social and intellectual dislocations taking place in early twentieth-century America that were threatening to undermine traditional Christian beliefs. These included the unease felt by many urban, white Americans as a result of the waves of newly settled non-Protestant immigrants from Southern and Eastern Europe. Fundamentalists were also alarmed by the rise of biblical criticism in the academy, and its implications for questioning the authority of the religious texts. Fundamentalists also condemned the teaching of Darwinian evolutionary theory in public schools, which they believed was undermining the literalness of the earth and its organisms as created in six days by divine acts. The evolutionists placed humanity on a par with other animals whose original change could be explained without reference to divinity. The fundamentalists perceived a broad-based conspiracy by the advocates of biblical criticism, Darwinian theory, and those who purveyed a new social order.

The response of *The Fundamentals* to these threats was to affirm five fundamentals of the faith. These are the strict and literal inerrancy of the Bible; the virgin birth and deity of Christ; the substitutionary view of the atonement; the bodily resurrection of Christ; and the imminent return of Christ. The first fundamental ensured that everything taught in the

Scripture, whether pertaining to science, religion, or history, was absolutely and categorically true. It was a fundamental tenet that marked the true believer from the conservative evangelical, earning the former the label "come-outers" especially after they decided to abandon mainline denominations and establish their own churches where they could worship away from (what they considered as) their corrupted brothers and sisters.[2] Interestingly, many Roman Catholics also embraced these fundamentals, a reality that suggests that belief in the fundamentals was not solely a Protestant feature. Moreover, the concerns of the Protestant fundamentalists were not only doctrinal in nature. Inspired by the evangelical revivalist movement of the nineteenth century, fundamentalists believed in the need to link religious orthodoxy with social and political action.

After World War I, Christian fundamentalists in the United States embarked on a crusade to resist the moral revolution then sweeping American society.[3] They campaigned to ban the production and sale of alcoholic beverages and to enforce Victorian standards of personal behaviour. Although the former battle was won, the latter was not. Consequently, and by the 1930s, Christian fundamentalists had withdrawn from American cultural and political life. Political activism was replaced by the organization of a subculture of fundamentalist publishing houses, radio stations, missionary bands, Christian day schools, and institutes. These activities were considered essential preparatory work in anticipation of Christ's imminent return. All this would change in the 1960s and 1970s, however. By then many Christian fundamentalists had become suspicious that a secular conspiracy targeting the nation's Judeo-Christian foundational values was underway. The Supreme Court, which had banned prayer in public schools in 1963 and permitted abortion in 1973, was a favourite target for the fundamentalists. These concerns ultimately give birth in the late 1970s to a number of Christian political action groups. Reverend Jerry Falwell's Moral Majority was one such group. These groups became prominent during the presidency of Ronald Reagan, lobbying against what they identified as the enemies of Christian America: namely abortion, pornography, and feminism. In the 1990s, Christian activism in the United States was spearheaded by Pat Robertson's Christian Coalition. Its grassroots activism on behalf of the Republican Party would prove decisive in the 1994 congressional elections, when 56 House seats, 10 Senate seats, 472 state legislature seats, and 11 governorships went from the Democratic to the Republican Party. The 1990s saw the emergence of a novel and influential force on the American political scene: the New Right, which combines populist conservatives and religious fundamentalists, allied with neoconservative intellectuals. The supporters of the New Right often engage in single-issue politics, such as abortion, and have an uneasy relationship with the Republican Party.

COMPARING FUNDAMENTALISTS

Fundamentalists from all religious persuasions typically share a number of common characteristics. They approach their social and political agenda in a militant manner. Their aim is to establish a new religious and political order, one based on their idiosyncratic interpretation of the religious texts. They also perceive the world in binary images: a site of contestation between the forces of good and the forces of evil, between *us* and *them*. In this contest, the enemy does not include only those who belong to another religious tradition. Rather, it includes members of your own religious community who may not interpret or practise the religion in a manner similar to yours. Often gathering individuals trained in the physical sciences—engineers, chemists, and doctors—fundamentalist movements share a number of common ways of thinking about their convictions.[4] They tend to be highly selective in their relation with tradition and modernity. They are selective in their choice of which religious texts to emphasize, and which not to. Moreover, they approach modern institutions and technologies in a selective manner: they will form political parties, contest elections, use cell phones and fax machines, yet at the same time reject the secularism and liberties that often accompany modernity. Fundamentalists also believe that their ideas are not open to reform or alternative interpretations, and insist that they are free from any error. Finally, fundamentalists tend to be millenarian: for example, the members of the Jewish

THE FIERY RISE OF HINDU FUNDAMENTALISM

by Michael Fischer in Bombay

Every year for the past two decades, veteran missionary Graham Staines of Australia conducted five-day open-air "jungle camps" in villages of the eastern Indian state of Orissa, teaching, preaching, and singing to Santal tribal members.

After one such meeting on January 23 in Manoharpur, a village 600 miles southeast of New Delhi, the 58-year-old Staines and his two sons, 10-year-old Philips and 7-year-old Timothy, were murdered. They had been sleeping in a vehicle parked outside a local church when militant Hindus, allegedly from the Bajrang Dal group, doused the vehicle with gasoline and set it afire. . . .

Police arrested 53 people in connection with the killings. Staines, secretary of the Evangelical Missionary Society, an independent missionary organization based in Brisbane, had been operating a hospital and clinic for lepers in India for 34 years. Two days after the murders, lepers dug the graves for the family while Gladys Staines consoled them as they wept. . . .

Indian President K.R. Narayanan denounced the "barbarous killing" of Staines and indicated it is not representative of his country's behavior. . . .

Prime Minister Atal Behari Vajpayee called the murders "a blot on our collective consciousness." In a televised speech, he said, "Such violence violates the country's tradition and culture of tolerance."

India has a long history of violence between the Hindu majority that makes up 82 percent of the population and a Muslim minority, which composes 12 percent. Until recently, Christians, only 2.5 percent of the 980 million people in India, have never been a target of violence. . . .

The Rise of Hindu Fundamentalism

The answer lies largely in the surge of Hindu fundamentalism during the past decade. It began with a

television campaign in the late 1980s to evoke and assert a self-conscious collective Hindu identity by the Rashtriya Swayamsevak Sangh (RSS). The RSS, an India-based organization of Hindu leaders, functions as the principal guardian of Hindu ideology. In 1991, present Interior Minister L.K. Advani followed up with a historic "chariot journey" from a Hindu temple in Somnath in Gujarat to Ayodhya in the north, the legendary birthplace of the Hindu god Ram. The symbolic journey helped establish the transformation of the Bharatiya Janatha Party (BJP) from a marginal group with only two seats in Parliament a decade ago to the ruling party today.

In 1992, Muslims became the chief targets of Hindus with the destruction of the sixteenth-century Babri mosque in Ayodhya. . . .

In India, the BJP government that came to power last year promised "one nation based on one culture" with a future linked to its Hindu heritage. The practical implications of "one nation and one culture" is that minority groups—including Christians—must accept the Hindu way of life. "We want all minorities to come into the Hindu mainstream, only then can we build a powerful Hindu nation," says 24-year-old RSS cadet Vasantrao Munde. "We should be proud of being Hindu. The RSS teaches us that we are unique". . . .

Despite the recent setbacks to Christians, India continues to be an open society with a relatively free press and a right to free expression. Indian journalist M.J. Akbar says, "India is secular because by far the greater majority of India's 80 percent Hindu population is secular with a high level of tolerance for other religions." The Indian Constitution, devised after independence from the British in 1947, gives Christians the right to freedom of conscience, and to profess, practice, and propagate their religion. . . .

Source: From Michael Fischer, "The Fiery Rise of Hindu Fundamentalism," *Christianity Today*, March 1, 1999, Vol. 43, no. 3, p. 46. Reprinted with permission.

fundamentalist movement Gush Emunim (Bloc of the Faithful) await the appearance of the Messiah, who will defeat the enemies of the Jewish people, and whose reign will usher justice on earth. Other fundamentalist groups strive to establish God's rule on earth, which they consider a matter of time, and believe that the use of violence to expedite this process is not only necessary but also justifiable. Having said this, it is also important to underscore the roots of many fundamentalist movements in socio-economic ills and injustices. For example, many Muslim fundamentalist movements emerged as a reaction to the economic and political failures and perceived injustices experienced by their societies. Similarly, Hindu fundamentalism has attracted many adherents, even among non-Hindus, because it has championed a campaign against corruption in India.

However, it would be wrong to assume that all religious movements are fundamentalist. Many religious movements are neither violent nor political. They are rather concerned with the spiritual and moral reform of the community. Indeed, this impulse of **religious reformism** has been at the heart of most nineteenth- and twentieth-century religious movements. Their appeal is to invoke a romanticized, sometimes "invented," version of past purity, one considered unsullied by the variable promiscuities of modern life.[5] Whether one surveys Muslim, Christian, or Jewish reformist movements in the contemporary era, the reaction to what are perceived as the social, moral, and cultural ills of modernity has shaped many of these movements. For example, among Muslim reformers, perhaps no one has represented the reformist impulse and preoccupation with the rejuvenation of the Muslim world better than the Egyptian Muhammad 'Abduh (1849–1905).[6] At the core of 'Abduh's intellectual concerns was what he diagnosed as the Muslim world's condition of inner decay, and the consequent need for inner revival. 'Abduh recognized that, faced with a plethora of overlapping social, moral, and political crises, the Muslim world could not regain its strength and prosperity without a process of inner reform, namely the reinterpretation of the religious law and its adaptation to the needs of the modern age. To this end, he spent much of his energy and time demonstrating how Islam could be reconciled with modern thought and the exigencies of the modern age. 'Abduh's early efforts ultimately inaugurated a necessary tradition of critical re-evaluation of religious thought in the Muslim world, one that remains till this day the ideational source of similar contemporary attempts.[7]

RELIGION AS POLITICS BY OTHER MEANS

Why do religious movements ultimately emerge and play a powerful role in politics? Is religion a camouflaged means for a political end? Are religious movements a monolithic band? Moreover, is there something inherently religious about religious movements or are they better understood as social movements deploying the language and symbols of religion to achieve their political ends? The following discussion uses these questions as a guide to an analysis of the causes of the emergence of contemporary Islamist movements in different parts of the world, but especially in the Middle East.[8] Although these movements cannot claim a monopoly over this subject, they do tend to be overrepresented in the international media, though almost always misunderstood. The terrorist attacks of September 11 have accentuated this dilemma. Consequently, a sober look at these groups, their causes, and variety is in order.

In general, there are at least two conventional explanations of the rise of Islamist movements in the late 1970s.

JEWISH FUNDAMENTALISM

Gush Emunim is a contemporary Jewish fundamentalist movement based primarily in Israel and numbering some 6000 members. The uniqueness of this movement rests in its ability to combine traditional religious doctrines with modern nationalism in the form of a syncretic "mystic-messianic" worldview.[9] As religious Zionists, the members of this movement believe that Zionism, albeit originally conceived as a secular ideology, is actually the realization of a messianic ideal, and as such is religiously inspired. Moreover, Gush Emunim members contend that the founding members of Zionism, though secular intellectuals, are in actuality agents of divine intervention, inspired by God to create a political movement guiding Jews back to Zion. The many victories Israel has achieved over the neighbouring Arab states are interpreted as proof of the divine power guiding Zionism. In this view, occupation and annexation of Palestinian land is considered legitimate, given that Yahveh promised this land to the Jewish people in the Book of Genesis. These ideas have inspired the Israeli settlement movement, with Gush Emunim advocating greater annexation of Palestinian lands.

The Political Cultural Approach

The political cultural approach assumes that the re-emergence of "Islam" in the 1970s is a manifestation of Muslims' disillusionment with modernization processes and with modernity in general. In this view, Islam is considered to be incompatible with modern institutions and ways of life. There is thus something natural about the explosion of Islamist movements into the political scene in the 1970s: they are a traditional society's way of rejecting the ways of the West.[10] Of course, the problem with this approach is that it is essentialist and ahistorical: it assumes that Muslims are congenitally mad at the "West"; it also uncritically accepts the tradition/modernity binary. After all, what is so traditional about contemporary Islamist movements such as *Hizbullah* (Party of God) in Lebanon, the Islamic Salvation Front in Algeria, *Hamas* in Palestine, or the Moslem Brotherhood in Egypt? All tend to operate in very modern political and national landscapes, those of the modern territorial state.

The Non-Cultural Approach

A second view underscores non-cultural explanations for the emergence of Islamist movements. In this view, there are a number of variables that explain not only the causes behind the emergence of these groups, but also the timing of their emergence. These variables include the following.

THE LANGUAGE OF ISLAM

Because Islamist movements tend to use the language of Islam as a substitute for tangible socio-economic and political platforms—for example, "Islam is the solution"—they naturally resonate with a broad spectrum of Muslims. After all, for Muslims, Islam provides a complete political and ethical blueprint for life. However, Islam has always been present in the imaginative and sociopolitical landscapes of the region's peoples. Consequently, focusing on the language of Islam alone does help us explain the popularity of Islamist movements, but not the timing of their emergence. Other variables need to be explored.

THE 1967 ARAB–ISRAELI WAR AND THE FAILURE OF SECULAR, REVOLUTIONARY REGIMES

This variable suggests that the turn to Islam in the 1970s, socially and politically, was triggered by the defeat of the Arab armies at the hands of Israel in the 1967 war. After all, the radical regimes that came to power after the 1948 war were considered secular and revolutionary, and promised the political and economic millennium. Consequently, their crushing defeat in 1967 exposed the futility of the secular option and opened the way for the emergence of Islamist movements as a critique of the existing order. Indeed, there is much merit to this argument. However, it fails to explain why it was Islamist groups that emerged after 1967 and not other groups. To do so, we need to look at some additional political economic variables. In many ways, support for Islamist movements in the Arab world derives primarily from economic and political variables rather than cultural and religious ones.[11] These variables include the following.

High urban unemployment rates, interrupted education, and inadequate housing among urban youth
These conditions blocked the prospects for upward socio-economic mobility for the urban middle and lower classes, thus alienating them from the existing status quo, and pushing them into the hands of other, sometimes radical, alternatives.

Income gaps and consumerism In many parts of the Middle East, economic liberalization policies introduced in the 1970s exacerbated, rather than ameliorated, the gap between the rich and the poor. They also unleashed a culture of consumerism and moral laxity among the upper classes. For the urban poor and the rural migrants swelling the belts of miseries surrounding the urban centres, the upper classes had become a parasitic class, enriching themselves off state resources at a time when most of the population was barely making ends meet. Moreover, their moral corruption was a threat to the religious and cultural identity of the society. Cut off from the stabilizing effect of kinship ties in their villages, these urban-based rural migrants found in religious communities the safety net and solace they were yearning for. It was thus natural for them to drift toward those religious firebrands advocating a greater measure of social equality and moral rectitude.

THE POST-INDEPENDENCE POLITICAL ORDER
Most of the regimes that assumed power in the post-independence period turned to authoritarianism, closing almost all avenues of political participation and contestation. In the process, they crushed secular and other types of legal opposition. Consequently, the mosques and the diverse religious charities emerged as the only sites for oppositional political activity. The fact that Islamist sympathizers could disguise themselves as charitable organizations meant that they were not obliged to work underground. This allowed Islamist movements an organizational capacity and space denied to other oppositional groups, most of which were co-opted or jailed. The result was that Islamist movements emerged as the only viable alternative to what were perceived as corrupt and unrepresentative regimes. Little wonder, then, that when these states began experiencing acute fiscal crises and responded with political openings, many citizens voted against the ruling regimes and for Islamist movements. In so doing, they were voting in an instrumental manner: a vote cast for the Islamic Action Front in Jordan, *al-Nahda* (Renaissance) in Tunisia, or the Islamic Salvation Front in Algeria, was not necessarily one cast in support of establishing an Islamic order in these countries. Rather, it was a vote against the corruption and political economic bankruptcy of the ruling regimes.

REGIONAL REVERBERATIONS
Two towering events have inspired both moderate and radical Islamist movements alike in the late twentieth century. The 1978–79 Islamic Revolution in Iran had a direct impact on the radicalization of religious groups throughout the Muslim world. It did so by exposing the power of religious discourse and symbolism. Although the revolution itself was waged by an alliance of secular and religious groups, Ayatollah Khomeini's ability to consolidate power and claim the mantle of the revolution empowered and inspired Muslim religious movements everywhere. At last, and after decades of defeat, first at the hands of colonial powers and then secular regimes, Islamists felt that Islam was striking back. The war in

Afghanistan, beginning immediately after the Soviet invasion of that country in 1979, was the other formative event. The ability of the disparate **Mujahideen** (fighters) groups to defeat the Soviet army was no mere achievement in the annals of Islamist history. This victory, with American intelligence and material support, was tantamount to a settling of scores with a mighty atheist superpower. Many of those non-Afghanis who fought in this war would return to their homelands—in the Middle East, South Asia, Africa, and even Europe—and create the nucleus of new radical cells bent on settling the score with their one-time ally: the United States. Rejected by their societies as militants, and hounded by the authorities, they sought sanctuary in Afghanistan, from which they planned their next move.

THE IMPACT OF STATE POLICIES

State policies have also played an important role in the emergence of religious movements and the radicalization of religious identities. For example, many states in the Muslim world supported religious groups, mainly to shore up their power domestically as well as regionally. Even Israel at one time encouraged the emergence of *Hamas*, chiefly to counterbalance the popularity of the Palestine Liberation Organization in the occupied territories. In Pakistan, the policies of the Zia ul-Huqq (1977–1988) regime led to a heightening of sectarian conflict, namely between the Sunni and the Shi'a Muslims.[12] Lacking a popular base for his regime, Zia exploited Islamic ideology to legitimize his rule. To do so, he championed the cause of the Islamization of Pakistan. This involved organizing Islamic courts to Islamize Pakistan's laws and enforce the Sunni variant of the *Shari'a* (Islamic Law) in 1980. However, by enforcing and spreading the Sunni Muslim legal code, Zia intimidated Pakistan's 20 percent–strong Shi'a population, not to mention the Hindus, Christians, and Ahmadiyyas. Indeed, Zia's Islamization policies triggered greater activism on the part of the Shi'a community in an attempt to defend their rights and to demand the application of the Shi'a legal code on themselves in Pakistan. The result was increased sectarian tensions that exploded in the form of ethnic rioting in the Punjab in September 1986.

In sum, then, popular support for Islamist movements, and the timing of their entry as oppositional groups into the political arena, may be viewed as primarily the result of economic, political, and sociological factors, rather than the cultural and religious traditions of Muslims or Arabs. Nor are these movements monolithic. Despite their sometimes-common discourse and symbolism, they span a broad spectrum. Some, such as the Islamic Action Front in Jordan, Hizbullah in Lebanon, and the Moslem Brotherhood in Egypt, have accepted to enter into the political arena, and play by the rules of the game set by the regime.

RELIGION AS LIBERATION

Contrary to common belief, religion is not always a reactionary force. Indeed, in Latin America religion, in the form of liberation theology, has played an emancipatory role.[13] Historically, the Roman Catholic Church in Latin America had been a bastion of social and political conservatism, siding with the economic and political elites. In the 1960s, a reform movement at the parish level began to take hold. Many priests and sisters began raising questions pertaining to their role in society. But these questions remained haphazard, as no systemic role for the Church in politics was yet articulated. All this would change after Vatican II, however.

The Second Vatican Council, convened by Pope John between 1962 and 1965, changed radically the mission of the Catholic Church. Hitherto the Church had tended to steer away from involvement in earthly matters. Vatican II now saw human progress as the hand of God

ISLAMIC SALVATION FRONT

The Islamic Salvation Front, commonly known by its French acronym, FIS, is an example of an Islamist movement that emerged as a non-violent socio-political and cultural protest movement but turned violent as a result of state policies. FIS was formed in March 1989. Like all Islamist movements, it comprised different factions, with the moderates led by Abbasi Madani and the radicals led by Ali Belhadj. By this time, the ruling National Liberation Front (FLN) in Algeria had begun a controlled process of political liberalization. This was mainly in response to the explosion of socio-economic tensions in the country during the October 5, 1988 riots. In turn, the riots had exploded in reaction to years of widespread unemployment and shortages of essential goods. But they were also a demonstration of public anger against the hypocrisy of the economically privileged ruling elite in Algeria. In the early decades after independence, the elite siphoned off national wealth through state capitalism, and was, in the 1980s, reaping the rewards of an economic liberalization policy launched to contain the state's growing fiscal crisis.[14] To the regime's horror, FIS swept the municipal and provincial elections held in June 1990, ones that were marketed as part and parcel of the regime's political liberalization process. For the ruling FLN, the election results registered a major defeat.

Elections for the National Assembly were scheduled for December 26, 1991. In the first round of voting, FIS won 188 out of 430 seats, and was leading in 150 additional ridings. FIS was poised to secure a majority in the National Assembly in the upcoming second round of voting scheduled for January 16, 1992. However, on January 11, 1992 senior army officers forced then-President Chadli Benjedid's resignation, declared a "state of siege," and assumed power through a higher council of state. The Council annulled the results of the December 1991 elections, cancelled the second round, cracked down on FIS supporters, and arrested at least 9000 Islamists. On March 4, 1992 the Council officially dissolved FIS as a legal political party. The consequence was the radicalization of FIS, whose armed wing, the Islamic Salvation Army (AIS), would henceforth engage the regime in a bloody confrontation, one that lasted until 1999. Only on June 12, 1999 did FIS and the AIS approve a peace accord with the Algerian government. On 3 July 1999, a new president, Abdelaziz Bouteflika, declared an amnesty for thousands of prisoners, one that was followed by the release of most of the FIS leadership. Since then, Bouteflika has steered Algeria toward domestic stability and peace.

in human history and, as such, invited Catholics to engage in social praxis. The implications of Vatican II for the Latin American Church were far reaching. In 1968, Latin American bishops convened a conference in Medellín, Colombia. The conclusions of the conference would amount to the Magna Carta of liberation theology. The bishops called for a greater role for the Church in social transformation and consciousness raising among the poor. Most importantly, the bishops committed themselves to defend human rights, democracy, and social justice in Latin America. In so doing, they opened the way for a radically new pastoral approach. At the heart of this new approach was the attempt to reinterpret the biblical narrative in a manner conducive to the empowerment of the poor and their ultimate liberation from their oppressive rulers. Instead of crying over past injustices and for deliverance, the believers were now invited to overcome these injustices and change the world. For example, the story of Moses' exodus from Egypt, traditionally interpreted in a manner that underscores its miraculous elements, is reinterpreted to stress the oppressive rule of the pharaoh, and the role played by Jewish leaders in liberating their people.[15]

This transformation in the role of the Catholic Church was transpiring at a time when Latin America was undergoing a hard turn toward greater authoritarianism. In Chile, Argentina, Brazil, and Uruguay, repressive military regimes, apprehensive of radical socioeconomic transformations and supported by external powers, had deposed popularly elected, sometimes socialist, governments. Military regimes were also in control in much of Central America and the central Andes. Armed with its new brand of liberation theology, the Church emerged in the mid-1970s as the strongest critic of the human rights abuses of Latin American military regimes. Moreover, the Church played a cardinal role in organizing the poor in what were known as *communidades eclesiales de base*, or Church Base Communities (CEBs). Conceived as base-level cells responsible for enhancing the social and political consciousness of the poor, many of these CEBs would prove to be agents for socio-political mobilization, and would spearhead popular protests against military dictatorships. Ironically, however, the political role of the Catholic Church has declined on the morrow of the democratic transitions that swept through Latin America in the 1980s. The establishment of civilian governments and the ability of opposition groups to operate openly have denied the Church the political clout and functions it assumed during the era of military authoritarian regimes.

TALIBAN, OSAMA BIN LADEN, AL-QAEDA, AND 9/11

The Taliban originated in the network of madrasas (schools) established in Pakistan by Zia ul-Haqq. During the Cold War, Zia's regime was the conduit for CIA aid to the Afghan Mujahideen in their war against the Soviet Union. The Taliban represented the elite students graduating from Zia's madrasas. Moreover, it was the most radical and fanatical of all the nationalist Afghan groups waging war against the pro-Moscow regime and its Soviet protectors. With the withdrawal of Soviet troops from Afghanistan in 1989, the Taliban gradually and brutally established its control over Afghanistan, with the exception of the northern areas. Like many other Arab and Asian Muslims, Osama bin Laden, a one-time Saudi citizen of Yemeni extraction, had participated in the Afghan war on the side of the Mujahideen. With the establishment of Taliban control over most of Afghanistan, bin Laden now acquired the sanctuary and organizational freedom he sought for himself and his followers. In 1991, and on the morrow of Iraq's occupation of Kuwait in August 1990, the United States led a coalition of states to war against Iraq. American troops remained in the Arabian peninsula after the war's end, and after Iraq was expelled from Kuwait. The permanent stationing of American troops in the peninsula—an area considered by Muslims as the holiest of sites—raised bin Laden's ire against America. The terrorist attacks on 9/11 against the World Trade Center and the Pentagon were the culmination of a campaign aimed at expelling American troops from Islam's holiest site, which included separate attacks on American troops in Saudi Arabia and Yemen. Al-Qaeda represents a new form of religious radicalism in the world: a network of transnational fundamentalism, crossing borders and ethnic identities, bent, at a minimum, on eliminating America's presence in the Muslim world and its support for Israel. However, most Muslims neither share bin Laden's interpretation of Islam, nor agree with his tactics. Bin Laden has nevertheless successfully tapped into a reservoir of Muslim resentment against the perceived injurious implications of American foreign policy in Afghanistan and the Middle East.

The U.S.–led invasion of Afghanistan was launched in October 2001, in part, to topple the Taliban regime, capture bin Laden, destroy Al-Qaeda's terrorist bases, and deny terrorist groups sanctuary in that country. It was followed by another U.S.–led invasion against Iraq on March 20, 2003, under the questionable pretext of destroying Saddam Hussein's weapons of mass destruction (WMD) program. In the run-up to the invasion, George W. Bush's administration also suggested a link between Saddam and terrorist organizations, namely Al-Qaeda. Both invasions have failed to contain terrorist groups and end terrorist attacks, however. Bin Laden remains at large, despite the heavy damage suffered by his terrorist network. Afghanistan is not terrorism free; and terrorists have struck back in many European cities. Moreover, the invasion of Iraq has sapped the resources of the American army, deflecting it away from the "war on terrorism" declared by Bush immediately after 9/11. It has also created a vacuum of power in Iraq into which terrorist groups have slipped, especially that led by the Jordanian Abu Musab al-Zarqawi. On the other hand, 9/11 has forced many states, especially in the Middle East, to launch a domestic war against terrorist groups and their radical ideas. Many terrorist cells have been destroyed in the Arab world, Pakistan, and Southeast Asia; others have been uncovered in Europe. Arab regimes have encouraged religious leaders to emphasize the tolerant, moderate nature of Islam. The Saudi monarchy has launched a public campaign against religious extremism, and has called upon Muslim scholars to debunk the radical ideas propagated by terrorist groups, and preach pluralism and a dialogue of civilizations. The battle against terrorism is bound to be costly and protracted. In the meantime, the threat of terrorist attacks persists.

ENDNOTES

1. For a discussion see William O. Beeman, "Fighting the Good Fight: Fundamentalism and Religious Revival," in *Anthropology for the Real World*, ed. J. MacClancy (Chicago: University of Chicago Press, 2001).

2. On this issue, the early Protestant fundamentalists are not very different from their Muslim counterparts in the late twentieth century. For example, the Egyptian group *al-Takfir wa-l-Hijra* (Excommunication and Holy Flight), condemned Egyptian society as un-Islamic, and called upon its members to abandon it and establish their own society, one that would be organized around Islamic values and principles, and where God's *hakimiyya* (sovereignty) would be established.

3. See the discussion in R. Scott Appleby, "Fundamentalism," in *Encyclopedia of Politics and Religion*, ed. Robert Wuthnow, 2 vols. (Washington, DC: Congressional Quarterly, Inc., 1988), 280–88.

4. For a discussion see Appleby, "Fundamentalism."

5. See Eric Hobsbawm and Terence Ranger, eds., *The Invention of Tradition* (Cambridge, MA: Cambridge University Press, 1983).

6. See Albert H. Hourani, *Arabic Thought in the Liberal Age* (Cambridge, MA: Cambridge University Press, 1968), 130–60.

7. See, for example, Fazlur Rahman, *Islam and Modernity: The Transformation of an Intellectual Tradition* (Chicago: University of Chicago Press, 1982).

8. The term "Islamist" is used rather than "Islamic" to underscore the social movement nature of these groups.

9. Gideon Aran, "Redemption as a Catastrophe: The Gospel of Gush Emunim," in *Religious Radicalism and Politics in the Middle East*, ed. Emmanuel Sivan and Minachem Friedman (New York: State University of New York Press, 1990), 161, and more generally 157–75. See also Appleby, "Fundamentalism."

10. See Bernard Lewis, "The Roots of Muslim Rage," *The Atlantic Monthly* (September 1990): 47–60.

11. For an excellent analysis see Mark Tessler, "The Origins of Popular Support for Islamist Movements: A Political Economy Analysis," in *Islam, Democracy, and the State in North Africa*, ed. John P. Entelis (Bloomington: Indiana University Press, 1997), 93–126.

12. See Hamza Alavi, "Pakistan and Islam: Ethnicity and Ideology," in *State and Ideology in the Middle East and Pakistan*, ed. Fred Halliday and Hamza Alavi (New York: Monthly Review Press, 1988), 64–111.

13. For a comprehensive account see Phillip Berryman, *Liberation Theology: The Essential Facts about the Revolutionary Movement in Latin America and Beyond* (New York: Pantheon Books, 1987).

14. For a discussion see Dirk Vandewalle, "Islam in Algeria: Religion, Culture, and Opposition in a Rentier State," in *Political Islam: Revolution, Radicalism, or Reform?* ed. John Esposito (Oxford: Oxford University Press, 1997), 33–51.

15. A similar dynamic transpired in Iran before the 1978 revolution. For example, the martyrdom of Imam Husayn in 680 A.D. in the struggle against the unjust Umayyad ruler Yazid, traditionally invoked to inspire acquiescence in the face of suffering, was reinterpreted to invite believers to rise, like Husayn, against injustice, now incarnated in the form of Shah Mohammad Reza Pahlavi.

READINGS

This chapter looked at the symbiotic relation between religion and politics in different parts of the world. It opened by exploring the North American origins of the fundamentalist phenomenon. Different forms of fundamentalism were discussed, including the violent and the non-violent ones. The rise of Islamist movements was explored in the context of their varying socio-economic and political contexts. The chapter closed with a discussion of liberation theology in Latin America. The political deployment of religion is the theme running across all these movements. This theme is well reflected in the first reading for this chapter. Howard Handelman's excerpt explores a variety of religious movements among Christians, Hindus, Sikhs, and Muslims. Handelman's comparative approach allows the student to appreciate the socio-economic and political causes of religious politics across different societies and world religions. It offers an antidote to the otherwise frequently misinformed media analysis of this important topic.

After offering a workable definition of fundamentalism, the reading explores this theme among Christians, Hindus, Sikhs, and Muslims. Students should pay special attention to the discussion of the multiple, but often political and economic, causes of religious politics in different parts of the world. They should also think comparatively of the different manifestations of religious groups. Moreover, the reading presents many examples, culled from different parts of the world, which together constitute an excellent panorama of different religious groups and their activities.

The second reading by F. Gregory Gause, III, problematizes the relation between democracy and terrorism in the Middle East. Gause debunks the Bush administration's claim that the promotion of democracy in the Middle East will make America a safer place. Gause argues that the thesis that democracy reduces terrorism is questionable if not empirically false. Moreover, he warns that democratic transformations in the Middle East will most probably lead to the electoral victory of Islamist parties. America, Gause suggests, should rather take the longer and more demanding road: prepare the ground for future democratization, and hold democratic elections only when it is confident that non-Islamist political forces can win them. Gause's sober Machiavellian argument merits a serious debate.

As you finish reading the following selection, you may wish to think about the following related questions. What has caused the rise of religious movements in the Muslim world? What are the differences between Muslim and Hindu fundamentalism? What was the role of the Catholic Church in political transformations in Latin America? How has the world changed after 9/11? What is the best way to defeat terrorist groups and radical ideas? And what is the best way to empower secular, liberal forces in Muslim countries?

RELIGION AND POLITICS

Howard Handelman

... since the 1970s much of the Third World, and the developed world too, for that matter, has experienced a religious resurgence intensifying the role of religion in the political arena.[1]

Nowhere is that more apparent than in the Middle East and parts of Asia, where a renewal of Islamic fundamentalism (or *Islamism*, the term preferred by many analysts) has had a dramatic political impact on Afghanistan, Iran, Lebanon, Algeria, Egypt, and Pakistan. The seizure of American hostages in Iran and Lebanon, the assassination of Egyptian President Anwar Sadat, the

bombings of a U.S. military housing installation in Saudi Arabia and of two U.S. embassies in East Africa, and, especially, the attacks on the World Trade Center and the Pentagon have all focused Western attention on "religion and politics." In fact, with the collapse of Soviet communism and the end of the Cold War, many politicians and journalists labeled radical (militant) Islamic fundamentalism as the greatest threat to Western security. Even before the 1991 Gulf War, a Gallup Poll survey revealed that 37 percent of British respondents expected a war in the 1990s between

Muslims and Christians.[2] The war in Afghanistan and Al Qaeda have revived such sentiments. While these perceptions are often based on prejudice and misunderstanding, the discussion of Islamic and Hindu fundamentalism later in this chapter indicates some valid reason for concern.

THE MEETING OF CHURCH AND STATE

Many of our preconceptions about religion and politics are based on serious misunderstandings, both of our own government and of political systems elsewhere. Americans generally accept a constitutional separation between church and state as natural. Such formal barriers, however, do not exist in many industrial democracies or LDCs. Moreover, even in the United States, religious organizations and beliefs continue to influence political behavior. Black Baptist churches, for example, have always been in the forefront of the American civil rights movement. Recently, conflicts over issues such as school prayer and abortion have led one expert to observe that "far from rendering religion largely irrelevant to politics . . . the structure of [American] government . . . may actually encourage a high degree of interaction."[3] Most Western European nations, though more secular than the United States in most aspects of everyday life, have not built walls between religion and politics. In Britain, for example, the Anglican church (or Church of England) is the official state religion. The Catholic church was closely linked to the Italian Christian Democratic Party, once that nation's leading party.[4]

Religion is more firmly embedded in most Third World cultures, and its impact on politics is correspondingly more pronounced than is ours. Indeed, religion is so central to traditional values that we often identify national or regional cultures by the predominant religion: Buddhist culture in Thailand, Confucian culture in China and Korea, Hindu culture in much of India and Nepal, and Islamic culture in North Africa and the Middle East.[5]

The blending of religion and politics is most apparent in theocratic states such as Iran where, since that nation's 1979 Islamic revolution, public policy has been shaped by the Shi'ite clergy. But it is also significant in Islamic fundamentalist states like Sudan, and more moderate Muslim nations such as Pakistan and Saudi Arabia. Afghanistan's Taliban government was a religious movement that made politics totally subservient to religion. In Brazil and Nicaragua, the theology of liberation,

espoused by progressive members of the Catholic church, motivated priests and nuns to organize the poor against economic and political injustices. And in India, the Bharatiya Janata Party (BJP), currently the country's largest political party and head of its governing coalition, carries the torch of Hindu fundamentalism.

STRUCTURAL AND THEOLOGICAL BASES OF CHURCH–STATE RELATIONS

The extent to which religions influence political attitudes and behavior and the degree of political involvement by organized religions vary considerably from place to place. Just as the separation of church and state in Western Europe has historically been more clearly defined in predominantly Protestant nations (for example, Denmark and Britain) than in Catholic ones (Italy and Spain), the political impact of the Third World's four major religions also differs. Two factors are particularly relevant: the particular religion's theological view on the relationship between temporal and spiritual matters, and the degree of hierarchical structure within the religion. The second factor refers to how well organized and centrally controlled a religion is.

Donald Smith distinguishes two different types of religio-political systems: the organic and the church. In the first case, the *organic* system, the clergy is insufficiently organized to challenge the country's political leaders who are, consequently, less restricted by religious institutions. Examples of organic systems include the Hindu and most Sunni Islamic cultures. *Church* religio-political systems, on the other hand, have a well-organized ecclesiastical structure that exercises considerable authority over politics. Such churches include Catholicism, Shi'ite Islam, and sometimes Buddhism (in countries such as Tibet and Burma). All have more formalized relations between church and state, with greater potential for religious challenges to the political order or political domination of the church than in organic systems. In some church systems, the state dominates the religious order; in others, the church dominates; and yet in others, there is an equal partnership.[6]

Islam

From its inception in seventh-century Arabia, Islam was a "religio-political movement in which religion was integral to state and society."[7] Perhaps more than any other great religion, traditional Islam usually recognized no border-line between religion and politics. On the one hand, the Islamic faith and its clergy legitimized the state. At the same time, however, the political leadership recognized the supremacy of Islamic law, called the *Shariah* (path of God). Thus, prior to the intrusion of colonialism, Muslims assumed that they lived in an Islamic state. Since religious Muslims believe that God wants them to live in a community governed in accordance with the Quran (divinely revealed law, much of it temporal), the very concept of separating church and state is alien to their culture. This does not mean that traditional Islamic culture and theology were inhospitable to other religions. Perhaps because it accepted Jewish and Christian scriptures and drew from both of those religions since its inception, Islam was often highly tolerant of other faiths. During the Middle Ages, for example, the large Jewish community in Muslim-controlled Spain enjoyed perhaps their greatest period of freedom and influence anywhere in Europe.[8] But even then, ultimate political authority remained Muslim.

The bond between Islam and politics remains strong in most Muslim societies today, though there is considerable variation. John Esposito distinguishes three types of Islamic regimes: the secular state, the Islamic state, and the Muslim state.[9] Turkey is perhaps the most noted *secular state* in the Islamic world. Starting in the 1920s, Mustafa Kemal Ataturk (the father of modern Turkey) ousted the sultan of the Ottoman Empire, abolished the basis of the sultan's religious authority, emancipated women, closed seminaries, and westernized Turkish society in many ways. Today, Turkey is not fully secularized because its constitution still endorses belief in God, but the political system offers Islam no special status and, in fact, prohibits certain traditional Islamic practices.[10]

During the 1980s and 1990s, however, an Islamic political party, the Refah (Welfare) Party steadily gained strength, particularly among residents of Turkey's urban slums, who had migrated from the countryside to large cities and had found modern, secular culture difficult, corrupt, and oppressive. As its name indicates, the Welfare Party gained considerable support among the poor by offering them social services that the government had failed to provide. In the 1995 parliamentary elections, Refah won the largest number of seats, setting off a frantic effort by Turkey's other major parties to exclude it from power. When those parties were unable to put together a stable governing coalition, Refah formed the new government. Despite its sometimes radical and inflammatory rhetoric, the Welfare Party's policies in office were relatively moderate when compared to those of many other Islamic parties in the region. Still, its program of religious reforms—including a proposed amendment eliminating the constitutional ban on religious dress so as to allow female students to cover their hair with scarves at school—was unacceptable to the powerful Turkish military, which views itself as the guardian of the country's secular tradition. In 1998, the military forced parliament to remove the Welfare Party from office and dissolve it as a legal political party.[11]

At the other end of the spectrum, *Islamic states* base their governing philosophies on the Quran and other Islamic law. Taliban Afghanistan, Iran, and Saudi Arabia are among the best-known examples, but Sudan, Pakistan, and Libya also fall in this category. These regimes can be quite distinct from each other. Whereas Iran subscribes to Shi'ite Islam, the other countries are all primarily Sunni. Afghanistan (until the recent war), Libya, Iran, and Sudan have pursued militantly anti-Western foreign policies and have supported terrorism, while Saudi Arabia is quite conservative and closely allied to the West. The new, post-Taliban government in Afghanistan is likely to be Islamic, moderate, and somewhat tied to the West. Thus, the term *Islamic state* (like the concept of fundamentalism) must be used carefully to avoid creating artificial categories that hide more than they reveal.

Finally, *Muslim states*, such as Egypt and Morocco, occupy an intermediate position on church–state relations and the role of religion. Unlike secular states, they identify Islam as the official religion and require the head of state to be Muslim. However, the impact of religion on politics is far more limited than in Islamic states. For example, unlike Taliban Afghanistan and Iran, political leaders are not clerics, and some are even non-Muslims.

Catholicism

More than any other major religion, Catholicism has a well-defined and hierarchical ecclesiastical structure that enables it to have a great impact on the political order. At the Church's apex is the Pope, whose authority is unchallenged and whose pronouncements on matters of faith and morals are believed to be infallible. Consequently, papal declarations can carry considerable political weight. For example, many of the twentieth-century, Catholic-based reform movements in Latin America can be traced to Pope Leo XII's 1891 encyclical, *Rerum Novarum*, which included an indictment of early capitalism's exploitation of the working class. Within each country, the Church hierarchy is headed by bishops, who often have tremendous political influence in Latin America and in Catholic countries such as the Philippines.

Like Islam in the Middle East, Catholicism used to be the state religion in most Latin American countries. For example, in Colombia as recently as 1953, government treaties with the Vatican gave the Church special authority in areas such as education.[12] Over the years, however, most Latin American nations either ceased having an official state religion or have rendered the link unimportant. Still, Church doctrine has generally supported the established political regime and helped legitimize it. "The ruling powers," said one encyclical, "are invested with a sacredness more than human. . . . Obedience is not the servitude of man to man, but submission to the will of God."[13]

That does not mean, however, that the Church has always supported the government. Over the years, there have been periodic clashes between the two, most notably when the state challenged Church authority in areas such as education. In the Philippines, Church support of Corazón Aquino's political reform movement helped topple the dictatorship of Ferdinand Marcos. Similarly, Catholic authorities opposed conservative military dictatorships in Brazil and Chile during the 1970s and 1980s. Church relationships with Marxist regimes in Cuba and Nicaragua were often tense, though relations with Castro's government have improved substantially since the Pope's visit to Cuba.[14] And in El Salvador, Archbishop Romero spoke out forcefully against the regime's severe human-rights violations in the 1980s. Shortly after one of his most powerful pronouncements, Romero was assassinated by the military. In other countries, however, the local hierarchy has been far more cautious about criticizing the government.

Hinduism and Buddhism

Asia's organic religions, Hinduism and Buddhism, generally have been less directly involved in politics than have Catholicism and Islam. (India's powerful BJP, a Hindu party, is not a part of the Hindu religious order.) Of course, Hinduism's cultural and philosophical values, most notably the caste system, have affected Indian and Nepalese politics profoundly. For example, the king of Nepal is worshiped as the incarnation of the god Vishnu.[15] But the religion is so diverse, composed of local religious groups, cults, and sects loosely tied together by a common set of beliefs, that there is no centralized political influence. Moreover, although there are gurus, holy men, temple priests, and even a priestly caste (Brahmans, though most of them no longer choose to be priests), there is no ecclesiastical organization.

Buddhism grew out of the Hindu religion in the sixth century B.C., emerging from the teachings of a Nepalese prince, Siddartha Gautama, who later came to be known as the Buddha (Enlightened One). Though greatly influenced by Hinduism, Buddhism rejects one of its basic tenets, the caste system. Indeed, as Buddhism spread through Asia, one of its great appeals was its egalitarian outlook. Today, many of India's untouchables continue to leave Hinduism for Buddhism, a religion far more hospitable to them.[16] Buddhism differs from Hinduism in having an organized ecclesiastical organization, namely the *sangha* (the monastic orders). In some countries, such as Myanmar, each sangha has its own leader, providing a hierarchical structure. Still, when compared to the Roman Catholic church or the mullahs of Shi'ite Islam, Buddhism's religious structure is less centralized and, thus, less able to impact the political system.

To be sure, Buddhist and Hindu groups sometimes have strongly influenced their nation's politics. During the early 1960s, Burma was declared a Buddhist state, though that was terminated after a few years. Protests led by Buddhist monks during that decade also helped topple three successive South Vietnamese leaders in a short period of time.[17] Monks have led major protests against government human-rights violations in Tibet, Myanmar, and Thailand as well. The modern liberator of India, Mahatma Gandhi, drew upon reformist Hindu theology when demanding greater equality for untouchables and the lower castes. Conversely, the Bharatiya Janata Party (BJP), currently heading the Indian government, and other contemporary fundamentalist Hindu groups support the traditional caste system.

In addition to having less hierarchically organized ecclesiastical orders, Eastern religions are less theologically oriented toward political involvement than are Catholicism and Islam. Their otherworldly philosophy places less emphasis on such temporal matters as politics; hence, the remainder of this chapter focuses more heavily on the political impact of Islam and Catholicism in the Third World.

Defining and Explaining Fundamentalism

Fundamentalism is the effort to define the fundamentals of a religious system and adhere to them. One of the cardinal tenets of Islamic fundamentalism is to protect the purity of Islamic precepts from the adulteration of speculative exercises. Related to Islamic fundamentalism is revival or resurgence, a renewed interest in Islam. Behind all this is a drive to purify Islam in order to release all its vital force.[18]

The precise meaning of fundamentalism varies somewhat from religion to religion.[19] But revivalists do share certain points of view across religions. To begin with, they all wish to preserve their religion's traditional worldview and resist the efforts of religious liberals to reform it. They also desire to revive the role of religion in private and public life, including politics, lifestyle, and dress.

In the developing world, fundamentalism usually appeals particularly to people who are disgusted by the inequalities and injustices in their country's political-economic system. This disgust reflects popular revulsion against local political and economic elites, against pervasive corruption and repression. In Lebanon the radical Hizbullah grew out of Shi'ite resentment against the economically powerful Christian community, as well as anger against Israel and the West. In India, the BJP attracts much of its support from voters (including some non-Hindus) embittered by government corruption. And in Algeria, Egypt, and the Sudan, militant fundamentalists expanded their support as a result of the government repression directed against them.[20] Ironically, then, many Muslims and Hindus are attracted to radical fundamentalism for the same reasons that drew Latin Americans to Marxist movements.

Radical fundamentalists also tend to be nationalist or chauvinistic, rejecting "outside" influences they feel challenge or pollute their culture and their true faith. Western culture is perceived as particularly deleterious, with its immodest dress, films, and music that allegedly promote promiscuous sex, drugs, and the like. But Western values are rejected for another reason. For years government leaders such as the Shah of Iran and Egypt's President Anwar Sadat promoted Western-style modernization as the route to national development. After decades of failed development in the Middle East, North Africa, and other parts of the Third World, however, many of those regions' citizens feel that they were deceived and must look elsewhere for answers to their problems.

Fundamentalists: Radical and Conservative

Finally, a distinction must be made between radical and conservative fundamentalists. Radicals, inspired by a "sacred rage," feel that they are conducting a holy war against forces that threaten to corrupt their fundamental religious values.[21] As a Hizbullah manifesto declared, "We have risen to liberate our country, to drive the imperialists and the invaders out of it and to take our fate in our own hands."[22] Holy war was first waged by Islamic mujahadeen in Afghanistan against the country's Soviet occupiers as well as the Afghan Marxist government, which Soviet troops defended.[23] Iran's Ayatollah Khomeini declared a *jihad* (holy war) against both the United States ("the great Satan") and Soviet communism. Elsewhere, the battle has been waged against internal enemies as well. Having been denied an almost certain electoral victory in 1992 (the military canceled the elections after the first round), Algeria's fundamentalist Islamic Salvation Front (FIS) attacked the nation's armed forces, police, and secular politicians, as well as foreigners.[24] More violent militants, most notably the Armed Islamic Group (GIA), also launched massive terrorist attacks on civilians, often mixing banditry with supposed religious warfare. From 1992 through early 2001, more than 100,000 people were killed either by armed Islamic groups or by the Algerian military and its allied civilian militias, which reacted with equal savagery. In India, Hindu fundamentalists have periodically directed their rage against the country's Muslim minority. . . . Because these are perceived to be holy wars against a grave threat, religious radicals feel justified in attacking their Muslim neighbors in India, or killing 3,000 people in New York

City, or pronouncing a *fatwah* (religious edict) sentencing author Salman Rushdie to death for having written *The Satanic Verses*.

Such radical militancy contrasts with the views and behavior of conservative fundamentalists, including Hasidic Jews and Saudi Arabian princes, who do not envision themselves in such a battle. They too wish to shield their flocks from unwanted outside influences, but they do not view adherents of other religions or nonfundamentalist members of their own faith as enemies.[25]

Reading Notes

1. Emile Sahliyeh, ed., *Religious Resurgence and Politics in the Contemporary World* (Albany, NY: SUNY Press), pp. 1–16.

2. Jeff Haynes, *Religion in Third World Politics* (Boulder, CO: Lynne Rienner Publishers, 1994), p. 3.

3. Kenneth D. Wald, "Social Change and Political Response: The Silent Religious Cleavage in North America," in *Politics and Religion in the Modern World*, ed. George Moyser (New York: Routledge and Kegan Paul, 1991), p. 240.

4. The Christian Democratic Party was the dominant party in Italian politics for decades but was devastated in the early 1990s by scandal. It has since changed its name to the Italian Popular Party.

5. One of the most influential and controversial books using the framework of clashing, religiously based cultures is Samuel P. Huntington, *The Clash of Civilizations and the Remaking of World Order* (New York: Simon & Schuster, 1996); see also Bernard Lewis, "The Roots of Muslim Rage," *Atlantic Monthly* 226, no. 3 (September 1990). Leonard Binder, a leading specialist on the Middle East, is critical of such terminology, arguing, for example, that Islam is only one part of Middle Eastern culture; see *Islamic Liberalism* (Chicago: University of Chicago Press, 1988), pp. 80–81.

6. Donald Eugene Smith, *Religion and Political Development* (Boston: Little Brown, 1970), pp. 57–84.

7. John L. Esposito, *Islam and Politics*, 2nd ed., (Syracuse, NY: Syracuse University Press, 1987), p. 1.

8. Contemporary hostilities between Jews and Muslims in the Middle East, as well as Islamic fundamentalist hostility toward the West, are relatively recent phenomena that are not rooted in Islam's core beliefs.

9. John L. Esposito, *The Islamic Threat: Myth or Reality?* (New York: Oxford University Press, 1992), pp. 78–79.

10. Anthony H. Johns, "Indonesia: Islam and Cultural Pluralism," in *Islam in Asia*, John L. Esposito, ed. (New York: Oxford University Press, 1987), p. 203.

11. In 2001 the Welfare Party tried to reorganize under a new name.

12. Donald Eugene Smith, *Religion, Politics and Social Change in the Third World* (New York: Free Press, 1971), pp. 12–22.

13. Smith, *Religion and Political Development*, p. 54.

14. At the same time, however, many parish priests and nuns supported the revolution in Nicaragua, and several priests served in the first Sandinista cabinet.

15. Ibid., pp. 57, 34–39; Haynes, *Religion in Third World Politics*, p. 146.

16. Janet A. Contursi, "Militant Hindus and Buddhist Dalits: Hegemony and Resistance in an Indian Slum," *American Ethnologist* 16, no. 3 (August 1989): 441–457.

17. Donald Eugene Smith, "The Limits of Religious Resurgence," Emile Sahliyeh ed. *Religious Resurgence and Politics in the Contemporary World* (Albany, NY: SUNY Press, 1990). pp. 36–39.

18. Dilip Hiro, *Holy Wars: The Rise of Islamic Fundamentalism* (New York: Routledge and Kegan Paul, 1989), pp. 1–2.

19. William Montgomery Watt, *Islamic Fundamentalism and Modernity* (London: Routledge and Kegan Paul, 1988), p. 2.

20. Peter Woodward, "Sudan: Islamic Radicals in Power," in *Political Islam* (Boulder, CO: Lynne Rienner Publishers, 1997), ed. John Esposito.

21. Robin Wright, *Sacred Rage: The Crusade of Modern Islam* (London: Andre Deutsch, 1986).

22. Robin Wright, "Lebanon," *in The Politics of Islamic Revivalism*, in Shireen T. Hunter ed. (Bloomington: Indiana University Press, 1988), p. 66.

23. Naby, Eden, "The Changing Role of Islam, as a Unifying Force in Afghanistan," in *The State, Religion, and Ethnic Politics: Afghanistan, Iran and Pakistan*, Ali Banuazizi and Myron Weiner eds. (Syracuse: Syracuse University Press, 1986), pp. 124–154; Paul Overby, *Holy Blood: An Inside View of the Afghan War* (Westport, CT: Praeger, 1993).

24. For a discussion of the origins of the FIS and the nature of Algeria's violence since 1992, see Claire Spencer, "The Roots and Future of Islamism in Algeria," in *Islamic Fundamentalism*, ed. Abdel Salam Sidahmed and Anoushiravan Ehteshami (Boulder, CO: Westview Press, 1996), pp. 93–109; also Esposito, *Islam and Politics*, 4th ed., pp. 302–307.

25. To be sure, some Israeli "ultra-orthodox" Jews are radical fundamentalists who have carried out violent attacks against Muslims and secular Jews. The most notorious examples were the attack by an ultra-orthodox Jewish gunman against worshipers in a Hebron mosque and the assassination of Israeli Prime Minister Izhak Rabin by a Jewish fundamentalist who objected to Rabin's efforts to achieve peace with the Palestinian Liberation Organization (PLO). But they are exceptional.

CAN DEMOCRACY STOP TERRORISM?

F. Gregory Gause III

WHAT FREEDOM BRINGS

The United States is engaged in what President George W. Bush has called a "generational challenge" to instill democracy in the Arab world. The Bush administration and its defenders contend that this push for Arab democracy will not only spread American values but also improve U.S. security. As democracy grows in the Arab world, the thinking goes, the region will stop generating anti-American terrorism. Promoting democracy in the Middle East is therefore not merely consistent with U.S. security goals; it is necessary to achieve them.

But this begs a fundamental question: Is it true that the more democratic a country becomes, the less likely it is to produce terrorists and terrorist groups? In other words, is the security rationale for promoting democracy in the Arab world based on a sound premise? Unfortunately, the answer appears to be no. Although what is known about terrorism is admittedly incomplete, the data available do not show a strong relationship between democracy and an absence of or a reduction in terrorism. Terrorism appears to stem from factors much more specific than regime type. Nor is it likely that democratization would end the current campaign against the United States. Al Qaeda and like-minded groups are not fighting for democracy in the Muslim world; they are fighting to impose their vision of an Islamic state. Nor is there any evidence that democracy in the Arab world would "drain the swamp," eliminating soft support for terrorist organizations among the Arab public and reducing the number of potential recruits for them.

Even if democracy were achieved in the Middle East, what kind of governments would it produce? Would they cooperate with the United States on important policy objectives besides curbing terrorism, such as advancing the Arab-Israeli peace process, maintaining security in the Persian Gulf, and ensuring steady supplies of oil? No one can predict the course a new democracy will take, but based on public opinion surveys and recent elections in the Arab world, the advent of democracy there seems likely to produce new Islamist governments that would be much less willing to cooperate with the United States than are the current authoritarian rulers.

The answers to these questions should give Washington pause. The Bush administration's democracy initiative can be defended as an effort to spread American democratic values at any cost, or as a long-term gamble that even if Islamists do come to power, the realities of governance will moderate them or the public will grow disillusioned with them. The emphasis on electoral democracy will not, however, serve immediate U.S. interests either in the war on terrorism or in other important Middle East policies.

It is thus time to rethink the U.S. emphasis on democracy promotion in the Arab world. Rather than push for quick elections, the United States should instead focus its energy on encouraging the development of secular, nationalist, and liberal political organizations that could compete on an equal footing with Islamist parties. Only by doing so can Washington help ensure that when elections finally do occur, the results are more in line with U.S. interests.

THE MISSING LINK

President Bush has been clear about why he thinks promoting democracy in the Arab world is central to U.S. interests. "Our strategy to keep the peace in the longer term," Bush said in a speech in March 2005, "is to help change the conditions that give rise to extremism and terror, especially in the broader Middle East. Parts of that region have been caught for generations in a cycle of tyranny and despair and radicalism. When a dictatorship controls the political life of a country, responsible opposition cannot develop, and dissent is driven underground and toward the extreme. And to draw attention away from their social and economic failures, dictators place blame on other countries and other races, and stir the hatred that leads to violence. This status quo of despotism and anger cannot be ignored or appeased, kept in a box or bought off."

Bush's belief in the link between terrorism and a lack of democracy is not limited to his administration. During the 2004 presidential campaign, Senator John Kerry (D-Mass.) emphasized the need for greater political reform in the Middle East as an integral part of the war on terrorism. Martin Indyk, a senior Middle East policymaker in the Clinton administration, has written that it was a mistake for Clinton to focus on Arab-Israeli peace while downplaying Middle East democracy, and he has urged Washington to concentrate on political reform. In a recent book he co-authored, Morton Halperin, the director of policy planning in Clinton's State Department, argues that the roots of al Qaeda lie in the poverty and educational deficiencies of Saudi Arabia, Egypt, and Pakistan, and that these deficiencies were caused by the authoritarian nature of those states and can be combated only through democratization. The New York Times columnist Thomas Friedman has done more to sell this logic to the public than anyone else.

Despite the wide acceptance of this connection, the academic literature on the relationship between terrorism and other sociopolitical indicators, such as democracy, is surprisingly scant. There are good case studies and general surveys of terrorists and terrorist organizations, but few that try to determine whether more democracy leads to less terrorism. Part of the problem is the quality of the data available. The Western press tends to report terrorist incidents with a cross-border element more completely than homegrown terrorist attacks. Moreover, most of the statistics identify the location of an incident, but not the identity of the perpetrators—and much less whether they came from nondemocratic countries.

Given such incomplete information, only preliminary conclusions from the academic literature are possible. However, even these seem to discredit the supposedly close link between terrorism and authoritarianism that underlies the Bush administration's logic. In a widely cited study of terrorist events in the 1980s, the political scientists William Eubank and Leonard Weinberg demonstrate that most terrorist incidents occur in democracies and that generally both the victims and the perpetrators are citizens of democracies. Examining incidents from 1975 to 1997, Pennsylvania State University's Quan Li has found that although terrorist attacks are less frequent when democratic political participation is high, the kind of checks that liberal democracy typically places on executive power seems to encourage terrorist actions. In his recent book, *Dying to Win: The Strategic Logic of Suicide Terrorism*, Robert Pape finds that the targets of suicide bombers are almost always democracies, but that the motivation of the groups behind those bombings is to fight against military occupation and for self-determination. Terrorists are not driven by a desire for democracy but by their opposition to what they see as foreign domination.

The numbers published by the U.S. government do not bear out claims of a close link between terrorism and authoritarianism either. Between 2000 and 2003, according to the State Department's annual "Patterns of Global Terrorism" report, 269 major terrorist incidents around the world occurred in countries classified as "free" by Freedom House, 119 occurred in "partly free" countries, and 138 occurred in "not free" countries. (This count excludes both terrorist attacks by Palestinians on Israel, which would increase the number of attacks in democracies even more, and the September 11, 2001, attacks on the United States, which originated in other countries.) This is not to argue that free countries are more likely to produce terrorists than other countries. Rather, these numbers simply indicate that there is no relationship between the incidence of terrorism in a given country and the degree of freedom enjoyed by its citizens. They certainly do not indicate that democracies are substantially less susceptible to terrorism than are other forms of government.

Terrorism, of course, is not distributed randomly. According to official U.S. government data, the vast majority of terrorist incidents occurred in only a few countries. Indeed, half of all the terrorist incidents in "not free" countries in 2003 took place in just two countries: Iraq and Afghanistan. It seems that democratization did little to discourage terrorists from operating there—and may even have encouraged terrorism.

As for the "free" countries, terrorist incidents in India accounted for fully 75 percent of the total. It is fair to assume that groups based in Pakistan carried out a number of those attacks, particularly in Kashmir, but clearly not all the perpetrators were foreigners. A significant number of terrorist events in India took place far from Kashmir, reflecting other local grievances against the central government. And as strong and vibrant as Indian democracy is, both a sitting prime minister and a former prime minister have been assassinated—Indira Gandhi and her son, Rajiv Gandhi, respectively. If democracy reduced the prospects for terrorism, India's numbers would not be so high.

Comparing India, the world's most populous democracy, and China, the world's most populous authoritarian state, highlights the difficulty of assuming that democracy can solve the terrorism problem. For 2000–2003, the "Patterns of Global Terrorism" report indicates 203 international terrorist attacks in India and none in China. A list of terrorist incidents between 1976 and 2004, compiled by the National Memorial Institute for the Prevention of Terrorism, shows more than 400 in India and only 18 in China. Even if China underreports such incidents by a factor of ten, it still endures substantially fewer terrorist attacks than India. If the relationship between authoritarianism and terrorism were as strong as the Bush administration implies, the discrepancy between the number of terrorist incidents in China and the number in India would run the other way.

More anecdotal evidence also calls into question a necessary relationship between regime type and terrorism. In the 1970s and 1980s, a number of brutal terrorist organizations arose in democratic countries: the Red Brigades in Italy, the Provisional Irish Republican Army in Ireland and the United Kingdom, the Japanese Red Army in Japan, and the Red Army Faction (or Baader-Meinhof Gang) in West Germany. The transition to democracy in Spain did not eliminate Euskadi Ta Askatasuna (ETA) Basque separatist terrorism. Turkish democracy suffered through a decade of mounting political violence that lasted until the late 1970s. The strong and admirable democratic system in Israel has produced its own terrorists, including the assassin of Prime Minister Yitzhak Rabin. It appears that at least three of the suicide bombers in the London attacks of July were born and raised in the democratic United Kingdom. Nearly every day brings a painful reminder that real democratization in Iraq has been accompanied by serious terrorism. And a memorial in Oklahoma City testifies to the fact that even U.S. democracy has not been free of terrorism of domestic origins.

There is, in other words, no solid empirical evidence for a strong link between democracy, or any other regime type, and terrorism, in either a positive or a negative direction. In her highly praised post–September 11 study of religious militants, *Terror in the Name of God*, Jessica Stern argues that "democratization is not necessarily the best way to fight Islamic extremism," because the transition to democracy "has been found to be an especially vulnerable period for states across the board." Terrorism springs from sources other than the form of government of a state. There is no reason to believe that a more democratic Arab world will, simply by virtue of being more democratic, generate fewer terrorists.

FLAWED

There are also logical problems with the argument supporting the U.S. push for democracy as part of the war on terrorism. Underlying the assertion that democracy will reduce terrorism is the belief that, able to participate openly in competitive politics and have their voices heard in the public square, potential terrorists and terrorist sympathizers would not need to resort to violence to achieve their goals. Even if they lost in one round of elections, the confidence that they could win in the future would inhibit the temptation to resort to extra-democratic means.

The habits of democracy would ameliorate extremism and focus the anger of the Arab publics at their own governments, not at the United States.

Well, maybe. But it is just as logical to assume that terrorists, who rarely represent political agendas that could mobilize electoral majorities, would reject the very principles of majority rule and minority rights on which liberal democracy is based. If they could not achieve their goals through democratic politics, why would they privilege the democratic process over those goals? It seems more likely that, having been mobilized to participate in the democratic process by a burning desire to achieve particular goals—a desire so strong that they were willing to commit acts of violence against defenseless civilians to realize it—terrorists and potential terrorists would attack democracy if it did not produce their desired results. Respect for the nascent Iraqi democracy, despite a very successful election in January 2005, has not stopped Iraqi and foreign terrorists from their campaign against the new political order.

Terrorist organizations are not mass-based organizations. They are small and secretive. They are not organized or based on democratic principles. They revolve around strong leaders and a cluster of committed followers who are willing to take actions from which the vast majority of people, even those who might support their political agenda, would rightly shrink. It seems unlikely that simply being outvoted would deflect them from their path.

The United States' major foe in the war on terrorism, al Qaeda, certainly would not close up shop if every Muslim country in the world were to become a democracy. Osama bin Laden has been very clear about democracy: he does not like it. His political model is the early Muslim caliphate. In his view, the Taliban regime in Afghanistan came the closest in modern times to that model. In an October 2003 "message to Iraqis," bin Laden castigated those in the Arab world who are "calling for a peaceful democratic solution in dealing with apostate governments or with Jewish and crusader invaders instead of fighting in the name of God." He referred to democracy as "this deviant and misleading practice" and "the faith of the ignorant." Bin Laden's ally in Iraq, Abu Musab al-Zarqawi, reacted to the January 2005 Iraqi election even more directly: "The legislator who must be obeyed in a democracy is man, and not God. . . . That is the very essence of heresy and polytheism and error, as it contradicts the bases of the faith and monotheism, and because it makes the weak, ignorant man God's partner in His most central divine prerogative—namely, ruling and legislating."

Al Qaeda's leaders distrust democracy, and not just on ideological grounds: they know they could not come to power through free elections. There is no reason to believe that a move toward more democracy in Arab states would deflect them from their course. And there is no reason to believe that they could not recruit followers in more democratic Arab states—especially if those states continued to have good relations with the United States, made peace with Israel, and generally behaved in ways acceptable to Washington. Al Qaeda objects to the U.S. agenda in the Middle East as much as, if not more than, democracy. If, as Washington hopes, a democratic Middle East continued to accept a major U.S. role in the region and cooperate with U.S. goals, it is foolish to think that democracy would end Arab anti-Americanism and dry up passive support, funding sources, and recruiting channels for al Qaeda.

When it works, liberal democracy is the best form of government. But there is no evidence that it reduces or prevents terrorism. The fundamental assumption of the Bush administration's push for democracy in the Arab world is seriously flawed.

ANGRY VOICES

It is highly unlikely that democratically elected Arab governments would be as cooperative with the United States as the current authoritarian regimes. To the extent that public opinion can be measured in these countries, research shows that Arabs strongly support democracy. When they have a chance to vote in real elections, they generally turn out in percentages far greater than Americans do in their elections. But many Arabs hold negative views of the United States. If Arab governments were democratically elected and more representative of public opinion, they would thus be more anti-American. Further democratization in the Middle East would, for the foreseeable future, most likely generate Islamist governments less inclined to cooperate with the United States on important U.S. policy goals, including military basing rights in the region, peace with Israel, and the war on terrorism.

Arabs in general do not have a problem with democracy, although some Islamist ideologues do. The 2003 Pew Global Attitudes Project asked people in a number of Arab countries whether "democracy is a Western way of doing things that would not work here." Strong majorities of those surveyed in Kuwait (83 percent), Jordan (68 percent), and the Palestinian territories (53 percent) said democracy would work where they lived. Small minorities (16 percent of Kuwaitis, 25 percent of Jordanians, and 38 percent of Palestinians) thought it would not. According to a 2002 poll conducted by Zogby International, most of the people surveyed in Egypt, Kuwait, Lebanon, Saudi Arabia, and the United Arab Emirates (UAE) held a favorable attitude toward U.S. freedom and democracy, even while viewing U.S. policy in the Arab world very unfavorably. According to the same poll, respondents in seven Arab countries ranked "civil/personal rights" as the most important political issue, before health care, the Palestinian issue, and economic questions.

These pro-democracy views are borne out by behavior on the ground. Voter turnout in Arab states for legitimate elections is regularly very high. Some 53 percent of registered Iraqis voted in the January 2005 parliamentary election, despite threats of violence and the boycott by most Sunni Arabs, who make up about 20 percent of the population. Algerians turned out at a rate of 58 percent for their presidential election in April 2004. Official figures put Palestinian turnout for the January 2005 presidential election at 73 percent, despite Hamas' refusal to participate. Turnout in Kuwaiti parliamentary elections is regularly more than 70 percent. And 76 percent of eligible Yemeni voters cast their ballots in the 2003 legislative election. Although there certainly are antidemocratic forces in the Arab world, and some Arab elections have been characterized by low turnout or low voter registration, Arabs are generally enthusiastic about voting and elections. Arguments that Arab "culture" bars democracy simply do not stand up to scrutiny.

The problem with promoting democracy in the Arab world is not that Arabs do not like democracy; it is that Washington probably would not like the governments Arab democracy would produce. Assuming that democratic Arab governments would better represent the opinions of their people than do the current Arab regimes, democratization of the Arab world should produce more anti–U.S. foreign policies. In a February–March 2003 poll conducted in six Arab countries by Zogby International and the Anwar Sadat Chair for Peace and Development at the University of Maryland, overwhelming majorities of those surveyed held either a very unfavorable or a somewhat unfavorable attitude toward the United States. The Lebanese viewed the United States most favorably, with 32 percent of respondents holding a very favorable or a somewhat favorable view of the United States. Only 4 percent of Saudi respondents said the same.

The war in Iraq–which was imminent or ongoing as the poll was conducted—surely affected these numbers. But these statistics are not that different from those gathered by less comprehensive polls conducted both before and after the war. In a Gallup poll in early 2002, strong majorities of those surveyed in Jordan (62 percent) and Saudi Arabia (64 percent) rated the United States unfavorably. Only in Lebanon did positive views of the United States roughly balance negative views. In a Zogby International poll conducted in seven Arab countries at about the same time, unfavorable ratings of the United States ranged from 48 percent in Kuwait to 61 percent in Jordan, 76 percent in Egypt, and 87 percent in Saudi Arabia and the UAE. One year after the war began, a Pew Global Attitudes poll showed that 93 percent of Jordanians and 68 percent of Moroccans had a negative attitude toward the United States.

Although it is not possible to pinpoint from poll data the precise reasons for anti-Americanism in the Arab world, there are indications that it is U.S. policy in the region, not a rejection of American ideals, that drives the sentiment. In the Zogby International-Sadat Chair poll of February-March 2003, respondents in five of six Arab countries said that their attitudes toward the United States were based more on U.S. policy than on U.S. values. Forty-six percent of Egyptians polled identified U.S. policy as the source of their feelings, compared with 43 percent who stressed American values. No fewer than 58 percent of respondents in Jordan, Lebanon, Morocco, and Saudi Arabia also emphasized their opposition to U.S. policy.

In 2004, Arab publics were particularly cynical about Washington's policy of democracy promotion in the Middle East. In a May 2004

Zogby International-Sadat Chair poll, only in Lebanon did a substantial segment of the population surveyed (44 percent) believe that promoting democracy was an important motive for the Iraq war—compared with 25 percent of Jordanians and less than 10 percent of those in Morocco, Saudi Arabia, Egypt, and the UAE. The majority of people polled in most of the countries thought the war was motivated by Washington's desire to control oil, protect Israel, and weaken the Muslim world. And in a less extensive Pew Global Attitudes survey, also conducted in 2004, only 17 percent of Moroccans and 11 percent of Jordanians thought that the U.S. war on terrorism was a sincere effort, rather than a cover for other goals. And no poll is needed to show that U.S. policy on Arab-Israeli questions is very unpopular in the Arab world.

There is no doubt that public opinion can be a fickle thing. Anti–U.S. feelings in the Arab world could change markedly with events. But although it is possible that Arab anti-Americanism would decline if Washington no longer supported authoritarian Arab governments, there is little data to test the assertion, and anecdotal evidence suggests otherwise. Syrians, for example, do not hold strongly positive views of the United States, even though the Bush administration opposes the government in Damascus. Apparently, the United States is unpopular in the Arab world because of the full range of its policies, not simply because it supports authoritarian governments.

Even if democratization could reduce anti-Americanism, there is no guarantee that such a reduction would yield pro-American governments. Anecdotal evidence certainly seems to indicate, for example, that the public in non-Arab Iran has a better impression of the United States than does the Iranian government. The Iranian public's more pro-American stance did not, however, translate into votes for the candidate favoring rapprochement with the United States in the second round of the recent presidential election.

History also indicates that legitimate democratic elections in Arab states would most likely benefit Islamists. In all recent Arab elections, they have emerged as the government's leading political opposition, and in many of them they have done very well. In Morocco, the new Justice and Development Party, an overtly Islamist party, took 42 of the 325 seats in the parliamentary elections of 2002, its first contest. (Only two long-established parties, the Socialist Union of Popular Forces and

the Independence Party, won more seats: 50 and 48, respectively.) The same year, in Bahrain, Islamist candidates took between 19 and 21 of the 40 seats in parliament (depending on how observers classified some independent candidates). This success came even though the major Shia political group boycotted the elections, protesting changes in the constitution.

In the 2003 parliamentary election in Yemen, the Yemeni Reform Group (Islah), a combination of Islamist and tribal elements, won 46 of the 301 seats and now forms the opposition. That year, Islamists combined to win 17 of the 50 seats in the Kuwaiti parliament, where they form the dominant ideological bloc. In the 2003 parliamentary election in Jordan, held after three postponements and a change in the electoral laws to benefit independent candidates, the Muslim Brotherhood's political party won 17 of 110 seats and independent Islamists took another 3 seats, forming the major opposition bloc.

So far this year, the pattern has repeated itself. In the Saudi municipal elections, informal Islamist tickets won 6 of the 7 seats in Riyadh and swept the elections in Jidda and Mecca. Candidates backed by Sunni Islamists also won control of the municipal councils in a number of towns in the Eastern Province. In the Iraqi parliamentary elections, the list backed by Shia Grand Ayatollah Ali Sistani won 140 of the 275 seats, compared with 45 seats for the two more-secular Arab lists, headed by then Prime Minister Ayad Allawi and then President Ghazi al-Yawar, and 75 seats for the unified Kurdish list, which is not particularly Islamist.

In the Palestinian territories, Mahmoud Abbas, of the nationalist Fatah Party, won a convincing victory in the 2005 presidential elections, but that is partly because Hamas did not field a candidate. Hamas has, however, performed strongly in recent municipal elections: in the West Bank in December 2004, it took control of 7 town councils compared with Fatah's 12, and earlier this year in Gaza, Hamas captured control of 7 of the 10 town councils, as well as two-thirds of the seats. Some observers predict that Hamas will outpoll Fatah in the upcoming Palestinian parliamentary elections, which could be one reason that Abbas has postponed them.

The trend is clear: Islamists of various hues score well in free elections. In countries where a governing party dominates or where the king opposes political Islam, Islamists run second and form the opposition. Only in Morocco, where more secular, leftist parties have a long history and an established presence, and in Lebanon, where the Christian-Muslim dynamic determines electoral politics, did organized non-Islamist political blocs, independent of the government, compete with Islamist forces. The pattern does not look like it is about to change. According to the 2004 Zogby International-Sadat Chair poll, pluralities of those surveyed in Jordan, Saudi Arabia, and the UAE said the clergy should play a greater role in their political systems. Fifty percent of Egyptians polled said the clerics should not dictate the political system, but as many as 47 percent supported a greater role for them. Only in Morocco and Lebanon did anticlerical sentiment dominate pro-clerical feelings—51 percent to 33 percent in Morocco and 50 percent to 28 percent in Lebanon. The more democratic the Arab world gets, the more likely it is that Islamists will come to power. Even if those Islamists come to accept the rules of democracy and reject political violence, they are unlikely to support U.S. foreign policy goals in the region.

THE LONG HAUL

The Bush administration's push for democracy in the Arab world is unlikely to have much effect on anti-American terrorism emanating from there; it could in fact help bring to power governments much less cooperative on a whole range of issues—including the war on terrorism—than the current regimes. Unfortunately, there is no good alternative at this point to working with the authoritarian Arab governments that are willing to work with the United States.

If Washington insists on promoting democracy in the Arab world, it should learn from the various electoral experiences in the region. Where there are strongly rooted non-Islamist parties, as in Morocco, the Islamists have a harder time dominating the field. The same is true in non-Arab Turkey, where the Islamist political party has moderated its message over time to contend with the power of the secular army and with well-established, more secular parties. Likewise, the diverse confessional mix of voters in Lebanon will probably prevent Hezbollah and other Islamists from dominating elections there. Conversely, where non-Islamist political forces have been suppressed, as in Saudi Arabia and Bahrain, Islamist parties and candidates can command the political field. Washington should take no com-

fort from the success of ruling parties in Algeria, Egypt, and Yemen over Islamist challengers: once stripped of their patronage and security apparatus, ruling parties do not fare very well in democratic transitional elections.

The United States must focus on pushing Arab governments to make political space for liberal, secular, leftist, nationalist, and other non-Islamist parties to set down roots and mobilize voters. Washington should support those groups that are more likely to accept U.S. foreign policy and emulate U.S. political values. The most effective way to demonstrate that support is to openly pressure Arab regimes when they obstruct the political activity of more liberal groups—as the administration did with Egypt after the jailing of the liberal reformers Saad Eddin Ibrahim and Ayman Nour, and as it should do with Saudi Arabia regarding the May sentencing of peaceful political activists to long prison terms. But Washington will also need to drop its focus on prompt elections in Arab countries where no strong, organized alternative to Islamist parties exists—even at the risk of disappointing Arab liberals by being more cautious about their electoral prospects than they are.

Administration officials, including President Bush, have often stated that the transition to democracy in the Arab world will be difficult and that Americans should not expect quick results. Yet whenever the Bush administration publicly defends democratization, it cites a familiar litany of Muslim-world elections—those in Afghanistan, Iraq, Lebanon, the Palestinian territories, and Saudi Arabia—as evidence that the policy is working. It will take years, however, for non-Islamist political forces to be ready to compete for power in these elections, and it is doubtful that this or any other U.S. administration will have the patience to see the process through. If it cannot show that patience, Washington must realize that its democratization policy will lead to Islamist domination of Arab politics. It is not only the focus on elections that is troubling in the administration's democracy initiative in the Arab world. Also problematic is the unjustified confidence that Washington has in its ability to predict, and even direct, the course of politics in other countries. No administration official would sign on, at least not in public, to the naive view that Arab democracy will produce governments that will always cooperate with the United States. Yet Washington's democracy advocates seem to assume that Arab democratic transitions, like the recent democratic transitions in eastern Europe, Latin America, and East Asia, will lead to regimes that support, or at least do not impede, the broad range of U.S. foreign policy interests. They do not appreciate that in those regimes, liberalism prevailed because its great ideological competitor, communism, was thoroughly discredited, whereas the Arab world offers a real ideological alternative to liberal democracy: the movement that claims as its motto "Islam is the solution." Washington's hubris should have been crushed in Iraq, where even the presence of 140,000 American troops has not allowed politics to proceed according to the U.S. plan. Yet the Bush administration displays little of the humility or the patience that such a daunting task demands. If the United States really does see the democracy-promotion initiative in the Arab world as a "generational challenge," the entire nation will have to learn these traits.

KEY TERMS

Fundamentalism   A militant and exclusivist interpretation of religion, one that stresses a return to the so-called fundamentals of the faith.

Mujahideen   Muslim "freedom" fighters, frequently supporting Islamist causes. In Afghanistan, fighters resisting Soviet forces.

Religious Reformism   The longing to return to a purer form of social and religious organization.

FURTHER READINGS

Halliday, Fred. *Islam and the Myth of Confrontation*. New York: I.B. Tauris, 2003.

Hefner, Robert W., ed. *Remaking Muslim Politics: Pluralism, Contestation, Democratization*. Princeton, N.J.: Princeton University Press, 2005.

Marty, Martin E., and R. Scott Appleby, eds. *The Fundamentalism Project*, Vols. 1–5. Chicago: University of Chicago Press, 1991–1995.

Said, Edward W. *Covering Islam: How the Media and the Experts Determine How We See the Rest of the World*. New York: Pantheon Books, 1981.

Sigmund, Paul. *Liberation Theology at the Crossroads*. New York: Oxford University Press, 1990.

Tétreault, Marry Anne, and Robert A. Denemark, eds. *Gods, Guns, and Globalization: Religious Radicalism and International Political Economy*. Boulder, Colo.: Lynne Rienner Publishers, 2004.

WEB LINKS

Fundamentalism:
http://religiousmovements.lib.virginia.edu/profiles/listalpha.htm

The Pew Global Attitudes Project:
http://pewglobal.org

September 11 and Aftermath: International Resources on the Web:
www.september11news.com

World Religions:
www.mnsu.edu/emuseum/cultural/religion

CHAPTER 17

CITIZENSHIP AND POLITICAL COMMUNITY

Citizenship is a key notion in democratic thought and practice. It defines the relationship between the individual and the state as well as the relationship among members of a community. As citizens, the rights and obligations that define our political community shape our identities. In the past twenty years, the issue of citizenship has become an important area of debate for political scientists, theorists, and ordinary citizens. Questions regarding the condition of being a citizen and the responsibilities and rights this status entails are hotly contested in contemporary politics. Our understanding of **citizenship**, that is, a person's membership in an organized **political community**, is being challenged by a number of different forces, including globalization, nationalism, international migration, and multiculturalism. This chapter provides students with a general understanding of the concept of citizenship and addresses some of the key ideas and principles that are contained in the concept of citizenship. It also introduces some of the recent debates on the meaning and scope of citizenship in the era of globalization.

THE ORIGINS OF CITIZENSHIP

The notion of citizenship has changed over time, and its significance has also varied in different historical periods.[1] Citizenship as social membership and participation has its origins in the classical Greek city-state or *polis*. Many Greek city-states, particularly Athens, developed democratic institutions and values. At the height of Athenian democracy in the middle of the fifth century B.C., adult male citizens were eligible to hold office and were considered equal before the law. They debated and voted on key issues of the state in the assembly. The philosophical works of Plato and Aristotle deliberated on the benefits and corresponding duties of the citizen in the *polis*. Aristotle defined a citizen as one who "shares in the administration of justice, and in [public] offices." Greek citizenship, therefore, stressed a person's duty and responsibility to participate in the public life of the city-state and to look after its interests. It is important to note, however, that not everyone in the city-state was a citizen. The ownership of property was a central precondition for the status of citizenship. Moreover, women, slaves, and foreigners were excluded from full citizenship; therefore, they could not vote or hold public office.

During the Roman Empire, citizenship was at first limited to male residents of the city of Rome. Later, by A.D. 202, citizenship was extended to all free male inhabitants of conquered territories incorporated within the empire. The growth of jurisprudence under the Roman Empire helped transform citizenship from a political status to a legal status, giving legally defined rights and protections to all male subjects of the empire. The so-called citizens, however, were primarily subjects of the emperors and did not participate in the affairs of government. Roman citizenship bestowed on the individual legal protections of his person, property, and rights and immunity from torture or violence in the trying of any case against him.

The development of modern citizenship as a formal-legal status is tied to the transition from feudalism to capitalism and the rise of the nation-state. Capitalism, and the liberal ideas that legitimized it, gave rise to a new class of merchants and entrepreneurs primarily located in medieval city-states whose desire was not to achieve the "good life" or a "moral society" but rather to achieve personal wealth and advancement in this new marketplace.[2] Individual freedoms and rights protecting private ownership lent support to this new form of economic life. In the sixteenth and seventeenth centuries, the nation-state became the primary locus within which citizenship was expressed and practised. With the extension of the notion of citizenship to the national level, national identities and solidarities became the primary form of collective membership.

The French Revolution was a pivotal event in the development of national citizenship. The revolution was important because it linked the idea of citizenship rights with the principles of political equality and social fraternity. The Declaration of the Rights of Man and of the Citizen coupled the notion of individual freedoms with principles of universality, equality, and community.[3] Citizenship held by all males, in contrast with earlier conceptions, conformed to this egalitarian ideal. The Declaration also contributed to the development of national citizenship by recognizing the sovereignty of the nation. As Turner explains, "The French Revolution contributed to an important institutional development of the state as a separate entity with specific subjects called citizens."[4]

Today, the nation-state continues to be the predominant community of political membership in the contemporary world, and modern citizenship is generally understood in the context of the nation-state. As Hannah Arendt wrote, a citizen "is by definition a citizen among citizens of a country among countries. His rights and duties must be defined and limited, not only by those of his fellow citizens, but also by the boundaries of a territory . . ."[5]

RIGHTS-BASED CITIZENSHIP

The notion of citizenship in twentieth-century social and political theory has traditionally been understood within a liberal-democratic model of rights and entitlements. This conception of citizenship is closely associated with the work of British sociologist T.H. Marshall, who defined citizenship as a status conferred to individuals who enjoy certain important rights and entitlements as members of a community. The enjoyment of rights, therefore, is the defining feature of societal membership in this conception of citizenship. According to Marshall, citizenship comprises three types of rights: civil, political, and social. Civil rights are institutionalized in legal doctrines and are meant to protect and uphold the individual freedoms of members of a political community, especially vis-à-vis the state. In the United States civil rights, such as the equal treatment of all individuals before the law with respect to the enjoyment of life, liberty, and property, are guaranteed under the U.S. Constitution. In Canada, similar rights are codified in the Charter of Rights and Freedoms. Political rights typically refer to the right to vote and the right to hold or seek political office. These rights allow individuals to participate in the exercise of political power in their polity. Social rights of citizenship are closely associated with the welfare state of the post-war era. These rights guarantee a citizen a certain standard of living to share fully in the "social heritage of the community."[6]

Marshall's theory was based on his historical analysis of the expansion of citizenship rights in Britain in the last three centuries. Drawing on his analysis of the experience of

British working men, Marshall put forward an "evolutionary" perspective that regarded the development of citizenship rights as the natural and inevitable consequence of societies evolving into higher and more complex forms, specifically from feudal societies to capitalist societies. Citizenship rights developed in three historical stages. In eighteenth-century Britain, civil rights such as religious freedom and freedom of speech were granted to all male members of the community. In the late nineteenth and early twentieth centuries, political rights, specifically the franchise, were extended to all citizens, not just property owners. Once civil and political rights were secured, citizens were able to mobilize for social rights. Social rights of citizenship emerged with the development of the welfare state in the twentieth century. A central feature of Marshall's theory is that the development and expansion of citizenship rights (especially social rights) occurred in order to reduce class inequalities and conflict resulting from capitalism.

It is important to note, however, that the expansion of political and social rights in Britain and in other liberal democracies was at first circumscribed to white males. Certain segments of society, such as women and visible minorities, would gain citizenship rights later through political struggle. In Canada, women lobbied for and won the right to vote in the provincial elections of Manitoba, Saskatchewan, and Alberta in 1916 and in federal elections in 1920. Canadians of Japanese origins were granted the right to vote in provincial elections in 1949 while Aboriginal peoples won the right to vote in federal elections in 1960. In the United States, the civil rights movement of the 1960s strove to abolish the status of African Americans as "second-class citizens" and the barriers that prevented them from exercising their political and civil rights. Discrimination in voting would end with the Voting Rights Act of 1965. These examples of exclusion reveal that the granting of citizenship rights was not always, as Marshall described, a peaceful or evolutionary process; rather, these rights were fought for and won by several groups in society through political struggle.

Limitations of the Rights-Based Model

Marshall's rights-based model of citizenship has been criticized on a number of fronts. Several scholars argue that Marshall's evolutionary theory describes only the British experience with citizenship and therefore does not capture the historical development of rights in other countries. Moreover, it does not take into account the different traditions of citizenship found in different countries. Turner's comparative research distinguished between active and passive forms of citizenship among Western countries. Active citizenship, found in countries with a history of revolutionary struggle such as France and the United States, conceptualizes the citizen as "an active political agent" who has duties and responsibilities to the political community. Passive citizenship, on the other hand, which is found in Germany and Britain, regards the citizen as "merely a subject of an absolute authority," whereby individuals claim rights and entitlements due to them as members of a political community.[7] Turner also found that there existed private or public forms of citizenship in these countries, depending on whether state intervention in social spheres is regarded in a favourable or in a negative light. In the United States, emphasis on the rights of the individual and suspicion of state intervention has relegated the private sphere, that is, civil society and the market, as the primary site of citizenship activity. Conversely, the strong **state tradition** in France has led to a public form of citizenship in that country.

While Turner's typology rightfully recognizes that the construction of citizenship takes many forms across different countries, his analysis is limited to Western nations. His research, which links citizenship to Western traditions, ignores the fact that different notions of citizenship exist in non-Western societies. For example, in post-colonial states, family ties and kinship relationships continue to be the focal points for political loyalty and organization. Moreover, social, political, and civil rights in countries like Saudi Arabia and Jordan hinge on the familial position of the individual citizen.[8] Citizenship, therefore, can take numerous different forms depending on a country's unique social and cultural heritage. Another limitation of Turner's typology is that it does not recognize the existence of more than one form of citizenship within one country. Segments of the population, like immigrants and minority groups, can be denied certain citizenship rights or do not have the means to exercise their rights as members of the political community. For example, African Americans in the United States and the "**underclass**" in Britain practise a passive form of citizenship due to their political and economic disempowerment in their society. As Davis explains, "Gender, sexuality, age and ability as well as ethnicity and class are important factors in determining the relationship of people to their communities and states."[9]

Feminist scholars and activists argue that the model ignores gender differences in the experience of citizenship; the model wrongly assumes citizenship rights are equally available to all members of a political community. Feminist research on citizenship reveals how contested issues of sexuality and reproduction undermine women's ability to participate as citizens in public life.[10] Moreover, while women have gained access to some political rights, they generally participate less than men in most political activities, such as running for office, because of institutional, cultural, and social barriers. Researchers examining race and ethnicity make similar observations, arguing that minority groups often face numerous obstacles in realizing full democratic citizenship. Feminist critics argue that Marshall's rights-based model is built around the individual rights of men within a class-differentiated society, ignoring other sources of political and social struggles such as those involving race, ethnicity, and gender.

The issues of race and immigration have taken centre stage in the debate on citizenship, and touch on all aspects of citizenship—civil, political, and social. Current struggles and debates focus on the right to enter and/or the right to remain in a particular country. The right of ethnic minorities and immigrants to enter and settle in a new community oftentimes depends on the particular laws and regulations of both the country of origin and the country where they are living. For example, some countries do not allow or recognize dual citizenship, thereby forcing immigrants to renounce the citizenship of their country of origin. Sometimes, members of some minority groups (such as Turks and Iranians) choose not to forego their original citizenship, fearing that they would not be able to visit their relatives in their country of origin.[11] This limits the political and social rights they have in their new country.

Countries have also adopted various inclusionary and exclusionary criteria for citizenship status constructed along racial, ethnic, class, or gender divisions. For example, in Germany citizenship is granted not on the basis of *ius soli*—by place of birth—but rather is granted to an individual on the principle of *ius sanguinis*, that is, if born of German parents. Foreigners and their children can be naturalized only after they have established residency in Germany for at least eight years. Immigration policies also determine the parameters of citizenship. For instance, many countries adopt immigration legislation that sets up ". . . ideological, often racist constructions of boundaries which allow unrestricted immigration to some and block it completely to others."[12] Racial or national quotas are at times used to prevent certain minority groups from settling in a country. Sometimes these quotas can be overridden if immigrants show proof of sizeable bank accounts. In Canada, immigration policy is governed by certain objectives that are laid out in the Immigration Act. One of these objectives is the promotion of economic development. To meet this objective, the Canadian government developed the category of "business immigrants" under which immigrants can apply and qualify to become permanent residents of Canada. The right of entry of individuals under this category depends on their ability to make a sizeable investment in Canada once an immigrant visa has been issued. In this case, access to citizenship rights is contingent on an immigrant's financial means rather than any universal sense of justice or equality. Several analysts argue that the practice of admitting immigrants who can contribute a certain amount of capital to the receiving country essentially "commodifies" citizenship. Other conditions attached to the right of entry to a country also undermine the social rights of immigrants. For example, immigrants frequently have to agree that they and any members of their families will not claim any welfare benefits from the state. This is the case in Germany where immigrants are required to sustain themselves and their families for at least eight years before attaining citizenship status. These issues, and the struggles that accompany them, fall outside Marshall's right-based notion of citizenship.

Nevertheless, Marshall's research continues to influence today's conception of citizenship, which is understood as a collection of rights linked to the individual, based on the fundamental principles of liberty, equality, and universalism. However, in recent years, a number of theorists have rejected Marshall's rights-based model on several grounds. Proponents of civic republicanism contend that Marshall's model places too much emphasis on rights and not enough on the duties and responsibilities attached to citizenship that help generate civic virtues and strong civic identities. Cultural pluralists challenge the individual-rights conception of citizenship, arguing that it does not recognize cultural or ethnic identities and group rights. While the former approach regards citizenship as a political activity, the second approach regards citizenship as a form of identity. We now turn to a brief discussion on these two alternative conceptions of citizenship.

MULTICULTURAL CITIZENSHIP AND THE POLITICS OF IDENTITY

An important issue in the citizenship debate that has emerged in multicultural societies is how to reconcile universal citizenship, which requires equal treatment, with group-based differences, which require special treatment. In the past, the balancing act was between the rights of the individual versus the interests of the state. Today, the challenge of multiculturalism is how to balance the civil and political rights of the individual citizen with the social and cultural rights of different communities in a given society. Some social theorists argue that certain group rights should be created and that exceptions to laws and norms should be allowed in an effort to accommodate diversity.

Proponents of the multicultural citizenship perspective are critical of the individualistic conception of citizenship because it ignores differences among people in multicultural or pluralistic societies. The "citizenship-as-identity" approach contends that so-called universal citizenship marginalizes and suppresses social and cultural differences because it imposes a standard that inhibits minority groups from living their lives as members of a majority. Many analysts argue that people's fundamental identities and solidarities are attached to a variety of communities that are not defined by the territorial boundaries of a nation but are based on identity, gender, class, religion, and ethnicity.[13] The argument here is that the emphasis on the individual in the modern conception of citizenship ignores the collective affiliations and commitments that people maintain with their cultural communities. Multiculturalists, like Will Kymlicka, argue that social unity in multicultural countries like Canada and Belgium not only rests on liberal principles of justice but also is contingent on the recognition and accommodation of "deep diversity." "Differentiated citizenship" or "multicultural citizenship" would place value on minority rights, including cultural rights, rights of representation, and in some instances the right to self-government. Within this framework, Quebec language laws and cultural policies are justified because they strive to elaborate and protect a collective identity. In this conception of citizenship, members of certain groups would be incorporated into the broader political community as not only individuals, but also members of their particular cultural and social groups.

What does "differentiated citizenship" imply in practical terms? Proponents of this perspective are in favour of policies and institutional mechanisms that recognize and represent the perspectives of groups that are disadvantaged or oppressed. This could mean greater access and input on the part of disadvantaged groups in decision-making processes as well as assigning veto power on specific policies that directly impact a particular group; for example, reproductive rights for women or the development and use of reservation land for Aboriginal communities.[14] These practices would ensure group representation and therefore enhance the legitimacy of decision-making processes and outcomes in liberal democracies.

CIVIL SOCIETY THEORY AND ACTIVE CITIZENSHIP

In this model, citizenship is regarded less as a legal status and more as a mode of political activity and participation. The emphasis here is on the deliberative or participatory dimension of membership. This understanding of citizenship traces back to the ancient Greeks, and was later elaborated by modern political thinkers including Machiavelli, Rousseau, and de Tocqueville. Aristotle described the citizen as one who participates in the affairs of the state for the common good of the polis. The goal of debate and deliberation in the state's affairs was to ensure a "proper quality of character among the members." De Tocqueville also wrote of how citizen participation strengthened the character of individual members and fostered a commitment to the common good. Displaced in the past by liberal models concerned with the rights and status of the individual, this conception of citizenship has been revived in the past three decades.

Today, proponents of this model, such as civic republicans and participatory democrats, argue that we should abandon the notion and practice of passive citizenship denoted by the rights-based model in favour of a perspective that views the citizen as a political being actively involved in shaping a shared collective identity. The defining features of citizenship are therefore communality and participation.[15] By participating in political life, citizens learn about solidarity, social responsibility, and the common good. Civil society theorists argue that these virtues are best learned not in the market but rather in the voluntary associations of civil society, such as families, churches, unions, neighbourhood associations, and community organizations.[16]

POST-NATIONAL CITIZENSHIP AND THE CASE OF THE EUROPEAN UNION

As mentioned earlier in the chapter, the concept and practice of citizenship has been and continues to be associated with the nation-state. However, in recent years, a number of social theorists and political activists are claiming that citizenship is being practised and experienced beyond the territorial boundaries of the nation-state. These analysts argue national citizenship is declining in importance in what is becoming an increasingly "post-national world."[17] The rise of transnational political activity in the areas of environmental protection and human rights displaces the nation as the only possible site of identity and commitment. The transnational activism of non-governmental organizations and grassroots social movements suggests the possibility of a new form of "global citizenship."

The definition of rights outlined in the Marshallian model of citizenship is constantly being challenged as material and social conditions change. Several analysts argue that a new generation of rights is emerging, articulated, and fought for at the international level. Global forces are in the process of creating new rights that cut across all cultures and affirm the inherent worth of every human being. While the nation was the primary arena for the attainment and protection of "first" and "second generation" rights (i.e., civil, political, and social rights), international institutions and arenas are the sites in which third- and fourth-generation rights (i.e., group and cultural rights) are being created around the issues of environmental protection, human rights, peace, and development. For example, cross-cultural negotiations and mobilization of women's organizations during the 1995 Fourth World Conference on Women in Beijing, China, led to an international political consensus on women's reproductive rights. The international agenda on environmental protection and sustainable development is also providing a new conception of citizenship that embodies the rights of present and future generations to clean air and water. While it is true that strong legal and political institutions do not exist to protect these newly proposed rights, international efforts around these issues force us to consider new conceptions and practices of citizenship that go beyond territorial borders.

A large body of work is examining the possibility of post-national citizenship in the context of the European Union (EU). Several analysts contend that the national conception of citizenship in the EU is today being challenged by a number of global forces, including the internationalization of labour markets, increasing rates of migration, the creation of international political institutions like the EU, and the global discourse on human rights. The case of guest workers in Europe best illustrates how the line between citizen and noncitizen is increasingly being blurred. Guest workers are foreigners recruited by European nations to meet the labour demands of their economies. The expectation was that these workers would remain on a temporary basis, based on the needs of the national economy. Instead, guest workers have gradually been incorporated and integrated into the social and political spheres of the host country. Over time, they established permanent communities, raised families, paid taxes, and participated in welfare plans.

According to some analysts, the intensification of transnational migration is resulting in the formation of a "post-national citizenship." Soysal argues that countries are increasingly feeling the pressure to extend membership rights to migrant labourers due to the growing international demands for the protection of human rights. The intensification of transnational migration is undermining national citizenship and replacing it with a model of membership based on the premise of universal personhood and respect for human rights such as those institutionalized in international conventions like the United Nations Declaration of Human Rights. According to Soysal, "post-national citizenship" replaces nationhood with personhood and national rights with universal human rights. It transcends national and ethnic loyalties. Individuals are granted rights not because they are citizens of a nation-state but because of their membership in a transnational political community.[18]

The nature of citizenship in today's world is changing. Our traditional understanding of belonging and membership is being challenged by domestic and international forces. The political community, which was once associated with the nation-state, is being reconfigured by economic and cultural globalization, increased transnational migration, and the existence of nations without states (e.g., Quebecers and Aboriginal peoples). With the advent of supranational institutions, like the EU, the nation-state is no longer the primary focus of loyalty and allegiance. Some would argue that state citizenship is being replaced with a global conception of human rights. Others suggest that what we are witnessing is the emergence of multi-tier citizenship, with individuals participating and pledging loyalty to more than one political community. While it remains to be seen which forms of citizenship will emerge in the near future, what is certain is that they will influence the way we view rights, identity, and political representation.

ENDNOTES

1. Will Kymlicka and Wayne Norman, "Return of the Citizen: A Survey of Recent Work on Citizenship Theory," in *Theorizing Citizenship*, ed. Ronald Beiner (Albany: State University of New York Press, 1995).
2. Mary G. Dietz, "Feminism and Theories of Citizenship," in *Feminism and Politics*, ed. Anne Phillips (Oxford: Oxford University Press, 1998).
3. Bryan S. Turner, *Citizenship and Capitalism: The Debate over Reformism* (London: Allen & Unwin, 1986).
4. Ibid., 18.
5. Hannah Arendt, *Men in Dark Times* (New York: Harcourt, Brace & World, 1968).
6. T.H. Marshall, *Class, Citizenship and Social Development* (New York: Anchor, 1965).
7. Bryan Turner, "Outline of a Theory of Citizenship," *Sociology* 24 (1990): 209.
8. Nira Yuval-Davis, *Gender and Nation* (London: Sage Publications, 1997).
9. Ibid., 84.
10. Anna Shola Orloff, "Gender and the Social Rights of Citizenship: The Comparative Analysis of Gender Relations and Welfare States," *American Sociological Review* 58 (June 1993): 303–28.
11. Nira Yuval-Davis, "The Citizenship Debate: Women, the State, and Ethnic Processes," *Feminist Review*, no. 39 (1991): 58–68.
12. Ibid., 61.
13. Linda Bosniak, "Citizenship Denationalized," *Indiana Journal of Global Law Studies* 7 (2000): 447.
14. Iris Marion Young, "Polity and Group Difference," in *Feminism and Politics*, ed. Anne Phillips (Oxford: Oxford University Press, 1998).
15. See Benjamin Barber, *Strong Democracy* (Berkeley: University of California Press, 1984).
16. Kymlicka and Norman, 1995.
17. Bosniak, 2000.
18. Yasemin Soysal, *Limits of Citizenship: Migrants and Postnational Membership in Europe* (Chicago: University of Chicago Press, 1994).

READINGS

This chapter explored different conceptions of citizenship, from Marshall's rights-based perspective to alternative forms of membership that emphasize identity and participation. It also examined the possibility of a post-national citizenship in an era of globalization and international human rights. The readings selected for this chapter address alternative ways of understanding citizenship and political community that move beyond Marshall's right-based framework. Jane Mansbridge's piece, "Does Participation Make Better Citizens?" conceptualizes citizenship not as a legal status but as an activity that performs an educative function. Drawing from the classical works of a number of political theorists such as Aristotle, de Tocqueville, and John Stuart Mill, Mansbridge reveals the link between active citizenship and character development of individuals in a political community. Citizen participation is said to enhance our intellectual capabilities, promote a more virtuous character, and enhance our commitment to the broader social good. In practical terms, citizen participation also helps us develop and articulate our interests or perspectives on a given issue. Mansbridge laments that in recent years, the educative function of active citizenship has been underexamined due to difficulties in measuring the impact of citizen participation on "self-development." The practice of democratic participation has also dwindled in recent years due to an unfavourable political climate. In the end, Mansbridge suggests that more research is needed to better understand the educative functions of active citizenship.

The second reading is "Postnational Citizenship: Reconfiguring the Familiar Terrain" by Yasemin NuhogUlu Soysal. In this article, NuhogUlu Soysal examines how "multilevel" politics is altering notions of identity and rights as well as the practice of citizenship, and explores the possibility of a postnational citizenship. She uses the term "postnational citizenship" to capture recent changes in the discourses of citizenship and identity brought about by transnational processes and institutions. Soysal argues that the emergence of postnational citizenship does not mean the demise of the importance of the nation-state; rather, it recognizes the importance of local, national, and international institutions as sites for mobilizing identities that are not tied to national territorial boundaries. Post-national citizenship is distinguished from cosmopolitanism and globalization, which advance a universal and homogenous identity. Soysal asserts that while post-national citizenship appeals to international discourses and institutions of human rights, it continues to recognize the diversity of identities and interests.

DOES PARTICIPATION MAKE BETTER CITIZENS?

Jane Mansbridge

Participation does make better citizens. I believe it, but I can't prove it. And neither can anyone else. The kinds of subtle changes in character that come about slowly, from active, powerful participation in democratic decisions cannot easily be measured with the blunt instruments of social science. Those who have actively participated in democratic governance, however, often feel that the experience has changed them. And those who observe the active participation of others often believe that they see its long-term effects on the citizens' character.

The earliest theories about the effects of participation began in America with de Tocqueville; our own generation's version began in America with Arnold Kaufman on "participatory democracy." Subsequent theorists often assumed that their ideas derived from a long line of such theorizing, stretching farther back, often to the Greeks. In this, however, they were wrong. Although the idea that active participation in political life helps develop human faculties has been in some sense available in Western thought since the fifth century B.C., and is implicit in or derived from, certain arguments in Aristotle, Machiavelli, and Rousseau, none of these theorists explicitly made this claim. Conclusions to the contrary stem primarily from our own generation's growing conviction that human development is an important goal in the practice of democracy. That conviction, I believe, is built most heavily on our own experiences, although it appropriated threads from earlier philosophers.

ORIGINS

In a section of the *Politics* that has had extraordinary influence over the ages, Aristotle wrote that the end, or goal, of the state includes ensuring a "proper quality of character among the members." Any true polis "must devote itself to the end of encouraging goodness."[1] But Aristotle did not say anywhere that participating in the decisions of the state makes an individual develop character, justice, or goodness. The context of his writing implies instead that living under the laws of a good polity helps develop the justice, goodness, and proper quality of character that he sought. Other sections of Aristotle's *Politics* demonstrate how the participation of the man in a decision may make the decision better. Again, however, the text says nothing about how that participation may make the many [*sic*] better. The truncated section of the *Politics* on education raises the tantalizing question, "Which way of life is more desirable—to join with other citizens and share in the state's activity, or to live in it like an alien, absolved from the ties of political society?" Although the question's very language seems to require the first of the two choices, Aristotle concluded by seeming to recommend a version of the second. He never discussed the potential educative effects of "sharing in the state's activity."[2]

Aristotle's description of citizenship as deliberating and judging, and of taking turns in office as requiring consideration of "the interest of others"[3] provided material from which later thinkers could construct a theory of the educative value of participation. But he himself did not explicitly draw such modern conclusions.

As Hanna Pitkin points out, Machiavelli's "vision of manly Citizenship" placed a high value on internal political conflict, which brought productive results if it was "ended by debating" and "law," as in Rome, rather than "by fighting" with the result of "exile and death," as in Florence.

Machiavelli too has sometimes been thought to argue that "shared responsibility for the *nomos*" and an enlarged understanding of the self and one's interests, can be achieved only "through the actual experience of citizen participation."[4] Machiavelli was undoubtedly concerned with *educazione* in a broad sense.[5] He also undoubtedly believed that political experience

(e.g., the experience of being overrun by the enemy when one has not held to one's first principles) taught people valuable lessons. But he does not seem to have said explicitly that participation in decision-making, through debate and deliberation for example, changed participants either for the better or for the worse.

Rousseau agrees with Aristotle that the job of the civil state was to make men just. In his own post-Christian understanding, however, this justice required an internal moral transformation, "substituting justice for instinct" in man's conduct, and "giving his actions the morality they had formally lacked." In the transformation, "the voice of duty" supplants "appetite," reason supplants inclination, the faculties are "ennobled," the soul "uplifted,"[6] and a "partial and moral existence" replaces the independent existence conferred by nature.[7] In the good civil state, human beings can, by genuinely willing what is good for all, take up a new identity as part of a larger whole, and experience the laws that result not as coercion, but as emanations from the better part of their beings, which Rousseau identified both with reason and with the good of the whole.

What generates this transformative development of the faculties? First, good laws.[8] Second, a civil religion that will promote social unity and make each citizen "love his duty."[9] Finally, perhaps, the natural healthy instincts of humanity, which, when not subverted by bad institutions, lead human beings to develop in a way that is best for them. Reading the *Social Contract* carefully, I see no passage in which Rousseau says that participation in making political decisions will engender or even maintain this transformation.

Rousseau, to be sure, believed deeply in participation. Without participation, the citizens are not free[10] and the state is dead.[11] More crucially, willing the law oneself transforms the character of those who engage in the process. But this will does not entail deliberation, nor most of what we mean today by political participation. It means instead recognizing as an individual what is in the common good (not conceived as a problematic exercise for those of good will) and acting upon that recognition. Rousseau never stated that the act of making decisions in concert with others develops the faculties by directing each individual's will to the common interest. Instead, he explicitly opposed political deliberation.[12]

It was Alexis de Tocqueville, returning from America, who first claimed that participation in the process of governing developed individual character. De Tocqueville's claim derived not only from the intellectual currents of his time that exalted "the development of the faculties" but also from his own experience of the New England town meeting. Town meetings, he concluded, "are to liberty what primary schools are to science: they bring it within people's reach, they teach men how to use and how to enjoy it."[13]

The teaching takes place when a citizen "takes part in every occurrence in the place" and practices the art of government in the small sphere within his reach.[14] It develops, in de Tocqueville's description, a rather conservative character, with a taste for incrementalism, order, and the balance of powers, knowing one's duties and the extent of one's rights.

Like Rousseau, however, de Tocqueville is also interested in developing commitment to the common good. In town meeting democracy he sees "the passions that commonly embroil society change their character," a change he explains by the way power is distributed so as to interest the greatest possible number of persons in the common weal.[15]

Without explicitly spelling out the mechanism, de Tocqueville suggests that the transformation he sees derives primarily from acts that make a town or a nation one's "own." Power produces ownership, with its attendant responsibility. He writes, for example, that a centralized state will make a man "indifferent to the fate of the spot which he inhabits," and lead him to look upon the "condition of his village, the police of his street, the repairs of the church or parsonage" as things that "do not concern him and are unconnected with himself." Uninvolved in deciding about these matters, he will not develop "the spirit of ownership nor any ideas about improvement."

Along with ownership through power, de Tocqueville's description of voluntary associations suggest[s] another dynamic by which individuals make the common weal their own. Here he writes that "feelings and opinions are recruited, the heart is enlarged, and the human mind is developed only by the reciprocal influence of men upon one another."[16] By an "enlarged" heart he may well have meant one that took the common good into account, by "feelings and ideas" the emotions of solidarity, and by "the reciprocal influence of men upon one another" the kinds of deliberation and interaction that occur in town meetings as well as

in voluntary associations. Such an interpretation fits my own analysis of what often happens in town meetings and other collectives, but as a child of my times, I stress the deliberative features more than de Tocqueville.

John Stuart Mill, influenced by de Tocqueville, von Humbolt, and the German Romantics' preoccupation with the "right and duty of self-development,"[17] was the first to make the effect of participation on individual character a major argument for democracy. In *On Liberty*, Mill argues that liberty produces diverse human development, and that such diverse development is good both for the individual and for society. In his conclusion he contends, critical for our discussion, that people should make their own decisions because doing so promotes self-development:

> . . . *in many cases, though individuals may not do the particular thing so well, on the average, as the officers of government, it is nevertheless desirable that it should be done by them, rather than by the government, as a means to their own mental education—a mode of strengthening their active faculties, exercising their judgment, and giving them a familiar knowledge of the subjects with which they are thus left to deal.*[18]

This passage looks forward to *On Representative Government*. Continuing his transition from private to public interest, Mill suggests in the closing pages of *On Liberty* that in another work he will discuss more fully:

> . . . *the practical part of the education of a free people, taking them out of the narrow circle of personal and family selfishness, and accustoming them to the comprehension of joint interest, the management of joint concerns—habituating them to act from public or semi-public motives, and guide their conduct by aims which unite instead of isolating them from one another.*[19]

In this promised work, *On Representative Government*, Mill specifies a little more exactly the three forms of individual development— virtue, intellectual stimulation, and activity—that he expects political participation to produce. Mill contends that political participation promotes all three capacities. His argument runs as follows: because it is the most important task of government to promote the development of its citizens,[20] and because the distribution of power has a greater influence on self-development than any other influence except the religious,[21] the ideally best form of government is one in which citizens both have "a voice" (not an equal one) in the sovereign authority and, at least occasionally, are "called upon to take an actual part in the government by the personal discharge of some public function, local or general."[22] In this way, individuals may develop an unselfish concern with the public good.

But Mill advocated individual development in unselfishness primarily for its effect on government stability, and only secondarily for the good it might do to the individual. Although he has sometimes been misinterpreted on this point, Mill's ultimate goal was a social, not an individual one.

THE SIXTIES

In the twentieth century, Mill's stress on the educative function of participation gradually faded under the impact of a more rights-oriented approach to democracy. Moreover, after World War II, democratic theorists in the United States and Britain became concerned more with preventing the other European democracies from going the way of Germany, and with congratulating themselves at having remained democratic at all, than with moving their own democracies closer to the ideal.

Yet by the 1960s, criticism of the existing forms of democracy had, at least in the United States, moved closer to home. In 1960, Arnold Kaufman coined the term "participatory democracy," arguing in an influential article that the "main justifying function of [participatory democracy] is and always has been . . . the contribution it can make to the development of human powers of thought, feelings and action."[23] Kaufman here echoes Mill's tripartite goal of developing the powers of thought, feeling, and action. Yet he specified even less clearly than Mill what precise powers he had in mind. He called instead on this point for empirical investigation: "Much empirical study is required both *to prove that participation is beneficial* (emphasis mine) and to clarify the way in which it can best be implemented in specific spheres."[24]

Kaufman was an advisor to the radical students at the University of Michigan who in 1962 drew up the Port Huron Statement. This Statement brought the term "participatory

democracy" into the language, and served as the philosophical inspiration for the New Left in the United States. Focusing on how the structure of politics in America diminished the individual self, it argued that political participation would bring people "out of isolation and into community," and would encourage "independence," a respect for others, "a sense of dignity and a willingness to accept social responsibility."[25]

The explicit changes in character that the Port Huron Statement advocated got lost as the phrase "participatory democracy" was translated into practice. Participants in the thousands of participatory collectives that sprang up around the United States in the next ten years did not justify their insistence on democratic participation by appeals to its effects on their character.[26] The practice of these collectives, however, demonstrated a strong underlying commitment—in some cases, a self-indulgent commitment—to the end of individual development.

Ten years after Kaufman's "Participatory Democracy," Carole Pateman published in Great Britain her highly influential *Participation and Democratic Theory*, also arguing that participation in democracy produces individual development. Unlike Kaufman, however, she made the final target of change not the individual but the polity. For Pateman, the goal was democracy, seen as an end in itself. Participation in realms other than the governmental developed faculties required for participating in government.[27]

Stressing the instrumental function of citizen education for public democracy allowed Pateman to be more specific than Kaufman about the kinds of individual development participation should produce. Because Pateman believed that democratic self-government required "confidence in one's ability to participate responsibly and effectively, and to control one's life and environment,"[28] she made a sense of "political efficacy" the major psychological or characterological quality that participation should develop.

In 1975, Peter Bachrach argued that participation should develop the faculty of understanding one's interest. Bachrach had previously revealed that the power of one set of interests or perspectives might keep fundamental questions completely off the political agenda.[29] Following this logic to its conclusion, he later pointed out that dominant constellations of power could keep citizens themselves ignorant of their interests. Participation, in his view, could allow human beings to become "communicative beings, to reflect, communicate, and act on their reflections, and so become aware of their political interests, which frequently conflicted with those of the ruling class."[30]

Recognizing that political participation can obfuscate issues as well as make them clearer, Bachrach concluded that only with a "requirement that all participants in the formulation of issues and in the decision-making process possess approximately an equal amount of power resources" would participation be more likely to guide citizens toward their real interests rather than away from them.

Building on Bachrach, I too argued that participation in small face to face democracies can help citizens develop a clearer understanding of their real interests.[31] One key goal of participation is to reveal on any given issue whether one's interest complements the interests of others in the polity or conflicts with them. The goal of developing a better understanding [of] one's interests is promoted by decisions on matters in which citizens have 1) experiential knowledge, 2) the opportunity for extended deliberation, 3) a critical mass for mutual support in each area of conflicting interest, and 4) an ideology and set of institutions that makes possible the shift back and forth from ways of making decisions appropriate for common interests to ways of making decisions appropriate for conflict.

Recently the focus of many democratic theorists has shifted from the educative functions of democracy to its deliberative functions. Each is the means to the other's end. Good deliberation ought to educate the participants on their interests, clarifying both the underlying conflicts and the good of the whole. Educated participants, in turn, will be more likely to produce good deliberations, which takes the ideas of each into account, fosters commonality when appropriate, and indicates which issues the group should handle with the methods of conflict.

FADING FROM VIEW

The idea of the educative effect of democratic participation rose in the 1960s, flourished in the 1970s, and waned in the 1980s. The idea faded in impact, I believe, not only because of the usual half-life of all ideas and because for several long presidential regimes in the United States the federal government turned away from interest in participation, but also because the practice itself faded. The contagious excitement of the thou-

sands of collectives formed between 1965 and 1975, which infected many who never even belonged, let many experience—in their own lives, or in the lives of their children, students, or friends—the way that taking collective action or responsibility for a group did activate their powers of thought, feeling, and action. When the pace of political change began to slow and involvements shifted toward the private,[32] commitment to participation became ghettoized in the feminist and ecological movements, and faded even there. Theoretical interest in the educative effects of participation also waned because the third step in the triad of practice–thought–practice proved hard to take. In the academic discipline of political science, normative theory often influences empirical research. Yet in the case of the educative effects of participation, whose beneficial qualities Arnold Kaufman had said remained empirically to be proved, the postulated effects took subtle forms that could easily be captured in empirical studies of relatively small numbers of people. First, although cross-sectional studies showed that people who participated in democratic politics also had many other admirable qualities, it was hard to find situations for study in which a researcher could measure the qualities of people before and after the addition of participation to see if participation itself had any causal effect in producing those admirable qualities[.]

Second, changes in people's heads are hard to measure. It took forty years of research to amass enough before-and-after studies to demonstrate that psychotherapy, conducted specifically for the purpose of changing psyches, had any effect. Only a massive (and therefore prohibitively expensive) study would be likely to pick up the effects on the character of participation in politics—an act not designed for the purpose of characterological change.

Without the stimulating effect of empirical research indicating the type and extent of changes in individuals brought about by democratic participation, and with the demise of a receptive political climate, the educative theory of participation has gone the way of most theories. Most democratic theorists, including myself, simply believe, from their own experience, from the work that they aim at one another, and from reinterpretations of Aristotle, Machiavelli, and Rousseau, that participation does have a beneficial effect on the participants. We do not now inquire too deeply as to what that effect might be.

Reading Notes

1. Aristotle, *Politics*. 1280b. trans. Ernest Barker (Oxford: Oxford University Press, 1946).
2. Aristotle, 1324a.
3. Aristotle, 1279a.
4. Nanna Fenichel Pitkin, *Fortune Is a Woman: Gender and Politics in the Thought of Niccolo Machiavelli* (Berkeley: University of California Press, 1984), p. 96.
5. Pitkin, p. 310.
6. Rousseau, *Social Contract* (1762). G.D.H. Cole, trans. (1950), p. 18.
7. Rousseau, p. 38.
8. Rousseau, pp. 37–42 (Ch. 7: "The Legislator").
9. Rousseau, pp. 134, 138.
10. Rousseau, pp. 94–96.
11. Rousseau, pp. 87–96, esp. 93.
12. Bernard Manin, "On Legitimacy and Political Deliberation," *Political Theory* 15 (1987), trans. E. Stein and J. Mansbridge.
13. Alexis de Tocqueville, *Democracy in America*, (1835–40). v. I, p. 63.
14. de Tocqueville, v. I, pp. 70–71.
15. de Tocqueville, v. I, p. 70. See also pp. 82–83, 98.
16. de Tocqueville, v. II, p. 117.
17. John Stuart Mill, *Autobiography*, 1873 (New York: Columbia University Press, 1960), p. 179.
18. Mill, pp. 111–12. He points out that "these are not questions of liberty," but are questions of development.
19. Mill, p. 112.
20. Mill, p. 25.
21. Mill, p. 30.
22. Mill, p. 42.
23. Arnold Kaufman, "Human Nature and Participatory Democracy," in Carl Freidrich (ed.), *Responsibility: NOMOS III* (New York: Liberal Arts press, 1960), p. 184. See also pp. 188, 190, 198.
24. Kaufman, pp. 192, 193.
25. Port Huron Statement, 1962 (in James Miller, *Democracy Is in the Streets*), p. 156.
26. Jane Mansbridge, *Beyond Adversary Democracy* (Chicago: University of Chicago Press, 1983), p. 244.
27. Carole Pateman, *Participation and Democratic Theory* (Cambridge, MA: Cambridge University Press, 1970), p. 42.
28. Pateman, pp. 45–46.
29. Bachrach and Baratz, "Decisions and Non-Decisions: An Analytical Framework," *American Political Science Review* 57 (1963), pp. 632–42.
30. Peter Bachrach, "Interest, Participation, and Democratic Theory," in J. Roland Pennock and John W. Chapman eds. *Participation in Politics: NOMOS XVI* (New York: Lieber-Atherton, 1975), p. 43.
31. Jane J. Mansbridge, *Beyond Adversary Democracy* (New York: Basic Books, 1980), p. 292.
32. Albert O. Hirshman, *Shifting Involvements: Private Interest and Public Action* (Princeton: Princeton University Press, 1982).

POSTNATIONAL CITIZENSHIP: RECONFIGURING THE FAMILIAR TERRAIN

Yasemin NuhogUlu Soysal

Citizenship is back with a vengeance. Since the 1990s it has made its way in noticeable strides into the discipline of Sociology. If one point of entry is the comparative and historical studies either reconceptualizing the Marshallian concept of citizenship as a more dynamic and relational one (Turner 1989; Sommers 1993; Wiener 1998) or renarrating the development of welfare and women's rights in the right historical order (Barbalet 1988; Fraser and Gordon 1992; Orloff 1993; Skocpol 1996), the other entry has been a growing literature on immigration and citizenship (Kymlicka and Norman 1994). Immigration provides a productive viewpoint to study citizenship since it challenges the very premises of the nation-state model that we political sociologists take for granted in our work.

Our theories are stubborn in assigning the nation-state a privileged position as a unit of analysis, even when conversing about global processes such as immigration. By doing so, they axiomatically embrace the dichotomy of citizen and alien, native and immigrant. This not only generates analytical quandaries as transnational institutions and discourses become increasingly salient, but also renders invisible changes to national citizenship and new formations of inclusion and exclusion.

The predominant conceptions of modern citizenship, as expressed in both scholarly and popular discourses, posit that populations are organized within nation-state boundaries by citizenship rules that acclaim "national belonging" as the legitimate basis of membership in modern states. As such, national citizenship is defined by two foundational principles: a congruence between territorial state and the national community; and, national belonging as the source of rights and duties of individuals as well as their collective identity. Hence, what national citizenship denotes is a territorially bounded population with a specific set of rights and duties, excluding others on the ground of nationality.

In the postwar era, a series of interlocking legal, institutional, and ideological changes affected the concept and organization of citizenship in the European state system. A significant development regards the intensification of the global discourse and instruments on individual rights. This emphasis on rights has been expressed through a codification of "human rights" as a world-level organizing principle in legal, scientific, and popular conventions. Individual rights that were once associated with belonging to a national community have become increasingly abstract and legitimated at the transnational level and within a larger framework of human rights.

As legitimized and celebrated by various international codes and laws, the discourse of human rights ascribes universal rights to the person. Even though they are frequently violated as a political practice, human rights increasingly constitute a world-level index of legitimate action and provide a hegemonic language for formulating claims to rights beyond national belonging. This elaboration of individual rights in the postwar era has laid the ground upon which more expansive claims and rights are advanced. The definition of individual rights as an abstract, universal category, as opposed to being attached to an absolute status of national citizenship, has licensed a variety of interests (environmentalists, regional movements, indigenous groups, as well as immigrants) to make further claims on the state.

A complementary development is the emergence of multilevel polities. The gradual unfolding of the European Union, for example, suggests that political authority is increasingly dispersed among local, national, and transnational political institutions. The diffusion and sharing of sovereignty, in turn, enables new actors, facilitates competition over resources, and makes possible new organizational strategies for practicing citizenship rights. The existence of multilevel polities creates new opportunities for mobilizing identities and advancing demands within and beyond national boundaries.

These developments have significant implications for the notions of identity and rights, on the one hand, and the organization and practice of citizenship, on the other. In Europe today, conventional conceptions of citizenship are no longer adequate to understand the dynamics of rights and membership. National citizenship or formal nationality is no longer a significant construction in terms of how it translates to rights and privileges; and, claims-making and participation are not axiomatically concomitant with the national order of things.

In the following sections, I will focus on two key aspects of the changing models of citizenship: the decoupling of rights and identity, and the expansion of collective claims-making and mobilization. Here I expand on what I called "postnational citizenship" elsewhere (Soysal 1994).

RIGHTS AND IDENTITY

The postwar elaboration of human rights as a global principle, in international agreements and institutions but also in scientific and popular discourses, legitimates the rights of persons beyond national collectivities. This authoritative discourse of individual rights has been influential in the formalization and expansion of many citizenship rights to those who were previously excluded or marginalized in society: women, children, gays and lesbians, religious and linguistic minorities, as well as immigrants. Particularly in the case of immigrants, the extension of various membership rights has significantly blurred the conventional dichotomy between national citizens and aliens.

The erosion of legal and institutional distinctions between nationals and aliens attests to a shift in models of citizenship across two phases of immigration in the twentieth century. The model of national citizenship, anchored in territorialized notions of cultural belonging, was dominant during the massive migrations at the turn of the century, when immigrants were either expected to be molded into national citizens (as in the case of European immigrants to the US) or categorically excluded from the polity (as in the case of the indentured Chinese laborers in the US). The postwar immigration experience reflects a time when national citizenship is losing ground to new forms of citizenship, which derive their legitimacy from deterritorialized notions of persons' rights, and thus are no longer unequivocally anchored in national collectivities. These postnational forms can be explicated in the membership of the long-term noncitizen immigrants in western countries, who hold various rights and privileges without a formal nationality status; in the increasing instances of dual citizenship, which breaches the traditional notions of political membership and loyalty in a single state; in European Union citizenship, which represents a multitiered form of membership; and in subnational citizenships in culturally or administratively autonomous regions of Europe (e.g., Basque country, Catalonia, and Scotland). The membership rights of noncitizen immigrants generally consist of full civil rights, social rights (education and many of the welfare benefits), and some political rights (including local voting rights in some countries). In the emerging European system, certain groups of individuals are more privileged than others— dual citizens and the nationals of European Union countries have more rights than (non-European) resident immigrants and political refugees; they in turn have more rights than temporary residents or those immigrants who do not hold a legal resident status. Thus, what is increasingly in place is a multiplicity of membership forms, which occasions exclusions and inclusions that no longer coincide with the bounds of the nation(al).

Paradoxically, as the source and legitimacy of rights increasingly shift to the transnational level, identities remain particularistic, and locally defined and organized. The same global rules and institutional frameworks which celebrate personhood and human rights, at the same time naturalize collective identities around national and ethno-religious particularisms, by legitimating the right to "one's own culture" and identity. Through massive decolonizations in the post-war period and the subsequent work of the international organizations such as the United Nations,

UNESCO, and the Council of Europe, the universal right to "one's own culture" has gained increasing legitimacy, and collective identity has been redefined as a category of human rights. In the process, what we normally consider as unique characteristics of collectivities—culture, language, and standard ethnic traits—have become variants of the universal core of humanness or selfhood. Once institutionalized as a right, identities occupy a crucial place in individual and collective actor's narratives and strategies. In turn, identities proliferate and become more and more expressive, authorizing ethnic nationalisms and particularistic group claims of various sorts. Accordingly, even when previous nation-states are dissolving (for example, the Soviet Union and Yugoslavia), the "emerging" units aspire to become a territorial state with self-determination, and the world political community grants them this right. In national and world polities, identity emerges as a pervasive discourse of participation, and is enacted as a symbolic (and organizational) tool for creating new group solidarities and mobilizing claims.

Thus, while rights acquire a more universalistic form and are divorced from national belonging, at the same time identities become particularistic and expressive. This decoupling of rights and identity is one of the most elemental characteristics of postnational citizenship. Individuals attain rights and protection, and thus membership, within states that are not "their own." An immigrant in Germany, for instance, need not have a "primordial" attachment of cultural and historical kind to Germanness in order to attain social, economic, and political rights. Their rights derive from transnational discourses and structures celebrating human rights as a world-level organizing principle. The idea of nation, on the other hand, persists as an intense metaphor of identity, and at times an idiom of war. It is still the source of a pronounced distinctiveness, but divested from its hold on citizenship rights.

COLLECTIVE CLAIMS-MAKING AND MOBILIZATION: THE PRACTICE OF CITIZENSHIP

With the postwar reconfigurations in citizenship, along with dissociation of rights and identity, the old categories that attach individuals to national welfare systems and distributory mechanisms become blurred. The postwar reification of personhood and individual rights expands the boundaries of political community, by legitimating individuals' claims to rights beyond their membership status to a particular nation-state. This inevitably changes the nature and locus of struggles for social equality and rights. New forms of mobilizing and advancing claims emerge, beyond the frame of national citizenship.

Two features of these emerging forms are crucial:

First, while collective groups increasingly mobilize around claims for particularistic identities, they connect their claims to transnationally institutionalized discourses and agendas of human rights. Immigrant groups in Europe mobilize around claims for group-specific provisions and emphasize their group identities. Their claims, however, are not simply grounded in the particularities of religious or ethnic narratives. On the contrary, they appeal to the universalistic principles and dominant discourses of equality, emancipation, and individual rights.

When immigrant associations advocate the educational rights and needs of immigrant children in school, they employ a discourse that appropriates the rights of the individual as its central themes. They directly invoke the international instruments and conventions on human rights to frame their position. They forward demands about mother-tongue instruction, Islamic *foulard*, or *halal* food by asserting the "natural" rights of individuals to their own cultures, rather than drawing upon religious teachings and traditions. For instance, the issue of wearing the Islamic *foulard* in school, which erupted into a national crisis in France in early 1990s, was not only a topical contention over immigrant integration or French *laicism*, but entered into the public arena as a matter of rights of individuals (see Feldblum 1993; Kastoryano 1996; Kepel 1997). During the debates, the head of the Great Mosque of Paris (one of the highest authorities for the Muslim community) declared the rules preventing wearing scarves in school to be discriminatory on the grounds of individual rights. His emphasis was on personal rights, rather than religious traditions or duties: "If a girl asks to have her hair covered, I believe it is her most basic right" (*Washington Post*, October 23, 1989). As exemplified in this case, immigrants advance claims for difference which are affirmed by universalistic and homogenizing ideologies of human rights. And by doing so, they appropriate host country discourses,

participate in the host country public spaces, and exercise civic projects as they amplify and practice difference.

The second feature of the new forms of claims-making is that the organizational strategies employed by collective groups increasingly acquire a transnational and subnational character. Their participation extends beyond the confines of a unitary national community, cover multiple localities, and transnationally connect public spheres. In the case of immigrant groups, for example, we find political parties, mosque organizations, and community associations which operate at local levels but also assume transnational forms, and develop organizational connections between places of origin and destination. They carry back and forth institutional forms, bridging a diverse set of public spaces. An example of this is the Alevite groups (a subsect of Islam), organized both in Turkey and Germany. Based on their experience in, and borrowing models from the German education system, they have raised demands for the recognition of denominational schools in Turkey, which do not have a legal standing in the current system. In a similar vein, during the last local elections in Berlin, Turkish immigrant groups pushed for their local voting rights, while at the same time put pressure on the Turkish government to facilitate their rights to vote in Turkish national elections. As such, they envision their participation in multiple civic spaces, both in Berlin and in Turkey. Similar claims are being made by the Mexican and Central American immigrant communities in the United States. They demand dual citizenship and dual voting rights in their countries of origin and residence. And, indeed, the governments of Mexico, Columbia [*sic*], and the Dominican Republic recently passed legislation allowing dual nationality.

All of this implies that the public spheres within which immigrants act, mobilize, and advance claims, have broadened. In pursuing their claims, the mobilization of immigrant groups entails multiple states and political agencies, and they target trans- and subnational institutions, as much as the national ones. For example, the much debated Islamic *foulard* issue was not simply a matter confined to the discretion of a local school board, but has traversed the realms of local, national, and transnational jurisdictions—from local educational authorities to the European Court of Human Rights.

While the claims and mobilization of immigrant groups aim to further particularistic solidarities, paradoxically, they make appeals to universalistic principles of human rights and connect themselves to a diverse set of public spheres. As such, their mobilization is not simply a reinvention of cultural particularisms. Drawing upon universalistic repertoires of making claims, they participate in and contribute to the reification of host society and global discourses.

The experience of immigrant communities in Europe indicates a diversion from classical forms of claims-making and participation in the public sphere. Much of the decolonization and civil rights movements of the 1960s and the early women's movements were attempts to redefine individuals as part of the national collectivity. Similarly, labor movements were historically linked to the shaping of a national citizenry. It is no coincidence that the welfare state developed as part of the national project, attaching labor movements to nations (as in Bismarckian Germany). However, the emerging forms of collective participation and claims-making in Europe are less and less nationally defined citizenship projects. Individuals and collective groups set their agenda for realization of rights through particularistic identities, which are embedded in, and driven by, universalistic discourses of human rights. This shift in focus from national collectivity to particularistic claims does not necessarily imply disengagement from public spheres. Neither does it mean the disintegration of civic arenas. On the contrary, they are evidence for the emerging participatory forms, and multiple arenas and levels that individuals enact and practice their citizenship.

This new form of claims-making and participation, which discursively and organizationally goes beyond nationally demarcated parameters, highlights the other important aspect of postnational citizenship. Postnational citizenship is not simply a set of legal rights and privileges or a legal status attached to a person as implied in Marshallian definitions of citizenship. It signifies a set of practices through which individuals and groups activate their membership within and without the nation-state. Individuals and collectivities interact with and partake in multiple public spheres—hence, altering the locus of participation and setting the stage for new mobilizations.

In concluding, I would like to clarify three major confusions that discussions of postnational citizenship seem to raise. In so doing, my intention is to differentiate postnational citizenship from other theoretical constructs (such as cosmopolitanism and globalization), which are also deployed to account for the shifts in the national order of things. I also intend to rearticulate its theoretical expanse in depicting the new topography of rights and membership and the contemporary dynamics of exclusion and inclusion.

First, postnational citizenship does not refer to an identity or a unitary legal status. It is a sociological category to narrate the changes in the very institutions of rights and identity, which locate citizenship and its practice in multilevel discourses and multiple public spheres (and national is only one of these multiple scripts and arenas). It does not mark the emergence of a legal status or identity at the global level, ascribed by a single, unified world society and political structure. If anything, postnational citizenship projects that identities remain constructed at local levels and get more and more attached to local spaces (see also Gupta and Ferguson 1992; Malkki 1995).

Thus, it is superfluous to associate postnational citizenship with ideologies of cosmopolitanism, which profess a moral, universalistic individual and identity. Likewise, it is unproductive to conflate postnational citizenship with theoretical formulations regarding "transnational communities," which presumptively accept the formation of tightly bounded communities and solidarities (on the basis of common cultural and ethnic references) between places of origin and arrival (see Basch, Schiller, and Blanc 1994; Cheah and Robbins 1998; Portes 1998). Postnational citizenship does not imply the necessary advent of transnational solidarities or communal bonds, or the existence of individuals devoid of (local) commitments, identities, and interests. Rather, it emphasizes the multiconnectedness of public spheres and the increasingly universalistic conceptions and discourses of rights, which are no longer limited by national constellations.

Second, postnational citizenship does not imply the "withering of the nation-state." The same transnational rules and institutions reify the nation-state's agency and sovereignty as much as they celebrate human rights and foster postnational citizenship. The normative and institutional domain of the transnational is not host to a harmonious and coherent rule system. It accommodates a multiplicity of principles often with contradictory outcomes and effects. Inasmuch as they are contradictory, the principles of human rights and nation-state sovereignty are equally part of the same transnational discourse and institutional terrain. Thus, as the source and legitimacy of rights increasingly move to the transnational level, rights and membership of individuals remain organized within nation-states. The nation-state remains a persistent depository of cultures of nationhood and still the most viable political organizational structure. This is what leads to the incongruity between the legitimation and location of postnational citizenship, which has paradoxical implications for the exercise of citizenship rights. Nation-states and their boundaries persist as reasserted by restrictive immigration practices and sovereignty narratives, while universalistic personhood rights transcend the same boundaries, giving rise to new models and understandings of membership.

Hence, postnational citizenship is not a sign of a linear procession from national to transnational. That is, we cannot (should not) postulate postnational citizenship as a stage within the much assumed dichotomy of national and transnational, and the expected transition between the two. There is much confusion around this issue and much time and energy is spent in arguing whether we are approaching a transnational stage or not. Postnational citizenship confirms that in postwar Europe the national no longer has primacy but it coexists with the transnational, mutually reinforcing and reconfiguring each other. Into the analytical realm of postnational citizenship, the national and transnational determinants figure in as mutual variables and as concurrent levels, within which the current practices of citizenship and participation should be understood.

Postnational citizenship is also mistakenly associated with globalization. This oversight arises from misconstruing globalization as the world becoming a homogeneous and/or disorderly entity. This extremely rudimentary notion is hardly entertained by any proponent of globalization. Even the most unyielding proponents describe a much more differentiated process (see Sassen 1996, 1998). A more useful definition of globalization refers to world-level structural changes, which shorten distances and connect local articulations to social events and relations seemingly located afar (see Giddens 1990; Robertson 1992; and Appadduraï 1996). Although they signify correlated processes, postnational citizenship is not one and the same as globalization and does not singularly derive from it. The intensification of discourses and institutions of human rights at the global level, a novel development in the postwar era, indeed underline the development of postnational citizenship. But postnational citizenship itself does not assume or predict a uniform modality of citizenship in a converging world (citizenship institutions, although being transformed, still keep certain distinctiveness, based on their historical and institutional specificities at national level).

Lastly, postnational citizenship is not in itself a normative prescription, nor does it presume public spheres free of conflict or devoid of exclusions. That is to say, on the one hand, postnational citizenship reveals an ongoing process of definition and redefinition of rights and participation. On the other, it productively brings to the fore the fact that there are no longer absolute and clear-cut patterns of exclusion and inclusion which simply coincide with the bounds of the national. In today's Europe, access to a formal nationality status is not the main indicator of inclusion and exclusion. Rights, membership, and participation are increasingly matters beyond the vocabulary of national citizenship. Under the rubric of postnational citizenship, inclusions and exclusions shape simultaneously and at multiple levels—local, national, and European.

The increasingly expansive definition of rights may appear as a contradiction in the face of recent attempts to deregulate the welfare state and eliminate policy categories based on the collective (e.g., affirmative action and welfare provisions). However, the copresence of postnational citizenship and/with the breakdown of the welfare state is no coincidence. Both trends derive from the global dominance of the ideologies and institutions of liberal individualism. While these ideologies contribute to the dismantling of the welfare state project, at the same time, they enable various groups in advancing identity-based claims justified on the basis of individual rights. Thus, the same transnational processes that lead to new marginalizations and exclusions also create new grounds for and spaces of claims-making and mobilization, and facilitate the expansion of rights.

However, the new spaces of citizenship and claims-making are not necessarily free of conflict. By emphasizing the hegemony of discourses and strategies of human or personhood rights, which resolutely underlines postnational citizenship, one should not take a naive position and assume that individuals and groups effortlessly attain rights, or that they readily bond together and arrive at agreeable positions. Postnational rights are results of struggles, negotiations, and arbitrations by actors at local, national, and transnational levels, and are contingent upon issues of distribution and equity. And like any set of rights, they are subject to retraction and negation. Rather than denying the certitude of conflict and contestation for rights, postnational citizenship as a category and practice draws attention to the multilayered and diverse forms that they take and new arenas in which they are enacted.

Our dominant theories and conceptualizations have yet to catch up with the changes in the institutions of citizenship, rights, and identity. They have yet to respond to the challenge posed by emergent actors, border-crossings, and non-conventional mobilizations. Postnational citizenship is an attempt to capture and incorporate these changes by assigning transnational institutions and discourses a more predominant analytical role than it is usually granted in the prevailing studies. Otherwise, we will continue to have models that do not work, anomalies in existing paradigms, and incongruities between official rhetoric and institutional actualities.

Reading References

Appaduraï, A. 1996. *Modernity at Large: Cultural Dimensions of Globalization.* University of Minnesota Press.

Barbalet, J.M. 1988. *Citizenship: Rights, Struggle and Class Inequality.* Milton Keynes: Open University Press; University of Minnesota Press.

Basch, L., N.G. Schiller, and C.S. Blanc 1994. *Nations Unbound: Trans-national Projects, Postcolonial Predicaments, and Deterritorialized Nation States.* Langhorne, PA: Gordon and Breach.

Cheah, P. and B. Robbins (eds.) 1998. *Cosmopolitics: Thinking and Feeling Beyond the Nation.* Minneapolis: University of Minnesota Press.

Feldblum, M. 1993. "Paradoxes of ethnic politics: The case of Franco-Maghrebis in France." *Ethnic and Racial Studies* 16: 52–74.

Fraser, N. and L. Gordon 1992. "Contract versus charity: Why is there no social citizenship in the United States?" *Socialist Review* 22(3): 45–67.

Giddens, A. 1990. *The Consequences of Modernity.* Cambridge: Polity Press.

Gupta, A. and J. Ferguson 1992. "Beyond 'culture': Space, identity, and the politics of difference." *Cultural Anthropology* 7: 6–23.

Kastoryano, R. 1996. *Négocier l'Identité: La France, l'Allemagne et leurs Immigrés.* Paris: Armand Colin.

Kepel, G. 1997. *Allah in the West: Islamic Movements in America and Europe.* Stanford: Stanford University Press.

Kymlicka, W. and W. Norman 1994. "Return of the citizen: A survey of recent work on citizenship theory." *Ethics* (January): 352–81.

Malkki, L.H. 1995. *Purity and Exile: Violence, Memory, and National Cosmology among Hutu Refugees in Tanzania.* Chicago: University of Chicago Press.

Orloff, A.S. 1993. "Gender and the social rights of citizenship: The comparative analysis of gender relations and welfare states." *American Sociological Review* 58: 303–28.

Portes, A. 1998. "Social capital: Its origins and applications in modern sociology." *Annual Review of Sociology* 24: 1–24.

Robertson, R. 1992. *Globalization: Social Theory and Global Culture.* London: Sage Publications.

Sassen, S. 1996. *Losing Control? Sovereignty in an Age of Globalization.* New York: Columbia University Press.

———. 1998. *Globalization and Its Discontents.* New York: The New Press.

Skocpol, T. 1996. *Protecting Mothers and Soldiers.* Cambridge, MA: Harvard University Press.

Somers, M.R. 1993. "Citizenship and the place of the public sphere: Law, community, and political culture in the transition to democracy." *American Sociological Review* 58: 587–620.

Soysal, Y.N. 1994. *Limits of Citizenship: Migrants and Postnational Membership in Europe.* Chicago: University of Chicago Press.

Turner, B.S. 1989. "Outline of a theory of citizenship." *Sociology* 24: 189–217.

Wiener, A. 1998. *"European" Citizenship Practice: Building Institutions of a Non-State.* Boulder, CO: Westview Press.

KEY TERMS

Citizenship   A legal status bestowed to individuals who belong to a political community. It entails both rights (civil, political, and social rights) and responsibilities, such as paying taxes and active participation in public life. It defines the relationship between the state and citizens, and determines the conditions of inclusion and exclusion in a specific political community.

Political Community   A society of people who share common rights and privileges and live under the same laws and regulations. It is traditionally demarcated by territorial boundaries and characterized by mandatory membership and a governing structure.

State Tradition   Characterizes the links between the state and civil society and the autonomy of the state from political interests. It encompasses the role of the state in economic matters and social life.

Underclass   A term used to describe individuals and groups that belong to the lowest or least privileged stratum of society.

FURTHER READINGS

Beiner, R., ed. *Theorizing Citizenship.* Albany: State University of New York Press, 1995.

Soysal, Y.N. *Limits of Citizenship: Migrants and Postnational Membership in Europe.* Chicago: University of Chicago Press, 1994.

Voet, R. *Feminism and Citizenship.* London: Sage, 1998.

WEB LINKS

Citizenship and Immigration Canada:
www.cic.gc.ca

The Global Campaign for Ratification of the Convention on Rights of Migrants:
www.migrantsrights.org

International Council for Canadian Studies:
www.iccs-ciec.ca/pages/7_journal/b_issues/number14.html

GLOSSARY

Anthropocentrism   Based on the principle of a human-centred world, where humans are assigned a superior status in their relationship with nature. The natural environment exists to serve the needs of human beings.

Authoritative Allocation of Values   This phrase, coined by David Easton, refers to the binding decisions made by a government to distribute scarce resources.

Authority   The ability to command. It is vested in individuals by virtue of their office.

Bourgeoisie (Capitalist Class)   The dominant class, which owns the means of production.

Cabinet   Strictly speaking, the cabinet is the council of ministers, the members of which are responsible for given portfolios or departments of government activity and jurisdiction.

Catch-All Party   The type of political party that appeals to voters across the boundaries of ideological and social cleavages. In order to retain their support base, catch-all parties have to broker the manifold differences that divide their followers. Examples of catch-all parties include the Liberal Party of Canada, the Indian National Congress Party, or the Liberal Democratic Party of Japan.

Charismatic Authority   Authority based on the extraordinary qualities and mission of the charismatic leader. Legitimacy of this authority is possible because the followers believe in that mission and those qualities.

Citizenship   A legal status bestowed to individuals who belong to a political community. It entails both rights (civil, political, and social rights) and responsibilities, such as paying taxes and active participation in public life. It defines the relationship between the state and citizens, and determines the conditions of inclusion and exclusion in a specific political community.

Civic Nationalism   Nationalism where inclusion in the nation is a matter of choice.

Civil Society   A set of groups, institutions, and interactions located between the state, the market, and the private sphere.

Class   Members of a society who share a common economic or social position or, in Marxist terms, common relations to the means of production.

Classical Conservatism   Original version of conservatism, often associated with British theorist Edmund Burke, which emphasizes order, morality, and traditions. It also stresses the organic nature of society, adopts a paternalistic view of the state's role in society, and advocates slow and gradual, as opposed to radical, change.

Classical Liberalism   Original version of liberalism that emphasizes equality of rights, negative freedom, and a minimal role for the state in society.

Cleavage-based Party   The type of political party that seeks to appeal to specific groups along particular political cleavages. Examples of such parties include workers' parties or religious confessional parties.

Coalition   An alliance of multiple political actors with the express purpose of designing coordinated strategies among its members. For example, a coalition government brings together multiple political parties that harmonize and correlate their ideal policies.

Communism   An ideology and political system that seeks to establish a classless society through revolutionary action. It calls for the collective ownership of goods and property.

Confederation   A political unit composed of independent states that accept to cede some of their sovereignty to common institutions. In this system, a set of sovereign states decide to create a union for the realization of specific goals (e.g., economic, military, etc.). The sovereign states delegate a certain number of powers to the government of the union. The state reserves the power to secede from the confederal system.

Consociational Democracy A type of democracy characterized by a grand coalition, proportional representation, mutual veto, and segmental autonomy.

Cosmopolitan Democracy A transnational governance regime comprising international institutions, democratic states, and civil societies committed to protecting human rights and democratic public law both within national borders and at the regional and international levels.

Cross-Cutting Cleavages When horizontal and vertical divisions intersect in a society.

Cultural Approach to Nationalism Nationalism is explained by the overwhelming power of culture (especially language) and the identity it naturally fosters.

Deep Ecology A branch of environmentalism that views nature and wildlife as worthy of moral consideration, and believes that this principle should govern social, economic, and political relations. It calls for changes in basic economic, technological, and ideological structures in an effort to preserve and restore ecosystems.

Democratic Socialism Branch of socialist thought that accepts to work within a liberal-capitalist order, but seeks to soften the effects of the market through regulation and redistribution.

Dependent Variable The political phenomenon we are trying to explain.

Diachronic Comparisons Comparing within the same country but during different periods.

Ecocentrism An organic view of the world that recognizes the interdependence and interconnection between humans and nonhumans.

Economic Approach to Nationalism Nationalism is a consequence of the uneven development of capitalism.

Electoral System The set of rules and regulations according to which the electoral process is organized. Its most important components include rules on eligibility to vote; the number of votes that each voter can cast; the electoral formula according to which votes are converted into seats; the number of seats that can be won in each electoral district; and, in cases where voters have multiple votes, regulations about whether voters can cumulate the votes they are entitled to and whether they must use all votes or can abstain partially.

Environmentalism An ideology and political project that seeks to protect the quality and continuity of life through the conservation, preservation, or protection of the natural environment and its inhabitants.

Ethnic Nationalism Nationalism where inclusion in the nation is determined on the basis of objective criteria such as race and ancestry.

Fascism An extreme-right ideology that rejects the ideals of rationality and individual liberty and champions a collectivist ideology that focuses on the needs and aspirations of a national community. Anti-materialist and anti-democratic, fascism rejects basic human equality as an ideal and espouses government by an elite group.

Fascist Corporatism One way of organizing state–society relations in autocratic, capitalist societies. An economic system divided into state-controlled associations representing labour, business, and professionals. Each association has a monopoly of representation and organization in its respective field. The economic interests of labour and industry are subordinate to the needs and objectives of the state.

Federalism A principle of government that seeks to reconcile unity and diversity through the exercise of political power along multiple autonomous levels.

Federation A state in which two or more levels of government are sovereign within their own constitutionally specified jurisdictions.

Feminism An ideology and political project based on the belief that men and women are treated unequally socially, politically, and economically. It aims to identify and abolish the sources of women's oppression in all spheres of life.

Feminism Politics Politics conceptualized in terms of gender relations.

Fundamentalism A militant and exclusivist interpretation of religion, one that stresses a return to the so-called fundamentals of the faith.

Gender   As opposed to sex, which refers to physiological differences, gender refers to characteristics of men and women that are socially constructed.

Globalization   A set of processes that are transforming and reorganizing social relations and intensifying economic, social, and political interconnections among people across territorial boundaries.

Head of Government   The head of the council of ministers.

Head of State   The chief executive of a political system.

Hypothesis   A conjectural statement about the relationship between two variables. It gives a direction to a study before it has begun.

Independent Variable   A factor that affects or causes the dependent variable.

Labour Theory of Value   The value (i.e., price) of a commodity is equal to the quantity of labour time required to produce it.

Legal Authority   The rule of law determines who exercises power. The obedience of the citizens and their acceptance of governmental decisions are due to their loyalty to the constitution.

Legitimacy   The acceptance by citizens of a political system of governmental policies or of a set of public authorities as proper and deserving obedience. Legitimacy is a response to authority.

Liberal Democracy   The type of democracy that emphasizes the protection and unhindered practice of the political and civil rights and liberties of individual citizens.

Liberal Feminism   A branch of feminism that seeks equality between men and women. It focuses on equal rights, individualism, liberty, and justice.

Majoritarian Democracy   Type of democracy that concentrates political power in the hands of an electoral majority.

Marxist-Socialist Feminism   A branch of feminism that views women's oppression as rooted in both patriarchy and capitalism. Women's emancipation requires the reorganization of institutions found in both the public and private spheres.

Max Weber (1864–1920)   German sociologist famous for his definition of the state.

Means of Production   The instruments and raw materials used to produce a commodity, e.g., equipment, buildings, and labour.

Mixed-Member Electoral System   The type of electoral system that combines elements of PR and majority-plurality systems.

Model   A theoretical and simplified representation of the real world. An operationalized theory.

Mode of Production   The method used to produce the necessities of life. It includes both the means of production and the relations of production, i.e., the social relations through which goods and services are produced.

Modernism   The view that nations are constructed entities whose origins are European and rooted in the rise of the modern state.

Mujahideen   Muslim "freedom" fighters, frequently supporting Islamist causes. In Afghanistan, fighters resisting Soviet forces.

Nation   A human community united by a special sense of solidarity deriving from shared features, most importantly language, religion, ancestry (real or imagined), history, myths, and symbols, and that seeks, in the name of this solidarity, to gain or maintain a distinct political situation, usually autonomy or independence.

Nationalism   A movement that makes political claims on behalf of a nation and on the basis of a national identity.

National Socialism   (Nazism) An extreme branch of fascism that espouses extreme or radical nationalism based on race. State policies aim to preserve racial purity and establish a new world order based on racial nationalism.

Nation-State   That type of political organization where the territorially defined state overlaps with the idea of a nation.

Neoconservatism   Stream of conservative thought that sheds the organic view of society in favour of an individualist conception, and that advocates a minimal state, i.e., less government and a small bureaucracy.

New Institutionalism   Politics is seen as heavily shaped by political institutions.

Patriarchy   An institutionalized system of male domination and power that subordinates and marginalizes women. Patriarchy is maintained by a number of institutions and processes in society, including motherhood, compulsory sexuality, notions of femininity, and the traditional nuclear family.

Pluralism A form of state–society relations that assumes a dispersion of power among the state and different social interests.

Plurality and Majority Electoral Systems Types of electoral system that award seats to parties that have received either the plurality or the majority of votes in the electoral district. In contrast to proportional representation, the share of legislative seats that political parties receive under these electoral systems is not in proportion with their share of electoral votes.

Plural Society A society in which the population is divided along different ethnic, linguistic, religious, regional, and/or cultural lines.

Political Approach to Nationalism Nationalism is the product of manipulative elites and/or processes of state construction.

Political Community A society of people who share common rights and privileges and live under the same laws and regulations. It is traditionally demarcated by territorial boundaries and characterized by mandatory membership and a governing structure.

Political Culture The pattern of individual attitudes and orientations toward politics among the members of a political system. It is the subjective realm that underlies and gives meaning to political action.

Political Economy Politics is conceptualized in terms of state–market relations.

Political Party A team of individuals united for the common purpose of capturing government power and implementing a commonly agreed-upon policy agenda.

Political Party System A set of patterned relationships among political parties. The most important properties of a party system are its fragmentation, polarization, and institutionalization. The first refers to the number of parties in the system, the second to the degree of ideological difference among them, and the third stands for stability in both the identity of individual parties and the properties of the party system.

Political Science The study of politics, where politics is understood as the process of making binding decisions to allocate scarce resources within the society.

Politics An activity pertaining to the authoritative allocation of resources. Power and conflict are embedded in the activity of politics.

Polyarchy An ideal political system, which, according to Robert Dahl, is characterized by the full participation of the population in the electoral process, and full contestability of government. Democracy approximates this ideal type very closely.

Postmodernism Politics is constructed by discourse.

Power The ability of a person to make others do something that they might not otherwise do.

Primordialism The view that nations are natural entities whose existence pre-dates modernity and that respond to the fundamental need of humans to belong to a cultural community.

Proletariat (Working Class) The subject class, which lives from the sale of its labour power.

Proportional Representation (PR) The type of electoral system that provides a close correspondence between the percentage of votes and seats that political parties receive in a general election. PR systems normally have large electoral districts in terms of the number of seats that can be won. The most commonly used formulae that PR systems use are the highest average (for example, d'Hondt) and the largest remainder (such as Hare or Hagenbach-Bischoff) rules.

Radical Feminism A branch of feminism that regards patriarchy as the root of all forms of oppression. It focuses on the link between biology and women's status in society. Proponents call for radical social change.

Rational Choice Political outcomes are viewed as the product of strategic decision making.

Reform Liberalism Stream of liberal thought, articulated in the nineteenth century, that advocates equality of rights and opportunity, negative and positive freedom, and some degree of state welfarism and interventionism. Also known as modern liberalism or welfare liberalism.

Regime The nexus of alliances within and without the formal bureaucratic and public sectors that the leader forms in order to gain power and to keep it.

Religious Reformism   The longing to return to a purer form of social and religious organization.

Representative Democracy   A type of democracy in which the political will of the people is exercised through the decisions and choices of the agents whom they select to represent them. Representative democracy provides for indirect rule by the people. A parliamentary democracy is a form of indirect and representative democracy.

Shallow Ecology   A branch of environmentalism that seeks to achieve short-term environmental objectives within existing institutions and processes.

Social Democracy   A branch of socialism that aims to reduce economic and social equality and diminish class distinctions by democratic means. It supports some level of state ownership of the means of production to accomplish these goals. The type of democracy that emphasizes the importance of collective, as opposed to individual, rights and development.

Socialism   An ideology that seeks to eliminate class divisions and social and economic inequalities in society through the collective ownership of the means of production, distribution, and exchange.

Societal Corporatism   A way of organizing state–society relations in democratic, capitalist societies whereby compulsory, single, functional, hierarchical interest groups emerge from below. This system replaces mature pluralistic state–society relations.

Split-Ticket Voting   Some electoral systems provide voters with multiple votes to cast. If voters cast these multiple votes for candidates of different political parties, then they cast a split vote.

State   A compulsory political association with continuous organization whose administrative staff successfully upholds a claim to the *monopoly* of *legitimate* use of force in the enforcement of its order within a given territorial area.

State Corporatism   A way of organizing state–society relations in authoritarian states whereby the state creates compulsory, single, functional, hierarchical interest groups.

State Sovereignty   The absolute and final authority of a country to regulate internal matters without being subject to any power outside itself.

State Tradition   Characterizes the links between the state and civil society and the autonomy of the state from political interests. It encompasses the role of the state in economic matters and social life.

Structural-Functionalism   Political structures are viewed as developing in response to social needs.

Synchronic Comparisons   Comparing across countries but during the same period.

Systems Analysis (Theory)   Politics is conceptualized as a system with inputs, outputs, and feedback.

Taxonomy   A subject divided into classes that are distinct from one another.

Theory   A set of systematically related generalizations suggesting new observations for empirical testing.

Traditional Authority   Authority (power) based on the inheritance of position such as a hereditary monarchy; a system legitimated by the sanction and prestige of tradition.

Typology   A more advanced and complex taxonomy that involves classifying phenomena based on a number of variables.

Underclass   A term used to describe individuals and groups that belong to the lowest or least privileged stratum of society.

Unitary State   A state in which any powers exercised by subnational governments are delegated only by the centre. In other words, subnational governments are not sovereign in prescribed fields and the central state can change the territorial division of power without the consent of the subnational units.

Veto Player   A political actor whose consent is necessary, but not sufficient, to alter the status quo.

Vote of Confidence   A legislative vote that is called in order to test whether the executive enjoys the confidence of a working majority in the legislature. Sometimes the head of government may choose to designate the parliamentary vote of a given bill as a matter of confidence. This technique may allow the head of government to rein in potential defectors in the party who may otherwise vote against the party line on the given bill.

Vote of No Confidence Similar to the confidence vote, this is also called to test the ability of the cabinet to enjoy the support of a working majority in the legislature. However, a no-confidence vote is called by the opposition. Some parliamentary systems use the constructive no-confidence vote, which requires that the motion designates an alternative head of government to the one whose removal is sought.

Wave of Democracy Sudden increase in the number of democratic regimes.

Weblike Societies Developing countries societies composed of competing and autonomous social organizations.

Welfare State An interventionist state that seeks to promote some measure of social and economic equality among its citizens by redistribution attained through taxation and social programs.

COPYRIGHT ACKNOWLEDGMENTS

Pages 10–13: From Max Weber, "Politics as a Vocation," H.H. Gerth and C. Wright Mills, from *Max Weber: Essays in Sociology* (New York: Oxford University Press, 1958), pp. 77–80; 82–85. Reprinted by permission of Oxford University Press, Inc.

Pages 13–22: From Bernard Crick, "The Nature of Political Rule," from *In Defence of Politics* (Chicago: University of Chicago Press, 1993), Fourth Edition, Chapter 1, pp. 15–33. Reprinted with permission of Weidenfeld & Nicolson, an imprint of The Orion Publishing Group.

Pages 33–40: From Janine Brodie, "The Political Economy of Regionalism," in Wallace Clement and Glen Williams (eds.), *The New Canadian Political Economy* (Kingston: McGill-Queen's University Press, 1989), selected sections. Reprinted with permission of McGill-Queen's University Press.

Pages 42–48: From Alan C. Cairns, "The Government and Societies of Canadian Federalism," *Canadian Journal of Political Science*, 10:4, 1977, pp. 695–725. Reprinted with permission.

Pages 59–72: From Michael Sodaro, "Crital Thinking About Politics," in *Comparative Politics: A Global Introduction* (Boston: McGraw Hill, 2001), pp. 51–73. Reprinted with permission of The McGraw-Hill Companies.

Pages 87–91: From John Stuart Mill, *Consideration on Representative Government* (New York: Bobbs-Merrill Company, 1958), pp. 36–46.

Pages 92–93: From Edmund Burke, *Reflections on the Revolution in France* (Dent: London, 1964), pp. 6–7; 87–88.

Pages 103–8: From Henry Milner, "What Canadian Social Democrats Need to Know about Sweden, and Why," in John Richards, Robert D. Cairns and Larry Pratt (eds.), *Social Democracy without Illusions: Renewal of the Canadian Left* (Toronto: McClelland & Stewart, 1991), pp. 56–65. Reprinted with permission.

Pages 109–11: From "What Is to be Done?" in *The Lenin Anthology*, Robert C. Tucker, ed. (New York: W.W. Norton & Company, Inc. 1975), pp. 19–20; 76–79.

Pages 119–22: From Benito Mussolini, *Fascism: Doctrine and Institutions* (New York: Howard Fertig, 1968), pp. 7–11; 20–23.

Pages 135–39: From Mary Wollstoncraft, *A Vindication of the Rights of Woman*, Carol Poston, Ed. (New York: W.W. Norton & Company, Inc., 1975), pp. 3–6; 10–11; 14–15.

Pages 140–43: From bell hooks, "Feminism: A Movement to End Sexist Oppression," in *Feminist Theory: From Margin to Center* (Boston: South End Press, 1984), 17–31. Reprinted with permission of South End Press.

IMAGE CREDITS

This page constitutes an extension of the copyright page. We have made every effort to trace the ownership of all copyrighted material and to secure permission from copyright holders. In the event of any question arising as to the use of any material, we will be pleased to make the necessary corrections in future printings. Thanks are due to the following authors, publishers, and agents for permission to use the material indicated.

Page 3: Gianni Dagli Orti/Corbis

Page 4: Historical Picture Archive/Corbis

Page 77: Bettmann/Corbis

Page 82: Bettmann/Corbis

Page 96: Bettmann/Corbis

Page 114: Bettmann/Corbis

Page 125: Bettmann/Corbis

Page 152: AP Images

Page 156: AP Images

Page 158: Handout/Corbis

INDEX